LINGUISTIC ARCHEOLOGY:

UNEARTHING THE SECRETS OF GENESIS USING SCAN

To Chris,

[signature]

BY AVINOAM SAPIR

Linguistic Archeology
Uncovering the Secrets of Genesis Using SCAN
By Avinoam Sapir

Dedicated to the memory of my mother,

Chaya Sapir

Table of Contents

Introduction

I would like to introduce myself to the reader. In the last twenty-five years I have been teaching and training investigators from various US and other government and private organizations – law enforcement, security, and intelligence. The training is designed to prepare investigators to analyze "open statements" (see definition later) given by witnesses, suspects, victims, and informants. The technique that I developed over the years is called "Scientific Content Analysis" or "SCAN."

The course that I teach, which is four full days, morning to evening, brought me to teach in different countries, starting in the US and Canada in the North American continent, Mexico in Central America, and Brazil in South America. In addition, I have been teaching in the UK and Belgium in Europe, and in Australia, Indonesia, Singapore, and South Africa. I also taught my class in Dubai and Qatar. In all of these countries I trained police investigators, as well as security and intelligence organizations. I am pleased to say SCAN has helped solve thousands of cases over the years. In all of these places, without exception, I found that the rules of analysis are effective, regardless of society, country or any particular language. All the rules and statistical observations are true for all people.

I would like to add another point, and it has nothing to do with my professional life, but it has a direct connection to the analysis presented in this book. One year after I came to live in the US, around 1986, I began serving as the reader of the weekly Biblical Torah portion in the synagogue in Phoenix.

The first five books of Moses, or the Torah, is divided into 52 weekly portions, and each Saturday (the Jewish Sabbath) morning one portion is read aloud to the congregation. The Torah itself, written on a scroll, includes only the text. There is no punctuation to indicate where a sentence or verse starts or ends. Moreover, the Hebrew language, unlike English, does not have the vowels in the letters, but outside the letters. In other words, the way to read the word is given by signs above and below the letters to show the reader how to pronounce the word. But the Torah scroll does **not** include these signs at all. The reader faces a text that is void of all indications of a sentence, and even any way to pronounce the words. If this seems complicated, then there is still another component to the reading. The Biblical portion is not read but actually sung according to certain signs indicating how to do so. As there are signs showing the piano player how to play the music, so also are there signs indicating how to sing the text. But again, these signs are **not** in the scroll. Therefore, the reader of the Biblical portion needs to memorize beforehand how to divide the sentences, how to pronounce the words, and how to sing the text.

During all these years I found it a challenge to memorize the text and to perform in a way that will be pleasant to the ears, and accurate to the knowledgeable person. I am quite proud to say that I am doing quite well. This experience in my personal life, which I considered as important as my professional life, brought me to remember the text of the first five books of Moses quite well. Many times, during the analysis of the text I could consult my memory to see how a certain word shows up in other places. At times, I found myself going to sleep at night, only to get up in the morning with an answer to a certain linguistic problem that bothered me. I could see the words running in front of me exactly like the book that helps the Torah readers prepare for the job.

The combination of teaching and analyzing statements during the weekdays, along with preparing for reading the Torah on Saturday morning, brought to my attention many times linguistic points which I shared with people around me. In this book I plan to present the analysis of the Biblical text in the same way that I analyze statements given to me by students. The emphasis will be on the book of Genesis, but very quickly the reader will see that the analysis consults other books in the Bible.

When I embarked on this analysis I was amazed how much I lost in understanding the text when I read it in the synagogue. Today, since I started the analysis (and this book is not the end of the journey), I understand that if one wants to read the Bible, one cannot read it with the Hebrew of today. The language of the Bible does not use Modern Hebrew, and there are many places that reading the text with Modern Hebrew will send the reader light years away from the meaning of the text.

Over the years many students asked me why I don't write a textbook on SCAN. In the course I am teaching I use a workbook, which has an extensive section of lecture notes, but why not publish a textbook? In this book I am doing just that. I am presenting to you, the reader, the SCAN technique, while using the book of Genesis as the text to show the implementation of the rules.

If you want to know more about SCAN, beyond the contents of this book, you are more than welcome to access the SCAN webpage at www.lsiscan.com.

Scientific Content Analysis (SCAN)

The basic concept of the technique is that no human being can say everything that he has in his/her mind. Before a person can write or talk, the person needs to decide if the information or opinion present in mind at that specific moment is important enough to transmit to the listener or reader, or maybe the information or opinion is not important enough, and therefore the person will not transmit it. This editing process is the engine behind every statement.

Once the person decides that a certain bit of information is important enough to enter the statement, still, the information does not reach the paper (if it is a written statement) or the mouth (if it is a spoken statement). The person needs to go into another stage before delivering the information, and this stage is phrasing the statement. The person needs to take a picture in memory and transform it into words. The person needs to decide in which order the statement will be given, and how to build the sentences – a process that calls for using syntax. The person also needs to choose the words to use in building the sentences.

These two processes, the editing process and the phrasing process, are very quick. Physiologically, the speed of the human brain is measured in milliseconds (one thousandth of one second). The human brain has 300 billion cells, and they create 100 trillion connections, and there is nothing random in all of these. Even today there is not much knowledge about vast areas of the human brain. Recently, a national project to map the human brain was announced, as the human genome was mapped. Scientists estimate that 50% of the human brain is enlisted to accommodate the ability to talk. The other 50% is for all the rest of life, such as the heart, lungs, etc.

Recently, there was a news article that said scientists put several super-computers together and managed to simulate the brain of a cat. The same article said that the scientists do not foresee in the near future simulating the brain of a human. There are not enough super-computers to put together to simulate **one** human brain.

The speed of the human brain is such that the person who gives a statement cannot answer questions about his own statement. For example, at the end of a statement, we ask the person two questions. First, did you know at the time of the writing that you changed your language (used different words to describe the same thing)? And second, do you know now why you changed your language? In most cases the person will answer negatively. Sometimes, the person might say, "I was told in school not to be redundant." However, if the SCAN analyst suggests to the person the reason for the change in language, based upon the location of the change in the statement, the person would be able to confirm or to deny the suggested reason. And in most cases the person will confirm the reason. The bottom line is that we are not facing the subconscious. The person knows the past, as it is present in his memory. What the person cannot do is connect the language he used in his statement to the information in his memory. The lack of connection is only due to the high speed of the brain when he is giving the statement.

As the speaker or writer goes through this process, the listener or reader can step into the person's shoes, and reach conclusions about what was present in the person's mind at the time of delivery of the text.

SCAN Rule: The person is dead. The statement is alive!

The speed of the brain brings about this basic rule of SCAN. It means that the person's ability to explain his own statement, and the ability of the reader/SCAN analyst to explain the same statement are not the same. The focus should be the statement and not on the person giving the statement. We look to the statement to explain the way the person chose to build the statement (the order of sentences, the way the sentences were built, and the choice of words inside the sentences).

Often, I am asked: don't you need to know the person, to know who he is, to be familiar with his personality, his behavior, and to see his facial expressions at the time of giving the statement? The answer is categorically negative. The SCAN analysis does not deal with people, but with the **content** people give (the statement), and therefore we label it Scientific **Content** Analysis.

To emphasize the point, if the person cries at the time of giving the statement, or if the person has tears in the eyes, but there is no crying or tears in the statement, then the SCAN analyst cannot consider the crying and the tears during the analysis. If the person says in the statement, "I cried," then we take it into consideration in the analysis.

When an investigator wants to give me a statement to look at, there are times in which the investigator would like to give me background information on the case, or even on the person. I don't want to get any of that outside information, other than the statement. The analysis deals with only the statement, and nothing beyond it.

The analysis in this book uses Scientific **Content** Analysis. The reader should know that the analysis in this book does not use any information that is not in the text of the Bible, including any **religious** commentary on the Bible, such as the Mishnah, Gemara, Midrash, or any other scholarly or **academic** source relating to the Bible. Professionally, we do not consider any other information present in an investigation file from which we take a statement when we perform a SCAN analysis. Similarly, in the context of this investigation we will not consider any outside sources (religious or academic) that were added onto the Biblical text over the thousands of years since the text was set down in writing. We ignore for the sake of this analysis those sources that bring the reader today to understand the text in a certain way.

At first, it might seem that this policy restricts the analyst. However, it actually frees the analyst to stick only to the text, and to build knowledge from the text itself, without any bias from prior knowledge about the person or circumstances. One can define this policy of SCAN as "Just the Text Itself."

SCAN Rule: Total Belief in the Subject

When people ask me to give them the most basic point in the SCAN technique, the foundation of all other rules used in this analysis, my answer is, "Total Belief in the Subject."

At first, most investigators, who deal with so many deceptive people, receive this news with major skepticism, thinking how can it be? They know from their experience that so many people lied to them in the past, so how can I come to them and say that they should approach the "open statement" by accepting it at face value? And I even emphasize to them, that even if I know for a fact that the subject is lying, I still look upon the statement as if the statement is absolutely true.

This point actually brought me to move from polygraph (lie detection) into statement analysis. It didn't take me long into my polygraph experience to realize that for most subjects who came deceptive on the charts coming out of the machine, and later confessed to the crime, their confessions **did not contradict** their initial statements. The confession **complemented** the initial statement, but did not contradict it. And there were people who even said after their confession, "But I want you to know that I didn't lie to you in my initial statement." And in fact, when I share this experience of mine with my students, and some of them are polygraph examiners, I see many of them nodding their heads, and some of them even say openly that this is their experience as well.

Once one realizes that the initial open statement, in the worst-case scenario, is only an incomplete truthful statement, meaning, what the person says is true, but he does not say the whole truth, then we are on our way to analyzing the statement.

And if the reader/listener encounters a point in the open statement that the reader/listener does not understand, it does not mean that the statement is deceptive. It only means that the reader/listener does not understand it. And in fact, in many cases, the reader/listener needs to first understand the choice of words used in the statement, before moving any further.

In most cases the SCAN analyst should not focus on what the statement says, but on what the statement does not say. And at times, what the statement does not say might turn the story upside down, 180 degrees. For example, a wife who was suspected of killing her husband gave a very brief statement, "I was in the living room. I heard a shot and I went to see what happened and I saw that he was dead." If we read this brief statement correctly, we can see that the woman did not lie at all. She was in the living room. She heard a shot. If you shoot someone you hear a shot. After the shot she went to make sure that she indeed killed him. There is only one sentence she did not say: 'I shot him.' In this case, the investigator for six hours accused the suspect of being deceptive, and during these six hours she responded, "But I didn't lie to you. Everything I said was absolutely truthful." And indeed it was.

Here the reader might ask: why can't a person who killed lie? If someone already killed, what is the problem to lie? But the fact is that in the decisive majority of cases, people who commit such crimes prefer not to lie. At least, not to produce information which did not take place. Most people prefer to conceal existing information, but not to lie.

When a person swears "to tell the truth, the whole truth, and nothing but the truth," the person swears using the legal definition of a lie. But the social definition is different. There are situations in which we might be asked, "Why didn't you tell me?" And our answer is, "Because you didn't ask me. If you were to ask me, I would have told you." We defend ourselves by lying by omission and not lying by commission.

With this understanding, the reader of this analysis should know that the objective of this analysis is to find out what the text does not tell us. No different from any other statement in the present day.

And as in any other scientific field, there is no way to reach a conclusion based upon just one observation. Scientific methodology mandates that we corroborate our findings in **different ways**, and the more points we find, the more solid the conclusion is. The more we go into the text and find linguistic evidence of the same conclusion, the more we realize that the conclusion is accurate. And once enough different points lead to the same conclusion, we know we are facing a **definite** conclusion. And that is why it is **Scientific** Content Analysis.

I was asked once in regard to my analysis of the Biblical text, "And if you find one place which contradicts your explanation does it mean that the explanation is no good?" And my answer was, and still is, "Yes." If one place contradicts the explanation, the analyst needs to know that he/she is wrong. He/she needs to search for another explanation, or to fine-tune the explanation. There is no way inconsistency can be tolerated within SCAN.

It is not much different from a crossword or Sudoku puzzle. As the numbers in the Sudoku puzzle need to fit up and down, and left to right, so in the analysis of the text. And when a person finds a contradiction within the Sudoku puzzle the person knows that he/she made a mistake some time earlier. SCAN analysis is actually a verbal Sudoku. The same applies in the analysis of a text. It is words and not numbers, sentences and not squares, but otherwise the concept is the same. Everything must fit. And if something does not fit, we know that we are wrong, and quite likely we messed up a lot earlier.

When a detective sends me a statement, and I finish the analysis, and everything fits, I know that the analysis is accurate. And in fact, rarely if ever, does the detective report that the analysis sent him the wrong way. And in most cases, the analysis finds information that the detective didn't know, and after receiving the analysis, the detective continues his investigation, and confirms the points exposed in the analysis.

Just as scientific research calls for physical evidence (or empirical in scientific terminology), the SCAN technique calls for linguistic evidence, or evidence from inside the text, and not from outside the text.

One more concept I have to bring you before we can move on. This is the 'unity' of the text, and the 'unity' of the analysis. By this I mean that the analyst cannot explain one word in a certain way in one place, and give a different explanation of that same word in another place in the text. The writer has a copyright on the text, and the analyst cannot add anything or subtract anything. As the text is sacred, so should the analysis be: unity for the text, and unity for the analysis. Or, in other words, the analyst must maintain **consistency** in interpreting words and in applying SCAN rules.

The Open Statement

An open statement is information that a person gives without the listener guiding the person with questions that tend to lead the story in a certain direction. The only question the listener is allowed to ask is, 'What happened?' From this point of view the book of Genesis fits the requirement of being an open statement as the listener or reader did not lead the statement at the time of delivery.

The Perception of an Open Statement

The language used in an open statement is a "linguistic mirror" of reality. In other words, if we compare the language to the lens of a camera that takes a picture of reality, then the language of the text is the linguistic lens: how the person giving the statement perceives reality.

The Social Introduction of People

A statement is made of several components: people, objects, events (verbs), places, and times. Of these five components, people are the most important. People are the engine behind every event. The way the person introduces us to people who take part in an event constitutes a major component of the analysis of a text. One cannot analyze a text without checking the way the person relates to people in his/her language.

We should treat the open statement as if the writer/speaker were talking directly to the reader/listener. This means that if my wife and I walk on the road, and we encounter someone I know, but who does not know my wife, basic manners and politeness call on me to conduct an introduction between my wife and the third person. The question is how I would phrase this introduction. Would I say, "Please meet my wife," or "Please meet my wife Leah," or "Please meet Leah?"

The way I introduce my wife is a way to learn about the relationship between my wife and me. The same applies in an open statement, and in our case, the book of Genesis. We can learn from how the text conducts the social introduction of people.

Components of Social Introduction

There are four components of social introduction in an open statement. The first is the title the speaker or writer attributes to the person. For example, would the text label the person as "son" or maybe "boy," or even "child?" Would the text label the person as "man" or "guy?"

The second component is possession. Would the text label the person as "**the** son" or "**my** son," or "**the** wife" or "**my** wife?"

The third component is the name of the person. Would the text label the person as "the wife" or "my wife," or "my wife Leah," adding the name to the title?

The fourth component is the order of listing the various components of the introduction. Would the text say "my wife Leah" or "Leah my wife?"

This book concentrates on the various components of the social introduction in an open statement, and specifically in Genesis. Saying that, the reader will be able to find all the rules of analysis in the various chapters of this book. And as we go further into the analysis, the reader will see that even if we deal with different text, the approach will remain the same. We apply the rules **consistently**.

I invite the reader on a fascinating exploration that aims to expose secret information in the text of Genesis and to demonstrate the SCAN technique.

THE ORDER OF BIRTH

Introduction

In this chapter we will concentrate on one component of the social introduction: what title the text gives to the people mentioned in the events with respect to their order of birth in the family. Who is the first, the second, etc.

The reader should have in mind one important point. The objective, outside reality is not at issue. Even if I, the reader, know who the firstborn is, who the second is, and who the youngest is, the question still remains how the text relates to this order. In general, the linguistic description is a lot more important than the objective reality.

SCAN Rule: We need to analyze the text according to the extraordinary, not according to the usual or average and accepted way the language goes about describing the events.

This means that the analyst has to find the usual or average way the text goes about delivering the statement. Only after this average way is established in definite terms are we ready to find the deviation from the average way, and then to understand the meaning of the text. In other words, we need to establish average vs. deviation.

Background Information

This concept of "average vs. deviation" is accepted in all areas of research. For example, the polygraph examiner studies the charts coming out of the machine, looking for deviations from the baseline (polygraph language), or "average" as we are labeling it here.

The reader is called upon to have some patience at the beginning of this chapter, as the strategy is to establish the average way, and from there, to look for the deviation.

Cain and Abel

The text informs us of the birth of Cain in the verse, "And Adam[1] knew his wife Eve, and she conceived and bore Cain..." (Genesis 4:1). There are two components missing here. First, unlike other places in the text of Genesis where the birth of someone is mentioned using the formula, "...and she conceived, and bore a son, and she named him...," here the text does not talk of the birth of a son, or even of naming the newborn. Still, the text gives us the reason for the name: "...and said I have acquired a man from the Lord."

And second, the text continues to inform us of the birth of Abel: "And she again bore his brother Abel..." (4:2). While Cain is mentioned on his own merit, Abel is mentioned as "Cain's brother," and without giving the reason for his name, although the name[2] speaks for itself. We should note that in regard to Abel the text does not say, "...and she conceived..." which should bring us to suspect that we are dealing with twins.

Noah's Sons

Unlike Adam and Eve, for whom the text informs us that Eve "conceived and bore," for Noah's sons the text goes a different way. The text uses the formula, "And Noah fathered three sons, Shem, Ham and Japheth" (Genesis 6:10). It is the same formula the text uses to describe the history of humanity from Adam to Noah. One should note that Noah's wife is not mentioned at all, except by the title 'his wife.'

If we compare the language to the camera lens focusing on the subject of the picture, then we can easily see that the linguistic lens concentrates on one son of Noah, Ham. The text finds it necessary to mention the fact that the youngest son of Noah is "the father of Canaan" (Genesis 9:18). The text repeats this formula later on saying, "And Ham, **the father of**

---

[1] Although we read here "And Adam..." one should note that the text in Hebrew says, "And the Adam knew..." The tendency in English is to perceive "Adam" as the name of the first human being. However, in Hebrew, "Adam" means simply "human being," not only in modern language, but also in Biblical Hebrew. One should only refer to the following verse in Leviticus, "...if *adam* brings an offering to the Lord..." (Leviticus 1:2) and the English translation makes it "any man." But one should note that "Adam" not only relates to male, but also to female: "So G-d created **the adam** in His own image, in the image of G-d created He him, male and female He created them" (Genesis 1:27).

[2] "Abel" in Hebrew, or more precisely, *Hevel*, means "vanity." As we see in Ecclesiastes, "Vanity of vanities said Kohelet, vanity of vanities; all is vanity." (1:2) And the word "vanity" in Hebrew is *hevel*.

Canaan, saw…" (9:22). When Noah "…knew what his youngest[3] son had done to him…" (9:24), Noah does not curse Ham but Canaan: "…cursed be Canaan; a slave of slaves shall he be to his brothers" (9:25). And Noah continues and compares the good son, Shem, to the bad one; and again, the bad one is not Ham, but Canaan: "…blessed be the Lord of Shem; and Canaan shall be his slave" (9:26).

Moreover, when the text continues to describe the history of Noah's descendants and their dispersion upon the earth, the text distinguishes between Canaan and all the others by speaking of Canaan's border: "And the **border** of the Canaanites was from Sidon, as you come to Gerar, to Gaza, as you come to Sodom and Gomorrah, and Admah and Zeboim to Lasha" (10:19).

Although the text does not tell us the order of birth within the family at the time it mentions their birth, still we know that Ham is the youngest: "…knew what **his youngest son** had done to him" (9:24).

The text does tell us the order of birth in the family, but it is not done by attributing a title to the specific person, or even as an important issue to talk about. The reader needs to read all the text in order to dig out what the order of birth was. Later, we will find that Japheth was the oldest: "To Shem also, the father of all Eberites, the brother of Japheth the eldest…" (10:21). The text gives Japheth the title the 'eldest' but not the title of 'first born' or even the 'first.' Language-wise, the text does not deal with this issue when talking of Noah's family.

Moreover, we should note the fact that the text avoids attributing the title "the second" to the second son of Noah, Shem. By not doing so, the text distinguishes Shem from the other two sons by not giving him the title that tells us his place among the sons. This avoidance of using the title "the second" should bring us to ask if the text had any problem with the title "the second."

The Birth of Abraham

The formula the text used to describe the generations from Adam to Noah is the same formula used to describe the generations from Noah to

---

[3] "[Y]oungest son:" in Hebrew the exact word used to relate to Ham is not "youngest" but "little" (in Hebrew *katan*) while Japheth is not described as the "eldest" but as "big" (in Hebrew *gadol*).

Abraham. "…Terah fathered Abram, Nahor, and Haran, and Haran fathered Lot" (Genesis 11:27). As with Noah, so with Abraham; the text does not give us the reason for the names of Terah's sons, and therefore we don't have the reason for Abraham's name.

Moreover, the text does not tell us anything, not in one place, nor scattered around (as in the case with Noah's sons), about the order of birth in the family of Terah's sons (who is the oldest and who is the youngest). What should we conclude? Does the text list the sons in the verse according to the order of birth, and so Abraham is the firstborn? Or, maybe the order of appearance is according to their importance in the sequence of events. In order to answer this question we need to deal with one important word, "…And these are the *toldot* of Terah…" (11:27).

Introduction to Linguistic Journeys

From this point on, there will be places in which we will stop the discussion and divert our attention to a very long survey of the use of one particular word throughout the Tanach. This long survey, labeled a "Linguistic Journey," will help us understand the meaning of a particular word we are surveying.

This is not true only of Biblical language, but for every statement we receive in an investigation. The reader should take into consideration that the person giving the statement (the subject) might use the same words the reader does, but the subject gives these same words different meaning from the one the reader uses.

During this analysis, there were numerous times in which I started a linguistic journey in order to understand the meaning of one particular word. With this linguistic journey I copied all the verses in which that one particular word was present. It was a very tedious job that took hours, and at times even days. I did all of it without having any guarantee that I would reach new insight that would help me in the analysis.

After copying the verses, I started to divide them into groups, either by an activity, or according to a certain issue, situation, or an event. Gradually, I reached new insight into Biblical language.

People think that SCAN is 95% brains and 5% tedium. The fact is that SCAN is 95% tedium, and only 5% brains.

After our linguistic journey we will be able to return to this point in our discussion, the order of birth as it appears in the language of the text.

Linguistic Journey – the Meaning of *Toldot*

Introduction

In Hebrew, each verb and/or noun has a root of three letters, and from these three-letter root words, derivatives are created by adding prefixes or suffixes, or by changing the vowels to make words with closely related meaning. For example, the three-letter root word Y-L-D can create the word *yeled*, which means male child, while the word *yalda* is female child. At the same time, the **verb** *yalda* means gave birth (past tense). The idea is that the mother bore a child. The word *meyaledet* means midwife. The verb *holid*, which has the two letters L and D with the addition of H at the beginning, means he brought the woman to bear a child, or, in short, he fathered a child.

In the word *toldot* one can easily see two of the three-letter root word Y-L-D. While *toldot* is in plural, the word *tolada* in the singular, in much later Hebrew, means result or effect of one event on another. The word *toldot*, again, plural, comes to mean the effect or impact of an event or a person. If we are talking about a person it can mean offspring. But at the same time, the word *toldot* can easily mean heritage, history, or effect.

Note: to avoid confusion, in the following analysis, we will use the word *toldot* in Hebrew, without an attempt to translate it. This is to avoid the need to choose between competing meanings.

Linguistic Observation

We find in the entire Tanach[4] the phrase "These are the ***toldot*** of..." in relation to the following: heaven and earth (Genesis 2:4), Adam (5:1), Noah (6:9), Shem, Noah's son (11:10), Terah, Abraham's father (11:27),

---

[4] Tanach is an acronym made out of three letters, T, N, and K. The first letter starts the word *Torah*, the first five books of Moses. The second letter N starts the word *Nevi'im* meaning prophets, and the third letter K starts the word *Ketuvim* meaning writings. The Tanach includes 24 books from Genesis to Chronicles, and is an acronym for the Hebrew Bible.

Ishmael (25:12), Isaac (25:19), Esau (36:1,9), Jacob (37:2), Moses and Aaron (Numbers 3:1), and Peretz, son of Judah (Ruth 4:18).

Discussion

We can see that the word *toldot* is used for heaven and earth. One cannot translate *toldot* here as generations or offspring, unless one says that this verse is relating to the evolution of all life forms from the physical surroundings. It is likely that the *toldot* of heaven and earth should be more accurately translated as "the **history** of the world (heaven and earth)."

The word *toldot* is in use only from Adam, as the first human being, to Moses and Aaron. Moses and Aaron are the last ones to close this linguistic unit. Even the book of Ruth, relating to a much later time, does not say "These are the *toldot* of David…" but instead connects David to Peretz, the son of Judah from Tamar: "These are the *toldot* of Peretz." And Peretz was born before Moses and Aaron.

This linguistic unit – Adam to Moses and Aaron – should bring us to conclude that the text sees the era of Moses and Aaron as the ending of the time of the beginning of the nation. If Abraham and his son Isaac, and his grandson Jacob, were the founding fathers **biologically**, then Moses and Aaron, who led the people at the time of Mount Sinai, were the founding fathers of the nation **spiritually**. The Mount Sinai revelation was the event that separates the Tanach, at least in terms of the use of the word *toldot*, into two significant eras, before Mount Sinai, and after it.

The most glaring omission is the word *toldot* for Abraham. One might think that the forefather who is considered the father of the Hebrew nation would merit such a phrase. But the text does not. Instead, the text uses the same formula as for all others, "Such and such fathered so and so" in relating to Isaac: "These are the **toldot** of Isaac the son of Abraham: **Abraham fathered Isaac**" (Genesis 25:19).

If we look upon the common structure relating to the line of descent between Adam and Abraham, we can see the use of the formula, "…and such and such fathered so and so…" Thus, Abraham also merited this formula. It was not placed in a verse of its own as in "These are the *toldot* of Abraham, Abraham fathered Isaac," but instead was attached to "These are the *toldot* of Isaac…"

It is quite likely that the text wanted to avoid mentioning the fact that Abraham fathered two sons, Ishmael (first) from Hagar, Sarah's maidservant, and Isaac (second) from his wife. The text did not want to give Ishmael the honor of being mentioned in the same breath with Isaac. The text does give Ishmael the honor of "These are the **toldot** of Ishmael…" (25:12), but immediately continues with, "These are the **toldot** of Ishmael, Abraham's son, whom Hagar the Egyptian, Sarah's maidservant, bore to Abraham." To have no doubt that even though he is Abraham's son, still he is the son of a maidservant, not the son of a legitimate wife. Later on in our linguistic journey, we will see again that the text has an issue with someone who is a slave/servant.

The Strategy of the Analysis

The above-mentioned discussion illustrates the need of the SCAN analyst to study the text not only left to right in English (or right to left in Hebrew). At the same time as the analyst studies the text left to right, the analyst also needs to study the text from the top to the bottom. How the text relates to the same point by meaning or by choice of words in different places in the text.

There are times in which a student approaches me and quotes a sentence from a subject, either from a statement, or even from an interview in the news media. The student asks me what I think of the text in the sentence. My answer is always that I cannot relate to that specific sentence without seeing the whole statement (or the whole interview) at the same time. One cannot and should not analyze a sentence out of context.

And as the above analysis considered all the occurrences in the entire Tanach of the word *toldot* together, so the analyst needs to do. Take all the sentences in which the topic or the word shows up, and put them together to analyze them. Only then can the analyst search for patterns, and attempt to draw conclusions.

Going Over the Text More Than Once

This search of the text from top to bottom mandates that the analyst go over the text more than once. We can see at times that the end of the statement will clarify a certain word that the analyst didn't even think needed to be clarified. And the end of the statement will explain the beginning.

Therefore, after the first pass over the statement, the analyst should take a rest, and go over the text again, from the beginning to the end, to see if a certain point reveals a new understanding based upon the overall view of the text.

There are times in which I send my analysis to the investigator and the investigator asks me: "Why didn't I see it in the first place?" And my answer is that I didn't see it in the first place either. But I went over the text more than once. All in all, I found out that the second pass over the text produces around 40% more information. And the second pass over the text should not be the last one. The third pass adds more information as well.

I can reveal to the reader that the second time I went over the text I found a lot more information than I found in the first pass. Moreover, while the first pass I did in Hebrew, the second pass I did in English. It may sound strange, but it is easier to analyze a text in a foreign language than in the reader's own (first) language. The problem with one's own language is the reader falls into the linguistic trap of accepting the language of the text with the reader's own understanding of the words. This linguistic trap does not exist in a foreign language. The reader is aware that he/she is not in full control of a foreign language with all its nuances. After finishing the second pass in English, I returned to this pass in Hebrew, and then I got some additional information as well.

Returning to our Linguistic Journey – *Toldot*

The text says, "And Terah lived seventy years, and fathered Abram, Nahor, and Haran. Now these are the *toldot* of Terah. Terah fathered Abram, Nahor, and Haran, and Haran fathered Lot" (11:26-27).

Why does the text repeat itself, bringing us two verses that are almost identical? The second verse adds, "…and Haran fathered Lot." What was the need to repeat the birth of these three sons?

In order to understand this repetition we have to examine other places in which the text uses this word versus places in which it does not. And there is no better place to do so than the mention of the sons of Levi (the third son of Jacob), since there are two places in which the text mentions Levi's sons, one with the word *toldot*, and one without it.

In the book of Exodus the text says,

> These are the chiefs of their fathers' houses. The sons of Reuben the first born of Israel, Hanoch, and Pallu, Hezron and Carmi, these are the families of Reuben. And the sons of Simeon, Jemuel, and Jamin, and Ohad, and Jachin, and Zohar, and Saul the son of a Canaanite woman. These are the families of Simeon. And these are the names of the sons of Levi *le'toldotam* Gershon, and Kehath, and Merari… (Exodus 6:14-16)

We should note that the text does not use the word *toldot* in regard to the first two tribes (Reuben and Simeon), but only for the tribe of Levi. And a bit later the text adds the phrase "…these are the families of Levi *le'toldotam*…" (6:19) after mentioning the sons of Merari, although it continues speaking about the tribe of Levi, and tells us about the birth of Aaron and Moses to Amram.

We can also see that the text gives the number of years Levi lived: "…and the years of the life of Levi were a hundred and thirty seven years" (6:16), and the text gives us the number of years of Kehath: "…and the years of the life of Kehath were a hundred and thirty three years" (6:18). The text does not give us the length of life of Gershon or Merari. By omitting the lives of Gershon and Merari, the text comes to tell us that all this section and after that, until the verse, "These are those who spoke to Pharaoh king of Egypt, to bring out the people of Israel from Egypt, these are Moses and Aaron" (6:27), come to introduce us in the sequence of events to two people, Moses and Aaron. Therefore, there is a bias in mentioning the descendants of Levi: Kehath, who fathered Amram, who fathered Moses, is the only one to merit having the numbers of years he lived to be mentioned, as he serves the goal of introducing Moses and Aaron, while Gershon and Merari do not.

Later on, the text mentions the tribe of Levi: "And these are those who were counted of the Levites according to their families..." (Numbers 26:57), but the text does not use the word *le'toldotam*, as there is no bias in this counting. The goal of the text in Numbers is only to give the numbers of the Levites, and no more.

At this stage, we get the impression that word *le'toldotam* comes to tell the reader that the text does not go according to the sequence of events, but according to the **historical importance** of these people in the sequence of events. Let us check this conclusion in other places.

First, still with the tribe of Levi. In Numbers the text says, "These are the *toldot* of Aaron and Moses in the day that the Lord spoke to Moses in Mount Sinai" (Numbers 3:1). And the next verse says, "And these are the names of the sons of Aaron..." (3:2). But the text does not mention Moses' sons at all. The goal of this text is to introduce us to the sons of Aaron, Eleazar and Ithamar, who "ministered in the priest's office in the presence of Aaron their father" (3:4). Therefore, the text has to mention that the two older sons of Aaron, Nadab and Abihu, "...died before the Lord when they offered foreign fire..." (3:4).

However, when the text speaks of the chiefs of the Levites, the report is complete – according to the order of birth – and therefore there is no need for the word *le'toldotam*.

At this point we can go back to Noah, and the text says, "These are the *toldot* of Noah. Noah was a just and perfect man in his generations[5], and Noah walked with the Lord. And Noah fathered three sons, Shem, Ham and Japheth" (Genesis 6:9-10).

The word *toldot* used for Noah should not surprise us. From the text we know that the listing of Noah's sons does not go according to the order of

---

[5] While the translation of the word *toldot* is often "generations," here in the text the Hebrew word is *dorot*, which is plural for *dor*. *Dorot* should be translated correctly into "generations," even in Modern Hebrew. While the word *dor* or in plural *dorot* connotes time, the word *toldot* connotes offspring. We know that the offspring of a person is a future generation, but the emphasis is not on time but on lineage. This is an example of how the translation does not maintain consistency and actually merges two Hebrew words, *toldot* and *dorot* into one English word, "generations."

their birth. We know that Ham is the youngest: "...and knew what his youngest son..." (Genesis 9:24). Later on, the text introduces Japheth as the eldest: "...the brother of Japheth the eldest..." (Genesis 10:21), and we are left with Shem who is in the middle. By using the word *toldot* the text tells us that the listing is according to their historical importance, not according to the order of birth. Shem, who is the father of the children of Heber (whence "Hebrew"), merits first place. Ham, who is the father of Canaan, is listed second. It would be interesting to find out where Ham would have been listed if he were not the father of Canaan.

When the text lists for us the generations after Noah, it starts with, "These are the *toldot* of Noah..." (Genesis 10:1). The text starts with Japheth's children, as he is the big (eldest) one, but it devotes only three verses to him. Then the text moves on to talk about Ham's children, and it devotes fourteen verses to him, four times more than to Japheth. Quantity wise, we can easily see that Japheth is not the focus of attention in the text.

In relation to Ham the text tells us "And Kush fathered Nimrod" (10:8). The text says, "And the beginning of his kingdom was Babel..." (10:10), and the text mentions Assyria and cities in Assyria. In relation to Canaan the text says, "And the border of the Canaanites was from Sidon, as you come to Gerar, to Gaza, as you come to Sodom and Gomorrah, and Admah and Zeboim to Lasha" (10:19). Canaan is the only one of which the text mentions its border, as Canaan's border had historical importance to the text, unlike the others.

And the text continues with Shem and devotes eleven verses to him. It is less than the text devoted to Ham, but after the generation of the Tower of Babel, it continues listing the generations between Shem and Terah (father of Abraham) and devotes another fifteen verses to them.

In other places where the text uses the word *toldot*, "And these are the *toldot* of Isaac the son of Abraham; Abraham fathered Isaac" (25:19), Ishmael vanishes altogether. Later on, the text says, "These are the *toldot* of Jacob. Joseph was seventeen years old..." (37:2), and all the other brothers vanished from the picture at this point. Joseph is the *toldot* of Jacob.

We find the word *toldot* also in regard to Ishmael: "These are the *toldot* of Ishmael, Abraham's son who Hagar the Egyptian, Sarah's maidservant, bore to Abraham" (25:12), and in relation to Esau: "These are the *toldot* of Esau..." (36:1). For both of them we should ask if the listing is by birth order or by importance.

If we return to Shem, the middle son of Noah, the text says, "These are the *toldot* of Shem..." (11:10). We should conclude that the listing of the generations from Shem to Terah does not mean necessarily that each son mentioned in a certain generation is the first-born. The people mentioned are only those who bring us from Shem to Terah, and thus to Abraham, the father of the nation.

Back to Terah

At this point we can return to the point where we started this section: "And Terah lived seventy years and fathered Abram, Nahor, and Haran. These are the *toldot* of Terah. Terah fathered Abram, Nahor and Haran, and Haran fathered Lot" (11:26-27).

As we saw with Noah's sons we should conclude that the same applies to the sons of Terah: we are not facing a listing according to the order of birth. Abram is not necessarily the oldest but the first one to be mentioned due to his historical importance. Lot shows up in the verse also due to his historical importance. We should not forget that Lot fathered two nations, Moab and Ammon, who were important later on in history.

And when the text does not use the word *le'toldotam* we see that the order of birth guides the text. For example, "These are the names of the sons of Israel who came to Egypt, Jacob and his sons: Reuben, Jacob's firstborn" (46:8). Later on, we find "...and it was told to Abraham saying behold Milcah she has also born sons to your brother Nahor. Huz his firstborn and Buz his brother and Kemuel the father of Aram" (22:20-21).

In these two places the text uses the title "firstborn," and it comes to tell us that the birth order is dominant, and the word *le'toldotam* is not in use.

There is only one place in which the text uses the word *le'toldotam* while still using the title "firstborn" and this is in relation to Ishmael.

These are the **toldot** of Ishmael, Abraham's son whom Hagar the Egyptian, Sarah's maidservant, bore to Abraham. And these are the names of the sons of Ishmael by their names *le'toldotam*. The firstborn of Ishmael Nebioth… (25:12-13)

We should also note that this is also the only place in the Bible where the text uses a unique formula to list the offspring: "…**by their names** *le'toldotam*." The text already started with, "And these are the names of…" Why does the text add this unnecessary repetition, "…**by their names** *le'toldotam*…?"

We should compare the wording the text uses for Ishmael to the wording it uses for the sons of Israel. In the book of Numbers, talking of the census of the twelve tribes of Israel, the text says, "And the sons of Reuben, Israel's firstborn son, by their *toldot*, according to their families **by the house of their fathers**, according to the number of their names…" (Numbers 1:20).

The phrase "by the house of their father" is missing from Ishmael. Instead, the text says, "And these are the names of the sons of Ishmael, **by their names, according to their** *toldot*…" (25:13).

If we remember that the text avoided using the phrase "These are the *toldot* of Abraham" to avoid merging Ishmael, who was born to a slave (Hagar), with the son who was born to the legitimate wife (Sarah), into one verse, one can understand that the phrase "by the house of their father…" is missing from Ishmael for the same reason – to avoid any connection, even an implied one, to Abraham.

Two Descriptions of Creation

We can end our discussion of the word *toldot* by going back to the beginning of the book of Genesis: "These are the *toldot* of the heavens and of the earth…" (2:4). Later on, the text says, "This is the book of *toldot* Adam in the day when the Lord created Adam in the image of the Lord he made him" (5:1).

The use of the word *toldot* in these two places comes to tell us that the report in the second chapter, unlike the first chapter, does not go according to the order of time but according to the historical importance.

The first chapter relates to the physical creation of the world, ending with the creation of the human being. The second chapter (it is more of a section than a chapter) relates to the history of the human being upon earth, not only in the physical sense, but also with a description of the direct contact between the Almighty and the human being. One can see that the creation of the human being is mentioned twice, in the physical creation, and in the social creation. They are not a repetition as such, but two dimensions of the same story. Unlike any other creation of a life form, either plant, or animal, the only one who merits being mentioned twice, in two different descriptions dealing with two different dimensions, is the human being.

Summary

From this linguistic journey of the word *toldot* comes a very important conclusion: the text wants to be exact when it goes by the order of time, or when it goes by the order of importance. This means that the text wants the reader/listener to know the exact meaning of the text. This is assuming that the reader/listener is attuned to the language of the text. If the reader/listener is not attuned to it, then the information remains hidden. But by the **language** of the text, the information is **not hidden**.

Returning to the Birth of Abraham

If we compare the text for Noah's sons to the text for Terah's sons, we can ask the question: why does it tell us the order of birth of Noah's sons, even though not in one place, but spread all around, while it does not tell us anything about the order of birth of Terah's sons? Why do we have to conclude the Abraham was not Terah's firstborn only by going into a linguistic journey to understand the word *toldot*? Why doesn't the text help us to position Abraham among his brothers?

[Note: this chapter deals with the **language** of the text in relation to the order of birth. We will deal with Abraham and Lot regarding the **content** of the text in a later chapter.]

Summary

From the birth of Cain to the birth of Abraham, at least from the language point of view, the text does not concentrate on the order of birth of children, a subject that seems remote to the author, and not the focus of attention. However, the text concentrates, content-wise, but not language-wise, on Noah's youngest son, Ham, who is "the father of Canaan" (Genesis 9:18).

Ishmael's Birth

The linguistic picture that we saw at the birth of Cain repeats itself in the birth of Ishmael. Here the text says, "And Hagar bore Abram a son" (Genesis 16:15).

Before the birth of Ishmael Abram complains, saying, "…I go childless…" (15:2), and "…to me you have given no seed…" (15:3). But after the birth of Ishmael the text says, "And Hagar bore Abram a son; and Abram called his son's name, whom Hagar bore, Ishmael" (16:15). Hagar received Ishmael's name from the angel who appeared to her "…by the fountain of water in the wilderness, by the fountain in the way of Shur" (16:7), and the angel told her, "…You are with child, and shall bear a son, and shall call his name Ishmael…" (16:11). Still, after the birth of the son, Abram is the one to give Ishmael his name, and by doing so, Abram acknowledged fully his fatherhood of Ishmael. The text even emphasizes, "And Abram was eighty six years old when Hagar bore Ishmael to Abram" (16:16), no different from the birth of Esau and Jacob, "…and Isaac was sixty years old when she bore them" (25:26).

Note that the text does not give us Jacob's age at the time his first son Reuben was born.

When the Almighty appears to Abraham and informs him of the change of Sarah's name from Sarai to Sarah, Abraham says, "…O that Ishmael might live in your presence" (17:18). Abraham shows that he does not see himself as childless anymore, or one to whom G-d 'gave no seed.' Here, the Almighty corrects him and informs him that Sarah's son will be the one to continue the covenant: "…and I will establish my covenant with him for an everlasting covenant, and with his seed after him" (17:19).

The text continues:

> And Abraham was ninety-nine years old when he was circumcised in the flesh of his foreskin. And Ishmael his son was thirteen years

old when he was circumcised in the flesh of his foreskin. In the midst of this day was Abraham circumcised, and his Ishmael his son. (17:24-26)

The last sentence ("In the midst of this day...") seems at first glance unnecessary; however, two components show up. First, the phrase "in the midst of this day,"[6] and second, if the first two verses mention the fact of the circumcision of the two, each one separately, then the third verse comes to emphasize to the reader that the two of them did it **together**.

Lot's daughters

Between the birth of Ishmael ("And Hagar bore Abram a son..." (16:15)), and the birth of Isaac ("Sarah conceived and bore Abraham a son..." (21:2)), the text moves to concentrate on Lot who dwelled in Sodom, the destruction of Sodom and Gomorrah, and the daughters of Lot sleeping with their father. Content-wise, the appearance of the angels to Abraham to inform him of the upcoming birth of Isaac is directly connected to the destruction of Sodom. The two angels who continue their way from Abraham to Sodom are from the three angels who appeared to Abraham.

Lot's daughters are the first children in Genesis for whom the text uses **language** to label them according to the order of birth, unlike Cain and Abel, for example, where we only know who is older and who is younger by the order of **mentioning** their birth. Cain and Abel did not get a title indicating who is first and who is second. On the other hand, Lot's daughters did get such a title. For one reason or another, the text perceives Lot's daughters to be important enough to generate language that nobody before them received. In a way, we can say that the linguistic lens is opening at the time of Lot's daughters, to concentrate on the importance to the text of who among the two daughters is the older (firstborn female - *bechira*), and who is the younger (*tzeira*).

In the story of the two daughters after the destruction we see:

---

[6] The phrase "in the midst of this day" appears at the time Noah and his family entered the ark (Genesis 7:13), twice when Abraham and Ishmael were circumcised (17:23, 17:26), at the time of the exodus from Egypt (Exodus 12:17, 12:41, 12:51) and at the time of the festivals. This phrase comes to indicate that there was (or might be) opposition to the act mentioned. It is more accurately translated as "in broad daylight."

- "And the older[7] told the younger..." (19:31),
- "...and the older came..." (33),
- "...and the older told the younger..." (34),
- "...and the younger arose..." (35),
- "And the older bore a son..." (37), and
- "And the younger also bore a son..." (38).

We should note that the use of language of "older" and "younger" appears again in Genesis, in relation to Leah and Rachel, the two daughters of Laban. Laban told Jacob, "...it must not be so done in our place to give [for marriage] the **younger** before the **older**" (29:26).

The birth of Ishmael influences the linguistic lens in regard to the order of birth in the family. There is no significance or importance to birth order until Ishmael's birth. The fact that Lot's daughters are the first ones to merit attention to their position in the family should guide us to scrutinize this place very carefully. Although it is a secondary story in the sequence of events in the book of Genesis, from the perception of the language of the text, this story is important enough to bring to the front the order of birth of Lot's daughters.

Isaac's Birth

Neither Ishmael nor Isaac receives any title. Not "older," "big," or "firstborn." The two of them are mentioned only by their names. While Isaac, the son of Abraham, was the firstborn of Abraham's wife Sarah, Ishmael, although he was Abraham's son, was also Hagar's son. Indirectly, we can say that Ishmael was also Sarah's son. We should note that Sarah was the one who gave her slave to Abraham saying, "...come to my slave, it may be that I will be built by her..." (16:2) Saying so, Sarah expresses her intent to see the baby as her son, from whom she will be "built."

Everything is going smoothly in Abraham's household until the incident described by the text as, "And Sarah saw the son of Hagar the Egyptian,

---

[7] In Hebrew the word *bechor* means firstborn (male). If there were a female firstborn it would be *bechora*. However, there is no firstborn for female. The text does not label the older as *bechora* but as *bechira*. Note the minute but important difference, between the "o" and the "i." Indeed, Onkelos, the Aramaic translator of the Tanach around the end of the second Temple, does not translate *bechira* as "firstborn" but as "big" or "older."

whom she had born to Abraham, *metzahek*[8] (21:9). At this stage, Sarah demands Abraham to expel "…this slave and her son…" (21:10).

Hagar: A *Shifcha*[9] or an *Ama*?

When the text introduces us to Hagar for the first time, it says, "Sarai, Abram's wife bore him no children, and she had a **slave**, an Egyptian whose name was Hagar" (16:1). When Sarah addresses Abram with her request that he "come" to Hagar so she will have a son that "I might be built from her…" (16:2) Sarah calls Hagar "my slave." And the text continues, "And Sarai Abram's wife took Hagar **her slave**…" (16:3). When Sarah complains to Abraham about the fact that Hagar does not give her proper respect after Hagar becomes pregnant, Sarah says, "…I have given my **slave** to your bosom…" (16:5). And Abraham replies, "…your **slave** is in your hand…" (16:6). When the angel addresses Hagar in the wilderness, the angel says, "…Hagar, Sarai's **slave**…" (16:8).

Once Hagar bears Ishmael the title "slave" vanishes from the text: "And Sarah saw the son of Hagar the Egyptian who she had born to Abraham…" (21:9). And when Sarah talks with Abraham, she says, "…Expel this *ama*[10] and her son…" (21:10). Not only is Hagar not a "slave," but she is an *ama*, and not Sarah's *ama*: "…Expel **this** *ama* and her son…" (21:10). Not '**my** *ama*.'

When the Almighty addresses Abraham, "…Let it not be grievous in your sight because of the lad and because of **your** *ama*…" (21:12), we learn that Hagar came out from Sarah's domain and came under Abraham's: "**your** *ama*."

From Abimelech, "…And G-d healed Abimelech and his wife and **his** *amas* and they bore children" (20:17), we see that the *ama* is the

---

[8] The three-letter root word here is TZ-H-K. To "laugh" would be *litzhok*. Isaac, or in Hebrew *Yitzhak*, is the future tense of the verb "to laugh." However, the verb M-TZ-He-K although it comes from "laughing," is not "laughing" or "mocking." It shows up in the entire Tanach only in places where ritual sex or marital relations between husband and wife are involved. See for example Genesis 26:8.

[9] Calling a *shifcha* a "maidservant" or "maid" is wrong. One only needs to go to the place where Jacob describes his wealth to his brother Esau: "And I have oxen and asses, flocks and male slaves and female slaves" (32:6). The word *eved* is "slave," not "servant." A "servant" is *mesharet*. In this verse the text equates a *shifcha* (female slave) to an *eved* (male slave).

[10] The word *ima* in Hebrew is "mother." The word *ama*, which is written with the same letters as *ima* but pronounced differently, represents a woman who bears a child to the man of household instead of the legitimate wife who is childless. In modern times we might call her a surrogate mother. Today, the baby born can be the son of the childless wife genetically, but at that time, the technology was not available. The son born was not the biological son of the legitimate wife.

husband's possession not the wife's. We see the same in, "And Laban went into Jacob's tent, and into Leah's tent, and into the tents of the two *amas*…" (31:33).

From the case of Sarah and Hagar, Rachel and Bilhah, and Leah and Zilpah, we learn that *ama* is a slave who bears a child to the master, and by doing so serves the master's wife as a surrogate womb.

It should be noted that in ancient times the father was thought to be the important component to determine the genetics, and the woman had no contribution in creating the baby. The mother was only a vessel to give birth to the baby who was shaped solely by the father.

And the text continues in regard to Hagar, "And also the son of the *ama* will I make a nation because he is your seed" (21:13). And when Abraham sends Hagar away, the text says, "And Abraham rose up early and took bread and a bottle of water and gave it to Hagar…" (21:14), neither slave nor *ama*. Just Hagar.

We should note another change of language in the text. While Sarah asked Abraham to "expel" Hagar (21:10), Abraham did not "expel" her, but "**sent** her **away**."

Expulsion vs. Sending Away

The difference between "expulsion" and "sending away" is explained in the verse discussing the ending of the term of the slave, "It shall not seem hard to you when you **send him away free** from you…" (Deuteronomy 15:18) "Sending away" means releasing the slave from his slavery, while "expulsion" has a stronger connotation. As evidence we can look at the ten plagues in Egypt. Before the plague of slaying the firstborn the text says, "…Yet will I bring one plague more upon Pharaoh, and upon Egypt; afterwards he will **send you away** from here; when he will **send you away**, he shall certainly **expel** you from here" (Exodus 11:1). Not only will Pharaoh "send them away," but He will also "expel" them. It means that the master can "send away" the slave without expelling him. If we return to Abraham and Hagar (who is not *ama* but Hagar) Abraham "sends her away," but he does not expel her, as Sarah wanted.

We can understand now why the goal of the ten plagues in Egypt was not only to allow the Israelites to come out of Egypt, but to bring Pharaoh to "send them away," or in other words, to release them **legally** from their slavery.

Abraham and Ishmael

When Sarah asks Abraham to expel the *ama*, Abraham responds with, "And the thing was very grievous in Abraham's sight because of his son" (21:11). Ishmael was his son for all purposes. At this point the Almighty intervenes and says to Abraham, "…in all that Sarah has said to you, listen to her voice…" (21:12). And Abraham indeed sends Hagar (not the *ama* as before) and the child (not Ishmael as before). See more in the chapter dealing with the word "child."

This struggle over the inheritance in Abraham's household establishes one important point: the inheritance is dependent on the son being born not only to his father. Ishmael was the firstborn for Abraham. The inheritance is also dependent on the son being born to his mother. Isaac was the firstborn for Sarah. In a society in which men could marry more than one wife it had a lot of significance, as we will see later in the book of Genesis.

Genetically, it was a major revelation at that time. The baby born is not only the contribution of the father, as it was practiced until that time, but also the mother had no less importance than the father. The mother was not just a vessel to bring the child to the world, but her impact on shaping the baby biologically was very important. This detail seems trivial to us today, but in the ancient world this information was not known at all, and in a society in which the man rules as a dictator, and the wife is only his possession, as any other possession, this point was revolutionary.

The reader at this time might wonder if Ishmael, who was the *ama's* son in Sarah's language, shouldn't be the one to inherit, but the fact is that Abraham didn't see Hagar as *ama*. She was his son's mother.

After Sending Hagar Away

After Hagar was sent away the text continues with two stories, first, Abimelech's approach to Abraham to have a treaty between them, and second, the binding of Isaac. Here one can ask the question: what is the connection between the events described immediately before (the birth of Isaac and the sending away of Ishmael and his mother)?

The content of Abimelech's approach might establish the connection. Abimelech is quoted as saying to Abraham, "…swear to me here by G-d that you will not deal falsely with me, **nor with my son, nor with my grandson**, but according to the kindness that I have done to you, you shall do to me…" (21:23). After Abraham establishes that the next generation to inherit from him is Isaac, not Ishmael, Abimelech asks to include "his son and grandson" in the treaty with Abraham.

Even the binding of Isaac on the altar, as important as it was, is connected to the idea of establishing the inheritance: "…Take now your son, **your only son**, whom you love, Isaac…" (22:2), and at the end of the event, after Abraham passed the test, the angel says to Abraham, "…for because you have done this thing, and have not withheld your son, your only son…" (22:16).

As a secondary dimension to the binding we learn from the language of the text that not only is Isaac indeed Abraham's son, but by his being the son of Abraham **and** Sarah, he is considered "the **only** son" of Abraham.

The Letter From Aram

At this point, the text moves to what seems at first glance a minor issue, and it seems as if it is not connected to the sequence of events: the information that Abraham receives from Aram dealing with the birth of sons to Milcah, Nahor's wife.

SCAN Rule: Out-of-sequence information is only out-of-sequence to the reader. To the one who gives the statement it is in sequence, and the information is positioned at the right place. When the reader/listener understands the statement in full, the out-of-sequence information becomes in-sequence.

Background information: knowing that every statement is "edited," the reader/listener should not read the statement with the assumption that each activity mentioned in the statement follows immediately after the previous activity. For example, if a person says, "I got up, took a shower, and got dressed," one is **not** allowed to say that the person took a shower right after he/she got up, or that the person got dressed right after he/she took the shower. Between each two activities might be 5 minutes, 10 minutes, or even several hours. And the statement is still true. "I got up at 6. Took a shower at 8 and got dressed at 10."

What is the reason that brought the text to include this information **at this exact place**?

SCAN rule: The first sentence in an open statement is the most important sentence.

Background information: In many "open statements" we find that the first sentence includes the **reason** for the events that follow. The first sentence does not deal with the event itself, but with the **reason** for the event.

The first sentence in this case is: "And it came to pass after these things that it was told to Abraham saying, behold, Milcah, she also has born sons to your brother Nahor" (22:20).

The addition "also" comes to equate Sarah who bore a son to Abraham, to Milcah who bore sons to Nahor. The text reminds us that Nahor is Abraham's brother.[11]

We should note that the text positioned Milcah in the sentence before Nahor ("...Milcah, she has also born sons to your brother Nahor"), an order of listing which comes to indicate her importance. And indeed, later on when Rebecca introduces herself to Abraham's slave she is quoted as saying: "I am the daughter of Bethuel the son of Milcah whom she bore to Nahor" (Genesis 24:24). Rebecca does not say, "I am the daughter of Bethuel the son of Nahor." Rebecca relates herself to her father, not to her mother, but for the preceding generation, she relates herself first to Milcah and only then to Nahor. We should remember that Milcah, as Sarah, was the daughter of Haran, the firstborn son, even though he is listed at the end of the sentence. It is quite likely that Nahor is the youngest son, and

---

[11] The connection "also" might support Rashi's commentary to the verse: "And Abram and Nahor took wives, the name of Abram's wife was Sarai, and the name of Nahor's wife was Milcah the daughter of Haran, the father of Milcah and the father of Iscah." (11:29). Rashi says, "Iscah is Sarah..."

therefore, Milcah, by being the daughter of the firstborn is more important than her husband, the youngest son of Terah.

Now we can understand the "letter from Aram" Abraham received telling him of the birth of the sons of Milcah to Nahor. The text comes to tell us that it was established not only in Abraham's family that the inheritance was based upon the firstborn to the father **and** the mother **on an equal basis**, but also in Abraham's brother Nahor's family.

If we consider the first sentence in the "letter" as the reason for (or the significance of) what follows, then the second sentence comes to include the information itself: "Huz his firstborn and Buz his brother and Kemuel the father of Aram" (22:21).

Language-wise, Huz, the firstborn of Nahor is the first one in the book of Genesis, and thus the Tanach, to merit the title "firstborn." Japheth, Noah's son, is the "big" one. But Huz, the son of both Milcah and Nahor, is the **firstborn** of Nahor.

Jacob and Esau

There are two births in the book of Genesis in which the text tells us that the mother got pregnant but the text does not tell us that the mother delivered or gave birth. The first is the birth of Jacob and Esau, and the second is the birth of Peretz and Zerah, Judah's sons from Tamar.

In the birth of Esau and Jacob the text says, "...and Rebecca his wife conceived" (25:21). Later, the text says, "And when her days to be delivered were fulfilled, behold, there were twins in her womb" (25:24). But when the time of the actual birth came, the text says, "And **the first** came out red all over like a hairy garment, and they called him Esau. And after that his brother came out..." (25:25-26).

We should note that for the first time in the Tanach, the text attributes to Esau the title "the first." But, as in the case of Noah's son Shem, the text does not give Jacob the title "the second."

As with Esau and Jacob, so is the case with the birth of Peretz and Zerah to Tamar who got pregnant by Judah. The text informs us of the pregnancy by saying "and she conceived by him" (38:18). When the actual time of birth came, the text says,

> And it came to pass when she labored that one put out his hand, and the midwife took and bound upon his hand a scarlet thread saying this came out first. And it came to pass as he drew back his hand, and behold, his brother came out, and she said, what a breach you have made for yourself. Therefore he named his name Peretz. (38:27-30)

The root *p-r-tz* means "breach" in Hebrew.

The text does not use the title "the first," but quotes the midwife, saying, "...this came out **first**." The text does not use the title "the second," but the scarlet thread on his hand should remind us of the title "the second." Note that "scarlet thread" in Hebrew is *sh-a-ni*, while "second" is *sh-e-ni*, the same letters with different pronunciation.

The fact that these are the only two instances in Genesis that the text does not relate to the arrival of the children by "giving birth" or "bearing" but prefers to use instead the verb "came out" should bring us to ask if it is because Jacob is the father of the nation, and Peretz is the father of the future kingdom of Judah, that the text avoids using the word "gave birth." Does the text see the activity of "giving birth" as demeaning for the father of the nation (Jacob) and the father of the kingdom (Peretz)?

Jacob and Esau – The Birthright

The fact that Esau was "the first" should have ended the discussion in the issue of the birthright of the firstborn. However, the text reports to us an incident that opened the issue anew. When Esau came from the field and he was "famished"[12] (25:29), Esau asks Jacob to, "Feed me with this red pottage[13]..." (30). Jacob in response says, "...sell me this day your birthright" (31). Esau does not resist and he says, "...I am about to die and what profit shall this birthright do to me?" (32). The sale is done in exchange for "bread and pottage of lentils" (34). Moreover, not only did

---

[12] Famished: the word in Hebrew is *a'ayef* and in Modern Hebrew it means to be "tired." Checking the entire Tanach it comes across to mean "dehydrated" – well beyond "thirsty."
[13] It is more accurately translated as "**Pour** into me this red, red food..."

Esau sell his birthright, but the text also tells us, "... Esau despised the birthright" (34).

Again, language-wise, we should note that the language of the text attributes the title "the first" to Esau but does not attribute the title "the second" to Jacob. We should also note that the text does not attribute the title "firstborn" to Esau at the time he was born. The first time the word "birthright" entered the text is in the quote of the conversation between the brothers, a quote of what Jacob said when he initiated the sale of the birthright.

Isaac's Blessing of Jacob

When the text moves on to discuss the receiving of the blessing by Jacob while he pretends to be Esau, the text uses only the titles the "big" (*gadol*) for Esau and the "little" (*katan*) for Jacob. The text avoids taking sides linguistically regarding who the "firstborn" is, whether it is Esau by being the first to be born, or, if the sale is legitimate, then it is Jacob, even though he is not the "first."

The story starts with, "...he called Esau his big son..." (27:1). At this stage, the linguistic lens tells us that Isaac had to know of the sale of the birthright. Esau is not the "first born" but the "big" one. It is quite unlikely that Jacob kept the sale of the birthright by Esau a secret. Moreover, the text tells us that Esau "despised the birthright" (25:34). If Esau despised the birthright, he couldn't have done it secretly. On the contrary, Esau was proud that he got something concrete in exchange for an abstract birthright.

And the description continues, "And Rebecca heard when Isaac spoke to his son..." (27:5), and we should note that the title "big" vanishes from the text. Besides Rebecca not accepting that Esau was the "firstborn," she also didn't even accept that he was the "big" one. He didn't behave as one who merited such an acknowledgement.

We should also note that at this stage Esau is not even "her" son but "his" son.

And the story continues, "And Rebecca spoke to Jacob her son..." (27:6), and again we don't see the title "younger" or "little."

The titles "big" and "little" come into play only when both Esau and Jacob are mentioned in one sentence. Rebecca takes something from Esau and gives it to Jacob, "And Rebecca took the best garments of her big son Esau, which were with her in the house, and put them on Jacob her little son" (27:15). And immediately the text moves on to say, "And she gave the savory food and the bread, which she had prepared, to the hands of her son Jacob" (17).

The text returns to use the titles "big" and "little" when the two are mentioned in one sentence, "And these words of Esau her big son were told to Rebecca, and she sent and called Jacob her little son…" (27:42).

To sum it up, if the two, Jacob and Esau, are not mentioned in the same sentence, when each is acting on his own, then the language of the text does not use the titles "big" and "little," and quite likely it has no significance to the text.

Laban's Daughters

Rachel is the first daughter to enter the text content-wise by being the shepherdess arriving at the well with her father's herd. However, when the text mentions Rachel and Leah together in one sentence, it says, "And Laban had two daughters, the name of the big one was Leah, and the name of the little one was Rachel" (29:16).

When Jacob complains to Laban, "…what is this that you have done to me? Did not I serve with you for Rachel? Why then have you deceived me?" (29:25). Laban replies, "…It must not be so done in our place to give the **younger** before the **elder**" (29:26).

Note that the text, when "socially introducing" the two daughters, used the titles "big" and "little." However, now the text quotes Laban using the titles "younger" and "elder."

We should remember that the word "firstborn" showed up for the first time in the text in the "letter" Abraham received telling him of the birth of sons to his brother Nahor with his wife Milcah. And the concept of "birthright" shows up in a quote of a conversation between the twins Jacob and Esau. We should also remember that the words "elder" and "younger" show up in the text in the conversation between two sisters, Lot's daughters.

Should we understand that we might be facing two different languages? One is the language of the text conveying the story, and a second language, the language of the text bringing us the quotations? Quotations of a conversation between Lot's two daughters, or between two brothers, Jacob and Esau, or in the reply of Laban? Is it possible that the words "firstborn female" (*bechira*) and "birthright" (*bechora*) are actually two Aramaic words?

We should also note that later on in the Tanach the text relates to King Saul's two daughters, "...and the names of his two daughters were these: the name of the elder (*bechira*) Merab, and the name of the younger (*ketanah*) Michal" (1 Samuel 14:49). The text still uses the title *bechira* for the older one, but uses the title *ketanah* ("little"), not *tzeira* ("young") as in Genesis 29:26.

Jacob's Sons

Leah is the first one to give birth. The text uses the title "the first" for Esau, but then the picture gets blurry when it comes to inform us of the birth of Jacob's sons.

The text starts, "And Leah conceived and bore a son and she called his name Reuben..." (Genesis 29:32). The text does not use the title *bechor* (firstborn) or "the first." And the text continues with same formula in regard to three more sons. "And she conceived again and bore a son..." (33) for Simeon, for Levi (34) and for Judah (35). For these four the text does not attribute any number telling us their position in the order of birth. At this stage, the text says, "...and she ceased bearing" (35).

At this stage, Rachel gives her slave Bilhah to Jacob and she delivers Dan who does not get any number. The same formula the text used for the first four sons from Leah is used here as well. "And Bilhah conceived and bore Jacob a son" (30:5). When Bilhah delivers her second son, Naftali, the text changes its course and says, "And Bilhah Leah's slave conceived again and she bore Jacob a **second** son" (30:7). The text couldn't have said for the first son Bilhah had, "...and she bore Jacob a first son," since for Jacob, Reuben was the first. But the text could easily have given up on the title "second" as it did for Simeon. But the text has no problem to attribute Naftali the title "**second** son."

At this stage, Leah gives her slave Zilpah to Jacob and she delivers Gad: "And Zilpah Leah's slave bore Jacob a son" (30:10), and when she delivers Asher: "And Zilpah Leah's slave bore Jacob a **second** son" (30:12). Again, we see the title "second" for Zilpah's second son.

Up to this point in Genesis, the text does not attribute the title "the second" to Shem, Noah's second son, or to Jacob, Isaac's second son. Instead, the text "runs away" by using the formula "and then his brother came out." But here, when we encounter the sons of the slaves the text does not hesitate to use the title "the second" for each of the two slaves' sons.

The Title "the Second"

In Genesis we find the title "the second" again, and here for slaves. When Jacob prepares the gifts to please his brother Esau, "And he commanded the first saying when Esau my brother meets you..." (32:18). "And so commanded he the **second**, and the third..." (32:20).

We find the title "the second" also for women. In Genesis: "And Lemech took for himself two wives, the name of one was Adah, and the name of the **second** Zillah" (4:19). In other books, in regard to the Hebrew midwives in Egypt: "...and the name of one was Shiphrah and the name of the **second** Puah" (Exodus 1:15). For Elkanah, Samuel's father, and his two wives: "And he had two wives, the name of one was Hannah, and the name of the **second** was Peninna..." (1 Samuel 1:2). And for Job's daughters: "And he called the name of **one** Jemima, and the name of the **second** Keziah and the name of **third** Keren Happuch" (Job 42:14). And for Elimelech's sons who married Moabite women described in the book of Ruth: "...the name of one was Orpah and the name of the **second** was Ruth..." (Ruth 1:4).

We also find the title "the second" in the book of Ecclesiastes, and this time for a child: 'I saw all the living who walk under the sun, with the **second** child that shall stand up in his stead" (4:15).

Up to the birth of the sons of Bilhah and Zilpah, we find the title "the second" for women, slaves, and a child. The second time that the title "the second" appears for an individual not from these three categories is in Numbers: "And there remained two of the men in the camp, the name of one was Eldad, and the name of the **second** was Medad, and the spirit rested upon them…" (Numbers 11:26), and Joshua's response: "My Lord Moses arrest them" (28). Not only does Joshua perceive the prophecy of the two negatively, but we can see this negative attitude also in the language of the text by the use of the title "the second."

We should note that the word "second" entered the language of the text again in the book of Numbers. This time it is in regard to the tribe of Reuben, "All who were counted in the camp of Reuben were a hundred thousand and fifty one thousand and four hundred and fifty, throughout their armies, and they shall journey **second**" (Numbers 2:16).

The Title "the Second" for Sons

In regard to Samuel's sons the text says, "And the name of his firstborn was Joel and the name of **next** to him[14] Abijah…" (1 Samuel 8:2).

Here, the text finds a way to avoid using the word "the second," not by using the formula "his brother," as in "the name of his firstborn was Joel and name of his brother Abijah," as we saw with the birth of Jacob after Esau. Instead, the text goes out of its way to produce a substitute title to "the second" by using *mishnehu,* translated as "the next."

We find the same in regard to David's older brothers: "And the three eldest sons of Jesse went and followed Saul to the battle, and the names of his three sons who went to the battle were Eliab the firstborn, and next to him Abinadab, and the third Shammah" (1 Samuel 17:13). The same applies to David's sons:

> …and his **firstborn** was Amnon of Ahinoam the Jezreelitess. And **next to him** Kileab of Abigail the wife of Nabal the Carmelite, and

---

[14] In the Hebrew the text does not say *sheni* ("second") but uses a different form *mishnehu,* translated as "next to him." The word *mishnehu* is divided into two components. The first is *mishneh*, which is used for the **two** loaves of bread on the table in the Tabernacle. It comes from the same root word as *sheni* ("second") but it is not "second." The "u" at the end stands for the pronoun "his." Therefore, "his *mishneh*" puts the possession with the first son, not the father. In Modern Hebrew the word *mishneh* means the second in command, or the one to take over once the head is incapable of performing the duty.

the **third** Absalom the son of Maachah the daughter of Talmai king of Geshur. And the **fourth** Adonijah the son of Haggith, and the **fifth** Shephatiah the son of Abital. And the **sixth** Ithream by Eglah David's wife…. (2 Samuel 3:2-5)

In the three above-mentioned places the text changed its language when talking about "the second" who merits here a new title "next to him." The text has no issue with the title the third, or even the sixth (David's son).

Language-wise, we should note that if a text avoids using a certain word, over a long period of time, as in our case, where the text avoided using the title "the second," for one reason or another, we don't know the reason. However, when the text replaces a certain word with another, as in our case – "**next** to him" instead of "the second" – we should consider it as **linguistic evidence** that the text in fact does its best to avoid the title "the second." In other words, the level of reliability of a conclusion is a lot higher when the text goes by commission (changing a word) versus by omission (not using a certain word).

In later books of the Tanach the language changes back again. In the first book of Chronicles when talking about Jesse's sons the text says, "And Jesse fathered his firstborn Eliab and Abinadab the **second** and Shima the **third** Netanel the **fourth**, Radi the **fifth**, Otzem the **sixth**, and David the **seventh**" (1 Chronicles 2:13-15). And so with David's sons, "And these were the sons of David who were born to him in Hebron: Amnon the **firstborn** of Ahinoam the Jezreelitess, the **second** Daniel of Abigail the Carmelitess…" (1 Chronicles 3:1-3).

In summary, starting with Genesis and ending with Samuel 2, we find that the text has an issue with the title "the second." Quite likely, it was a social problem in attributing this title to anyone. Later on, this problem vanishes and doesn't exist. We see it in the book of Chronicles, which maintains linguistic unity throughout. Only the first merits a special title "firstborn."

Back to the Sons of Jacob and Leah

After the birth of the slaves' sons, Leah "hires" Jacob from Rachel for one night in exchange for her son Reuben's mandrakes. And Leah resumes giving birth. And now we face an interesting change in language. While Leah's first four sons did not get a number to indicate their place in the birth order, in the birth of the two additional sons, Issachar and Zebulun, the text brings us their number in the order of birth. Issachar is "fifth" (30:17) and Zebulun is "sixth" (30:19).

We know that the text avoids using the title "the second" for the order of birth when talking about high-ranking people, like Noah's son Shem and Jacob. Now we see that the text avoids not only the title "the second" but also the title "the third" and "the fourth."

From David's sons, mentioned later in the Tanach, we know that there is no problem in using the title "the third" or "fourth" or any other number. The problem focuses only on "the second." Therefore, by the text returning to number the sons only from the fifth son, we can conclude that the text is "running away" from using "the third" and "the fourth."

SCAN Rule: The location in the "open statement," or in the sentence, is connected to the change of language.

Background information: The analyst cannot remove himself/herself from the statement when trying to explain the change of language. The statement itself needs to explain the change of language. Therefore, the location in the statement, where the change of language occurred, is the most important point to explain the change of language.

Since this "running away" in the report of the birth of Leah's sons ends after the birth of the fourth, Judah, we should conclude that Judah is the one who brings this linguistic "running away" to its end. We should conclude that the language of the text goes out of its way not only in regard to "the second," but also when dealing with Judah, the language of the text does not want to disrespect him and therefore does not use even the title "the fourth."

We should note here that this bias of the text towards Judah fits well with the fact that the text compares the birth of Esau and Jacob to the birth of Peretz and Zerah, Judah's sons from Tamar. Since Peretz is the head of the line that will produce a son who will ascend to the throne, we can understand why the text quotes the midwife as saying "this one came out **first.**" Although the text does not attribute the title "the second" to Zerah, with a linguistic hint (the "scarlet thread" on his hand, *shani*, vs. *sheni*, "second"), the text gets close to doing so. Don't forget that Zerah didn't play any role in the tribe of Judah, concerning the kingdom, later on.

Rachel, Jacob's wife

Between the two sisters who married Jacob, Leah and Rachel, Rachel is the one who received the title of Jacob's "wife." We find it for the first time when Jacob tells Laban, "Give me **my wife** for my days are fulfilled..." (Genesis 29:21).

When Judah delivers a speech in front of Joseph, a speech that brought Joseph to reveal himself to his brothers, Judah quotes his father as saying to his sons, "You know that **my wife** bore me two sons" (44:27). When the text counts "all the souls of the house of Jacob..." (46:27), it says, "The sons of Rachel, **Jacob's wife**..." (46:19). In contrast to Rachel, Leah is described only as "These are the sons of Leah whom she bore to Jacob in Padan Aram..." (46:15). And Leah does not get the title "Jacob's wife." When Jacob tells his sons before his death of his wish to be buried in the Cave of the Patriarchs, the text quotes him saying, "There they buried Abraham and Sarah his wife; there they buried Isaac and Rebecca his wife, and there I buried Leah." (49:31). Again, no mention of the title "wife."

Joseph, Rachel's Son

Joseph appears for the first time in the sequence of events in,

> And G-d remembered Rachel, and G-d listened to her, and opened her womb. And she conceived and bore a son, and said G-d has taken away my reproach. And she called him Joseph and said the Lord shall add to me another son. (30:22-24)

We should note two points in this description. First, both Leah and Rachel get the same description "...and opened her womb." The other two foremothers do not get such description. For Sarah the text says, "And the Lord visited Sarah as he had said and the Lord did to Sarah as he had spoken. Sarah conceived and bore Abraham a son..." (21:1-2). For Rebecca the text says, "...and the Lord granted his prayer and Rebecca his wife conceived" (25:21). For Leah and Rachel, the text refers to the woman's womb.

Another point to consider. Joseph, the first son of Rachel does not receive any title, neither "firstborn" nor "first." No different from the way the text related to Reuben, Leah's first son.

Esau's Sons

After the birth of Joseph and the return of Jacob to Canaan with his twelve sons, the text informs us of Isaac's death, and his burial by his two sons Esau and Jacob. The listing of Esau before Jacob indicates that Jacob indeed accepted the fact that Esau was the first to be born.

At this stage, the text moves on to tell us of Esau's *toldot* from his three wives (36:1). Among all of the sons there is no title "first," "firstborn," or "second." Language-wise, the linguistic lens that opened after the birth of Ishmael in the description of Abraham's family is now closed. From the perspective of the text, there is no significance to these births and therefore there is no need to focus on them, at least from the point of view of the order of birth.

Only later, when the text moves to count the "Chiefs of the sons of Esau..." (36:15), does the text give Eliphaz the title "firstborn" without giving any title to the others. Does the fact that the text attributed to Eliphaz the title "firstborn" have anything to do with the text saying earlier, "And Timna was concubine to Eliphaz Esau's son, and she bore to Eliphaz **Amalek**..." (36:12)? This is the same Amalek that attacked the Israelites in the desert.

Joseph, Jacob and Rachel's Firstborn

The text says, "These are the *toldot* of Jacob, Joseph..." (Genesis 37:2). By Joseph being the firstborn to his mother, his father's wife, Joseph is the "firstborn," no different at all from Isaac who was born to Abraham from his wife Sarah and no different from Huz, Nahor's first born from his wife Milcah.

The text continues in establishing Joseph with his rights as the firstborn: "...He was shepherding his brothers with the sheep..." (37:2). Joseph is also the one who received from his father "...a coat with long stripes" (37:3).

A "coat with stripes" is mentioned in the Tanach one other time, in the story of Amnon and Tamar: "And she had a coat with stripes, for with such were dressed the king's daughters who were virgins" (2 Samuel 13:18). The "coat with stripes" testifies that Joseph was groomed for the throne. It is true that the text tells us that Joseph received such a coat because, "And Israel loved Joseph more than all his sons because he was the son of his old age..." (37:3), a sentence which might give the reader the idea that Joseph received "the coat with stripes" only because of unjustified fatherly preference, but in the background we have Joseph's full right to the family's inheritance after his father's death. And Jacob indeed related to Joseph in such a way. Later on, the text tells us that Jacob addressed Joseph, telling him, "...Are not your brothers shepherding in Shechem? Come, and I will send you to them. And he said to him, here I am. And he said to him, go please and see your brothers' well-being and the sheep's well-being, and bring word back to me" (37:13-14). Joseph who was "shepherding his brothers with the sheep, is sent by his father to see about his brothers' and the sheep's well-being, or, in other words, to supervise them and to report to Jacob.

After the father and the son are united in Egypt, Joseph brings his two sons to Jacob to be blessed. And Jacob tells Joseph, "And your two sons, Ephraim and Menashe, who were born to you in the land of Egypt before I came to you to Egypt are mine; as Reuben and Simeon they shall be mine" (48:5). Joseph gets twice what his brothers get. Later on, Jacob tells Joseph, "And I have given you one portion above your brothers, which I took from the hand of the Amorite with my sword and with my bow" (48:22).

From the perspective of rights and benefits, Joseph receives what is due to a firstborn, the son of both the father and the mother who is the father's wife (Rachel). There is one thing Joseph does not receive in the **language** of the text: he does not receive the title "firstborn." When Jacob blesses his sons before his death, he tells Reuben, "Reuben my firstborn, my might, and the beginning of my strength..." (49:3). It is true that Reuben is Jacob's firstborn as he was the first one to be born to Jacob, but he is only Jacob's firstborn ("**my** firstborn"). From the "family law" point of view he is not the firstborn of the family.

On the other hand, when he blessed Joseph, Jacob said, "...they shall be on the head of Joseph, and his brothers' laurel and crown of the head" (49:26). Indeed, he didn't receive the title "firstborn," but he received the title "crown of the head" and "laurel." He is head of the brothers, not only because he is the ruler of Egypt, but also because he is the son of both Jacob and Rachel.

The book of Chronicles says,

> The sons of Reuben, Israel's firstborn, for he was the firstborn, but since he defiled his father's bed, his birthright was given to the sons of Joseph the son of Israel, so that the genealogy is not to be considered after the birthright. For Judah prevailed above his brothers and from him came the chief ruler, but the birthright belonged to Joseph. (1 Chronicles 5:1-2)

Chronicles attributes the transfer of the birthright from Reuben to Joseph to the incident of Reuben and Bilhah. But **language**-wise and **content**-wise, we see that Jacob related to Joseph as his firstborn from the beginning. From a practical point of view he was the firstborn, although not by language.

Now we can ask the question: why does the language of the text avoid labeling Joseph as "firstborn" although by the content he is so? Why is there a gap between the **content** and the **language** of the text?

Menashe and Ephraim – Comparison

The text informs us of the birth of Joseph's sons in Egypt:

> And Joseph called the name of the firstborn Menashe, for G-d, he said, has made me forget all my toil, and all my father's household. And the name of the second he called Ephraim, for G-d has caused me to be fruitful in the land of my affliction. (41:51-52)

Joseph's two sons are the only men in the book of Genesis who get a straightforward description with regard to the order of birth. Menashe is the "firstborn" and Ephraim is the "second." We already saw that the title "the second" indicates some disrespect by the text, that only women, slaves, and children received. Therefore we should ask why Ephraim gets such disrespect in the language of the text.

When Joseph brings his two sons for them to get a blessing from his father, the text says, "And Israel stretched out his right hand, and laid it upon Ephraim's head, who was the younger, and his left hand on Menashe's head, changing his hands, for Menashe is the firstborn" (48:14).

Jacob explained himself: "...he also shall become a people, and he also shall be great, but truly his little brother shall be greater than he, and his seed shall become a multitude of nations" (48:19).

The question now gets stronger: why does the linguistic lens attribute to Ephraim the title "the second," which only women, slaves and children receive? Why does the linguistic lens attribute to Ephraim a title ("the second") used for two prophets who prophesy in the camp in the desert without any connection to the central leadership (Moses' leadership)? Why does Ephraim merit such linguistic disrespect?

Back to Joseph's Sons

Why does the text call Ephraim "the **younger** son" while Jacob calls him "his **little** brother"?

Language-wise, there are three places in Genesis that the title "younger" (either male or female) appears. One, in the story of Lot's daughters: "the elder" and "the younger," two, in the story of Rachel and Leah: "...It must not be done in our place to give the younger before the elder" (29:26), and three, in the story of Menashe and Ephraim. What is the common denominator of these three stories?

Onkelos translates these words as follows:

English	Biblical Hebrew	Aramaic
big (masculine)	gadol	rabba
big (feminine)	gedolah	rabta
little (masculine)	katan	zeira
little (feminine)	ketana	ze'erta
firstborn (masculine)	bechor	buchra

firstborn (feminine)	*bechira*	*rabta*
young (masculine)	*tzair*	*zeira*
young (feminine)	*tzeira*	*ze'erta*

We should note in Onkelos' translation two points: First, Onkelos distinguishes between *bechor* (firstborn male) and *gadol*, while he does not distinguish between *bechira* and *gedola*. Second, we can see how the word *tzair* in Hebrew is replaced with *zeir* in Aramaic. We are facing just one consonant change, the first letter from "tz" to "z."

It is difficult to understand why Onkelos does not distinguish between *tzair* (or *tzeira*) and *katan* (or *ketana*). This lack of distinction would be justified only if in Aramaic there are no synonyms for *tzair* or *katan*. But the likelihood that there are no synonyms for these two words is very slim. In many languages there are synonyms for these words.

The linguistic closeness along with the auditory closeness between *tzair* and *tzeira* in Hebrew and *zeira* and *ze'erta* in Aramaic, should bring us to ask if the use of *tzair* and *tzeira* in the three above-mentioned cases, Lot's daughters, Laban's daughters, and Joseph talking to his father Jacob in Egypt, are use of the Aramaic language, or a dialect close to it.

Moses' Sons

The text introduces us to Moses' son, "and she bore him a son, and he called his name Gershom; for he said, I have been an alien in a foreign country" (Exodus 2:22).

Later on, in Exodus, when Jethro, Moses' father-in-law, comes to visit Moses in the desert, the text says,

> And her two sons; and the name of **one** was Gershom, for he said I have been an alien in a foreign country. And the name of **one** was Eliezer, for the G-d of my father was my help and saved me from the sword of pharaoh. (Exodus 18:3-4)

Moses' two sons who are introduced together merit a unique "social introduction" in the Tanach. After our discussion of the title "the second" (to connote some disrespect) we can understand why the text avoided using the title "the second" for Eliezer. But this is the only place in the

Tanach in which both sons receive the title "one." Not only does Gershom not get the title "firstborn," but he also doesn't get the title "the first." The text could have used the familiar formula "…and his brother Eliezer," but it even avoided using "his brother" in relation to Gershom. How come? Were they not brothers, these two sons of Moses?

Moreover, we could understand why the first would be named Eliezer and the second Gershom, not the order we find in the text. The first was born close to Moses' rescue from the sword of Pharaoh, and it would have been understood if Moses were under the influence of his rescue at the time his son Gershom was born. But once his exile in Midian lengthened, we could understand if the experience of living in a long exile would bring him to name his second son Gershom. Why does Gershom's name relate to Moses' exile, while the name of Eliezer, the son who was born after Gershom, and labeled "the one" as well, relates to Moses' rescue?

Plus, since Moses was in exile in Midian, the name "Gershom" should be Gerpo, not Gershom.[15] Gershom was born in Midian, during Moses' exile from Egypt. Moses' point of view should be that he is a "foreigner" in Midian, not that he lives far from his exile.

Lot's Daughters

Since Lot's daughters "opened up the linguistic lens" in regard to the order of birth in the family (elder and younger) it should bring us to scrutinize the language in that story very carefully. Before we would be able to do so, we need to go on a long detour dealing with two important issues in Biblical language. First, Biblical language has two different "withs," and second, the text uses three different verbs for a sexual relationship.

Linguistic Journey – the Word "With" in Biblical Hebrew

Introduction

When a person wants to describe to us a certain activity the person and another person did in the past, the person has several ways to describe that activity. First, the person needs to "introduce" the other person in the language. Once the person already did the "social introduction," the person has the following ways (among others) to describe it:

---

[15] *Gershom* is the combination of two words *ger* ("foreigner") and *sham* ("there"). *Po* in Hebrew means "here."

We went…
We went together
My wife and I went…
I went with my wife…
I went with the wife…

These alternatives, though they describe the same activity, come to indicate a difference in the relationship between the two at the time of the activity.

The first: "we went…" – This is the best way to describe it, as it is the shortest way. The shortest way to describe something is the best way. And pronouns are the shortest way.

The second: "we went **together**…" – Here, the person is not going the shortest way, as the pronoun "we" already indicates that the two were together. In most cases, the addition of the word "together" comes to compare this activity to other instances in which this activity took place, but it was not together. The person comes to emphasize the togetherness in comparison to other times. In short, the word "together" indicates "unique," or "unusual."

The third: "my wife and I" – Even though they were together, they were not **that** together. The separation in the sentence between "my wife" and the pronoun "I" might reflect distance in the past between the two. It might be that the person giving the statement didn't want to go with his wife. Or the wife didn't want to go with him.

The fourth: "I went with my wife" – One should note the distance in the sentence between "I" at the beginning and "wife" at the end. The word "with" also indicates "distance" between the two. It might be that one of them was not with the other all the time. For example, in "I watched TV with my wife," in most cases we find that the two of them were sitting in front of the TV, but one of them wasn't watching. Note that the structure of the sentence does not tell us which one wasn't watching. Or, "I went shopping with my wife." In most cases one of them was away from the other while shopping.

The fifth: "I went with the wife." – The change from the possessive pronoun "my" to "the" in regard to the wife indicates strongly the negative emotions of the person towards "the wife" at that time.

In short, the word "with" indicates distance. However, it does not mean that there was a conflict between the two at the time. It is just that there was no "togetherness" at the time of the activity.

The Word "With" in the Tanach

In Biblical language we find two words used for the word "with." One is *im* and one is *et*. In spite of the fact that there is a tendency to consider these two prepositions identical in meaning, still we find that Biblical language is very strict in using these two words with a very distinct meaning for each, and it corresponds to the sequence of events, as they are described in the sentence. Generally speaking, we can see that the word *im* comes to indicate an intimate closeness between two people, while the word *et* comes to indicate some difficulty in the relationship between the two.

To Walk[16] With

As an example, there is a well-known story with Balaam mentioned in the book of Numbers. Balak, the king of Moab, sent his ministers to enlist the prophet Balaam to curse the Israelites who were at his border. Balaam consults the Almighty who orders him, "You shall not go with (*im*) them..." (Numbers 22:12). After Balak sent another delegation with higher-ranking ministers, the Almighty tells Balaam, "If the men come to call you, rise up, and go with (*et*) them..." (22:20). The text brings us Balaam's response: "And Balaam rose up in the morning and saddled his ass and went with (*im*) the ministers of Moab" (22:21). And the text continues, "And G-d was angry that he went..." (22:22). Why the divine anger? Is it because of one small difference between *im* and *et*?

We see the same in two other examples in the text. The first is in regard to Lot, Abraham's nephew: "And Abram went as the Lord had spoken to him and Lot went with (*et*) him..." (Genesis 12:4). One can ask, were there

---

[16] In Hebrew the verb H-L-KH literally means "to walk;" however, most Biblical translations alternate according to context between "to walk" and "to go." There is no word "to go" in Hebrew, and therefore, one cannot say, "I went in my car;" one can only say, "I drove in my car," or "I rode in my car." In this book we usually do not change the traditional translation when it uses "to go."

already signals that the relationship between Abraham and Lot was not that good? By the language of the text it seems so. The second example is with Jethro, Moses' father-in-law: "And Moses said to Hobab, the son of Reuel the Midianite, Moses' father-in-law, we are journeying to the place about which the Lord said I will give it to you, come with (*et*) us..." (Numbers 10:29).

On the other hand, when Rebecca's family asks her if she would like to marry Abraham's son, the text quotes them as saying, "...will you go with (*im*) this man..." (Genesis 24:58).

We find another preposition used with the activity of walking, a word indicating unequal relationship: "to walk after" (literally) or "to follow." For example, "And Rebecca arose, and her maids, and they rode upon the camels, and walked after the man..." (24:61). "And Moses rose up and went to Dathan and Abiram and the elders of Israel walked after him" (Numbers 16:25). And so for the connection with the Almighty, "You shall not go **after** other gods..." (Deuteronomy 6:14), and "You shall walk **after** the Lord your G-d and fear him..." (Deuteronomy 13:5).

To Speak With

For example, the verb "to speak with (*im*):"

- "And they said to Moses, speak with (*im*) us and we will hear; but let not G-d speak with (*im*) us, lest we die" (Exodus 20:16)
- "...this stone shall be witness to us; for it has heard all the words of the Lord which he spoke with (*im*) us" (Joshua 24:27)
- "Then said Eliakim the son of Hilkiah, and Shebna, and Joah, to Rabshakeh, speak, please to your slaves in the Aramean language; for we understand it; and speak not with (*im*) us in the language of Judah in the hearing of the people who are on the wall" (2 Kings 18:26)
- "And he strove with an angel and prevailed; he wept, and made supplication to him; he found him in Beth-El, and there he spoke with (*im*) us" (Hosea 12:5)

We find in the Tanach "to speak with (*et*)..." in the story of Joseph and his brothers: "And Joseph saw his brothers and he recognized them but made himself strange to them, and spoke roughly with (*et*) them..." (Genesis

42:7). When the brothers report to their father what happened to them in Egypt, "The man who is the lord of the land spoke roughly with (*et*) us..." (42:30). In both instances we find the word "roughly" along with *et*.

To Sit With

When Rebecca sends Jacob to Haran, to prevent Esau from killing him, she says, "And sit[17] with (*im*) him a few days until your brother's fury turns away" (Genesis 27:44). When Laban welcomes Jacob, the text quotes Laban saying, "...it is better I give her to you, than I give her to another man. Sit with (*im*) me" (29:19).

On the other hand, when Jacob's sons speak with Shechem and his father Hamor after Shechem abducted Dinah, Jacob's daughter, the text quotes them, "Then we will give our daughters to you, and we will take your daughters for us, and we will sit with (*et*) you, and we will become one people" (34:16). From their language one can understand that they are not talking of full and complete unity. The same applies to Shechem and Hamor, when they speak to the people of their city, they say, "Only thus the men will consent to sit with (*et*) us to be one people..." (34:22), and "Shall not their cattle and their wealth and every beast of theirs be ours? Only let us consent to them, and they will sit with (*et*) us" (34:23).

Later on, we find in the event of the "concubine in Gibeah" the verse, "And his father-in-law, the girl's father, made him stay and he sat with (*et*) him three days..." (Judges 19:4) and "to sit *et*..." is in conjunction with "made him stay," not according to his real will.

To Be With

The combination of "to be" in conjunction with the word "with" appears in the text in regard to the connection between the Almighty and the forefathers.

For Isaac:

---

[17] "...sit with him..." – the word *lashevet* is literally "to sit." However, it is also used with the meaning of "to dwell" and even "to settle."

- "Sojourn in this land and I will be with (*im*) you and will bless you..." (Genesis 26:3)
- "And they said, we saw certainly that the Lord was with (*im*) you..." (26:28)

For Jacob:

- "And the Lord said to Jacob, return to the land of your fathers and to your family and I will be with (*im*) you" (31:3)
- "And let us arise and go up to Beth-El and I will make there an altar to G-d who answered me in the day of my distress and was with (*im*) me in the way which I went" (35:3)
- "And Israel said to Joseph, behold I die but G-d shall be with (*im*) you and bring you back to the land of your fathers" (48:21)

For Moses:

- "And he said certainly I will be with (*im*) you and this shall be the sign to you that I have sent you..." (Exodus 3:12)
- "Now therefore go and I will be with (*im*) your mouth and teach you what you shall say" (4:12)
- "And you shall speak to him and put words in his mouth and I will be with (*im*) your mouth and his mouth and will teach you what you shall do" (4:15)

For Joshua:

- "And he gave Joshua the son of Nun a charge and said, be strong and of a good courage for you shall bring the people of Israel into the land which I swore to them and I will be with (*im*) you" (Deuteronomy 31:23)

From among the three forefathers, Abraham is the only one that the text does not say that G-d "was with" him. For Abraham we find something else: "for I **know** him..." (Genesis 18:19) as we find for Moses, "...you have said I **know** you by name..." (Exodus 33:12). This linguistic comparison between Abraham and Moses should remind us that the text quotes the Almighty talking to Abimelech after he took Sarah into his palace: "Now therefore restore the man his wife for he is a **prophet**..." (Genesis 20:7), and for Moses, "And there has not arisen since in Israel a

prophet like Moses whom the Lord knew face to face" (Deuteronomy 34:10). The word "since" comes to restrict this assertion to the time after Moses, to inform us that there was such a prophet before Moses – Abraham.

Joseph is the only one in the Torah that the text uses the word *et* (as opposed to *im*) in describing his connection to the Almighty: "And the Lord was with (*et*) Joseph and he was prosperous man and he was in the house of his Egyptian Master. And his Master saw that the Lord was with (*et*) him…" (Genesis 39:2-3).

In returning to the phrase "to be with (*im*)" we find it for the connection between man and his connection to his creator: "You shall be perfect with (*im*) the Lord your G-d" (Deuteronomy 18:13).

In the entire Tanach we find the phrase "to be with" applying to the relationship between humans in only two places. First, "The Hebrews who were with the Philistines before that time who went up with (*im*) them into the camp from the surrounding country they also turned to be with (*im*) the Israelites who were with Saul and Jonathan" (1 Samuel 14:21). And second, "They were a wall to us both by night and day all the while we were with (*im*) them keeping the sheep" (1 Samuel 25:16).

We can start from the second place. When David sent emissaries to Nabal the Carmelite asking Nabal to support David and his people with money and supplies, Nabal rebuffed them and sent them away. The servants of Nabal's wife, Abigail, commented to her that David and his people did help them day and night, and guarded them while taking care of the sheep. The servants' comment actually portrayed David and his people as brethren to them. And in the language we see "to be with (*im*)" indicating a close relationship.

The first place talks about the chaos in the Philistines' camp, when the Philistines were killing each other with "friendly fire." The verse tells us that during the chaos, the Philistines and the Israelites were in such proximity to each other that the Philistines could not distinguish between a Philistine and an Israelite. And, again, to describe this situation, the text uses the expression "to be with (*im*)" to indicate the closeness between the two camps.

Linguistic Journey – Sexual Relations in Biblical Language

The text uses four different linguistic forms to relate to the sexual relationship between a man and a woman: to know, to come to, to lie with (*et*), and to lie with (*im*).

To Know

The verb "to know" appears twice as a general assertion to state that a woman is a virgin. When Lot offers his two daughters to the angry mob surrounding his house in Sodom, Lot is quoted as saying, "Behold now I have two daughters who have not **known** man…" (Genesis 19:8). When Rebecca is introduced for the first time into the text, it is said, "And the girl was very pretty to look upon, a virgin and no man had **known** her…" (Genesis 24:16). The word appears again to rule out a relationship, and this time for Judah and Tamar, "…and he **knew** her again no more" (39:26).

After the war with Midian, which starts after the promiscuous behavior in Shittim, due to the appearance and guidance of Balaam, the text says, "…every woman that has **known** man…" (Numbers 31:17). And, "But all the young women who have not **known** man…" (31:18), and, "…of women that had not **known** man…" (31:35).

For a specific man and woman the text uses the word "to know" only three times, and only for Adam and Cain.

For Adam:

- "And Adam **knew** Eve his wife…" (Genesis 4:1)
- "And Adam **knew** is wife again…" (4:25)

For Cain:

- "And Cain **knew** his wife…" (4:17)

The fact that besides Adam and Cain, the text uses the word "to know" exclusively to relate to sexual relations between a man and a woman outside marriage is a signal to us that the institution of marriage did not exist at the time of Adam and Cain.

To Come to

The text uses the word "to come to" to describe to marital relations in a respectable context. When Sarah gives Hagar to Abraham, the text says, "And he came to Hagar and she got pregnant..." (Genesis 16:4). When Jacob asks Laban to give him Rachel as his wife, as it was agreed between them, the text quotes Jacob, "...Give me my wife for my days are fulfilled that I may come to her" (29:21). When Rachel is switched for Leah, the text says, "...he took Leah his daughter and brought her to him, and he came to her" (29:23). Later on, when he got Rachel for a wife, "And he came also to Rachel and he loved also Rachel more than Leah..." (29:30). When the text talks about Judah taking a wife it says, "And Judah saw there a daughter of a Canaanite whose name was Shuah, and he took her and came to her" (38:2).

The only time in which the text relates to sexual relations between husband and wife, without using the verb "to come to" is when Leah approached Jacob demanding the night with him after she bought the right to that night with her son's mandrakes. Here the text says, "...and Leah went out to meet him and said, you must **come to** me for I have hired you with my son's mandrakes. And he **lay with** (*im*) her that night" (30:16). We should note that while Leah is quoted as saying, "come to me," Jacob didn't "come to" her, but he "lay with" her. The change of language comes to testify to Jacob's displeasure about being "sold" by his beloved wife Rachel. Still, the respectable preposition *im* is in the picture.

While with Jacob we find that he "lay with" Leah, unlike our expectation that he should have "come to" her, we find a place in which we would have expected the verb "to lie with," but we do not find it. The text tells us that Judah saw Tamar on the side of the road and "...he thought her to be a **harlot**" (38:15). What would we expect a man approaching a prostitute for sex to say? The text quotes Judah saying to Tamar, "...and said, come please, let me **come to** you..." (38:16).

Judah is using the language that the text uses only for marital relations between husband and wife, very respectable language. Should we conclude that Judah was a gentleman? Or, should we conclude that we are facing language in the text that does not fit the atmosphere of the encounter? And if so, we have to conclude that we are facing a possible linguistic bias in favor of Judah.

To Lie With (*im*) vs. to Lie With (*et*)

We find the verb "to lie with (*et*) in the following places:

- "And Abimelech said, what is this you have done to us? One of the people might easily have lain with (*et*) your wife and you would have brought guilt upon us" (Genesis 26:10)
- "…because he had done a vile deed in Israel in lying with (*et*) Jacob's daughter…" (34:7)
- "…Reuben went and lay with (*et*) Bilhah his father's concubine…" (35:22)

In the above-mentioned examples we find the verb "to lie with (*et*) when it is not proper. But we also see places where the text uses "to lie with (*im*) – When King David lies with Bathsheba, the text says, "…and she came to him and he lay with (*im*) her…" (2 Samuel 11:4). When David tries to convince Uriah the Hittite to go and be with his wife, Uriah is quoted as answering, "…the ark, and Israel, and Judah remain in tents and my lord Joab and the servants of my Lord are encamped in the open fields, shall I then go into my house to eat and to drink and to lie with (*im*) my wife?" (2 Samuel 11:11). After the appearance of the prophet Nathan with the parable of the poor man's lamb, and the death of the child, the text says, "And David comforted Bathsheba his wife and he came to her and lay with (*im*) her…" (12:24).

We find "to lie with (*et*)…" also with Eli's sons, "And Eli was very old and heard all that his sons did to all Israel and how they lay with (*et*) the women who assembled at the door of the tabernacle of the congregation" (1 Samuel 2:22).

If we compare the incestuous relations mentioned in Leviticus (chapter 20) to the ones mentioned in Deuteronomy (chapter 27), we see that the ones mentioned in Leviticus use the preposition *et*. On the other hand, the ones in Deuteronomy, mentioned at the curse on Mount Eival, use the preposition *im*. We can conclude that the ones in Leviticus are not necessarily with the consent of both parties, while the ones in Deuteronomy relate to relationships where both parties consent to the act.

We find the same in, "If a man seduces a virgin who is not betrothed, and lies with (*im*) her..." (Exodus 22:15). When the text talks about seduction, and quite likely the woman consented, the text describes it as "to lie with (*im*)."

"To lie with her (*ota*)"[18]

There are three places in the text in which we find the phrase "to lie with her (*ota*)." Two of the three are identical. First is the case of Dinah, Jacob's daughter in Shechem, "And when Shechem the son of Hamor the Hivite, prince of the country, saw her, he took her and lay with her (*ota*)..." (34:2).

Second is the case of Amnon, David's son, and his sister Tamar. In this case, we find two expressions, "to lie with (*im*)," and "to lie with her (*ota*)."

Amnon, who desired Tamar, Absalom's sister, is pretending to be sick so Tamar will cook for him. When they are alone in the room, Amnon addresses her, "...come lie with (*im*) me, my sister" (2 Samuel 13:11). When she refuses and tells him to ask the king permission to ask for her, the text says, "But he would not listen to her voice but being stronger than she, forced her and lay with her (*ota*)" (13:14).

In these two cases, Dinah and Shechem, and Amnon and Tamar, we are dealing with rape, and the text in both of these cases uses the same expression, "lie with her (*ota*)."

The third place should bring us to wonder if rape is also in the picture. It is part of the recitation of laws dealing with bodily discharges, "... if any man lies[19] with her (*ota*), and her menstrual discharge is upon him..." (Leviticus 15:24). When the woman is menstruating, it is described as "lying with her (*ota*)." Does the text perceive the situation to be the woman refusing while the man imposes himself on her? Or, does the

---

[18] In Hebrew there is a difference between "he lay with her (*eta*)" as opposed "he lay with her (*ota*)." While the first sounds more direct, the second sounds more remote, and it even seems like objectifying the woman. The difference is only one letter, "e" vs. "o."

[19] "...*shacov yishchav*..." Here we find the verb *lishchav* ("to lie") twice. Whenever the Biblical text doubles a verb, it stresses the strength of the activity. One way to translate the doubled verb into English is to insert the adverb "strongly" or "forcefully."

language of the law, discussing a hypothetical situation, express the law codifier's attitude against such an activity: a man sleeping with a woman at the time of her menstruation calls for the same language used for rape?

Summary

While "to lie with (*im*)" relates to a good intimate relationship, the phrase "to lie with (*et*)" describes a relationship when something is not proper, such as Abimelech's guilt, and Reuben's lying with Bilhah, his father's concubine. It relates to a sexual relationship when one side does not consent to the act or when the act is not proper. The phrase "to lie with her (*ota*)" is used when talking about rape, or when there is a suspicion that the man imposes himself on the woman.

"To Lie With (*im*) his Fathers"

The phrase "lie with (*im*) his fathers," to describe the death and burial of a king, shows up for the first time in Genesis when Jacob speaks to Joseph before his death, "And I will lie with (*im*) my fathers and you shall carry me out of Egypt and bury me in their burying place" (Genesis 47:30). Throughout the book of Kings we find this phrase for the death of a king. There is only one place in which the text uses the phrase "to lie with (*et*) his fathers," when the prophet Nathan comes to King David and informs him that he will not be the one who will build a temple for G-d. The text says, "Go and tell my servant David thus said the Lord, shall you build me a house for me to dwell in?" (2 Samuel 7:5). And later the text says, "And your days are fulfilled and you shall lie with (*et*) your fathers, I will set up your seed after you who shall issue from your bowels and I will establish his kingdom. He shall build a house for my name..." (7:12-13). When the Almighty's response to David's request to build the temple is negative, the preposition *et* is in use.

Back to Lot's Daughters

The text says, "And the elder said to the younger, our father is old and there is no man on earth to **come to** us after the manner of all the earth. Come, let us make our father drink wine, and we will **lie with** (*im*) him, that we may preserve seed of our father. And they made their father drink wine that night; and the elder **came**, and **lay with** (*et*) her father; and he did not know when she lay down, nor when she arose. And on the next day, the elder said to the younger, behold, I **lay** last night **with** (*et*) my father; let us make him drink wine this night also; and you **come** and **lie with** (*im*) him that we may preserve seed of our father. And they made their father drink wine that night also, and the younger **arose** and **lay with** (*im*) him and he did not know when she lay down nor when she arose..." (19:31-35).

The elder brings up the idea while she uses the respectful verb "to come to," as we saw earlier in this linguistic journey. However, there are two changes in language between the elder and the younger.

The elder suggests the idea and she is quoted using the respectful word "to come to." However, when the text describes the act itself, there is a difference between the elder and the younger. While the elder "lay with (*et*) her father" and she even reports it this way the next day, the elder suggests to the younger "to lie with (*im*) him. The **language** of the text indicates that the elder did what she did out of necessity, and as such the distance between herself and her father. Her sister, on the other hand, didn't see any wrong in her activity, and from her point of view, it was no different from a marital relationship with any other man. Does the text know something about the relationship between Lot and his younger daughter?

We encounter another change in language between the two. For the elder the text says, "And the elder **came**..." using the respectable term "to come to," but for the younger the text says, "...and the younger **arose**..." It is evident from the **language** that the text attributes more strength to the younger ("she arose") in her activity. On the other hand, the elder is more careful – "she came" – a verb indicating respect and honor.

We can conclude that the **language** of the text distinguishes between the elder and the younger. While the elder receives a "discount" – she did it out of obligation – there is no such "discount" for the younger. We should look upon this double change in language as a "linguistic bias" towards the elder.

Linguistic Biases in the Language of the Text

Up to this point we are facing the following biases:

1. Peretz and Zerah, Judah's sons from Tamar, are compared linguistically to Isaac's sons Esau and Jacob.
2. The text wants to prevent disrespect towards Judah by not giving him the title "the fourth."
3. Although Joseph gets all the benefits of being the firstborn to Jacob and Rachel, the text does not give him the title "firstborn."
4. Ephraim, Joseph's younger son, is the only man in Genesis who gets a title indicating disrespect: "the second."
5. The elder of Lot's daughters, the one who gave birth to Moab, gets a "discount" in the language of the text; "she came" and "lay with" (*et*), while the younger "arose" and "lay with" (*im*).
6. There is a <u>possible</u> linguistic bias in favor of Judah due to use of respectable language ("…come please, let me **come to** you…") in an encounter between a man and a harlot.

Additional point in language to consider:

The connection to the Almighty is important for the text. The Mount Sinai revelation separates the Biblical text into two separate eras, at least from observing the use of the word *toldot*.

THE ORDER OF THE SOCIAL INTRODUCTION

Introduction

In this chapter we will deal with the order of appearance of the social introduction – which comes first, the name before the title, or the title before the name? For example, does the text label the person "my wife Rachel" or "Rachel my wife"?

General

In the vast majority of the cases in which the social introduction includes both the title and the name, we find that the name appears before the title. (See Appendix A: The Social Introduction.)

Two points will help us to find the common denominator behind the change of language from the formula "name + title" to the formula "title + name." First, most changes of language are due to emotions. Second, without any exception, the death of a king and the ascension to the throne of his son is described by the formula "name + title." For example, "And Nadab (or any other king's name) his son reigned in his place." If so, we have to conclude that this formula represents formal language (describing kings). And if this explanation is the right one, then the opposite formula of "title + name" must be personal (familiar) language, or emotional language, indicating a close connection between two people.

The Formula of "Title + Name"

We will start by checking the places where the formula of "title + name" is used. And we will start with a quote not from Genesis but from Exodus.

"My Son, My Firstborn Israel" (Exodus 4:22)

We are facing two titles, "my son" and "my firstborn," before the name "Israel." This formula testifies to the close connection between the Almighty and his people Israel. The content confirms it. At the beginning of the event of the burning bush the Almighty tells Moses, "I have surely seen the affliction of My people who are in Egypt..." (3:7), and "...that you may bring forth My people the sons of Israel out of Egypt" (3:10). And we can see again the formula of "title" ("my people") + "name" ("the sons of Israel"). The same formula appears in, "...and bring forth My armies My people the sons of Israel out of the land of Egypt..." (7:4). We should note that we cannot find in the entire Tanach the formula "name + title" for the sons of Israel, as in "the sons of Israel My people."

The Sin of the Golden Calf

When the children of Israel sin with the golden calf, the Almighty tells Moses, "Go down for **your** people whom you brought out of the land of Egypt have corrupted themselves" (32:7), and, "Arise, get down quickly from here for **your** people have corrupted themselves..." (Deuteronomy 9:12), and, "...I make a covenant; before all **your** people I will do marvels..." (Exodus 34:10). The fact that the Almighty is quoted as saying "**your** people" should remind us of a couple who talk about their misbehaving offspring. One parent says to the other, "Look how **your** son is behaving."

Generally speaking, the change of possessive pronoun is due to emotions. People have a tendency to avoid using the possessive pronoun "my" (in this case "my people") when there are anger and other negative emotions. The change of one noun to another noun reflects a change in the perception of reality. In a way, we can say that while a change of pronouns (for example "my" to "the") represents a change of emotions, and likely to be negative when the "my" is missing, a change of nouns represents a change in the way the person relates to reality. Or, in other words, while pronouns deal with emotions, nouns deal with logic. And one should note that while emotions can be temporary, the perception of reality is usually more permanent and constant.

Here also, the change of the formula from "title + name" to the opposite formula "name + title" would be a change of the perception of reality, something which is a lot more significant. And in fact, we don't find in the whole Tanach the formula of "name + title" for the sons of Israel as the people of G-d. This conversation between the Almighty and Moses is more like a couple who are parents of children, a more intimate relationship.

In summary, the use of "your people" instead of "my people" should not bring us to worry, as it only reflects the close connection between Moses and the Almighty.

And the play on possession moves to Moses' court, as he responds as expected from a concerned mother defending her son to her husband. The text quotes Moses responding to the Almighty, "…why does Your anger burn hot against **Your** people…" (Exodus 32:11), "…and repent of this evil against **Your** people" (32:12). And, "…consider that this nation is **Your** people" (33:13), "For where shall it be known here that I and **Your** people have found grace in Your sight?" (33:16). And in Deuteronomy we find Moses asks the Almighty, "…destroy not **Your** people and Your inheritance…" (9:26), and "And they are **Your** people and Your inheritance…" (9:29).

From these preliminary observations in Exodus, we now move back to Genesis.

The Order of the Generations

Cain and His Son Enoch

The text says, "And Cain knew his wife and she conceived and bore Enoch and he built a city and called the city after the name of his son Enoch" (Genesis 4:17). "His son Enoch," and not "Enoch his son." The text uses a formula indicating personal language. We can consider this use of personal language as Cain putting his personal signature on the city he built. We find here unity between the **content** and the **language** of the text.

This unity between the content and the language should bring us to perceive **the building of a city** as an important point behind the text. It is not a "bias" of the language, but it is definitely an issue to consider when later discussing the profile embedded in the text.

Noah

At the beginning of the flood the text tells us, "In the midst of this day came Noah and Shem and Ham and Japheth, the sons of Noah, and Noah's wife, and the three wives of his sons with them, into the ark" (Genesis 7:13). The text uses here the formula of "name + title." After the flood the text says, "And the sons of Noah, who went out of the ark, were Shem, and Ham, and Japheth…" (9:18), and here the text uses the formula of "title + name." The same we find later, "And these are the *toldot* of the sons of Noah, Shem, Ham and Japheth..." (10:1). Before the flood the text used formal and distant language, then after the flood the text used personal and emotional language. We can conclude that quite likely the stay in the ark brought closeness between Noah and his sons.

If the stay inside the ark brought closeness between Noah and his sons, this is not the case between Noah and his wife. Before the flood the text says, "...you shall come into the ark, you, your sons, and your wife, and your sons' wives with you" (6:18). Here we see that the sons are listed in the sentence before Noah's wife. We find the same in, "And Noah came and his sons and his wife and his sons' wives with him into the ark..." (7:7). We saw it above in 7:13 as well.

After the flood the Almighty tells Noah, "Go out from the ark, you and your wife and your sons and your sons' wives with you" (8:16). Here we see that Noah's wife was "upgraded" and she is listed before the sons. Did Noah accept this order of priorities expressed by the Almighty? The text answers this question by saying, "And Noah went out and his sons and his wife and his sons' wives with him" (8:18).

In summary, the stay in the ark brought closeness between Noah and his sons, as expressed by the change in formulas of "name + title" before the flood to an opposite formula of "title + name" after the flood. But in spite of the Almighty's expectation, as it comes across by the order of listing in the sentence, that the stay in the ark would bring closeness between Noah and his wife, it didn't actually happen.

Abraham

The text uses the formula of "name + title" for Isaac. For example, "Isaac his son." However, we see places in which the text uses the opposite formula. When Sarah demands that Abraham expel Ishmael she is quoted as saying to Abraham, "Expel this slave and her son, for the son of this slave shall not be heir with my son with Isaac" (21:10). We cannot expect the opposite formula when the text talks about a mother who defends the rights of her son. Moreover, we are facing a quote of a conversation between a wife and her husband, a conversation that can only be personal and not formal. This is assuming that the two are not in divorce proceedings.

We should also note that in this place we find a "split" introduction. Sarah is not saying "...with my son Isaac." Instead, she is quoted as saying, "with my son, with Isaac." The split introduction serves to emphasize something. We should not forget that when Sarah gave her slave Hagar to Abraham she expected that the baby born would be hers, an expectation that didn't materialize. Now Sarah says in this short split introduction: I have only one son, and in case you have any doubt who it is, it is Isaac.

When the text starts the event of the binding of Isaac on the altar, the text quotes the Almighty who guides Abraham, "Take please your son your only one whom you love, Isaac..." (22:2). We see here three titles, "your son," "your only one," and "whom you love" before the name "Isaac." The use of this formula of multiple titles before the name, indicating personal and emotional language, testifies to the close connection between Abraham and the Almighty. We should note that the Almighty was quoted as saying, "Shall I hide from Abraham that thing which I do?" (18:17). Not only does the content testify to the close connection, but also the linguistic formula the Almighty uses to talk to Abraham testifies to it.

When Abraham speaks with his slave and guides him to go to Haran to bring a wife for his son Isaac, the text says, "You shall go to my country and to my family and take a wife for my son for Isaac" (24:4).

We should note that as Sarah did before, here Abraham does the same. Instead of saying, "for my son Isaac" the text quotes Abraham using a split introduction, "for my son for Isaac." Again, coming to emphasize that there is only one son of Abraham. This is the only time in which Abraham is quoted using the formula of "title + name," a formula indicating personal language, close and intimate between the two.

The close connection between Jacob and Joseph does not come only in the content of the text which says, "And Israel loved Joseph more than all his children because he was the son of his old age..." (Genesis 37:3). We see the close connection also in the language. Joseph tells his brothers after he revealed himself to them, "Hurry back to my father and say to him thus said **your son Joseph**..." (45:9), and, "...the time drew nearer that Israel must die and he called **his son Joseph**..." (47:29), and, "...one told Jacob and said Behold **your son Joseph** comes to you..." (48:2). We do not find the formula "Joseph his son" ("name + title"), as this formula does not go along with the close connection between father and son.

Jacob and Esau

Both of them appear before their father to get the blessing, and the first is Jacob pretending to be Esau. Jacob tells his father, "I am **Esau your firstborn**..." (27:19). Jacob is quoted using the formula "name + title," indicating formal language. Esau, on the other hand, appears and tells his father, "I am **your firstborn Esau**" (27:33), and Esau is quoted using the formula "title + name" indicating closeness between the two.

The language of the text indicates that the connection between Esau and Isaac was closer than the connection between Isaac and Jacob. How come? In order to understand it we have to check the connection between Isaac and Jacob.

The Connection Between Jacob and Isaac

When we examined the places where the text uses the formula "name + title," we saw that Jacob did not receive the title "his son" in relation to Isaac. The text tells us that Terah took **Abram his son**. Abram circumcised **Isaac his son**. Isaac calls **Esau his big son**. Jacob talks with **his son Joseph** (the only one who receives the formula "title + name"). The only one who did not receive the title "his son" is Jacob. One place in which Jacob got close to receiving such a title, and even that was indirectly, was in, "And Isaac expired and died and was gathered to his people being old and full of days and Esau and Jacob **his sons** buried him" (35:29). When Isaac died Jacob merited to be described in the language of the text as Isaac's son, and even then only when the two brothers are mentioned together – "his sons" – in the plural.

We should note that there is one other place in which Jacob indirectly received the title "his son:" "And Isaac said to his son how is it that you have found it so quickly my son..." (27:20). But we should note that this title "his son" shows up when Isaac does not know that it is Jacob there and not Esau.

Was this distance between Isaac and Jacob a two-way street? The text tells us that Jacob tells his mother Rebecca:

- "**My father** perhaps will feel me..." (27:12)
- "...he came to **his father** and said, **my father**..." (27:18)
- "And Jacob went near Isaac **his father**..." (27:22)
- "And Isaac **his father** said to him..." (27:26)
- "...and Jacob had scarcely gone out from the presence of Isaac **his father**..." (27:30)

It can be said that during the meeting between the two, Isaac doesn't know that Jacob is the one who is facing him, and therefore we cannot consider these places as evidence. But we see additional places where the title "his father" appears, when Isaac knows that it is Jacob in front of him. For example, "And that Jacob obeyed **his father** and his mother and he went to Padan-Aram" (28:7).

And upon Jacob's return from his long stay in Aram we find:

- "...to go to Isaac **his father** in the land of Canaan" (31:18)
- "...and Jacob swore by the fear of **his father** Isaac" (31:53)
- "And Jacob came to Isaac **his father** to Mamre to the city of Arba which is Hebron..." (35:27)
- "And Jacob lived in the land where **his father** was a stranger, in the land of Canaan" (37:1)

We can compare the two places where the text uses the formula of "name + title," indicating formal language, "...to go to **Isaac his father** in the land of Canaan" (31:18), and, "...Jacob came to **Isaac his father** to Mamre to the city of Arba which is Hebron..." (35:27), and the one place where the text uses the personal and emotional language formula of "title + name:" "...and Jacob swore by the fear of **his father Isaac**" (31:53). When Jacob is taking an oath to Laban, just before ending the conflict with Laban and his sons, to be free to go on his way, the text uses personal and emotional language. The text exposes to us the high degree of emotion Jacob experienced at that time.

In summary, while Isaac is not quoted in the text using the title "his son," Jacob, on the other hand, is quoted as using "my father" as a direct quote by him, and even in the language of the text describing the events. We can see that the distance between the father and the son was from the father's point of view, but not from the son's. Jacob wanted the closeness with "his father" but didn't achieve it all his life.

Jacob and Esau

Upon his return from Haran, the text tells us, "And Jacob sent messengers before him to **Esau his brother** to the land of Seir the country of Edom" (32:4). Here the language of the text uses the formal and distant formula of "name + title."

The text continues, "And the messengers returned to Jacob saying, we came **to your brother to Esau**..." (32:7). The text quotes the messengers using the personal and emotional formula of "title + name." But it does not quote the messengers as saying, "We came to your brother Esau..." Instead, the text splits the formula, and the title "your brother" is separated from "Esau." Although the title "your brother" appears before "Esau," and that in itself should tell us that he is more "your brother" than "Esau," the split between the two components of the formula comes to emphasize quite likely the doubt the messengers had as to which way Esau was leaning.

The text says that Jacob prays, "Save me please from the hand of **my brother** from the hand of **Esau**..." (32:12). We can understand why Jacob is using here the personal and emotional formula of "title + name" when he is asking the Almighty for his life. And, again, we should note the split between the components of the social introduction, between the title and the name: "from the hand of **my brother** from the hand of **Esau**..."

When Jacob guides his slaves who are to be in charge of the gifts sent to Esau, the text says, "...when **Esau my brother** meets you..." (32:18), and the text returns to the formal language of "name + title." It should not surprise us, since Jacob is guiding his slaves, and formal language is expected in this situation. And in his address to the slaves Jacob is quoted saying, "And you shall say, they are **your slave Jacob's**. It is a present sent to my master Esau..." (32:19), and, "...say you also, behold, **your slave Jacob** is behind us..." (32:21). Jacob instructs his slaves to respond to Esau with the personal and emotional formula of "title + name."

"Title + Name" Using "My Slave X"

Abraham My Slave

The first one who merits the title "my slave" is Abraham. The text tells us of the appearance of the Almighty to Isaac after the war over the water wells: "And the Lord appeared to him that night and said, I am the G-d of Abraham your father, fear not, for I am with (*et*) you and will bless you and multiply your seed for **Abraham My slave**" (26:24).

We should note two points: first, the text uses the formal language of "name + title," "Abraham My slave." This goes in harmony with the "introduction" of Abraham earlier in the sentence, "Abraham your father," and with the use of the word "with" (*et*) indicating some distance. Second, this title of Abraham, "My slave," comes after the text told us earlier, "And Abraham expired and died in a good old age, an old man, and full of years, and was gathered to his people" (25:8).

Isaac

We should note that out of the three forefathers, Abraham, Isaac, and Jacob, Isaac is the only one who did not merit the title "my slave." Neither "Isaac My slave," nor "My slave Isaac."

Jacob

The title "My slave Jacob" (as well as "Jacob My slave") appears in the prophets in relation to the people of Israel, not to Jacob, the individual person. Out of eight times in which the title appears, seven times it appears as "My slave Jacob" and only one time as "Jacob My slave."

When it is in regard to a general address calling for attention from the people of Israel, the prophet says, "Yet now hear O **Jacob My slave**, and Israel whom I have chosen" (Isaiah 44:1), and we find here the formal language formula of "name + title."

However, when the text talks about comfort and encouragement to the people, we can see the personal and emotional language using the formula "title + name." For example,

- "...Fear not O **My slave Jacob** and Jeshurun whom I have chosen." (Isaiah 44:2)
- "For My slave Jacob's sake and Israel My elect..." (Isaiah 45:4)
- "Therefore do not fear O **My slave Jacob** says the Lord nor be dismayed O Israel for behold I will save you from afar..." (Jeremiah 30:10)
- "And do not fear O **My slave Jacob** and be not dismayed O Israel for behold I will save you from far away..." (Jeremiah 46:27)
- "Do not fear O **My slave Jacob** says the Lord for I am with (*et*) you..." (Jeremiah 46:28)
- "...when I shall have gathered the house of Israel from the people among whom they are scattered and shall be sanctified in them in the sight of the nations, then shall they dwell in their land that I have given **to My slave to Jacob**" (Ezekiel 28:25)
- " ...they shall dwell in the land that I have given to **My slave Jacob**, where your fathers have dwelt..." (Ezekiel 37:25)

"For **My slave Jacob**'s sake and **Israel My elect**..." (Isaiah 45:4)

In this verse we should note that Jacob gets the personal and emotional formula of "title + name," "My slave Jacob" while Israel gets the formal and distant formula of "name + title," "Israel My elect." If we read the beginning of the chapter in Isaiah we can understand the difference. The chapter starts with, "Thus says the Lord to his anointed Cyrus..." (Isaiah 45:1). We should note that Cyrus receives the personal and emotional formula of "title + name." On the other hand, Israel does not receive this formula. Knowing that Cyrus is a tool used by the Almighty, and at the time Cyrus is ruling over Israel and Israel is in exile (as punishment for its behavior in the past), we can understand why the prophet uses the formal and distant formula ("name + title") for Israel, "Israel My elect."

Moses the Lord's Slave

As we find with Abraham, so with Moses. The text says, "And Moses the Lord's slave died there in the land of Moab according to the word of the Lord" (Deuteronomy 34:5). In conjunction with mentioning Moses' death, Moses receives the title "the Lord's slave," and the text uses the formal formula of "name + title." This formula repeats itself 31 times in the Tanach:

Joshua 1:1, 1:2, 1:7, 1:13, 1:15, 8:31, 8:33, 9:24, 11:12, 11:15, 12:6, 13:8, 14:7, 18:7, 22:2, 22:4, 22:5
1 Kings 8:53, 8:56,
2 Kings 18:12,
Malachi 3:22,
Psalms 105:26,
Daniel 9:11,
Nehemiah 1:7, 1:8, 9:14, 10:30,
1 Chronicles 6:34,
2 Chronicles 1:3, 24:6, and 24:9.

My Slave Moses

There are only two places in the Tanach in which the personal and emotional formula of "title + name" is used for Moses, "My slave Moses."

The first, when Miriam and Aaron are complaining to Moses, "...Has the Lord indeed spoken only by Moses? Has he not spoken also by us?" (Numbers 12:2). The text gives us the Almighty's response,

> Hear now My words; if there is a prophet among you, I the Lord will make Myself known to him in a vision, and will speak to him in a dream. Not so with **My slave Moses**, for he is the trusted one in all My house. With him I speak mouth to mouth, manifestly, and not in dark speech; and he behold the form of the Lord. Why then were you not afraid to speak against **My slave Moses**? (Numbers 12:6-8)

There are three components factoring into this event. First, we are facing a direct quote from the Almighty. It is not the language of the text describing the events, but what the Almighty said. And the formula of "title + name" testifies to the high degree of closeness between the Almighty and Moses, as the Almighty sees it.

The second component is that we are dealing with a conversation within the family. The complainants are Miriam and Aaron who are Moses' siblings, and it can be understood that personal and emotional language will be used.

The third component is the rarity existing in Moses, who receives the title "My slave Moses" while still alive, in contrast to Abraham who received this title only after his death.

The second place where we see the phrase "My slave Moses" is in the book Kings, and again, in a quote from the Almighty's words speaking to David and Solomon.

> And he [King Menashe] set a carved idol of the Ashera that he had made in the house, of which the Lord said to David and to Solomon his son, in this house, and in Jerusalem, which I have chosen from all tribes of Israel, will I put My name forever. Neither will I make the feet of Israel move any more from the land which I gave to their fathers; only if they will observe to do according to all that I have commanded them, and according to all the Torah that **My slave Moses** commanded them. (2 Kings 21:7-8)

The text contrasts the abominations of King Menashe described in 2 Kings Chapter 21 with the closeness that King David and his son Solomon enjoyed with the Almighty. Their closeness was due to their adherence to the teachings relayed by "My slave Moses." The closeness of Moses to the Almighty was based upon the teachings of the Torah, and anyone who follows the teachings of the Torah enjoys the same closeness that Moses had with the Almighty. And the opposite is also true. One who does not act according to the teachings of the Torah, like king Menashe, distances himself from the Almighty.

Moses My Slave

The text says at the beginning of the book of Joshua, "And it was after the death of Moses the slave of the Lord that the Lord spoke to Joshua the son of Nun, Moses' servant, saying **Moses My slave** is dead..." (Joshua 1:1-2). The message we receive from the language of the text is that life goes on. Even the loss of such a great leader as Moses does not mean it is the end of the road. Moses is "Moses the Lord's slave" and Joshua is "Joshua the son of Nun, Moses' servant." Both of them received the formal language formula of "name + title." Moreover, even for Moses, the formal language formula is back in use. Not "My slave Moses," but "Moses My slave."

We see the phrase "Moses My slave" immediately after that: "Only be strong and very courageous that you may observe to do according to all the Torah, which **Moses My slave** commanded you..." (Joshua 1:7). Twice the formula repeats itself to testify that the concept was decided. There is a new leader, and the previous leader, with all his glory as "the Lord's slave," is "Moses My slave."

The phrase "Moses My slave" returns in the book Malachi: "Remember the Torah of **Moses My slave** which I commanded him in Horeb for all Israel, with the statutes and judgments" (Malachi 3:22).

Moses and Joshua

The text relates to the relationship between Moses and Joshua three times. First, when Moses ascended to Mount Sinai: "And Moses rose up, and **Joshua his servant** and Moses went up to the mount of G-d" (Exodus 24:13). In this place the text uses the formal language formula of "name + title." The text does the same later on in Numbers, when two elders, Eldad and Medad, started prophesying in the camp. The text says, "And **Joshua the son of Nun, the servant of Moses, one of his young men,** answered and said, My Lord Moses stop them" (Numbers 11:28). (Here we see "name + title + title+ title.")

But there is one place in which the text changes the language to the personal and emotional formula of "title + name." The text says, "And the Lord spoke to Moses face to face as a man speaks to his friend. And he returned to the camp and **his servant Joshua the son of Nun, a young man,** did not depart from the tent" (Exodus 33:11). When Joshua is inside the tent, Joshua receives a "promotion" to enjoy the enhanced closeness between the Almighty and Moses that exists in the tent. The enhanced closeness is projected on Joshua, via the language of text changing the formula to "**title** + name + title + title," for one who is present in the tent.

Joshua, like Moses, received the title "the Lord's slave" after his death: "...Joshua the son of Nun, the slave of the Lord died being one hundred and ten years old" (Joshua 24:29). The same verse repeats itself in the book Judges (2:8). We do not find the phrase "My slave Joshua" using the formula "title + name."

Moses and Jethro

After Jethro gives his daughter Zipporah to Moses (Exodus 2:21), the text says, "And Moses shepherded the sheep of **Jethro his father-in-law, the priest of Midian**..." (3:1). The text uses the formal language formula of "name + title." Jethro received two titles, "his father-in-law," and "the priest of Midian." We should note that the order of listing of the two titles indicates to us the relative importance of the first title, "Moses' father-in-law," over his position as "the priest of Midian."

After the burning bush event the text says, "And Moses went and returned to Jethro his father-in-law..." (4:18), and again, we see the formal language formula of "name + title."

After the exodus from Egypt the text says, "And Jethro the priest of Midian Moses' father-in-law heard..." (18:1). Although the text used the same formal language formula of "name + title," still we face a change in language. Before the exodus the title "Moses' father-in-law" appeared before the title "the priest of Midian." Now, after the exodus, the order reversed itself, and the title "the priest of Midian" appeared before the title "Moses' father-in-law." Since Jethro came to Moses in the desert after Moses had sent Zipporah away (18:2), should we conclude that the situation between the two changed? The title "Moses' father-in-law" became secondary to Jethro.

And the text continues with the formal language formula of "name + title" thus: "And Jethro, Moses' father-in-law took..." (18:2), and "...Jethro, Moses' father-in-law, came..." (18:5). Jethro sends a message to Moses before his arrival: "I your father-in-law Jethro..." (18:6). Here we find that Jethro addresses Moses with the personal and emotional formula of "title + name."

The text continues, "And Moses went out towards his father-in-law..." (18:7), and, "...Moses told his father-in-law..." (18:8) The name Jethro vanishes from the language of the text. Should we conclude that Moses went out towards Jethro only because he is "his father-in-law?" That is, to fulfill the familial obligation, but not because he is Jethro.

And the text continues, "And Jethro rejoiced because of all the goodness..." (18:9), and "And Jethro said blessed be the Lord..." (18:10).

In these two places the name showed up and the title vanished. When the two are by themselves, Jethro's title vanishes. The story talks about two people – Moses and Jethro – having a conversation between them. However, when the two return to the public arena the text says, "And Jethro, Moses' father-in-law, took a burnt offering and sacrifices for G-d..." (18:12). The text returns to the formal language formula of "name + title." And the text continues, "...and Aaron came and all the elders of Israel to eat bread with Moses' father-in-law before G-d" (18:12). When Aaron and the elders of Israel appear, the name vanishes. From the language of the text it becomes clear that they honored him only by his position as "Moses' father-in-law."

My Slave Caleb

Like Moses, who received the title "My slave Moses" while still alive, Caleb the son of Jephunneh from the tribe of Judah also received it. After the affair of the spies, the Almighty said, "Surely they shall not see the land which I swore to their father, nor shall any of them who provoked me see it" (Numbers 14:23). And the text continues,

> "And **My slave Caleb,** because he had another spirit with him and has **fulfilled (*lemaleh*) after** me, I will bring him into the land where he came there and his seed shall inherit it" (14:24).

Linguistic Journey - the Verb *Lemaleh*

The verb *lemaleh* appears four times in the Tanach. After Laban cheats Jacob and gives him Leah as a wife instead of Rachel, Laban suggests, "*maleh* this week and we will give you this also..." (Genesis 29:27). When Jacob kept his commitment to the deal, the text says, "And Jacob did so, and he *maleh* this week..." (29:28).

In the book Judges we read, "And the man Micah had a house of gods and made an ephod and *teraphim* and **va'yemaleh** the hand of one of his sons and he became a priest for him" (Judges 17:5). We see it also in "And Micah **va'yemaleh** the hand of the Levite and the young man became a priest for him..." (17:12). When King Saul offers a reward for whoever brings him 200 foreskins of the Philistines, and David does so, the text says,

David arose and went he and his men and slew of the Philistines two hundred men, and David brought their foreskins, and they [the foreskins] served to **vayemaloom**[20] [fulfill the requirement] of the king, to marry in the king [into the king's family], and Saul gave him Michal his daughter for a wife. (1 Samuel 18:27)

In summary, the verb *lemaleh*, which literally in Hebrew means to "fill up," as in filling up a bucket with water, serves here to mean to fulfill an obligation. And as with the Levite becoming a priest, the phrase "*lemaleh* the hand of" means to appoint officially.

"*Lemaleh* after"

The phrase "*Lemaleh* after" appears in only two places in the Tanach: first, in the sin of the spies, as we saw above in the case of Caleb, and second, in the case of King Solomon. The text says, "And Solomon did evil in the sight of the Lord, and did not *lemaleh* after the Lord, as did David his father" (1 Kings 11:6). Language-wise, the text equates Caleb the son of Jephunneh to King Solomon. There are many places in the Tanach in which the sins of the people are mentioned. But only to two does the text attribute the phrase "*lemaleh* after." The text attributes this phrase to Caleb the son of Jephunneh in a positive way, that he indeed "*maleh* after the Lord." On the other hand, the text attributes this phrase to King Solomon in a negative way, that he did not do so, because he sinned by idolatry. We can see this comparison as bestowing regal honor on Caleb the son of Jephunneh.

Caleb and Saul

As we saw, Caleb the son of Jephunneh is compared **language**-wise to King Solomon. Here Caleb is also compared **content**-wise to another king, to King Saul.

In the book Joshua we find, "And Caleb said, he who strikes Kiriath-Sepher, and takes it, to him I will give Achsah my daughter for a wife" (Joshua 15:16). Caleb's daughter is offered as a reward to the victor in the

---

[20] This is a good example of how the Hebrew language is very concise, in which one word to be translated into English will create a whole sentence. For example, the word *Vayemaloom*: the *va* at the beginning is "and;" the *ye* is the future "will;" the *lemaleh* is to fulfill a requirement, and the *oom* at the end serves as the pronoun "them." However, in biblical Hebrew the combination of *va* at the beginning of the verb and the future tense is usually understood to be past tense.

battle. No different from King Saul who offered his daughter as a reward to the one who will strike the Philistines.

After Othniel the son of Kenaz took Kiriath-Sepher, the text continues and says, "And when she came to him, she urged him to ask her father for a field; and she alighted from her ass; and Caleb said to her, what is going on with you? And she said, Give me a blessing for you have given me the land of the Negev; give me also springs of water. And Caleb gave her the upper springs and the lower springs" (Judges 1:14-15). As Joshua gave Hebron to Caleb the son of Jephunneh for an inheritance, so Caleb gives his daughter the upper and the lower springs. We can deduce that Caleb rules the area strongly enough to be able to give his daughter an area for herself.

Othniel, the son of Kenaz, and Caleb's brother and son-in-law, is the first judge, and starts the era of judges after the death of Joshua, "And the spirit of the Lord came upon him and he judged Israel…" (Judges 3:10). And his era ends with, "And the land had rest for forty years and Othniel the son of Kenaz died" (Judges 3:11).

Caleb and Saul – Summary

As Caleb the son of Jephunneh offered his daughter as a reward to the victor in the battle, to the one who would take Kiriath-Sepher, so did Saul as king offer a reward to the one who would slay Goliath who cursed the G-d of Israel. King Saul announced, "…and it shall be that the man who kills him, the king will enrich him with great riches, and will give him his daughter, and make his father's house free in Israel" (1 Samuel 17:25). And, "…Saul said to David, behold my elder daughter Merab, her will I give you for a wife, only be brave for me and fight the Lord's battles…" (1 Samuel 18:17). And the text tells us that this offer was not meant by Saul in the best interest of David: "…And Saul said, let not my hand be upon him, but let the hand of the Philistines be upon him" (18:17).

Saul, as king, offered his daughter to the victor, as Caleb did many years before him. Should we deduce that Caleb functioned as a king for all practical purposes, although without the title of "king," at least not in the language of the text?

Back to My Slave Caleb

We should note that equating Caleb to Moses, the only two men in the first five books of Moses who received this honor, and while alive, is so rare, that we should relate to it as a **linguistic bias** in favor of Caleb the son of Jephunneh from the tribe of Judah. Moreover, this rare title, which only Moses received, comes with the phrase, "because he had **another spirit** with him."

And what did Caleb do? Right after the frightening report of the spies, "Nevertheless the people who live in the land are strong..." (Numbers 13:28), the text says, "And Caleb quieted the people before Moses and said let us go up at once and possess it; for we are well able to overcome it" (13:30).

It is interesting to note that the text uses only Caleb's first name, assuming that we already know who Caleb is. Before the spies embarked on their mission, the text says, "For the tribe of Judah Caleb the son of Jephunneh" (Numbers 13:6). Saying that, we should note the linguistic form in front of us, "And **Caleb** quieted the people before **Moses**..." As Moses appears in the text throughout with only his name, so here the text grants Caleb the same treatment.

Joshua and Caleb

The congregation responds with a complaint against Moses and Aaron, and they tell each other, "...Let us choose a chief and let us return to Egypt" (14:4) because the spies brought forth the slander of the land (13:32). At this point, the text says,

> And Joshua the son of Nun and Caleb the son of Jephunneh, which were of those who spied the land, tore their clothes. And **they** spoke to all the congregation of the people of Israel saying, the land that we passed through to spy is an exceedingly good land. If the Lord delights in us, then He will bring us into this land, and give it to us, a land which flows with milk and honey. Only do not rebel against the Lord... (14:6-9)

First we should note that both men are mentioned with their full names. If earlier Caleb appeared with only his first name, here the text returns to mention both his name and his father's name, as it does for Joshua. The return to use the full name should testify that the use of only the first name earlier for Caleb, in proximity to Moses, was not accidental.

The text tells us that both Joshua the son of Nun and Caleb the son of Jephunneh defended the idea of going into the land. Moreover, in their appeal to the people the text lists Joshua before Caleb, indicating his importance in this instance. But we should not forget that until the point the people asked to return to Egypt, the text does not tell us that Joshua intervened. On the other hand, Caleb the son of Jephunneh intervened immediately, even before the people responded to the frightening report of the spies. Caleb tried to nip the problem in the bud. Joshua, on the other hand, intervened only after the conflict was raging out of control. And Caleb the son of Jephunneh received the title "My slave Caleb" as Moses did.

There are four additional places in the first five books of Moses in which Joshua and Caleb are both mentioned in one breath. Out of these four times, only once is Joshua mentioned before Caleb, in the language of the text, "And Joshua the son of Nun and Caleb the son of Jephunneh who were of the men who went to spy the land, lived still" (Numbers 14:38).

The other three places are in a quote of the Almighty's words, or Moses quoting the Almighty's words. (1) The Almighty is quoted, "...save Caleb the son of Jephunneh and Joshua the son of Nun" (14:30). (2) The Almighty is again quoted, "And there was not left a man of them, save Caleb the son of Jephunneh and Joshua the son of Nun" (26:65). And (3) Moses quotes the Almighty, "Save Caleb the son of Jephunneh and Joshua the son of Nun for they fulfilled after the Lord" (32:12).

In Deuteronomy the two are mentioned, but not together:

> Save Caleb the son of Jephunneh, he shall see it, and to him will I give the land that he has trodden upon, and to his children, because he has fulfilled after the Lord. Also the Lord was angry with me for your sakes saying you also shall not go in there. Joshua the son of Nun who stands before you, he shall come in there, encourage him, for he shall cause Israel to inherit it. (Deuteronomy 1:36-38)

We should note several points from this passage:

First, the distance between Caleb the son of Jephunneh who is mentioned in the first verse and Joshua the son of Nun who appears in the third verse. In between them we have the verse, "Also the Lord was angry with me for your sakes…"

Second, while for Caleb the son of Jephunneh the text says, "he shall see it," for Joshua the son of Nun the text says, "he shall go in there." From the practical point of view in the outside reality the result is the same; both men will come into the land and both of them will inherit it. But from the language point of view we are facing a change in language. The phrase "he shall see it" should remind us of several verses at the end of Deuteronomy where the text relates to Moses and the prohibition on his entering the land: "Because from across you **shall see** the land before you but you shall not go there to the land that **I give** to the people of Israel" (Deuteronomy 32:52). And, "…**I will give** it to your seed. **I have made you see** it with your eyes and you shall not cross there" (34:4).

We can see the combination of the verb "to see" and the verb "to give" for Caleb: "…he shall see it, and to him will I give the land…" And for Moses, "Because from across you **shall see** the land… … that **I give**…" as well as, "…**I will give** it to your seed. **I have made you see** it…"

Thus, language-wise, the text equates Caleb with Moses, but with a twist. Caleb "will see" and the Almighty will "give" him the land. However, Moses will "see" but the Almighty will not "give" him the land. Unlike Caleb, Joshua will not "see" but will "come." The Almighty will not "give" him the land, but he will make the people of Israel inherit it.

Choosing Joshua to Lead

When Moses asks the Almighty to appoint a leader to succeed him, the text quotes Moses as saying, "Let the Lord, **the G-d of the spirits** of all flesh, set a man over the congregation" (Numbers 27:16). The title "G-d of the spirits" appears earlier, at the time of the Korach rebellion: "…O G-d, **the G-d of the spirits** of all flesh shall one man sin and will you be angry with all the congregation?" (Numbers 16:22).

The Almighty responds to Moses and guides him, "…Take Joshua the son of Nun, a man **in whom is spirit**, and lay your hand upon him" (27:18).

And indeed, at the end of Deuteronomy the text says, "And Joshua the son of Nun **was full of the spirit of wisdom** for Moses had laid his hands upon him…" (Deuteronomy 34:9).

There are other men to whom the text attributes "the spirit." First, Eldad and Medad: "And there remained two of the men in the camp, the name of the one was Eldad, and the name of the second is Medad, **and the spirit rested upon them**, and they are in the writings, and they did not come out to the tent and they prophesied in the camp" (Numbers 11:26). The text tells us that Joshua tells Moses, "My Lord Moses arrest them" (11:28), only to find out that it didn't bother Moses at all: "Let it be that all the Lord's people will be prophets for G-d will give **his spirit** upon them" (11:29).

We should remember that in proximity to the title "My slave Caleb" the text says, "…because he had another **spirit** with him…" (Numbers 14:24). And the text equates Caleb to Moses in two ways, use of the first name only: "And **Caleb** quieted the people before **Moses**…" (Numbers 13:30), and the combination of the two verbs "to see" and "to give" that appears for both Moses and Caleb.

All these linguistic comparisons should bring us to ask if Moses wanted Caleb the son of Jephunneh to be his successor only to find out that the Almighty commanded him to appoint Joshua?

Another question we can ask: are we facing a linguistic bias of the text in favor of Caleb the son of Jephunneh from the tribe of Judah, while Joshua the son of Nun is from the tribe of Ephraim?

Caleb, the Son of Jephunneh, and Joshua

In the book Joshua we read, "And the sons of Judah came to Joshua in Gilgal, and Caleb the son of Jephunneh the Kenazite said to him, you know the thing that the Lord said to Moses the man of G-d concerning me and you in Kadesh-Barnea" (Joshua 14:6). We should note that Caleb does not say, "…concerning **us**…" Instead, he puts distance between him and Joshua. Moreover, generally speaking, just to be polite, it is customary for the speaker to list himself last. And here Caleb says, "…concerning **me** and **you**…" and he lists himself first. Should we conclude that Caleb has something in his heart against Joshua?

And the text continues Caleb's words to Joshua – "Forty years old was **I** when Moses the Lord's slave sent **me** from Kadesh-Barnea to spy out the land; and **I** brought him back word as it was in **my** heart" (14:7). Although we know that Caleb was one out of twelve, and we know that both Caleb and Joshua defended Moses from the people, still Caleb talks only of himself.

The Sons of Aaron

We find changes in the order of the social introduction in regard to Aaron's sons. Nadab and Abihu offered before the Lord "strange fire which they were not commanded to do" (Leviticus 10:1). The text brings us their names, "And the sons of Aaron Nadab and Abihu took each of them his censer..." (10:1), and the text uses the personal and emotional formula of "title + name." This formula fits the fact that they did a "personal job," noy one which they were commanded to do.

When Moses guides the people to take out the bodies, the text says, "And Moses called Mishael and Elzaphan the sons of Uzziel the uncle of Aaron..." (10:4). Here we see the formal language formula of "name + title." The events return to their normal course.

Note: this book focuses mainly on Genesis. See more about the formula of "title + name" as it appears in the rest of the Tanach in Appendix A: The Social Introduction.

Linguistic Biases in the Language of the Text

Up to this point we are facing the following biases:

1. Caleb the son of Jephunneh from the tribe of Judah is equated language-wise to Moses: "Moses My slave" and "Caleb My slave."
2. Caleb the son of Jephunneh from the tribe of Judah is equated language-wise to King Solomon: "*Lemale* after."
3. Caleb the son of Jephunneh from the tribe of Judah is equated language-wise to King Saul: offering his daughter to the victor in the battle.

Additional points in language to consider:

1. Building a city is an important point for the text. This is due to the unity between the content and the language in regard to this point.
2. The connection to the Almighty is important issue in the language of the text. This is due to the "promotion" in language in regard to Joshua.
3. The use of "personal language" vs. "formal language" might indicate that the author has a public persona along with a personal one.

SOCIAL INTRODUCTION – THE TITLE ITSELF

In this chapter we will deal with the choice of words to describe the person active in the event. We will deal with two words that are in extensive use in the language of the text in the book of Genesis and the rest of the Tanach.

"Child[21]" vs. "Lad"

We encounter the word "child" for the first time in, "And the child grew and was weaned, and Abraham made a great feast the day that Isaac was weaned" (Genesis 21:8).

Why is Isaac described as a "child?" The text could have very easily described the event thus: "And Isaac grew and was weaned…" Another question we can ask: why did Abraham make a great feast "the day Isaac was weaned?" What is the importance of having the feast on that day? Couldn't Abraham wait a day or two?

> "…and Abraham made **a great feast**
> the day Isaac was weaned" (Genesis 21:8).

Linguistic Journey – Having a Feast

Introduction

The word "feast" in Hebrew is *mishteh,* which is derived from the three-letter root word *SH-T-H* that stands for the verb "to drink." Although we see in the text a *mishteh* including eating, one should note that the main component of *mishteh* is drinking. It is a social event.

Having a *Mishteh*

In Genesis we find several places in which a feast is mentioned. Lot made a feast for the two people/angels who came to visit him: "…and he made them a feast, and baked unleavened bread, and they ate" (19:3). Isaac made a feast for Abimelech and Phichol his military captain who came to

---

[21] Unlike in English, in which the noun "child" applies to both male and female, in Hebrew, the ending of the noun indicates the gender. Adding the sound "ah" at the end of the noun indicates female. The word *yeled* ("child") applies to male while the word *yalda* applies to female.

visit him: "And he made them a feast, and they ate and drank" (26:30). Laban celebrated the day of his daughter's wedding (Leah replacing Rachel): "And Laban gathered together all the people of the place and made a feast" (29:22). And Pharaoh on his birthday, "… made a feast for all his slaves…" (40:20).

There are only two places in the whole Tanach in which the text mentions "a great feast." The first is in our place where Abraham makes "a great feast" on the day Isaac was weaned. And the second, in the book of Esther, "And the king made a great feast for all his ministers and his slaves, it was Esther's feast…" (Esther 2:18).

Back to Abraham

We should conclude that the feast Abraham made was something special and unique. What was unique about the "day Isaac was weaned?" These questions should bring us to check the meaning of the word "growth" and "weaning" as they are used in the Tanach.

Linguistic Journey – "Weaning" and "Growing"

In regard to Samuel's mother Hanna, the text says,

> And Hanna did not go up, for she said to her husband, I will not go up until the **lad** is weaned, and then I will bring him, that he my appear before the Lord, and sit there forever. And Elkanah her husband said to her, do what seems to you good, remain until you have weaned him; only the Lord establish his word. So the woman sat and nursed her son until she weaned him. (1 Samuel 1:22-23)

Both Isaac and Samuel were "weaned." But Isaac is labeled a **child**, and Samuel is labeled a "**lad**" ten times, and elsewhere a "son" (or "her son").

There are other Biblical figures who "grew." First, for Moses the text says, "And the **child** grew and she brought him to Pharaoh's daughter, and he became her son. And she called him Moses,[22] and she said because I drew him out of the water" (Exodus 2:10).

---

[22] Moses – in Hebrew the name is *Moshe* from the verb *limshot*, which means to take out of the water.

Moses got the title "child." Moses "grew," but the text does not say that he was "weaned," at least not in the language of the text.

We find another case of a child who "grew" but was not "weaned" with the Shunammite woman and the prophet Elisha.

> "And the **child grew**, and the day came and he went out to his father to the reapers. And he said to his father, my head, my head. And he said to a lad, carry him to his mother. And he carried him and he brought him to his mother, and he sat on her knees till noon and he died" (2 Kings 4:18-20).

Here, we find that the "child" "grew" but he was not "weaned," and time passes, and the child died. And what about Moses? In his encounter with the Almighty at the burning bush he said, "...O my lord, I am not a man of words neither yesterday nor the day before yesterday nor since you have spoken to your slave, because I am with weighty mouth and a weighty tongue" (Exodus 4:10). In response, the Almighty says, "Who has put a mouth to human, or who makes the dumb, or deaf, or the seeing, or the blind, is it not I the Lord?" (Exodus 4:11).

From the text, it is clear that Moses had some disability. His speech was not regular. Again, we find the lack of "weaning" in the context of some weakness or disability.

There is another Biblical figure who was not "weaned." "And the woman bore a son, and called him Samson and the lad grew and the Lord blessed him" (Judges 13:24).

The story of Samson will give us insight into the process of "growing" in ancient times. In regard to Samson we find,

> And the Angel of the Lord appeared to the woman and said to her, behold, you are barren and bear not, and you shall conceive and bear a son. And now beware please, and drink not wine and alcohol and eat not any unclean food. For behold, you shall conceive and bear a son, and no razor shall come on his head, for the lad shall be a Nazirite to G-d from the womb, and he shall begin to save Israel from the hand of the Philistines. (Judges 13:3-5)

The Angel told the woman "the **lad** will be a Nazirite to G-d from the womb." He will start as a "lad" (even in the womb) and not as a "child." One can deduce that a "lad" is stronger and healthier than a "child." This explains why Samson was not "weaned." There was no need for it as he was not in danger.

Taking into consideration the high mortality rate of infants in ancient times (and up to a hundred years ago) one can understand the concern that parents had for their children during infancy. At the beginning of his life the "child" was in danger. When the danger passed, the "child" turned into a "son" or "daughter" and the parents could connect emotionally to their children.

The "growing" process is expressed in Isaiah, "For to us a **child** is born, to us a **son** is given..." (Isaiah 9:5). He is **born** as "child" and later is **given** as a "son."

We can return to the birth of Isaac, "And the child grew and was weaned, and Abraham made a great feast the day that Isaac was weaned" (Genesis 21:8). The day Isaac was declared as being out of danger, that day, was important enough to call for "a great feast." On the other hand, in the story of Hanna and Samuel, who is labeled a "lad," his mother Hannah calls for him to be "weaned."

Up to his point we have seen several cases:

- A "child" (in danger) who "grows" and gets "weaned" (coming out of danger).
- A "child" who "grows" but is not "weaned" (weak, with disability, or still in danger).
- A "lad" (healthier, not in danger) who "grows" but is not "weaned" (does not need to come out of danger, since no danger exists).

And now back to Samuel. We find that he is labeled a "lad" and his mother wants to "wean" him. Why does Hannah need to "wean" Samuel if he is out of danger (a "lad")?

The answer is that Hannah was barren and she prayed for a son. She took a vow that if G-d would give her "seed of men," then she would give him to G-d for all his life. However, after Samuel was born, his mother did not rush to give him up so quickly. She wanted to wait and enjoy her son. Therefore, she did not want to go up to the Tabernacle in Shiloh for the festival, as she did in the past. If she were to go on pilgrimage, she had to leave her son with the priest. This is the reason that Hannah says to her husband, "I will not go up until the **lad** is weaned, and then I will bring him, that he may appear before the Lord, and sit there forever" (1 Samuel 1:22). In spite of her knowledge that Samuel is a "lad," she needs to "wean" him, only to get some more time with him.

Her husband replies, "And Elkanah her husband said to her, do what seems to you good," but reminds her of her vow, "…only the Lord establish his word" (1:23). Hannah didn't forget her vow and we read, "And she took him up when she weaned him, with three bulls and one ephah of flour and one pitcher of wine, and she brought him to the house of the Lord in Shiloh…" (1:24).

Knowing that "child" means "to be in danger" while a "lad" is not in danger, we can ask now: what was the danger that Isaac was in before he got "weaned?"

In order to understand it, we have to deal with the issue of a woman being barren, as it shows up in the text.

Three of the foremothers started out "barren." For Sarah, the text says, "But Sarai was barren; she had no child[23]" (Genesis 11:30). For Rebecca the text says, "And Isaac prayed to the Lord for his wife because she was barren…" (25:21). For Rachel, "…and Rachel was barren" (29:31). The only one to whom the text does not attribute the word "barren" is Leah, who indeed bears six sons and one daughter. For Leah the text says, "…He opened her womb…" (29:31), as the text does later on for Rachel, "And G-d remembered her and G-d listened to her, and opened her womb" (30:22).

We should note that the text says about Leah that after bearing four sons, "And she stopped bearing[24]" (29:35).

---

[23] The text in Hebrew does not really say the word "child" (*yeled*) but uses instead the word *valad*. It is still a word coming from the three-letter root word Y-L-D, but not the same. While the word *yeled* refers to the baby itself, the word *valad* refers to the baby as coming from the mother, more in the sense of being a "descendant."
[24] Stopped bearing – literally in Hebrew it is said that she "stood" (using the verb *Laamod*) indicating that until this point she was "running."

There are two other barren women in the Tanach. The first is Samson's mother. For her the text says, "And there was one man from Zorah, of the family of the Danites whose name was Manoah; and his wife was barren, and bore not" (Judges 13:2). We should note that the text adds for her "and bore not," almost as it does for Sarah. The second is Hannah, Samuel's mother. For her the text changes the language and does not attribute the word "barren" to her. Instead, the text uses two expressions: one, "...and Hannah had no children" (1 Samuel 1:2), and two, "...and the Lord had closed her womb" (1:5), and "...because the Lord had closed her womb" (1:6).

The Lord's angel appears to Samson's mother and tells her, "...you are barren and bear not, but you shall conceive and bear a son" (Judges 13:3). And, indeed, later on the text says, "And the woman bore a son and called his name Samson, and the lad grew and the Lord blessed him" (13:24).

Hannah, Samuel's mother, prays to the Almighty in Shiloh, and the text says, "...And Elkanah knew Hannah his wife and the Lord remembered her. And in due course Hannah conceived and bore a son..." (1 Samuel 1:19-20). Hannah got pregnant after the Almighty "remembered her." The same description we find in regard to Rachel, Jacob's wife, "And G-d remembered Rachel and G-d listened to her, and opened her womb" (Genesis 30:22).

Sarah is the only one of the three barren foremothers that the text changes the language with respect to the Almighty's intervention, which brings upon her pregnancy, "And the Lord *pakad*[25] Sarah as he had said, and the Lord did to Sarah as he had spoken. And Sarah conceived and bore Abraham a son..." (Genesis 21:1-2). The text does not say that the Almighty "remembered" her as is the case with Rachel and Hannah. The text does not say that the Almighty "opened her womb" as with Leah and Rachel. Instead, the text uses the verb *pakad*.

Two facts will explain this linguistic rarity. First, the only other woman for whom the text uses the word *pakad* is Hannah. After Hannah had Samuel, and brought him to the Tabernacle in Shiloh, the text says, "And the Lord *pakad* Hannah and she conceived and she bore three sons and

---

[25] *Pakad* – this verb is used extensively in the text to refer to the census of the people in the desert. At this point the word is left without translation. The objective of this research is to determine the exact meaning of the word *pakad* as it is used in this context.

two daughters…" (1 Samuel 2:21).   From Hannah we learn that when the Almighty *poked* (the verb *pakad* in the present tense) a woman, it is after she already bore a child before.   This will allow us to understand why Sarah said to Abraham, "…the Lord stopped[26] me from bearing please come to my slave…' (Genesis 16:2).   One cannot say that one "stopped" unless one was in movement before.   A woman cannot say that the Almighty "stopped" her from bearing, unless she bore before.

Now we can understand why the text says in regard to Sarah, "But Sarai was barren; she had no child" (Genesis 11:30).   Sarah indeed bore a child, but it is quite likely that the baby did not survive, and died in infancy. This is very likely the reason that the text uses the word *valad* instead of the word *yeled*.   When Isaac was born there was a major concern that his fate would be the same fate as the previous child.   It is no wonder that Abraham made "a great feast" when Isaac was declared as being out of danger, or, in the language of the text, he was "weaned."

We will now examine other places where child and lad appear.   The first one, Hagar, Sarah's slave, is in the desert with her son Ishmael, after Sarah expelled her from her house.

Hagar and Ishmael in the Desert

> And G-d said to Abraham, let it not be grievous in your sight because of the **lad**, and because of your slave; in all that Sarah has said to you listen to her; for in Isaac shall your seed be called. And also the slave's son will I make a nation because he is your seed. And Abraham rose up early in the morning and took bread, a pitcher of water, and gave it to Hagar, put it on her shoulder, and the **child**, and sent her away, and she went and wandered in the wilderness of Beersheba. And the water in the pitcher ended and she threw the **child** under one of the shrubs. And she went and sat down opposite him a distance of a range of a bow for she said, let me not see the death of the **child**, and she sat opposite him, and raised her voice and cried. And G-d heard the voice of the **lad** and the angel of G-d called to Hagar from heaven and said to her, what is going on Hagar? Fear not, for G-d heard the voice of the **lad**

---

[26] In Hebrew the verb used is *laatzor*. We find this verb in "For the Lord had *atzar* from the wombs of the house of Abimelech because of Sarah Abraham's wife" (Genesis 20:18). We find it also in, "And he stood between the dead and the living and the plague stopped (*neetzara*)" (Numbers 17:13).

where he is. Arise, carry the lad and hold him with your hand for I will make him a great nation. And G-d opened her eyes and she saw a well of water and she went and filled the pitcher with water and gave the **lad** to drink. And G-d was with the **lad** and he grew and lived in the wilderness and became an archer. (Genesis 21:12-20)

The "child" is in danger, but "G-d heard the voice of the **lad**." We should note that the story started with the Almighty appearing to Abraham telling him, "...Let it not be grievous in your sight because of the **lad**..." and the Almighty promises Abraham, "And also the slave's son will I make a nation." When there is hope and future, the word "lad" appears.

Back to Moses

And the woman conceived and bore a son and she saw that he was good and she hid him three months. And she could not hide him any longer, and she took for him an ark made of reeds and daubed it with slime and with pitch, and put the **child** in it, and she put it in the rushes on the Nile's bank. And his sister stood from afar to know what would be done to him. And Pharaoh's daughter came down to wash on the Nile and her maidens walked along the Nile, and she saw the ark among the reeds and she sent her slave and she took it. And she opened it and she saw the **child**, and behold a **lad** was crying, and she had compassion on him and said, this is from the Hebrews' children. And his sister said to Pharaoh's daughter, should I go and call for you a nurse from the Hebrew women that she may nurse the **child** for you? And Pharaoh's daughter said to her go, and the maiden went and called the **child**'s mother. And Pharaoh's daughter said to her, take this **child** and nurse him for me and I will give you your wages, and the woman took the **child**, and nursed him. And the **child** grew, and she brought him to Pharaoh's daughter, and he became a son for her and she called his name Moses and she said because I drew him out of the water. (Exodus 2:2-10)

When Pharaoh's daughter opens the ark she sees a "child," but the "lad" is crying. The change of language does not come to tell us that Moses grew up instantly. The change of language tells us he is out of danger; he is becoming a "lad."

We should note that once Pharaoh's daughter gives Moses to his mother to nurse him, he returns to be a "child" in the language of the text. With his mother he is still in danger, as he returns to the Hebrews' quarters. At that time, any Egyptian can kill him with no guilt, without knowing that he has the immunity of Pharaoh's daughter.

David and Bath-Sheba

King David desires a married woman Bath-Sheba. To get her, he sends her husband Uriah to the war front so he will get killed. David marries Bath-Sheba and she bears him a son. The prophet Nathan tells David that the Almighty decided to punish him, and therefore the baby will die.

And David said to Nathan I have sinned against the Lord. And Nathan said to David the Lord has put away your sin; you shall not die. But because you have given great encouragement to the enemies of the Lord to blaspheme by doing this deed, the **child** who is born to you shall die. And Nathan went to his house, and the Lord struck the **child** that Uriah's wife bore to David and he was in mortal danger. And David prayed to G-d for the **lad**, and David fasted and came in and slept all night and lay on the ground. And the elders of his house arose to raise him from the ground but he would not, neither did he eat bread with them. And on the seventh day the **child** died, and David's slaves feared to tell him that the **child** died, for they said, behold while the **child** was yet alive we spoke to him and he didn't want to listen to us, and how could we tell him the **child** died and he will do evil. And David saw that his slaves were whispering and David understood that the **child** died and David said to his slaves, did the **child** die? And they said he died. And David arose from the ground and washed and oiled himself and changed his garment, and came to the house of the Lord and bowed down and he came to his house and he asked for and they set bread before him and he ate. And his slaves told him, what is this thing that you have done? You fasted and you cried for the live **child**, and when the **child** died you arose and ate bread. And he said, while the **child** was yet alive I fasted and cried for I said who knows if G-d will be gracious with me, and the **child** will live. But now he is dead, why should I fast? Can I bring him back again? I am going to him but he shall not return to me. (2 Samuel 12:13-23)

In this example we find only once the word "lad," when David prays to the Almighty to save him. When there is hope, and David prays to the Almighty and hopes for the best, he is a "lad." On the other hand, when the danger is imminent, and the situation is hopeless, he is a "child."

Elijah and the Widow

Another "child" is in danger. The prophet Elijah stayed at the house of a widow who fed him. The widow's son got sick, and the text tells us, "And after these things the son of the woman, the mistress of the house, fell sick, and his sickness was so severe, until there was no breath left in him" (1 Kings 17:17).

We should note that the text does not say that the child "died," but that "there was no breath left in him."

> And she said to Elijah, what have I to do with you, O you man of G-d? You came to me to remind me of my sin and kill my son. And he said to her, give me your son, and he took him from her bosom, and carried him to the loft where he was sitting there, and laid him upon his bed. And he called to the Lord and said, O Lord my G-d, have you brought evil upon the widow with whom I sojourn, by slaying her son? And he stretched himself upon the **child** three times and called the Lord and said, O Lord my G-d, please let this **child**'s soul return into him. And the Lord listened to Elijah and the soul of the **child** returned into him and he lived. And Elijah took the **child** and brought him down from the loft into the house and gave him to his mother and Elijah said, see your **son** lives. And the woman said to Elijah, now by this I know that you are a man of G-d and the word of the Lord in your mouth is true. (1 Kings 17:18-24)

We should note that when Elijah returned the child's soul to him he is still labeled a "child;" he is still in danger. Only when the prophet gives him back to his mother and tells her, "See your **son** lives," is he out of danger. He turned into a "son."

A "Lad" Who is in Danger

The son of Jeroboam, a king of Israel, fell sick. Earlier, Jeroboam had ordered the people of Israel to rebel against the Lord's words and to bring idolatry back into the land. Once his son fell sick, Jeroboam wanted to ask the prophet Ahijah about his son's fate. Jeroboam knew that his deeds in the past would not make the prophet want to help him. Therefore, he asked his wife to conceal her identity so the prophet would not recognize her, and to go and talk with the prophet instead of him. However, the prophet knew in advance that Jeroboam's wife was coming. "And the Lord said to Ahijah, behold, the wife of Jeroboam comes to ask you for her son, for he is sick, thus and thus shall you say to her, and when she comes, she shall feign herself to be another" (1 Kings 14:5).

And the prophet Ahijah informs Jeroboam's wife of the Lord's tough words:

> Go tell Jeroboam, thus said the Lord G-d of Israel, since I exalted you from among the people and made you ruler over My people Israel. And I tore the kingdom away from the house of David and gave it to you, and yet you have not been as My slave David, who kept My commandments and who followed Me with all his heart, to do only what is right in My eyes. But you have done evil above all who were before you, for you went and made you other gods and molten images, to anger Me, and you have thrown Me behind your back. Therefore, behold, I will bring evil to the house of Jeroboam, and will cut off from Jeroboam any who pisses against the wall, and he who is arrested and abandoned in Israel, and will eradicate away the remnants of the house of Jeroboam, as a man eradicates the dung till it is fully gone. He who dies of Jeroboam in the city shall the dogs eat, and he who shall die in the field the birds of the sky will eat, for the Lord has spoken. Arise therefore and go to your house, and when your feet enter the city the **child** will die. (1 Kings 14:7-12)

And the text continues: "And Jeroboam's wife arose and went and came to Tirzah, and when she came to the threshold of the door the **lad** died" (1 Kings 14:17).

Up to this point we saw that only a "child" is in life threatening danger. And here, for the first time, we find the word "lad" is used in the context of danger and death. How come?

"…and came to Tirzah…"

The text does not talk about Tirzah as the place where King Jeroboam located his palace, and the center of his kingdom. It is quite safe to assume that Jeroboam's wife took the prophet's words literally: "…and when your feet enter the city the child will die." These words brought her to avoid going home. In order to save her son's life she decided not to enter the city and to go instead to Tirzah. This diversion brought the "child" to feel better and to become a "lad." When the danger passed she went to visit her son. However, "…when she came to the threshold of the door the lad (who had overcome his illness) died," with no apparent reason other than the prophet Ahijah's words to his mother.

Elisha and the Shunammite Woman

We can find another case in the Tanach where a "lad" is in life-threatening danger: the story of the prophet Elisha and the Shunammite woman, found in 2 Kings 4:8-37.

After the woman invited Elisha to be her guest in a small loft at her house, the prophet asked the woman what he could do for her. The prophet's servant said, "she has no son and her husband is old" (4:14). The prophet calls the woman and tells her, "At this festival in the coming year you shall embrace a son" (4:16). Indeed, "And the woman conceived, and bore a son at that festival in the following year that Elisha had said to her" (4:17).

> And the **child** grew and one day he went out to his father to the reapers. And he said to his father, my head, my head, and he said to a lad, carry him to his mother. And he carried him and he brought him to his mother, he sat on her knees till noon, and he died. (4:18-20)

The **child**'s mother laid him on the bed of the man of G-d in the loft and she ran to the prophet on Mount Carmel. When the prophet saw the woman, he said to his servant, "…run please towards her and tell her, is it well with you, is it well with your husband, is it well with the **child**, and she said, it is well" (4:26).

By using the word "child" it is clear that the prophet suspected that something was wrong with him. Otherwise, why would the woman come to see him? The woman tells the servant "it is well;" however, when she reaches the prophet, she holds his feet, a behavior which tells the prophet that indeed there is a problem with the child. And he tells his servant who wants to push the woman away, "Don't hold her for her soul is grieved and the Lord hid it from me, and did not tell me" (4:27).

> Then he said to Gehazi, belt up your waist, and take my staff in your hand, and go, if you meet any man, greet him not, and if anyone greets you, don't answer him, and lay my staff upon the face of the **lad**. And the mother of the **lad** said, as the Lord lives, and as your soul lives, I will not leave you, and he arose and went after her. And Gehazi passed on before them, and laid the staff on the **lad**'s face, but there was no voice and no listening, and he returned towards him and told him saying, the **lad** did not wake up. And Elisha came into the house and behold, the **lad** was laid dead upon his bed. And he came and he closed the door upon the two of them and he prayed to the Lord. And he went up and lay upon the **child** and put his mouth upon his mouth, and his eyes upon his eyes, and the palm of his hands on his palms, and he stretched upon him and the flesh of the **child** got warm. And he returned and walked inside the house back and forth, and he went up, and stretched himself upon him, and the **lad** sneezed seven times, and the **lad** opened his eyes. And he called Gehazi, and said, call this Shunammite, and he called her, and she came to him, and he said, carry your **son**. And she came and she fell at his feet and she bowed to the ground, and she carried her **son** and she went out. (4:29-37)

At first, in verse 26, the prophet used the word "child" indicating danger and death. However, the story continues using the word "lad," by the mother, the prophet's servant, and even the prophet himself. One might ask: why is the word "child" used in the beginning, then changing to "lad," and then changing back to "child" in verse 34?

Verse 33, preceding the change of language from "lad" to "child," explains the change of language: "…and he prayed to the Lord." At first, the prophet was confident in himself and his ability to save the "child." The prophet himself used the word "lad," influencing all the people around him – his servant, and the child's mother. The prophet thought that just putting his staff on the child would create the miracle – that the source of the miracle was the prophet himself and his staff. And when Gehazi put the staff on the "lad" and the "lad" still didn't revive, Elisha understood that he was not omnipotent, and he could not replace the Almighty. When he came to this realization, the "lad" was not a "lad" anymore, but a "child," and that he should pray to the one who could really save the "child." And, indeed, after his prayer, the "child" turned into a "lad" when he returned to life and opened his eyes.

Dinah in Shechem

The text tells us that when Dinah, Jacob's daughter, goes to be with the daughters of the land, she is taken by the son of the ruler, who takes her, sleeps with her, and hurts her. The text says, "…he took her and lay with (*ota*) her…" (Genesis 34:2).

We saw earlier in our linguistic journey dealing with the two Biblical forms of the preposition "with" that *im* indicates closeness, and *et* indicates distance. We also saw that the phrase "to lay with (*ota*) her" appears three times in the entire Tanach – here in the case of Dinah in Shechem, in the case of Amnon raping his sister Tamar, and the case of a man lying with a woman while she was menstruating. Therefore, we should note that from the beginning the text describes the events in Shechem with the language reserved for rape or suspected rape.

And the text continues, "And his soul was drawn to Dinah Jacob's daughter and he loved the **lass**, and spoke to her heart" (34:3).

At this stage, one might think that the young man is really in love with Dinah, and when he slept with her earlier, he might have done so with good intentions towards her, and only the text perceives it as rape, but not the young man himself.

However, the text continues, "And Shechem spoke to his father Hamor saying, take for me this **child** for a wife" (34:4).

By the text quoting Shechem using "child" when talking to his father we can conclude that Shechem knew that his behavior was improper, and he knew that Dinah was in danger by being with him.

The language of the text even shows us that Shechem talked to his father differently from the way he was talking to Dinah's father. When talking to Jacob, the text quotes him as saying, "Put on me as much dowry and gift and I will give according to what you say to me, and give me the **lass** for a wife" (34:12).

Did Shechem talk to his father differently (using "child") because he knew that he did wrong to Dinah, or, did he talk like that because his father expected him to mistreat women? Either way, the language of the text confirms to us that we should disregard the fact that Shechem loved Dinah. She was in fact in danger.

Judah, Benjamin, and "The Lad"

When Judah addresses "Israel his father" (Genesis 43:8) in a second attempt to get Benjamin to go with the brothers to Egypt to face the ruler (Joseph), the text quotes Judah saying, "…send the lad with (*et*) me, and we will arise and go, that we may live and not die, we, and you, and our little ones" (43:8).

When Judah used the word "lad" (and not "our brother" as in 43:4), Judah sends the message that he is confident that Benjamin is not in danger.

Judah's Speech to Joseph

At this point we should go over what Judah experienced. Judah knew that the ruler demanded that he bring Benjamin to him. When Benjamin came in front of the ruler, the ruler blessed him with, "G-d be gracious to you, my son" (Genesis 43:29). When the brothers sat down to eat lunch with Joseph, the brothers and Joseph ate different food from the Egyptians sitting with them. This point exposed that Joseph the ruler was not an Egyptian by origin. During the lunch, the ruler positioned the brothers at the table, "…the firstborn according to his birthright, and the young according to his youth…" (43:33). And the brothers' response, "…and the men looked at one another in amazement" (43:33). When the ruler gave the brothers gifts he gave Benjamin five times more, "...but Benjamin's portion was five times as much as any of theirs..." (43:34). And then, the ruler's cup was found in Benjamin's bag, and Judah had no doubt that Benjamin did not steal the cup, and it was a false accusation. But what could be the objective of the false accuser?

When "Judah and his brothers" return and stand in front of the ruler, Judah says, "...what shall we say to my lord? What shall we speak? Or how shall we clear ourselves? G-d has found out **the iniquity of your slaves**..." (44:16). Judah is talking here of the iniquity of everyone and not of the iniquity of one, Benjamin. "The iniquity of your slaves" in the plural can relate only to the sale of Joseph to slavery. And Judah says this to Joseph. Up to this point, Joseph was listening to their conversations. Yet "... they knew not that Joseph understood them for he spoke to them by an interpreter" (42:23). This is not true in this conversation. Judah talks directly to Joseph and relates to "the iniquity of your slaves" without specifying which iniquity. The cup? Or the sale of Joseph, so many years earlier?

When Judah suggests to the ruler that all of them be slaves, the ruler answers, "...G-d forbid that I should do so, but the man in whose hand the cup was found he shall be a slave to me, and as for you, go up in peace to your father" (44:17). Since the ruler demands only Benjamin, whom Judah knows didn't steal the cup, the same Benjamin who received "five portions," it is quite likely that Judah knows that he is facing one who wants Benjamin to stay with him. Judah knows now that the ruler is emotionally connected to Benjamin, and who can that be? One who is not originally an Egyptian? And now Judah "came near" (44:18) to Joseph to talk with him. It is quite likely that Judah knows that he is dealing with Joseph. But knowledge is not enough. Joseph might continue playing the role of the ruler of the land, to prevent Benjamin from returning to his father, and by doing so would force Judah to renege on his promise to his father.

Judah starts his speech by detailing the events that brought everyone to this point:

My lord asked his slaves saying have you a father, or a brother? And we said to my lord, we have a father, an old man, and a child of his old age, a little one, and his brother died, and he alone is left of his mother, and his father loves him. And you said to your slaves, bring him down to me, that I may set my eyes upon him. (44:19-21)

Linguistic Journey - To Go Down (*Laredet*)

This is not the only place in which the book of Genesis describes the act of traveling from the land of Canaan to another country as the act of "going down," and by doing so, attributes holiness to the land of Canaan.

First, we find it with Abraham: "And there was a famine in the land, and Abram **went down** to Egypt to sojourn there, for the famine was severe in the land" (12:10). When there is a famine in Isaac's time, the Almighty appears to Isaac saying, "...Do not **go down** to Egypt, live in the land of which I shall tell you" (26:2). In the time of Jacob, we find the act of "going down" mainly in regard to Joseph: "And Joseph's ten brothers **went down** to buy grain in Egypt" (42:3). When Jacob argues with his sons about taking Benjamin down to Egypt: "...my son shall not **go down** with you..." (42:38). And after Jacob agreed to let Benjamin go with them: "And the men took this present, and took double silver in their hand, and Benjamin, and rose up, and **went down** to Egypt and stood before Joseph" (43:15). And the brothers appear before "the man who is in charge of Joseph's house" and say, "...oh my lord, we **came indeed down**[27] the first time to buy food" (43:20).

When Judah talks to Joseph after Benjamin is caught with the cup, and Benjamin is in danger of being enslaved, Judah tells Joseph of the brothers' conversation with their father in the land of Canaan, "And we said, we cannot **go down**, if our little brother is with us, then will we **go down**..." (44:26). Earlier, Judah quoted Joseph's demand to see Benjamin saying, "And you said to your slaves, if your little brother will not **go down** with you, you shall see my face no more" (44:23).

We should note that the text does not use the verb "to go down" when Joseph demands Benjamin. "And **bring** your little brother to me..." (42:20). Joseph, the Egyptian ruler, does not use the verb "to go down" when it relates to Egypt. As an Egyptian ruler who appears before the brothers, he cannot use such a verb, a verb that dishonors the position of

---

[27] "...[W]e came indeed down..." – Again, in the Hebrew we find that the verb is doubled for emphasis. Literally, the text says, "...**coming down** we **came down**..."

Egypt as the great superpower of the era. Only when Joseph acknowledges himself to his brothers as Joseph does the text quote him as saying to his brothers, "And you shall tell my father of all my glory in Egypt, and of all that you have seen, and you shall hurry and bring my father **down** here" (45:13).

If we accept that the verb "to go down" from the land of Canaan to Egypt attributes holiness to the land of Canaan, and dishonor to the land of Egypt, we should expect that Joseph's brothers would adjust their language to the language used in Egypt, only to assure that the Egyptian ruler, or any other man in Egypt, will be not be offended by such dishonor. Moreover, if this is the language that Joseph's brothers used while talking to Joseph, or the man who is in charge of Joseph's house, we should expect that Joseph, or the man under him, would correct them, and put them in their place. And if Joseph and the man in charge of his house did not correct them, shouldn't that alone trigger a red flag in the brothers' minds that something is not right?

And Judah misquoted Joseph as saying to the brothers, "...bring him **down** to me, that I may set my eyes upon him" (44:21). It is possible that Judah is using here language that sends a message to Joseph: I know that you understand the meaning of "to bring down" or "to come down." Correct me if you wish. And if you do not correct me, you confirm that you are a member of a family that attributes holiness to the land of Canaan, and there is only one family like that: Jacob's family.

The text says, "...bring him down to me, that I may **set my eyes upon him**" (44:21). If we check Joseph's words when he demanded they bring Benjamin in front of him, we do not find this phrase, "that I may set my eyes on him." Joseph phrased his demand to bring Benjamin as follows: "Hereby you shall be tested, by the life of Pharaoh, you shall not go from here, unless your little brother comes here" (42:15). And later Joseph said, "And bring your little brother to me **so your words shall be verified**, and you shall not die, and they did so" (42:20).

Judah added a phrase, "that I may set my eyes upon him," which does not show up at all in Joseph's words. Such a phrase contradicts the demand to bring Benjamin as a test to verify the brothers' words, and positioned Joseph's demand of bringing Benjamin to Egypt, as the means to verify Benjamin's well-being.

Moreover, "that I may set my eyes upon him," is more guarding Benjamin, in a very positive way. We can find in the Tanach the concept of eyes upon someone/something as supervising from close by in the following verse: "A land which the Lord your G-d cares for, **the eyes** of the Lord your G-d **are** always **upon it**, from the beginning of the year to the end of the year" (Deuteronomy 11:12).

At this stage we could expect that Joseph would express resistance to this concept of caring for Benjamin. Joseph would say that he didn't say such a thing. Joseph presents himself as one who interrogates the brothers under suspicion of being spies. But Joseph is silent and allows Judah to continue with his speech.

Interrogators know, when they attempt to get a confession from a suspect under interrogation by using a long persuasion speech, that there is a stage in which the suspect is silent. This silence confirms to the interrogator that the suspect is ready to confess. The suspect's silence tells the interrogator that the confession is not far away in time.

And Judah continues recounting the events, "And we said to my lord, the **lad** cannot leave his father, for if he should leave his father, his father would die" (44:22).

If earlier, Judah presented Benjamin as a "child" (…we have a father, an old man, and a **child** of his old age…), then after Joseph's silence, and lack of resistance to the idea that he only wanted Benjamin to guard him, Judah knows that his suspicion, that he in fact is talking to Joseph, is verified, and if so, Benjamin is out of danger. Benjamin becomes a "lad" and not a "child." The danger passed.

For comparison, Judah said to his father, "If you send **our brother** with us…" (43:4). In his speech to Joseph, Judah quotes himself talking to his father, but adding the adjective "…our **little** brother…" Judah is playing with Joseph's emotions.

And Judah continues, "And when we **went up** to your slave **my father**, we told him the words of my lord. And **our father** said, return and buy us a little food" (44:24-25).

In his speech, Judah uses the title "your slave my father" several times. Now, we are facing a double change of language. From "my father" to "our father," and from "your slave our father" to only "our father." It is interesting to notice that in this verse Judah quotes accurately Jacob's words, "...their father said to them, return, buy us a little food" (44:25). This fact should bring us to ask, in the other places where Judah uses "your slave my father" or "your slave our father," if he is quoting his father's words inaccurately.

And Judah continues, "And we said, we cannot go down, if our **little** brother be with us, then we will go down, for we may not see the man's face unless our **little** brother be with us" (44:26).

And Judah continues,

> And your slave my father said to us, you know that my wife bore me two. And the one went out from me, and I said surely he was torn to pieces, and I saw him not since. And you take this one also from me, and disaster befall him, and you will bring down my old age in evil to Sheol. (44:27-29)

The opening "And your slave my father" which might indicate inaccuracy (to say the least) when Judah quotes his father, should bring us to ask what Jacob actually told his son.

"And Jacob their father said to them, you made me bereaved, Joseph is not present, and Simeon is not present, and you will take Benjamin, all these things are upon me" (42:36).

When Reuben came with the proposal to kill his two sons if Benjamin did not return, Jacob said, "...my son shall not go down with you, for his brother died, and he is left alone, and disaster will befall him on the way that you are going to walk in, and you will bring down my old age with sorrow to Sheol' (42:38).

In the two times that Jacob talks to his sons he does not say, "you know that my wife bore me two." And we should not expect that Jacob would say something like that to his sons. Why should he state the obvious? Judah added this sentence, which Jacob didn't say, to send a message to Joseph that Rachel, Joseph's mother who died giving birth to Benjamin, is still Jacob's wife, and not Leah, Judah's mother. If Joseph has any doubt of his position in Jacob's household, then after such a sentence, it is clear to Joseph that he is the firstborn to Jacob's preferred and beloved wife.

As for the conclusion of Joseph's fate, Jacob used two words, (1) "not present" when he also mentioned Simeon was not present (42:36), and (2) "he died" (42:38) when he was talking about Joseph. Judah, on the other hand, prefers to quote Jacob from the time immediately after Joseph disappeared, "...and I said surely he was torn to pieces, and I saw him not since" (44:28). "And he recognized it and said, it is my son's coat, an evil beast has devoured him, Joseph is surely torn in pieces" (37:33).

The addition, "and I saw him not since," which Jacob also did not say, comes to tell Joseph that Judah knows that Joseph is not dead and that he is not missing, as he stands right there in front of him. And if there is one who didn't see Joseph "since," it is Jacob, but definitely not Judah.

We should also note that Jacob did not say the word "also" in, "And you take this one **also** from me..." Jacob only said, "And you will take Benjamin..." But Judah added this word "also" and by saying it, he admits "the iniquity of your slaves" from years past, that the brothers were the ones who took Joseph away from his father, and that there was no order by the father to get rid of Joseph, in case such an option was in Joseph's mind.

And Judah continues, "And now when I come to your slave my father, and the **lad** is not with us, and his soul is bound with his soul. And when he will see that the **lad** is not with us, and he will die, and your slaves will take our father's old age in sorrow to Sheol" (44:30-31).

The phrase "And **now**..." which is a "connection" phrase, comes to tell us that Judah ended his message he wanted to give Joseph, and he moves now to the end of his speech, in which he expects a "confession" from the ruler.

The combination of "your slave my father" and the word "lad" constitutes a contradiction between the **language** and the **content**. While the use of the phrase "your slave my father" might indicate that Judah is not telling the truth, the word "lad" indicates that Judah knows at this stage that Benjamin is not in danger. If so, what is the deception in the sentence?

Judah knows that the chance that he will need to come back to his father without Benjamin is very slim, and therefore, there is no chance his father will die as a result, but he continues with the idea, only to play on Joseph's emotions.

And Judah turns to end his speech with his strongest card yet, "his word is his word."

> Because your slave became surety for the **lad** to my father saying, if I bring him not to you, then I shall sin to my father forever. And now, please let your slave sit instead of the **lad** as a slave to my lord, and let the **lad** go up with his brothers. For how shall I go up to my father, and the **lad** is not with me? Lest perhaps I see the evil that shall come on my father. (44:32-34)

In this section, in which Judah talks of his strongest trait, keeping a promise, and "his word is his word," Judah repeatedly uses the title 'my father" and not "your slave my father." If there is truth in Judah's words, it is in this section.

And Joseph's reaction to the speech is, "And Joseph could not refrain himself before all those who stood in front of him…" (45:1). Joseph, like his father Jacob, knows Judah well enough to accept that if Judah is willing to replace Benjamin, that he actually means it. Judah does not talk just for talking, and this knowledge breaks Joseph.

Summary

One can read Judah's speech not knowing the inner thoughts of Judah, and perceiving the speech as pleading with Joseph for mercy. However, if one is tuned to the language, and one knows that the word "child" means danger, while the word "lad" means safety, along with comparing Judah's words to Jacob's words in the past, one can easily see that Judah is talking from a position of strength, and not from weakness. If one looks upon the two – Joseph and Judah – and perceives Joseph to be the "interrogator," and Judah the "subject," one loses. If we read the text correctly by the **language**, we can see that, in fact, Judah "interrogates" Joseph, and not vice versa.

Isaac and the Binding on the Altar

We can return now to Isaac, the Biblical figure with whom we started this chapter. Abraham is commanded by the Almighty to take his son, his only one, Isaac, and to raise him as a burnt offering "on one of the mountains which I will tell you" (22:2).

And the text continues,

> And Abraham rose up early in the morning, and saddled his ass, and took two of his lads with him, and Isaac his son, and broke the wood for the burnt offering, and rose up, and went to the place of which G-d had told him. On the third day Abraham lifted his eyes and saw the place from afar. And Abraham said to his lads, stay here with the ass, and I, and the **lad**, will go here and bow down and return to you. (22:3-5)

Abraham is not using the word "child" which indicates danger and death. Instead, Abraham used the word "lad" indicating that Isaac is not in danger. One might ask: if Abraham knew that he was going to sacrifice Isaac his son, why didn't he use the word "child" here?

There are two possibilities to explain it. First, Abraham wanted to mislead the two lads, out of fear they would rebel and prevent him from obeying the Almighty's directive. Therefore, he could not show anything on the outside, not even in his language, that there was a danger to Isaac.

The second explanation, which is more realistic, is that Abraham knew that the directive to offer Isaac as a burnt offering contradicted the Almighty's promise to him from an earlier time, "...and I will establish my covenant with him (Isaac) for an everlasting covenant, and with seed after him" (17:19). This promise brought Abraham to understand that the Almighty was only testing him: "And after these things, G-d tested Abraham..." (22:1). Abraham was confident that the Almighty would intervene at the last moment, and would not let him sacrifice Isaac. This understanding expressed itself in Abraham's language, and his confidence that he indeed would return to the two lads with Isaac, "...and we will return to you" (22:5).

And the text continues,

And Isaac spoke to Abraham his father, my father, and he said, here I am my son. And he said, behold here is the fire and the wood and where is the lamb for a burnt offering? And Abraham said, G-d will provide himself the lamb for a burnt offering, my son, so they went both of them together. (22:7-8)

In reading the text with the cantillations[28] that determine the right division of the sentence into its components, there is a comma between "burnt offering" and the phrase "my son." Moreover, in the previous sentence Abraham ended his words to Isaac with "my son" as well. "My son" is only an ending to the sentence, and not necessarily part of the message. Therefore, we should read the sentence as saying not more than G-d will provide himself the lamb. The traditional commentary looks at this sentence as saying, G-d will provide himself with the lamb, and if not my son will be offered for a burnt offering. This apologetic approach is only to defend Abraham by saying that Abraham did not mislead his son. But the fact is that by accurately reading the sentence, knowing that the address "my son" is not part of the message, but only a term of endearment the father uses towards his son, we see that Abraham only expresses again his confidence that Isaac is not going to be a burnt offering.

If we listen to the information expressed in the language describing the events, as well as listening to the content of the story, then we can see that Abraham was confident that the Almighty would bring a lamb to him. He knew all along that he would not need to sacrifice Isaac.

And the story ends with,

And Abraham stretched out his hand and took the knife to slay his son. And the angel of the Lord called to him from heaven and said, Abraham, Abraham, and he said, here I am. And he said, lay not your hand upon the **lad**, nor do anything to him, for now I know that you fear G-d, seeing that you did not withhold your son, your only son from me. (22:10-12)

And now we can see that the "lad" is not in danger.

---

[28] The cantillations are the signs that determine the way the text is to be sung aloud in the synagogue. They determine the division of the sentence into its components, and the way to sing it.

Modern Perspective of Child vs. Lad or Son or Daughter

The understanding that "child" means grave danger to the offspring, in contrast to the word "lad," which indicates no danger, is not only applicable in Biblical language. Even today, we can use these meanings to understand the perception of reality by the subject who gives a statement. Investigators who deal with child abuse, either verbal, physical, or sexual abuse, can testify that it is rare to find a parent who abuses his/her own children and still uses the words "son" and "daughter." Not only in an "open statement" over a page or two, but constantly in their everyday language. We can explain it as a mental process of detachment. This process enables the person to abuse his/her offspring. A human being cannot abuse his/her own son or daughter. The person needs to say first, "This is not my son," and "This is not my daughter" before they can cross the line from being a parent who educates a son or daughter, to a parent who abuses them.

This phenomenon is seen in so many cases, to the point that an investigator who receives an "open statement" from a suspect in child abuse, and encounters the words "son" and "daughter" even once, should take into consideration that the parent might not be an abusive parent. Statistically, we can consider it very strong linguistic evidence to exonerate the parent.

It is a fact that in many cases we find that an abusive parent uses the child's first name, or the words "child," and "boy/girl." This should guide the interviewer in the conversation with the parent. Even if the interviewer does not know if any abuse took place, the interviewer should not use the titles "your son" and "your daughter" in their questions. Not even the words "son" and "daughter" without the possessive pronoun "your." Such language might influence the parent's language, and might bring the parent to use such language. Instead, the interviewer should use only the child's first name.

ELIEZER AND REBECCA

The text starts the sequence of events of sending Abraham's slave to Haran to get a wife for Isaac by saying, "And Abraham said to his slave the oldest in his household who ruled over all that he had…" (Genesis 24:2).

Abraham's slave is mentioned for the first time several chapters before that:

> After these things the word of the Lord came to Abram in a vision saying, fear not Abram, I am your shield, and your reward will be great. And Abram said, Lord G-d, what will you give me, and I am walking childless, and the son of my household is Eliezer of Damascus." And Abram said, to me you have given no seed, and the son of my household is inheriting me. (15:1-3)

In this earlier story Eliezer of Damascus is described as "the son of my household" and he might even inherit from Abraham, since Abraham had no seed. However, if we return to the story of Eliezer and Rebecca in Genesis 24, we should note that throughout the chapter, which is the longest chapter in Genesis at 67 verses, the text does not mention the slave's name. From the text itself we do not know that the slave is indeed Eliezer. To say that it is "the story of Eliezer and Rebecca" is only our assumption.

The fact that Eliezer of Damascus receives two different titles (assuming we are dealing with the same person) testifies to his importance. He is not only a "slave" but also "the son of the household" and he is even a potential heir. Even in the story in front of us, Eliezer receives an honorific title, "slave the oldest in his household." This same title appears in the funeral of Jacob: "And Joseph went up to bury his father, and with him went up all Pharaoh's slaves, the elders of his house, and all the elders of the land of Egypt" (50:7). We should note that "Pharaoh's slaves the elders of his house" are listed before "the elders of the land of Egypt," and by being listed first, the text makes Pharaoh's slaves more important.

Moreover, if we return to the verse that starts the sequence of events dealing with Eliezer and Rebecca, we find, "And Abraham said to his slave the oldest in his household, who ruled over all that he has, please **put**

your hand under my thigh" (Genesis 24:2). We see an identical event in, "And the time drew nearer that Israel would die, and he called to his son Joseph and said to him, if I found grace in your sight please put your hand under my thigh…" (47:29).

To sum it up, Eliezer, who was Abraham's slave, the oldest of his household, the son of his household, and even a potential heir to Abraham, was an important person in Abraham's household. It is no wonder that Eliezer introduced himself to Rebecca's family by saying, "… I am Abraham's slave" (24:34). He was very proud of being a slave to a person such as Abraham.

From the beginning of the story the text attributes the title "slave" to Eliezer: "And Abraham said to his **slave**…" (24:2), "And the **slave** said to him…" (24:5), "And the **slave** put his hand under the thigh of Abraham his master…" (24:9), "And the **slave** took ten of his master's camels…" (24:10), "And the **slave** ran towards her and said, please pour me a little water from your water jar" (24:17).

And the text continues to describe the course of events:

> And she said, drink my lord, and she hurried and took down her water jar into her hand and gave him to drink. And when she finished giving him to drink, she said, I will draw water for your camels also until they have finished drinking. And she hurried and she emptied her water jar into the trough, and ran back to the well to draw water, and drew water for all his camels. (24:18-20)

When Rebecca did exactly what Eliezer asked in his prayer to the "Lord G-d of my master Abraham" (24:12), the text promotes Eliezer and attributes to him the title "man" "And the **man** wondering at her held his peace to see whether the Lord had made his way successful or not" (24:21).

We should note here that we are not facing a "promotion" given in a quote attributed to one of the people in the story. It is a "promotion" in the **language** of the text describing the course of events. When it becomes clear that the slave's appeal to the Almighty was answered immediately, the slave received the same title that Abraham, Isaac, Jacob, and Moses received: man.

Linguistic Journey - Important People in Genesis and the Title "Man"

Most of the important people in Genesis received the title "man" (*ish*). If we go by the order in the book, then the first one to receive this title is Noah: "These are the *toldot* of Noah, Noah was a righteous and perfect **man** in his generations…" (6:9). Also, "And Noah the **man** of the earth began and planted a vineyard" (9:20).

We find the same in Lot, Abraham's nephew, who sat in Sodom: "And they said stand back and they said, this one came in to sojourn and he wants to be a judge, now we will do to you more harm than to them. And they pressed hard upon the **man**, and came near to break the door" (19:9).

Abraham himself received the title, when the Almighty talked to Abimelech after Abimelech took Sarah into his house, "And now return the **man**'s wife for he is a prophet and he shall pray for you and you shall live…" (20:7).

We should note that Abraham received the title "man" only in conjunction with Sarah his wife, "the man's wife."

Eliezer, Abraham's slave, also receives the title "man" in his meeting with Rebecca by the well. First by the text itself,

- "And the **man** is wondering…" (24:21)
- "And the **man** bowed down his head…" (24:26)
- "…and Laban ran out to the **man**…" (24:29)
- "…and he came to the **man**…" (24:30)
- "And the **man** came into the house…" (24:32)

Second, the text brings Rebecca's words when she ran to her brother to tell him what happened, "…thus spoke the **man** to me…" (24:30). And third, Rebecca's family asks her, "…will you go with this **man**…" (24:58).

Isaac received the title "man" in a quote of Abimelech, "And Abimelech commanded all his people saying, he who touches this **man** or his wife shall surely be put to death" (26:11). And he received the title "man" from the text itself, "And the **man** became rich, and gained more and more, until he became very wealthy" (26:13).

Jacob and Esau: "And the lads grew and Esau was a **man** knowledgeable of hunting, a **man** of the field, and Jacob was an innocent **man** living in tents" (25:27). Later on, Jacob himself says, "And Jacob said to Rebecca his mother, behold, Esau my brother is a hairy **man** and I am a smooth **man**" (27:11). The text describes Jacob's wealth, "And the **man** extended significantly and he had many sheep and female slaves and male slaves and camels and asses" (30:43).

When Jacob's sons introduce themselves to Joseph, they say, "We are all one **man**'s sons, we are honest..." (42:11), and also, "And they said your slaves are twelve brothers, the sons of one **man** in the land of Canaan..." (42:13).

Joseph as well receives the title "man" while still in the house of Potiphar his master, "And the Lord was with Joseph and he was a successful **man**..." (39:2). When his master's wife talks to the people of her household, she says, "...see he has brought us a Hebrew **man** to *letzahek*[29] us" (39:14).

When the brothers report their experience in Egypt to their father Jacob, they say, "The **man** who is the lord of the land spoke roughly to us..." (42:30), and, "And the **man**, the lord of the land said to us..." (42:33).

In the following chapter we find Joseph's brothers and their father Jacob relate to the ruler of the land as a "man" several times:

- "...the **man** did solemnly protest unto us saying..." (43:3),
- "...for the **man** said to us..." (43:5),
- "And Israel said, why did you harm me to tell the **man**..." (43:6),
- "And they said the **man** asked us extensively about us, our homeland, saying...' (43:7),
- "...and carry down a present to the **man**..." (43:11),
- "...and arise and return to the **man**" (43:13), and finally,
- "...And God Almighty give you mercy before the **man**..." (43:14).

---

[29] The verb *letzahek*, which is derived from the three-letter root TZ-H-K is not the same verb as "to laugh" (*litzhok*). Isaac (*Yitzhak* in Hebrew) is the future tense of "to laugh." We leave *letzahek* without translation for now, and we will see more about in a coming chapter.

Joseph related to himself as a "man" in the following, "And Joseph said to them, what deed is this that you have done? Do you not know that such a **man** as I can certainly read the future?"[30] (44:15).

There are several important people in the rest of the Tanach who receive the title "man." One to be noted especially is Moses, "...the **man** Moses was very great in the land of Egypt..." (Exodus 11:3), "...as for this Moses the **man** who brought us out of the land of Egypt..." (Exodus 32:1, 23), and, "And the **man** Moses was very humble, more than all of the people who were upon the face of the earth" (Numbers 12:3).

Back to Eliezer and Becoming a "Man"

The text says, "And the **man** wondering at her held his peace to see whether the Lord had made his journey **successful** or not" (24:21).

The combination of a "man" with being "successful" appears once more in Genesis: "And the Lord was with Joseph and he was a **successful man**..." (39:2). "Success" appears in Genesis only in relation to a "slave." On the other hand, when the text relates to a free man, the text uses different language. For Abraham, "And the Lord has blessed my master greatly and he has become **great**..." (24:35). For Isaac, "And the man became **rich**, and gained more and more, until he became **very wealthy**" (26:13). And for Jacob, "And the man **extended significantly** and he had many sheep and female slaves and male slaves and camels and asses" (30:43).

In the curse section in Deuteronomy, the verb "to be successful" appears in the negative form, "And you shall grope at noonday, as the blind gropes in darkness, and you shall not succeed in your ways..." (Deuteronomy 28:29). The blind in darkness is as the slave in the darkness of slavery.

And the text continues the story of Eliezer, "...and the **man** took a golden earring..." (Genesis 24:22), "And the **man** bowed down..." (24:26), "...and Laban ran out to the **man**..." (24:29), and "And the **man** came into the house..." (24:32).

---

[30] In the Hebrew the word *lenachesh* is used. In Deuteronomy this act of *lenachesh* is used to illustrate the opposite of being complete with the Almighty. Another example is reading cards.

And the text brings us Eliezer's words to Rebecca's family. Eliezer starts by introducing himself, "And he said, I am Abraham's slave" (24:34). Although the text "promoted" Eliezer to the same rank as the forefathers and Moses, Eliezer shows his pride as "Abraham's slave."

At the end of his words, when Laban and Bethuel agree that Rebecca will become a wife to his master's son, the text continues, "...when Abraham's slave heard their words he bowed to the ground to the Lord" (24:52). The text does not call him "the slave," as the story began with, but "Abraham's slave," as Eliezer introduced himself.

If we have any doubt that the title "Abraham's slave" comes to adjust the language of the text to Eliezer's language, then the text continues, "And they called Rebecca and said to her, will you go with this **man** and she said, I will go" (24:58). Eliezer perceives himself as "Abraham's slave" but not so Rebecca's family. For them he is a "man."

And the text continues, "And they sent away Rebecca their sister, and her nurse, and Abraham's slave and his men" (24:59). After they bless Rebecca upon embarking on her journey, the text says, "And Rebecca arose and her lasses and they rode upon the camels and they went after the **man**, and the **slave** took Rebecca and went" (24:61).

In Hebrew the sentence starts with the title "man" and just one (Hebrew) word is a buffer between the "man" and the word "slave," "and he took." The act of "taking," which is the act of marriage, turned Rebecca into his master's wife, and the text returns to use the title "slave" as it did in the beginning of the story. Thus Rebecca took charge of the "slave."

Rebecca

The connection to the Almighty, as seen in the ability to ask something from the Almighty and get a positive response from the Almighty to the request, justifies the change in the language of the text from slave to man. This connection to the Almighty is important to the text and is also expressed in the case of Rebecca.

Rebecca is the foremother who takes first place for the number of times she is mentioned in the text. Compare Rebecca with 50, Rachel with 46, Leah with eight, and Sarah with 16. If we take into consideration that an average chapter in Genesis is around 30 verses, then Rebecca makes up about two full chapters.

Rebecca is the only one among the foremothers that the text introduces her on the stage of history at the time she was born,

> And it happened that after these things it was told to Abraham saying behold Milcah she has also borne sons to Nahor your brother. Huz his firstborn and Buz his brother and Kemuel the father of Aram. And Kesed and Hazo and Pildash and Jidlaph and Bethuel. And Bethuel fathered Rebecca. These eight Milcah bore to Nahor Abraham's brother. (22:20-23)

The text does not mention the birth of the other foremothers Sarah, Rachel and Leah, even though we know of them. By mentioning her birth, the text equates Rebecca to the forefathers, Abraham, Isaac, and Jacob.

If we examine Genesis, which lists the different lineages, we see lineage from Adam to Noah, and then from Noah to Abraham. Thereafter, we have a more detailed account of the birth of the sons to Abraham, Isaac, and Jacob. We also have a detailed account of the lineage of Esau in chapter 36. In addition, in the text in front of us we have Rebecca's birth, and we have the birth of the two sons to Judah from Tamar, Peretz and Zerach, at the end of chapter 38.

Rebecca stands out as an exception in the description of lineage in the entire book. What is so unique about Rebecca? If we are guided by the change in language in the story of Eliezer and Rebecca from "slave" to "man," which testifies to the importance of the connection with the Almighty, then it is clear that Rebecca is the only one who appeals to the Almighty, and the Almighty answers her **immediately and directly**, and tells her of upcoming events.

> And the sons struggled inside her, and she said, if so, why am I thus? And she went to ask the Lord. And the Lord said to her, two nations are in your womb, and two peoples shall be separated from your bowels, and the one people shall be stronger than the other people, and the elder shall serve the younger. (25:22-23)

The text describes another event related to Rebecca, and quite mysterious. "And Esau hated Jacob because of the blessing which his father blessed him, and Esau said in his heart, when the days of mourning for my father are at hand then I will kill Jacob my brother" (27:41). Rebecca was told what Esau said in his heart. How come?

When we compare Rebecca to Sarah, we see that the Almighty also talked to Sarah, but only briefly, and not about the future, but about her denial that she laughed when she heard she was going to have a son. "And Sarah denied saying I laughed not, for she was afraid and He said, no, you did laugh" (18:15).

It is true that the Almighty tells Abraham, when Abraham struggles with Sarah's demand to expel Ishmael, "...in all that Sarah has said to you, listen to her..." (21:12), but Rebecca does not need such help. When the problem arises that Isaac wants to bless Esau, Rebecca takes the fate of the family in her hands, and encourages Jacob to go and receive the blessing from his father. When Jacob asks what will happen if his father will expose the fraud, and curse him instead of blessing him, Rebecca said with full confidence, "Upon me be your curse my son..." (27:13).

After the blessing Rebecca counsels Jacob to go to Haran, and she even gets for him Isaac's blessing. And now in the open, with no need for any fraud, "And Rebecca said to Isaac I am weary of my life because of the daughters of Heth. If Jacob takes a wife of the daughters of Heth, such as these who are the daughters of the land, what good shall my life be to me?" (27:46).

And the text tells us, "And Isaac sent away Jacob, and he went to Padan-Aram to Laban, son of Bethuel the Aramean, the brother of Rebecca, **Jacob's and Esau's mother**" (28:5).

If we follow the development of Rebecca as a Biblical figure, then the reason for this sentence starts to become clear. At the beginning of Isaac and Rebecca's marriage, the text says, "And Isaac was forty years old when he took Rebecca for a wife, the **daughter** of Bethuel the Aramean of Padan-Aram, the **sister** to Laban the Aramean" (25:20). At the beginning of her marriage, Rebecca is listed as "Laban's sister."

However, once her plan materializes, and Jacob indeed gets the blessing, and now in the open, with no fraud, and Isaac sends Jacob to Haran to get a wife, Rebecca gets promoted in the text. She is not "Laban's sister" anymore. Laban the son of Bethuel the Aramean becomes "Rebecca's brother." And indeed, when Jacob met Rachel at the well, the text tells us, "When Jacob saw Rachel the daughter of **Laban his mother's brother**, and the sheep of **Laban his mother's brother**..." (29:10). Rebecca is above Laban, and not as it was when she started on her way in the Biblical story.

Moreover, the title "Jacob's and Esau's mother" (28:5) comes to tell us that the text favors the implementation of Rebecca's plan. She gave the younger one (of the twins) to receive the blessing, and so it happened. And Jacob is listed before Esau.

By changing the language in regard to Rebecca's "social introduction," the text expresses its admiration of Rebecca, the one who started out as "Laban's sister" and ends up as "Jacob's and Esau's mother." This admiration expressed in the text should bring us to further examine Rebecca and her personality.

Rebecca vs. Rachel

Two foremothers, Rebecca and Rachel, each appear at the water well, in a meeting that will determine the fate of their marriages later on. For Rebecca, the text says, "And before he had finished speaking, and behold, Rebecca came out[31] who was born to Bethuel the son of Milcah Nahor's wife Abraham's brother, with her water jar on her shoulder" (Genesis 24:15). On the other hand, for Rachel the text says, "And while he still spoke with them and Rachel came with her father's sheep for she was a shepherdess" (29:9). While Rebecca "came **out**," Rachel just "came" (two different verbs in Hebrew). This change of language should encourage us to make a thorough comparison of these two meetings.

In the case of Rebecca we find a sentence which does not appear for Rachel, "And the lass was very pretty to look upon, **a virgin, and no man had known her**..." (24:16). And if the text didn't say it, might we suspect Rebecca not to be a virgin?

---

[31] "came out" – it should be noted that in the Hebrew text the verb has a missing letter (aleph).

Rebecca is described as a "lass."[32] But if we read the text as it shows up in the scroll, we find out that the word is written differently from the way we read it, in an example of *Keri* ("read") versus *Ketiv* ("written"). The word *naarah* ("lass") shows up with the last letter *ah* missing, and actually in the text we find the word *naar* ("lad"). Is it a coincidence? A misprint?

Throughout the description of the events the word *naar* ("lad") is used. Even before Rebecca appears the text tells us that Eliezer sets for himself "the test of charity" as the way to choose the young woman, saying, "And the *naar* to whom I shall say let down your water jar please that I may drink and she shall say drink..." (24:14). And in the rest of the story, four more times (verses 16, 28, 55, and 57) the text uses the male form of the noun, *naar*. Only when Eliezer speaks with Rebecca's family is there a full change of language. Not only does Eliezer not use *naar* or even *naarah*, but he also uses a different word altogether, "...and it will happen that **the young lady** (*almah*) who comes out to draw water, and I say to her give me please a little water from your water jar to drink" (24:43). Is it a coincidence?

The word *almah* shows up four times in the entire Tanach, first, in this place, second, in the encounter between Pharaoh's daughter and Moses' sister. "And Pharaoh's daughter said to her, go. And the *almah* went and called the child's mother" (Exodus 2:8). Third, in Isaiah, "Therefore the Lord himself shall give you a sign; behold the *almah* conceives and bears a son, and shall call his name Immanu-El"[33] (Isaiah 7:14). And fourth, in Proverbs, "The way of the eagle in the sky, the way of a serpent on a rock, the way of a ship in the midst of the sea, and the way of man[34] with *almah*" (Proverbs 30:19).

These four places together show us the difference between *naarah* and *almah*. Both of them are likely to indicate the same young age, as Rebecca didn't get older just because Eliezer labeled her differently. But the examples from Isaiah and Proverbs clearly indicate that *almah* has to do with fertility (Isaiah) and courtship of a couple (Proverbs). The

---

[32] The word "lad" in Hebrew is *naar*, and the word "lass" is *naarah*. In many cases in Hebrew, adding the letter "ah" at the end of the noun makes it feminine.

[33] *Immanu* is "with us" and *El* is "G-d." The name is "G-d is with us."

[34] In Hebrew the word *gever* is used and not *ish*, which is generally understood in translation as "man." The word *gever* is made out of three-letter root word of G-B-R that stands for "strong." The verse talks about the eagle (the king of the birds) in the sky, the serpent on the ground, the ship in the sea, and the *gever* with *almah*; all four metaphors deal with strength and control of the environment.

example in Exodus uses the word *almah* in proximity to Pharaoh's daughter, which indicates to us that it is an honorific title. It is quite likely that Eliezer, in talking to Rebecca's family used an honorific title, while stressing to her family that she is at a marriageable age, so they wouldn't tell him that she was too young to marry.

Back to *naarah*. We find in the text several more times in which the word *naarah* is written without the ending *ah*, in other words actually using the word *naar* in the masculine form, "lad" and not "lass." The first example is with the story of Dinah, Jacob's daughter, being taken by the ruler's son in Shechem. The text uses the word *naar* three times: "And his soul was drawn to Dinah the daughter of Jacob, and he loved the *naar*, and spoke to the *naar*'s heart" (Genesis 34:3). Later on, when Shechem speaks with Jacob and his sons, and asks for Dinah's hand, the text says, "...give me the *naar* for a wife" (34:12).

In two additional places the word *naarah* appears as *naar*. The first is the case of the one who "brings an evil name" (Deuteronomy 22:14) upon a *naarah*. The text says, "The father of the *naar* and her mother take and bring forth the *naar*'s virginity to the elders of the city at the city gate" (22:15). When the text speaks of the punishment of the man, we find, "And they shall fine him a hundred shekels of silver and give them to the father of the *naarah* because he has brought up an evil name upon a virgin of Israel..." (22:19). When it becomes clear that she indeed was a virgin, and all the man's claim was deceptive, the text uses the feminine form of the word, *naarah*. And immediately after the text says, "And if this thing was true, there were no virginity signs found for the *naar*. And they shall bring out the *naar*..." (22:20-21). When she is not a virgin, she is *naar* in the masculine form.

The text later says, "If a *naar* virgin and bethrothed to a man, and a man finds her in the city and lies with her, then you shall bring them both out to the city gate and you shall stone them with stones that they may die, the *naar* because she cried not..." (22:23-24). And, again, we see the word *naar* twice in the masculine form.

In summary, in the Bible we see the word *naarah* (feminine) four times as *naar* (masculine) referring to a young woman. Three of these cases deal with rape: Dinah, a married woman whose husband claims she is not a virgin, and a bethrothed woman found with another man who doesn't cry out in the city. And the fourth is Rebecca who "comes out" to the well with her water jar on her shoulder.

The case of Dinah in Shechem also starts with the verb to "come out." "And Dinah the daughter of Leah whom she bore to Jacob came out to see the daughters of the land" (34:1).

It is no wonder that the text finds it necessary to add for Rebecca, unlike for Rachel, who came out to the well, the sentence, "And the lass was very pretty to look upon, **a virgin, and no man had known her...**" (24:16). Otherwise, the reader encountering the word *naar* in the masculine form might think that Rebecca was not a virgin.

We can ask, if Eliezer is quoted using the word *naar* in the masculine form even before meeting Rebecca, does it mean that the young women of Haran had a reputation of being "free?" This point can be examined in the text.

When Eliezer asks Rebecca's family for Rebecca's hand so he can take her to his master's house, and by doing so he will complete his mission, Rebecca's family answer, "We will call the *naar* and inquire at her mouth" (24:57). Even if we had a "time machine" that would take us from that time to the present, we would not find in the Middle East, in very conservative societies such as the society of Haran (Iraq and Turkey today), that a father would ask his daughter whom she wants to marry. In most of the Moslem societies of today, the daughter is actually "sold" to her future bridegroom. And if we go back four thousand years, even much more so. But not for Rebecca. One can say that the family's response was meant to slow the process of Rebecca marrying Isaac. But if we take Rebecca's personality into consideration, it is easy to see that she would not have gone against her will.

We cannot end the discussion about Rebecca without mentioning an event that connects Rebecca to Tamar, Judah's daughter-in-law, who bears two sons to him. The two of them covered themselves with a veil. For Rebecca it is said, "And she said to the slave who is this man who walks in the field towards us, and the slave said he is my master, and **she took the veil and covered herself**" (24:65). For Tamar the text says, "And she took off her widow's garments, **and covered herself with a veil** and made herself look tired[35] and sat in an open place..." (38:14). Tamar wanted Judah to think that she was a prostitute and so covered herself with a veil, and Rebecca covered herself in front of her future husband.

Now we can return to the beginning of the Biblical description of the sequence of events that introduces us to Rebecca.

"And the lass was very pretty to look upon, **a virgin, and no man had known her**..." (24:16). The text had no choice but to mention this fact. Her behavior, as the behavior of the other young women of the place, to the outside was very "free," but internally, Rebecca was different.

Points in language to consider:

1. The connection of the human to the Almighty is an important issue for the text – the ability to ask something from the Almighty, and the immediate positive response by the Almighty to the request, changed the language of the text in regard to **Abraham's slave** from him being a "slave" to being a "man."
2. The connection of the human to the Almighty is an important issue for the text – the ability to ask something from the Almighty, and the immediate positive response by the Almighty to the request. **Rebecca** is the only foremother who appeals to the Almighty, and the Almighty answers her **immediately and directly**, and tells her of upcoming events.

---

[35] The verb used here, *vatitalaf*, is used one other place in the Tanach, in the book of Jonah, "...G-d brought a hot east wind and the sun beat down upon the head of Jonah so that he *vaitalaf* (translated as "fainted") and wished to die..." (Jonah 4:8).

JOSEPH IN EGYPT

"And Joseph was taken down to Egypt…" (Genesis 39:1)

SCAN Rule: The first sentence in an "open statement" is the most important sentence. In many cases the first sentence includes the reason for the events that follow.

Let us return to Chapter 37, where "And the *medanim*[36] sold him to Egypt to Potiphar, an officer of Pharaoh, and captain of the guard" (37:36). The description of the events in the story of Joseph going down to Egypt is cut in the middle by Chapter 38, which is an "out-of-sequence" chapter dealing with Judah and Tamar, and the birth of Peretz and Zerach. Peretz is the forefather of David's kingdom. Chapter 38, like chapter 39, which deals with Joseph in his Egyptian master's house, starts with the verb "to go down. "At that time Judah **went down** from his brothers…" (38:1), and now the text says, "And Joseph **was taken down**…"[37]

The Verb *Laredet*

Throughout Genesis we find the verb "to go down" in regard to the act of traveling from the land of Canaan to Egypt, and the opposite is true, using the verb "to go up" for traveling from Egypt to Canaan.

When Abraham returns from Egypt after the famine, the text says, "And Abram **went up** from Egypt…" (13:1). After Isaac lived for a while in the land of the Philistines, the text says, "And he **went up** from there to Beersheba" (26:23). When Judah talks to Joseph before the latter acknowledged himself to his brothers, the text quotes him as saying, "Now therefore let your slave sit instead of the lad a slave to my lord, and let the lad **go up** with his brothers" (44:33). When the brothers go back to their father Jacob, the text says, "And they **went up** from Egypt and came to the land of Canaan to Jacob their father" (45:25). When Joseph goes to Canaan to bury his father Jacob, "And Joseph **went up** to bury his father and with him **went up** all the slaves of Pharaoh…" (50:7).

---

[36] Medanim – there is a tendency to read this word as Midianites, but the Hebrew word is not *Midyanim* but *medanim*. We find the word *medanim* in three places in the book Proverbs – "Perverseness is in his heart, he plots evil continually, he sows *medanim*" (Proverbs 6:14), "A false witness who speaks lies and he who sows **medanim among brothers**" (Proverbs 6:19), and "Hatred stirs up *medanim*, but love covers all sins" (10:12).
[37] In both instances the text in the Hebrew uses the same verb, *laredet*. In the case of Joseph it is the passive form *huRaD*, and for Judah it is the active form *va-yeReD*.

In summary, for the land of Egypt and the land of the Philistines the text relates to traveling to and from there with "going down" and "going up," respectively, indicating their lower status in relation to the land of Canaan. This is not the case in regard to Haran, the place of Abraham's origin.

In regard to Abraham immigrating to the land of Canaan, the text says,

> And Abram took Sarai his wife, and Lot his brother's son, and all their possessions that they had gathered and the souls that they had gotten in Haran, and they **went forth** to go to the land of Canaan, and they **came** to the land of Canaan. (12:5)

Abraham did not "go up" to the land of Canaan. When Abraham's slave goes to Haran to bring a wife to his master's son, the text says, "And the slave took ten of his master's camels and **went** and all the goods of his master in his hand, and he arose and **went** to Aram Naharayim to the city of Nahor" (24:10). Again, the slave "went" but did not "go down." When Rebecca tells Jacob to run away from his brother Esau, she is quoted as saying, "Now therefore my son, obey me, and arise and **flee** to Laban my brother to Haran" (27:43). And Jacob did indeed go to Haran, the text says, "And Jacob **went** out from Beersheba and **went** towards Haran" (28:10).

We do **not** find the words "down" and "up" for Haran, but for Egypt. One might ask, if the words "down" and "up" indicate higher status of the land of Canaan over Egypt, is it due to holiness? And, if so, why doesn't the land of Canaan get higher status than Haran? Language-wise, we find that the text equates Haran with Canaan. How come?

"And Joseph **was taken down** to Egypt..." (Genesis 39:1)

There is one other place in the five books of Moses in which the verb *laredet* ("to go down") is used in the passive form, *ve-huRaD* ("to be taken down"), "And the tabernacle **was taken down** and the sons of Gershon and the sons of Merari traveled, carrying the tabernacle" (Numbers 10:17). Earlier, we find the commandment to take down the cover of the ark before the journey, "...and they shall take down the covering veil and cover the ark of Testimony with it" (Numbers 4:5).

The fact that the text uses the same passive form of the verb "to be taken down" (*vehurad*), both for Joseph going down to Egypt and for the tabernacle, should bring us to ask if there is a component of reduction in holiness in regard to Joseph in Egypt. We should wait and see if there are other points in the language of the text to corroborate this apparent reduction in holiness.

> "…and Potiphar, an officer of Pharaoh, captain of the guard,
> an Egyptian man, **bought him**[38]…" (39:1)

At the end of Chapter 37 the text says, "And the *medanim* **sold** him to Egypt to Potiphar, an officer of Pharaoh and captain of the guard" (37:36). If the *medanim* "sold" him to Potiphar, then it is understood that Potiphar "bought" him. If so, what is the big news here that the text needs to tell us that Potiphar "bought" him? This question brings us to a "linguistic journey" dealing with commerce and trade as they are expressed in Biblical language. This "linguistic journey" will answer our question why the text had to say that the *medanim* "sold" Joseph, and also to say that Potiphar "bought" Joseph.

Linguistic Journey – Deals and Commerce in Genesis

In Genesis we find several deals described between people, when one person sells something to another, either property, or service. We will examine these deals **language**-wise.

Buying the Cave of the Patriarchs

Abraham addresses the people of Heth and tells them, "…**give** me possession of a burying place with you…" (Genesis 23:4). The sons of Heth respond, "…in the choice of our tombs bury your dead…" (23:6). This response is not satisfactory to Abraham, and he asks to speak with Ephron the Hethite, "…And he will **give** me the cave of Machpelah which he has, which is in the end of his field, for full value[39] he will **give** me…" (23:9). If at first, Abraham said, "give me possession of a burying place," now he clarifies that he wants to buy the place, and not to receive it free, as a present. We should note that the text does not quote Abraham as

---

[38] In Biblical Hebrew the verb usually appears before the subject of the sentence. In the text we read literally, "…and bought him Potiphar…" Therefore, we start the linguistic journey with the verb "to buy."
[39] Full value – in the Hebrew it is "full silver."

saying, "…and he will **sell** me the cave of Machpelah…" Instead, the text uses the verb "to give" in exchange for "full value." In reality, Abraham is talking of buying and selling, but the text does not use the verb "to sell." Even after Ephron agreed to Abraham's request and he sets a price, the text says, "…and Abraham weighed to Ephron the silver…" (23:16). At the end of the deal, the text says,

> And the field of Ephron which was in Machpelah which was before Mamre, the field, and the cave which was in it, and all the trees that were in the field, that were in all the borders around were made over to Abraham for a possession in the presence of the sons of Heth… (23:17-18)

If we wonder whether it is a coincidence that the text tells us that the cave became a possession of Abraham without telling us that Ephron **sold** him the cave, then, at the end of Genesis, when Jacob gives his will to his sons before his death, the text quotes him as saying,

> …bury me with my fathers in the cave that is in the field of Ephron the Hittite. In the cave that is in the field of Machpelah, which is before Mamre, in the land of Canaan which Abraham **bought** the field of Ephron the Hittite for a possession of a burying place. (49:29-30)

And then when Jacob is buried the text says, "…and buried him in the cave of Machpelah which Abraham **bought** the field for a possession of burying place from Ephron the Hittite before Mamre" (50:13).

In summary, the text uses the act of "buying" and not the act of "selling."

Jacob in Shechem

The text tells us that Jacob comes "to Shalem a city of Shechem" (33:18), and he buys a plot of land. The text describes the deal as, "And he **bought** a parcel of a field where he had spread his tent, from the hand of the sons of Hamor, Shechem's father, for a hundred pieces of money" (33:19). Again, we see that Jacob "bought" but Hamor's sons did not "sell," at least not language-wise.

Judah and Tamar

When Judah sees Tamar and thinks she is a prostitute, he addresses her with the request, "...let me please come to you..." (38:16). Tamar answers, "What will you **give** me that you may come to me?" (38:16). Again, the text deals with a payment in exchange for a "service," but the verb "to sell" is not used in the language.

Joseph in Egypt

When Joseph buys the lands of the Egyptians for the food he collected during the time of plenty, the text says, "And Joseph gathered up all the money that was found in the land of Egypt and in the land of Canaan for the grain which they got..." (47:14). **Content**-wise, we are facing an act of "selling," but the text refrains from using the verb "to sell." Instead, the verb uses the verb *lishbor.*[40] Joseph does not sell food to the Egyptians. He only "collects" the money in exchange for the food (literally, the break they are breaking) he gives them.

And when they don't have any more money, Joseph says, "**Give** your cattle and I will **give** you for your cattle..." (47:16), and "...and Joseph **gave** them bread in exchange for horses..." (47:17), and the text uses the same verb, "to give," as in the previous deals described. When the Egyptians didn't have anything to offer in exchange for the food, they came to Joseph and said, "...**buy** us and our land for bread..." (47:19), and, indeed, "And Joseph **bought** all the land of Egypt for Pharaoh..." (47:20). Only after the text said that Joseph "bought," can the text say, "...for the Egyptians **sold** every man his field..." (47:20). When the text relates to the priests' land, it says, "Only the land of the priests he did not **buy**, because it is the law for the priests from Pharaoh, and they ate their portion that Pharaoh gave them, therefore they did not **sell** their land" (47:22). We should note that the text lists first that Joseph "did not **buy**" because they did not **sell**. The order of listing in the sentence shows us the importance of the "buying" over the "selling." Even if it shows up in the negative, "did **not** buy" and "did **not** sell."

In **summary**, we find a gap between the objective reality and the way the language of the text describes the event. While in reality we understand

---

[40] *Lishbor* – literally, "to break." It is quite likely used due to the fact that they are "breaking" their hunger, as in the word "breakfast" in English.

that we are facing a transaction of a sale and a purchase, in the **language** of the text there is a preference of the verbs "to give" and "to buy" over the verb "to sell." This preference should bring us to check in which contexts the verb "to sell" shows up in the Bible.

The Verb "to Sell"

The verb "to sell" shows up in four circumstances in Genesis. The first circumstance is in the transaction that Jacob initiated by asking his brother Esau to sell him the birthright in exchange for the food he would give him. Twice we find the verb "to sell;" first, "And Jacob said, **sell** me this day your birthright" (25:31). And second, the text describes finalizing the transaction by saying, "...and he **sold** his birthright to Jacob" (25:33).

The second circumstance is when Rachel and Leah speak to Jacob responding to his request to leave Haran, their homeland, and to return to Canaan. They said, "Are we not counted by him as foreigners? For he has **sold** us..." (31:15).

The third circumstance is in regard to Joseph's brothers selling him into slavery. "Come, and let us **sell** him to the Ishmaelites..." (37:27), "...and they **sold** Joseph to the Ishmaelites for twenty pieces of silver..." (37:28). "And the *medanim* **sold** him to Egypt..." (37:36), "I am Joseph your brother whom you **sold** into Egypt" (45:4), and "Now therefore be not grieved not angry with yourselves that you **sold** me here..." (45:5).

The fourth circumstance is in regard to Joseph buying the lands of the Egyptians (except the lands of the priests), "And Joseph bought all the land of Egypt for Pharaoh, for the Egyptians **sold** every man his field..." (47:20), and, "Only the land of the priests he did not buy, because it is the law for the priests from Pharaoh, and they ate their portion that Pharaoh gave them, therefore they did not **sell** their land" (47:22).

In both the case of Rachel and Leah speaking to Jacob, and the case of Joseph's brothers selling him to slavery, we can easily see the negative attitude of the text toward "selling." It is safe to assume that in both the case of Esau selling the birthright and the case of the priests not selling their land to Joseph, the attitude of the text is negative as well.

Back to Joseph

The fact that the text starts the story in Joseph by mentioning that Potiphar "bought" Joseph indicates to us that Chapter 37 is written from the perspective of taking Joseph down to Egypt. By Joseph being sold, the act of taking him down to Egypt is finished, from the top to the bottom, from being a free man to being a slave. On the other hand, Chapter 39 starts from the perspective of Potiphar and how the events took their course in Potiphar's household; hence "And he bought him."

> "...and Potiphar, a eunuch of Pharaoh, the minister of *tabachim*,[41] an Egyptian man **bought him**..." (39:1)

Realizing that the text uses the verb "to buy" to describe acquiring Joseph as a slave by his master, we should reach the conclusion that the text looks upon Joseph entering the house of Potiphar in a positive way. Nothing was wrong with Potiphar getting Joseph as his slave, as opposed to the brothers and the Ishmaelites "selling" him.

> "...and Potiphar, a **eunuch** of Pharaoh, the minister of *tabachim*," an Egyptian man bought him..." (39:1)

Linguistic Journey – the Broader Meaning of "Eunuch"

The title "eunuch"[42] is known to us from the book of Esther:

- "...the seven eunuchs who served in the presence of the king Ahasuerus" (Esther 1:10),
- "...Shaashgaz, the king's eunuch who guarded the concubines" (2:14), and
- "...Hatach one of the king's eunuchs whom he appointed to attend on her" (4:5).

But eunuchs were not necessarily only in the position of guarding the king's women. There are places in the Tanach in which eunuchs are

---

[41] *Tabachim* – even in Modern Hebrew it is a problem to translate this word. We know that the three-letter root *T-B-CH* stands for slaughtering an animal, or making a feast. For example, Joseph tells the man in charge of his household, "...bring these men home and *teboach tebach* and make ready for these men shall dine with me at noon" (Genesis 43:16). It is quite likely that the doubling of the verb (in Biblical Hebrew, an emphatic form) means that Joseph instructed him to make a big feast and slaughter a lot. We will translate this Biblical Hebrew to Modern Hebrew later.

[42] Eunuch – *saris* in Hebrew.

mentioned as serving in very high-ranking positions. When the people ask the prophet Samuel to appoint a king to lead them, Samuel tells the people the law of the king, "And he will take the tenth of your seed, and of your vineyards, and give to his eunuchs and slaves" (1 Samuel 8:15). From this place we learn that eunuchs were not slaves. They were free men.

The book Chronicles describes the event in which King David convened all the important people in Jerusalem. The text says,

> And David assembled all the ministers of Israel, the ministers of the tribes, and the ministers of the companies who served the king, and the ministers of the thousands, and the ministers of the hundreds, and the ministers of all property and livestock of the king and his sons, with the eunuchs and the mighty warriors, and all the successful mighty men in arms to Jerusalem. (1 Chronicles 28:1)

And in this description the eunuchs are listed before the mighty warriors.

When King Hezekiah showed the Babylonian king's delegation all the treasures in his palace, the prophet Isaiah told the king, "And your sons who will come out of you whom you will father they will be taken away, and they shall be eunuchs in the palace of the king of Babylon" (Isaiah 39:7). Not only will the wealth of the kingdom vanish, but the seed of the king will vanish as well, and the House of David will cease to exist.

Why would a king of that time prefer eunuchs to serve in high-ranking positions? It is quite likely that the eunuch, who is described by the prophet Isaiah as a "dry tree" (56:3), would not be a threat to the king, and he would not rebel against the king, knowing that even if he did take over the kingdom, he would not have anyone of his own flesh and blood to inherit it.

In the time of King Hezekiah we find the following description, "And the king of Assyria sent Tartan and master-eunuch and Rabshakeh from Lachish to King Hezekiah with a great army against Jerusalem" (2 Kings 18:17). Here we see the position of "master eunuch."

When Nebuchadnezzar king of Babylon sent Nebuzaradan, his *rav-tabachim*,[43] to Jerusalem after it was conquered, the text describes his activities,

> And from the city he took one eunuch who was set over the men of war and five men who were in the king's presence who were found in the city and the scribe of the commander of the army who ruled over the people of the land, and sixty men from the elite of the people who were in the city. (2 Kings 25:19)

This description testifies that the eunuch was in charge of the "men of war." And it made sense. If there is a threat to a king and his kingdom, the one who is in charge of the "men of war" is definitely a greater threat, since he has the means to stage a rebellion.

Back to Joseph

Up to this point we discussed why a king would choose a eunuch to run the war, or his kingdom, for him. But there was a personal impact on the life of the eunuch; he couldn't have children. In this one title among the several Potiphar received, the text is setting the stage for the internal politics inside Potiphar's household.

> "…and Potiphar, a eunuch of Pharaoh, **the minister of *tabachim*,** an Egyptian man bought him…" (39:1)

The only thing we know from the book of Genesis about the position of "minister of *tabachim*" is that he is the one who is in charge of the prison, "a place where the king's prisoners were confined" (Genesis 39:20), in other words, political prisoners. Although the text brings us the position of "master of the prison" (39:22), we still know that the minister of *tabachim* was in charge of this prison. After Pharaoh's dream, the minister of the butlers told the king, "Pharaoh was angry with his slaves, and put me in custody of the minister of *tabachim*, both me and the minister of the bakers" (41:10). Therefore, the minister of *tabachim* was in charge of the defense of the kingdom.

In the book 2 Kings, chapter 25, we see that the title *rab tabachim* is reserved for the one who was in charge of the war pressed by King

---

[43] *Rav tabachim* – Remember that Potiphar, Joseph's master, is described as the minister of *tabachim*.

Nebuchadnezzar of Babylon against the Judean kingdom. While Potiphar was in Egypt and Nebuchadnezzar was in Babylon, it is still quite likely that Potiphar was in a very high-ranking position in the Egyptian kingdom. And if his position equaled the one of the Babylonian *rab tabachim*, then Potiphar was in charge of the war campaigns of Pharaoh. In other words, **he was often absent from home**.

> "…and Potiphar, a eunuch of Pharaoh, the minister of *tabachim*,
> **an Egyptian man** bought him…" (39:1)

We should note that in the Tanach we encounter another man who receives the title, "an Egyptian man." After Moses rescued Reuel's daughters from the shepherds, the daughters returned home. The text says that their father asked them, "How is it that you have come so soon today" (Exodus 2:18), and they answered, "**An Egyptian man** rescued us from the hand of the shepherds…" (2:19). Potiphar in Genesis and Moses in Exodus receive the same a title. Should we understand from this linguistic **equivalence** that Potiphar had some religious role in the Egyptian establishment? We should not forget that later on the text tells us that Pharaoh gives Joseph a woman to be his wife, "…and he gave him to wife Asenath the daughter of **Potiphera priest of On**" (Genesis 41:45).

Joseph in his Master's House

> "And the Lord was with (*et*) Joseph, and he was a prosperous
> man, and he was in the house of his master the Egyptian.
> And his master saw that the Lord was with (*et*) him…"
> (Genesis 39:2-3).

The only one in the five books of Moses whom the Lord was with (*et*) and not with (*im*) is Joseph. This linguistic rarity should bring us to ask why there is distance between the Almighty and Joseph, at least from the point of view of Biblical **language**.

We should not forget that the story of Joseph in Egypt started with the verb "taken down" (*huRaD*) which indicates some reduction of holiness.

Potiphar's Social Introduction

In the first verse the text introduces Joseph's master for the first time as "Potiphar, Pharaoh's eunuch, the minister of *tabachim*, an Egyptian man." In the second verse the text shortens its language and introduces Joseph's master as "his master the Egyptian."

SCAN Rule: The shortest way to give a sentence is the best way. Any deviation from the shortest way is meaningful.

We should note here that if the text really wanted to shorten its language, the text could have used the name Potiphar, which is the first component of the initial social introduction. However, the text chose to use a new social introduction, "his master the Egyptian." All the other components vanished from the picture: "Potiphar," "Pharaoh's eunuch," "the minister of *tabachim*," and even "man."

In the next verse (verse 3) the text continues to shorten its language, and now Joseph's master is introduced only as "his master." The title "Egyptian" vanished as well. Should we conclude that the Egyptian society surrounding them retreats into the background, and the relationship between them gets to be more personal? No more "Egypt" and "Egyptian," but just the two of them, "Joseph," and "his master."

In the next verse (verse 4) the text continues to shorten its language, and now the text moves to use pronouns: "And Joseph found grace in **his** eyes, and he served **him**, and **he** appointed him over **his** house, and all the things that belong to **him he** put into his hand" (Genesis 39:4).

SCAN observation: It is generally accepted in language, that after the first "social introduction" of a person inside the "open statement" the one who gives the statement moves on to use pronouns. Pronouns shorten the language and facilitate and enhance the delivery of the information.

The text does it in the fourth verse. But we should note that the text could have done so earlier, in the third verse. The verse could have been very easily phrased as, "And **he** saw that the Lord was with him..." The fact that the text did not do so in the third verse emphasizes to the analyst that the "Egyptian" component of the master's social introduction vanished.

Continuing to read the text, we should note that the next verse, the fifth verse, starts with what seems like repeating the activity described in the fourth verse. The fourth verse says, "…and he made him overseer over his house, and all that he had he put into his hand." The fifth verse starts with, "And from the time that he had made him overseer in his house, and over all that he had…"

SCAN observation: At times we encounter in an "open statement" repeating an activity. In other words, we find that in one spot in the text the subject mentioned twice one particular activity, for example, "…I got dressed. After I got dressed…" or, "I took a shower. After the shower…" Repeating or "doubling" an activity indicates that at the time of delivering the information the subject stopped for a while. The subject stopped to think how to proceed with the statement. During this short break, that can last 10-15 minutes, the subject might be seen as holding the pen/pencil and looking into his memory. At the end of the short break, the subject returns to delivering the information, but since the subject continues after a break, the subject would return to where he was stopped and therefore "double" the activity.

During this short break the subject reviews the event in memory, without putting into the "open statement" the information the subject reviewed. Such a point can be equated to "a blackout in the neighborhood," a situation in which a person sits in front of the TV screen watching a show. Then there is a blackout in the neighborhood with no electricity and no TV for ten minutes. When the electricity and the TV come back on, the viewer continues to watch the TV show; however, he lost ten minutes of the show. The TV station still continued to broadcast the show without the viewer being able to watch it due to the blackout. The same applies to the "open statement." Doubling an activity indicates that the person was "broadcasting;" however, due to the "blackout" in the "open statement" the reader lost the information that was "broadcast" in the subject's mind, without it reaching the paper.

SCAN Rule: Doubling an activity in an "open statement" indicates a signal of concealing information.

Concealing Information – Discussion

Concealing information is not deception. Concealing information is a strong signal that memory is guiding the statement. How one can conceal if there is nothing in memory to conceal? Concealing information gives credibility to the statement as it indicates that the statement is not fabricated from scratch, and we are not facing an event that did not occur at all. It is true that concealing information poses a challenge to the reader of the statement, as the reader needs to go back and interview the subject in order to get the missing information. But from the perspective of credibility, the reader/listener can reach a conclusion that the statement cannot be dismissed altogether. Memory is behind the information.

Back to Joseph's Master

> "…and he made him overseer over his house,
> and all that he had he put into his hand." (39:4)

> "… from the time that he had made him overseer in his house,
> and over all that he had, the Lord blessed
> the Egyptian's house …" (39:5)

Are we facing a simple repetition of an activity? Checking the language indicates changes in language in describing the activities. These two verses talk about two kinds of property, but in different ways. The first kind is Potiphar's household, and the second is everything else he owned. However, while in verse four the text says that Potiphar made Joseph overseer **on** (*al*) his house, and all the rest he "gave in (*b'*) his hand," in verse five there is a reversal. For the house, the text says that "…he made him overseer **in** (*b'*) his house…" and the text used the preposition letter *b'* (Hebrew "in") instead of the preposition *al* (Hebrew "on"). And the text uses the preposition *al* ("on") to deal with all the rest. The appointment of Joseph in the fifth verse indicates that **Joseph was brought inside the house**, a closer relationship than the one described in the fourth verse.

In addition, in the fifth verse there is a change in the language of the text in regard to Potiphar. In this verse Potiphar is not described as "his master the Egyptian" or even as "his master," but the text talks about "the Egyptian's house," as in "…the Lord blessed the Egyptian's house for

Joseph's sake…" (39:5). The "master" component of Potiphar vanished from the language of the text.

The following are the people in the book of Genesis who receive a blessing from the Almighty:

Adam and Eve: "And G-d **blessed** them saying be fruitful and multiply…" (1:22), "And G-d **blessed** them…" (1:28), and "Male and female created he them and **blessed** them…" (5:2)
Noah and his sons: "And G-d **blessed** Noah and his sons and said to them be fruitful and multiply and fill the earth" (9:1).
Abraham: "That I will strongly[44] **bless** you…" (22:17), and "…and the Lord had **blessed** Abraham in all things" (24:1).
Isaac: "And after the death of Abraham G-d **blessed** Isaac his son…" (25:11).
Jacob: "And G-d appeared to Jacob again when he came back from Padan-Aram and **blessed** him" (35:9).

"…the Lord blessed the Egyptian's house for Joseph's sake…" (39:5)

Laban and Potiphar are the only two in the book of Genesis mentioned as receiving the blessing of the Almighty **because of someone else**. For Laban the text says, "…the Lord has blessed me for your sake[45]" (30:27). And Jacob responds to Laban saying, "…and the Lord has blessed for my sake[46]…" (30:30).

In Laban's case we encounter a change in language between Laban's language and the language of Jacob. While the text quotes Laban as saying *biglalcha* (30:27), the text quotes Jacob as saying *leragli* (30:30). The word *leregel* in the context of giving a reason (similar to *biglal*) shows up in the entire Tanach only once, in Jacob's language in talking to Laban. Why this change of language?

Linguistic Journey – the Word *Biglal*

Besides Laban and Potiphar, we find the word *biglal* in the following places:

---

[44] "…strongly bless…" – the verb is doubled for emphasis in the Hebrew text, literally, "blessing I will bless you."
[45] "…for your sake…" – in the Hebrew the word used is *biglali*.
[46] "…for my sake…" – in the Hebrew the word used is *leragli*.

- "Please say that you are my sister that he may be well with me for you, and my soul shall live *biglalech*[47]" (Genesis 12:13).
- "And the Lord was also angry with me *biglalchem*[48] saying you also shall not come there," (Deuteronomy 1:37).
- "You shall surely give him, and your heart shall not become evil when you give to him, because *biglal*[49] this thing the Lord your G-d shall bless you..." (Deuteronomy 15:10).
- "For all that do these things are abomination to the Lord, and *biglal* these abominations..." (Deuteronomy 18:12).

The first quote deals with Abraham's preparations before going to reside in Egypt due to the famine that ravished the land of Canaan. The second quote relates to the sin of the golden calf after the revelation on Mount Sinai. In order to understand the third quote, we need to go to the beginning of that section, "Beware that there be not a thing with your wicked heart saying..." (Deuteronomy 15:9), and the verse starts the section dealing with the "wicked heart." It is quite clear that in the fourth quote the word *biglal* comes in proximity to "these abominations" describing all the ways the other nations worshipped idols.

In all these four quotes we find that two deal with Egypt (Abraham, and the sin of the Golden Calf imported from the idolatry of Egypt), and "wicked heart" and "abominations" relating to idolatry.

Gilulim

The related word *gilulim* describing idolatry can be found in the following places, among others:

- "And I will destroy your high places, and cut down your images, and put your dead bodies on your dead *gilulechem*, and my soul shall loathe you" (Leviticus 26:30).
- "And you have seen their abominations and *gilulechem*, wood and stone, silver and gold which were among them" (Deuteronomy 29:16).

---

[47] "...*biglalech*..." – the ending *ech* indicates the pronoun "you feminine."
[48] "...*biglalchem*..." – the ending *chem* indicates the pronoun "you masculine plural"
[49] "...because *biglal*..." literally *ki biglal* – this is the only place where we find both words being used in the same place – "because" and *biglal* indicating to us that *biglal* cannot be "because."

- "And he expelled the male cult prostitutes from the land and all the *gilulim* that his father had made" (1 Kings 15:12).
- "And he did very abominably in following the *gilulim* according to all things as did the Amorites…" (1 Kings 21:26).
- "Because Menashe king of Judah has done these abominations, and has done more wickedly than the Amorites did who were before him and had made Judah also sin with *gilulav*[50]" (2 Kings 21:11).
- "…her idols are put to shame, *giluleah*[51] are broken in pieces" (Jeremiah 50:2).

And we find it many times in the book Ezekiel. If we wonder why idolatry is called *gilulim*, we need only to go to the prophet Ezekiel who said, "Then he said to me behold I have given you cow's dung instead of *gelelei* humans (translated as "human excrement") and you shall prepare your bread with it" (Ezekiel 4:15).

The Biblical text relates to idolatry as *gilulim*, in a very disgusting way as "human excrement." As the word *gilulim* comes to demean idolatry in the strongest linguistic way possible, so the word *biglal* resonates in a similar way regarding Egypt, the wicked heart, and abominations.

We should not end this linguistic journey without mentioning the clarification of the word "abominations" in the text. The section in the book Leviticus dealing with all the incestuous relations starts with, "As the doings of the land of Egypt where you dwelt, shall you not do, and the doings of the land of Canaan where I bring you shall you not do…" (Leviticus 18:3). The section ends by saying, "…and shall not commit any of these **abominations**…" (18:26), "For all these **abominations** have the people of the land done…" (18:27), and "For whoever shall commit any of these **abominations**…" (18:29).

In summary: the abominations related to in the book Leviticus, described as "abominations," and said to have been done in Egypt and in the land of Canaan, have to do with incestuous activities among close relatives.

Back to Joseph's Master

"…the Lord blessed the Egyptian's house *biglal* Joseph…" (39:5)

---

[50] *gilulav* – the ending *av* indicates the third person masculine possessive pronoun.
[51] *giluleah* – the ending *ah* indicates the third person feminine possessive pronoun.

The "Egyptian's house" received the Almighty's blessing, but only *biglal*. The use of the word *biglal* comes to send us the message that we are dealing here with Egyptian idolatry in the background. Therefore, Potiphar is not the one to receive the blessing, but rather his house. This also explains why there is distance between the Almighty and Joseph; the Almighty is with (*et*) and not with (*im*) Joseph. This also explains why the story of Joseph in Egypt starts with the verb *huRaD* ("being taken down"), indicating some reduction in holiness.

Reaching Conclusions

Scientifically, when we reach a conclusion, we cannot base ourselves upon one point, or one linguistic signal. One signal is only speculation. We need at least two signals corroborating each other before we can say we have a conclusion. At this stage, we have three signals. Therefore, we can say quite confidently that there is reduction in holiness in the case of Joseph in Egypt. Still, we will continue to look for additional signals that will confirm this conclusion. After all, the more signals we get, the more confident we can be that the conclusion is the right one.

> "And Joseph found grace in his eyes, and he **served him**, and he **appointed** him **over** his house, and **all the things that belong to him** that he had, he put into his hand." (Genesis 39:4).

It is interesting to compare this verse to a verse in the beginning of Numbers that deals with the Levites serving in the Tabernacles,

> And you shall **appoint** the Levites **over** the tabernacle of Testimony, and over all its utensils, and over **all the things that belong to it**, they shall carry the tabernacle, and all its utensils, and they shall **serve it**, and shall camp around the tabernacle. (Numbers 1:50)

There are three identical components in these two verses, the one in Genesis dealing with Joseph in his Egyptian master's house, and the verse in Numbers dealing with the Levites and the Tabernacle. First, "appoint over," second, "all the things that belong to him/it," and third, "to serve." And the suspicion that Joseph's master brought Joseph into Egyptian idolatry is strengthening.

Note: At this stage we are facing several signals indicating that Joseph was involved in Egyptian idolatry. The next stage is to find more linguistic signals to confirm it.

Joseph and Idolatry

Introduction

At this point we will deviate from the sequence of events as described by the text, and go forward in the story of Joseph in Egypt, to see if we can find confirmation of the linguistic message by the words (not by the content) that Joseph was involved in Egyptian idolatry in Potiphar's house. Let's examine some verses from the event between Joseph and his master's wife.

> "And it came to pass **as this day**[52] Joseph came into the house to do his work…" (Genesis 39:11)

Linguistic Journey – "<u>As</u> This Day"

Besides our place here, the phrase "as this day" appears the Tanach in the following places:

- "And the Lord commanded us to do all these statutes, to fear the Lord our G-d, for our good always, that he might preserve us alive, **as** it is at **this day**" (Deuteronomy 6:24).
- "And the Lord will not longer bear, because of the evil of your doings, and because of the abominations which you have committed, therefore is your land a desolation, and an astonishment and a curse without an inhabitant **as** at **this day**" (Jeremiah 44:22).
- "Since the days of our fathers to this day we have been exceedingly guilty, and for our iniquities we, our kings, and our priests, have been delivered into the hand of the kings of the lands, to the sword, to captivity, and to plunder, and to utter shame **as** it is **this day**" (Ezra 9:7).

---

[52] In Hebrew the phrase is *ke-hayom hazeh*. The letter *ke* starting the word *ke-hayom* is the word "as." The word *hayom* means "the day." The word *hazeh* means "this."

- "O Lord G-d of Israel, you are righteous for we are left a remnant that has escaped, **as** it is **this day**…" (Ezra 9:15).
- "And You gave signs and wonders against Pharaoh, and all his slaves, and all the people of the land, for You knew that they acted intentionally against them. So You made a name for Yourself **as** it is **this day**" (Nehemiah 9:10).

In four places the phrase "as this day" appears in the context of G-d. Even in the place where G-d is not mentioned (the third in the list), the passive verb "have been delivered" can only relate to G-d. In summary, the phrase "as this day" is a phrase used only in relating to G-d.

"And it came to pass **as this day** Joseph came into the house to do his work…" (Genesis 39:11)

The fact that the event between Joseph and his master's wife starts with the phrase "as this day" tells us that we are likely dealing with something that has to do with god in Egypt.

"And it came to pass as this day Joseph came **into the house**[53] to do his work…" (Genesis 39:11)

Linguistic Journey – "Into the House"

The use of *habaytah* ("into the house") appears in four more places in Genesis and once in Exodus. When the text talks about the angels/men defending Lot from the mob who wanted to raid the house, the text says, "And the men put forth their hand and brought Lot to them into the house (*habaytah*) and the door they closed" (Genesis 19:10). When Eliezer comes into house of Rebecca's family, the text says, "And the man came into the house (*habaytah*) and he ungirded his camels, and gave straw and provender for the camels, and water to wash his legs and the legs of the men who were with him" (24:32). When the brothers return to Egypt, "And Joseph saw Benjamin with them, he said to the man in charge of his house, bring these men into the house (*habaytah*) and slaughter a beast

---

[53] In Hebrew the word "house" is *bayit*. Adding the letter *ha* at the beginning of a word adds the word "the" in English. In Biblical Hebrew, adding the same letter *ha* (in this case pronounced "ah") at the end of a place comes to add the word "to" or "toward," which in English would be before the word. For example, when the text says that Jacob came out of Beersheba and went to Haran, the text does not use the word "to." Instead, the text says that Jacob went *Haranah*, and the *ah* at the end means "to Haran." Here, the text says that Joseph came *habaytah*, meaning "into the house."

and make ready for these men shall dine with me at noon" (43:16). "And when Joseph came into the house (*habaytah*) they brought him the present which was in their hand into the house (*habaytah*) and bowed to him to the earth" (43:26). And in Exodus,

> Send therefore now and gather your cattle and all that you have in the field for upon every man and beast that shall be found in the field and shall not be brought into the house (*habaytah*), the hail shall come down upon them, and they shall die. (Exodus 9:19)

Except for Eliezer, Abraham's slave, who is described as a "man" (discussed in a previous chapter), all the other places deal with the owner of the house: Lot, Joseph who hosts his brothers, and the Egyptian man in the field in the book of Exodus. Even Eliezer enters the house of Abraham's family. Again, we find evidence that Joseph was a member of the household, if not the owner.

When Joseph refuses the request of his master's wife, the text quotes Joseph as saying,

> "There is none greater in **this house** than I..." (39:9).

The word "this" cannot show up in language unless the speaker has in mind another. The word "this" (or "that") comes to distinguish between "A" and "B." And now one can ask, to which other house does Joseph relate when he says "this house?"

Linguistic Journey – "This House"

Moreover, except for this place, where Joseph is speaking to his master's wife, the phrase "this house" appears in the whole Tanach only in reference to the Temple in Jerusalem.

The first time we find the phrase "this house" is when the Almighty talks to King Solomon during the time of building the Temple, "Concerning **this house** which you are building, if you will walk in my statutes and execute my judgments..." (1 Kings 6:12). Later on, when King Solomon stands in front of the altar at the time of the dedication of the Temple, he says, "...**this house** that I have built" (1 Kings 8:27). Later on, King Solomon uses the phrase several more times in his address:

- "That your eyes may be open toward **this house** night and day..." (8:29),
- "...before your altar in **this house**" (8:31),
- "...and shall return again to you and thank your name and pray and beg you in **this house**" (8:33),
- "...and spread his palms towards **this house**" (8:38),
- "...he shall come and pray toward **this house**" (8:42), and
- "...and that they may know that **this house** which I have built..." (8:43).

When the Lord responds to King Solomon's address:

- "...I have hallowed **this house** which you have built..." (9:3), and
- "And **this house** will be superior..." (9:8).

The prophet Jeremiah also relates to the Temple:

- "Is **this house** which is called by my name become a den of robbers..." (Jeremiah 7:11),
- "Then they shall come by the gates of **this house**..." (22:4),
- "...that **this house** shall become a desolation" (22:5),
- "Then I shall make **this house** like Shiloh..." (26:6),
- "Why have you prophesied in the name of the Lord saying **this house** shall be like Shiloh..." (26:9), and
- "...the Lord sent me to prophesy against **this house**..." (26:12).

And so the prophet Haggai:

- "...while **this house** lies in ruins" (Haggai 1:4),
- "Who is left among you who saw **this house** in its first glory..." (2:3),
- "...and I will fill **this house** with glory..." (2:7), and
- "The glory of **this** latter **house** shall be greater than that of the former..." (2:9).

And so the prophet Zechariah:

- "The hands of Zerubbabel have laid the foundation of **this house**..." (4:9).

There is no other place in the entire Tanach in which the phrase "this house" is used to mean any place other than the Temple in Jerusalem, except the verse in front of us, dealing with Joseph speaking to his master's wife: "There is none greater in **this house** than I..." (39:9).

Should we conclude that, in this place as well, the phrase "this house" relates to a temple? And if Joseph says "this house" should we conclude that the conversation between them is being held in an Egyptian temple?

> "And it came to pass as this day Joseph came into the house
> **to do his work**[54]..." (Genesis 39:11)

Linguistic Journey – "To Do Work"

The combination of words *la'asot* ("to do") and *melacha* ("work") appears in the Torah in the following places:

The **Creation**:

- "And on the seventh day G-d ended his work (*melachto*) which he did (*asah*)" (Genesis 2:2),
- "...because in it He had rested from all his work (*melachto*) which G-d created to do (*la'asot*)" (2:3).

The **Sabbath**:

- "Six days shall you labor and do (*ve'asita*) all your work (*melachtecha*)" (Exodus 20:9),
- "You shall keep the Sabbath for it is holy to you; every one who defiles it shall surely be put to death for whoever does (*ha'oseh*) any work (*melacha*) on it..." (31:14),
- "Six days may work (*melacha*) be done (*ye'aseh*) and in the seventh day is the Sabbath of Sabbath holy to the Lord..." (31:15),
- "Six days shall work (*melacha*) be done (*te'aseh*) but on the seventh day there shall be to you a holy day, a Sabbath of rest..." (35:2), and

---

[54] "...to do his work" – the verb "to do" in Hebrew is *la'asot* and "work" is *melacha* and "his work" is *melachto*. The ending -*to* adds the third person masculine possessive pronoun.

- "Six days you shall labor and do (*ve'asita*) all your work (*melachtecha*)" (Deuteronomy 5:13).

The **Tabernacle**:

- "...to do (*la'asot*) in all work (*melacha*)" (Exodus 31:5),
- "...to bring for all the work (*hamelacha*) which the Lord had commanded to do (*la'asot*) by the hand of Moses..." (35:29),
- "...to do (*la'asot*) in all thoughtful work (*melechet*)" (35:33),
- "...to do (*la'asot*) all work (*melechet*) of the engraver..." (35:35),
- "...to know how to do (*la'asot*) all work (*melechet*) for the labor of holy..." (36:1),
- "...to come to the work (*hamelacha*) to do (*la'asot*) it" (36:2),
- "...for doing (*la'asot*) the work (*limlechet*) for the labor of holy to do it..." (36:3),
- "And all the wise men that did (*ha'osim*) all the work (*melechet*) of holy..." (36:4),
- "...the people bring much more than enough for the labor of the work (*lamelacha*) which the Lord commanded to do (*la'asot*)" (36:5),
- "...Let neither man nor woman do (*yasu*) any more work (*melacha*) ..." (36:6),
- "...and the work (*hamelacha*) was sufficient for all the work (*hamelacha*) to do (*la'asot*) it and more" (36:7),
- "And every wise hearted man among them that did (*vaya'asu*) the work (*hamelacha*) of the tabernacle..." (36:8),
- "All the gold that was done (*he'asuy*) for the work (*lamelacha*) in all the work (*melechet*) of the holy..." (38:24),
- "And Moses saw all the work (*hamelacha*) and behold they had done (*assu*) it as the Lord had commanded so had they done (*assu*) it..." (39:43), and
- "...all who come into the army to do (*la'asot*) work (*melacha*) in the Tent of Meeting" (Numbers 4:3).

The **sacrifice** of peace offering: "...may be used (*ye'aseh*) for all work (*melacha*)..." (Leviticus 7:24).

Impurity: "...whatever utensil it is where any work (*melacha*) is done (*ye'aseh*)" (Leviticus 11:32).

With only one exception, the combination of the two words *melacha* ("work") and *la'asot* ("to do") appears in relating to holiness: the creator of the world, the Sabbath (vs. the secular work week), the Tabernacles and the sacrifice of peace offering, and alternately with the issue of impurity.

The one exception – Leviticus 11:32 – discussing "impurity" should bring us to wonder if the "impurity" the text talks about in Leviticus has anything to do with holiness, or anything to do with the tabernacle and/or the temple. After all, the book Leviticus is labeled "The book of Priests" (*Torat Kohanim*) as it relates mainly to worship and sacrifices in the tabernacle.

And in the context of Joseph, "And as this day Joseph came into the house **to do his work**[55]..." (Genesis 39:11), we should wonder what holiness, or alternatively impurity, the language of the text relates to.

"And she caught him by **his garment**..." (39:12)

Although this verse is taken from the encounter between Joseph and his master's wife, still we should deal with it now, before we even deal with the encounter itself.

The text attributes a lot of importance to Joseph's garment, as this same word repeats itself several times:

- "...and he left **his garment** in her hand..." (39:12),
- "And when she saw that he had left **his garment** in her hand..." (39:13),
- "...that he left **his garment** with me..." (39:15),
- "And she laid down **his garment** by her..." (39:16), and
- "...that he left **his garment** with me..." (39:18).

Moreover, the text devotes one full verse to the fact that his master's wife kept the garment, "And she laid up his garment by her until his master came home" (39:16).

What is the significance of Joseph's garment in the events?

---

[55] "...to do his work" – the verb "to do" in Hebrew is *la'asot* and "work" is *melacha* and "his work" is *melachto*. The ending *to* adds the third person masculine possessive pronoun.

The fact that Chapter 39, which deals with Joseph and his life in Egypt, starts with the Hebrew letter *vav* (meaning "and") should guide us to examine if the text equates the story in Chapter 38 that deals with Judah and Tamar to the story of Joseph and his master's wife. In both stories we read about marital relations (or proposed relations) that are not within marriage. In the entire book of Genesis there are three examples of it: Lot's daughters with their father, and the two stories in front of us. In the two stories, Judah and Tamar in Chapter 38, and Joseph and his master's wife in Chapter 39, the woman is the one who initiated the contact (so it is in the story of Lot's daughters and their father as well). In the two stories the woman holds in her hand proof of the contact. In the story of Judah and Tamar, Tamar asks for a guarantee, "your signet, your bracelets, and your staff" (38:18). Judah indeed gave her these items, which later saved her from death. In the story of Joseph and his master's wife, the woman holds the garment to show it to Potiphar. It is justified to compare the importance of the signet, the bracelets and the staff in the case of Judah (signs of Judah's importance) to the importance of Joseph's garment. As important as the items are to Judah, so we can conclude was this item (the garment) important to Joseph and to his master's wife.

The importance of the garment comes to the fore in another verse that at first reading seems unnecessary: "And she laid up his garment by her until his master came home" (39:16). What is the news in this verse? We already know from the two previous verses that Joseph left his garment in her hand, and if so, she had the garment, and therefore the text does not need to generate an "unnecessary" verse for us.

SCAN Rule: In an "open statement" there is no "unnecessary" sentence. It is only "unnecessary" for the reader/listener, but it is the "necessary for the subject. When the reader/listener encounters an "unnecessary" sentence, the reader/listener should realize that the sentence is extremely important.

The "unnecessary sentence" adds two points to the story, adding important details.

> "And she **laid**[56] down his garment by her
> until his master came home" (39:16).

---

[56] In Hebrew the verb *le'aniach* is used. In this verse, the form is *vatanach*.

Linguistic Journey – "to Lay Down"

Except for one place that raises a question, the verb *le'aniach* ("to lay down") appears in the Tanach only about some holiness. After the rebellion of Korach, when Moses laid down the staffs of the tribes as a testimony in the Tent of Meeting, the text says,

- "And Moses *vayanach* the staffs before the Lord in the Tent of Testimony" (Numbers 17:22).

When Joshua instructs the Israelites to take one stone per tribe as a testimony that

- "...the waters of the Jordan were cut before the Ark of the Covenant of the Lord..." (Joshua 4:7), the people "...carried twelve stones... *vayanichum* there" (4:8).

When the people address the prophet Samuel asking him to anoint a king for them,

- "And Samuel spoke to the people the law of the kingdom, and wrote it in a book, and *vayanach* it before the Lord..." (1 Samuel 10:25).

When King Solomon brought the utensils into the Temple,

- "*Vayanach* Solomon all the utensils unweighed because they were very many..." (1 Kings 7:47).

We find the same when King Solomon brought tables into the sanctuary,

- "He made ten tables *vayanach* in the sanctuary..." (2 Chronicles 4:8).

When the text talks about the body of "the man of G-d" who rebelled against the Almighty,

- "And the prophet carried the carcass of the man of G-d *vayanichehu* upon the ass and brought it back..." (1 Kings 13:29), and

- "*Vayanach* his carcass in his grave..." (13:30).

The only place that seems as if it does not deal with holiness is when the prophet Elijah runs away from King Ahab and his wife Jezebel: "And he saw and he arose and went for his soul and he came to Beersheba which is in Judah *vayanach* his lad there" (1 Kings 19:3). The fact that the verb *vayanach* is used in regard to the prophet's lad should bring us to wonder if either the lad was another prophet, or if Elijah *vayanach* the lad there as a testimony for something.

> "And she laid down his garment **by** her
> until his master came home" (39:16).

Up to this point the text twice uses the expression "...he left his garment **in her hand**..." (39:12-13). However, when she addresses the people of her household she says, "he left his garment **by me**" (39:15), and she does so twice more, in the "unnecessary" sentence (16), and when she speaks with Potiphar (18).

While the expression "in her hand" expresses actual contact between the woman and the garment, the word "by her" expresses some distance between the woman and the garment.

We find the word "by" (*etzel*) in regard to the altar several times in the Torah:

- "...and throw it by the altar, by the place of the ashes" (Leviticus 1:16),
- "...and raise the ashes which the fire consumed with the burnt offering on the altar, and he shall put them by the altar" (6:3),
- "...and eat it without leaven by the altar..." (10:12),
- ...who live in the Arabah, opposite Gilgal, by (*etzel*) the terebinths of Moreh" (Deuteronomy 11:30), and
- "You shall not plant yourself an Ashera of any tree by the altar of the Lord your G-d, which you shall make" (Deuteronomy 16:21).

In the fourth example above, we find the word "by" (*etzel*) with no **mention** of an altar. But note that the terebinth of Moreh **is** the first place where Abraham built an altar to the Almighty after his arrival in the land of Canaan (Genesis 12:7).

If we accept the claim of Potiphar's wife that Joseph tried to rape her, or to sleep with her, she didn't have to change her language to distance herself from the garment. The opposite would be expected. She had to show that Joseph indeed got close to her, as much as he could and therefore she could hold the garment "in her hand." That would have been the strongest evidence that he indeed tried to sleep with her. Does this change of language indicate that the woman knew that she was not supposed to hold the garment "in her hand?"

Let's not forget the comparison between the two verses – the one in Genesis, "And Joseph found grace in his eyes, and he **served** him, and he **appointed** him over his house, and **all the things that belong to** him he put into his hand" (Genesis 39:4), and the one in Numbers, "And you shall **appoint** the Levites **over** the tabernacle of Testimony, and over all its utensils, and over **all the things that belong to it**, they shall carry the tabernacle, and all its utensils, and they shall **serve it**, and shall camp around the tabernacle" (Numbers 1:50). In both verses we find three identical components – "to appoint," "to serve," and "all the things that belong to." This comparison should bring us to assume that the garment that Joseph had on was **a priestly garment**, and quite likely Potiphar's wife was not allowed to have direct contact with it.

We find in the Torah that the priestly garments had their own holiness, "…and sprinkle it upon Aaron, and upon his garments, and upon his sons, and upon the garments of his sons with him, and he shall be sanctified and his garments and his sons and his sons' garments with him" (Exodus 29:21). And, "…and sprinkled it on Aaron and on his garments, and on his sons and on his sons' garments with him, and sanctified Aaron and his garments, and his sons and his sons' garments with him" (Leviticus 8:30).

In Exodus, the text says, "And the garments of holiness of Aaron shall be to his sons after him to be anointed in them, and to fulfill the requirement to be appointed by them[57]" (Exodus 29:29). And, indeed, at the time of Aaron's death we find, "And strip Aaron of his garments and put them upon Eleazar his son…" (Numbers 20:26). "And Moses stripped Aaron of his garments and put them upon Eleazar his son…" (20:28). We do not find any other act of anointing Eleazar to priesthood after his father.

---

[57] In the Hebrew the text goes – "to be anointed by them and to *lemaleh* with them their hands." The same verb *lemaleh* we saw earlier to indicate in one verb the meaning of fulfilling a requirement.

Putting on the garments, which had holiness in them, was enough to give the holiness of the position to Eleazar.

Summary

We saw language-wise that the text started Joseph's life with the verb *huRaD* which is to "take down" in the passive form, and noted that this is the same verb used to take the tabernacle down before going on a journey. From this point alone we should suspect that we are dealing with some reduction in holiness. We also saw that the Almighty was with (*et*) Joseph, unlike all the others that the Almighty was with (*im*) in Genesis, indicating some distance between the Almighty and Joseph.

We also saw several points in the language indicating that quite likely the distance is due to idolatry. This is confirmed by the following:

1. Using the word *biglal* (for the sake of Joseph), and the word *biglal* is used in the Tanach for idolatry, reminding us of the word *gilulim* used for it.
2. The similarity in the way Joseph's master appointed him, which includes the three components, "to appoint," "to serve," and "all the things that belong," to the appointment of the Levites to serve in the Tabernacle.
3. The use of the phrase "as this day" that is used solely in relation to the Almighty.
4. The use of the word *habayta* ("into the house") indicating that Joseph was a member of the family, if not "the man of the household."
5. The use of the phrase "this house" that is otherwise used in the Tanach solely in relation to the Temple in Jerusalem.
6. The combination of the words "to do" (*la'asot*) and "work" (*melacha*), which is used almost exclusively for holiness, and once for impurity.
7. The change in the woman's language from having the garment "in her hand" to having it "**by** her," indicating the holiness of the garment.
8. The use of the verb "to lay down" (*vatanach*) the garment, also a verb used almost exclusively for holiness.

Conclusion: Eight points are strong evidence that Joseph was indeed involved in the idolatry going on in Potiphar's household.

> "...the Lord blessed the Egyptian's house
> for the sake of (*biglal*) Joseph..." (39:5)

The omission of the word "his master" (In Hebrew it is one word as the possessive pronoun is part of the noun), and the use of only "the Egyptian's house" should guide us to a different way of reading the verse. Maybe at this stage Joseph's master didn't see himself as "his master" anymore. Maybe at this stage Joseph's master had released him from his slavery, and brought him into the house as a member of the family.

We will continue to read with the assumption that quite likely that's what happened (Joseph was adopted by Potiphar as a son), but we are still looking for corroborating evidence to this point, beyond one change of language.

Did all family members accept this change of language? It seems that they didn't. The text continues and introduces us in verses 7 and 8 to "his master's wife," and that's the way it is throughout the story. When Joseph refused her request the text quotes Joseph saying to her "my master." His master's wife refused to recognize this change in Joseph's status. We find evidence of it in the change of language between the way she talked to the people of her household, and the way she talked to Potiphar. While to the people of her household she says, "See, he has brought in a Hebrew **man**..." (39:14), to Potiphar she is quoted as saying, "...The Hebrew **slave**..." (39:17). The people of her household knew that Joseph was a "man" (quite likely free), while she saw him as a "slave."

At this point we should note that nowhere in the **language** of the text do we find that Potiphar was her husband. She is always introduced as "his master's wife."

What Did the Egyptian Pagan Religion Include?

The description in Exodus of the sin of the golden calf gives us a window into the pagan practices.

> "And they rose up early on the next day and offered burnt

offerings and brought peace offerings, and the people sat
down to eat and drink and rose up *letzahek*" (Exodus 32:6).

Besides burnt offerings, peace offerings, eating, drinking, and *letzahek*, the text says more about the events there. When Moses went down from the mountain we find, "And Joshua heard the noise of the people as they shouted, he said to Moses, there is a sound like war in the camp" (32:17).

Moses responded, "…it is not the voice of affliction (*aanot*[58]) from strength, and it is not the voice of affliction from weakness, it is the voice of affliction that I hear" (32:18).

There are several places in the Biblical text that give us the meaning of the word *aanot*. In their conversation, at their meeting at Mount Gilead, Laban says to Jacob, "If you shall afflict (*te'aneh*) my daughters…" (Genesis 31:50). In Exodus we find, "You shall not afflict (*te'anun*) any widow or an orphan. If you afflict (*te'aneh*) him…" (Exodus 22:21-22). In Leviticus we find in regard to the Day of Atonement, "For whatever soul who shall not be afflicted (*te'uneh*)…" (Leviticus 23:29). The prophet Isaiah says, "Is such the fast that I have chosen? A day for a man to afflict (*aanot*) his soul?…" (Isaiah 58:5).

In summary, the word *aanot*, along with the verb *le'aanot* deal with self-affliction of the body. One should note that even today we see some zealots who take chains and afflict themselves to the point of ecstasy.

Besides "shouting" and "affliction," the text added one more component. When Moses got closer to the camp, "…and he saw the calf and the **dancing**…" (Exodus 32:19).

But shouting, affliction, and dancing were still not the full picture. There was also the component of *letzahek*.

The wife of Joseph's master is quoted as saying to the people of her household, "See, he has brought in a Hebrew man *letzahek* us…" (Genesis 39:14).

---

[58] We find in Isaiah the following verse, "Is such the fast that I have chosen? A day for a man to afflict (*aanot*) his soul…" (Isaiah 58:5). The word *aanot* is the name of the verb *le'aanot*, which is "to afflict." For the day of Yom Kippur (the day of Atonement) it is said, "…you shall afflict (*ve'initem*) your soul…" (Leviticus 16:31).

Linguistic Journey – the Verb *Letzahek*

The verb *letzahek* comes from the three letter root word, *TZ-H-K. Litzhok* means "to laugh." And indeed Abraham's and Sarah's son is called *"yiTZHaK"* (Isaac in English) which means "he will laugh." When Abraham is told by the Almighty that Sarah will have a son, the text says that Abraham "laughed" (*vaitzhak*) (Genesis 17:17). This is the same reaction of Sarah: "Sarah laughed (*vatitzhak*) within herself..." (18:12). When Yitzhak was born, Sarah is quoted as saying, "G-d has made laughter (*TzeHoK*) of me, all those who will hear will laugh (*yitzhak*) at me" (21:6).

Does the verb *letzahek* mean "to laugh?"

At this point, we will check if a different form of the verb taken from the three-letter root word *TZ-H-K* indicates a different meaning. Is *litzhok* ("to laugh") different in meaning from *letzahek?*

The verb *letzahek* appears in the following places:

- "And Lot went out and spoke to his sons-in-law who married his daughters and said, arise and get out from this place for the Lord will destroy this city, and he appeared to his sons-in-law as *metzahek*"[59] (19:14),
- "And Sarah saw the son of Hagar the Egyptian whom she had born to Abraham *metzahek*" (21:9),
- "And when his time there lengthened, Abimelech King of the Philistines, looked out the window, and saw that Isaac was *metzahek* his wife Rebecca" (26:8), and
- "And they rose up early in the morning on the next day and offered burnt offerings and brought peace offerings, and the people sat down to eat and drink and rose up to *letzahek*" (Exodus 32:6).

From the use of the verb *letzahek* between Isaac and Rebecca, activity that indicated to King Abimelech that they were a married couple, contrary to Isaac's claim that she was his sister, we learn that the verb *letzahek* deals with the intimate and sexual relationship between a man and a woman.

---

[59] *Metzahek* – present tense of the verb *letzahek*.

With this understanding of the meaning of the verb *letzahek* we can understand why Sarah was so adamant in her demand to expel Ishmael and his mother Hagar, once she saw that Ishmael was *metzahek*. When Sarah told Abraham, "...expel this slave and her son..." (Genesis 21:10), Abraham's reaction was, "And the thing was very grievous in Abraham's eyes because of his son" (21:11). The Almighty told Abraham, "...in all that Sarah has said to you, listen to her voice..." (21:12). Not only was it objectionable in Sarah's eyes, but the text tells us that the Almighty also sees this sexual activity as a red line which should not be crossed.

The text brings us Ishmael's behavior by adding "unnecessary" information that is already known to us from earlier – that Ishmael was the son of Hagar **the Egyptian**.

Is it "unnecessary?" Let's examine the report in the text of the sin of the Golden Calf, a sin of idolatry, quite likely brought by the people from Egypt.

The Golden Calf

The text says that the people did "a mask of a calf" (*egel masecha*) (Exodus 32:4). The people announced, "These are your gods, O Israel, which brought you up out of the land of Egypt" (32:4). The story continues with Aaron building an altar and declaring "Tomorrow is a festival to the Lord" (32:5).

Throughout the story idolatry takes over the people, and the Almighty sits idle as if nothing is happening. The text continues, "...and offered burnt offerings and brought peace offerings" (32:6), and the Almighty is still silent. The people sit down to eat and drink, and the Almighty is still silent.

"...[A]nd they arose *letzahek*," and here we see a dramatic change: "And the Lord said to Moses, go down for your people whom you brought out of the land of Egypt have corrupted themselves" (32:7). As long as the people only declared the "mask of calf" as the god of Israel, and even offered sacrifices to it, and started celebrating (eating and drinking), the Almighty did not intervene. But when the people arose *letzahek*, "they corrupted themselves," the red line was crossed, and there was a need to act.

155

Both Ishmael (the son of Hagar the Egyptian) and the people sinning with the Golden Calf sinned with *letzahek*. If we have any doubt that the verb *letzahek* deals with sexual activities, we need to go to Chapter 18 in Leviticus, and we find there, "After the doings of the land of Egypt where you dwelt you shall not do…" (Leviticus 18:3), and the text moves on to list the incestuous relationships between members of the same family, between parents and children, between siblings, etc.

Lot and His Sons-in-Law

Before we go back to Joseph in Egypt we should examine the story of Lot. The text says, "And Lot went out and spoke to his sons-in-law who married his daughters and said, arise and get out from this place for the Lord will destroy this city, and he appeared to his sons-in-law as *metzhahek*" (19:14).

If we read the verse while tuning in to the pronouns used in the text, we see that Lot does not say, "Arise and let **us** get out of the city." Instead, he said, "Arise and [**you**] get out of the city." Lot encourages them to leave the city without committing himself to leave the city as well. Now it is clear why his sons-in-law perceived him as *metzahek*. They understood that Lot saw them as the ones who took his daughters from him, and that he would like to *letzahek* with his daughters all to himself. Realizing this point we can see the daughters' behavior (initiating the sexual encounter with their father after the destruction of Sodom) as apples that didn't fall far from the tree.

Back to Joseph and his Master

In the beginning the text tells us that Joseph's master appointed him over his house, and "all that belonged to him" he gave in his hand. Later the text brings us an additional development: Joseph's master "left" (39:6) everything in his hand, without close supervision.

> "…and he knew not anything with him
> **except for the bread which he ate…**" (39:6)

There is another place in Genesis in which the bread is mentioned as a point to distinguish between Joseph and the Egyptians,

...and he said, set on bread. And they set for him by himself, and for them by themselves, and for the Egyptians who ate with him, by themselves, because the Egyptians cannot eat bread with the Hebrews, for that is abomination to the Egyptians. (43:31-32)

The text tells us specifically when Joseph hosted his brothers (and at that time they were not supposed to know that he was their brother, only the ruler of the land) that Joseph kept a distance from the Egyptians who were under his rule, with respect to bread.

It is quite likely that from the beginning of his time in his master's house Joseph ate separately from his master. For the Egyptians, the wife was no more than property. On the other hand, the food on the table testified to the importance that Potiphar was not willing to grant Joseph.

"And Joseph was handsome and good looking" (Genesis 39:6)

Once we realize Joseph's master "left" everything in the hands of Joseph, including his wife, and we realize his role in Egyptian idolatry, we see that sex is moving to the center of events. The text prepares the reader by saying how good-looking Joseph was.

The fact that the text used the phrase "the Egyptian's" house instead of "his master's," and the possibility that Joseph's master freed him of his slavery and brought him into the house, should bring us to be concerned for Joseph's fate. The higher he goes in rank in his master's house, along with his involvement with the Egyptians' idolatry, the more likely that sexual activity (*letzahek*) will come into play.

The Incident Between Joseph and his Master's Wife

This incident starts with the phrase, "After these things..." (39:7).

"After these things" is a connecting phrase between two different events.

SCAN Rule: A word, a sentence, or a phrase that connects two different events might indicate that there was a stop in the delivery of the information, and might indicate that some information was ejected from the statement at this point of time.

Background information: The assumption in an "open statement" is that each event happens after another. And the assumption is that the person giving the statement lists the events according to the order they happened. Therefore, a connecting word, or phrase, seems unnecessary.

Generally speaking, in an "open statement" a connecting phrase indicates that at the time of the writing the statement, the subject pauses for a while, still holding the pen, and looks into memory to review the event. The event still shows up on the "screen" in the subject's memory. The subject quite likely decides not to include this part of the event in the statement, and returns to writing at the point where he/she paused. Therefore, the subject puts a connecting phrase to indicate that he/she is resuming the writing after the pause. Such a connecting phrase can be equated to a "blackout" in the reader/listener's neighborhood, while the TV station (the subject's memory) is still broadcasting the event. However, due to the "blackout" (the pause in delivery) in the reader/listener's neighborhood (statement) the reader/listener loses this segment.

One should note that the fact that the subject decided to eject something from the statement is not a bad signal at all. It signifies that memory is the engine behind the statement. How one can conceal without having something in memory to conceal? And the fact is that many truthful people (estimated at around 70%) do conceal information.

Linguistic Journey – "After These Things"

We find we find the phrase "After these things" in Genesis six times. After the victory of Abraham over the kings who captured the people of Sodom including Abraham's nephew Lot, Abraham met the king of Sodom. The text tells us the king of Shalem appears at this meeting as well. At the end of the meeting Abraham reaches an understanding with the king of Sodom that only the people who joined him in the war – Aner, Eshkol, and Mamre – will get their share from the spoil of war. Immediately after this event the text continues, "After these things..." (Genesis 15:1) and the text brings us the word of G-d to Abraham, "Fear not Abram..." and the text continues with the covenant of the splits, the covenant in which the Almighty informs Abraham that his seed will live in a land they don't own for 400 years, and that they will be enslaved, and that at the end of that period the Almighty will deliver them to the land of Canaan, and will punish the nation that enslaved them.

The second place where we find the phrase "After these things" is in Genesis 22:1, which introduces the binding of Isaac at the altar. This phrase shows up after the covenant Abraham reached with Abimelech, the king of the Philistines. We should note that the binding ends with the phrase "After these things" (22:20), as it started, which is the third place in the book. This place starts the section bringing us the news about the birth of Rebecca.

The fourth place (39:7) starts the incident between Joseph and his master's wife. This phrase appears after the text says that Joseph's master "left" in his hand "everything that belonged to him," which can be understood as a "covenant" between these two men.

At the end of the incident Joseph is put in prison, and he reaches an understanding with the prison warden (39:22-23). Immediately, the text continues with the fifth place where we find the phrase, "After these things" (40:1). This place starts the section reporting the dreams of Pharaoh's two ministers.

The sixth place, and the last one in Genesis, appears after Jacob asks Joseph to take an oath that he will not bury him in Egypt. The text continues, "After these things one told Joseph, behold your father is sick..." (48:1).

Except for the last place, all the other five places in which the phrase "After these things" appears, the text puts this phrase after the Biblical figure, either Abraham or Joseph, comes to an understanding with some foreign ruler, when the Biblical figure relies upon the foreign figure's word. In the case of Abraham it is the king of Sodom and the king of the Philistines. In the case of Joseph it is Joseph's master, and later the prison warden. The text perceives this reliance on the word of the foreign ruler as contradictory to the course of events guided by the Almighty.

The fact that the phrase "After these things" appears in the Biblical text in very distinct places – only after one of the Biblical figures makes a pact with a Gentile king, or with a Gentile authority – exposes the approach of the text to historical events. The text perceives that everything that goes on in history is divinely guided. Therefore, when the Almighty promises something to a human, that human should trust the promise of the Almighty, and not rely upon a pact with another human to guarantee the results promised by the Almighty. When Abraham made a pact with Abimelech, the king of the Philistines, Abraham neglected the promise he received from the Almighty that the land would be his seed's. Therefore, the text continues with, "After these things the Almighty tested Abraham." There is a need for a test, as the pact with Abimelech showed lack of trust.

In **summary**, the phrase "After these things..." represents the text signaling the reader the following: I am showing you what man is doing, but don't forget that the Almighty is still behind the scene, guiding the course of events. The phrase "After these things" echoes the verse from Proverbs: "There are many thoughts in a man's heart, and the counsel of the Lord shall prevail" (Proverbs 19:21).

We could also consider the understanding that Jacob reached with Joseph concerning his burial in the land of Canaan as an understanding with a foreign ruler, meaning Joseph the ruler of Egypt. We should not forget that before Jacob went down to Egypt the Almighty promised him, "I will go down with you to Egypt and I will also surely bring you up again..." (Genesis 46:4). If the Almighty already promised Jacob, before he left the land of Canaan on his way to Egypt, that He would bring him back to Canaan, then why does Jacob need to ask Joseph to take an oath that he will bury him in the land of Canaan?

The six places where we find the phrase "After these things" relate to four events: the covenant of the splits, the binding of Isaac, Joseph and his master's wife, and the oath Joseph took before Jacob. From these four events we have two events that the phrase "After these things" starts **and** ends the report: the binding of Isaac, and Joseph and his master's wife. Because these two events have this phrase both at the beginning and at the end, we will consider them separate from the others.

SCAN Rule: when a certain event in an "open statement" is surrounded by two "unnecessary connections" the reader/listener should relate to that event as extremely sensitive. In an "open statement" of modern times the SCAN analyst should guide the investigator to focus on this point in the follow-up investigation, even if the analyst does not see anything sensitive, according to his/her point of view.

Abraham and Joseph

The fact that these two events, the binding of Isaac and the story of Joseph and his master's wife, are both surrounded by the unnecessary connection "After these things" should bring us to the conclusion that the text perceives these two events as equivalent in some way.

We should also note that in Genesis the title "Hebrew" is given to only two men. First, Abraham, when he is informed of Lot being taken captive, "And the refugee came and told Abram **the Hebrew**…" (14:13). Second, Joseph, when his master's wife says, "…he has brought us a **Hebrew** man *letzahek* us…" (39:14). Later on, when she talks to Potiphar, "**Hebrew** slave" (39:17), and thereafter three more times, all referring to Joseph: 40:15, 41:12, and 43:32.

Joseph is **linguistically** connected to Abraham in two ways. First, the fact that both the binding of Isaac, and Joseph's experience with his master's wife are surrounded by the two unnecessary connections, "After these things," and second, the fact that the two men are labeled "Hebrew."

We should remember that these two events deal with two of the three points that constitute the most egregious offenses in Judaism – spilling blood (murder) in the binding of Isaac, and "exposing sexual organs"[60] in the story of Joseph and his master's wife. In the latter we also have the third point – idolatry. However, it does not show up in the **content**, but in the **language** of the text. As we saw that the event of the binding came to test Abraham, "After these things G-d tested Abraham…" (22:1), so the story of Joseph and his master's wife came to test Joseph, although the text does not say it specifically. We should also note that unlike Abraham where the text specifically says that he passed the test, "…for now I know that you fear G-d…" (Genesis 22:12), the text does not say anything about Joseph passing the test, although it is clear from the content that he passed it with flying colors.

"…and his master's wife **raised her eyes** to Joseph…" (39:7)

---

[60] In Hebrew it is literally labeled *giluy* (uncovering) *aarayot* (sexually intimate places, typically translated as "nakedness" in English). See Leviticus chapter 18.

Linguistic Journey – "Raising the Eyes"

The activity of "raising the eyes" appears several times in Genesis. In all of them it has the meaning of looking at something or someone from afar and focusing on it. For example,

- "And Lot **raised his eyes** and saw the valley of the Jordan that it was well watered everywhere..." (13:10),
- "And the Lord said to Abram, after Lot was separated from him, **raise your eyes** and see from the place where you are to the north, and to the south, and to the east, and to the west" (13:14),
- "On the third day Abraham **raised his eyes** and saw the place from far away" (22:4),
- "And Abraham **raised his eyes** and looked and behold behind him a ram caught in a thicket by his horns..." (22:13),
- "And he **raised his eyes** and saw the women and the children..." (33:5),
- "And he **raised his eyes** and saw his brother Benjamin, his mother's son..." (43:29), and
- "And Balaam **raised his eyes** and he saw Israel abiding in his tents according to their tribes..." (Numbers 24:2).

We also find places where the one who looks sees the object or the person getting closer from afar –

- "And he **raised his eyes** and looked and behold three men stood by him..." (Genesis 18:2),
- "And Jacob **raised his eyes** and looked and behold Esau came..." (33:1),
- "And they sat down to eat bread and they **raised their eyes** and looked and behold a company of Ishmaelites came from Gilead..." (37:25), and
- "And Pharaoh drew near, the people of Israel **raised their eyes** and behold Egypt riding after them..." (Exodus 14:10).

Back to Joseph and his Master's Wife

As Joseph was "promoted" in the Egyptian's house, especially after the Egyptian "left" "everything that belonged to him" in his hands, his master's wife "raised her eyes" to Joseph. In other words, he was far from her until this point, but now he got closer. And the more he got closer, and entered the house, the more he entered her thoughts.

What Did the Master's Wife Ask of Joseph?

> And it happened after these things his master's wife raised her eyes to Joseph and said **lie with (*im*) me**. And he refused and said to his master's wife, my master knows not what is with me in the house, and everything that belongs to him he gave in my hand. There is none greater in this house than I, nor has he kept back anything from me but you because you are his wife, how then can I do this great evil and sin to G-d? And it came to pass she spoke to Joseph day by day and he didn't listen to her to **lie by her** to be with (*im*) her. (39:7-10)

Did she ask him to have sexual relations as we understand them between a woman and a man? Or is there maybe something deeper here than meets the eye?

We already discussed earlier the difference in Biblical Hebrew between the two "withs:" *im* which indicates closeness, and *et* which indicates distance. And the woman asked Joseph to lie with (*im*) her.

There are two ways to explain the woman's language. First, we can use this quote to understand that we are talking here about an act similar to the daughters of Lot having sex with their father. Having sexual relations within the family, or in other words, incest. If so, Joseph was indeed adopted by Potiphar as a son, and brought into the family. Second, we can see the "with" (*im*) testifies to the woman's innocence, a woman who lived in Egyptian society that was ridden with incest ("And the doings of the land of Egypt where you dwelt shall you not do" (Leviticus 18:3)). The woman did not see anything wrong with it.

Once Joseph refused her initial request the text changes the language and says that the woman wanted him to "lie down **by** her" and not "with" (*im*) her (39:10). We should note that this is the only place in the entire Tanach where we find the verb "to lie down" (*lishkav*) with the preposition "by" (*etzel*). All the other places it is with the preposition "with," either *im* (closeness), or *et* (distance).

(We should remember here the discussion of the verse where the woman "laid down the garment **by** her.")

The woman was willing to compromise and to have Joseph lying down "by" her and not "with" her. If this was her wish after his refusal, assuming she wanted to make it easier for him to accept the seduction, why did Joseph panic?

The verse does not end with her wanting him to lie down "by" her. The verse adds one more component, "to lie down by her **to be with (*im*) her**" (39:10).

We already saw in the chapter on birth order that the verb "to be with (*im*)" appears in Genesis only in regard to the connection between the forefathers (Isaac and Jacob) and the Almighty, and later on, in Exodus, in regard to the connection between the Almighty and Moses. The woman did not want just sex. She wanted sexual relations within the religious rituals practiced in Egypt. She wanted the closeness with the priest who served her gods.

Joseph did not only reject the woman's advances. By rejecting the woman, Joseph rejected the Egyptian religion. With this understanding we can now move on to read the woman's complaint to the people of her household, and later on to Potiphar.

To the people of her household she is quoted as saying,

> See, he has brought us a Hebrew man *letzahek* us, he came to me to lie with (*im*) me and I called (*va'ekra*) with a loud voice. And when he heard that I raised my voice he left his garment by me and fled and came outside. (39:14-15)

One should note that by the narrative of the text he "came to her" before she raised her voice. However, in the second component of the sentence, when she talks about Joseph running away from her, she attaches his fleeing to her raising her voice. Raising her voice was the trigger, in her view, for him to flee.

We should compare the woman's report to a section in Deuteronomy that deals with rape: "And if the man finds the betrothed girl in the field, **and**

the man holds her and lies with her…" (Deuteronomy 22:25). And the text continues, "…and the betrothed girl **cried for help** (*tzaaka*) and there was no one to rescue her" (22:27). [See all the places in the Torah in which crying for help is described by the verb *litzok* in Appendix B.]

The text in the above verses brings us two components that need to be present before we say that we are dealing with rape: the man "holds" the woman (against her will), and the woman cries for help, two components that are missing in the case of the report by the wife of Joseph's master to the people of her household.

But what is interesting in the woman's report is not only what she didn't say ("being held" and "crying for help") but also what she did say.

> "**See**, he has brought us a Hebrew man *letzahek* us,
> he came to me to lie with (*im*) me
> and I called (*vaekra*) with a loud voice" (39:14).

As we will see later in this chapter, calling in a loud voice is not the same thing as crying for help.

Linguistic Journey – the Command "See"

We have several places in Genesis in which a statement is preceded by the word "see." When Isaac blessed Jacob, he started the blessing with, "…and he blessed him and said, **see**, the smell of my son is like the smell of a field which the Lord has blessed" (27:27), When Laban makes a pact with Jacob, "…there is no man with us, **see**, G-d is witness between me and you" (31:50), "And Pharaoh said to Joseph, **see**, I have set you over all the land of Egypt" (41:41). We can see that the word "see" starts a very important public statement that is a blessing (Isaac to Jacob), an appointment (Pharaoh to Joseph) or witness to evidence (Laban and Jacob).

We can see the word "see" starting Moses' appeal to the Almighty to show his face to Moses, "And Moses said to the Lord, see, you say to me bring up this people and you have not let me know whom you will send with me…" (Exodus 33:12). So Moses is looking for confirmation, or evidence, or an appointment of another person to send with him.

"**See**, he has brought us a Hebrew man *letzahek* us..." (39:14)

It is clear that the woman starts a very significant statement. We know it is not a blessing and it is not an appointment. If so, is it evidence that she is bringing them? And if it is evidence, evidence of what?

SCAN Rule: the first sentence in an "open statement" is the most important sentence. In many cases it might include the reason for the events that follow.

"...he has brought us a Hebrew man *letzahek* us..." (39:14)

We should note that she does not start the "open statement" by saying, "...he came to me to lie with (*im*) me..." For her, the events started with Potiphar bringing Joseph *letzahek* us.

Moreover, the fact that she labels Potiphar only as "he" without giving him a title might express her anger with Potiphar. We should not forget that not even once does the text label her as "Potiphar's wife." She is always labeled as "his master's wife." Only two times does the title "his wife" appear. First, when Joseph refused her by saying that she is "his wife" and how can he do such a thing (39:9), and second, after she reports to Potiphar, the text says, "When his master heard the words of **his wife**..." (39:19). So if she is directing her anger towards Potiphar, why wouldn't she show any anger towards Joseph?

Question: Is it possible that the word "see" comes to bring evidence that a "Hebrew man" is not the right one to *letzahek* us?

"...he **came to** me to lie with (*im*) me..." (39:14)

We know that "coming to" is a word used for a proper marital relationship between husband and wife. Jacob is quoted as telling Laban, "...give me my wife for my days are fulfilled that I may **come to** her" (29:21). Leah tells Jacob, after she "bought" the night from her sister with her son's mandrakes, "You are to **come to** me..." (30:16). Potiphar's wife uses the same respectable verb as a wife would say to her husband. This is not language expected from a woman talking about a man who tried to rape her.

"...and I **called** in a loud voice" (39:14)

In the Hebrew we find that the verb used here is *va'ekra,* which is translated into "and I called." The text does not use the verb *va'etzak,* which is the verb used throughout the Torah for "crying for help." See Appendix B listing all the places where crying for help is described using the verb *litzok.*

The verb *likro* in Hebrew comes from three-letter-root word *K-R-A.* It is used to mean both to call and to read, in Biblical Hebrew as well as in Modern Hebrew.

Summary of Appendix C: *Likro* – to Call

We see many places where the verb *likro* is used to name a person at birth, or to name a location. When it comes to calling someone we find that depending on the preposition letter/word going with the verb, the verb *likro* might be "to call somebody to come to you" or "to call" in the sense of raising your voice. In most cases the text used "to call *el*" (*el* means "to"), which means to call from afar, which entails raising the voice. There are places where the text uses "to call *l*" (a contraction of *el*) and in these cases it seems that it means to summon one to come to you. There are five places where the text uses "to call *et.*" Realizing from the previous discussion that *et* means distance while *im* means closeness, it seems that it applies with the verb *likro* as well.

There are a few places that the verb *likro* is used without any preposition. However, the text brings us the content of the call, and then we know that we are dealing with a declaration.

There are only two places in the entire Torah in which the verb *likro* comes without any preposition letter/word, without saying to whom the call is addressed, and without saying what the content of the call is. These two places are in the story of Joseph and his master's wife: "...and I **called** in a loud voice. And when he heard that I raised my voice and I **called**..." (39:14-15).

The story of Joseph and his master's wife contains the only two places in which a person calls but without indicating the content of the call and without indicating to whom the call is addressed. These two characteristics should bring us to scrutinize this place very carefully.

"…and I **called in a loud voice**." (Genesis 39:14)

Linguistic Journey – "to Call in a Loud Voice"

We find in the Tanach the activity of calling in a loud voice in the following places:

When the prophet Elijah challenges the priests for Baal, the pagan god on Mount Carmel, the text says, "And it happened at noon and Elijah mocked them and said **call in a loud voice** for he is a god…" (1 Kings 18:27), and "…they **called in a loud voice**…" (18:28).

We find the phrase "calling in a loud voice" relating indirectly to idolatry in the prophet Ezekiel as well. After talking about "…the abominations that they committed," and "filling the land with evil" (Ezekiel 8:17), the prophet says, "Therefore I too will deal in fury, my eye shall not spare, nor I will have pity and even if they would **call** in my ears **in a loud voice**, I will not hear them" (Ezekiel 8:18). When the punishment comes the people will attempt to return to the true G-d, but they will do it in the way they did their abominations and their evil ways by calling in a loud voice. The following chapter starts with, "And he **called** in my ears **in a loud voice**…" (Ezekiel 9:1), and again, the chapters discuss the abominations done in Jerusalem.

We also find the phrase "to call in a loud voice" used not in the context of idolatry, but still used by a foreigner and someone not from the Israelite culture:

"And Rabshakeh stood and **called with a loud voice** in the language of Judah…" (2 Kings 18:28 and Isaiah 36:13), and, "And they **called with a loud voice** in the language of Judah to the people of Jerusalem who were on the wall to frighten them and to trouble them so that they might take the city" (2 Chronicles 32:18).

Taking into consideration that Moses could hear "the voice of affliction" from the camp upon his descent from Mount Sinai, meaning a voice loud enough to be heard from afar, we should conclude that the pagan practice was to worship by "calling in a loud voice." There was no idolatry conducted in silence, or even in a whisper, or even in a normal voice. It had to be "in a loud voice."

In comparison, the text brings the words of the Almighty to the prophet Elijah,

> And he said, go out, and stand upon the mount before the Lord. And, behold, the Lord is passing by, and a great and strong wind tore the mountains, and broke in pieces the rocks before the Lord, **but the Lord was not in the wind**, and after the wind an earthquake, but **the Lord was not in the earthquake**. And after the earthquake a fire, but **the Lord was not in the fire**, and after the fire a sound of thin silence.[61] (1 Kings 19:11-12)

"And when he heard that I **raised my voice** and I called…" (39:15)

When the text relates to the covenant on Mount Eval and Mount Gerizim, the text says, "And the Levites shall answer and say to all the men of Israel **in a high[62] voice**" (Deuteronomy 27:14).

When Isaiah talks about the king of Assyria, the text quotes the prophet Isaiah saying, "Whom have you taunted and blasphemed? And against whom have you **raised your voice**…" (2 Kings 19:22, Isaiah 37:23). When the time of judgment is to come, the prophet Isaiah says, "Lift up a banner upon the high mountain, **raise a voice** to them, wave a hand that they will come in the entrances of the nobles" (Isaiah 13:2).

"Cry aloud (in Hebrew, "with your throat") spare not [referring to the throat] **raise your voice** like a shofar and tell my people their transgressions and to the house of Jacob their sins" (Isaiah 58:1). When talking about the Day of Atonement, "Behold, you fast for strife and debate and to strike with the fist of wickedness, you shall not fast as you do this day to make your **voice** be heard **up high[63]**" (Isaiah 58:4), and on the first time the temple was used, "…and many in joy **to raise the voice**" (Ezra 3:12).

---

[61] "…thin silence" – often translated as a "still small voice," but "thin silence" is a closer translation.

[62] Unlike the places where we find *kol* ("voice") *gadol* ("loud"), here we find *kol ram* ("high"). The word *ram* ("high") has the same root as "to **raise** the voice" – *leharim*.

[63] Up high – in the Hebrew the word *marom* is used, from the same root as *leharim* ("to raise").

Summary

While idolatry is described with a "**loud** voice," the worship of the Almighty is described with a "**high** voice," or with "**raising** the voice."

Back to the Wife of Joseph's Master

We find that in all the places in which "raising the voice" is mentioned, it has to do with some religious occasion. And the wife of Joseph's master said, "And when he heard that I **raised my voice** and I called…" (39:15).

We should note that the text itself says what happened between the two was only, "And she caught him by his garment saying lie with me and he left his garment in her hand and fled and came out" (39:12). What she said later to the people of her household is not in the sequence of events that the text said happened.

However, one should note that the report the woman gave to her people, regardless of the fact that it didn't happen according to the text, is loaded with idol worship terminology and meaning.

And now what she does not say is even more meaningful. She does not say that Joseph "held" her, as we see in the case of rape mentioned in Deuteronomy. And she did not cry for help (*litzok*).

Summary

She started her report by saying that the objective of Joseph being brought into the house was *letzahek*, which means having sexual relations within the Egyptian pagan religious practice. She presented it that Joseph came to lie with her, using language ordinarily used between husband and wife ("came to"). She "called in a loud voice when he **came** to lie with (*im*) her. She presented it as she was "calling" to her gods within the religious ritual as was expected of her to do. And Joseph left his garment and fled. She presented it as if Joseph quit on her in the middle of her attempt to connect to her gods. It is very easy to read it as if she is saying to the people: Joseph was brought for the purpose of *letzahek*, and he didn't do what he was supposed to do. No wonder she emphasized that he was a Hebrew, meaning, a foreigner who didn't accept the social norms of Egypt. Actually, by saying, "See **he** brought us a Hebrew man *letzahek* us," she is expressing her anger at her stupid husband who should have known better; for the activity of *letzahek* he should have brought an **Egyptian** man who would have been able to perform his duties as expected.

When she reported the event to Potiphar upon his returning home, the text says, "And when his master heard the words of his wife which she spoke to him saying **as these things** your slave **did** to me and he became angry" (39:19). The combination of the two, "as these things" (*ka'devarim haeleh*) with the verb "to do" (*aasah*) is found once more in the Tanach. In the book of Samuel it is said that the sons of Eli the priest who served at the Tabernacle in Shiloh were doing the following, "And Eli was very old, and heard all this his sons did to all Israel, and they lay with the women who assembled at the entrance of the Tent of Meeting" (1 Samuel 2:22). Eli confronted his sons by saying, "Why do you do (*taasoon*) as these things (*ka'devarim ha'eleh*)?" (2:23).

Eli is quoted using the exact same words Potiphar's wife used when speaking to Potiphar, "*ka'devarim ha'eleh aasah* your slave to me." And Eli was talking about his sons the **priests** having **sex** with women who came to the tabernacle.

Eli added, "If one man sins against another, and the *elohim* will judge him, and if a man sins against the Lord, who shall entreat for him?" (2:25). Eli is not talking about sexual harassment, or even sexual assault. Eli is talking with his sons about a sin against the Lord. Having sex within the environs of the tabernacle, a practice known to be part of the Egyptian culture, is a sin against the Lord.

We should note one other word that shows up both in the book of Samuel and in the book of Exodus when the text is talking about the construction of the Tabernacle. In Exodus the text says, "And he made the basin of bronze and its pedestal of bronze from the **assembled'** (*tzoveot*) mirrors who assembled at the entrance to the tent of meeting" (Exodus 38:8). The same word is used in the book Samuel, "…they lay with the women who assembled (*tzoveot*)…" (1 Samuel 2:22).

At the entrance to the tabernacle there was the basin in which the text says, "For Aaron and his sons shall wash their hands and their feet. When they go into the Tent of Meeting they shall wash with water..." (Exodus 30:19-20).

In a very conservative society of the time in which women were fully covered (as it is today in some areas in the Middle East), the women were exposing their hands and feet. This was the circumstance in which Eli's sons took advantage of the opportunity to "lie with" the women.

Back to Joseph

Upon the completion of the woman's report to Potiphar of Joseph's behavior, the text says, "And when **his master** heard the words of his wife..." Earlier we saw that the title "his master" vanished from the text, indicating the close relationship between Joseph and his master, and maybe even Joseph's adoption into the family as a son, but now we see that the title "his master" returns to the language of the text. Their relationship returns to the way it was at the time Joseph was bought by "his master."

If we were facing a simple case of sexual assault by an underling we would have expected a lot more repercussions. But the text gives us a very mild reaction, "And Joseph's master took him, and put him in the prison, **a place where the king's prisoners were confined**..." (39:20). Joseph was not sent to a regular prison where regular criminals were confined. Joseph was in a prison where the king's prisoners were confined. The text tells us that Joseph's master did not perceive Joseph as a regular criminal. He was one who violated the king's trust, to be sent to be with other political prisoners. Joseph's crime was that he was a **Hebrew** and not an **Egyptian**. He didn't go along with the Egyptian culture when it really mattered. He was serving his master in his master's idolatry as long as it didn't call for him to perform the real abomination of the Egyptian culture. But when the time came, he refused, and stayed with his own people, his own culture, and his own religion.

Question: Language-wise, the text equates the binding of Isaac to the incident of Joseph and his master's wife. Both start and end with the phrase "After these things..." However, the text describes to us the "test" that Abraham went through in the binding of his own son, and the fact that Abraham was willing to go to the extreme and slaughter his son. Only the intervention of the angel prevented the killing of Isaac. The text also comments on the fact that Abraham passed the test with flying colors. Joseph also went through a "test," although the text does not comment on the fact that Joseph passed the test with flying colors. All the information that we have on the success of Joseph in this test is not in the **content** but in the **language**. We have to "dig" very seriously throughout the text to find out that we are not facing a simple encounter between a woman and a man, but actually a very serious struggle between the Egyptian culture, and the budding Hebrew culture. Why does the text conceal this success of Joseph? Why doesn't the text give Joseph the "reward" that he so deserves?

We should look upon this concealment as a major "linguistic bias" by the text against Joseph.

The "Social Introduction" of the Almighty

The text says,

> And he refused and said to his master's wife, behold, my master knows not what is with me in the house, and he gave all that belongs to him in my hand. There is none greater in this house than I, nor has he kept back anything from me but you because you are his wife, and how then can I do this great evil and sin to *elohim* (G-d). (39:8-9)

At this stage we should examine the way the text relates to the Almighty language-wise.

Introduction

In Biblical Hebrew we find two main ways to relate to the Almighty. First is *elohim,* which literally means "gods" in plural. The same word is used in a section of Exodus to relate to the judge in court. Second is the four-letter word (the tetragrammaton) that is a combination of the three tenses (past, present, and future) of the verb "to be." In English it is often rendered "Jehovah." From now on, the word here will be *Y-H-V-H* to adhere to the strong Biblical prohibition of using the name of the Almighty.

Note: As earlier in this analysis, the word "G-d" is hyphenated, so it is here with the word *Y-H-V-H*.

Joseph and Potiphar

The sequence of events starts with, "And *Y-H-V-H* was with Joseph..." (39:2), "And his master saw that *Y-H-V-H* was with him and that everything he does Y-H-V-H makes it successful in his hand" (39:3), "...and *Y-H-V-H* blessed the Egyptian's house for Joseph's sake and the blessing of *Y-H-V-H* was upon all that he had in the house and in the field" (39:5).

From the beginning of the description of what happened, the text uses the name *Y-H-V-H* that is the name of the Almighty, the G-d of Israel. Moreover, the text shows us that Potiphar understood that *Y-H-V-H* (the G-d of Joseph) was the one who brought him the blessings in his affairs, "And his master saw that *Y-H-V-H* was with him..." After the incident between Joseph and Potiphar's wife, and Joseph was thrown into prison, the text continues to use the name of *Y-H-V-H*, "And *Y-H-V-H* was with (*et*) Joseph..." (39:21), and, "...because *Y-H-V-H* was with (*et*) him, and that which he did, *Y-H-V-H* made it prosper" (39:23).

However, when Joseph refuses the request of Potiphar's wife, the text does not quote him as using the name of *Y-H-V-H*, the G-d of Israel, but the general name of *elohim*. Later on, in the rest of Genesis, we can see that Joseph uses only the name of *elohim* or *ha'elohim* (the gods).

When Joseph brought his two sons to be blessed by his father Jacob, his father is quoted as saying, "*El Shaddai* (G-d Almighty) appeared to me at Luz in the land of Canaan and blessed me" (48:3). When Jacob blessed Joseph, the text quotes him as saying, "...*ha'elohim* (the G-d) which shepherded me from the time I was born to this day" (48:15). Jacob in speaking to Joseph had to specify which god he meant.

Leah and Her Six Sons

We find the same change of language between *Y-H-V-H* and *elohim* in Leah's language after the birth of her sons.

And Leah conceived and bore a son and she called his name Reuben for she said because *Y-H-V-H* saw my affliction, now my husband will love me. And she conceived again and bore a son and said, because *Y-H-V-H* has heard that I am hated, and He gave me this one also, and she called him Simeon. And she conceived again and bore a son and said, now this time my husband will accompany me because I have born him three sons, therefore he called him Levi. And she conceived again and bore a son, and she said, now I will thank *Y-H-V-H*, therefore she called his name Judah and stopped bearing. (Genesis 29:32-35)

In the story with the mandrakes in which Leah "hires" Jacob for the night, she approached him and said, "to me you will come" (30:16). Instead he "lay with (*im*) her that night." From that point on, the text changes its language, "And *Elohim* listened to Leah and she conceived and bore Jacob a fifth son. And Leah said *Elohim* has given me my reward because I gave my slave to my husband…" (30:17-18). After the birth of Zebulun, "And Leah said, *Elohim* has endowed me with a good endowment…" (30:20).

While for the birth of the first four sons the text quotes Leah as using the name *Y-H-V-H*, the name of the G-d of the house of Abraham, at the time Leah still hoped that the birth of the sons would raise her ranking in her husband Jacob's eyes. However, that night, when she asked him to "come to" her and he only "lay with" her, she understood that there was no hope for any closeness between them, even if she bore him six sons and one daughter. At that point, she returned to her previous god, the gods of Nahor and the gods of Laban her father ("why did you steal my gods?" (31:30)).

Back to Joseph

Returning to Joseph's refusal to his master's wife,

And he refused and said to his master's wife, behold, my master knows not what is with me in the house, and he gave all that belongs to him in my hand. There is none greater in this house than I, nor has he kept back anything from me but you because you are his wife, and how then can I do this great evil and sin to *Elohim*. (39:8-9)

We should note the order of listing in Joseph's words. He started with his relationship with his master, and the trust between them. Only at the end of his words did he say, "…and sin to *Elohim*." By the order of appearance we can see that at that point his master was more important to him than *Elohim*.

The connection between Joseph and *Elohim* (even though it is not *Y-H-V-H* as at the beginning of the description) goes through an evolution in Joseph's language. During his refusal to his master's wife, *Elohim* is at the end of his words. Then when he is in prison and he meets Pharaoh's ministers, he is quoted as saying, "Do interpretations not belong to *Elohim*? Please tell them to me" (40:8). At this stage, *Elohim* is first and the "me" is last. Later on, when Joseph appears before Pharaoh, after he had his double dream, the text quotes Joseph as saying, "It is not I. *Elohim* will answer Pharaoh's well-being" (41:16). At this point the "I" is erased ("It is not I") and only *Elohim* is in the picture.

Linguistic Journey – Refusal in Biblical Language

Since a major component of the incident between Joseph and his master's wife is Joseph's refusal, we need to examine the way the text relates to a refusal. We find out that Biblical language uses three different words to describe refusal: didn't *avah*,[64] didn't *shamaa* (listen[65])," and *lema'en* (to refuse).

Immediately we can see that while *lema'en* is the positive form, the other two come in the negative form (didn't + verb). This positive form may make *lema'en* stronger than the other two. So, what is the difference between *avah* and *shamaa*?

Two verses from Deuteronomy indicate that the verb "didn't *avah*" relates to the stage before "didn't *shamaa*" (didn't listen). First, "Do not *avah* to him, nor listen to him, nor shall your eye pity him, nor shall you spare him, nor shall you conceal him" (Deuteronomy 13:9). Second, "And *Y-H-V-H* did not *avah* to listen to Balaam…" (Deuteronomy 23:6). It is clear

---

[64] As you can see we have a translation for two of them, but not for *avah*. It is due to the fact that we don't use this verb in Modern Hebrew.

[65] Although the traditional translation of the verb *lishmoa* is "hear," we use "listen" here because in English it conveys the additional meaning of acceptance of what is heard. For example, a person might say, "I told him but he didn't listen to me."

from these two verses that *lo avah* is different from "didn't listen." If so, what is the exact meaning of "did not *avah*?"

The first time we encounter the verb "did not *avah*" is in the conversation between Abraham and his slave, when Abraham tells his slave to go to Haran to bring him a wife. The slave asks, "Perhaps the woman will not *avah* (*lo toveh*) to follow me to this land..." (Genesis 24:5). We should note that the slave does not ask, "Perhaps the woman *lo toveh* to marry Isaac? The refusal deals with one specific issue. Even if the woman is willing to marry Isaac, what would happen if she does not agree to relocate from her place of residence? The slave did not have any doubt that any woman would like to marry his master's son, but the difficulty was the place of residence.

Can we conclude then that the verb *lo avah* relates to a specific disagreement while there is agreement on other issues? Is there any word in English to relate to this particular situation? The closest word would be "to acquiesce" that means agreement, with some component of disagreement in the picture.

Let's examine this hypothesis in other places in the text.

The text says, "And I stood in the mount according to the first days, forty days and forty nights, and *Y-H-V-H* listened to me at that time also, and *Y-H-V-H lo avah* to destroy you" (Deuteronomy 10:10). The text talks of the agreement of the Almighty to Moses' request not to destroy the Israelites. The text does not talk about total forgiveness. We know this because in the original story in Exodus the Almighty says to Moses, "Therefore now go, lead the people to the place about which I have spoken to you, behold, my Angel shall go before you, nevertheless in the day when I punish I will punish their sin upon them" (Exodus 32:34). Actually, the text does not rule out some punishment other than destruction. We see confirmation of it in the following verse, "*Y-H-V-H lo yoveh* forgive him because the anger of *Y-H-V-H* and his jealousy shall smoke against that man..." (Deuteronomy 29:19). While the "...*lo avah* to destroy you" speaks of lack of destroying, we understand that it also relates to lack of forgiveness.

Two more places in the Torah will help us to see more about the exact meaning of *lo avah*. First, the story of Sihon the king of Heshbon.

The text informs us that Moses sent messengers to Sihon, king of Heshbon, with "words of peace, saying..." (Deuteronomy 2:26). The content of the message was,

> Let me pass through your land, I will go along by the high way, I will neither turn to the right hand nor to the left. You shall sell me food for money, that I may eat, and give me water for money, that I may drink, only I will pass through on foot. (2:27-28)

Sihon's response is described as, "But Sihon king of Heshbon *lo avah* let us pass by him..." (2:30).

A similar story shows up in Numbers, and this time with the king of Edom. Moses sent messengers to the king of Edom with the request,

> Please let us pass through your country, we will not pass through the fields, or through the vineyards, nor will we drink of the water of the wells, we will go by the king's high way, we will not turn to the right nor to the left, until we have passed your borders. (Numbers 20:17)

Unlike Sihon, the text describes the exchange between Israel and Edom, "And Edom said to him, you shall not pass by me, lest I come out against you with the sword" (20:18). In return, Israel sent back, "We will go by the high way, and if I and my cattle drink of your water then I will pay for it, not a thing will happen only I will pass through by foot" (20:19). Edom responded, "You shall not go through, and Edom came out towards him with many people and with a strong hand" (20:20). And the text summarizes, "And Edom **refused** (*vayema'en*) to give Israel passage through his border therefore Israel turned away from him" (20:21).

Edom's response of "And Edom came out towards him with many people and with a strong hand" is described as "to refuse" (*lema'en*) and indeed Israel "turned away from him. Sihon, on the other hand, *lo avah,* and a war started between Israel and Sihon. *Lo avah* seems to be a less-than-emphatic refusal, one that might even be ambiguous.

The second example can be seen in the case in which a man does not want to marry the widow of his dead brother, an event that is called *yibum* in

Biblical Hebrew. The idea of *yibum* is that if the widow is childless, the brother of the deceased will marry the widow, and the child born from this marriage will be considered the child of the deceased, and will continue the family line of the deceased.

The text describes the complaint of the widow who shows up to the court saying, "My husband's brother **refused** to build his brother a name in Israel, he *lo avah* marrying me for the sake of his brother" (Deuteronomy 25:7).

The brother's lack of will to build a name for his deceased brother is described by the verb *lemaen* (to refuse), while his lack of will to marry the widow is described as *lo avah*. It is clear from the woman's words that she perceives the lack of the brother's will to marry her as not deriving from a personal reason relating to her. She perceives that she is secondary to his lack of will to build a name for his deceased brother, which is the main problem here.

The verb "to refuse" (*lema'en*) appears in Genesis in the following places:

- Jacob mourning his lost son Joseph, "And all his sons and all his daughters rose up to comfort him, and he refused (*vayema'en*) to be comforted…" (37:35),
- Joseph refusing the wife of his master, "And he refused (*vayema'en*) and said to his master's wife, behold, my master knows not what is with me in the house, and he has committed all that he has to my hand" (39:8), and
- Jacob who refused Joseph's request to prefer for the blessing the firstborn son over the younger son, "And his father refused (*vayema'en*) and said I know it my son, I know it, he also shall become a people, and he also shall be great…" (48:19).

"Not Listening"

We find the activity of "not listening" in the sense of refusing in the following places.

- In regard to the manna in the desert, "And they **listened not** to Moses…" (Exodus 16:20),

- When the Almighty refused Moses' request to enter the land, "And the Lord was angry with me for your sakes, and **did not listen** to me…" (Deuteronomy 3:26),
- "You shall **not listen** to the words of that prophet…" (Deuteronomy 13:4),
- You shall not acquiesce (*lo toveh*) to him, **not listen** to him, nor shall your eye pity him…" (Deuteronomy 13:9),
- "And the man who will act presumptuously and will **not listen** to the priest…" (Deuteronomy 17:12),
- "And it shall come to pass that whoever will **not listen** to my words…" (Deuteronomy 18:19),
- "If a man has a stubborn and rebellious son, who will **not listen** to the voice of his father or the voice of his mother…" (Deuteronomy 21:18), and
- "And the Lord did **not acquiesce** (*lo avah*) **to listen** to Balaam…" (Deuteronomy 23:6).

Moses, Pharaoh and the Plagues in Egypt

At the start of his mission the Almighty says to Moses, "And Pharaoh will **not listen** to you…" (Exodus 7:4). After Aaron transforms his staff into a serpent, and Aaron's staff swallows the staffs of the Egyptian sorcerers, the text says, "And he hardened Pharaoh's heart and he **didn't listen** to them as *Y-H-V-H* said" (7:13). Before the first plague, the plague of blood, the Almighty tells Moses to say to Pharaoh, "Let my people go that they may serve me in the wilderness and behold **you didn't listen** until now" (7:16). After the plague of blood, "And Pharaoh's heart was strengthened and he **didn't listen** to them as *Y-H-V-H* said" (7:22).

Before the second plague, the plague of the frog, the Almighty says to Moses to tell Pharaoh, "And if you **refuse** (*lema'en*) to let them go behold I will plague all your borders with frogs" (7:27). The plague of blood ended not only with Pharaoh not listening to them, but in addition, "And Pharaoh turned and came to his house and he didn't set his heart to it." This description brought the text to "upgrade" Pharaoh's refusal. The text does not attribute to him "not listening," but attributes to him the verb *lema'en*, "to refuse," a much stronger reaction.

The plague of frogs brought Pharaoh to react: "And Pharaoh saw that there was respite and he **made his heart weighed down** and **didn't listen** to them" (8:11).

We should note a change in language in regard to Pharaoh's reaction. At first, when the Almighty instructs Moses to approach Pharaoh the text says, "And I will **harden** Pharaoh's heart..." (7:3). After the plague of blood, "and Pharaoh's heart **strengthened**" (7:22) without stating that the Almighty is the one who strengthened his heart. By the text, Pharaoh's heart strengthened on its own. On the other hand, after the plague of the frogs the text says, "...and he made his heart **weighed down**..." The text does not use the verb "to harden" nor the verb "to strengthen." Should we understand that the plague of frogs weakened Pharaoh's heart? The noise of the frogs weighed down Pharaoh's heart, or in other words, it was too much for him.

After the third plague, the plague of lice, the text says, "...and Pharaoh's heart was strengthened and he **didn't listen** to them..." (8:15).

After the fourth plague, the plague of flies, the text says, "And Pharaoh weighed down his heart at this time as well and he did not send away the people" (8:28). Here, we see a change in the way the text described Pharaoh's attitude. The formula of "he didn't listen to them" vanished from the description. After four plagues Pharaoh indeed listened, but he still didn't send the people away.

At this stage, after the fourth plague in which the formula "he didn't listen" vanished, Moses is told by the Almighty to go to Pharaoh and say, "...if you **refuse** (*lema'en*) to send them away and you still hold them..." (9:2). The text tells us that Pharaoh's inner-thought process is secondary. If he "listens" or he "does not listen" is secondary to the fact that he is not sending the people away.

After the fifth plague, the plague of the livestock, the text says, "And Pharaoh's heart was weighed down and he did not send away the people" (9:7). Again, we see that the formula of "he didn't listen" is missing.

After the fourth, the fifth, and the sixth plague, the plague of boils, one could have expected Pharaoh to reach total implosion. But here the text says, "And *Y-H-V-H* strengthened Pharaoh's heart and he **didn't listen** to them…" (9:12). This is the first time in the course of the plagues that Pharaoh's heart is not strengthening on its own. This is the first time that the text says that there was need of intervention by the Almighty to strengthen Pharaoh's heart. And indeed the formula "he didn't listen to them" returns to the description.

After the seventh plague, the plague of hail, the text says, "…and he **weighed down** his heart, he and his slaves. And the heart of Pharaoh was **strengthened** and he didn't send away…" (9:34-35). The formula "he didn't listen to them" does not show up, but we face, for the first time, a change in the language of the text. The text describes Pharaoh's reaction in two ways, "weighed down" and "strengthened." The plague of hail did, in fact, leave a major impression on Egypt and on Pharaoh.

After the eighth plague, the plague of locust, the text says, "And *Y-H-V-H* strengthened Pharaoh's heart and he didn't send away…" (10:20). The formula "he didn't listen" is not there, but there is a need for the Almighty's intervention to prevent total implosion at this stage.

After the ninth plague, that of darkness, the text says, "And *Y-H-V-H* strengthened Pharaoh's heart and he *lo avah* to send them" (10:27). Here, too, there is a need of intervention by the Almighty to strengthen Pharaoh's heart, but there is a change in Pharaoh's attitude. Pharaoh is not refusing (*lema'en*) to send them away. Pharaoh is not "didn't listen to them." The text uses the word *lo avah*. Knowing that *lo avah* means willing to do A while refusing to do B tells us that at this point Pharaoh indeed wanted to get rid of the Israelites, but he didn't want to "send them away" willingly, at his order. That was too much for him.

After this plague the Almighty tells Moses, "And *Y-H-V-H* said to Moses, yet I will bring one more plague on Pharaoh and on Egypt and afterwards he will send you away from here, and when he will send you away he will strongly[66] expel you from here" (11:1). Not only he will **send** you away. He will also strongly **expel** you.

Back to Joseph

The text says that his master's wife asks him "lie with me" (39:7). The text brings us Joseph's reaction, "And he **refused** (*vayema'en*)…" (39:8).

---

[66] The word in Hebrew for "expel" is *legaresh*. Here it is *garesh yegaresh*, doubled for emphasis.

The text continues in the next verse, "As she spoke to Joseph day by day and he **didn't listen** to her…" (39:10).

Should we understand that as time passed, with the woman consistently attempting to persuade him, Joseph's refusal eroded over time? It might very well be that Joseph had to run away. Otherwise, his master's wife would have succeeded in bringing him to do what she wanted him to do.

A Scale of Sensitivity

Before we can end the analysis of the story of Joseph in Egypt we need to take a long detour and discuss a point that is guided by the editing process governing the "open statement."

An "open statement" means that the person giving the information is not guided by the listener/reader as to the extent and character of the information. The listener/reader asks an open question, "What happened?" and leaves the decision of what to say and what not to say to the person giving the information. When we read an open statement, even if we do not know what the question was that prompted the information, we still can safely assume that the question was, "What happened?" in one form or another.

[Note: in investigations there are two types of "open questions" to start the flow of information. One, "What happened?" and two, "What happened from the time you got up in the morning until you went to sleep?" While the first leaves to the person the decision where to start and where to end, the second dictates to the person the starting and ending points.]

The person giving the information can branch out of the question "What happened?" in two ways. One, at a certain point the text might include "a negative sentence," (what did not happen). Generally speaking, such a sentence will include the word "no" or "not" in one form or another.

A Negative Sentence

We should realize that while at a certain point in time in a statement only one event can occur, the possibilities for what did not happen at a certain point in time are limitless. The question is, why would the one who gives the information choose to include in an open statement one of the unlimited options for what could have happened, but did not happen? The conclusion has to be that such information is important for the person. If it is important for the person who gives the information, it should be important to the person receiving the information. There will be times that such information does not seem important for the listener/reader, but the reader/listener should not be guided by his/her own logic, but by the logic guiding the text.

Giving a Reason

The second way to branch out of the question "What happened?" is to give a reason for the event. Again, we should be guided by the fact that the reader/listener is only asking, "What happened?" and not "Why did it happen?" For one reason or another, the person giving the information feels the need to explain and/or justify a certain event. By doing so, the person branches out of the question, "What happened?" on his own initiative. As a result, the reader/listener should perceive this information as **sensitive**.

The Text vs. Quotations in the Text

We should distinguish in an open statement between information about events that occurred in the past, and quotations that are included in the open statement relating to what other people said in the past. While we can assume that the person who gives the information about events uses his own language, the reader/listener should be careful when encountering quotations. Assuming the quotation is accurate, and the words were indeed said by the person in the past, the language used in the quote is not necessarily the language of the person giving the open statement, but the language of another person.

For example, the sentence, "And Sarai was barren she <u>had no</u> child," (Genesis 11:30) is information given by the narrator. On the other hand, the sentence, "And Pharaoh called Abram and said, what is this that you have done to me? Why <u>did you not</u> tell me that she was your wife?" (Genesis 12:18), is a sentence that brings us a quote of what Pharaoh told Abraham. While the two examples are negative sentences, the first sentence that tells us what did not happen to Sarah is more important to us than the second sentence. The second sentence should be considered secondary in importance for the analysis of the text.

A Cluster of Negative Sentence and Giving a Reason

When the reader/listener encounters a certain point in the text in which the person giving the information twice branches outside of the question of "what happened?" – first, by giving a sentence in the negative (what did not happen) and second, by giving a reason (why something happened), we are facing a **cluster** of two points branching outside of the question at the same time. The reader/listener should perceive this point in the statement as an **extremely sensitive** point.

See the list of double and triple clusters in Appendix D: Clusters of Negative and Reason Sentences.

Quadruple Clusters

There are two places in the book of Genesis in which there is a quadruple cluster of negatives in a sentence (what did not happen) in conjunction with reasons.

The first cluster deals with Judah and Tamar. After it was exposed that Tamar got pregnant, Judah ordered her executed. Tamar in return sent Judah his signet, his bracelets and his staff that he gave her as a guarantee that he would send her the sheep for the "sexual services" she gave him. When Judah saw these items, the text quoted him, "And Judah recognized them and said, she has been more righteous than I **because** I did not give her to Shelah my son and he knew her again no more" (Genesis 38:26).

[In the Hebrew we find two expressions for this "because" in the same spot – *ki* (because) and *al ken* (because). If we were to translate it literally the sentence would be "...because because I did not give her..." As we saw before with *ki biglal*, with SCAN there are no synonyms. This means that the two words used for "because" cannot have the exact same meaning. However, unlike *ki biglal*, we will leave the linguistic journey to find the subtle difference in meaning between *ki* and *al ken* for another time. The distinction between the two is likely as nuanced as that between "because" and "since" in English.]

In this place we find that the text starts with two words indicating "giving a reason" and the text continues with two negative components, "I did not give her," and "he knew her no more." It can be said that this sentence has two parts. The first part deals with the fact that Tamar was not given to Shelah – (reason-reason-negative), and for this point we face a triple cluster. On the other hand, the second part of the sentence deals with one negative sentence, dealing with the relationship between Judah and Tamar after she bore the two sons.

The only place that is a quadruple cluster, and for one issue, deals with Joseph's reign in Egypt: "Only the land of the priests he did not buy **because** the priests had a portion assigned to them from Pharaoh, and ate their portion which Pharaoh gave them **therefore** they did not sell their lands" (47:22). Here, we see a negative sentence "he did not buy" followed by giving a reason ("because"). Then the sentence continues with giving a reason ("therefore") followed by a negative sentence ("they did not sell"). This verse gives us a cluster of "negative-reason-reason-negative" which testifies to its extreme sensitivity, the highest in Genesis. One can say that the first part of the sentence deals with Joseph's point of view, while the second parts deals with the priests' point of view. Still, these two parts deal with the same issue – sparing the priests of Egypt the humiliation of losing their land, as the rest of the Egyptians did.

If we have any doubt that this is the highest sensitivity in the text, then a few sentences later the text says again, "…only the land of the priests by themselves did not become Pharaoh's" (47:26), and we face another negative sentence on the same issue.

By the scale of sensitivity based upon clusters of negative sentences in conjunction with giving a reason, it becomes clear that the fact that Joseph did not buy the lands of the priests is the most sensitive point in the book of Genesis. And we will have to conclude that the text knows that there is at least one more reason, other than the one stated, which brought Joseph to spare the Egyptian priests: the fact that Joseph belonged to the priesthood in Egypt. The text knows about it, but prefers to conceal it. It does not show up in the **content**, but in the **language** of the text.

Summary

From the beginning of Chapter 39 that starts with "Joseph was brought down (*huRaD*) to Egypt (reduction of holiness), until the end of Genesis we can see that the language of the text exposes the fact that Joseph was a priest in the Egyptian establishment. The incident with his master's wife is loaded with connotations of the component of *letzahek* (sex in Egyptian idolatry). As Abraham was tested with the binding of Isaac on the altar, and was called "Hebrew," so Joseph, the only other person to be called "Hebrew," was tested on his faithfulness to his heritage. Abraham passed his test, and Joseph passed his.

The question is: why did the text conceal this major component of the story that we can find only via the **language**, and not via the **content**? This should be considered an important "linguistic bias."

Linguistic Biases in the Language of the Text

In this chapter we note the following biases:

1. The text conceals the fact that Joseph was priest of Egyptian idolatry.
2. The fact that Joseph did not buy the lands of the Egyptian priests at the time of the famine is the most sensitive point in the book of Genesis.
3. The text does not perceive Haran, or Aram, as equivalent to Egypt, a place to where people "go down" from the Land of Canaan, or from where they "go up" to Canaan. Going to Haran is no different from going from place to place within Canaan.

Points in Language to Consider:

1. The text perceives that the flow of history is divinely guided. "After these things" shows us that when the Almighty promises something to a human, the human should trust the promise of the Almighty, and not rely upon a pact with another human to guarantee the results promised by the Almighty.

BROTHERS

Introduction

In this section we will deal with linguistic issues relating to sibling rivalry, a point that is prominent in Genesis. We will see pairs of brothers – Cain and Abel ("Am I **my brother**'s guard?"), Abraham and Lot ("We are men, **brothers**"), Jacob and Esau ("**my brother** keep what you have to yourself") – and we will end with Joseph and his brothers ("**our brother** our flesh").

CAIN AND ABEL

"And Cain said to Abel his brother, and when they were in the field Cain rose up against Abel his brother and killed him." (Genesis 4:8)

The first murder in the Bible. Is it?

It is accepted that Cain killing his brother Abel was 'murder.' However, two points contradict this characterization. First, the text itself does not label it as 'murder' but as 'killing.' "...Cain rose up against Abel his brother and **killed** him" (4:8), and later, "And Adam knew his wife again and she bore a son and called his name Seth because G-d gave me another seed instead of Abel whom Cain **killed**" (Genesis 4:25). Second, Cain was not punished by death, the punishment prescribed throughout the Biblical text for spilling blood. Instead, Cain was punished by expulsion, the punishment prescribed in the Bible for one who kills someone unintentionally.

We find in Numbers the conditions prescribed for sending someone to a city of refuge after killing someone:

If he suddenly pushed him without enmity or threw on him any tool without lying in wait, or with any stone that he may die without seeing him and dropped on him and he died and he is not his enemy, nor seeking his harm. (Numbers 35:22-23)

If so, what really happened between Cain and Abel?

"And Cain said to Abel **his brother**, and when they were in the field

Cain rose up to Abel **his brother** and killed him." (Genesis 4:8)

From the beginning of the chapter we know that Adam and Eve had two sons, Cain and Abel, and if so, we know that they are two brothers. What is the reason that the text says 'Abel **his brother**' twice? What is the news? The answer is quite likely that the text comes to emphasize to us that there was no real conflict between the two brothers, to the extent that would bring them to act in a way not becoming 'brothers,' as we will see later in Genesis. Cain and Abel did act as 'brothers.'

"And Cain **said** to Abel his brother…"

SCAN Observation – 'Talking' in an Open Statement

We should note that an open statement does not include all the events that happened in the past. In an open statement, the one who gives the statement needs to decide what is important and what is not. When two people get together it is assumed that they talk; they do not look at each other without saying a word. Whenever a conversation enters the language of the open statement it indicates that the person giving the statement considered the conversation important enough to enter the text.

"And Cain **said** to Abel his brother…"

The text uses the verb 'said' (*vayomer*) and not 'spoke' (*vayedaber*). Generally speaking, whenever the verb 'said' is in use, we expect to find the quote following it. However, here we find the verb 'said' without saying what exactly Cain said to Abel.

What did Cain say to Abel? This sentence comes immediately following the report of the conversation between Cain and the Almighty, in which the Almighty reacted to Cain's anger over the lack of acceptance of his offering to the Lord. Was this 'saying' the report of that conversation? And if it was not, what was in the conversation that elevated it to enter the text? Moreover, why it was elevated to enter the text, without telling us what was said?

"And Cain said to Abel his brother, and when they were in the field Cain rose up to Abel his brother and killed him." (Genesis 4:8)

The order of the events in the sentence could have been "And when they were in the field Cain said to Abel his brother, and Cain rose up to Abel his brother and killed him."

SCAN Rule: The sequence of events inside the sentence should reflect the sequence of events in reality in the past.

This means that if a person says, "I got up, took a shower, and got dressed," that we should understand the person took a shower **after** he got up, and that he got dressed **after** he took a shower.

The order of events in the sentence in front of us, the way we have it in the text, positions the fact that Cain 'said' to Abel his brother **before** 'and they were the field.' If so, this conversation between the two took place before they were in the field. This point is important to understand the events that follow, as there was no conversation taking place in the field that was important enough to enter the text at that point.

"…and when they were in the field…"

The place where the event took place seems at first glance like 'unimportant information.' After all, the event could have taken place anywhere, and it would have the same meaning.

SCAN Rule: 'Unimportant information' is only 'unimportant' to the reader/listener, but it is important for the one who gives the statement, since only what is 'important' will enter the open statement. When the reader/listener encounters 'unimportant information' it should be considered by the reader/listener as 'extremely important.'

"…and **when they were**[67] in the field…"

Besides this place we find the word 'when they were' (*bihyotam*) in the following places in the Tanach:

- "And on the third day when they were (*bihyotam*) in pain" (Genesis 34:25),

---

[67] "…[W]hen they were…" – in Hebrew is only one word: *biheyotam*. The *bi* at the beginning means 'when;' the component *heyot* means 'were;' and the component *tam* at the end means the pronoun 'they.'

- "And yet for all that when they were (*bihyotam*) in the land of their enemies I did not cast them away, nor did I loathe them to destroy them utterly…" (Leviticus 26:44),
- "And a man of G-d came to Eli and said to him thus said the Lord, did I not appear to the house of your father when they were (*bihyotam*) in Egypt in Pharaoh's house?" (1 Samuel 2:27), and
- "When they were (*bihyotam*) a few in number and barely residers there" (Psalms 105:12).

In all these places the word *bihyotam* appears at the time the person is in trouble. In the case of the city of Shechem it was when the men were hurting after their circumcisions, a fact that weakened them in defending themselves. In Leviticus, the word appears in the context of the people in the land of their enemies. The same applies with the quote in Samuel; the people of Israel were in slavery in Egypt. The same applies in Psalms in talking about the forefathers in the land of Canaan surrounded by other nations threatening them.

Back to Cain and Abel, 'when they were' (*bihyotam*) in the field they were in some trouble. Were they surrounded by hostility?

"…and when they were **in the field**[68]…"

What is the significance of them being in the field? Moreover, why it is in '**the** field' (known) and not in '**a** field' (unknown)?

'The Field' in Ancient Times

Let's examine now other places in the Tanach in which 'the field' is mentioned. The first one we encounter who is 'in the field' is Isaac: "And Isaac went out *lasuach* in the field before the evening…" (Genesis 24:63). Statistically, out of the 35 places in the Tanach where the word *lasuach* is used, 19 places (54%) are in the book of prayers, the Psalms.

Isaac 'went out' to the field to pray. The field was a place where Isaac he.could pray, and not in the house or the city, or in his place of residence. And in fact this verse is preceded by giving us the location where Isaac

---

[68] "…[I]n the field…" – in Hebrew it is only one word, *basadeh*. The *ba* at the beginning is 'in the' and *sadeh* is 'field.' The way the letter *b* at the beginning is pronounced determines if it is known or unknown. A known (definite) one is *ba*, while an unknown (indefinite) one is *be*.

was, "And Isaac came from the way of the well *lahairoi*, for he settled in the land of the Negev" (Genesis 24:62). It is quite likely that the place Isaac had settled was a place of idolatry, and he had to get out of there for his prayer.

The fact that one cannot appeal to the Almighty in a place of idolatry appears in the case of Moses in Egypt. When Pharaoh asks Moses to pray for him after the plague of the flies, Moses says, "…behold I go out from you and I will appeal to the Lord…" (Exodus 8:25). The same we see after the plague of hail, "And Moses said to him, as soon as I am gone from the city I will spread my palms to the Lord" (Exodus 9:29).

> "And Isaac went out *lasuach* in the field
> **before the evening**…" (Genesis 24:63)

We should note two points: first is the fact that the evening is the time in which people can go out in most of the Middle East, where the temperatures in desert areas are elevated to the point that nobody can be outside during the day. Before the advent of air conditioning, there were places in the Middle East in which people had to sit in containers of water to cool themselves down. The fact that Isaac came from the way of the well only tells us that he was in an oasis in the desert, where the existence of the well allowed life. No different from the area of Haran (Iraq, between the two rivers, the Tigris and the Euphrates) in which the evening is the time of the day for all outside activities, including drawing water from the wells.

Second, we see a change in language. While Abraham's slave came to the well at the time of the evening, when the sun was already going down, Isaac went outside 'before' the evening. It should indicate to us that quite likely the temperatures in the land of Canaan were not as extreme as those in Haran. One should note that the land of Canaan is mostly desert, but it has the sea to the west. The breeze from the sea makes the temperatures milder.

This distinction between the two places, the lands of Canaan and Haran, is evident by this change of language, as the text shows us in the meeting between Abraham's slave and Rebecca, and the meeting between Isaac and Rebecca.

The field, or the place outside the city, was not only a place for prayer, but also a place for hiding. When David talked with Jonathan, King Saul's son, he is quoted as saying, "…that I may hide myself in the field…" (1 Samuel 20:5). In another place, we find the meeting between King Jeroboam and the prophet Ahijah, "…and the two were alone in the field" (1 Kings 11:29).

The field was also a place to hide valuable items. For example, we find in Jeremiah, "…do not kill us for we have hidden stores in the field…" (Jeremiah 41:8).

With this knowledge we can understand a passage in the account of the attack on the city of Shechem to rescue Dinah. When Simeon and Levi raid the city and loot it, the text says, "They took their sheep, and their oxen, and their asses, and that which was in the city, and **that which was in the field**" (Genesis 34:28). It is clear that the text is not talking about harvesting the field. After their victory in battle, we do not expect warriors to cut grain in the field. There were important things in the field, important enough to be looted. It is very likely "that which was in the field" relates to hiding places where the people of the city had hidden their possessions.

We should read the text with the eyes of one who lived at that time. Places of habitation were small; a person had no privacy at all; everyone knew everything about everyone. So if someone wanted to meet someone else, to talk about something without anyone knowing about it, the field was the ideal place for it. The field was the place to hold secret meetings. For example, when Jacob wanted to consult his wives before running away from Haran, the text says, "And Jacob sent and called Rachel and Leah **to the field** to his flock" (31:4). For possessions, the field was the 'bank' of the time. The field, unlike how it might seem at first glance, was not a public place where everyone could see what was going on, but the place to conceal and to hide.

Summary

"…and when they were **in the field**…"

In these few words we have something which seems 'not important' (and therefore 'very important') that includes two components. First, Cain and

Abel were quite likely in some trouble. Second, they wanted to conceal or to hide.

"…Cain rose up **to** Abel his brother and killed him" (Genesis 4:8)

In several places in the Torah we find the act of 'rising **on**' someone in order to kill him. For example, "If any man hates his fellow man, and lies in wait for him, and rises up **on** him and strikes his soul and he dies…" (Deuteronomy 19:11), "…as when a man rises up **on** his fellow man and slays his soul…" (Deuteronomy 22:26), and, "The Lord shall cause your enemies who rise up **on** you to be defeated before you…" (28:7).

In other books in the Tanach we find the act of 'rising up on.' For example,

- "And you have risen up **on** my father's house this day, and have slain his sons…" (Judges 9:18),
- "…the enemies of my lord the king, and all who rise **on** you for evil…" (2 Samuel 18:32),
- "…there are many who rise up **on** me" (Psalms 3:2),
- "For strangers have risen up **on** me…" (Psalms 54:5), and
- "…people with bad intentions have risen up **on** me…" (Psalms 86:14).

The only place in the entire Tanach in which we find the verb 'to rise up' in the context of killing, but with the preposition word 'to' (*el*) instead of 'on' (*al*) is in the case of Cain killing Abel: "…Cain rose up **to** Abel his brother and killed him." We have to conclude that Cain's intention was not to kill Abel, as he didn't 'rise up **on**' him, but 'rose up **to**' him. Moreover, from the act of 'rising up to' we understand that Cain's position was lower than Abel's. Cain had to rise up **to** Abel.

At this point we can connect together what we have already found:

Cain and Abel were in some trouble.
They were in the field to hide or to conceal something.
Cain 'rose up **to**' Abel and not 'on' Abel.

Question: is it possible that Cain was digging in the field to get to some hidden treasure, while Abel was beside him, and when Cain rose up "to"

Abel, the digging tool he was using struck Abel unintentionally and killed him?

> If he suddenly pushed him with no enmity **or threw on him any tool without targeting him**, or, with any stone that he may die, without seeing him, and dropped on him and he died, and he is not his enemy, nor sought his harm. (Numbers 35:22-23)

According to Mosaic law, these are the conditions that exist before the killer can be punished only by expulsion and not by death.

ABRAHAM AND LOT

Introduction

> "And these are the *toldot* of Terah. Terah fathered Abram,
> Nahor and Haran, and Haran fathered Lot." (Genesis 11:27)

When Terah starts traveling towards the land of Canaan, Lot is mentioned as "Lot the son of Haran, the son of his son" (11:31). When Abram goes to the land of Canaan, Lot is mentioned only by his name Lot, "...and Lot went with him..." (12:4) In the next verse Lot is mentioned thus: "And Abram took... and Lot his brother's son..." (12:5). What is the news in giving Lot a new title? We already know that Lot is the son of Abram's brother.

We should remember that for purposes of this analysis, actual reality is **not** what counts. The **language** of the text is what counts.

If we continue with the course of events, we should notice that Lot vanished from the text from the time Abram arrived in Canaan until Abram returned from Egypt ("And there was a famine in the land and Abram went down to Egypt to reside there..." (12:10)). When Lot returns to the text, he appears with his name only, without a title: "And Abram went up from Egypt, he and his wife, and all that he had, and **Lot** with him to the Negev" (13:1).

Later on, when the text tells us about the war between the four kings fighting the five kings, the text says, "And they took Lot, and his possessions, the son of Abram's brother and they went..." (14:12). When the refugee came and informed Abram that Lot was taken captive, the text says, "And Abram heard that **his brother** was taken captive..." (14:14). Here Lot got a new title, **Abram's brother,** and not the "son of Abram's brother." He is not even mentioned by name. Coincidence? Later on, we find, "And he brought back all the possessions, and also brought **his brother Lot** and his possessions..." (14:16). From this point on, Lot appears in the text only by name, without any title.

The fact that we have changes in regard to the titles Lot receives from the text should tell us that there is something going on in the background behind the content. Quite likely, this background event has to do with

Lot's relationship with Abraham. To understand these changes in language we need to go back to the beginning of the sequence of events.

Terah's Family

The text says, "And Terah lived seventy years and fathered Abram, Nahor, and Haran" (11:26). In the very next verse the text says, "And these are the *toldot* of Terah. Terah fathered Abram, Nahor and Haran, and Haran fathered Lot" (Genesis 11:27). Abraham and Lot appear on the stage almost simultaneously.

It seems that these two sentences come to say the same thing. However, there are differences between them. First, the first sentence continues the lineage from Noah to Abram:

- "...Shem was hundred years old and fathered Arphaxad..." (11:10),
- "And Arphaxad lived thirty five years and fathered Salah" (11:12),
- "And Salah lived thirty years and fathered Eber" (11:14),
- "And Eber lived thirty four years and fathered Peleg" (11:16),
- "And Peleg lived thirty years and fathered Reu" (11:18),
- "And Reu lived thirty two years and fathered Serug" (11:20),
- "And Serug lived thirty years and fathered Nahor" (11:22),
- "And Nahor lived twenty nine years and fathered Terah" (11:24),
- "And Terah lived seventy years and fathered Abram, Nahor, and Haran" (11:26).

The second sentence, on the other hand, brings us the *toldot* of Terah, "These are the *toldot* of Terah..." (11:27), and the text starts to focus more on Terah's life. By doing so, the text equates Terah to

- Noah: "These are the *toldot* of Noah..." (6:9),
- Noah's sons: "These are the *toldot* of Noah's sons..." (10:1), and
- Shem: "These are the *toldot* of Shem..." (11:10).

The second difference is that while the first sentence mentions the birth of three sons to Terah, the second sentence mentions their birth under the title *toldot*, a title that indicates that the order of listing in the sentence is not according to their birth, but according to their importance in the course of events, as we saw earlier with the word *toldot*.

If we go by the order of appearance in the sentence in regard to Noah's sons, Shem, Ham, and Japheth, when Japheth was the firstborn, Shem was the second, and Ham is the youngest, then it is quite likely that Haran was the firstborn, Abram the second, and Nahor is the youngest. The likelihood that Nahor is the youngest can be confirmed by the fact that he is named after his grandfather (Terah's father) who died before he was born. One should note that this custom is alive among Jews today – to name a baby after a deceased grandparent of the baby.

As Japheth was not active in the course of events, and therefore is mentioned last among Noah's sons, so is the case with Haran who died at a relatively young age, and was not active in the course of events.

The third difference is that the second sentence informs us of the birth of Lot, Haran's son. And the text continues, "And Haran died *al penei*[69] his father Terah in the land of his birth, in Ur of the Chaldeans" (11:28).

What is the significance of Haran's death, which brought it to be elevated to enter the Biblical open statement?

The phrase *al penei* might bring us to understand the importance of this point.

We find the phrase *al penei* in the following place: "And Jacob finished commanding his sons, he gathered his feet into the bed, and expired, and was gathered unto his people. And Joseph fell ***al penei*** his father..." (Genesis 49:33-50:1).

We find the phrase *al penei* in another place: "And Nadab and Abihu died before the Lord when they offered foreign fire before the Lord, in the wilderness of Sinai, and they had no children, and Eleazar and Ithamar ministered in the priest's office ***al penei*** Aaron their father" (Numbers 3:4). At this point, it is clear that the death of the older sons of Aaron brought his two remaining sons to inherit their position at the tabernacle. If so, it is quite likely that the phrase *al penei* relates to inheritance. When Joseph fell *al penei* his father, the text comes to tell us that Joseph

---

[69] The word *panim* in Hebrew means 'face.' *Al penei* literally is 'on the face of' or 'in front of' or simply 'before.'

inherited the position of head of the family after the death of the family's head.

When the text informs us of the laws of inheritance, it says, "And at the day he makes his sons inherit that which he has, that he may not give preference to the beloved wife *al penei* the son of the hated one" (Deuteronomy 21:16). Here the text comes to inform us that although the firstborn is the son of the hated wife, still it is his right to inherit the birthright.

Now we return to the sentence, "And Haran died *al penei* his father Terah in the land of his birth, in Ur of the Chaldeans" (Genesis 11:28). The objective of the sentence is not only to inform us of Haran's death. The sentence comes to inform us that Haran, likely the firstborn, had the right of inheritance after the death of the father Terah, and Haran died before being able to take his position as the head of the family. The death of the firstborn had direct implication on the inheritance of Terah. Who would be the one to inherit from Terah? Would it be the second son by order, Abram? Or would it be the firstborn of the dead firstborn son, Lot?

The fact that Haran is the oldest son explains why later Rebecca introduced herself as, "I am the daughter of Bethuel the son of Milcah whom she bore to Nahor" (24:24). The text does not say, "I am the daughter of Bethuel the son of Nahor…" Milcah appears before Nahor as she is the daughter of the oldest son, while Nahor is the youngest son. From the perspective of the family, the oldest brother (Haran) and his offspring (Lot, Iscah/Sarai, and Milcah) take preference.

The text continues, "And Abram and Nahor took wives. The name of Abram's wife was Sarai, and the name of Nahor's wife Milcah the daughter of Haran, the father of Milcah and the father of Iscah" (11:29).

The tendency to marry one's offspring with the offspring of the father's brother is common even today in the Middle East. Statistics show a 30% rate of marriage between relatives. And in fact, Nahor takes for a wife Milcah, the daughter of the firstborn son, the same Milcah that later on had Bethuel who fathered Laban and Rebecca. Abram takes Sarai for a wife. And what about Iscah, the second daughter of Haran? If Nahor took Milcah as a wife, then Iscah, naturally, was destined to be a wife for Abram.

The fact that Sarai is quite likely to be Iscah appears later on in the text. When Abimelech complains to Abraham that he introduced Sarah as his sister while she was really his wife, Abraham responded by saying, "And yet indeed she is my sister, she is the daughter of my father, but not the daughter of my mother, and she became my wife" (20:12). If 'my father' relates to the father of the family, and at the time Terah was in this position, then Sarah is indeed the offspring (albeit the granddaughter) of Abraham's father, Terah.

And if Sarah is indeed Iscah, Haran's daughter, then Sarah and Lot were brother and sister, a fact which is not emphasized at all in the text, although we can find confirmation of it later on.

But the main question is this: assuming Sarah is indeed Iscah, why does the text replace her name from the original to a new one, and why is she **the only such one** in the entire book of Genesis? Why does the text move **actively** to conceal Sarah's identity?

The text continues, "And Sarah was barren she had no child[70]" (11:30).

Again, we can ask the same question we asked earlier about Haran's death: what is the significance of the fact that Sarah is barren, that it is elevated to enter the Biblical open statement, and at this specific point?

We should understand that the sentences in this section come to inform us of the tension regarding the inheritance of Terah's estate. And if we know the firstborn Haran is dead, then if the second son, Abram, has no offspring, the issue of inheritance is settled. The candidate is Lot, the son of Haran.

And the text continues,

> And Terah took Abram his son, and Lot the son of Haran the son of his son, and Sarai his daughter-in-law his son Abram's wife, and they came out with them from Ur of the Chaldeans to go to the land of Canaan, and they came to Haran, and settled there. (11:31)

---

[70] We should note here that the word "child" in the Biblical Hebrew is *yeled*. Here, we find a variation of the word, *valad*. It is only place in the entire Tanach where this variation of the word appears.

First, the one who is missing here is Nahor. He just vanished and does not exist. He will show up later when Abraham is told of the birth of Rebecca. However, the order the people are mentioned tells us their importance. The order shows us that the text positions Lot before Sarai, Abram's wife. Lot is a buffer between Abram and his wife. Why not to list the couple together: And Terah took Abram his son, and Sarai his daughter-in-law his son Abram's wife, and Lot the son of Haran the son of his son...? If we know that Lot and Sarah are brother and sister, then we can understand why the text lists the older brother before his younger sister. The fact that Sarai is Abram's wife is secondary, when the order goes according to the inheritance rights within the family.

Summary

At this point, we can conclude that Lot is the son of the oldest son of Terah, and as such, is entitled to inherit the family fortune. Abram, the second son, married the daughter of the oldest son Haran, and thus Sarah is higher than her husband Abram in the hierarchy of the family.

Abraham's Journey to Canaan

The journey starts by the text saying, "And the Lord had said to Abram get out of your country, your homeland, **and from your father's house**..." (12:1). Abram, being the second son, will not be able to establish himself in a new country if he does not separate himself from his father's house. In order for him to be "a great nation" (12:2) he needs to become independent, on his own, and not be relegated to second place as the second son in a large family.

The text continues,

> And Abram went as the Lord had spoken to him and Lot went with him, and Abram was seventy-five years old when he came out of Haran. And Abram took Sarai his wife and Lot his brother's son, and all their possessions that they had gathered, and the souls that they had gotten in Haran, and they came out to go to the land of Canaan, and they came to the land of Canaan. (12:4-5)

As we saw with Terah, again we encounter two similar sentences. Here also, it seems that these two sentences constitute "unnecessary" duplication.

The first sentence comes to inform us that Abram did what the Lord told him to do, and he went to the land to Canaan. The sentence adds the facts that Lot joined Abraham, and that Abraham was advanced in age at seventy-five years. And remember that his wife 'had no child' (11:30). The claimant to the throne sees the future as belonging to him. Terah is still alive, and as such the issue of inheritance is in deep freeze.

The second sentence comes to change the picture altogether: "And Abram took Sarai his wife and Lot his brother's son…" (12:5). The order of listing tells us that from Abram's point of view, unlike his father Terah, Sarai his wife is more important than Lot, even if she 'has no child,' and Lot is relegated to second place. Moreover, positioning Lot in third place in the sentence, along with giving him the new title 'his brother's son,' comes to tell us that as concerning Abram, the inheritance issue is settled. By Abraham leaving Haran, and leaving his father's house, Abraham establishes a new line of family, detached from Terah's. Abraham is becoming the head of a new family, and as such, Lot is not 'Haran's son' anymore, but the son of Abram's brother.

Abraham and Lot in Canaan

Once Abraham arrives in Canaan, Lot disappears from the text. For the text he simply does not exist. Abraham arrives in Shechem, and receives a promise from the Almighty that his seed will inherit the land. Abraham builds an altar, and when he arrives in Beth-El[71] he builds an altar again "and calls in the name of the Lord" (Genesis 12:6-8).

The text continues with Abraham going to Egypt due to the famine. Abraham asks his wife to say "you are my sister" (12:13); Sarah is taken to Pharaoh's palace; Pharaoh and his house suffer great afflictions, and Pharaoh releases Sarah and allows Abraham and Sarah to go away free (12:14-20).

---

[71] Beth-El is a name of a place but literally *beth* means 'house,' and *el* means 'G-d.' So Beth-El means house of G-d.

At this point, the text continues, "And Abram went up from Egypt, he, and his wife, and all that he had, **and Lot with him** to the Negev" (13:1).

Lot, who was not mentioned at all once they arrived in Canaan, and was not mentioned during the journey to Egypt, or during the time in Egypt, is now returning to the text. However, there is one major difference in the relationship between Abraham and Lot at this time. If we compare the time they traveled to Canaan (the last time Lot was mentioned) to the time after returning from Egypt, we can see that at the time they traveled to Canaan the text said, "And Abram took Sarai his wife and Lot his brother's son **and all their possessions…**" (12:5). Upon returning from Egypt the text said, "And Abram went up from Egypt, he, and his wife, **and all that he had**, and Lot with him to the Negev" (13:1). On the journey to Canaan Lot is mentioned **before** the possessions, while upon returning from Egypt Lot is mentioned **after** the possessions, at the end of the sentence.   The change of location in the sentence constitutes downgrading or demotion in Lot's importance. What caused Lot to be demoted at the time of their stay in Egypt? Can we connect it to the fact that on the journey to Canaan Sarah is mentioned as 'Sarai his wife,' while upon returning from Egypt, she is mentioned only as 'his wife' without mentioning her name?

If we have any doubt that something did happen in Egypt, the text continues describing the course of events thus: "And Abram was very rich in cattle, in silver and in gold" (13:2). This sentence does not say what happened. It only states a fact. We should note that this sentence comes right after the text ended the previous sentence by saying, "…and Lot with him to the Negev."

And the text continues,

> And he went on his travels from the Negev to Beth-El, to the place where his tent had been at the beginning, between Beth-El and Hai. To the place of the altar which he had made there at the first, and there Abram called in the name of the Lord. (13:3-4)

Upon returning from Egypt Lot is mentioned at the end of the list, with the possessions being a buffer between Abraham and Lot. At the time Abraham is back in Canaan, Lot is not even mentioned in the sentences detailing Abraham's travels. Lot appears in a separate sentence, "And Lot also, who went with (*et*) Abram, had flocks and herds and tents" (13:5).

Upon the return from Egypt, Lot is at the end of the sentence, and there are two full sentences separating Lot from Abraham. Moreover, Lot receives his own sentence, and is not mentioned in the intervening sentences about Abraham.

And the text continues, "And the land **was not able to bear them** that they might settle together **because** their possessions were great, and they **could not settle together**" (13:6).

We are facing a triple cluster of 'negative + reason + negative.' According to the scale of sensitivity based upon negative sentences in conjunction with giving a reason (discussed earlier), we are facing information of extreme sensitivity.

Moreover, the two negative components of the sentence deal with two different issues. While the beginning of the sentence deals with the land, the ending of the sentence deals with the two men, regardless of the land.

We should compare this sentence to a similar sentence dealing with Jacob and Esau: "…and went to another country away[72] from his brother Jacob. **Because** their possessions were more than to settle together and the land where they resided **could not bear** them **because** of the cattle" (36:6-7).

The text dealing with Jacob and Esau deals with two components of the separation, the possessions, and the land they resided in. The text dealing with Abraham and Lot also brings two components, one being the possessions. However, the second component is the fact that the two could not live together. We should note that Jacob and Esau made peace between them upon Jacob's return to Canaan after his long stay in Haran. Therefore, there was no need to bring the lack of brotherhood as a reason for separation. This is not the case with Abraham and Lot.

---

[72] "[A]way" – the text uses *mipnei*. The *mi* at the beginning is 'from' and *pnei* is 'face,' which literally means, 'from the face of.'

Summary

Throughout the text, from the time they embarked on their journey from Haran to the land of Canaan, up to this point in the text, we face gradual erosion in the relationship between Abraham and Lot. It is not mentioned in the **content** of the text, but is brought to us via the **layout** of the sentences, or, in other words, the way the text builds the sentence – what comes first, what comes second, and so on.

SCAN – the Context Channel of Communication

Up to this point we saw two different channels of communication – the content, and the language. Now, we are facing another channel of communication – the context channel. This channel includes the layout of the sentences – which sentence comes after which one, the layout of the sentence itself – how the text lays out the various components of the sentence. In other words, which comes first, second, third, and so on.

The order of the different components inside the sentence might indicate the importance the text attributes to these components.

Back to Abraham and Lot

And the text continues, "And there was *riv* ('strife') between the shepherds of Abram's cattle and the shepherds of Lot's cattle, and the Canaanite and the Perizzite settled then in the land" (13:7).

The *riv* mentioned between the shepherds of Abraham and the shepherds of Lot was not a simple quarrel. We find in Genesis that the text uses the same word for the struggle going on between the shepherds of Isaac and the shepherds of the Philistines over the water wells (Genesis 26:20-21). One does not expect that the struggle between the shepherds of two strangers will be described linguistically the same as the struggle between shepherds of one family. If we want to know what such a *riv* is likely to include, we only need to go to another place in the text, "And if men quarrel and one strikes another with a stone, or with his fist..." (Exodus 21:18).

If it was only a quarrel between the shepherds, what prevented their masters, Abraham and Lot, from simply ordering them to behave themselves? Abraham's approach to Lot says openly that it was not only a quarrel between the shepherds. The text quotes Abraham as saying to Lot, "Please, let there be no strife **between me and you**, and between my shepherds and your shepherds because we are men brothers" (Genesis 13:8).

Abraham talks of two different issues that are the cause of the quarrel, listing first the quarrel between the two of them, and only second the quarrel between the shepherds.

There was a quarrel between the two, Abraham and Lot. And it started from the time they returned from Egypt. Something brought the text to gradually demote Lot by relegating him to the end of the sentence, and later to another sentence altogether, separated from Abraham by two sentences.

Men vs. Brothers

In his approach to Lot, Abraham said, "because we are **men brothers**." Why mention both 'men' and 'brothers?' Wasn't it enough to just say "...because we are brothers?" And why list 'men' before 'brothers?' And on top of it, Abraham and Lot were not brothers. Lot was the son of a brother[73] and not a brother.

The use of these two words, 'men' and 'brothers,' is a very important milestone in the relationship between Abraham and Lot. There is no more talk about Lot being the son of Abraham's brother, a very close family connection. The relationship is described as 'men' (quite likely honorable) who are also relatives. And indeed, from this point on, Lot does not receive the title 'brother's son' but only 'brother.'

And Abraham continued his words to Lot, "All the land is before you. Separate yourself please from me. If you will take the left then I will take the right, and if you take the right I will take the left" (13:9).

Very openly, yet politely, Abraham says to Lot, echoing the rabbi in *Fiddler on the Roof*, "May G-d bless and keep you ... far away from me." What brought Abraham to want such distance?

---

[73] In Biblical Hebrew there is no word for 'nephew' or 'niece.' It is 'son/daughter of a brother/sister.'

The text brings us a hint as to the reason. Where did Lot choose to live? "…and Lot settled in the cities of the plain, and pitched his tent toward Sodom. And the people of Sodom were exceedingly wicked and sinners to the Lord" (13:12-13).

And the text continues,

> "And the Lord said to Abram **after
> Lot separated from him**…" (13:14).

The phrase "…after Lot separated from him…" is an 'unnecessary' repetition of the fact that they separated. However, there is no 'unnecessary' detail in an open statement. The most we can say that it is 'unnecessary' for the reader, but it is not 'unnecessary' for the speaker/writer. As we saw earlier in regard to the 'unnecessary connection' in the case of Joseph in Egypt ("After these things…"), an 'unnecessary connection' indicates an attempt to conceal information. We have to conclude that the separation between Abraham and Lot was very meaningful, and quite likely not relating to one minute, or even one day.

The departure of Lot brought another promise to Abraham by the Almighty, that the land would be given to him and to his seed.

We remember the promise Abraham received upon arrival in the land of Canaan, "To your seed will I give this land" (12:7). However, "after Lot separated from him" the promise was much richer in content:

> Raise up your eyes and look from the place where you are to the north, and to the south, and to the east, and to the west. Because all the land which you see to you will I give it and to your seed forever. And I will make your seed as the dust of the earth, so that if a man can count the dust of the earth, then shall your seed also be counted. Arise and go through the land in its length and in its breadth, for I will give it to you. (13:14-17)

The richness of the promise testifies faithfully that the text sees the separation between Abraham and Lot, initiated by Abraham, as a positive step that allows Abraham to enjoy a promise richer in content.

From the time Abraham told Lot, "we are men brothers" we constantly view the layout of the information in the sentence as a demotion of Lot. After the end of the war between the four kings and the five kings, the text says, "And they took Lot and his possessions, the son of Abram's brother and they went" (14:11).

The text positioned the component 'the son of Abram's brother' far from Lot, inserting between Lot and this title the words 'and his possessions.' The text tells the reader with whom we deal, but we should notice that Lot has no closeness to the title 'the son of Abram's brother' anymore.

If we have any doubt that the distance between the name of Lot and his title as 'the son of Abram's brother' is a coincidence, then Abraham's reaction to Lot falling in captivity constitutes confirmation: "And Abram heard that his brother was taken captive…" (14:14). Abraham reacts only because Lot is a 'brother,' meaning, a relative, and not because he is Lot, or even the son of his brother.

And when Abraham rescues Lot, "And he brought back all the goods, and also brought back Lot his brother…" (14:16). Again, we see that the 'goods' appear first, and Lot is relegated to second place, accompanied by the title 'brother.' Lot was not Abraham's nephew for a long time already.

Lot and Egypt

These two points, Lot and Egypt, will enable us to know what happened in Egypt that brought the separation between Abraham and Lot. We will start with Lot.

Lot is the father who tells the public of Sodom surrounding his house, "I have two daughters who have not known man. Let me bring them out to you and do to them as is good in your eyes, only to these men do nothing, seeing that they have come under the shadow of my roof" (19:8).

Lot's honor as a host was more important to him than the honor of his family, and the honor of his daughters, not to mention their physical safety.

We already saw earlier that Lot's sons-in-law thought that Lot might want *letzahek* when he asked them to get out of the city without saying that he himself was going to get out as well. And his sons-in-law received a double title. Not only are they his sons-in-law, but they are also "the ones who took his daughters."

The text brings us the event after the destruction of Sodom in which Lot's two daughters initiated sex with their father so they could get pregnant. The two daughters brought their father to get drunk and then had sex with him. And, in fact, they bore two sons to their father, and these two sons became two nations.

Did Lot know what happened during the night? Or was he so drunk that he didn't know?

If we examine the denial produced in the text as to Lot's lack of knowledge of what happened that night, we see a very specific denial, "And he knew not when she lay down nor when she arose" (19:33 and 35).

We can ask the question: is it possible that this denial is accurate and yet Lot still knew what was going on? And the answer is in the affirmative. He didn't know the time she came into bed, and he didn't know the time she left the bed. But he definitely knew what happened in between those two points of time. He knew and he didn't protest!

Egypt

We already established earlier, in the section dealing with Joseph in Egypt, that sexual relations were common between close relatives in Egypt. History even tells us that there were Pharaohs who married their sisters and/or their mothers.

The text in Leviticus talks about the "doings of the land of Egypt" (Leviticus 18:3) and then the text lists all the permutations of forbidden sexual relations between family members. Among them, "The nakedness of **your sister**, the daughter of your father, or daughter of your mother, whether she was born at home, or born abroad, their nakedness you shall not uncover" (18:9).

To summarize points in the report in the text, we should remind ourselves of the following:

- Lot was Sarah's brother, although the text does not come out and say it openly.
- Sarah is the only one in the book of Genesis whose name throughout the text does not match the name she received at birth.
- Lot chose to live in Sodom where the people were 'extremely wicked and sinners.'
- Lot offered his daughters to the crowd surrounding his house.
- Lot was perceived by his sons-in-law as someone who wanted *letzahek* ('to have sex'), and quite likely with his daughters.
- Lot knew of his daughters having sex with him, although he didn't know when they came or when they left the bed.
- By the layout of the sentences Lot is gradually distanced from Abraham after the stay in Egypt.
- Abraham asks Lot to maintain a distance from him.

Question: Is it possible that while in Egypt, a country whose culture saw sex within the family as natural, Lot attempted, or maybe even brought himself to either 'expose the nakedness' of Sarah, or *letzahek* with her?

At the moment, this is only a suspicion, although quite a strong one, as it will connect all the dots coming out of this part of the narrative. It explains the events in the layout of the narrative, the gradual demotion of Lot after Egypt, and Abraham's request from Lot to keep a distance from him. It also explains why Sarah is the only one in Genesis who has a problem with her name, as the text switches from the name she received when she was born to a name given to her later, without saying anything about this switch.

We should note that for us to learn of this event in Egypt we need to dig deeply into the language and the way the text builds the sentences – the context. There is nothing about this event in the **content** of the text. On the contrary, the text presents it to us as separation between the two due to a quarrel between the shepherds of the two men.

Question: assuming Lot indeed attempted or did 'something' with Sarah, why does the text conceal it from the reader? The text does not have any issue with presenting to us the account of Lot's daughters initiating sex with their father. The Tanach doesn't have any issue with bringing us the account of Amnon, David's firstborn son, raping his half-sister Tamar, a rape that resulted in Absalom, Tamar's brother, killing Amnon. Why then does the text have an issue with Lot doing 'something' with Sarah? By not telling us of Lot's behavior, are we facing an attempt by the text to guard the honor of Sarah? Or are we facing an attempt by the text to guard the honor of Lot? (And if so, why would the text like to guard the honor of Lot?) We should consider it a 'linguistic bias' of the text by attempting to guard the honor of Sarah and/or Lot.

JACOB AND ESAU

Introduction

As we saw earlier, in the chapter dealing with the order of birth in the family, the text equates the birth of Jacob and Esau to the birth of Peretz and Zerach, Judah's two sons from Tamar. In both cases, the text does not use the verb 'she bore' (*vateled*). Instead, the text uses the verb 'came out' (*vayetze*).

The birth of Jacob and Esau is unique in another way. The text relates to the birth of a baby by relating to the baby as 'his brother' in only three cases: the birth of Cain and Abel, the birth of Esau and Jacob, and later on, the birth of Peretz and Zerach. For Cain and Abel, "And she again bore **his brother** Abel..." (Genesis 4:2). For Esau and Jacob, "And the first came out red, all over like a hairy garment, and they called his name Esau. And after that came **his brother** out..." (25:25-26). For Peretz and Zerach, "...as he drew back his hand, that behold **his brother** came out, and she said what a breach you have made for yourself. Therefore he called his name Peretz. And afterwards came out **his brother**..." (38:29-30).

Cain is the firstborn son to humanity. Jacob, and later on, Israel, is the father of the nation. Peretz, Judah's son, is the father of the part of the Judean tribe that later on got the kingdom.

We know that Cain killed Abel. We know that Esau wanted to kill Jacob, after Jacob got the blessing from Isaac instead of him (27:41). Here, we should ask the question if something similar happened between Peretz and Zerach. The text does not say anything about it. Is it because the text does not want us to know anything about it? Or is it because they are Judah's two sons, the same Judah who told his brothers not to kill Joseph, "...for he is our brother our flesh..." (37:27)?

There is an additional point that connects the birth of Jacob and Esau to the birth of Peretz and Zerach. For Jacob and Esau, "And her days to deliver were fulfilled and behold there were twins in her womb" (25:24). For Peretz and Zerach it says, "And it came to pass in the time of her labor and behold twins were in her womb" (38:27). For Cain and Abel, it does not say that they were twins, but the text hints at it, "...and she conceived and bore Cain... And she again bore his brother Abel..." (4:1-2). We should note that no conception is mentioned for Abel.

"And the lads **grew**..." (25:27)

The verb 'to grow' appears in Genesis with two meanings. First, to grow in age. For example, "And the child grew and was weaned..." (21:8), "And Judah said to Tamar his daughter-in-law, remain a widow at your father's house, till Shelah my son will **grow**..." (38:11).

The second meaning of the verb 'to grow' is to grow in wealth or good name (reputation). For example, Eliezer, Abraham's slave, says to Rebecca's family, "And the Lord has blessed my master, and he **grew**..." (24:35). For Isaac it says, "And the man **grew** and went on **growing** until he **grew** a lot" (26:13). Jacob says to Joseph, at the time he blessed Joseph's sons, "I know it my son, I know it, he also shall become a people and he also shall **grow**, but his little brother will **grow** more than him and his seed shall become a multitude of nations" (48:19).

In the case of Jacob and Esau both meanings might be valid. One, they grew in age, and, two, when they grew they established themselves, each one according to his own personality.

"And **the lads** grew..." (25:27)

The word 'the lads' appears in two more places in Genesis. When Abraham relates to his people who went to war with him to rescue Lot, "...only that which **the lads** have eaten, and the share of the men who went with me..." (14:24). Later on, when Jacob blesses Joseph's sons, "The Angel who redeemed me from all evil will bless **the lads**..." (48:16).

In the case of Abraham, the text relates to the ones who went to war, and in Jacob's blessing the text relates to the preference of the younger brother over his older brother. As it was during the pregnancy, "...two nations are in your womb, and two peoples shall be separated from your bowel..." (25:23), so it is in their lives.

In summary, it seems that the word "the lads" is used, at least in the book of Genesis, in the context of quarrel and strife.

> "…and Esau was a man knowledgeable of hunting, a man of the field,
> and Jacob was a perfect man living in tents" (25:27).

The text distinguishes between the two. For Esau the text says, "…a **man** knowledgeable of hunting, a **man** of the field, using the word 'man' for each point. For Jacob, on the other hand, the text does not say, '…a perfect **man,** a **man** living in tents.' Instead, the text says the word 'man' only once, combining the two points into one, '…a perfect **man** living in tents.' It is quite likely that the text used the word 'man' twice for Esau, to emphasize that it relates to two different traits that are not connected to each other.

"…a man **knowledgeable of hunting**…"

Several occupations are mentioned in Genesis. First, Cain and Abel: "…And Abel was a shepherd and Cain was tiller of the ground" (4:2). When Pharaoh asks Joseph's brothers, "What is your occupation," they answer, "…your slaves are shepherds" (47:3). "The father of those who settle in tents and of those who have cattle" (4:20) is mentioned a lot earlier about Jabal, the son of Lemech. And we find "And Noah began to be a farmer and planted a vineyard" (9:20).

We find also other occupations: Jubal, "…he was the father of all who handle the harp and pipe" (4:21) and Tubal-Cain who was "forger of every sharp instrument in bronze and iron" (4:22). For hunting, we find Nimrod: "He was a mighty hunter before the Lord. Therefore, it is said, as Nimrod the mighty hunter before the Lord" (10:9). Later on, it is said about Ishmael, "…and became an archer" (21:20).

Esau is the only one that the text attributes to him the title "**knowledgeable** of hunting." Does the text come to tell us that although Esau was knowledgeable of hunting, it was not necessarily his occupation?

We find in the Tanach, although later on in time, another occupation that comes with the addition "knowledgeable:" music, in regard to David who played music before King Saul, "…to seek out a man who **knows** how to play a lyre…" (1 Samuel 16:16), and "…who **knows** how to play…" (16:18). And we know that although David knew how to play, he was a shepherd.

"…a man of the field…"

If we compare Esau to Nimrod who is also mentioned as a "mighty hunter," we find that the text does not say that Nimrod was a hunter 'in the field.' It is clear for the reader that hunting was done in open areas and not in places where people resided. If so, what is the reason to mention that Esau was "a man of the field?"

We already saw in Cain and Abel ("When they were in the field…") that the field was a place to have privacy in an ancient culture when people lived very close to each other. It is quite likely that "a man of the field" comes to say that Esau was a man who took care to conceal his activities from others. Therefore, his place was in the field, away from city people.

"…and Jacob was a perfect man living in tents" (25:27)

The text used the word 'man' for Esau twice, but it used the word 'man' only once for Jacob, with the addition of the word 'perfect' (*tahm*).

The word *tahm* appears once more in Genesis, in the case of King Abimelech who took Sarah to his palace. Abimelech defended himself saying that he didn't know that Sarah was a married woman, "But he said to me she is my sister, and she, even she herself said he is my brother in the *tahm* of my heart and the cleanliness of my hands have I done this" (20:5). From the use of the two terms 'innocence (*tahm*)[74] of the heart' and 'cleanliness of the hands' it seems that Abimelech distinguishes between the act and the intent. While '*tahm* of the heart' relates to the inner world of the person, to the intent, 'cleanliness of the hands' relates to the outside, to the act of the hands. In both, Abimelech defends himself by saying he was not guilty for taking Sarah, as both of them misled him.

The response of the Almighty shows that Abimelech's claim about intent is accepted, but not about the act itself: "I know that you did this in the innocence of your heart…" (20:6). 'Innocence of the heart' was there, but not 'cleanliness of the hands.'

---

[74] Tahm – This word does not translate easily into English; it connotes perfection, innocence, completeness, unity.

Returning to Jacob who was an 'innocent man,' compared to Esau, it can be said that Jacob was a man for whom 'what you see is what you get.' His inside was the same as his outside.

"…living in tents" (25:27)

The word 'tents' appears once more in Genesis, in relating to Lot, "And Lot also, who went with Abram, had flocks, and herds, and **tents**" (13:5). We find the word 'tent' in proximity to cattle also with Jabal, Melech's son, "…he was the father of those who settle in a **tent**, and those who have **cattle**[75]" (4:20). The fact that 'tents' appears in proximity to 'sheep and cattle' might tell us that while Esau was 'a man of the field,' Jacob was a shepherd. Later on in life, Jacob shepherded Laban's sheep.

"And Isaac loved Esau because he had hunting in his mouth
and Rebecca loves Jacob (25:28).

If 'hunting' means 'lying in wait' for prey to appear, then 'hunting in his mouth' means that Esau was 'lying in wait' for the prey to show up, so he could 'jump' on his prey with his 'mouth,' not with his weapon. If we had any doubt about the dual traits of Esau, this verse clarifies that the 'hunting' the text talks about was not actual hunting, but 'hunting in his mouth,' more likely concealing and hiding his true self from others.

There are two times in Genesis in which the text gives us a reason for love. Isaac's love of Esau here, and Jacob's love of Joseph, "And Israel loved Joseph more than all his sons because he was the son of his old age…" (37:3). The text does not bring us any reason for Rebecca's love of Jacob.

"And Isaac loved (vaye'ehav) Esau because he had hunting in his mouth
and Rebecca loves (ohevet) Jacob (25:28).

Linguistic Journey - Love Relationships in the Tanach

Introduction

The Biblical text uses two different tense forms to relate what happened. One is the regular past tense, for example, "he **went**…" The second, a

---

[75] In the Hebrew text it says literally, "…father of tent dweller and cattle."

future tense preceded by the letter *vav*, which is usually considered to be the 'turning *vav*,[76]' turning the future into the past, for example, literally, '**and** he **will** go' is understood to be 'he went.'

The word 'love' in Hebrew comprises the three-letter root word A-H-B, with the letter 'B' pronounced as a 'V' in English. The regular past tense, used also today in modern Hebrew is *ahav*, the present tense is *ohev* and the future tense is *yohav*, and the *yo* in the beginning adds the future to the verb. The Biblical form using the 'turning *vav*' is *vaye'ehav*, where the *va* at the beginning is the 'and,' and the following *ye* is the future tense.

Love Between a Couple

There are several times in the text where love is mentioned. For example, when Isaac takes Rebecca to be his wife, "...and took Rebecca and she became his wife *vaye'ehaveha*..." (24:67). We also find a married woman expecting love from her husband. The text says about Leah, "And Leah conceived and bore a son and she called his name Reuben for she said for the Lord has looked upon my affliction now therefore my husband will *ye'ehavani* [77]" (29:32).

The text mentioned Isaac's love for Rebecca **after** she became his wife, and the expected love for Jacob by Leah **while** they were married, but the text mentioned Jacob's love for Rachel **before** their marriage: "Jacob *vaye'ehav* Rachel..." (29:18).

Later on in the Tanach, we find love between a couple in the following:

- Samson and Delilah: "...*vaye'ehav* a woman in the Valley of Sorek whose name was Delilah" (Judges 16:4).
- Michal and David: "Michal, Saul's daughter *vate'ehav* David..." (1 Samuel 18:20)
- Rehoboam and Maachah: "Rehoboam *vaye'ehav* Maachah the daughter of Absalom more than all his wives and concubines..." (2 Chronicles 11:21)
- King Ahasuerus and Esther: "And the king *vaye'ehav* Esther more than all the women..." (Esther 2:17)

---

[76] The letter *vav* is the sixth letter in the Hebrew alphabet. When it starts a word, it translates to the word 'and' in English.
[77] The suffix *ani* adds the pronoun 'I/me' to the verb.

Up to this point we saw 'love' between a married couple, either before or after the marriage. But we also see 'love' without marriage:

- Shechem and Dinah: "And his soul was drawn to Dinah the daughter of Jacob *vaye'ehav* the lass…" (Genesis 34:3)
- Amnon and Tamar: "…*vaye'ehaveha* Amnon, David's son" (2 Samuel 13:1)

We find the word 'love' relating to two, but not a man and a woman.

- "And David came to Saul and stood before him and *vaye'ehavehu* greatly and he became his armor bearer" (1 Samuel 16:21)
- "And it happened when he had finished speaking to Saul that the soul of Jonathan was tied with the soul of David, *vaye'ehavehu* Jonathan as his own soul" (1 Samuel 18:1)
- "And Solomon *vaye'ehav* the Lord to go in the statutes of David his father, only he sacrificed and burned incense in the high places" (1 Kings 3:3)
- "*Vaye'ehav* cursing so let it come to him…" (Psalms 109:17)

The verse dealing with King Saul comes in the following context,

And David came to Saul and stood before him and *vaye'ehavehu* greatly and he became his armor bearer. And Saul sent to Jesse, saying please let David stand before me, for he has found grace in my sight. And it happened when the spirit of G-d was upon Saul, that David took a lyre and played with his hand and Saul had a respite and he felt good and the evil spirit moved from upon him. (1 Samuel 16:21-23)

It is clear from the text that Saul suffered from emotional instability. He could have reached very strong emotions ("*vaye'ehavehu* greatly"), and on the other hand, he could go down to an emotional abyss that only David's music could help him out of.

For David and Jonathan, it is enough to quote David eulogizing Jonathan after he got killed in the battle: "I am distressed for you, my brother Jonathan, very dear have you been to me, your love for me was wonderful more than the love for women" (2 Samuel 1:26).

The verse relating to King Solomon comes in the following context,

> And Solomon married[78] Pharaoh the king of Egypt, and he took Pharaoh's daughter as a wife, and brought her to the city of David, until he finished building his own house, and the house of the Lord, and the surrounding wall of Jerusalem. Only the people sacrificed in the high places because there was no house built to the name of the Lord until those days. And Solomon *vaye'ehav* the Lord to go in the statutes of David his father, only he sacrificed and burned incense in the high places. (1 Kings 3:1-3)

King Solomon's order of priorities was first, he married Pharaoh the king of Egypt. Second, he took Pharaoh's daughter as a wife. Third, he brought her to the city of David. Fourth, he finished building his own house. Fifth, he built the house of the Lord. Sixth, he built the surrounding wall of Jerusalem.

It is understandable that King Solomon's marriage to Pharaoh's daughter was to defend his country from attacks from the south, a marriage based upon a clear and logical political interest.

"And Solomon *vaye'ehav* the Lord to go in the statutes of David his father..." (1 Kings 3:3)

Although his marriage to Pharaoh's daughter was based upon logic, his connection to the Almighty was more emotional. Does the text compliment Solomon on such a connection? If we compare David's words to his son Solomon before David's death, to what the text says here, we can see this is more criticism than compliment.

David said to Solomon, "And keep the charge of the Lord your G-d to go in his ways, to keep his statutes, and his commandments, and his judgments, and his testimonies, as it is written in the Torah of Moses..." (1 Kings 2:3). And the text, in regard to what King Solomon did, says, "...to go in the statutes **of David his father**...," and not 'in the statutes of **Moses.**'

---

[78] Married in the sense of entering into a political marriage alliance.

It should be noted that the use of the grammatical form of the verb *vaye'ehav* for King Solomon's connection to the Almighty, explains quite well the book Song of Songs. This book, considered an allegory of the love between the Almighty and the people, talks in very explicit terms about love making between a man and a woman.

The verse from Psalms, "*Vaye'ehav* a curse and let it come to him..." (Psalms 109:17) speaks for itself. Is there anyone who 'loves' a curse? Is there any logic in it? It seems that the verse talks about emotional love that has no basis.

'Love' With the Form *Ahav/Ohev*

Parental Love:

- "...please take your son, your only one, whom you *ahavta*, Isaac..." (Genesis 22:2)
- "...and Rebecca *ohevet* Jacob" (25:28)
- "And Israel *ahav* Joseph more than all his sons because he was the son of his old age..." (37:3)
- "...and his father *ahevo*" (44:20)

Slave's Love for his Master:

- "And if the slave will strongly say *ahavti* my master..." (Exodus 21:5)

Loving Your Fellow Man and the Foreigner:

- "...ve'ahavta your fellow man as yourself..." (Leviticus 19:18),
- "*Va'ahavtem* the foreigner..." (Deuteronomy 10:19).

Love Between Man and the Almighty:

- "And because He *ahav* your fathers..." (Deuteronomy 4:37),
- "*Ve'ahavta* the Lord your G-d with all your heart, and with all your soul, and with all your might" (6:5),
- "...the faithful G-d which keeps covenant and mercy *leohavav*..." (7:9),
- "...and *ohev* the foreigner..." (10:18),

- "...the Lord your G-d tests you to know whether you *ohavim* the Lord your G-d" (13:4)

Public Love:

- "And all Israel and Judah *ohev* David..." (1 Samuel 18:16)
- "...for Hiram was *ohev* David all the time" (1 Kings 5:15)
- "And King Solomon *ahav* many foreign women..." (1 Kings 11:1)

The fact that the form *ahav* indicates some distance (as opposed to the form *vaye'ehav*) shows up in the account of Amnon and Tamar.

The description started with, "...Absalom the son of David had a beautiful sister whose name was Tamar, *vaye'ehaveha* Amnon the son of David" (2 Samuel 13:1). Jonadab, the son of Shimeah David's brother, Amnon's friend asked Amnon, "Why are you, being the king's son, so wasted every morning please tell me..." (13:4), and Amnon responded, "Tamar, Absalom's sister I *ohev*" (13:4).

The text presented Amnon's feelings towards Tamar using the form of the verb *vaye'ehaveha*, still, Amnon himself says that he *ohev* Tamar. Does Amnon reduce the intensity of his feelings towards Tamar in his language when talking to Jonadab because he wants to conceal the fact that his love is the love between man and woman?

We should note that the text in Genesis does not attribute the word 'love' to Judah. Not towards his Canaanite wife (Genesis 38:2), nor towards Tamar (38:15-16), nor even after the birth of the twins.

We should also note that the text does not attribute any love by King David to any of his wives.

'Soul' Between Two People

When we find the word 'soul' relating to the relationship between two people, we find it in conjunction with the verb 'to tie' (*liKSHoR*). For example, When Judah speaks to Joseph, before Joseph acknowledged himself to his brothers, and Judah mentioned the connection between Jacob the father and Benjamin the son, "...and his soul is tied (*KeSHuRa*) to his soul" (44:30). In the case of David and Jonathan, "...and the soul of

Jonathan was tied (*niKSHeRa*) to the soul of David…" (1 Samuel 18:1). In both cases the text relates to either love of a father for his son, or love between friends.

The word 'soul' (*nefesh*) relating to love between a couple appears in conjunction with the word 'love' (*ahava*) only in the Song of Songs:

- "By the night on my bed I sought him whom my soul (*nafshi*) loves (*she'ahava*)…" (Song of Songs 3:1),
- "…I seek him whom my soul (*nafshi*) loves…" (3:2),
- "…have you seen him whom my soul (*nafshi*) loves?" (3:3), and
- "…when I found him whom my soul (*nafshi*) loves…" (3:4).

The fact that the combination of 'soul' and 'love' is found in the whole Tanach only in the Song of Songs confirms that the 'love' we face in the book is quite likely to be spiritual love and not earthly love. It goes along with the fact that the text describes King Solomon's love for the Almighty by the verb form *vaye'ehav*, which is the form used almost entirely between a man and a woman. This might explain why the graphic description of physical love portrayed in Song of Songs is interpreted by traditional commentary as spiritual and emotional love and not physical love. King Solomon, who wrote the Song of Songs (Song of Songs 1:1), expressed his love for the Almighty in the language that a man uses to express his love for a woman. Therefore the form of love is *vaye'ehav*.

One last point: we find the word soul (*nefesh*) in Jacob's words to Simeon and Levi before his death, "In their counsel my soul (*nafshi*) should not come…" (Genesis 49:6). He is expressing his disgust and revulsion for the cruelty they showed in their attack on Shechem, and as a result he does not want to be close to them. Or, in other words, he expresses the opposite of love for them in this context.

The Verb 'to Desire' Between Two People

The verb 'to desire' (*lachashok*) relating to the connection between two people is found in the Tanach in only three places. First, in the case of Dinah in Shechem, when Shechem's father speaks with Jacob and his sons, "…my son Shechem, his soul desires (*chashka*) your daughter…" (Genesis 34:8).

The second time, in Deuteronomy, "And you will see among the captives a beautiful woman and desire (*chashakta*) her…" (Deuteronomy 21:11).

The third place is in the case of King Hezekiah who, lying in his deathbed, is informed by the prophet Isaiah that the Almighty granted him fifteen more years to live. King Hezekiah is quoted as saying, "…and you desired (*chashakta*) my soul not to have my soul in the pit of destruction…" (Isaiah 38:17).

In the last two places, the captive woman, and King Hezekiah, it comes across that the combination of the verb to desire (*lachashok*) with the word soul' is in the context of danger (beautiful woman in captivity), and King Hezekiah (danger of death). With this understanding we need to realize the extent of the danger that Dinah faced while in captivity in Shechem.

Back to Jacob and Esau

"And Isaac *vaye'ehav* Esau…" (25:28)

Now that we ended our linguistic journey into the verb 'to love' in the Tanach, we can return to Isaac and his relationship with Esau. The use of the form *vaye'ehav* tells us that this is not simple 'love' that we are facing between a father and a son. After all, this form of the verb is used almost entirely between a husband and a wife.

We should note that the text describes Joseph with the same words as it used to describe his mother Rachel. For Rachel, the text said, "…and Rachel was beautiful (*yefat to'ar*) and beautiful to look upon (*yefat mareh*)" (Genesis 29:17). For Joseph the text says, "…and Joseph was beautiful (*yefeh to'ar*) and beautiful to look upon (*yefeh mareh*)" (39:6).

We should remember that Esau was red-haired: "And the first came out red (*admoni*), all over like a hairy garment…" (Genesis 25:25). If so, we should ask the question: is it possible that Isaac saw in Esau his wife Rebecca when she was young? Is it possible that Rebecca was a redhead as well?

We should note that the adjective *admoni* (red) appears in the Tanach only once more, in regard to David: "And he sent and brought him in. And he was red haired (*admoni*) with beautiful eyes (*yefeh einayim*) and good looking (*tov r'oi*)…" (1 Samuel 16:12).

Back to Isaac and Esau. Learning from the case of King Saul and his relationship with David, which was very emotional and more of a roller coaster than a steady relationship, and knowing that the text described the love between the two as *vaye'ehav*, we should wonder if the relationship between Isaac and Esau (*vaye'ehav*) was more like King Saul and David (*vaye'ehav*) than the one between Jacob and Joseph (*ahav*).

Linguistic Journey – 'Call (*et*)'

We find a linguistic signal that indeed Isaac was not completely content with Esau and his behavior. Earlier, in the case of Joseph and his master's wife, we went into a linguistic journey into the word 'to call.' We found out that mostly the text in the Tanach uses to call *el* or to call *l*.' However, there are five places in which the text uses the form of 'to call (*et*).'

We will start from the last place:

> And the Lord said to Moses behold your days approach to die call (*et*) Joshua and present yourselves in the Tent of Meeting that I may give him a charge and Moses and Joshua went and presented themselves in the Tent of Meeting. (Deuteronomy 31:14)

We find several places in the text relating to the relationship between Moses and Joshua, in terms of Joshua being the successor.

The text says, "And the Lord said to Moses, **take** Joshua the son of Nun a man in whom is spirit, and lay your hand upon him" (Numbers 27:18), and Moses indeed did so, "And Moses did as the Lord commanded him, and he **took** Joshua and set him before Eleazar the priest, and before all the congregation. And he laid his hands upon him and gave him a charge…" (27:22-23).

It is a point to note that Moses did not call Joshua. He didn't need to. In another place we find that Joshua was with Moses practically all the time: "And the Lord spoke to Moses face to face, as a man speaks to his friend. And he turned again into the camp, and his servant Joshua the son of Nun, a lad, **did not move from inside the Tent**" (Exodus 33:11).

Later on in Deuteronomy, we find again that Joshua was with Moses constantly: "Joshua the son of Nun who stands before you…" (Deuteronomy 1:38). When there is a need to command Joshua, there is no need to call him: "And charge Joshua and encourage him and strengthen him…" (Deuteronomy 3:28). The same is true in, "…Joshua, he shall go over before you…" (31:3).

When there is a need to call Joshua, the text used the formula, "And Moses called to (*l'*) Joshua…" (Deuteronomy 31:7). Only when the text quotes the Almighty saying to Moses, "…Behold your days approach to die…" do we find "…call *et* Joshua…" It seems that the language of the text perceives some distance between the two, very close to Moses' death. Is it because Moses begged the Almighty in vain to let him enter the land and continue on with his mission?

There are two places where we find 'call *et*' in regard to Pharaoh. One, after his dream about the starving cows swallowing the fat cows, and the same with the wheat, the text says, "And in the morning his spirit was troubled and he sent and called *et* all the sorcerers of Egypt and all its wise men…" (Genesis 41:8). From the use of *et* we can understand that Pharaoh already had a problem with his sorcerers and wise men who didn't satisfy him with their interpretations of his dreams. We find the same when Pharaoh is calling Joseph from the dungeon, "And Pharaoh sent and called *et* Joseph and they rushed him out of the dungeon…" (41:14). It is also clear here that Pharaoh had a problem with calling a Hebrew slave from a dungeon to interpret his dream.

From the above-mentioned examples we can see that 'calling *et*' appears when someone does something even though he or she doesn't want to do it.

The fourth place presents a challenge for us. It is in regard to Moses, the baby who was put in the basket on the Nile to guard him from the Egyptians who were killing all the Hebrew baby boys. Moses' sister was guarding the basket from afar. Pharaoh's daughter came to the Nile and saw the basket, opened it and saw Moses. Moses' sister approached Pharaoh's daughter and asked her if she wanted her to call a nursing woman from the Hebrews to nurse the baby. When Pharaoh's daughter approved, the text says, "…and the maiden went and called (*et*) the child's mother" (Exodus 2:8).

Why there would be distance between Moses' sister and her own mother?

If we read the text by the **language**, we see two changes in language. First, while earlier, Moses' sister is referred to by her relationship to Moses, "his sister," now she is called the "maiden" (*almah*). Second, the "maiden'" called "the child's mother." But when the deal between Pharaoh's daughter and the child's mother is sealed, the text does not call her "the child's mother" but "the woman." From these two changes of language, "his sister" to the "maiden," and "the child's mother" to "the woman," along with the fact that the text describes calling the mother as 'calling *et*,' we can understand that Moses' sister, along with her mother, concealed from Pharaoh's daughter that the woman to nurse the baby was really the child's mother. If they were to expose it, it is quite likely that Pharaoh's daughter would not have let the child's mother do the job, out of fear that she would not see the child again. After all, she wanted him for herself.

Back to Isaac and Esau

"And when Isaac was old and his eyes were dim so that he could not see he called (*et*) Esau his big son…" (Genesis 27:1).

The fact that the text uses 'call *et*' for Isaac summoning Esau to get the blessing should tell us that Isaac didn't really want to bless Esau. He knew very well that Esau's behavior did not merit a blessing. He quite likely knew that Esau 'sold' the birthright. The text tells us that Esau despised the birthright (25:34). And he couldn't have done this despising in secret. But then, Esau was the first to be born, and tradition says that the first to be born is the 'firstborn,' and as such he should be the one to inherit his position as head of the family. Isaac, the conflicted father, 'called *et*' Esau to bless him.

We have confirmation that Isaac really didn't want to bless Esau. When Esau showed up with the food he prepared and asked Isaac to bless him, Isaac responded, "…Who then is he who hunted the prey and brought me and I ate of all before you came and have blessed him, **moreover he shall be blessed?**" (27:33). Before knowing all the details of how Jacob fooled him, Isaac approved of the blessing in retrospect. He realized that it was not meant for Esau to get the blessing. He had doubts about Esau from the beginning, and when the results became clear, he was relieved.

Back to Rebecca and Jacob

> "And Isaac *vaye'ehav* Esau because he had hunting in his mouth
> and Rebecca loves (*ohevet*) Jacob (25:28).

The text used the form of *vaye'ehav* for the love of Isaac for Esau, and we went into a long linguistic journey to see the meaning of this love. Now we can move to deal with the love of Rebecca for Jacob, for which the text uses the form *ohevet*.

Mother's Love for Her Children

The fact that a mother loves her son is not something that should be mentioned in an open statement. It is taken for granted. And, indeed, there is no other place in Genesis where the love of a mother for her son is mentioned. If so, what does the text tell us by bringing up this taken-for-granted news? It is true that this fact comes as a comparison between Isaac's love for Esau and Rebecca's love for Jacob. Still, for this point to enter an open statement means it is doubly important. The suspicion is raised that there is something in this love that is not the regular love that we assume exists between a mother and her son. If so, what is this love?

In our linguistic journey into the different forms of the verb 'love' [A-H-B(V)] we found that the form *vaye'ehav* is usually for love between man and woman, while *ahav* is between father and son (Abraham and Isaac, Jacob and Joseph).

But the text does not say, "...and Rebecca *ahava* ('loved' in the past tense) Jacob." Instead, the text said "...And Rebecca *ohevet* ('loves' in the present tense) Jacob."

Did Rebecca prefer Jacob over Esau, as Jacob did with Joseph?

At the beginning of the account of Isaac's blessing, the text says, "When Isaac was old, and his eyes were dim for him to see, he called Esau **his big son**..." (Genesis 27:1). Then the text says, "And Rebecca hears Isaac's speaking to Esau **his son**..." (27:5), and "And Rebecca said to Jacob **her son**..." (27:6).

The fact that Esau is labeled as 'his (Isaac's) son' and Jacob is labeled as 'her (Rebecca's) son,' should bring us to wonder if there was any distance between Isaac and Rebecca at this point of time. We might even conclude that there was also a major rift between Rebecca and Esau. In continuing, the text says, "And Rebecca took the best garments of Esau **her** big **son**, which were with her in the house, and put them on Jacob **her** little **son**" (27:15). Here, for the first time, we see that Rebecca is acting with the recognition that Esau is 'her son' and not only Isaac's son.

After the blessing the text says, "And Rebecca was told the words of Esau **her** big **son** and she sent and called Jacob **her** little **son**..." (27:42). And later, Rebecca shows that her love for her two sons is the same, "...Why should I lose you both in one day?" (27:45). And if we doubt her love for both of them, the text says, "And Isaac sent away Jacob, and he went to Padan-Aram, to Laban son of Bethuel the Aramean, the brother of Rebecca, **the mother of Jacob and Esau**" (28:5). Although the text listed Jacob first as he was first for her, still she was the mother of both of them.

"...And Rebecca *ohevet* Jacob"

If we connect the fact that the form of the verb 'love' appearing in the present tense (*ohev*) appears in Deuteronomy in discussing the love of the Almighty for mankind, and the love of the Almighty for the foreigner, with the fact that the account of the birth of Jacob and Esau appears after the Almighty says to Rebecca, "Two nations are in your womb, and two peoples shall be separated from your bowels, and the one people shall be stronger than the other people, and the elder shall serve the younger" (25:23), then we can understand why the text uses the verb love in the present tense (*ohevet*) for Rebecca's love for Jacob. We are not dealing here with regular motherly love for her son, but with reliance upon the Almighty's word to her. This explains why the text even mentioned Rebecca's love for Jacob in an open statement. It deserves mentioning, in the open statement (the Tanach) as this love testifies to Rebecca's connection to the Almighty. It also testifies to the importance the text attributes to such a connection that would bring it to include such love in the open statement.

It is no different from the fact that the text changed the language in regard to Abraham's slave, from 'slave' to 'man,' once his request from the Almighty was answered, and very quickly. The conclusion we can draw is that the language of the text testifies to the importance of this issue to the text. Although it is not a 'linguistic bias,' it is an important inherent characteristic of the text.

Selling the Birthright

Introduction

The first event in Jacob and Esau's life is the selling of the birthright. In this description the text does not attribute to the two the title 'brother.' The two of them appear with only their names,

- "…and **Esau** came from the field…" (25:29),
- "And **Esau** said to **Jacob**…" (25:30),
- "And **Jacob** said…" (25:31),
- "And **Esau** said…" (25:32),
- "And **Jacob** said…" (25:33),
- "…and he sold his birthright to **Jacob**" (25:33),
- "And **Jacob** gave **Esau**…" (25:34), and
- "…and **Esau** despised the birthright" (25:34).

The selling of the birthright starts with

"And Jacob cooked pottage…" (25:29)

SCAN Rule: The first sentence to start an open statement is the most important sentence. It is the point at which the subject decided to start the statement. In many statements the first sentence might include the reason for the events that follow.

Social Journey – 'Cooking' in Genesis

The activity of 'cooking' is mentioned in the following places:

First, Abraham hosts the three angels:

And Abraham hurried to the tent to Sarah, and said, rush three measurements of fine meal, knead it, and **make** cakes. And Abraham ran to the herd, and took a calf tender and good, and gave it to the lad, and he hurried to **make** it. And he took butter and milk, and the calf that he had **made**, and set it before them, and he stood by them under the tree, and they ate. (Genesis 18:6-8)

We should note that Abraham expects Sarah to knead the dough and make the cakes. As for the calf, Abraham gave it to the lad who was the one to make it. The text does not say that Abraham did the cooking himself, but arranged for and served the food.

Second, cooking is also mentioned when Lot hosts the angels visiting him, "…and he **made** them a feast,[79] and **baked** unleavened bread (*matzot*), and they ate" (19:3).

We should note that the text specifies that Lot served his guests *matzot*, a food that we can consider 'fast food.' Abraham, on the other hand, started with making cakes, and slaughtering the calf and cooking it, activities which take a long time.

Third, the text mentions 'cooking' in the account of Isaac blessing Jacob instead of Esau. The text starts with Isaac instructing Esau, "And **make** me savory food…" (27:4). Later on, Rebecca says to Jacob, "Go please to the flock, and take for me two good baby lambs and I will **make** them into savory food for your father such as he loves" (27:9), and then, "…and his mother **made** savory food…" (27:14), and, "And she gave him the savory food and the bread which she **made**…" (27:17).

The text mentions 'eating' without mentioning 'cooking' in the case of Abraham's slave visiting Rebecca's family, "And they ate and drank, he and the men who were with him…" (24:54). We find the same with Abimelech and his military commander visiting Isaac, "And he made them a feast and they ate and they drank" (26:30). So for Jacob and his brother on Mount Gilead, "And Jacob said to his brother, gather stones, and they took stones, and made a heap, and they ate there upon the heap" (31:46), and, "…and called his brothers to eat bread, and they ate bread…"

---

[79] 'Feast' in Hebrew is *MiSHTeH* which comes from the three-letter root word of *SH-T-H* which is 'to drink.' The word *mishteh* connotes more of a 'drinking event' than an 'eating event' (a meal).

(31:54). The same for Joseph's brothers who ate while Joseph was in the pit, "And they sat down to eat bread…" (37:25).

Joseph is quoted as saying to the one who was in charge of his house, "…bring these men home, and slaughter a lot, and **prepare** for these men shall dine with me at noon" (43:16).

From Abraham and Rebecca we see that the common verb to relate to cooking food is 'to **make**.' As for the use of the verb 'to prepare' in regard to Joseph, it is clear from the text that Joseph does not expect the one who is in charge of his house to be the one to do the cooking. Therefore, the text uses the verb 'to **prepare**' and not 'to **make**.'

The only two men in Genesis who are mentioned as 'cooking' are Lot with 'baking' (*matzot*), and Jacob 'cooking' the pottage.

"And Jacob cooked (*vayazed*) pottage (*nazid*)…" (25:29).

What is unique about the case of Jacob that brought the text to use a unique verb to describe the act of cooking – *vayazed*?

Linguistic Journey – the Verb *Z-D-H*

The verb *Z-D-H* appears in the following places in the Torah:

Jethro, Moses' father-in-law, responds to Moses telling him of all the miraculous events that happened at the time of the exodus, "Now I know that the Lord is greater than all gods, for in the thing that they *zadu* about them" (Exodus 18:11).

The verb *zadu* is from the root word *ZaDaH*, where the last letter 'H' falls out and is replaced by the letter 'u' standing for the pronoun 'they.' How should we translate this word *zadu*? 'Spoke' about them? And to whom does Jethro refer by saying 'them?'

Since Jethro is comparing the Almighty to the other gods, it is quite likely that the pronoun 'them' refers to the other gods. But then, what is it that 'they' *zadu* about the other gods?

We have only to go to the text dealing with the false prophet to understand the word *zadah* or *zadu*. The text says, "But the prophet who shall *yazid* to speak a word in my name which I have not commanded him to speak…" (Deuteronomy 18:20), and, "…that is the thing which the Lord has not spoken, *bezadon*[80] the prophet spoke…" (Deuteronomy 18:22), and, "… the man who will do *bezadon* to not listen to the priest…" (Deuteronomy 17:12).

It becomes clear that the text is talking about doing something with the knowledge that what one does is not proper. The word *zadon* and the verb *Z-D-H* do not deal with intent, but with the criminal knowledge at the time of the act itself. The text is ruling out someone who does something out of ignorance.

Back to Jethro: "Now I know that the Lord is greater than all gods, for in the thing that they *zadu* about them" (Exodus 18:11). Jethro says to Moses that now he realizes that what the priests of idolatry said about their gods was not something they said out of ignorance, but they said it knowing that what they said was untrue.

The idea that the person has the knowledge that what he/she is doing is something that should not be done, is the idea of *zadon*.

With this understanding we can read the following:

- "If a man will *yazid* to treacherously kill his fellow man…" (Exodus 21:14)
- "And I spoke to you and you did not hear, and you rebelled the commandment of the Lord, and *vatazidu* and went up the mountain" (Deuteronomy 1:43)
- "And all the people shall hear and fear and will not *yezidun* any more" (Deuteronomy 17:13)

*"**Vayazed** Jacob nazid"* (25:29)

It is true that the word is pronounced as *vayazed* and not as *vayazid*, (just one tiny vowel difference) but one should know that the vowels in the Hebrew language are not in the letters, but outside the letters. In the text, we find the same letters for *vayazid* and for *vayazed*. It is only tradition

---

[80] While the verb is *Z-D-H*, the noun is *zadon*. The *be* at the beginning of *bezadon* means 'with.'

that tells us how to read and pronounce, and to make a distinction between identical words written the same and pronounced differently.

Even if the word *vayazed* is different in meaning from *vayazid*, we know that the language of the Biblical text uses the sound of words to send messages. We already saw it from the word 'second' (*sheni*) as opposed to 'scarlet thread' (*shani*) in the birth of Zerach, Judah's second son from Tamar, "And afterwards came out his brother, who had the scarlet thread (*shani*) upon his hand and he called his name Zerach" (Genesis 38:30). Or the word *biglal* ('because'), used for idolatry, which in Biblical Hebrew is labeled *gilulim*. It seems that it is not different at all from our case where the text labels Jacob's 'cooking' with a verb used elsewhere to relate to knowing that one is doing something that should not be done.

The text sends messages to the listener not only by the **content** of the text and/meaning of the words, but also by the **sound** of the words registering in the listener's ear. One might wonder if the biblical text was more often read aloud to listeners than read silently to oneself.

Question: Does the text send us a message with the word *vayazed* that Jacob is plotting something, knowing that he is doing something that he should not do? We should not forget that after Esau found that Jacob got the blessing instead of him, the text quotes Esau telling Isaac his father, "And he said, is he not rightly named Jacob? For he has followed (*vayaakveni*[81]) me twice now, he took my birthright, and now he took my blessing..." (27:36).

It is no different from a couple of modern English idioms, 'he is **cooking** something up,' meaning hatching some devious plan, or 'he is **cooking** the books,' meaning falsifying accounts.

"*Vayazed* Jacob *nazid*" (25:29)

The word *nazid* (pottage) is mentioned in the Tanach two more times. The first is in regard to the prophet Elisha, when talking about the sons of the prophets: "And Elisha came again from Gilgal, and there was a famine in the land, and the sons of the prophets were sitting before him, and he said

---

[81] The word *aakev* in Hebrew is 'heel.' Jacob got his name because when he came out his hand was holding his brother's heel, and therefore, 'Yaakov.' One should note that this is the only place where the word *akev* functions as a verb. The word *ekev* is used many times to mean 'following this...'

to his lad, set on the great pot and boil *nazid* for the sons of the prophets" (2 Kings 4:38). The second is, "If one carries holy meat in the skirt of his garment, and with his skirt touches bread, or *nazid*, or wine, or oil, or any food, shall it become holy…" (Haggai 2:11-12). Although in this second place the holiness is reserved to the meat and not to the *nazid*, still the word *nazid* comes in the context of holiness.

Content-wise, this preparation of food by Jacob, a man cooking, is found only once more in Genesis, when Lot baked the *matzot* for the angels (motive of holiness). And the fact that Jacob prepared *nazid* for itself also has the built-in motive of holiness. This event is unique also language-wise because of the fact that the text uses the word *vayazed* for cooking.

Back to Selling the Birthright

We already saw in our linguistic journey into deals and commerce in Genesis that the text prefers to use the words 'to give' and 'to take' to describe a transaction. And for finalizing the transaction, the text prefers to use the word 'to buy' over the word 'to sell.'

When Jacob says to Esau, "**Sell** me this day your birthright" (Genesis 25:31), instead of 'Let me **buy** your birthright,' or even 'Give me your birthright' (in exchange for the pottage), we should realize that the text is using a word that it avoids using in other transactions. If so, the conclusion should be that the language of the text does not view positively the fact that Jacob wants to '**buy**' the birthright from Esau. And when the text says at the end of this transaction that "…and he (Esau) sold his birthright to Jacob" (25:33), the text does not view positively that Esau sold his birthright.

The content gives us additional messages.

Finalizing the Transaction

The text describes the transaction by saying, "…and he **sold** his birthright to Jacob. And Jacob **gave** Esau bread and pottage of lentils…" (25:33-34).

Esau 'sold,' and Jacob 'gave.' The text does not say that Jacob 'bought' the birthright. The same formula that the text used to finalize the transaction of the purchase of the Cave of the Patriarchs, "to Abraham for a possession (*miknah*[82]) in front of the eyes of the Hittites..." (23:18), the same verb the text used for Jacob's buying the land from the people of Shechem, and the same verb that the text used for Joseph's buying the land and the Egyptian people, regarding the birthright the formula for ending the transaction, 'And Jacob bought the birthright,' is missing. We have a **sale** but not a **purchase**. We should conclude that the text sees a flaw in this transaction.

There are additional points to indicate that the transaction of transferring the birthright was deficient, that Esau sold it, but Jacob didn't buy it.

Linguistic Journey – 'Eating' in Genesis

Introduction

Generally speaking, in an open statement, the time of food (breakfast, lunch, and supper) should be considered a 'promising activity,' promising in the sense of generating more information, especially about people whom the subject didn't mention, but who were still present during the activity. Relating to the time of food in an open statement enables the reader/listener to learn about relationships between people.

In Genesis we find several times in which 'eating food' is mentioned.

The first time is right at the beginning, with eating the forbidden fruit. The serpent entices the woman to eat in spite of the prohibition. The serpent starts by saying to the woman that they are not allowed to eat from the fruit of the garden. The woman responds with, "...**we** may **eat** of the fruit of the trees of the garden" (3:2). We should note that at this point the woman is using the pronoun 'we' in relation to herself and Adam.

However, when the actual time came to eat the fruit, the text says, "And the woman saw that the tree was good for food, and that it was pleasant to the eyes, and a tree to be desired to make one wise, she took of its fruit, **and ate**, and gave also to her husband with her, **and he ate**" (3:6).

---

[82] The verb 'to buy' is from the three-letter root word *K-N-H*, and the word *miKNaH* is a derivative.

We note that there is no 'we' between Adam and Eve at the time of eating the fruit. The woman ate first, and only then gave it Adam to eat. We should also note that the text emphasizes that her husband was 'with her.'

Once each one of them ate from the fruit, and separately, the text continues, "And the eyes of **the two of them** opened, and **they** knew that **they** were naked, and **they** sewed fig leaves and **they** made **themselves** belts" (3:7).

We should note that at the time of 'opening the eyes' the text does not say, "And their eyes opened…" Instead of "they" the text uses 'the two of them' (*shneihem*, which is *sheni* ('two'), plus *hem* ('they')). By saying 'the two of them' the text comes to say that their eyes didn't open at the same time. After all, she ate the fruit before him. Once their eyes were opened, the knowledge they acquired brought them back together, as they were before eating the fruit ("…**we** may eat of the fruit…").

When the Almighty confronted them about their behavior, Adam said, "…the woman whom you gave to be with me, she gave me from the tree and I ate" (3:12). The tendency is to see Adam as running away from responsibility, by blaming the woman for everything, but the fact is that Adam's response expresses exactly what the text said in the narration of the events.

The second 'meal' we encounter, is the one Abraham offers his three guests, "And I will take a slice of bread and you will **help** your hearts…" (18:5).

One should note that in Hebrew, even in Modern Hebrew, to eat a meal is *lisod*. And the verb *lisod* comes from the three-letter-root word of *S-AA-D*,[83] which is to help. *Se'udah* is 'meal' and *misaadah* is 'restaurant.' The idea is that when a person 'eats,' the person **helps** himself/herself. English has at least two equivalents; one puts food on the table accompanied by the sentence, 'Help yourself,' and one might have an extra 'helping' on occasion.

And the text continues with the meal Abraham set up for his guests, "…and set it before them, and he stood by them under the tree, **and they**

---

[83] The letter 'AA' stands for the letter *ayin*, which is the sound 'ah' but comes from deep in the throat and not from the front of the mouth. The English alphabet has no equivalent letter.

ate" (18:8). We should note that Abraham is not eating with them. One might wonder if the reason is that Abraham, as a human, didn't feel he should eat with angels.

We find the same with Lot and the angels visiting him, "And he pressed upon them greatly and they turned in to him, and came to his house, and he made them a feast, and baked unleavened bread, **and they ate**" (19:3). And now we should wonder if 'they ate' refers only to the angels, or is Lot included? Quite likely 'they ate' refers only to the angels.

The next meal is with Abraham's slave visiting Rebecca's family. The text says, "And there was set food before him to eat, and he said I will not eat until I have said my words, and he said speak on" (24:33).

The fact that Abraham's slave did not want to eat before dealing with the mission he was sent for ('business first') testifies to the fact that eating together means an 'agreement.' As long as he did not secure their agreement to let Rebecca marry his master's son, he didn't want to give them the feeling that he was with them, even though he was employed by their relative.

Once he spoke his words, and Laban and Bethuel (Laban is listed first before his father) said, "The matter proceeds from the Lord… Rebecca is in front of you, take her…" (24:50-51), and Abraham's slave gave presents to Rebecca and her brother and her mother (Bethuel vanished), only then does the text say, "and they ate and they drank he and the men who were with him…" (24:54). It is interesting that the text does not say that Rebecca's family ate as well, although it is assumed.

We see people eating together also in the following:

When Isaac makes a pact with Abimelech and Phichol, "And he made them a feast **and they ate and they drank**" (26:30). After Jacob and Laban made a non-belligerence pact, "And Jacob said to his brothers, gather stones, and they took stones, and made a heap and **they ate** there upon the heap" (31:46), and, "Jacob offered sacrifice upon the mount, and called his brothers to eat bread, and **they ate bread** and slept the night at the mount" (31:54).

We see the same with Joseph's brothers, after they threw Joseph into the pit, "And they took him and threw him into the pit, and the pit was empty, there was no water in it. And **they sat down to eat bread**..." (37:25). One should wonder how heartless they could be when their brother was in the pit, quite likely crying for help, and they just sat to eat. But the mention of their eating comes to tell us that once Joseph was 'out of the picture' the brothers could relax and get together. There was too much turmoil when he was there. And now there was none.

When Joseph's brothers go down to Egypt, the text mentions food several times. "And Joseph saw Benjamin with them, he said to the one in charge of his house, bring these men home and slaughter a lot, and prepare, for **these men shall eat with me** at noon" (43:16). Eating together is a major signal that Joseph sends them that he is pleased. And the brothers got the message, "...because they heard that **they will eat bread there**" (43:25).

And the text goes on to elaborate on the way the meal went. Although they ate at the same time, the text wants us to know that there was no togetherness among them: "And they served him by himself, and for them by themselves, and for the Egyptians **who ate with him** by themselves, because the Egyptians **cannot eat bread** with the Hebrews because it is abomination to the Egyptians" (43:32). And in fact, the text ends the description by saying, "...and they drank and got drunk with (*im*) him" (43:34).

We should note two points: First, the text does not say that they 'ate.' Only that they 'drank.' Second, the text uses the word 'with' (*im*), a preposition that does not appear in other places where it says, "and they ate and they drank." The text comes to tell us that although they agreed to drink, there was no 'togetherness' between them (even though it was the close 'with').

The significance of food comes in the account of the blessing Isaac gave Jacob. Isaac says to Esau, "And make me savory food such as I love and bring it to me **and I will eat** so my soul will bless you before I die" (27:4). Isaac explains that the reason for the meal is to influence the 'soul' that will do the blessing. Not just outward blessing, but inward as well. Thus, the need for 'savory food' (*mataamim* in Hebrew; *taam* is 'taste'; literally, it is 'tasty foods' in the plural) was to have a powerful impact on the soul, to guarantee a great blessing.

We can understand why Isaac eats by himself, while Jacob is serving him the food. The one who eats is the father who intends to bless the son. There is no need for the two of them to reach an 'agreement' or to reach 'togetherness.' The only reason was to guarantee to easy flow of the blessing from the father's soul to the son.

We can understand why Abraham and Lot did not eat with the Angels. One does not expect a human to eat with an angel. And although the text says that Eve ate from the fruit before Adam, still it also says that Adam was 'with her' (3:6).

Back to Jacob and Esau

The only one we see who eats by himself while we know that his equal is present is Esau, when Jacob served him the food, "And Jacob gave Esau bread and pottage of lentils, **and he ate and drank**, and rose up, and went, and Esau despised the birthright" (25:34). We should note that the text talks about Esau eating alone although Jacob is serving him the food.

The fact that the text says that Esau 'ate and drank' comes, quite likely, to tell us that there was no agreement between them. No togetherness. Esau 'sold' his birthright, but the rift between them remained as strong as before.

Additional Evidence for 'Selling' the Birthright Without 'Buying' it

The **content** shows us in two additional ways that Jacob knows that he is not the 'firstborn' even though Esau 'sold' the birthright. The first is when Rebecca says to Jacob to go and get the blessing, Jacob says, "…Behold Esau my brother is a hairy man and I am a smooth man. My father perhaps will feel me and I shall be in his eyes as a deceiver and I shall bring a curse upon me, and not a blessing" (27:11-12). Jacob does not claim the birthright. Jacob knows that if he wants to receive the blessing he needs to deceive his father, and his fear is to be caught pretending to be Esau.

The second is when Jacob appeared before his father with the food Rebecca prepared, and his father asks him, "…who are you my son?" (27:18).

It is quite likely that Isaac's being blind ("...and his eyes were dim..." (27:1)) made his hearing very strong to compensate. Later on, Isaac said, "...the voice is Jacob's voice..." (27:22). When Jacob addressed his father by saying, "My father..." (27:18), Jacob exposed himself to his father as being Jacob, even if his voice was similar to Esau's voice because they were twins. The human capacity to distinguish voices is very strong. When we answer the phone and the speaker on the other side of the line says one word, we can identify the speaker right away. This is even more true for a blind man.

Jacob answers, "I am Esau your firstborn; I have done according to what you told me," (27:19). Isaac's question dealt only with his identity, and not with his status in the family. Jacob could have said, 'I am Esau I have done according to what you told me,' but Jacob added the title, 'your firstborn.' Jacob knows very well that although Esau sold the birthright, Jacob didn't buy it, and if so, Esau is still the firstborn, just by the mere fact that he came out first.

The phenomenon that Jacob added information in his answer that the question didn't ask is found also in the case of Joseph's brothers who appeared before Joseph, the ruler of the land. Joseph asked them, "From where did you come?" (42:7), and they answered, "...from the land of Canaan to buy food" (42:7). He did not ask them **why** they came. Due to the famine in the neighboring countries it was understood that people came to buy food. If so, the brothers added information that was not asked, just as did Jacob who said, "I am Esau **your firstborn**."

The **language** of the text also testifies to the fact that Esau 'sold' and Jacob didn't 'buy.'

Isaac asks Esau to make him savory food before he will give him the blessing. The text starts with, "When Isaac was old, and his eyes were dim for him to see, he called Esau his **big** (*gadol*) son..." (27:1). We should note that the text does not use the title 'the **firstborn**.' Later on, the text says, "And Rebecca took the best garments of Esau her **big** (*gadol*) son, which were with her in the house, and put them on Jacob her **little** son" (27:15). And at the end of this event, the text says, "And

Rebecca was told these words of Esau her **big** son, and she sent and called Jacob her **little** son…" (27:42).

Twice, when the two brothers are mentioned in the same sentence, the language of the text uses the title 'big' (and not '**firstborn**') for Esau, and the title '**little**' (again, not '**firstborn**') for Jacob. The language of the text testifies that Esau 'sold' his birthright; therefore, he does not merit the title 'firstborn.' At the same time, Jacob didn't 'buy' the birthright, and therefore he does not merit this title either.

The Use of the Title 'Brother'

The account of the blessing is a narrative in which one of the sons pretends to his father that he is the other son, and by doing so he takes from his brother fraudulently: "And he said your brother came **with cunning** and has taken away your blessing" (27:35), the blessing that his father wanted to give him. For such an account we would not expect to see the title 'brother' used.

'Esau Your Brother'

At the beginning of the account Rebecca says to Jacob, "I heard your father speak to **Esau your brother**…" (27:6). It is expected that a parent speaking to his/her son would use the name of the other son, or use the title 'your brother.' However, it is not expected that a parent would use both ('your brother' + name) when there are only two brothers. This should bring us to wonder if Isaac and Rebecca had more children than these two twins. One should remember that when Esau complained to his father Isaac about Jacob taking the blessing from him, Isaac answered, "…I have made him thy master, and all his **brothers** (in the plural) I have given to him for slaves…" (27:37). It might be that the word 'brothers' relates to real brothers, or might relate to the extended family, not necessarily to real brothers. The text does the same later on for Jacob, "…and called **his brothers** to eat bread…" (31:54).

And at this point, Rebecca tells Jacob her plan to bring Jacob to be the one to receive the blessing and not Esau.

'Esau My Brother'

Jacob's response to Rebecca was, "...Behold Esau my brother is a hairy man and I am a smooth man" (27:11). Again, we do not expect that a son talking to his father and/or mother would use the title 'my brother.' The listener, and in this case the parent, knows to whom the speaker refers. But the use of the title 'my brother' comes to tell us, quite likely, that Jacob does not see himself as being in conflict with Esau his brother, and therefore not only does he not want to cheat his father, but he also does not want to cheat his brother.

Rebecca persuaded Jacob to act according to her plan and present himself as Esau. So Jacob appeared before his father, "And he did not recognize him because his hands were hairy, like Esau **his brother**'s hands, and he blessed him" (27:23). Throughout the account the text uses the title 'brother.' For example, "And it happened that as soon as Isaac had finished blessing Jacob, and Jacob had scarcely gone out from the face of Isaac, Esau **his brother** came in from his hunting" (27:30).

'Jacob My Brother'

Even when Esau intends to kill Jacob the text says, "...and Esau said in his heart, when the days of mourning for my father are at hand, and I will kill Jacob **my brother**" (27:41). Rebecca says to Jacob to run away to her brother Laban in Haran, "...behold Esau **your brother** comforts himself by planning to kill you" (27:42). And she says, "And you remain with him a few days until **your brother**'s fury turns away. Until **your brother**'s anger turns away from you..." (27:44-45).

Jacob

After Isaac blessed Jacob for the second time, and this time knowing it was Jacob, the text says, "When Esau saw that Isaac had blessed Jacob..." (28:6), and now the title 'brother' vanishes from the language of the text. Up to this point, Esau who saw himself hurt that Jacob got the blessing fraudulently, still perceived Jacob as 'his brother,' even though he wanted to kill him. However, once Jacob received the blessing from his father, knowing that he was Jacob, the rift between the two was complete.

'Esau His Brother'

Upon his return from Haran to the land of Canaan, the text says, "And Jacob sent messengers before him to **Esau his brother** to the land of Seir, the country of Edom" (32:4). When the text quotes Jacob instructing the messengers before they went on their way, the text says, "Thus shall you say to my master Esau…" (32:5), "…and I have sent to tell my master that I may find grace in your eyes" (32:6). Jacob goes out of his way to flatter Esau by using the title 'my master.'

'To Your Brother to Esau'

Upon their return, the messengers report to Jacob, "…we came to your brother to Esau and also he goes towards you and four hundred men with him" (32:7). We should note here that the text does not say, 'We came to your brother Esau…' Instead, the text splits the title 'your brother Esau' into two, by putting the word 'to' (*el*) between the two. This separation in the title is very meaningful. The messengers' report is not decisive. They put the title 'your brother' first, before the name, and by doing so, they say that it is possible that Esau will behave as 'your brother.' However, they are not sure, and it is quite possible that he will behave as 'Esau.'

Jacob's reaction to the report was, "And Jacob was greatly afraid and distressed…" (32:8). When he addressed the Almighty in a prayer, he said, "Save me please from the hand of my brother from the hand of Esau for I fear him…" (32:12), and here, too, we see the split in the title. Jacob was not sure of Esau's intent either.

'Esau His Brother'

After his appeal to the Almighty, it seems from the text that Jacob felt more confident in himself, "And he slept there on that night and he took of that which came to his hand a present for **Esau his brother**" (32:14). Jacob instructs his slaves, "…when Esau my brother meets you…" (32:18). Although there is no split in the title, still 'Esau' appears before the title 'his brother'/'my brother.'

'Esau'

After the fight with the angel during the night, the text says, "And Jacob raised his eyes and saw and behold **Esau** came and with four hundred men…" (33:1). At this point the suspense is growing. Jacob sees Esau from afar ("And Jacob raised his eyes") and with 400 men, a picture that explains why Jacob is afraid of what might happen.

'His Brother'

When Jacob gets closer to Esau and he can see his facial expressions, the text says, "And he passed over before them and bowed to the ground seven times until he came near to **his brother**" (33:3).

'Esau'

It seems that Jacob was mistaken in his assessment of 'his brother.' The text continues and says, "And **Esau** ran to meet him and embraced him and fell on his neck and kissed him and they wept" (33:4). We should note that the title 'his brother' is not present in the language of the text. Esau remained 'Esau.' The fact that the title 'his brother' vanished should help us to resolve the debate if Esau's intent in embracing Jacob was positive or negative.

The conversation between the two starts by Esau asking Jacob, "Who is this to you, all this drove which I met?" (33:8). Jacob answers, "…to find grace in my master's eyes" (33:8). And the text quotes Esau, "I have enough **my brother** let be yours what is yours" (33:9).

The fact that Esau uses the title 'my brother' in talking to Jacob should remind us of Abraham's conversation with Lot before their separation, "Let there be no strife between me and you and between my shepherds and your shepherds **for we are men brothers**" (13:8). The title 'brothers' appears in Abraham's language upon separation. And here we find that Esau uses the title 'my brother.'

It would be wrong on Jacob's part to relax at this point; indeed, the text continues, "And Esau said let me introduce you to some from the people who are with me…" (33:15), and Jacob answers, "Why do I find grace in my master's eyes?" (33:15). And their visit ends with, "And Esau returned that day to his way to Seir" (33:16). The omission of the title 'his brother' in verses 33:15 and 33:16 should tell us that although their encounter ended peacefully, the rift between the two did not end. Esau remained 'Esau.'

Jacob's Sons

Jacob's sons appear for the first time as a group when Esau asks Jacob, during their meeting when Jacob was on his way back to Canaan, "Who are those to you?" (Genesis 33:5). And Jacob answers, "The children whom G-d has graciously given your slave" (33:5). Note that the text says that Esau saw 'the women and the children' (33:5), which brought him to ask Jacob about them. However, Jacob answers only about 'the children' and does not answer about the women.

Dinah in Shechem

The next time Jacob's sons appear as a group, and this time as 'active participants' in the event, is in the case of Dinah in Shechem. The text says, "And Jacob heard that he had defiled Dinah his daughter, and **his sons** were with his cattle in the field, and Jacob held his peace until they came" (34:5). We can understand that Jacob's sons are not 'the children' Esau met on the way. Jacob even waits for them before deciding what step to take. From this point alone, we can conclude that this event was a significant period of time after Jacob's arrival in Shechem, and after he bought "a parcel of the field, where he had spread his tent, from the hand of the sons of Hamor, Shechem's father, for a hundred pieces of money" (33:19).

And the text continues, "And Hamor the father of Shechem came out to Jacob to speak with (*et*) him" (34:6). Note that we already saw the difference between *et* and *im* in Biblical Hebrew, and *et* indicates distance.

And the following verse, "And **the sons of Jacob** came from the field when they heard it..." (34:7). By the order of the verses it can be understood that Hamor, Shechem's father, went to speak with Jacob **before** his sons 'came from the field.' If so, the sons show up when Jacob and Hamor are already sitting down to talk about the events. And at the time of their arrival at this meeting they are labeled as 'Jacob's sons.'

And the verse continues, "...and **the men** were grieved and they were very angry because he had done a vile deed in Israel in lying with Jacob's daughter, which thing ought not be done" (34:7). Since the subject of the sentence from its beginning is 'Jacob's sons' the text could have continued with, "…and **they** were grieved and were very angry…" and we would still know that the pronoun 'they' relates to "Jacob's sons."

SCAN Rule: The shortest way to give a sentence is the best way. Any deviation from the shortest way is very meaningful.

Note: Pronouns are the shortest way to relate to people after the initial "social introduction." When the text avoids using a pronoun, and instead, uses another "social introduction" (changing the language), the text comes to send us a message of a change, and quite likely a change in emotions and/or attitude.

What happened between their arrival, when they are labeled as 'Jacob's sons,' and immediately after that when the text labels them as 'the men?' It is clear that the use of the title 'the men' comes to reject the idea of 'Jacob's sons.' Why wouldn't Jacob's sons see themselves as his 'sons' right after their arrival?

Moreover, the description of their emotions lists first their 'grief' ("…and the men were grieved…") before their 'anger' ("…and they were very angry…"). We can understand their anger, and even desire for revenge, but what brought them to grieve?

If we add the order of their emotions ('grief' before 'anger') to the fact that text changes its language from 'Jacob's sons' to 'the men,' we should wonder if Jacob's behavior brought 'the men' to detach themselves from being 'Jacob's sons.' What do we know about Jacob's behavior that would bring such a reaction from his sons?

Jacob's Personality

In the account of the blessing Jacob received from his father while pretending to be his brother Esau, the text quotes Rebecca as telling Jacob,

> Behold, I heard your father speak to Esau your brother saying, bring me prey and make me savory food that I may eat, and bless you before the Lord before my death. Now my son, obey me to what I command you. Go please to the sheep and take for me from there two good baby goats, and I will make them into savory food for your father such as he loves. And you shall bring it to your

246

father that he will eat, and that he will bless you before his death (27:6-10).

Reading the text correctly, Rebecca does not say to Jacob to pretend to be Esau. She only tells him to bring the savory food that she will cook to Isaac, and then Jacob will receive the blessing. According to Rebecca, the blessing is dependent on the savory food, and if Jacob will bring it to his father before Esau, then his father will bless him.

Jacob's response to Rebecca's idea brings forth for the first time the idea of fraud: "Behold, Esau my brother is a hairy man and I am a smooth man. My father perhaps will feel me and I shall seem to him as a deceiver, and I shall bring a curse upon me and not a blessing" (27:11-12). It is very easy to read Rebecca's instructions to Jacob thus: to go to his father Isaac, present himself as Jacob, give him the savory food, and ask for the blessing, since he sees himself more suitable to get the blessing than his brother. However, this idea does not enter Jacob's mind – to confront his father **openly** and **directly** to receive the blessing. Instead, Jacob turns to the idea that he will present himself as Esau, an idea that Rebecca did not raise. Rebecca continues with her plan to enable Jacob to receive the blessing, even if Jacob is not able to go to his father in the open.

The lack of will for an open and direct confrontation appears later on in Jacob's life, and this time at the end of his stay in Haran. The text says that Jacob heard "the words of Laban's sons saying, Jacob has taken away all that was our father's and from that which was our father's he has gotten all this honor" (31:1). Would Jacob turn to Laban and talk with him about their relationship, in order to smooth all the rough points? Not Jacob. Instead, Jacob calls his two wives to the field, and secures their support in escaping from Haran. And indeed the text says, "And Jacob **stole** the heart of Laban the Aramean in that he did not tell him that he was running away" (31:20). The use of the word 'stole' in the language of the text testifies that the text sees Jacob's running away in a very negative way – running away without talking to Laban about what Laban's sons said, and without taking proper leave from him. Moreover, one would expect that Jacob would allow the grandparents of his children to say goodbye before they go to a far away country, with the strong likelihood that they might not see them ever again. And, indeed, later on Laban complained, "And why did you not let me kiss my sons and my daughters?" (31:28).

At the time of the encounter between Jacob and Esau, the text says that Jacob "...passed over before them and bowed to the ground seven times until he came near to his brother" (33:3). Did Jacob need to bow down to the ground seven times in submission to Esau, or did he maybe bow down so he would not need to look Esau straight in the eyes? And when they finally met, the text says, "And Esau ran to meet him and embraced him and fell on his neck and kissed him and they wept" (33:4). Even the 'falling on the neck' prevents Jacob from looking straight into Esau's eyes.

Later on, Jacob gave Joseph the title "the crown of the head who was separate from his brothers" (49:26) and he gave him all the benefits of a 'firstborn' (two tribes instead of one), without giving him the title 'firstborn.' This behavior fits Jacob's lack of will to confront the fact that Reuben was indeed '**his** firstborn,' while Joseph is the firstborn of him **and** his wife Rachel.

The bottom line is that we can conclude that Jacob is described as a man who does not like open conflicts, and instead prefers to do all in his power not to be in a situation of open conflict. Jacob prefers to act **indirectly**.

"And Jacob heard that he had defiled Dinah his daughter, and his sons were with his cattle in the field, and Jacob held his peace until they came" (34:5). Jacob is not in a rush to act and prefers to wait for the arrival of his sons.

Back to Jacob Facing Hamor and Shechem

"And Hamor the father of Shechem went out to Jacob to speak with (*et*) him" (34:6). Jacob is facing a very pressing problem; Dinah is captive in Shechem, and the father of the one who took his daughter is now visiting him to talk about the events. From what we know of Jacob's personality, Jacob would have preferred to be in any other place in the world, just not to sit across from the father of the man who 'defiled his daughter.'

Can we understand from Jacob's past behavior that Jacob would be firm in his dealing with Hamor the father of Shechem? Or, maybe there is consistency in Jacob's behavior, and he would lean towards compromising as much as possible with Hamor to avoid a confrontation? The change of language from 'Jacob's sons' to 'the men' along with listing 'grief' before 'anger' raises the prospect that Jacob was willing to compromise with Hamor.

We should also add the words of the 'men' before their attack on Shechem, "…because he had done a vile deed in Israel in lying with Jacob's daughter, which thing ought not be done" (34:7) to their words after the attack on Shechem, "…should he deal with our sister as with a harlot?" (34:31). Their words indicate that the second generation, Jacob's sons, were the firm ones during the course of events.

"…because he had done a vile deed in **Israel**…" (34:7)

Up to this point, the text 'introduces' to us the father of the family as 'Jacob' thus:

- "And Dinah the daughter of Leah whom she bore to **Jacob**…" (34:1),
- "And his soul was drawn to Dinah the daughter of **Jacob**…" (34:3),
- "And **Jacob** heard…" (34:5),
- "…and **Jacob** held his peace…" (34:5), and
- "And Hamor the father of Shechem came out to **Jacob**…" (34:6).

However, the 'men' do not talk about the daughter of 'Jacob,' but of 'Israel.' The change of name from 'Jacob' to 'Israel' took place for first time during the struggle with the angel at night (32:28). The Almighty appears to Jacob after the events with Dinah and Shechem, and informs him, again, of the change of name (35:10). The men's words are the first time, after the struggle with the angel, that the concept of 'Israel' is expressed **during an event**. [See the title 'the children of Israel' in regard to the "sinew of the vein" (32:33).] The use of 'Israel' in the men's words indicates that while Jacob saw the event as a 'private' one, a father whose daughter was kidnapped by a local ruler, the 'men' tell him that it is not a **private** event ('Jacob'), but a **national** event ('Israel').

And the text continues,

"And Hamor talked with (*et*) **them** saying…" (34:8).

At this stage, the language of the text tells us that Hamor addresses them, Jacob and his sons, as one united group – 'them.'

Hamor's Offer

"…**Shechem my son,** his soul desires your daughter
please give her to him for a wife" (34:8).

As we saw in the order of the 'social introduction,' we find that the text quotes Hamor using the formal language formula of 'name + title.'

"…Shechem my son, **his soul desires** your daughter
please give her to him for a wife" (34:8).

As we saw earlier in our linguistic journey into love in Biblical language, the combination of 'soul' (*nefesh*) and 'desire' (*chashka*) indicates danger, and even a life-threatening situation.

"…Shechem my son, his soul desires your daughter
please **give** her to him for a wife" (34:8).

As we saw earlier in our linguistic journey into trade and commerce in Biblical language, the verb 'to give' is in use for a commercial transaction. When Abraham's slave addresses Rebecca's family, he does not use the verb 'to give' but the verb 'to take' (24:48). When Rebecca's family answers the slave they also use the verb 'to take' (24:51). The verb 'to give' is not in use in the description of the negotiations between Abraham's slave and Rebecca's family. Shechem's father addresses Jacob using the verb 'to give,' using commercial language, cheapening the situation.

And the text continues Hamor's offer to Jacob,

"And you shall live with us, and the land shall be before you,
settle, trade in it, and possess there" (34:10).

If we remember the purchase of the Cave of the Patriarchs by Abraham from Ephron the Hittite, then we realize the purchase of land, unlike receiving it as a gift, granted the purchaser the rights of a resident, including the right to bury his dead. If so, the text already informed us, before the account of Dinah being taken into Shechem, that Jacob purchased "a parcel of the field where he had spread his tent, from the hand of the sons of Hamor, Shechem's father..." (33:19). This purchase meant that Jacob and his family were not only residents of the place but also landowners. Moreover, they purchased the land from the same Hamor who now offers them to settle in the place. Actually, Hamor offers Jacob and his sons the same thing they already received by the earlier purchase. **In other words, Hamor does not offer them anything.**

At this stage, the text does not say anything about the reaction of Jacob and his sons to Hamor's offer. It will be safe to assume that their reaction was not positive, since if it were positive Shechem himself didn't need to enter the conversation and to say what he had to say.

"And Shechem said **to her father and to her brothers**..." (34:11)

We should note the following points: First, when Hamor said his words, the text says that he talked to 'them,' meaning, as one unit. Here, on the other hand, the text says that Shechem speaks to 'her father and her brothers' – two different entities – there is a split in the family. The family is not acting here with a united front.

Second, the fact that the father is mentioned before the brothers might be due to politeness, but it might also be due to the fact that Jacob was willing to agree while the brothers were not.

Third, the text says that Shechem talked to "her father and **her brothers**" and not to "her father and **his sons**." The sons are perceived as Dinah's brothers, and not as Jacob's sons.

The words of Shechem were, "Let me find grace in your eyes and what you shall say to me I will give. Ask me ever so much as dowry and gift, and I will give according as you shall say to me, but give me the lass for a wife" (34:11-12).

Note what Shechem does not say in his words. He does not say that he wants Dinah because of his love for her. Shechem talks only about money – 'dowry and gift.'

Compare Shechem's behavior here to the behavior of Abraham's slave who asks Rebecca's hand from her family, and even Jacob's behavior when he asked Rachel's hand from her father Laban.

The text says about Abraham's slave, "And it came to pass as the camels finished drinking that the man took a golden ear ring of half a shekel weight, and two bracelets for her hands of ten shekels weight of gold" (24:22). Abraham's slave gives Rebecca great gifts, even before he talks with her to find her identity, and definitely before talking to her family. Jacob, since he was penniless, came to Laban and offered, "I will serve you seven years for Rachel your little daughter" (29:18). Neither Abraham's slave nor Jacob say, "Ask me ever so much as dowry and gift." Such an offer turns the marriage contract into a simple commercial transaction and diminishes its importance. Although it is clear to all, and it is true even today in very conservative societies in the Middle East, that the father expects the bridegroom to 'pay' for the daughter, still, nobody calls the spade a spade. Shechem's offer was insulting. It would have been interesting to know how the events would have developed if Shechem hadn't opened his mouth, and had left the stage to his father.

After Hamor's offer the text doesn't tell us the family's exact reaction, but after Shechem's words the family reacted, "And **the sons of Jacob** answered Shechem and Hamor his father deceitfully…" (34:13).

We should note two points of language. First, when they came from the field they were 'the sons of Jacob.' When they are 'grieved' they are described as 'men.' Now, they are returning to be 'the sons of Jacob.' The fact that they received this title by the language of the text should tell us that at this point of time Jacob and his sons were with one mind for the planned move ahead. We can see confirmation of this united front in their words:

"We cannot do this thing, to give **our sister** to one who is uncircumcised, for that would be a reproach to us. But in this will we consent to you. If you will be as we are, that every male of you be circumcised. Then we will give our daughters to you, and we will take your daughters for us, and we will settle with you, and we will become one people. But if you will not listen to us, to be circumcised, then we will take **our daughter**, and we will be gone" (34:14-17).

The message starts with 'our sister,' which fits 'the sons of Jacob' as the ones who are doing the talking. But the message ends with 'our daughter,' a title that can only refer to Dinah at that point of time, and such a title fits only Jacob.

The second point is that the text says, "And the sons of Jacob answered **Shechem and Hamor his father**…" (34:13), listing Shechem before his father. By doing so, the text comes to tell us that the answer they gave was addressed first and most of all to Shechem. His father Hamor, was relegated to second place and with secondary importance.

The Retaliation

"And it came to pass on the third day, when they were hurting, that two of the sons of Jacob, Simeon and Levi, brothers of Dinah, took each man his sword, and came upon the city boldly and slew all males" (34:25).

Here, we face a split 'social introduction,' using a formula of title ('the sons of Jacob') + name ('Simeon and Levi') + title ('the brothers of Dinah'). Such a formula might indicate different objectives, when the primary one is 'the sons of Jacob,' and the secondary one 'the brothers of Dinah,' secondary as this title is listed last.

If the attack by Simeon and Levi was with them being 'the sons of Jacob,' what was the reason for Jacob's grievance against them later on?

If we read the description of the attack, we can see that there were two stages to it. First, "…and came upon the city boldly and slew all males. And they slew Hamor and Shechem his son with the edge of the sword, and took Dinah out of Shechem's house and went out" (34:25-26). In this part of the attack the brothers rescue Dinah and they come out of Shechem's house.

But there is a second part to the attack, and this part starts with the title 'the sons of Jacob.' No more 'Simeon and Levi the brothers of Dinah.' Only 'the sons of Jacob' – Dinah was rescued and out of danger.

The second part was,

The sons of Jacob came upon the slain and plundered the city because they had defiled their sister. They took their sheep, their oxen, and their asses, and that which was in the city and that which was in the field. And all their wealth and all their little ones and their wives they took captive, and carried off all that was in the houses. (34:27-29)

This part of the attack did not relate to the rescue of Dinah. This part describes plundering and looting for the sake of revenge ("...because they had defiled their sister"). For this part Jacob complained:

"...You have **shamed me** (*AACHaRtem oti*) to make me odious among the inhabitants of the land, among the Canaanites and the Perizzites..." (34:30).

The verb *la'AA-Ch-oR* appears in the Torah only once, in Jacob's complaint to his sons. The next time we encounter this verb is in the case of Achan the son of Carmi who committed trespass[84] in regard to the devoted property..." (Joshua 7:1). His behavior brought about the defeat in the battle at Ai. The text quotes Joshua who says, "What great shame you brought upon us (*AACHaRtanu*), the Lord will shame you (*yAACHeRcha*) this day..." (7:25). The text continues, "Therefore he called the name of the place the Valley of *AAChoR* to this day" (7:26).

When Jacob accuses his sons Simeon and Levi saying '*AACHaRtem* me' he talks about the plundering and the looting that took place in Shechem. No different from the looting of Achan the son of Carmi many generations later on.

"...You have shamed me **to make me odious** (*lehavyisheni*) among the inhabitants of the land, among the Canaanites and the Perizzites..." (Genesis 34:30).

The verb *B-A-SH* appears three times in Exodus in the context of the rotten stinking smell of dead animals. After the plague of blood, "And the fish that is in the river shall die and the river shall stink (*bash*)..." (Exodus 7:18, 21) After the plague of the frogs, "And they gathered them together upon heaps and the land stank (*vativash*)" (8:10). And in regard to the

---

[84] The word in Hebrew for 'trespass' is *maal*. In Modern Hebrew this word means 'embezzlement,' theft by an employee who is in charge of property.

manna in the desert, "…but some of them left of it until the morning and it bred worms and stank (*vayivash*) (16:20).

We find the verb *le'avish* in the meaning of losing good name and/or reputation in the eyes of someone. For example, the elders of Israel accuse Moses and Aaron of the deterioration in the situation after Moses and Aaron talked to Pharaoh, "…because you have made us loathsome (*hivashtem et recheinu*[85]) in the eyes of Pharaoh…" (5:21). When David reports to Achish the King of Gat on his attacks on the Canaanites as attacks on the Israelites, the king is quoted as saying, "And Achish believed David saying, he has made himself completely loathsome (*havesh hivish*) to his people to Israel…" (1 Samuel 27:12). Ahitophel advises Absalom, David's son, during the revolt against King David, "…come to your father's concubines, whom he has left to keep the house, and all Israel shall hear that you have made yourself odious (*nivashta*) to your father…" (2 Samuel 16:21).

Since the second phase of the attack on Shechem starts with, "The sons of Jacob came upon **the slain**…" (Genesis 34:27), we should take the combination of the two verbs, *la'aachor* and *le'avish* to relate to the fact that the sons of Jacob raided the dead bodies to take all the valuables that were on them. It was not the attack on Shechem to rescue Dinah that was Jacob's complaint. After all, it is quite likely that he was in favor of launching this attack. It was the fact that the two sons didn't even mind making themselves stink by touching the dead bodies after they killed them.

'The Sons of Jacob'

The report about the attack on Shechem ends with, "…and the fear of G-d was upon the cities that were around them, and they did not pursue after **the sons of Jacob**" (35:5).

'The sons of Jacob' are mentioned again after the death of Rachel, and after the brief mention of Reuben sleeping with Bilhah, his father's concubine. The text counts the verse with, "…and Israel heard and **the sons of Jacob** were twelve" (35:22).

---

[85] *[H]ivashtem et recheinu – Re-ach* in Hebrew is 'smell.' Literally, the phrase means "you made our smell stink." One should note that the phrase should not be taken literally, as the verse continues, "…you made our **smell stink in the eyes** of…" Of course, 'the eyes of' does not mean 'eyes' literally, but more 'the perception of.' The word 'eyes' and 'to see' will be dealt with in a later analysis.

'The Sons of Jacob' and Joseph

The text starts the narrative about Joseph with, "These are the *toldot* of Jacob, Joseph…" (Genesis 37:2). Thus the picture changes in regard to 'the sons of Jacob.' The linguistic lens focuses on Joseph, and as a result 'the sons of Jacob' are presented in the text as 'Joseph's brothers.'

- "…he was the shepherd of **his brothers** with the sheep…" (37:2),
- "And **his brothers** saw that their father loved him more than all **his brothers**…" (37:4)
- "And Joseph dreamed a dream and he told it to **his brothers**…" (37:5)
- "And **his brothers** said to him…" (37:8)
- "And he dreamed another dream and told it to **his brothers**…" (37:9)
- "And he told it to his father and to **his brothers**…" (37:10)
- "And **his brothers** envied him…" (37:11)
- "And **his brothers** went…" (37:12)
- "…are not **your brothers** shepherding in Shechem…" (37:13)
- "…go please see whether it is well with **your bothers**…" (37:14)
- "And he said I seek **my brothers**…" (37:16)
- "…and Joseph went after **his brothers**…" (37:17)
- "And it came to pass when Joseph came to **his brothers**…" (37:23)

The Linguistic Lens – Judah and Reuben

When Joseph is already in the pit and awaits his fate, the text says, "And Judah said to **his brothers**…" (37:26). At this point, the linguistic lens moves to focus on Judah for a little bit, when Judah suggests selling Joseph to slavery instead of killing him, "And **his brothers** [Judah's] listened to him" (37:27).

When Reuben returns to the pit and finds out that Joseph is missing, the linguistic lens moves to focus on Reuben, "And he returned to **his brothers**…" (37:30).

We should note that there are three sons that the linguistic lens focuses on. The first is Joseph, and the majority of the narrative is written from his perspective. However, there are two more sons that the linguistic lens focuses on – Judah (twice) and Reuben (once). This focus of the lens will have great importance later on.

Once Joseph is sold to the Egyptian Potiphar, the text takes a detour, leaves Joseph aside for a while, and moves to tell us about Judah and Tamar, and the birth of Peretz and Zerach. And the detour involving Judah starts with, "And it came to pass at that time that Judah went down from **his brothers**…" (Genesis 38:1), and the linguistic lens describes 'the sons of Jacob' as 'Judah's brothers.'

'The Sons of Jacob'

Time passes, and after Joseph's rise to power in managing the grain during the seven years of plenty, famine comes to the land, and the text returns to tell us about 'the sons of Jacob,' saying, "When Jacob saw that there was grain in Egypt, Jacob said to **his sons**…" (42:1).

And the text continues, "And Joseph's ten brothers went down…" (42:3), and, again, the text moves to focus on Joseph when they go down to Egypt. However, when they arrive in Egypt, the text says, "And the sons of **Israel** came to buy grain among those who came…" (42:5).

This is the first time in Genesis that 'the sons of Jacob' are labeled 'the sons of Israel,' as they will be called later on during their time in Egypt. Their arrival in Egypt brings the language of the text to change the title and to look upon them in a **national** way and not in a **private** one, as 'the sons of Jacob.'

And the text continues, "…and Joseph's brothers came…" (42:6), "And Joseph saw his brothers…" (42:7), and "And Joseph recognized his brothers…" (42:8). And the text continues with Joseph demanding to bring Benjamin to him, arresting Simeon, and sending the brothers back to Canaan with food, the money for the food having been sneaked back into their food bags.

Reuben's Conversation With Jacob

During the discussion with their father Jacob about taking Benjamin with them, Reuben said, "Slay my two sons if I bring him not to you, give him to me and I will return him to you" (42:37).

Many wonder: what is the logic in killing Reuben's two sons that might bring Jacob to give him Benjamin? Is not enough for Jacob to have already suffered the loss of one son (Joseph), the imprisonment of another son in a foreign country (Simeon), and the concern of losing the only son left from his beloved wife Rachel, that killing two grandsons would persuade him to give Benjamin? What is the logic that Reuben applies? In order to answer this question we need to go back in time and deal with two important events in Jacob's life: first, the death of Rachel, and second, the incident in which Reuben slept with Bilhah, his father's concubine.

Linguistic Journey – Mourning in the Tanach

There are several places in the Biblical text where the loss of a dear one is described. First is Cain killing his brother Abel. The text does not tell us how the parents reacted to this loss. However, later on in the text, we find the following, "And Adam knew his wife again, and she bore a son, and called his name Seth, for G-d has appointed another seed instead of Abel, whom Cain slew" (Genesis 4:25). Eve missed Abel, and once she got another son, she saw him as a substitute for the one she lost.

The next instance is Abraham dealing with his wife Sarah's death. The text says, "And Sarah died in Kiriath-Arba which in Hebron in the land of Canaan and Abraham came to mourn for Sarah and to weep (*livkotah*) for her" (Genesis 23:2). This is the first time we find 'crying' as an act of mourning.

The text does not tell us that Abraham was comforted after Sarah's death, but it says, "And Abraham continued and he took a wife and her name was Keturah" (25:1).

The next one who had to deal with the loss of a dear one is Isaac, who mourned for his mother. The text says, "And Isaac brought her [Rebecca] to the tent of Sarah his mother, and he took Rebecca, and she became a wife to him, and he loved her, and Isaac was **comforted** after his mother's death" (24:67).

The next one is Jacob mourning for the loss of his son Joseph. The text says, "And Jacob tore his clothes, and put sackcloth upon his waist, and mourned for his son many days. And all his sons and all his daughters rose up to comfort him **and he refused to be comforted** and his father wept for him" (37:34-35).

Here, we find more than 'crying.' First, we find the tearing of the clothes, and then second, putting sackcloth upon his waist. We also find the act of relatives coming to comfort the bereaving father, who in this case, refused to be comforted. And at last, we find the act of crying by 'his father.' It is a point to note that the text says "his father," and if the title 'his father' means Isaac, then we have a problem with the sequence of events, as the text mentions that Isaac died two chapters earlier, "And Isaac expired and died…" (Genesis 35:29). It is more likely that 'his father' refers to Jacob himself, being the father of Joseph, and the 'his' means 'Joseph's.'

The next one mentioned dealing with a loss is Judah, losing his first wife. The text says, "And in the process of time the daughter of Shuah, Judah's wife, died, and Judah was **comforted**…" (Genesis 38:12).

We should not be surprised that Judah got comforted so quickly after his wife's death. The relationship between them had deteriorated very quickly, right after the wedding. The text says, "And she conceived and bore a son and **he** called his name Er. And she conceived again and bore a son and **she** called him Onan. And she conceived again and bore a son and **she** called his name Shelah, **and he was at Kezib when she bore him**" (38:3-5).

The change in pronouns testifies to the rapid deterioration. With the firstborn, **he** (Judah) called him the name. With the second, **she** called him the name. With the third, not only did **she** call him the name, but Judah was not even there for the birth. He was in Kezib; the text goes out of his way to emphasize Judah's absence.

Even when she died, we should note that the text lists her title as "the daughter of Shuah" first, and only second, the fact that she was Judah's wife. So, Judah got comforted quickly, and the text continues, "…and Judah was comforted and went up to his sheep shearers in Timnath…" (38:12). Knowing that the annual event of shearing the sheep was a major event in the life of shepherds, equivalent today to the state fair in the summer or fall, one realizes why the text specifies this fact; Judah didn't even mourn for his wife.

Judah also lost his two sons who died. The text does not say anything about Judah's mourning for them. Still, Judah's behavior after the death of his two sons indicates that he was affected by it. The text says that after they died, regarding his third son Shelah, Judah told the widow Tamar to go back to her father's house, "...for he said, lest perhaps he die also, as his brothers did" (38:11).

The next one to lose two sons is Aaron who lost his two oldest sons by fire. The text says that Moses says to Aaron upon their death, "This is what the Lord spoke saying I will be sanctified by my *kerovai*,[86] and before all the people I will be weighed..." (Leviticus 10:3). These words of Moses are an attempt to comfort Aaron. And the text brings us Aaron response, "And Aaron held his peace" (10:3).

Can we assume that Aaron did not mourn for his two dead sons? Continuing the text, we realize that Aaron, the public figure, had to deal differently with his private disaster. The text says, "And Moses said to Aaron and to Eleazar and Ithamar his sons, uncover not your heads, nor tear your clothes..." (10:6). And the text continues, "...and let your brothers the whole house of Israel **cry**..." (10:6).

And here we find, again, the tearing of the clothes and crying as acts of mourning. For Aaron and his sons the priests, we also find the commandment not to uncover their heads, as their hats were part of their uniforms.

And later on, when Moses inquired why the sacrifice was not eaten by the priests, Aaron said, "...and such things have befallen me..." (10:19). Aaron defended his decision not to eat the sacrifice by saying that he is mourning due to the "such things" that had befallen him.

Crying as an act of mourning is found also in public mourning. When Jacob died, the text says, "...and the Egyptians cried for him seventy days" (Genesis 50:3). When Aaron and Moses died, the text says, for Aaron, "And all the congregation saw that Aaron died, they **cried** for Aaron thirty days, all the house of Israel" (Numbers 20:29). For Moses, "And the people of Israel **cried** for Moses in the plains of Moab thirty days..." (Deuteronomy 34:8).

---

[86] [K]erovai – the word karov means 'near'/'close.' In Modern Hebrew the word karov means 'relative.' Literally, the text says, 'I will be sanctified by those who are **close/near** to me...'

Jacob's Mourning for Rachel's Death

Unlike all the others mentioned, for whom the text attributes the act of 'crying,' we find out that the text does not mention 'crying' by Jacob for the loss of Rachel. On the other hand, the text does not say that Jacob was 'comforted' as Judah was, nor does the text say that Jacob was 'not comforted' as with the loss of Joseph. At least by the content, it seems we are at a loss to find out Jacob's emotions towards the loss of Rachel.

Even without mentioning 'crying' or being 'comforted'/'not comforted,' the text, in two places, gives us an accurate picture of Jacob's mourning.

"And Rachel died, and was buried in the way of Ephrath, which is Beth-Lehem. And Jacob set a pillar (*matzevah*) upon her grave, that is the pillar of Rachel's grave to this day" (Genesis 35:19-20).

Setting up a *matzevah* is very significant act. There are three other places in which the text says that Jacob set up a *matzevah*. The first is after the Almighty talks with him and promises him he will be with him wherever he goes, and will bring him to safety. Jacob's reaction is quoted as, "How awesome is this place! This is no other but the house of G-d, and this is the gate of heaven" (28:17). The text continues by saying that Jacob "…took the stone that he had put under his head, and set it up for a *matzevah*…" (28:18). The second place is where Jacob set up a *matzevah* when he made the pact with Laban (31:45). The third place is when the Almighty appears to Jacob, changes his name, and promises him and his seed the land. "And Jacob set up a *matzevah* in the place where he talked with him, a *matzevah* of stone…" (35:14). From these examples we can see that the *matzevah* is made for remembrance and for worship.

We find that before going up the mountain for 40 days, Moses built an altar and a *matzevah*, "And Moses wrote all the words of the Lord and rose up early in the morning and built an altar under the mountain, and twelve *matzevah* to the twelve tribes of Israel" (Exodus 24:4).

We find several times the commandment to break the *matzevot* of the other nations,

- "…and break down their *matzevoteiem*" (Exodus 23:24),

- "But you shall destroy their altars and break their *matzevotam*..." (34:13),
- "...and you shall break their *matzevotam*..." (Deuteronomy 7:5), and
- "...and break their *matzevotam*..." (12:3).

The prohibition to set up a *matzevah* is also repeated,

- "You shall not make for yourselves idols, nor a statue, and you shall not set up a *matzevah* for yourselves (Leviticus 26:1), and
- "And you shall not set up a *matzevah* which the Lord your G-d hates" (Deuteronomy 16:22).

"And Jacob set a *matzevah* upon her grave, that is the *matzevah* of Rachel's grave to this day" (35:20).

'On Me'

In his conversation with Joseph, Jacob mentions the death of Rachel, Joseph's mother, "And as for me, when I came from Padan Rachel died **on me** (*alai*) in the land of Canaan in the way, when yet there was but a little way to come to Ephrath, and I buried her there in the way of Ephrath which is Beth-Lehem" (48:7).

In all the places where Jacob uses the word *alai* ('on me') it is the context of a curse. Jacob says to Rebecca, "My father perhaps will feel me and I shall seem to him as a deceiver, and I shall bring a curse on me (*alai*) and not a blessing" (27:12). Rebecca answered, "On me (*alai*) be your curse..." (27:13).

Later on, Jacob uses the word *alai* when he reprimands Simeon and Levi for their behavior during the attack on Shechem, "...and they shall gather together *alai* ('on me') and slay me and I shall be destroyed, I and my house" (34:30).

And when Jacob expresses total despair when talking to his sons who want Benjamin to go with them to Egypt, "...me have you bereaved, Joseph is not, and Simeon is not, and you will take Benjamin, all of these are *alai* ('on me')" (42:36).

Joseph also uses the word *alai* in the context of evil, "But as for you, you thought *alai* ('on me') evil, but G-d meant it to good..." (50:20).

Abimelech, when talking to Abraham, complaining about him not saying that Sarah was his wife, "...what have you done to us? And in what have I offended you that you have brought *alai* ('on me') and on my kingdom a great sin?" (20:9).

And the word *alai* appears also in the context of payment. Laban says to Jacob, "Appoint your wages *alai* ('on me') and I will give" (30:28). Shechem when speaking to Jacob and his sons, asking them to give him Dinah, says, "Make *alai* ('on me') a lot dowry and gift and I will give according as you shall say to me..." (34:12).

When Jacob says to Joseph, "And as for me, when I came from Padan Rachel died **on me** (*alai*) in the land of Canaan..." (48:7), it is quite likely that Jacob **blamed himself** for her death due to the curse he put on her unwittingly. When Laban complained that Jacob stole his idols, Jacob said, "With whom you will find your gods, let him not live. Before our brothers point out what is yours with me and take it with you. And Jacob did not know that Rachel had stolen them" (31:32). This curse pursued him the rest of his life; "...Rachel died **on me**..." Not only did he lose his beloved wife, but he also understood that her death was a 'payment' for his words to Laban at the time of the search for the stolen idols. The setting up of the *matzevah*, quite likely, allowed Jacob to be alone with his mourning, and with his part in Rachel's death.

This heavy mourning by Jacob for Rachel's death had an immediate impact on Jacob's ability to lead the family. The text says, "And Israel traveled[87] and spread his tent beyond the Tower (*migdal*) of herd (*eder*) (Genesis 35:21).

"And Israel traveled..."

This is the first time in the text in which the narrator uses the new name 'Israel' for Jacob. The change of the name by the Almighty (not by the angel earlier) took place after the attack on Shechem, "And G-d said to him, your name is Jacob; your name shall not be called any more Jacob, but Israel shall be your name..." (Genesis 35:10).

---

[87] "...traveled..." – this verb *linsoaa* is often translated 'to journey.' Here we use 'to travel.'

We saw earlier that Jacob's sons used the name 'Israel' when they express their anger about what happened to Dinah: "And the sons of Jacob came from the field when they heard it, and the men were grieved and they were very angry because he had done an evil in **Israel** in lying with Jacob's daughter…" (Genesis 34:7). In this instance we find the use of 'Jacob' and 'Israel' in the same verse, to indicate that Jacob acted as a **private** man while his sons ('the men') were thinking on the **national** level.

However, once Jacob built the *matzevah* on Rachel's grave, an act described using his old (personal) name Jacob, the text moves to relate to his activity thereafter, "And **Israel** traveled…" using his **national** name.

"And Israel traveled…"

Linguistic Journey – Traveling in Genesis

There are many travels mentioned in the book of Genesis. However, in the language of the text, the verb 'to travel' (*linsoaa* with the root *N-S-AA*) is rarely used. Instead, the text prefers to use mostly the verb 'to go' (*lalechet*[88]), and some other verbs which are more intent oriented, like to 'run away,' 'to pursue,' 'to pass,' among others.

If anyone should get an Olympic medal for traveling, Abraham should. Starting with the Almighty saying to him to "…**go** for yourself from your country…" (12:1). The text says, "And Abram **went** as the Lord spoken to him…" (Genesis 12:4). Later, the text says, "…and they **went** out to go to the land of Canaan and they came to the land of Canaan" (12:5). Then we see that the text says, "And Abram **passed** through the land…" (12:6). "And he **moved** from there to a mountain…" (12:8).

Even when Abraham is forced to go to Egypt due to the heavy famine, the text says, "…and Abram **went** down to Egypt…" (12:10), "And it came to pass when he **came near** to come to Egypt…" (12:11), "And it came to pass when Abram **came** to Egypt…" (12:14). Upon his return from Egypt, "And Abram **went** up from Egypt…" (13:1), "And he **went** on to his travels…" (13:3).

---

[88] *Lalechet* – this verb's original meaning is 'to walk,' but we use its broader practical meaning 'to go,' which is a very commonly used translation.

After the separation from Lot, the Almighty said to Abram, "Arise, **go** through the land…" (13:17), and, "And Abram packed up his tent and he **came** and settled in the plain of Mamre…" (13:18).

When Abram chased Lot's captors, the text says, "and he **pursued** them to Dan" (14:14).

When the Almighty ordered Abraham to take his son Isaac to Mount Moriah and put him on the altar, the text says, "…and rose up and **went** to the place of which G-d had told him" (22:3).

There are only two places in Abraham's life in which the language of the text attributes to him the verb 'to travel.' This is a ratio of 8 times 'go' or 'went' (plus some other intent-oriented verbs) as compared to only twice 'traveled.'

First, upon his arrival in Canaan, the text says, "And Abram **traveled going and traveling** towards the Negev" (12:9). We should note that the text starts with using the verb 'travel' and then moves on to elaborate and to say that he was both 'going and traveling.'

SCAN Rule: Change of language reflects a change in reality.

Language does not change without a reason. Since the language of the text uses both verbs, the text comes to tell us that "going" is not "traveling." The two of them were applicable to Abraham's situation in his traveling throughout the land of Canaan.

Question: What is the difference between the two verbs?

SCAN observation: Emotions are the engine behind most changes in language. When the reader/listener encounters a change in language, the reader/listener should take into consideration that quite likely the emotional dimension is behind the change of language.

Background information: Note that the structure in the human brain that stores long-term memory is also the center of emotions. This is the reason that people are advised, if they want to remember something, to attach some emotion to it. It is a fact that people in the U.S. recall the day of

9/11 very easily, and all the events of that day from morning to evening, as it was a very emotional day.

The second place where the text used the verb 'to travel' for Abraham is his going to the Philistine land controlled by Abimelech. The text says, "And Abraham **traveled** from there to the Negev and settled between Kadesh and Shur and resided[89] in Gerar" (20:1).

Is the verb 'to travel' in the second place due to what happened when Sarah was taken into Abimelech's palace? If so, why, when Abraham went down to Egypt and Sarah was taken to Pharaoh's palace, doesn't the text use the same verb 'to travel?' Both places, Egypt and the Philistine land, fit the description that Abraham gives to Abimelech, "...because I thought surely the fear of G-d is not in this place..." (20:11). There was no fear of G-d in Egypt, and yet Abraham's going down to Egypt is not described as 'traveling.'

Is it possible that the verb 'to travel' found in the language of the text is due to what happened **before** that in the text? After all, the sequence of events before this second use of 'travel' brings us the sexual relations between Lot and his two daughters, and they bore sons to their father Lot. Is it possible that the language of the text exposes the fact that this event was too much for Abraham, and therefore, he had to distance himself from the land of Canaan?

And if this is the case, then the first place where the text says that Abraham 'went and traveled' – the two verbs at the same time – tells us that 'going' is a neutral verb while 'traveling' is a verb with a negative connotation.

What was the reason that brought the text to use the two verbs – 'to travel' and 'to go' at the same time? It has to be something that happened before the text uses these two verbs.

When the text says, "And Abram **passed** through the land..." (12:6), the text adds, "...and the Canaanite was then in the land" (12:6). Right after this statement of fact (that the Canaanite was then in the land), the text brings us the Almighty's promise to Abraham. "...to your seed will I give this land..." (12:7). It is quite likely that Abraham looked for a place to

---

[89] Resided – this word is often translated 'sojourned' from the Hebrew verb *lagur*.

settle. But it was not that simple. The Canaanites didn't welcome the foreigner who just showed up from afar. And it is quite likely that there were people in places that expelled Abraham from their midst. This is the reason that the Almighty is telling Abraham, 'It is not easy for you as a new immigrant, but you should know that it will be easier for your offspring.' Abraham thanks the Almighty for this promise by building an altar "…to the Lord who appeared to him" (12:7). But still, Abraham does not have a place to settle, "And he moved from there to a mountain…" (12:8), and again, Abraham builds an altar, "…and called upon the name of the Lord" (12:8). Here comes the text to summarize it for us, in its language, "And Abraham **traveled** and **went** to the Negev" (12:9). There were 'ups and downs' upon arrival at the land of Canaan. The absorption of the new immigrant didn't happen easily. There were some places that accepted Abraham better than other places, but Abraham still had to be a nomad – 'traveling and going.'

Isaac

Unlike Abraham, where we find the verb 'to travel' twice, Isaac did not 'travel,' at least not in the language of the text, although in reality he did.

When there was a famine in Isaac's time, the text says, "…and Isaac **went** to Abimelech king of the Philistines to Gerar" (26:1). When Isaac left Gerar the text says, "And Isaac **went** from there…" (26:17).

Jacob

Among the three forefathers – Abraham, Isaac, and Jacob – Jacob also does his share of 'traveling,' according to the language of the text. Suspecting now that the verb 'to travel' indicates some negativity, we can connect it to Jacob's words to Pharaoh, the king of Egypt, "…few and evil have the days of the years of my life been…" (Genesis 47:9).

After Jacob receives the blessing from his father Isaac while pretending to be his brother Esau, his mother Rebecca tells Jacob to run away. The text quotes Rebecca as saying, "…and arise, **flee** to Laban my brother to Haran" (27:43). We should note that it was a long trip, and even more dangerous to embark on such a trip by himself. However, on the way to Haran, and on the way back, some twenty years later, Jacob did not 'travel,' at least not in the **language** of the text.

When Jacob goes to Haran, the text says, "And Jacob **went** out from Beersheba and **went** to Haran" (28:10). After his dream with the ladder of the angels, and his encounter with the Almighty, the text says, "And Jacob picked up his feet and **went** to the land of the people of the east" (29:1). When Jacob started his way back from Haran to Canaan, the text says, "And he **fled** with all that he had, and he rose up and crossed the river and set his face to the Mount Gilead" (31:21). After his encounter with Laban, the text says that Laban, "...kissed his sons and his daughters and blessed them, and Laban **went** and returned to his place" (32:1). As for Jacob, "And Jacob **went** on his way..." (32:2).

After the encounter with brother Esau, the text says that, "...Esau **returned** that day to his way to Seir" (33:16). And as for Jacob, "And Jacob **traveled** to Succoth..." (33:17). And then, "And Jacob **came** to Shalem..." (33:18).

We find the verb 'traveled' right after Jacob's encounter with his brother Esau. Again, we see that quite likely it is what happened **before** the verb is used that causes the verb to show up in the language of the text. No different from Abraham 'traveling' after Lot's daughters had sons by having sexual relations with their father.

This explanation of the verb 'to travel' (negative feelings; wanting to get away from what happened before) also comes into play after the attack on Shechem, when the Almighty instructs Jacob to build an altar for him. The text says, "And they **traveled** and the terror of G-d was upon the cities that were around them, and they did not pursue after the sons of Jacob" (35:5).

But the verb 'to travel' does not enter immediately after the attack on Shechem; instead the Almighty told Jacob to build an altar at Beth-El. And in response, Jacob collected all the idols from his household, and buried them "under the oak which was by Shechem" (35:4). **Then** "they traveled..." This proximity of the verb 'to travel' coming right after burying the idols, should bring us to wonder if the sensitivity before the 'travel' (in the language) is caused not by the attack on Shechem, but by the burying of the idols. If so, what is there in this event that would cause this negativity, and the desire to distance himself?

The next time the verb 'to travel' appears is right after the appearance of the Almighty to Jacob, changing his name from Jacob to Israel, and promising the land to him and to his sons thereafter. Jacob built a *matzevah*, "…and he poured a drink offering on it and he poured oil on it. And Jacob called the name of the place where G-d spoke with (*et*) him there Beth-El" (35:14-15).

Immediately after, the text says, "And they **traveled** from Beth-El, and there was but a little way to come to Ephrath and Rachel labored and she had difficult labor" (35:16).

Both burying the idols in Shechem, and building the *matzevah* in Beth-El caused the verb 'to travel' to appear. We will deal with this point later on in this analysis, in the section dealing with the names of the Almighty used in the Tanach.

Not surprisingly, after the death of Rachel the text says, "And Israel **traveled** and spread his tent beyond the Tower (*migdal*) of herd (*eder*) (35:21). We can conclude that the use of the verb 'traveled' comes to reflect the trauma Jacob experienced after Rachel's death.

Later on in the text, when Esau leaves the land of Canaan and goes away from Jacob, the text says, "…and he **went** to another country away from his brother Jacob" (36:6).

Jacob's Sons

When the brothers go down to Egypt to buy food, the text says, "And Joseph's ten brothers **went** down to buy grain in Egypt" (42:3). When they go back to Canaan, "…and they **went** from there" (42:26). When Jacob gives permission for Benjamin to join the brothers, the text says, "…and they rose, and they **went** down to Egypt…" (43:15). When Joseph orders that his cup be put in Benjamin's food-bag, the text says, "They **came out** of the city and not yet far off…" (44:4). And once the cup was found in Benjamin's food-bag, "…they **returned** to the city" (44:13). When Joseph tells his brothers to go back to Canaan and bring their father to Egypt, Joseph says, "**Hurry back** to my father…" (45:9), "And he sent his brothers and they **went**…" (45:24). "And they **went** up from Egypt and they came to the land of Canaan to Jacob their father" (45:25).

For the funeral procession from Egypt to Canaan the text says, "And Joseph **went** up to bury his father…" (50:7), "…and with him **went** up all the servants…" (50:7), and after the burial, "And Joseph **returned** to Egypt…" (50:14).

The verb 'to travel' appears in the events dealing with Joseph and his brothers in the following places:

When Joseph was on his way to seek his brothers, per his father's direction, he met a man on the way. He asked the man if he knew where his brothers were. The man's answer was, "…they have **traveled** from here for I heard them say, let us **go** to Dothan, and Joseph **went** after his brothers…" (37:17).

Note that the man describes them going by using the verb 'to travel' while the man quoted the brothers as saying, "…let us **go** to Dothan…" Should we conclude that the man saw something wrong going on with the brothers, even if the brothers themselves did not see anything wrong?

It is no surprise the verb 'to travel' appears when Jacob goes down to Egypt to meet Joseph. The text says, "And **Israel traveled** with all that he had…" (46:1). We should note that here the language of the text uses the national name of Jacob – Israel – and not his private name – Jacob.

If we had any doubt that this is not a coincidence, the text continues a few verses later saying, "And **Jacob** rose up from Beersheba and **the sons of Israel carried Jacob** their father…" (46:5). While the sons were 'the sons of Israel,' Israel himself was 'Jacob.' They were a national unit, while he was just the private person.

Beersheba was the turning point. After Beersheba Jacob is 'Jacob' a private man, while his sons are 'the sons of **Israel**.' The language of the text tells us that Jacob returned to be a private man, while his sons are rising to the stage of history on their way to become a people, the sons of Israel, a term used extensively thereafter in the Tanach to relate to the nation of the Israelites.

Back to Jacob after Rachel's death

> "And Israel traveled *vayet* his tent…" (Genesis 35:21).

Two additional places give us the meaning of the verb *vayet*. Both of them appear in the account of Judah and Tamar, "And it came to pass at that time that Judah went down from his brothers and turned in (*vayet*) to an Adullamite man whose name was Hirah" (38:1). And when Judah met Tamar sitting on the side of the road, "And he turned in (*vayet*) to her to the road…" (38:16).

When Judah 'went down' from his brothers he actually leaves them (*vayet*) and he connects himself to the Adullamite man. And when he diverts from the road upon which he traveled, and goes to talk with Tamar, he *vayet*.

It is quite likely that when the text says that Jacob traveled and *vayet* his tent that he did as Judah did later, leaving his brothers, or Judah leaving the road, and turning to the side to talk with Tamar. Jacob left the family and *vayet* his tent at some distance from them.

"…beyond (*mehalah*) the Tower (*migdal*) of herd (*eder*) (Genesis 35:21).

We should note that the text does not say the exact place that Jacob positioned his tent. From the text we only know the distance to a certain place, *Migdal Eder* (Tower of Herd). The word *halah* appears in Genesis in the account of Lot and the Angels in Sodom. When the people of Sodom surrounded the house, they said to Lot, "*Gesh halah*" (19:9). The word *gesh* is the command form of the verb *lageshet*, which means 'to get close to' and the word *halah* is 'away.' The people of Sodom said to Lot, 'get out of the way.'

In other books we see the word *halah*:

- "When a bull, or a sheep, or a goat, is born, then it shall be seven days with its mother, and from the eighth day and on (*vahalah*) it shall be accepted for an offering…" (Leviticus 22:27)
- "All that the Lord has commanded you by the hands of Moses, from the day that the Lord commanded Moses, and onward (*vahalah*) to your generations" (Numbers 15:23)
- "…and scatter the fire yonder (*halah*) for they are sanctified" (Numbers 17:2)

- "For we will not inherit with them on the other side of the Jordan and beyond (*vahalah*), because our inheritance has fallen to us on this east side of the Jordan" (Numbers 32:19)

In the rest of the Torah the word *halah* or *vehalah* is used in the context of distance – either time or place. We should note that in the text in regard to Jacob, "*mehalah* to the Tower of Herd," the word *halah* comes with the prefix *me* ('from'), a combination that appears twice in the Tanach, and in very late books.

- "He shall be buried with the burial of an ass, drawn and thrown out from beyond (***mehalah***) the gates of Jerusalem" (Jeremiah 22:19).
- "And I will cause you to go into exile from beyond (***mehalah***) Damascus, says the Lord…" (Amos 5:27).

In these two additional places where the word *mehalah* appears, it is in the context of burial (Jeremiah) and exile (Amos). And Jacob "…turned his tent from beyond (*mehalah*) to Migdal Eder." Jacob, in his very heavy mourning over Rachel's death, went to exile himself from the family, and practically buried himself in his grief.

Rachel's death was a devastating blow to Jacob, and he mourned heavily over her death, blaming himself for her death, due to his words to Laban that whoever took his idols should not live. This heavy mourning explains his behavior over the loss of Joseph, when his brothers sold Joseph to slavery. It is quite likely that Jacob was afraid that the curse that was put on Rachel was still projecting itself on Joseph. This also explains why he did his best to guard Benjamin, and not to let him go down to Egypt: "Me have you bereaved, Joseph is not, and Simeon is not, and you will take Benjamin, all of these are on me" (Genesis 42:36). Does 'all of these' refer also to Rachel?

Jacob himself summarized his life when he met Pharaoh:

And Jacob said to Pharaoh, the days of the years of my residence (*megurai*) are a hundred and thirty years, few and evil have the days of the years of my life have been, and have not attained to the days of the years of the life of my fathers in the days of their residence (*megureihem*). (Genesis 47:9)

Jacob's words sound more like a 'eulogy' than a 'summary of life.' While his father lived 180 years and his grandfather lived 175 years, Jacob notes that he lived only 130 years. The reader might wonder how Jacob can compare his age to the age of his two fathers. After all, he is still alive, and his life does not end then. After his present age of 130, he can still live another 50 years, and reach the age of his father. But Jacob does not see it this way. Jacob talks as if his life has ended. Not only that his years were 'few,' but also they are even 'evil.' Jacob talks as if he is a 'dead man walking.' Later on, we will see that it is not only Rachel's death that brought about this feeling.

The text continues to describe Jacob's situation after Rachel's death, "And it came to pass, when Israel **was present** (*biSHKoN*) in that land…" (35:22).

Realizing that the text refers to the national figure (Israel), the text says that Jacob, in his capacity as Israel was practically not present physically. He was 'present' and not 'settling' (*vayeshev*) or even 'residing' (*lagur*).

"…when Israel **was present** in that land…" (35:22)

Linguistic Journey – to Reside / to Live

The text in Genesis uses several verbs to describe the act of residing at a place.

The Verb *Lashevet*

First, the verb *lashevet* is from three-letter root word *Y-SH-V*.[90] Literally, it means 'to sit.' For example, "And the Lord appeared to him in the plains of Mamre and he was **sitting** (*YoSHeV*) at the entrance to the tent in the heat of the day"(18:1). Or, "And it shall be when he **sits** (*keShiVto*) upon the throne of his kingdom…" (Deuteronomy 17:18).

The common translation of the verb *lashevet* when it relates to 'residing' it is to use the English verb 'to live.' But we should be aware that in English the verb "to live" has two meanings, one, is to live life, and the second is to reside. In Biblical Hebrew there are two different verbs for each meaning. The meaning of 'to live life' is expressed by the verb *lichyot*,

---

[90] *Y-SH-V* – The 'V' is actually a 'B,' but it is a soft 'B,' pronounced as a 'V.'

which is from the three-letter root *CH-Y-H*, while the verb 'to reside' is expressed by the verb *lashevet*, 'to sit.' To distinguish the two meanings of 'live,' in this analysis we translate *lashevet* to 'settle,' which is closer in meaning to 'sit,' and still conveys the meaning of residing.

The discussion between Jacob and his sons and Shechem and his father Hamor in regard to the fate of Dinah, Jacob's daughter, after she was taken into Shechem, gives us the true meaning of the verb *lashevet*.

Jacob's sons "answered Shechem and Hamor his father deceitfully" (Genesis 34:13). Their offer was to ask the people of Shechem to circumcise, and only then would the family be able to merge with the people of Shechem through marriage, "...and we will settle (*veyaSHaVnu*) with (*et*) you and we will become one people" (34:16). We can see that the verb *lashevet* is used in the context of people residing in a place as part of the community, "...and we will become one people." And, indeed, when Hamor and Shechem talk to their own people, they are quoted as saying, "These men are peaceful with us, they will settle (*veyeSHVu*) in the land and trade in it..." (34:21), and "...let us take their daughters to us for wives and let us give them our daughters" (34:21).

It is quite likely that Biblical Hebrew used the verb 'to sit' to indicate 'residing with full rights,' as the metaphor of 'sitting' illustrates that the person is putting all his weight in the place he sits.

The Verb *Lagur* – 'to Reside'

If the verb *lashevet* means living as a citizen with full, equal rights as part of the community, then the verb *lagur* means something less.

That *lagur* is less than *lashevet* comes across in the words of the people of Sodom to Lot, when Lot hosted the two angels at his house, "...And they said, this one came in to reside (*lagur*) and he wants to be a judge..." (19:9). The people of Sodom say that one who lives only with the status of *lagur* cannot be a judge, a position that requires the status of a citizen with full rights and duties.

When there is a famine in the land, and Abraham is forced to go to Egypt, the text says, "...and Abram went down to Egypt to **reside** (*lagur*) there..." (12:10). Taking into consideration that Abraham was told by the

Almighty to go to the land of Canaan, then we should understand that the verb *lagur* connotes the meaning of residing in a place, but not as a citizen, and definitely not with equal rights. For example, the Israelites in slavery in Egypt are described as *GeRim*, for example, "You shall not wrong the *ger* nor oppress him for you were *gerim* in the land of Egypt" (Exodus 22:20). Or, "One law shall be both for you of the congregation and to the *ger* who **resides** with you..." (Numbers 15:15). Thus it is clear that the *ger* is not a 'member of the congregation.' It might help us understand the meaning of *ger* to know that in the Arabic of today the word *gar* means 'neighbor.'

Borrowing from the American terminology of today, the resident alien, one who is not a 'citizen' but has a permanent permit to reside in the country, without the right to vote, we will use the verb 'to reside' for the Biblical Hebrew word *lagur*.

'To Settle' vs. 'to Reside'

We know that time is not the factor that determines if someone *yoshev* ('settles') or *gar* ('resides') in a place. When Rebecca tells Jacob to run away from his brother Esau, and to go to her brother Laban in Haran, she is quoted as saying, "And settle (*veyashavta*) with (*im*) him a few days..." (Genesis 27:44). Later on, the text says that upon Jacob's arrival in Haran, and before Jacob went to work for his uncle as a shepherd, "...and he settled (*vayeshev*) with him a month" (29:14). It was not the amount of time that determined that the text used the verb *lashevet*, but the fact that Jacob was at his uncle's house, part of the family, equal to all the others. Not as a stranger, for which the text would use the verb *lagur*.

When Joseph instructs his brothers to go back to the land of Canaan and bring their father to Egypt to reside, the text quotes Joseph as saying, "And you shall **settle** (*veyashavta*) in the land of Goshen, and you shall be near me..." (45:10). Again, we see that the verb *lashevet* is used in conjunction with one being 'near' to the locals.

Although Joseph called upon his father and his brothers to live in Egypt, they didn't see it this way. When the brothers appear before Pharaoh, they are quoted as saying, "They said to Pharaoh, to **reside** (*lagur*) in the land we have come..." (47:4). The brothers didn't see themselves as part of the Egyptian community. They were 'residents' in the land of Egypt, in spite of the fact that their brother Joseph was the acting ruler of the land. They were willing to 'settle' only in the land of Goshen, "...please let your slaves **settle** (*yeshvo*) in the land of Goshen" (47:4).

Pharaoh tells Joseph, "The land of Egypt is before you, let your father and brothers **settle** (*hoshev*)[91] in the best of the land, in the land of Goshen let them **settle** (*hoshev*)..." (47:6). And, indeed, later on the text says, "And Joseph *vayoshev* his father and brothers, and gave them a possession (*achuza*[92]) in the land of Egypt, in the best of the land, in the land of Ramses..." (47:11).

The text summarizes the settlement of the family in Egypt by saying, "And **Israel settled** (*vayeshev*) in the land of Egypt in the land of Goshen and they had possessions in it..." (47:27). In the following verse, the text says, "And **Jacob** lived (*vayechi* – note the different verb in the Hebrew used here) in the land of Egypt seventeen years..." (47:28).

We should note two points. First, while the first verse talks about 'Israel' the national entity, the second verse talks about 'Jacob' the private man. Second, while the first verse uses the verb *vayeshev* ('to settle' or literally as we saw, 'to sit'), the second verse uses the verb *vayechi* ('to live life').

Question: Does the text mean to tell us that, while the family as a whole accepted their 'settling' in Goshen/Egypt, Jacob did not? And although he did not accept it, he still didn't have a label for his stay in Egypt. He couldn't call it *lashevet*, nor could he call it *lagur*.

Or, maybe the text comes to tell something else in using the verb *lichyot* ('to live life'). In the beginning of Genesis, when the text goes quickly over the generations from Adam to Noah, and then later from Noah to Abraham, the text uses the formula of, "And Adam lived a hundred and thirty years and fathered..." (Genesis 5:3). And we see this formula in use through Terah, "And Terah lived seventy years and fathered..." (11:26).

Not long after the text says "And Jacob lived (*vayechi*) in the land of Egypt seventeen years..." (47:28), it moves to deal with the 'rebirth' of two tribes in the family, Menashe and Ephraim, Joseph's two sons, whom

---

[91] *Hoshev* is the command form of the verb *lashevet*.
[92] *Achuza* is also translated elsewhere as 'inheritance.' It is the same word used for the Land of Canaan as belonging to the Israelites.

Jacob elevated from being 'grandsons' to being 'sons' to him; "And now your two sons who were born to you in the land of Egypt before I came to you to Egypt **are mine**, Ephraim and Menashe as Reuben and Shimon they **shall be mine**" (48:5).

The Verb *Lishkon*

The verb *lishkon* comes from the three-letter root word *SH-K-N*. At times, the letter 'K' is a soft one, and then it is transliterated as 'ch' and pronounced more as the 'ch' of 'chrome' or the 'X' in Spanish. Besides the place where the text speaks about Jacob after his wife Rachel's death, the verb appears in Genesis several times:

First, the refugee from the war tells Abraham that Lot was taken captive, "And there came one who had escaped and told Abram the Hebrew for he *SHoCHeN* in the plains of Mamre the Amorite…" (Genesis 14:13).

Second, the Angel says to Hagar about the upcoming delivery of her son Ishmael, and his future, "And he will be a wild man, his hand will be against every man, and every man's hand against him, and he shall *yiSHKoN* in the presence of all his brothers" (16:12).

Third, the Almighty appears to Isaac and says to him, "…do not go down to Egypt, *SHeCHoN* in the land of which I shall tell you" (26:2).

Fourth, Jacob blesses his sons before his death, and addresses Zebulun, "Zebulun *yiSHKoN* at the shore of the seas and he shall be for the shore of ships, and his hall shall be to Sidon" (49:13).

Guiding us as to the meaning of the verb *lishkon* should be the place in Exodus, "And let them make me a sanctuary and I will **dwell** (*veshachanti*) among them" (Exodus 25:8). It is clear from this verse that the Almighty's presence is not going to be a physical one, but a spiritual one. If we maintain consistency in the meaning of any word throughout the language, then the verb *lishkon* would mean in Biblical language 'to be present,' although not always or even necessarily physically.

If we check this meaning throughout Genesis, and we start with Zebulun, then it is clear that Zebulun, who was a seafarer, was not present in his place of residence all the time. His place of residence was more of a place where one goes home now and then. It was not a place that one could find him all the time. The same applies to Ishmael, "and he shall *yiSHKoN* in the presence of all his brothers." The text talks of being around others, but definitely not of being in one place permanently. When the Almighty says to Isaac, "…do not go down to Egypt, *SHeCHoN* in the land of which I shall tell you," the Almighty does not talk of permanent living or of settling the land or merging with the local population.

As for Abraham, we are facing a change in language in regard to his living in the land. Earlier, right after the separation of Lot from Abraham, the text labeled Abraham residing as, "…and he came and *vayeshev* in the plains of Mamre…" (Genesis 13:18); however, there was a change in Abraham's status later. By the time Lot was taken captive, "…Abram the Hebrew for he *SHoCHeN* in the plains of Mamre the Amorite…" (14:13).

The Status of the Forefathers in the Land of Canaan

Abraham

When Abraham first came to the land of Canaan from Haran, the text says, "And Abram **passed** through the land…" (12:6), and the text ends this verse with, "…and the Canaanite then in the land" (12:6).

We should note that the text relates to the status of the Canaanites residing in the land without using any verb, "…the Canaanite **then** in the land." Not the verb *lashevet*, nor *lagur*, nor even *lishkon*. Unlike later, when talking about the conflict between Abraham's and Lot's shepherds, "And there was a strife between the shepherds of Abram's cattle and the shepherds of Lot's cattle and the Canaanites and the Perizzites **settled** (*yoshev*) then in the land" (13:7). From the difference in language from the time Abraham first entered the land ('then'), until the strife with Lot ('settled'), we can conclude that at the time Abraham entered the land, it was also the beginning of the Canaanites' settlement in the land. They strengthened their settlements as time went by, and by the time the strife between Abraham and Lot was going full steam, the Canaanites were already entrenched and they were 'settled' (*yoshev*) in the land.

The text continues to describe Abraham's movements in the new land, "And he **moved** from there to a mountain in the east of Beth-El and he

pitched (*vayet*) **his tent** having Beth-El on the west, and Hai on the east..." (12:8).

We should note that during all this time the text does not attribute to Abraham any label regarding his status in the land. He 'passed,' and he 'moved,' and he 'pitched his tent.' At this stage, Abraham is not described with either of the two verbs *lashevet* or *lagur*.

The first time the verb *lagur* ('reside') appears in Abraham's life is when Abraham goes down to Egypt due to the famine: "And there was famine in the land, and Abram went down to Egypt to reside (*laGuR*) there..." (12:10).

After Abram went up from Egypt, the text says, "And Abram was very rich in cattle, in silver, and in gold" (13:2). The text moves on to describe the separation of Lot from Abraham, after which it says, "Abram settled (*yashav*) in the land of Canaan and Lot settled (*yashav*) in the cities of the plain and pitched his tent toward Sodom" (13:12). The separation from Lot brought an upgrade to Abraham's status in the land of Canaan.

At this stage the Almighty appears to Abraham and promises the land to him and to his seed, and instructs Abraham to "Arise, go through the land in its length and in its breadth for I will give it to you" (13:17), and the text continues with, "Abram removed his tent and came and settled (*vayeshev*) in the plains of Mamre which is in Hebron..." (13:18).

As we saw earlier, this 'settling' (*vayeshev*) did not last for long. By the time Lot was taken captive, the text says that Abraham was *ShoCHeN* in Mamre, meaning, he was not there all the time. He was there only once in a while. One should wonder what brought Abraham to weaken his hold at Mamre.

Later on, the text says, "And Abraham traveled from there to the Negev and **settled** (*vayeshev*) between Kadesh and Shur and **resided** (*vayagar*) in Gerar" (20:1). The text describes Abraham and his wife Sarah in the land of the Philistines, how Sarah was taken to the king's palace, and her return. Then it describes the birth of Isaac, and the pact Abraham made with the king of the Philistines. The text ends with, "And Abraham **resided** (*vayagar*) in the Philistines' land many days" (21:34).

We should note two points. One, the text attributes to the land of the Philistines the same language as to the land of Egypt – the verb *lagur*. Two, Abraham is described as 'living' (*lashevet*) in the land of Canaan, only when it describes the distance that was put between Abraham and Lot. For this 'living' the text uses the regular past tense form of the verb, *yashav*. The only two times the text uses the commonly-used form of the verb *vayeshev* are when Abraham settled "…in the plains of Mamre which is in Hebron…" (quite likely Hebron, which is on the southern side of the mountain ridge, was not part of the land of Canaan), and "…between Kadesh and Shur…" in the desert.

Isaac

The text says that after Abraham's death, "G-d blessed his son Isaac and Isaac settled (*vayeshev*) by the well Lahairoi" (25:11). We do not know the exact location of this place, but taking into consideration that the text talks about a "well," then it is quite likely to be an oasis in the desert.

When there was a famine in the land, the Almighty appeared to Isaac and said to him, "…do not go down to Egypt, *shechon* in the land of which I shall tell you. **Reside** (*gur*) in this land and I will be with you…" (26:2-3). Later on, the text says that "Isaac settled (*vayeshev*) in Gerar" (26:6), which is in the land of the Philistines. There is no mention of Isaac being in the Land of Canaan. There is only one place where the text says that Isaac was in Hebron, upon the return of Jacob from Haran, after more than 20 years with his uncle Laban: "And Jacob came to Isaac his father to Mamre, the city of the four which is Hebron, where Abraham and Isaac resided (*gar*) (35:27). And here the text in one word explains to us the status of Abraham (and Isaac) in relation to his living in Mamre – not *lashevet* and not *lishkon*, but *lagur*. This should tell us that although Abraham bought the land to bury Sarah, still he did not become a citizen of the place. He was relegated to a second-class resident.

The fact that Isaac was not a full citizen in Canaan comes across when the text talks about the separation between Jacob and Esau, still during the life of their father Isaac, "…and the land where they **resided** (*megureihem*) could not bear them…" (36:7).

Jacob

After the text reports the kings of Edom, the text says, "And Jacob **settled** (*vayeshev*) in the land where his father **resided** (*megurei*) in the land of Canaan" (37:1).

The text tells us that Jacob was different from his father Isaac. While Isaac **resided**, Jacob **settled**.

Back to Jacob after Rachel's death

"…when Israel **was present** in that land…" (35:22)

It is quite likely that Jacob, being 'Israel,' was not present physically. At this time, the text attributes to him the verb 'to be present' (*lishkon*), and not the verb 'to settle' (*lashevet*) or the verb 'to reside' (*lagur*). Israel was there and not there at the same time. One cannot describe him as being in one place. Could the family contact him at any given time? Quite likely not.

"…when Israel was present **in that land**…" (35:22)

The phrase 'in that land' appears twice more in the Torah. First, in regard to Isaac, after the king of the Philistines, Abimelech, returns Rebecca his wife to him. And the text says, "And Isaac sowed **in that land** and reaped in that year a hundredfold, and the Lord blessed him" (26:12). One might consider the fact that Isaac reaped a hundredfold and that the Almighty blessed him as a good context. But if we realize that the text ended the previous verse by saying, "And Abimelech charged all the people saying, **he who touches this man or his wife shall surely be put to death**" (26:11), will realize that the text comes to tell us that the blessing was in spite of the fact that the land was no good – '**that** land.'

The second place where we find the phrase '**that** land' is in Deuteronomy, "And the anger of the Lord was kindled **in that land** to bring upon it all the curses that are written in this book" (Deuteronomy 29:26).

If 'that land' indicates a bad situation, then the phrase 'this land' indicates the opposite. The Almighty appears to Isaac and says to him, "Reside **in this land** and I will be with you…" (Genesis 26:3). Even when Moses talks to the people before his death saying, "Because I die **in this land**, I am not crossing the Jordan, and you shall cross and possess **that** good **land**" (Deuteronomy 4:22), Moses is not saying anything bad about the land where he is about to die. After all, earlier in the text, he is very proud of the fact that he conquered the land from the two kings who opposed the Israelites, Sichon and Og.

In summary, it is quite likely that the text is re-emphasizing, language-wise, that the lack of Israel's physical presence in running the family was due to his heavy mourning over Rachel's death. His mourning was aggravated by the fact that he saw the effect of the curse he put on whoever had Laban's idols with him, and it happened that it was Rachel, his beloved wife. And, quite likely, he felt guilty that he brought on Rachel's death.

Into this vacuum of leadership that was created in the family, Reuben, the firstborn, moved to act.

"Reuben went and lay with Bilhah his father's concubine…" (35:22)

Linguistic Journey – Marriage in Biblical Language

In general, we found that the text uses the verb 'to take' (*lakachat*) for the act of marriage.

In **Genesis**

- "And Lemech **took** for himself two wives…" (4:19)
- "…and they **took** as wives all those whom they chose" (6:2)
- "And Abram and Nahor **took** wives…" (11:29)
- "And Isaac brought her to his mother Sarah's tent, and **took** Rebecca and she became his wife…" (24:67)
- "And again Abraham **took** a wife…" (25:1)
- "And Esau was forty years old when he **took** a wife…" (26:34)
- "And Judah saw there a daughter of a Canaanite man whose name was Shua and he **took** her and came to her" (38:2)
- "And Judah **took** a wife for Er his firstborn whose name was Tamar" (38:6)

In **Exodus**

- "And Amram **took** Jocheved his father's sister for himself for a wife…" (6:20)
- "And Aaron **took** Elisheva, daughter of Amminadav, sister of Nachshon to wife…" (6:23)

In **Deuteronomy**

- "And who is the man that has betrothed a wife and has not **taken** her…" (20:7)
- "If any man **takes** a wife, and comes to her…" (22:13)
- "A man shall not **take** his father's wife…" (23:1)
- "If a man has **taken** a wife and had marital relationship with her…" (24:1)
- "…or if the latter husband dies who **took** her to be his wife" (24:3)
- "Her former husband which sent her away many not **take** her again to be his wife…" (24:4)
- "If a man **takes** a new wife…" (24:5)
- "…her husband's brother will come to her and **take** her for himself as a wife…" (25:5)
- "And if the man does not wish to **take** his brother's wife…" (25:7)
- "…and if he says I do not wish to **take** her" (25:8)

Two Unique Cases in Genesis

Jacob is unique. While the text uses the verb 'to take' in regard to Abraham and Sarah and to Isaac and Rebecca (although Rebecca was already inside the family's household – in Sarah's tent), the text does not use the verb 'to take' in regard to Jacob marrying Leah, or Rachel thereafter.

The text quotes Jacob as saying to Laban, "**Give** me my wife, for my days are fulfilled…" (Genesis 29:21). Did Jacob 'take' Rachel? The text does not use this verb for Leah or for Rachel. For Leah, the text uses the verb 'to take' for Laban, Jacob's future father-in-law, "And it came to pass in the evening that he **took** Leah his daughter and brought her to him…" (29:23). One could say that the text could not use the verb 'to take' for Leah as Jacob did not 'take' her. He thought she was Rachel. But we find the same for Rachel as well, "…and he gave him Rachel his daughter for him as a wife" (29:28).

The fact that Jacob did not 'take' the two sisters to be his wives, and instead they were given to him, might explain why later on the text quotes Jacob explaining to Laban why he ran away without formally departing from him, "…because I was afraid for I said perhaps you would steal your daughters from me" (31:31). Jacob was not secure that the two were his, as he did not 'take' them.

The second unique case in which we see the verb 'to take' is in the case of Dinah in Shechem. The text says, "And Shechem the son of Hamor the Hivite, prince of the country saw her, he **took** her, and lay with her and defiled her" (34:2).

The common understanding is that Shechem abducted Dinah. However, we should always ask ourselves if the text of a statement could have said something in a much shorter way. And in this case, the text could have very easily said that Shechem lay with Dinah, and defiled Dinah. Why did the text need to say that Shechem 'took' Dinah? Is it possible that Shechem married Dinah according to the law of their country?

The Verb 'Went' in Conjunction With 'Took'

There are two cases in the Torah in which the verb 'to take' a wife is preceded by the act of 'going' ('went'). The first is with Esau, "And Esau **went** to Ishmael and **took** Mahalath the daughter of Ishmael the son of Abraham the sister of Nevaioth to be his wife besides the wives he had" (Genesis 28:9). The second is with Moses' father marrying Jocheved his aunt, "And a man of the house of Levi **went** and **took** a daughter of Levi for a wife" (Exodus 2:1).

The common practice in the society of that time was for a man to marry the daughter of the older brother, like Abraham and Nahor, who married the daughters of Haran, or to marry a cousin, like Jacob marrying Leah and Rachel who were his first cousins (Laban and Rebecca were brother and sister).

However, in the two cases in which the text uses the verb 'went' the man marries a wife out of his immediate family. Esau married the daughter of

Ishmael, and although she was his cousin, still, Ishmael was sent away from the family, being the son of Abraham (as the text specifies) without being the son of Sarah.

Amram, Moses' father, married his 'aunt' and not his cousin, and although quite likely she was his age, still, she was not from the expected line of marriage – a man marrying a 'cousin' (not an aunt), or a niece.

Back to Reuben and Bilhah

"Reuben **went** and lay with Bilhah his father's concubine…" (35:22)

The fact that the text starts the account of Reuben laying with Bilhah with the verb 'went,' a verb that elsewhere starts the act of marriage out of the regular expected family circle of a cousin or a niece, should bring us to wonder if the text deals here with Reuben publicly laying with his father's concubine for everyone to know of this act. And if so, why would he do it publicly?

The act of 'coming to' (having a marital relationship) the king's concubine is discussed in the Tanach twice. The first example is with King Saul's concubine, Rizpah the daughter of Aiah. After the death of King Saul and his son Jonathan in the battlefield, the text says,

> And it came to pass while there was war between the house of Saul and the house of David, Abner (Saul's military commander) made himself strong in the house of Saul. And Saul had a concubine, whose name was Rizpah the daughter of Aiah, and Ish-Bosheth (Saul's son) said to Abner, why have you come to my father's concubine? (2 Samuel 3:6-7)

The fact that Abner made himself strong in the house of Saul went along with the act of Abner 'coming to' the late king's concubine. By doing so, Abner made a public statement that he was the strongman in the household. No wonder the son of the late king complained about this act.

The second example is with Absalom's rebellion against his father David, a case that will help us understand Reuben's act.

The text says,

And Ahitophel said to Absalom, Come to your father's concubines, whom he has left to keep the house, and all Israel shall hear that you have made yourself odious to your father; then shall the hands of all who are with you be strengthened. So they spread Absalom a tent upon the roof and Absalom came to his father's concubines in the sight of all Israel. (2 Samuel 16:21-22)

We can assume that Reuben's act of laying with Bilhah, Jacob's concubine, was akin to what Abner did with Rizpah, and what Absalom did with King David's concubines. As Abner wanted to exhibit his status in the late king's household, and as Absalom wanted to seize the reign from his father David, so did Reuben who took the reign of the family during the vacuum in leadership created by the heavy mourning of Jacob for his late wife Rachel.

Corroborating evidence to the fact that Reuben acted only due to the incapacitation of Jacob can be found in Jacob's words to Reuben before his death. If we compare Jacob's words to Reuben to his words to Simeon and Levi, it becomes clear that his anger towards Simeon and Levi was above and beyond what he felt towards Reuben. Jacob did not start his words to Reuben with a curse, as he did to Simeon and Levi ("Cursed be their anger…" (Genesis 49:7), and he does not disperse him among the other tribes. He starts his words by saying, "Reuben, you are my firstborn, my might and the beginning of my strength, the excellency of dignity and the excellency of power" (49:3).

At most, Jacob accuses Reuben with, "Rushing as water, you shall not excel because you went up to your father's bed, then you defiled it, he went up to my couch" (49:4). Jacob attributes Reuben's act to 'haste,' and not to actual rebellion. It is quite likely that Jacob understood that his behavior contributed to Reuben's act.

Sensitivity of the Text

If indeed Reuben took the reins during the time Jacob mourned over Rachel's death, then we can ask the question: why does the text diminish this event by giving it only one verse? Just the mere mention of this event testifies to the importance of the event. After all, in the editing process of an open statement, only what is important enters the text, and what is not important does not enter. This event – Reuben replacing Jacob during this time – was important enough to be included in Genesis, but also important enough to actually be concealed, as if the text is saying it and not saying it at the same time. Concealing the event of Reuben taking control of the family affairs testifies to the sensitivity of the text concerning this issue.

Back to Reuben

With this new understanding of Reuben's behavior – stepping up to fill the void the father created by abdicating his responsibility as head of the family – we can examine Reuben's behavior in relation to Joseph with a very different understanding.

First, we will examine the event when Joseph comes to meet his brothers, a meeting which will result in Joseph being sold to slavery. The brothers wanted to kill him,

> And they saw him from far away, even before he came near to them, they conspired against him to slay him. And they said one to another, behold, this dreamer comes. And now, go and let's slay him and throw him into some pit and we will say some evil beast has devoured him, and we shall see what will become of his dreams. (37:18-20)

And Reuben's reaction was,

> And Reuben heard it and he saved him from their hands and said we will not kill him. And Reuben said to them, shed no blood, throw him into this pit that is in the wilderness, and lay no hand upon him, that he might rescue him from their hands to return him to his father. (37:21-22)

Twice Reuben addresses his brothers. In his first address he said, "We will not kill him." The prohibition to kill him was not accepted by the brothers. If they cannot do so, they have to return to live with the problem called 'Joseph.' As a result, Reuben suggested a compromise. Not to kill him, but at the same time not to release him, but to throw him into the pit. And the text brings us Reuben's thought process, 'to rescue him' and 'to return him to his father.' We should note that the text does not give the credit for the attempt to rescue Joseph to Reuben because of Joseph. The reason is 'to return him to his father.' Reuben knew that he would be the main guilty party for what would happen to Joseph. He was the one who wanted to take control of the family, as the firstborn, and he would be the primary suspect of wanting to get rid of Rachel's firstborn. Reuben only wanted to rescue Joseph with the objective of not aggravating his father beyond what he already had.

We can compare Reuben's approach to Judah's approach:

> And Judah said to his brothers, what profit is it if we slay our brother, and conceal his blood. Come and let us sell him to the Ishmaelites and let not our hand be upon him, for he is our brother and our flesh. And his brothers listened. (37:26-27)

Reuben does not even mention Joseph's name. The text only quotes him, "We shall not kill **him**," "throw **him**," and "and lay no hand upon **him**." Judah, on the other hand, relates to Joseph as 'our brother,' and even emphasizes that he is 'our flesh.' While Reuben has to struggle with the implications of his past behavior, Judah is free to relate to the problem that the brothers want to get rid of Joseph and they cannot continue to live with him being around. Still, Judah does not deny the fact that Joseph is a 'brother' for all purposes.

Reuben's Offer to Kill His Sons

When the family was discussing the Egyptian ruler's (Joseph's) command to bring him Benjamin, Reuben addresses his father Jacob and says, "Slay my two sons if I bring him not to you, give him to my hand and I will return him to you" (42:37).

Reuben's offer deals with a solution to one concern that Jacob expressed, the fear that Benjamin would be lost like Joseph. Reuben only addresses the issue of Benjamin returning to his father. Moreover, Reuben's offer is divided into two. The first part speaks in the negative: "…if I bring him not to you," and the second part speaks in the positive: "I will return him to you." The order of listing of the two parts of the sentence tells us Reuben's set of priorities. Reuben's concern was that he would be suspected that he would not return Benjamin.

Moreover, Reuben does not relate to Benjamin by name. Reuben's concern was focusing only on himself and his image in his father's eyes. Not different from his behavior when he tried to defend Joseph when the brothers wanted to kill him.

But Reuben's offer to kill his two sons if he would not return Benjamin testifies to a lot more.

Killing Sons

At a time in which the kingdom was transferred from father to son, and an orderly transfer of the government from one generation to another secured the stability of the kingdom, the fate of the king's sons was extremely important to governmental stability.

In different eras in the kingdom of Israel we find that the killing of the previous king's sons came to secure government stability. For example, when Jehu ascends to the throne, he sent a message to kill Ahab's seventy sons. The text says, "And it came to pass, when the letter came to them, that they took the king's sons, and slew seventy persons, and put their heads in baskets, and sent them to Jezreel" (2 Kings 10:7). It was an extremely cruel act, but necessary to secure Jehu's reign. We find the same with King Zedekiah's fate, the last Judean king. When he was captured by the Babylonian king, the text says, "And they killed the sons of Zedekiah before his eyes…" (2 Kings 25:7).

Even at the time of King David we find a similar event. When Absalom killed Amnon for raping his sister, the rest of the king's sons ran away. The text says,

> "And it came to pass, while they were in the way, that news came to David saying, Absalom has killed all the king's sons, and there is not one of them left. And the king arose, and tore his garments, and lay on the earth, and all his slaves stood by with their clothes torn" (2 Samuel 13:30-31).

If it were true, and Absalom indeed killed all the king's sons, then the meaning was that it was an attempt to have a revolution to throw David off his throne.

And the text continues,

> "And Jonadab, the son of Shimeah David's brother, answered and said, let not my Lord suppose that they have killed all the lads the king's sons, for only Amnon is dead, for by the command of Absalom this has been ordained from the day that he raped his sister Tamar. And therefore let not my lord the king take the thing to his heart to think that all the king's sons are dead, for only Amnon is dead" (2 Samuel 13:32-33).

Jonadab says to David, "And therefore let not my lord the king take the thing to his heart to think that all the king's sons are dead..." as the meaning of such an event meant a revolution, "...for only Amnon is dead." Jonadab comforted David by saying that the death of one son, although he was David's firstborn, and quite likely the heir to the throne, is still not the end of the world, or, more accurately, not the end of the kingdom. Killing the king's sons has political implications beyond the personal ones.

We find another way, more humane, to bring about the end of a kingdom, a way that does not call for killing the king's sons. Instead, castrate them, to ensure that there is no future to the kingdom. The prophet Isaiah says to King Hezekiah, "And of your sons that shall issue from you, which you will father, shall they be taken away and they shall be **eunuchs** in the palace of the king of Babylon" (2 Kings 20:18; Isaiah 39:7).

Reuben's Offer

"Slay my two sons if I bring him not to you, give him to my hand and I will return him to you" (Genesis 42:37).

Such an offer sounds very cruel. Does Reuben suggest killing his sons? However, if we read the offer with the knowledge that killing sons was an accepted behavior in ancient time, when a kingdom was transferred from one king to another who was not his son, and if we read the offer knowing that Reuben was suspected of wanting to get rid of Rachel's second son, after the firstborn Joseph vanished, then we can understand what Reuben promises his father. In many words, Reuben's offer says: you suspect that I want to take Benjamin in order to get rid of him. But you should know that I have no intent to use this opportunity to open my way to inherit as

Leah's firstborn. If Benjamin vanishes while he is under my supervision, then my sons, who are due to be my heirs, will not gain anything.

The Meaning of Reuben's Offer

If indeed this is the meaning of Reuben's offer, preventing Reuben from taking the reins of the rule of the family from Benjamin, the only son left by Jacob's wife Rachel, then we have a second point to confirm that Jacob's family acted like a kingdom for all purposes. The first signal is Reuben's sleeping with his father's concubine, another accepted behavior in ancient times for one who wants to take the kingdom from a previous king. Even if the text does not grant Jacob the title 'king,' still Jacob (or 'Israel') functions according to all the rules of kingdoms practiced at that time.

Note: at this point of time we have two signals that Jacob functioned as a king. We will continue our journey into the language of the text to see if we can find other confirmations of this point.

Judah's Conversation With Jacob

Judah's words to Jacob are divided into two sections. At first, the text says that Judah addresses his father, "If you send our brother with us, we will go down and buy you food" (Genesis 43:4).

From the beginning, we can see that Judah had positive expectations that his father Jacob would give him Benjamin to take to Egypt. The words are divided into two, and the positive form, "If you send" appears before the negative one, "And if you do not send..." (43:5).

Moreover, Judah, as the text quoted him before the sale of Joseph to slavery, "What profit is it if we slay **our brother**... for he is **our brother** and our flesh..." (37:26-27), recognizes the fact that Benjamin is "our brother," a title missing from Reuben's words.

We also face a significant change in language. Before Reuben's offer the text says, "And **Jacob their father** said to them, me have you bereaved, Joseph is not, and Simeon is not, and you will take Benjamin, all of these are *alai* (on me)" (42:36). Jacob's words express complete despair, accompanied by the text relating to him as "Jacob their father." And

Reuben's offer to kill his two sons starts with, "And Reuben said to his father…" (42:37). And, in fact, Reuben's offer does not succeed in taking Jacob out of his despair.

The text continues, "…**their father** said to them, go again and buy us a little food" (43:2). Then comes Judah's first address which includes the magic title "our brother," and the text continues, "And **Israel** said, why did you deal so ill with me…" (43:6). Judah's words brought the text to change its language relating to Jacob and to 'upgrade' him from the personal 'Jacob' to the national 'Israel.' Language-wise, Judah's words succeed in uplifting Jacob's mood to make him 'Israel.' He is not yet ready to reach the decision to send Benjamin with his brothers, but he is already 'Israel' and not 'Jacob.'

And the text continues with Judah's second address to Jacob. This one starts with, "And Judah said to Israel his father…" (43:8). If we read the narrative as one unit, it is clear that the same figures are acting, Judah and Jacob. At this point, the text does not need to grant Jacob a different title, unless something changed in the relationship between the two. The text says now that Jacob is not only 'Israel,' but he is even 'Israel his father' when talking about Judah. Language-wise, the text granted Judah a major and very significant linguistic 'upgrade.' Not only did Judah succeed in taking Jacob out of his despair, but the text also recognizes that Jacob's future as 'Israel' is connected to Judah.

The text quotes Judah as saying, "…send the lad with me and we will arise and go, that we may live and not die, both we, and you, and also our little ones" (43:8).

We should note two points, one linguistic, and one relating to content. First, if Judah was quoted as calling Benjamin 'our brother,' now he calls him 'the **lad**.' Throughout the book of Genesis we can see that the status of 'brother' does not guarantee personal safety. Cain kills Abel 'his brother.' Abraham asks Lot to separate from him by saying "We are men brothers" (13:8). Esau wants to kill Jacob 'his brother.' Judah suggested selling Joseph to slavery saying, "he is **our brother** our flesh" (37:27). At this point, Judah calls Benjamin 'the lad,' and language-wise he takes Benjamin out of danger, at least from the practiced behavior between brothers in Genesis.

Second, content-wise, Judah does not see taking Benjamin as the important point in solving the problem. For him, Benjamin is only the means to reach the goal that is 'let us live and not die.' By saying so, Judah shows that his thought process is not focusing on Benjamin, but on the problem the family is facing.

And the text continues Judah's offer, "I will be surety for him, from my hand shall you require him, if I bring him not to you, and present him before you, then let me bear the blame forever" (43:9). Judah enlists his main trait to aid him: 'his word is his word.' He promises and he delivers.

'Surety'

The word 'surety' appears in the Torah only in regard to Judah. In the account of Judah and Tamar we find that Judah promised her, "I will send a kid-goat from the flock..." (38:17), and she says, "If you give a **surety** till you send it" (38:17). In response, Judah asks, "What **surety** shall I give you?" (38:18). Later on, Judah sends his friend, "...to take the **surety** from the woman..." (38:20).

In talking to his father, Judah is quoted as saying, "I will be surety for him..." (43:9). Later on, when Judah speaks to Joseph, the text quotes Judah as saying, "For your slave became **surety** for the lad..." (44:32).

Back to Judah's Words to Jacob

Judah continues his words by saying, "For if we had not delayed, we would now have returned twice" (43:10).

At this point, the text says, "And their father Israel said to them, if it must be so now, do this..." (43:11). Now, 'Israel' is not only Judah's father. He is the father of all the sons. Judah's words brought Jacob to a complete withdrawal from his despair, and to return to functioning, to lead his sons by instructing them how to behave. After his instruction to take a gift to the man, and to return the money, 'Israel their father' says, "And take **your brother** and arise and go back to the man" (43:13). Jacob accepted that now there is brotherhood between the sons of the two mothers Rachel and Leah.

Reuben and Judah

We can see the words of the two brothers, Reuben and Judah, each one with his own offer, as a discussion of the conditions that will allow Benjamin to go with the brothers to Egypt. At the same time, we can see the two offers as a very intense struggle for the status of the family's leader. Will it be Reuben the firstborn? Reuben proved twice that he could not solve a problem the family faced. First, with the brothers' wish to kill Joseph, and now with Jacob's refusal to allow Benjamin to go to Egypt. On the other hand, Judah proved himself twice, in the same two cases in which Reuben failed. Will Judah's success in bringing Jacob to be 'Israel their father' sit quietly among the brothers? The language of the text reveals to us what went on 'behind the scenes.'

'The Men'

As we saw in the case with Dinah in Shechem, when the text changed its language from the brothers being 'Jacob's sons' to being 'the men,' so does the text from the time 'Israel their father' agreed to give Benjamin. From this point on, the word 'the brothers' vanished from the language of the text:

- "And **the men** took this present..." (43:15)
- "Bring **these men** home..." (43:16)
- "and the man brought **the men** into Joseph's house" (43:17)
- "And **the men** were afraid..." (43:18)
- "And the man brought **the men** into Joseph's house..." (43:24)
- "Fill **the men**'s sacks with food..." (44:1)
- "As soon as the morning was light **the men** were sent away..." (44:3)
- "Arise, pursue **the men**..." (44:4)

Is it a coincidence that from the time the brothers went down to Egypt until Joseph's cup was found in Benjamin's sack, the text avoids using the title 'the brothers?' Or, are we maybe facing a response to the struggle that took place between Reuben and Judah over Jacob's agreement? It is quite likely that Judah's status was not accepted by all the brothers, and certainly not by Reuben.

However, when the cup is found in Benjamin's sack, and the brothers are facing another crisis as serious as the first two – selling Joseph instead of killing him, and getting their father to give Benjamin, – the text says, "And **Judah and his brothers** came to Joseph's house..." (44:14). At this stage, it is clear, and accepted by all brothers, that the leadership is in Judah's hands. He is the one who gave the surety to his father. He is the one who needs to deliver on his promise. And, indeed, the text says, "And Judah said, what shall we say to my Lord? What shall we speak? And how shall we show our righteousness? God has found the iniquity of your slaves..." (44:16). Judah took the leadership. He is the one to talk to Joseph. He is the one who brought Joseph to reveal himself to his brothers.

JOSEPH AND HIS BROTHERS

From the time Joseph revealed himself to his brothers the linguistic lens returns to focus on 'Joseph and **his brothers**.' We find in the text,

- "…and there stood no man with him while Joseph made himself known to **his brothers**" (45:1)
- "And Joseph said to **his brothers**…" (45:3)
- "…and **his brothers** could not answer him…" (45:3)
- "And Joseph said to **his brothers**…" (45:4)
- "And he kissed all **his brothers** and wept on them and after that **his brothers** talked with (*et*) him" (45:15)
- "…**Joseph's brothers** have come…" (45:16)
- "And Pharaoh said to Joseph, say to **your brothers**…" (45:17)

'The Sons of Israel'

When the brothers went down the first time to Egypt to buy food, the text said, "And **the sons of Israel** came to buy grain among those who came…" (42:5). We see the same now, after Pharaoh's instructions; the text says, "And the sons of Israel did so and Joseph gave them wagons according to the commandment of Pharaoh…" (45:21).

We see the same when the family goes down to Egypt, "…and **the sons of Israel** carried Jacob their father and their little ones and their wives in the wagons which Pharaoh had sent to carry him" (46:5). In conjunction with going down to Egypt, or in conjunction with Pharaoh, the brothers are described as 'the sons of Israel.'

Back to Joseph and his Brothers

The text continues with

- "And he sent **his brothers** away…" (45:24)
- And Joseph said to **his brothers**…" (46:31)
- "And he took some of **his brothers**…" (47:2)
- "And Pharaoh said to **his brothers**…" (47:3)
- "And Joseph placed his father and **his brothers**…" (47:11)
- "And Joseph nourished his father and **his brothers**…" (47:12)

After Jacob's death, when they went up to the Land of Canaan to bury Jacob, the text says, "And all the house of Joseph and **his brothers** and his father's house…" (50:8). However, when they got to the land of Canaan, the text says, "And **his sons** did to him according as he commanded them" (50:12), and, "And **his sons** carried him to the land of Canaan…" (50:13).

In the land of Canaan they are not 'Joseph's brothers;' they are 'Jacob's sons.' They relate to Jacob and not to Joseph. And when they return to Egypt, "And Joseph returned to Egypt, he and **his brothers**…" (50:14). We should note that the text could have returned to the same linguistic formula of "And Joseph and his brothers returned to Egypt…" Instead, the text actively comes to create a linguistic split between Joseph and his brothers, "And Joseph returned to Egypt, **he** and his brothers…"

Something happened during the journey to the land of Canaan at the time of Jacob's burial that brought about this split. Does this language change come from the fact that it was in the land of Canaan, or, was the reason for it deeper? Was there any argument between the brothers and Joseph?

If we have any doubt that something did take place in Hebron, and quite likely an argument between Joseph and the brothers, then the text brings us the following event after the return to Egypt: "And **Joseph's brothers** saw that their father was dead, they said, Joseph will perhaps hate us…" (50:15), and the brothers want to make peace with Joseph. If the reason for peace is that they sold him to slavery, couldn't they have made peace before their father's death? Or maybe an incident at the time of the burial, in which the language of the text labels them as 'his sons' instead of 'Joseph's brothers,' brought them to reach out for peace.

From now on, they are indeed 'Joseph's brothers:'

- "And **his brothers** also went…" (50:18),
- "And Joseph said to **his brothers**…" (50:24).

There is only one place where they are not 'Joseph's brothers.' Instead, they are labeled again as 'the sons of Israel:' "And Joseph took an oath from **the sons of Israel**, saying God will surely redeem you…" (50:25). Again, when they are in Egypt and before Joseph's death they are 'the sons of Israel.'

Brothers - Summary

Throughout the text of Genesis we saw language-wise that the word 'brother,' either in the singular or in the plural, is **not** used in a positive context.

When the Almighty asked Cain as to the whereabouts of Abel, after Cain had killed Abel, Cain responded with "Am I **my brother's** keeper[93]?" (Genesis 4:9).

When Abraham suggested to his nephew Lot to separate, Abraham is quoted as saying, "We are **men brothers**" (Genesis 13:8), and we should note that Abraham listed 'men' before 'brothers.'

When Judah suggested to his brothers to sell Joseph, their half-brother to slavery, Judah is quoted as saying, "**our brother** our flesh" (Genesis 37:27).

The only one whom the text describes as close to his brother (reality-wise), and at the same time uses the title 'my brother' (language-wise): "**my brother** keep what you have to yourself" (Genesis 33:9), is Esau, when at the meeting with his brother Jacob, the text brings the sequence of events: Esau embraced Jacob and kissed him, and Esau is quoted as saying 'my brother.' This is the only place in Genesis where the content merged with the language to reflect the use of 'my brother' in a positive context.

All in all, we see that the titles 'my brother' and 'our brother' are predominantly used in a negative context. We should consider this a linguistic bias of the text.

In this chapter we are facing the following biases:

1. The text conceals the fact that Reuben took the leadership while his father Jacob was absent due to his heavy mourning for Rachel's death.
2. The text avoids giving Jacob the title 'king,' although Jacob (Israel) functioned according to all the rules of kingdoms commonly used in that era. We learn it from quotes by Jacob, Judah and Reuben.

---

[93] "Keeper" – traditional translation; this analysis normally uses the translation 'guard.'

Points in language to consider:

1. The language of the text uses the **sound** of words to send messages – *vayazed* vs. *vayazid, sheni* vs. *shani,* and *biglal* vs. *gilulim.*
2. The fact that the text uses the **sound** of the words the way they register in the listener's ear should bring us to wonder if the text was more read to **listeners** than read silently.
3. Throughout the text of Genesis the word 'brother,' either in the singular or in the plural, is **not** used in a positive context.

THE STATUS OF JACOB/ISRAEL

Introduction

When we come to evaluate the position of Jacob/Israel, we should consider the two points we already found. Reuben's offer to kill his sons represents a custom in ancient times of killing the sons of a previous king. This offer was related to the fact that Reuben slept with his father's concubine, Bilhah, when his father was mourning for Rachel and didn't function. Sleeping with the concubine of a king was also a practice in ancient times by one who took over a kingdom from a previous king, to illustrate to the people his strength. These two points combined together lead us to the idea that Jacob and his family functioned as a 'kingdom' with all the practices and customs associated with this status.

Now we will continue our journey to see if there is confirmation of this under-the-radar point.

The Sons of Israel

Language-wise, we can see that the title 'the sons of Israel,' used extensively in the book of Exodus, appears in the book of Genesis when "Joseph's brothers" (42:3) go down to Egypt to buy food. When they enter Egypt they change to become 'the sons of Israel' (42:5). This title appears a long time before Joseph's death and the beginning of slavery. We should also note that this title appears when Jacob is still in the land of Canaan with Benjamin, while the rest of his sons are in Egypt.

We should not forget that the title 'the sons of Israel' appears for the first time in an off-hand remark, when the text says after the struggle between Jacob and Esau's angel, "Therefore **the sons of Israel** do not eat the sinew of the vein which is the hollow of the thigh to this day, because he touched the hollow of Jacob's thigh in the sinew of the vein" (Genesis 32:33).

We can see that Joseph's brothers or Jacob's sons receive the title 'the sons of Israel' twice when they arrive in Egypt, in chapter 42 verse 5, and chapter 46 verse 5.

Jacob and Pharaoh

When Jacob's family is in place in Egypt, the text says, "And he took some of his brothers, five men, and **presented** them to Pharaoh" (47:2). We find the same when the text quotes Judah in his second address to his father, in his attempt to convince him to give him Benjamin, "I will be surety for him, from my hand shall you require him, if I bring him not to you, and **present** him before you, then let me bear the blame forever" (43:9).

The word the text uses to describe the appearance of the five brothers before the Egyptian king – 'to present' – is the same word the text uses to quote Judah when he addresses his father: "And Judah said to **Israel** his father…" (43:8). This identical language equates these two events; Israel (the national name of Jacob) has the same status as Pharaoh.

Jacob Before his Death

There are two places in which Jacob is quoted regarding his upcoming death. First, Jacob asks Joseph to take an oath that he will bury him in the land of Canaan, "**And I will lie with my fathers** and you shall carry me out of Egypt and bury me in their burying place…" (Genesis 47:30).

When Jacob talks to all his sons before his death, the text quotes him as saying, "…I am to be gathered to my people…" (49:29).

When talking to all his sons, the text quotes Jacob using the regular formula in the book of Genesis. The text says:

- For Abraham, "And Abraham expired and died in a good old age, an old man, and full of years, **and was gathered to his people**" (25:8)
- For Ishmael, "…and he expired and died, **and was gathered to his people**" (25:17)
- For Isaac, "And Isaac expired and died, **and was gathered to his people**, being old and full of days…" (35:29)
- For Jacob, "…and expired **and was gathered to his people**" (49:33)

The point to notice about Jacob is the change in language from the time he talked to Joseph to the time he talked to all his sons. When talking to Joseph, "**And I will lie with my fathers** and you shall carry me out of Egypt and bury me in their burying place..." (Genesis 47:30).

The phrase 'lie with my fathers' is the Biblical formula used to describe the death of a king, starting with David, Solomon, and other kings. By using this formula, Jacob uses the language of a king to describe his death. This language vanishes when he talks to all his sons. But when he talks to another king, or in this case, the second to a king (his son Joseph), Jacob uses the language of a king.

We should still note that while the text brings us a quote by Jacob using the language of a king, the text itself uses language that is non-kingly language to describe Jacob's death, the same language used to describe the death of Abraham and Isaac.

Summary

To the points that we found earlier, Reuben's offer to kill his sons, and Reuben's move to lay with his father's concubine, two activities associated with a kingdom in ancient times, we can add now two additional points. First, the text uses the same language for Pharaoh the king of Egypt as for Jacob; and second, the text quotes Jacob using the formula for the death of a king regarding his own upcoming death.

We also saw that the title 'the sons of Israel,' a title used extensively starting from the book of Exodus to relate to the people of Israel, is used quite early, at the time Jacob is still in the land of Canaan, and at least on the surface we do not know of any existence of the nation of Israel.

Jacob – the First King of Israel

Before his death Jacob says to Joseph, "And I have given you one portion above your brothers which I took from the hand of the Amorite with my sword and with my bow" (Genesis 48:22). Jacob is talking about his conquests in the land of Canaan.

The fact that Jacob/Israel was the first king of Israel explains the insertion of the section dealing with kings of Edom, "And these are the kings who reigned in the land of Edom before there reigned any king over the sons of Israel" (Genesis 36:31). The text lists several kings who reigned in Edom. It should be noted that none of them appears in the books Joshua, Judges, Samuel 1 or 2, or Kings 1 or 2. These kings are listed only in Genesis. And their listing appears between the verse informing us of the death of Isaac, "And Isaac expired and died and was gathered to his people, being old and full of days, and his sons Esau and Jacob buried him" (Genesis 35:29), and the verse stating, "And Jacob lived in the land where his father sojourned, in the land of Canaan" (37:1).

The section dealing with the Kings of Edom brings many to wonder: what is this section doing in the book of Genesis? At first glance this section seems to be 'out-of-sequence.'

SCAN Rule: 'Out-of-sequence' information is only 'out-of-sequence' to the reader/listener. However, it is 'in-sequence' for the writer/speaker, and the writer/speaker positioned it at the place it should be. When the reader/listener understands the statement completely, everything will be 'in-sequence.'

SCAN Rule: 'Out-of-sequence' information indicates that the writer/speaker took some significant information out of the 'open statement,' but left in the 'open statement' the effects of the missing information. Once the missing information is brought back into the 'open statement,' everything will be 'in-sequence.'

Summary: There is no 'out-of-sequence' information without the writer/speaker concealing information.

Back to the Kings of Edom

Since the section dealing with the kings of Edom comes before the announcement that Jacob was in the land of Canaan with a higher status than his father (Jacob 'lived' while his father 'resided'), we can understand that the digression about the Edomite kings prepares the stage for the ascension of the first king of Israel onto the historical stage, "These are the *toldot* of Jacob Joseph…" (Genesis 37:2).

The End of the First Kingdom of Israel

Joseph's Proposal to Settle in Egypt

After identifying himself to his brothers, Joseph outlined his proposal to move to Egypt. His proposal is described in three verses. The first one is like a subject line: "Hurry back to **my father** and say to him, thus said your son Joseph, G-d has made me the lord of all Egypt; come down to me; delay not." (45:9).

We should note that this verse starts with Joseph talking to his brothers saying 'my father.' Joseph does so also in the other verses, "And you shall tell **my father** of all my glory in Egypt..." (45:13), and, "...and you shall hurry and bring down **my father** here" (45:13).

For one to talk to his siblings saying 'my father' or 'my mother' is very rare and unexpected. It is as if the speaker says, 'I am the son and not you.'

Does Joseph say 'my father' because he cherishes the renewed connection he now has with his father? Or, is Joseph maybe responding to Judah's words when he talked to Joseph to bring him to reveal himself?

In his speech Judah used the title 'my father' seven times, and 'our father" only twice :

- "And it came to pass when we came up to your slave **my father**..." (44:24),
- "And **our father** said..." (44:25),
- "And your slave **my father** said to us..." (44:27),
- "Now therefore when I come to your slave **my father**..." (44:30),
- "...and your slaves shall bring down the gray hairs of your slave **our father**..." (44:31),
- "For your slave became surety for the lad to **my father** saying if I bring him not to you then I shall bear the blame to **my father** for ever" (44:32),
- "For how shall I go up to **my father** and the lad be not with me lest perhaps I see the evil that shall come to **my father**" (44:34).

But Judah was talking to Joseph at a time that Joseph had not yet revealed himself as their brother. The most we can say is that by Judah using 'my father,' he was slighting his other brothers standing beside him, and not Joseph. But Joseph is talking in a different context, in the open, once everyone knows who everyone else is.

Should we conclude that 'my father,' used by Joseph, came to emphasize to Judah that now Joseph is in the picture, and he is asserting leadership and the connection with the father?

Or, is there some other reason – hidden altogether in the text?

> "…thus said **your son Joseph**…" (45:9)

We should note that the text quotes Joseph using the personal language formula of 'title + name' when relating to his connection to his father.

The second verse of Joseph's proposal to move to Egypt is actually talking about settling in the land of Goshen, "And you shall **live** in the land of Goshen and you shall be near me, you and your sons and your grandsons, and your flocks and your herds, and all that you have" (45:10). By using the verb 'to live' (*veyashavta*), Joseph is actually talking about total resettlement from the land of Canaan to Egypt. If the settlement of Jacob in the land of Canaan started with "And Jacob **lived** (*vayeshev*) in the land where his father **sojourned**…" (37:1), a description which comes to signal the idea that Jacob lived in the land of Canaan as a landlord, or, in other words, as a king, then Joseph is quoted using the same verb, *veyashavta*, to tell his father to move his operation to Egypt.

If the second verse of the proposal is talking about a 'permanent' resettlement, then the third verse is talking about the move to Egypt in temporary terms, "And there I will nourish you, **for yet there are five years of famine**, lest you and your household and all that you have come to poverty" (Genesis 45:11). This last verse leaves open the option of returning to Canaan after the famine is over.

The text ends Joseph's proposal with, "And he fell upon his brother Benjamin's neck and cried, and Benjamin cried upon his neck. And he kissed all his brothers and cried on them, and after that his brothers talked with (*et*) him" (45:14-15).

Linguistic Journey – Crying

We find the activity of 'crying' in the book of Genesis many times and in different situations.

The first one to be mentioned as 'crying' is Abraham, after the death of Sarah his wife, "And Sarah died in Kiriath-Arba which is Hebron in the land of Canaan, and Abraham came to eulogize Sarah and to **cry for her**[94]" (Genesis 23:2).

'Crying **for**' someone as part of the process of mourning for the death is also mentioned after Joseph 'vanished' as a result of his brothers presenting it to their father that he was prey for wild animals, "And all his sons and all his daughters rose up to comfort him, but he refused to be comforted, and he said, for I will go down to Sheol to my son mourning, and his father **cried** for him" (Genesis 37:35).

We find the same after the death of Jacob, "…and the Egyptians **cried for him** seventy days" (Genesis 50:3).

We find the activity of 'crying' also in the following places:

- After Esau found out that Jacob got his blessing, "…and Esau raised up his voice and cried" (Genesis 27:38).
- When Jacob met Rachel by the well, "And Jacob kissed Rachel and raised up his voice and **cried**" (Genesis 29:11).
- At the meeting between Jacob and Esau upon Jacob's return from Haran, "And Esau ran to meet him and embraced him and fell on his neck and kissed him and they **cried**" (Genesis 33:4).

The activity of 'crying' is mentioned quite often for Joseph. When he listened to his brothers expressing remorse over what they did to their brother Joseph, "And he turned himself away from them and **cried**…" (Genesis 42:24). When the brothers brought Benjamin with them, "And Joseph made haste for his emotions yearned to his brother and he wanted to **cry** and he came to the room and **cried** there" (Genesis 43:30). After

---

[94] "…to cry for her" – one should note that in Hebrew the format is *li'bkotah,* which actually means, 'to cry her' without the preposition 'for.'

Jacob's death the brothers ask forgiveness from Joseph, "…and Joseph **cried** when they spoke to him" (Genesis 50:17).

We find three places where the activity of 'crying' is mentioned along with the activity of 'falling on the neck' of the person, and both are in a reunion between two people, after a very long time without seeing each other. The first reunion is between Jacob and Esau, "And Esau ran to meet him and embraced him **and fell on his neck** and kissed him and they **cried**" (33:4). The second reunion is between Joseph and Benjamin, "And he **fell upon his brother Benjamin's neck** and **cried** and Benjamin **cried upon his neck**" (Genesis 45:14). The third is the reunion between Joseph and his father Jacob, when Jacob came to Egypt, "And Joseph made ready his chariot and went up to meet Israel his father to Goshen, and presented himself to him, and **he fell on his neck** and **cried** on his neck a good while" (Genesis 46:29).

We should note that we do not find 'falling on the neck' when Joseph is revealing his true identity to his brothers.

Moreover, there are only two times in which 'crying' is mentioned with the preposition 'on.' The first time is after Joseph revealed himself to his brothers, "And he kissed all his brothers and **cried on them** and after that his brothers talked with him" (Genesis 45:15). The second time is immediately upon Jacob's death, "And Joseph fell upon his father's face and **cried on** him and kissed him" (Genesis 50:1).

Question: why would the text use the same language for crying on a dead person (a father), and crying on his brothers after revealing himself to them? Should we conclude that the brothers were "dead" to his proposal?

If this is not enough, let's check the way the text describes Joseph kissing his brothers.

Linguistic Journey – to Kiss

The verb 'to kiss' in Hebrew comes from the three-letter-word root verb *N-SH-K*. Because 'N' is the first letter, the verb is an irregular verb, where in most cases the first letter 'N' drops, and is not written or pronounced.

We find it in the following:

- When Jacob approached his father Isaac to get the blessing instead of his brother Esau, "And he came near and he kissed (*vayishak*) him..." (Genesis 27:27).
- When Jacob met Rachel at the well upon his arrival in Haran, "And Jacob kissed (*vayishak*) Rachel..." (Genesis 29:11).
- When Jacob and Esau meet upon Jacob's return from Haran, "And Esau ran to meet him and embraced him and fell on his neck and kissed (*vayishakehu*) him and they cried" (Genesis 33:4).
- When Joseph brought his two sons to get a blessing from his father Jacob, "...and he brought them near to him and he kissed (*vayishak*) them and embraced them" (Genesis 48:10).
- When Jacob died, "And Joseph fell upon his father's face and cried on him and kissed (*vayishak*) him" (Genesis 50:1).

In the rest of the Tanach we find the verb 'to kiss' with the letter 'N' dropping in the following places:

- "And Moses went out to meet his father-in-law and did obeisance and kissed (*vayishak*) him and they asked each other about their welfare..." (Exodus 18:7).
- When Samuel anointed Saul to be king, "And Samuel took a vial of oil and poured it upon his head and kissed (*vayishakehu*) him..." (1 Samuel 10:1).
- When David and Jonathan met before David had to run away from Jonathan's father, King Saul, "...and they kissed (*vayishku*) one another and cried one with another until David exceeded" (1 Samuel 20:41).
- When David made peace with Absalom, "...and the king kissed (*vayishak*) Absalom" (2 Samuel 14:33).
- When David kissed one of his supporters, "...and the king crossed over, and the king kissed (*vayishak*) Barzilai..." (2 Samuel 19:40).

We find it also later in the Tanach:

- "...let the men who sacrifice kiss (*yishakun*) the calves" (Hosea 13:2).
- "He who gives a right answer kisses (*yishak*) the lips" (Proverbs 24:26).

- "Let him kiss (*yishakeni*) me with the kisses of his mouth…" (Song of Songs 1:2).

However, there are times in which the text uses the verb 'to kiss' without dropping the letter 'N.' In Genesis, we find four places, out of which three places are used for Laban, "And it came to pass when Laban heard the tidings of Jacob his sister's son that he ran to meet him, and embraced him, and kissed (*vayenashek*) him…" (Genesis 29:13). Note it is *vayenashek* and not *vayishak*. The fact that the text says that Laban 'ran to' meet Jacob, should remind us that Laban, upon seeing the jewelry his sister Rebecca received from Abraham's slave, also ran out to greet the man. We should note the change of language between these two places. While for Abraham's slave it is said that Laban 'ran **outside**,' for Jacob it is said that Laban 'ran **to**.'

The sequence of events in regard to Laban and Abraham's slave does not necessarily mean that Laban knew of the jewelry before he ran outside. The text positioned the verses in the following order:

1. "And the girl ran and told those of her mother's house these things" (24:28).
2. "And Rebecca had a brother and his name was Laban, and Laban ran out to the man" (24:29).
3. "And it came to pass, when he saw the earring and bracelets upon his sister's hands, and when he heard the words of Rebecca his sister saying, thus spoke the man to me, that he came to the man…" (24:30).

In this third verse we witness a change in language regarding Rebecca. The change occurs between mention of the jewelry and the words that Rebecca said ("thus spoke the man to me…). While for the jewelry the text introduces Rebecca as 'his sister,' for the quote of Rebecca the text re-introduces Rebecca as 'Rebecca his sister.' Since we are dealing with the same verse, the text could have easily use a pronoun – '**her** words.' By re-introducing her, and this time using the formal language formula "name + title," the text indicates Laban's displeasure about the report of what the man had said, unlike his attitude towards the jewelry.

By the order of the verses, Laban ran outside before he knew of the earring and bracelets. On the other hand, when Jacob, Rebecca's son, arrives, Laban remembered the event, many years earlier, and therefore Laban 'ran to' Jacob. The fact that the text uses the form of the verb *vayenashek* (without dropping the letter 'N') comes to indicate that Laban had an ulterior motive in this kiss.

When Laban chased Jacob, after Jacob fled from him, Laban wanted to harm Jacob. However, Laban himself quoted the Almighty who appeared to him during the night and forbade him from harming Jacob. So, when Laban eventually met Jacob he complained, "And why did you not let me kiss (*lenashek*) my sons and my daughters…" (Genesis 31:28). This is the same Laban about whom his own daughters complained, saying, "Are we not counted by him as strangers? For he has sold us and has quite devoured also our money" (Genesis 31:15).

Laban and Jacob made a pact of not harming each other, and the text ends the event by saying, "And early in the morning Laban rose up, and kissed (*vayenashek*) his sons and his daughters…" (Genesis 32:1).

The fourth place is reserved to Joseph, when he revealed himself to his brothers, "And he kissed (*vayenashek*) all his brothers and cried on them…" (Genesis 45:15).

Realizing from our earlier search into the verb 'to love' in which the different forms of the verb are used to describe different kinds of love, one should wonder if we are not facing the same situation here. If so, without searching any further, it would be a good bet to say that the majority of cases in which the verb 'to kiss' is used in the proper way (dropping the first letter 'N') would indicate a kiss with good intentions, while the form including the 'N' would be the opposite – a kiss without a good intention.

Joseph would be a good example to check this hypothesis. When he kissed his father upon his father's death, the text used the form dropping the 'N,' while when he kissed his brothers the text did **not** drop the 'N,' indicating to us the internal world of Joseph, who still had to struggle with the fact that his brothers who sold him to slavery were standing right there in front of him.

At this point we will go to check in the rest of the Tanach if this explanation for the verb 'to kiss' (with the letter 'N') is valid elsewhere.

The first place is with Absalom, King David's son. The text tells us that Absalom, in order to lure people to his side, waited outside the palace for the people who came to the king for judgment. Absalom wanted to bring the people to his camp, and to distance the people from the king. And, indeed, the text says, "And it was so that when any man came near to him to bow down to him, he put forth his hand, and took him and kissed (*venashak*) him" (2 Samuel 15:5). And the text concludes this account by saying, "...so Absalom stole the hearts of the men of Israel" (2 Samuel 15:6). It is clear from this place that the kiss Absalom gave the people was self-serving and not a good one.

Before Joab, David's military commander killed Amasa, who was Absalom's military commander during the rebellion, the text says, "And Joab said to Amasa, are you well my brother? And Joab took Amasa by the beard with the right hand **to kiss** (*lineshok*) him. And Amasa took no heed of the sword that was in Joab's hand so he struck him with it in the belly..." (2 Samuel 20:9-10). This kiss was before killing him.

We find the verb 'to kiss' with the letter 'N' in the context of idolatry, "Yet I have left me seven thousand in Israel, all the knees that have not bowed to Baal, and every mouth that has not kissed (*nashak*) him" (1 Kings 19:18).

The most obvious example is in Proverbs, and the text speaks for itself:

> And behold there met him a woman dressed as a harlot and wily of heart. She is loud and stubborn; her feet do not remain in her house. Now she is outside, now in the streets and lies in wait at every corner. She caught hold of him and kissed (*venashka*) him...
> (Proverbs 7:10-13)

If indeed the verb to 'kiss' with the letter 'N' contains some bad feelings towards the person being kissed, then we should wonder about the following: "Loving kindness and truth meet together, righteousness and peace kissed (*nashaku*) each other" (Psalms 85:11).

Does the text tell us that righteousness and peace have bad feelings upon their meeting, as these two have a track record of not living together?

Back to Joseph and his Brothers

When Joseph kissed his brothers, it was not the same kiss that he gave his dead father. After all, Joseph was closer to his father than to his brothers who sold him to slavery because they were jealous of him.

And the text gives the reader a signal to know that this is the case; Joseph was still struggling with the past.

Did the brothers know Joseph's internal feelings? The text continues, "And he kissed (*vayenashek*) all his brothers, and cried on them, and **after that** his brothers talked with (*et*) him" (Genesis 45:15).

After the kiss (without dropping the letter 'N'), and after the crying (with the preposition 'on'), the text adds the phrase 'after that.'

The phrase 'after that' (in Hebrew it is one word) is a connection phrase, which seems 'unnecessary,' and it comes to connect two different parts of the events.

SCAN Rule: An 'unnecessary connection' comes to indicate that some information might be missing at this point of time.

Background information: One can describe an 'unnecessary connection' as a 'temporary blackout.' One watches a favorite television show. Suddenly, there is a blackout, no electricity, and no television, and no show. After a few minutes the electricity is back on, and the television is back on, but the person lost the part of the show during the blackout. After all, the television station is still broadcasting regardless of a blackout in a certain neighborhood.

The same happens during the delivery of an 'open statement.' The person stops the delivery for a while. When the person is writing an 'open statement,' one can observe that the person stops for a short while, still holding the pen in hand and looking into memory, but does not write anything. When the person returns to writing ('broadcasting'), the person puts in an 'unnecessary connection,' which is not 'unnecessary' at all. It signals that there was a pause during the delivery of the statement.

In Genesis we find the phrase 'after that' in the following additional places:

- When the Almighty foretells the future to Abraham at the Covenant of the Splits, "And also that nation whom they shall serve will I judge, and **after that** they will come out with great wealth" (15:14).
- After the purchase of the plot in which Abraham would later bury his dead wife Sarah, "And **after that** Abraham buried Sarah his wife…" (23:19).
- After the birth of Esau, "And **after that** came his brother out…" (25:26).
- When Jacob instructs his slaves to bring the present to his brother Esau, "And say you, behold, your slave Jacob is behind us, for he said, I will appease him with the present that goes before me, and **after that** I will see his face, perhaps he will forgive me" (32:21).

In these events we can see that the text perceives the prior activity as a break in the sequence of events. The stay and slavery in Egypt is only a break in the residence of the forefathers and their offspring in the land. Abraham had to negotiate the purchase of the land before we could bury his wife, and the text comes to tell us that this negotiation, with all of its importance of buying land in Canaan; was only a break in the sequence of events – between the death of Sarah and her burial. The birth of Esau is perceived by the text as a break before the birth of the more important baby – Jacob. Even the present that Jacob is sending ahead of him to his brother Esau is only a break before the two will meet.

Back to Joseph and his Brothers

"And he kissed (*vayenashek*) all his brothers, and cried on them, and **after that** his brothers talked with (*et*) him" (45:15).

The text perceives the kiss, and the crying, as a necessary break, before the brothers could even talk with Joseph.

One only needs to compare the reaction of Benjamin to the other brothers' reaction. For Benjamin, the text says, "And he fell upon his brother Benjamin's neck, and cried, and Benjamin cried upon his neck" (45:14).

But for his brothers, it was a one-sided 'crying' – Joseph on his brothers, but not they on him. Moreover, with his brother Benjamin, the two cried on each other's **neck**, which is missing from the text with the other brothers. We just need to compare the two other 'reunions' described in Genesis. The first reunion is between Jacob and Esau. Here, the text says, "And Esau ran to meet him and embraced him **and fell on his neck** and kissed (*vayishak*) him and **they** cried" (33:4). Esau, who earlier wanted to kill Jacob for Jacob receiving the blessing instead of him, now is ready to make peace.

The second reunion is between Jacob who went down to Egypt and his long-lost son Joseph. And the text says, "And Joseph made ready his chariot and went up to meet Israel his father to Goshen and presented himself to him, **and he fell on his neck** and cried on his neck a good while[95]" (46:29).

We should note that by the text it comes across that Joseph did the crying while Jacob did not. Still, Joseph 'fell on Israel his father's neck.' Later on, we might find the reason why Jacob did not reciprocate with crying, as he did with Esau.

If we compare the two reunions, Jacob with Esau, and Jacob with Joseph, to the one between Joseph and his brothers, we can see that this last reunion, Joseph and his brothers, was lacking. It was not a complete reconciliation.

And if the 'crying' and the 'kissing' is not enough, let's check the rest of the verse, "…and after that his brothers talked with (*et*) him" (45:15).

We already established in an earlier linguistic journey that Biblical language has two different 'withs' – *im*, indicating closeness, and *et*, indicating distance. And here, for the brothers talking to Joseph, the language of the text uses the 'with' indicating distance, *et*. The brothers were distant from Joseph.

Summary: three points indicate distance between Joseph and his brothers (excluding Benjamin) after Joseph revealed himself to his brothers, 'crying **on them**' as if they are dead people, using the form of the verb 'to kiss' that indicates something is not right, and using the distant 'with.'

---

[95] "a good while" – in the Hebrew literally it says 'more.'

One might expect that after the brothers sold him to slavery – very harsh treatment – Joseph might be able to forgive, but not to forget. But is there any other reason why there was distance between them?

In order to find the reason for this distance, we need to go and check Joseph's proposal to the brothers, what is there **and what is not there**.

> "…thus said your son Joseph, G-d has made me lord of all Egypt, come on to me, delay not" (45:9)

Linguistic Journey – to Come to a Country

Introduction

The verb 'to come' in Hebrew comes from the three-letter root word *B-V-A* and the second letter is dropped so the word *Ba* means 'came' in the third person, singular, masculine.

One should also note that unlike in English, where there are two different words for 'coming' and 'bringing,' in Hebrew the verb 'to bring' shares the same three-letter root word as the verb 'to come.' In Hebrew the causal form of the verb 'to come,' *lehavi*, is used to mean 'to bring.' In other words, in Hebrew 'to bring' is actually literally "to cause to come."

We already saw that the verb 'to come to' is a nice way for the text to describe the intimate relationship between a husband and his wife. We also find that 'to bring a woman into the house' is the prelude to marriage. The text says that when Rebecca came to the land of Canaan, "And Isaac **brought** her to his mother Sarah's tent, and took Rebecca and she became his wife…" (Genesis 24:67).

We also find that the verb 'to come' is used to indicate a close relationship, when someone invites another to come to his house. For example, Abraham's slave found that Rebecca was the one who answered his prayer, and she gave water to him and to all his camels. Abraham's slave gave her gifts, and she ran home to tell her family. The text continues with her brother Laban running outside to meet the man, "And he said, **come in**, you blessed of the Lord, why do you stand outside? For I have prepared the house, and room for the camels. And the man **came**

into the house..." (Genesis 24:31-32) We find that the same Laban, later on, invited Jacob into his house, "And it happened when Laban heard the tidings of Jacob his sister's son that he ran to meet him and embraced him and kissed him and **brought** him to his house..." (Genesis 29:13).

When Joseph's brothers brought Benjamin with them to Egypt, the text says, "And Joseph saw Benjamin with them and he said to the one overseeing his house **bring** these men into the house..." (Genesis 43:16).

And the text repeats this event several times, indicating how important this activity was:

- "And the man did as Joseph said and the man **brought** the men into Joseph's house" (Genesis 43:17),
- "And the men were afraid because they were **brought** into Joseph's house..." (Genesis 43:18),
- "And the man **brought** the men into Joseph's house..." (Genesis 43:24).
- "And Joseph **came** into the house..." (Genesis 43:26).

This is the same 'coming into the house' that the text mentions before the wife of Joseph's master approached him asking him to lay with (*im*) her, "And it happened about this time that Joseph **came into** the house to do his work..." (Genesis 39:11).

As it is for 'coming into the house,' or inviting someone to 'come into the house,' or 'bringing a woman into the house before marriage' (Rebecca), so is the activity of 'coming' to a country.

Note: we will now survey the way the text relates **language-wise** to the arrival of people in various places. We should remember that for this analysis the issue is not the **content**, or the outside reality, or the sequence of events, but the way the text describes the events **language-wise**.

Terah

The text says that Terah, Abraham's father 'came out' of Ur of the Chaldeans, "to go to the land of Canaan and they **came till** Haran and lived there" (Genesis 11:31). We should note that the text does not say that they 'came to' Haran, but that they came 'till' Haran. This indicates to us that their objective was not Haran, but the land of Canaan.

Abraham

Unlike his father Terah, when the Lord instructed Abraham to leave his family and his country, the text says, "…and they went out to go to the land of Canaan, and they **came to** the land of Canaan" (Genesis 12:5).

Not long after Abraham's arrival in Canaan, there was a famine in the land that forced Abraham to go to Egypt. Unlike the land of Canaan that relies on rain for water, Egypt relies on the Nile that flows constantly.

The text says about Abraham's journey to Egypt,

> And there was a famine in the land and Abram **went down** to Egypt to reside there, for the famine was severe in the land. And it happened, when he came near **to come** to Egypt, that he said to Sarai his wife behold I know that you are a pretty woman to look upon. (12:10-11)

Realizing that Abraham went 'to reside' in Egypt and not just to visit, one can understand why Abraham would be described as 'coming to' Egypt. And the text even emphasizes it, "And it happened that when Abram **came to** Egypt…" (Genesis 12:14).

However, when Pharaoh returned Sarah to Abraham, and sent him away, the text says, And Abram **went up** from Egypt, he, and his wife, and all that he had, and Lot with him, to the Negev" (Genesis 13:1). The text does not say that upon his return Abraham 'came to' the Negev. It seems from this that one can 'come to' to the land only once, and if one leaves the land even for a while, then the text does not say that the person 'came to' it again.

Isaac

The text says that there was a famine in the land of Canaan at the time of Isaac, Abraham's son, "And there was a famine in the land besides the first famine that was in the days of Abraham. And Isaac **went to** Abimelech king of the Philistines to Gerar" (Genesis 26:1). The text does not say that Isaac 'came to' Gerar, but that he 'went to.' And indeed, the text says, "And the Lord appeared to him and said, do not go down to Egypt; be present in the land which I shall tell you" (Genesis 26:2).

From that point on, the text talks about Isaac's movements using the following language,

- "And Isaac **settled in** Gerar" (Genesis 26:6),
- "And Isaac **departed from there** and pitched his tent in the valley of Gerar and settled there" (Genesis 26:17),
- "And he **went up** from there to Beersheba" (Genesis 26:23).

Throughout the life of Isaac, the text does not say that Isaac 'came to,' not to the land of the Philistines, and not to Beersheba, which was in the land of Canaan. Later on, when Jacob returns to the land of Canaan, we learn that Isaac moved his place to Hebron, "And Jacob came to Isaac his father to Mamre, to the city of Arba, which is Hebron, where Abraham and Isaac resided" (35:27). For this movement by Isaac, not only does the text not say that Isaac 'came to' Hebron, but the text also does not say anything about Isaac's movement to Hebron, and it shows up only in connection with Jacob's life.

Jacob

When Jacob fled to Haran because his brother Esau wanted to kill him after Esau's blessing, the text relates to Jacob's journey. At first, the text says, "And Jacob went out from Beersheba and went to Haran" (Genesis 28:10). After the Almighty appeared to Jacob and promised him He would guard him wherever he goes, the text brings us the following, "And Jacob lifted his feet and went to the land of the people of the east" (Genesis 29:1). However, the text does not say that Jacob 'came to' Haran. The text moves on to describe Jacob's encounter with the shepherds, "And he saw and behold a well in the field…" (Genesis 29:2).

One can conclude that Jacob was not going to Haran to live there permanently. His mother Rebecca told him, "And settle with him a few days until your brother's fury turns away" (Genesis 27:44). 'A few days' means no 'coming to' Haran. Not like Abraham who came to 'reside' in Egypt.

However, upon Jacob's return to his homeland, the land where his parents lived, and where he was born, the text says, "And Jacob **came** to Shalem, a city of Shechem which is in the land of Canaan when he **came** from Padan-Aram and pitched his tent before the city" (Genesis 33:18).

Although the translation brings us the activity as 'came to,' the text does not actually use the preposition 'to' as it does everywhere else. In this place, the text says that Jacob "...came *shalem* a city of Shechem..." It is true that there is a place east of Shechem that is today called 'Salem' and it might refer to this place that Jacob came to. But if we know that *shalem* also means 'complete' or 'without flaw,' then it might be that the text actually refers to the Almighty's promise that he would guard him on his way until he returned to the land.

After the raid on Shechem due to the abduction of Dinah, the text says, "And Jacob **came to** Luz which is in the land of Canaan that is Beth-El, he and all the people who were with him" (Genesis 35:6), and later on, the text says again, "And Jacob **came to** Isaac his father to Mamre, to the city of Arba, which is Hebron where Abraham and Isaac resided" (Genesis 35:27).

We should note that for Abraham the text does not say that he 'came to' the land upon his return from Egypt, as he already 'came to' the land earlier, upon his migration from Haran. However, for Jacob the text does say that he 'came to' places (Shechem and Luz) in the land of Canaan upon his return from Haran after a very long stay in Haran. Not a few days or months, but over twenty years. And as Jacob described it, "...for with my staff I passed over this Jordan and now I have become two camps" (Genesis 32:11). Penniless he went, and a rich man he returned.

Conclusion: as it is for people, and as it is for a couple, so it is for 'coming to a country.' One who comes to visit is not one who 'comes to that country.' 'Coming to a country' is an activity which unites the comer with the country. The comer becomes a resident (as Abraham in Egypt), or even naturalizes to live there permanently with full rights.

Jacob and his Sons Going Down to Egypt

The only 'coming to a country' that is repeated many times in the text is the journey of Jacob and his sons from the land of Canaan to Egypt/Goshen.

The text says, "…and they **came to** Egypt, Jacob and all his seed with him" (Genesis 46:6). Then the text moves to detail what it means by all his seed: "His sons, and his grandsons with him, his daughters, and his sons' daughters, and all his seed…" (46:7), and the text ends the verse by saying, "**brought**[96] he with him to Egypt" (46:7).

In the immediately following verse the text says, "And these are the names of the sons of Israel who **come to** Egypt…" (46:8). After detailing all the people, the text continues with, "All the souls who **come to** Jacob to Egypt…" (26). Both times, the text uses the present tense. We should also note that the text does not say, 'All the souls who came to Egypt **with** Jacob…' Instead, the text put it as, "All the souls who come **to** Jacob to Egypt…" It seems as if the 'souls' came to Egypt, but not with Jacob. Jacob seems like he is out of the picture. He is more a figurehead that an actual leader.

After detailing Joseph and his sons, the text, again, says, "…all the souls of the house of Jacob who **come to** Egypt seventy" (46:27). And if this is not enough, the text continues with, "…and they **came to** the land of Goshen" (46:28).

In total, the text says **six times** that they "**came to** Egypt" and once that they came to the land of Goshen. Just by the mere number of repetitions we can see the importance the text attributes to this transfer of the family from Canaan to Egypt. A lot more than Abraham's moving from Haran to settle in the land of Canaan. A lot more than Abraham going down to Egypt to reside there, due to the famine in the land of Canaan. A lot more than Jacob returning to the land of Canaan after his long stay in Haran. No other journey from one country to another received this preoccupation **in the language** of the text as this one, Jacob going down to Egypt with 'all his seed.'

---

[96] "brought" – don't forget that 'brought' in Hebrew is 'caused to come.'

Back to Joseph's Proposal

> "...Thus said your son Joseph, G-d has made me lord of all Egypt,
> **go down** to me, delay not" (45:9)

We should note that Joseph does not say, "...**come** down **to** me..."
Instead, Joseph talks only about 'going down' to Egypt.

If we have any doubt that Joseph was not talking about 'coming to' Egypt,
then let's visit another place. After his family arrived in Egypt, the text
says, "And Joseph said to his brothers, and to his father's house, I will go
up and tell Pharaoh and say to him, my brothers and my father's house
who were in the land of Canaan have **come to me**" (46:31). Joseph is not
talking about his family 'coming to' Egypt. They only came to 'him.'

And when Joseph talked with Pharaoh, the text quotes him as saying,
"...my father and my brothers and their flocks and their herds and all that
they have, **have come from the land of Canaan**, and behold they are in
the land of Goshen" (47:1).

We should note how Joseph avoided saying that his family '**came to**
Egypt.' He bypassed this problematic description for him by saying that
they came '**from** the land of Canaan' and they are in the land of Goshen,
without even saying that they came to the land of Goshen. They 'landed'
in the land of Goshen as if from a vacuum.

And if we continue to read Joseph's proposal we see how his proposal
deals with a very temporary relocation for the time of the famine, "And
there I will nourish you, for yet there are five years of famine, lest you and
your household and all that you have, come to poverty" (45:11). It is clear
that Joseph is talking about a five-year program, for the rest of the famine,
after which the family will go back to the land of Canaan.

If this was Joseph's proposal, why did the brothers respond as if they were
'dead?' Remember, he 'cried **on** them' and the distance between them, the
unique form of the verb to kiss, and talking with (*et*)?

In order to understand the brothers' reaction we need to go back to the
beginning of the account, even before the brothers went down to Egypt to
get food for the first time.

The Famine

The text 'introduces' us to the famine by saying, "And the seven years of famine began to come as Joseph said; and the famine was in all lands, but in all the land of Egypt there was bread" (41:54). But when the famine got to Egypt, Pharaoh sent the people to Joseph and he sold grain to the Egyptians, and still, "the famine grew severe in the land of Egypt" (41:56). At this point, the text is focusing on the famine in Egypt.

But the famine was not only in Egypt. The text continues, "And **all the land** came to Egypt to Joseph to get food because the famine was severe in **all the land**" (41:57). By saying 'all the land,' the text refers to all the nearby countries, and east of Egypt was the land of Canaan.

We should note that the text could have easily described it as, "And all the land came to Joseph to get food…" and we would have known that 'all the land' came to Egypt, as Joseph was in Egypt. But the text specifies to us that first 'all the land came **to Egypt**.' Knowing that 'coming to a country' was not just a journey to visit or to do business, we have to conclude that the famine caused a major **migration** from nearby countries into Egypt. There was no way people could have gone to Egypt to buy food and return back to their places, as a person today goes to the supermarket. The road was long and difficult, and a donkey ride would have taken several days to get there.

With this background of major migration to Egypt going on, we can move on to read about the impact of the famine on Jacob and his family.

We don't know how long the interlude was between the first trip the brothers took to Egypt and the second trip in which they brought Benjamin with them. However, we know that when Joseph revealed himself to his brothers, he said that there were going to be five more years of famine. This means that Jacob and his sons waited at least a year, and maybe a year and a half into the famine before they moved to get food from Egypt.

Question: What delayed them so long? It can be understood that when a famine starts it takes a while for people to realize that they are in the midst of a famine. And the first reaction of anyone is to hope that it is temporary, and the trouble will pass, and life will return to normal. But to wait over a year before acting? And if they were shepherds, it necessitates starting to kill their herds, gradually but surely. And even the slaughtered animals will not provide relief for very long. We should remember that there was no refrigeration at the time. Animals were slaughtered for a meal, and right before the meal. Still, Jacob and his sons were immobile, waiting close to two years before moving.

We should wonder if the answer to this question is the same answer to the question why Joseph, after ascending to be vice-royal, didn't go visit his father. Or at least send a message that he was alive.

And the text starts the issue of the impact of the famine in Jacob's family with, "And Jacob saw that there was grain in Egypt, and Jacob told his sons, **why do you look one upon another**" (42:1).

In English the phrase "why do you look one upon another?" is actually just two words in Hebrew, '*lama* ('why') *titra'u*?'

The verb *titra'u* comes from the three-letter root word R-A-H, 'to see.' But the grammatical structure[97] used here indicates that the activity is geared inward and not outward.

It is a unique structure for the verb 'to see' and it is found in the entire Tanach in only two instances, here, when Jacob spoke to his sons, and in another place in 2 Kings (and repeated again in Chronicles) in an encounter between the king of Judah and the king of Israel. "Then Amaziah sent messengers to Jehoash, the son of Johoahaz son of Jehu, king of Israel, saying, let us look one another in the face" (2 Kings 14:8). In Hebrew the text says, *nitra'eh panim* where *nitra'eh* is the verb, and *panim* means 'face.' But what does it mean when one king sends another a request to have an encounter in which both of them look at each other in the face?

Continuing to read the text we realize that this is not simply "one looking at another." The king of Israel responded with, "…the thistle that was in Lebanon sent to the cedar that was in Lebanon saying, give your daughter to my son for a wife, and there passed by a wild beast that was in Lebanon and trampled down the thistle" (2 Kings 14:9).

---

[97] In Hebrew there are seven "structures" to a verb, and each one indicates a different angle of the activity.

The metaphor compares the king of Judah to a thistle and the king of Israel to the cedar, a comparison that leaves no doubt who is the stronger.

And indeed, the king of Israel didn't send only the parable in his message. He went on to give his translation and commentary: "You have indeed defeated Edom, and your heart has lifted you up, keep your glory, and remain at home, for why should you provoke trouble, that you should fall, you, and Judah with you?" (2 Kings 14:10).

Now it is clear that the initial 'request' of the Judean king was not just to 'look one upon the other in the face.' The Judean king, after his victory over the Edomites, felt confident enough to challenge the northern kingdom to a duel, "to look one upon the other in the face."

And the text continues, "And Amaziah did not listen, and Jehoash king of Israel went up and he and Amaziah looked one another in the face (*vayitra'u panim*) at Beth-Shemesh which belongs to Judah. And Judah was defeated by Israel…" (2 Kings 14:11-12).

To translate *vayitra'u panim* or *titra'u* (in our case with Jacob's sons) 'to look one upon another' is to translate language literally without realizing we are facing an idiom here meaning 'to challenge one to a duel,' which really means 'facing each other,' but in a very hostile situation, a 'face-off.' It actually talks about a war between these two kings, a war that brought the defeat of the Judean king.

Back to Jacob and his Sons and the Famine

> "And Jacob saw that there was grain in Egypt, and Jacob told
> his sons, **why do you look one upon another**" (42:1)

After consulting the language in the second book of Kings, we should translate the verse as follows: **'why do you challenge each other?'**

A personal note: I must admit that it is not only difficult to translate Biblical Hebrew into English. The same difficulty exists in translating Biblical Hebrew into Modern Hebrew. I read this verse many times, and it didn't dawn on me that I was facing here an idiom meaning 'challenging one to a duel.' I saw it more as meaning, 'Why are you afraid?' since the word *titra'u* is close to the word *tira'u* meaning 'you are afraid.' Only during this analysis, when I went to check the text **literally,** did I find this meaning. The bottom line: It is news to me as it is to the reader.

Moreover, this place is a classic example that reading the Biblical text with Modern Hebrew means to read it the wrong way. As we will progress with this analysis, we will realize how this is true of all Biblical language.

What were the two factions among the brothers? The next verse will expose one faction, and by default we will know the other. In the next verse, Jacob took sides.

The text says, "And he said, behold, I have heard that there is grain in Egypt, go down **there** and get for us food **from there**, that we may live, and not die" (42:2).

We should note the emphasis in Jacob's word repeating the word 'there.' After all, the text could have easily quote Jacob as saying, "go down and get for us food that we may live, and not die." By adding the word 'there' and later 'from there,' Jacob is saying that we are 'here' and the food is 'there,' and we need to bring the food 'from there' to 'here.'

What would the other option be? Remaining in the land ravished by the famine without doing anything was not an option. No food meant sure death. And as Jacob ends his words, 'that we may live, and not die.' The only other option was to move the family completely to Egypt and live there for the time of the famine.

Let's examine now if this understanding is confirmed by the text.

In the following verse the text says, "And Joseph's ten brothers **went down** to get grain **from** Egypt" (42:3). We should note two points. First, their journey is described as 'going down' and their mission is not to get grain 'in' Egypt, but to get grain 'from' Egypt, exactly as Jacob said.

The next phrase interrupts the sequence of events by stating that Jacob did not send Benjamin with the others out of fear that something bad would happen. It is quite likely that this verse explains the earlier verse in which their numbers were stated: ten. It also explains why the 'social introduction' is shifting to 'Joseph's brothers,' as Benjamin, the only full-brother of Joseph, is staying behind.

The next verse looks, at first glance, repetitive:

> "And the sons of Israel came to get food among those who came,
> for the famine was in the land of Canaan" (42:5).

There are several points in this verse that distinguish it from the earlier one. First, the 'social introduction' changes. If they were 'Joseph's brothers' earlier, now they are 'the sons of Israel.' This is the first time ever that this title is used for them, the title that later on came to mean the Hebrews in the other books, Exodus, Leviticus, Numbers, and Deuteronomy. The text uses the national title. Just by this social introduction we should be on alert that something very significant is happening.

Second, the earlier verse said that they 'went down,' but now they are 'coming.' And we know that 'to come to a country' is not just to visit or to do business. It is at least to 'reside' (as Abraham did) or even to settle.

Third, the verse added one more component: they came 'among those who came.' What is the big news? Of course they were not the only ones to come to Egypt. However, the others were **migrating** to live in Egypt, while the brothers were going on a mission authorizing them to get food **'from** Egypt' and transport it back to their country. The additional phrase 'among those who came' is quite likely the point that changed their perception of their mission. At this point, they 'came,' and quite likely the faction advocating migration to Egypt took over.

We find confirmation of this change of heart in the first encounter between Joseph, who was in charge of all the food in Egypt, and the brothers.

Getting to Joseph

> "And Joseph was the governor over the land, and he was the one who sold food to all **the people of the land**…" (Genesis 42:6).

The words 'the people of the land' in Hebrew is *aam ha'aretz* where the word *aam* stands for 'people' with the meaning 'nation' and the word *ha'aretz* standing for 'the land.'

In order to understand this term, we need to go to an earlier place in Genesis, when Abraham is negotiating the purchase of a burial plot in order to bury his dead wife Sarah. There, the text says, "And Abraham rose up and bowed to ***aam ha'aretz***, to the sons of the Hittites" (Genesis 23:7). The same 'bowing down' to the *aam ha'aretz* is repeated later in 23:12. And when Abraham insists on getting the land for money, and not as a gift, the text says, "And he spoke to Ephron in the hearing of ***aam ha'aretz...***" (23:13).

It is clear from the text relating to Abraham that *aam ha'aretz* relates to the elite of the people. One does not bow to people under him. And the text tells us that Joseph was "...the one who sold food to all ***aam ha'aretz...***"

Incidentally, in Modern Hebrew the term *aam haaretz* comes to relate to someone who is simple with no education, or ignorant. This is the exact opposite meaning from the Biblical Hebrew. It presents a problem for Hebrew speaking people to read this text, as they will relate to the verse as saying that Joseph was in the retail business, running a 'grocery store,' or even a 'supermarket' selling food.

One would not expect the governor of all the food in the country to be the one who stands behind the counter at a grocery store, or even at a supermarket. Joseph was in charge of all the food in the country, and quite likely he had stations throughout the land to provide the necessary food for the citizens, and even from people coming from abroad. What Joseph kept for himself was dealing with the elite of the country, either Egyptian, or those of nearby countries. The text reveals to us here that the ten brothers, 'the sons of Israel' showed up before the governor because they were distinguished people from a nearby country. And they came 'among the people who came,' and Joseph was there to meet them – the vice-royal facing ten distinguished people from the land of Canaan.

The Encounter With Joseph

The text says, "...and he said to them from where do you come..." (Genesis 42:7). We should note that Joseph did not ask them why they came. The reason is understood. Joseph was in charge of the food, and he was dealing only with the elite, and quite likely only the elite who wanted to **migrate** to Egypt due to the famine.

The brothers answered with, "...from the land of Canaan **to buy food**" (42:7).

It is true that their initial mission was to buy food. However, the text changed its language to say that they came 'among those who came' and this was the reason that brought them before Joseph. To say that they came 'to buy food' would be a misleading statement in the context of them facing Joseph.

Joseph accused them saying, "...you are spies; to see the nakedness of the land you have come" (42:9). If they were there only 'to buy food' they wouldn't have reached Joseph. This answer simply didn't make any sense. No wonder Joseph accused them of being spies.

We should note that Joseph charged them with two separate issues: one, that they were spies, and two, that they came to see "the nakedness of the land." The brothers responded with, "...your slaves are not spies" (42:11). We should note that they **did not deny** the second charge, 'to see the nakedness of the land.'

Joseph continued with, "No, to see the nakedness of the land you have come" (42:12). At this point, Joseph dropped the charge of being 'spies' as they denied it, but he stayed with the second charge, they came to see 'the nakedness of the land.' And the brothers responded with, "And they said, your slaves are twelve brothers, the sons of one man in the land of Canaan, and behold the youngest is this day with our father and one is not" (42:13). At this point of time it is clear that the brothers do not deny the second charge. They could not. It was a true charge. They 'came' to the land 'among those who came.'

After arresting and holding them for three days, Joseph relented and offered them the following:

If you are honest, let one of your brothers be confined in the house of your prison, you go and bring food for the hunger of your houses. And bring your little brother to me; so shall your words be verified, and you shall not die. And they did so. (42:19-20)

The Misleading Report to Jacob

When the brothers returned to their father in the land of Canaan they quoted Joseph's demand to bring Benjamin to Egypt in the following way: "And bring your little brother to me then shall I know that you are no spies, but that you are honest men, so I will deliver you your brother **and you shall trade in the land**" (42:34).

But Joseph did not say the words 'and you shall trade in the land.' An offer 'to trade in the land' is mentioned earlier in Genesis. After Jacob's daughter Dinah was abducted into the city of Shechem, the father of the young man who abducted her approached Jacob and made an offer: "...and you shall live with us, and the land shall be before you, live **and trade in it**, and get possessions in it" (Genesis 34:10). The offer to 'trade in the land' was preceded by the verse saying, "And make you marriages with us, and give your daughters to us, and take our daughters for you" (34:9).

Hamor's offer to Jacob was to live in the land and to merge the two groups into one. So the brothers are adding words he did not say to Joseph's words. They are misleading the father, and quite likely the ones who are doing the misleading are the faction advocating migration to Egypt to live there, and not to be traveling back and forth for food.

The Heads of the Two Factions

Who was heading the faction advocating migration to Egypt? We learn it from the conversation between Jacob and Judah, a conversation that persuaded Jacob to allow Benjamin to go down to Egypt. The text quotes Judah, saying, "If you will send our brother with us, we will go down and get **you** food" (43:4). We should note that the text does not quote Judah as saying, "...and get **us** food." By using the second-person pronoun 'you,'" Judah clearly puts himself with the faction advocating migration. Judah is saying, we are doing it only to get **you** food. We could have easily stayed there in Egypt and solved the problem of food for good. But we are willing to go down to Egypt, and come back with food, **only for you**.

We can even go earlier to the conversation between the brothers when they were in custody. The text says, "And they said one to another, we are truly guilty concerning our brother, in that we saw the anguish of his soul, when he besought us, and we did not listen, therefore is this distress come upon us" (42:21).

Why would the demand to produce Benjamin take them back in time to when they sold Joseph to slavery? The one who suggested selling him into slavery (instead of killing him) was Judah. And Judah also had already established himself as one who was willing to admit mistakes. We only need to go back to Judah and Tamar, when Judah admitted that Tamar was more righteous than him (38:26). Judah is also the one who used the word 'our brother' when he suggested selling Joseph to slavery, "Come, and let us sell him to the Ishmaelites and let not our hand be upon him for he is **our brother** and our flesh…" (Genesis 37:27).

However, if Judah headed the faction advocating migration, then we understand that this demand stands in the way of their relocation to Egypt. They need to go back to Jacob and ask for Benjamin. Joseph is in Egypt, and now there is a demand for Benjamin to be in Egypt. One son of Rachel is already in Egypt against his will, and now the other son of Rachel is requested, again, against his will. No wonder that triggered the memory of the sale of Joseph to slavery in Judah.

Reuben's response, "And Reuben answered them saying, did I not tell you saying do not sin against the child and you did not listen? Therefore, behold, also his blood is demanded" (42:22).

Although the text does not say it, it is quite likely that the struggle for leadership of the family was re-ignited right then and there, between Reuben the firstborn and Judah the fourth son of Leah.

It should not be a surprise to us that Reuben the firstborn, who is due to inherit the position of head of the family, would be for the option of staying in the land of Canaan. If they are going to leave for Egypt what would he inherit? On the other hand, Judah, as the fourth son, is very likely to be the one who would advocate migrating. It should remind us of

Abraham, the second son of Terah, who immigrated to the land of Canaan, so could make a name for himself by separating himself from the family and the home land.

And Joseph is privy to all of this, as the text tells us, "And they knew not that Joseph understood them for he spoke to them by an interpreter" (42:23).

Linguistic Biases

At this point, we are heading to a conclusion that Judah headed the faction advocating migration to Egypt while Reuben headed the faction advocating staying in the land of Canaan. We also have the conclusion that Joseph is suggesting a third option, different from the first two - temporary relocation in Egypt, and returning to the land of Canaan after the famine is over.

We should note that this information is not in the **content** of the text. It is in the **language** used in the text. We should consider this information a 'linguistic bias' of the text, to **conceal** the fact that Judah was for migration, while Joseph was for the land of Canaan, although having to deal with the famine on a temporary basis.

We will continue our search into the text for verification of the above-mentioned conclusions.

Back to Joseph's Proposal

Knowing this background information we should revisit Joseph's proposal. We can understand now why Joseph is using the title 'my father' and not talking to the brothers directly. It is quite likely that Joseph suspected that the brothers were misleading their father. After all, they did not deny that they came to see 'the nakedness of the land.' And Joseph knew his father well enough to believe that his father would not want to leave the land of Canaan.

This should bring us to wonder if the demand to bring Benjamin down to Egypt was a way for Joseph to send a message to his father. If he suspected that the brothers were acting against the interest of the father, how could he warn him? He could not ask the brothers to talk against themselves. And we know that he did not maintain contact with his father and his family, even after he became vice-royal.

And Joseph's proposal brought about a third option that the two factions of the brothers did not consider: to move to Egypt **temporarily**, for only the five-year duration of the famine, and then to return to the land of Canaan. The brothers could not come up with this option, moving temporarily to Egypt, as they did not know what Joseph knew – that the famine was going to last seven years. For the family, and for the brothers, the famine was strong enough to bring them to total despair.

Joseph's proposal did not serve either faction. And their response was total silence, at least at that time. No wonder the text uses the form of the verb 'to kiss' indicating that the situation was not that friendly. No wonder the text tells us that Joseph cried **on** them, as if they were 'dead.' No wonder the text uses the unnecessary connection 'afterwards' to indicate that the kissing and the crying were only meant to pave the way for a meaningful conversation. And no wonder the text tells us that even when they talked with him, it was with the preposition *et* indicating distance.

What did the brothers do? Accept the situation as is? Remain dead silent? The text says,

> "And **the voice was heard** in Pharaoh's house saying
> Joseph's brothers have come and it pleased Pharaoh well
> and his slaves" (Genesis 45:16).

Linguistic Journey – to Inform Someone

There are a few verbs in Hebrew to indicate the activity of 'telling' someone some information. One verb that is used is the verb *lehagid*, which comes from the three-letter-word *N-G-D* (in most cases the first letter 'N' drops in the different variations). This linguistic journey will not concentrate on the meaning of the verb, but on the forms in which it is used, either active or passive.

SCAN Analysis: One should note that when a reader reads a statement he/she should always ask himself/herself, "Do I know who did what?" When the reader does not know who did the activity described in the sentence, then he/she should ask himself or herself why didn't the speaker/writer want the listener/reader to know? Is it because the speaker/writer did not know the identity, or is it because the speaker/writer did not want the listener/reader to know?

Note that in the active form we know the identity of the one who did the activity, but in the passive form we do not know. And it is a fact that the passive form of a verb is used many times to conceal identity.

Active

Throughout the Torah we find the active form of the verb to tell (*lehagid*) in the following places:

- "And Ham, the father of Canaan, saw the nakedness of his father and told (*vayaged*) his two brothers outside" (Genesis 9:22)
- "And there came the refugee and told (*vayaged*) Abram the Hebrew…" (Genesis 14:13)
- "And it came to pass that day that Isaac's slaves came and told (*vayagidu*) him concerning the well which they had dug…" (Genesis 26:32)
- "And Jacob told (*vayaged*) to Rachel that he was her father's brother…" (Genesis 29:12)
- "And Joseph dreamed a dream and he told (*vayaged*) to his brothers…" (Genesis 37:5)
- "And told (*vayagidu*) him saying Joseph is yet alive…" (Genesis 45:26)
- "And Joseph said to his brothers and to his father's house, I will go up and tell (*ve'agidah*) to Pharaoh…" (46:31)
- "And Joseph came and told (*vayaged*) to Pharaoh and said…" (Genesis 47:1)
- "And Moses told (*vayaged*) to Aaron all the words of the Lord…" (Exodus 4:28)
- "…and Moses told (*vayaged*) the words of the people to the Lord" (Exodus 19:9)
- "And the lad ran and told (*vayaged*) to Moses and said Eldad and Medad are prophesying in the camp" (Numbers 11:27)
- "And He told (*vayaged*) to you his covenant…" (Deuteronomy 4:13)

- "...ask your father and he will tell (*veyagedcha*) you...")
  (Deuteronomy 32:7)

We find one place in which the text uses the active form of the verb to tell although we don't know the identity of the speaker, "And one[98] told (*vayaged*) to Jacob and said behold your son Joseph comes to you..." (Genesis 48:2).

Passive

We find the passive form of the verb 'to tell' in the following places:

- "And it came to pass after these things that it was told (*vayugad*) to Abraham saying behold Milcah she has also borne sons to your brother Nahor" (Genesis 22:20)
- "And these words of Esau her elder son were told (*vayugad*) to Rebecca..." (Genesis 27:42)
- "And it was told (*vayugad*) to Laban on the third day that Jacob had fled" (Genesis 31:22)
- "And it was told (*vayugad*) to Tamar saying behold your father-in-law goes up to Timnath to shear his sheep" (Genesis 38:13)
- "And it came to pass about three months after that it was told (*vayugad*) to Judah saying Tamar your daughter-in-law..." (Genesis 38:24)
- "And it was told (*vayugad*) to the king of Egypt that the people fled..." (Exodus 14:5)

> "And **the voice was heard** in Pharaoh's house saying
> Joseph's brothers have come and it pleased Pharaoh well
> and his slaves" (Genesis 45:16)

In all other places in which the text used the passive form of the verb (*vayugad*) to relate to delivering a message, indicating that the text either didn't know the identity, or didn't want to give the identity of the speaker, the text still relates to the activity from the point of view of the **speaker** (the telling). The only place in Genesis in which the text relates to the activity not from the **speaker's** point of view, but from the **listener**'s point

---

[98] In the original Hebrew there is not even the word 'one,' which is added in the translation to indicate that the teller is unknown. In Hebrew it is said, "and he told (*vayaged*) to Jacob..." We know that it is the pronoun 'he,' as in Hebrew the pronoun is part of the verb.

of view (the hearing) and still does not identify the speaker, is right here in this place.

"Listening to the Voice"

The question is: does the text here talk about a 'voice,' relating to an unknown person, or are we facing here an idiom in Biblical Hebrew?

If we transform the text here from its **passive** form to the **active** form we will get the phrase 'listening to the voice.[99]' Take into consideration that this phrase in Biblical Hebrew does not relate to just the registration of the sound in the listener's ears. This phrase means 'to agree, to go along, and to obey.'

Just in the book Genesis alone we find that the Almighty tells Abraham to go along with Sarah's demand to expel Ishmael, "…in all that Sarah has said to you **listen to her voice**…" (Genesis 21:12) And the Almighty is quoted as talking about Abraham who is the one who followed the guidance of the Almighty, "And in your seed shall all the nations of the earth be blessed because you have **listened to my voice**" (Genesis 22:18). And, "Because Abraham **listened to my voice** and kept my charge, my commandments, my statutes, and my laws" (Genesis 26:5).

In the account of Jacob getting the blessing from his father Isaac, instead of his brother Esau, the text three times quotes Rebecca as saying to Jacob, "Now therefore my son, **listen to my voice** according to that which I command you" (Genesis 27:8), "And his mother said to him upon me be your curse my son, only **listen to my voice** and go fetch me" (Genesis 27:13), and "Now therefore my son **listen to my voice** and arise flee to Laban my brother to Haran" (Genesis 27:43).

After a going childless long time, and after her maid gave birth to a son, the text quotes Rachel, "And Rachel said, G-d has judged me and also **listened to my voice**, and has given me a son…" (Genesis 30:6).

---

[99] Technically, transforming 'being heard' from passive to active yields 'hearing,' not 'listening.' For now please accept that listening is 'close enough.' This is a point that will be covered in a future book on verbs dealing with communication in the Bible. See also footnote 66.

Realizing that 'listening to (or hearing) a voice' means 'agreeing' or 'obeying,' one should wonder what prompted the house of Pharaoh to 'listen to a voice.'

> "And the voice was heard in **Pharaoh's house** saying
> Joseph's brothers have come and it pleased Pharaoh well
> and his slaves" (Genesis 45:16).

Pharaoh's House

There are two incidents in which Joseph wants to reach Pharaoh to tell him something. However, there is a difference in the way Joseph approached Pharaoh. The first time, Joseph is quoted as telling his family, "...I will go up and I will tell **Pharaoh** and say to him my brothers and my father's house who were in the land of Canaan have come to me" (Genesis 46:31).

At this point, the text shows that Joseph had a direct connection to Pharaoh. However, after Jacob's death, the text says, "...Joseph spoke to **the house of Pharaoh** saying if I have found grace in your eyes speak please in the ears of Pharaoh saying" (Genesis 50:4).

It comes across that during the time from the arrival of Joseph's family until Jacob's death, Joseph lost his direct approach to Pharaoh, and he had to go through 'the house of Pharaoh.' In other words, 'the house of Pharaoh' is the administration that ran the palace and the kingdom.

And from the sentence, "And the voice was heard in **Pharaoh's house** saying Joseph's brothers have come and it pleased Pharaoh well and his slaves" (Genesis 45:16), it comes across that 'the house of Pharaoh' was a layer beneath Pharaoh himself and his slaves. We find 'the house of Pharaoh' also when Joseph revealed himself to his brothers as he cried, "...and the Egyptians heard, and **the house of Pharaoh** heard" (Genesis 45:2).

> "And the voice was heard in Pharaoh's house saying
> **Joseph's brothers have come** and it pleased Pharaoh well
> and his slaves" (Genesis 45:16)

The message that the house of Pharaoh received was that 'Joseph's brothers have come.' But how did they receive that message?

According to the text, before Joseph revealed himself to his brothers, it says, "…and he called cause every man to go out from me. **And there stood no man with him** while Joseph made himself known to his brothers" (45:1).

The following verse says, "And he cried aloud and the Egyptians heard and the house of Pharaoh heard" (45:2). The fact that his loud crying was heard can be explained by the fact that the people standing outside the room where Joseph revealed himself to his brothers could hear his loud crying. But how would they understand what he told his brothers? It is very unlikely that Joseph talked to his brothers in the Egyptian language. Up to this point the text specified that there was an interpreter (translator) between Joseph and the brothers: "And they knew not that Joseph understood them, for he spoke to them by an interpreter" (42:23).

It is quite likely that in revealing himself to the brothers he talked to them in their (his and their) language – the language they used in the land of Canaan. If so, it is very unlikely that the people standing outside the door, even if they were to eavesdrop, could understand what he said. Then how was 'the voice … heard' at the 'house of Pharaoh' with a very clear message, 'Joseph's brothers have come?'

There are three options: Joseph himself, the brothers, or the interpreter.

It is very unlikely to be Joseph. Up to this point, Joseph acted with his brothers, and with the rest of Egypt, according to the authority Pharaoh gave him initially, "And Pharaoh said to Joseph, I am Pharaoh, and without you shall no man lift his hand or foot in all the land of Egypt" (Genesis 41:44). Upon revealing himself to his brothers, Joseph is quoted saying to his brothers, "So now it was not you who sent me here but G-d, and He has made me **a father to Pharaoh and the lord of all his house, and a ruler throughout all the land of Egypt**" (45:8).

And, indeed, in the course of events, since the first arrival of the brothers to buy food, Joseph was acting without consulting Pharaoh. He accused the brothers of being spies. He arrested one of the brothers. He ordered the money the brothers paid into their food bags returned (acting outside the budget, with no transparency as we would say in modern times), framing his brother Benjamin by planting his cup in Benjamin's food bag, and all of these things were done according to his wishes. No Pharaoh was in the picture.

Moreover, Joseph, upon his own authority, told the brothers to tell his father, "And you shall live in the land of Goshen and you shall be near me... And there I will nourish you..." (45:10-11). And all this plan without consulting Pharaoh.

From Joseph's point of view, there was no need to ask Pharaoh again for authority to settle his father in Egypt or even to feed him from the kingdom's resources. He had that authority already.

Pharaoh intervened for the first time since Joseph took over, right after the text tells us, "**And the voice was heard** in Pharaoh's house saying Joseph's brothers have come..." (45:16), the text says. "And Pharaoh said to Joseph..." (45:17).

If it was not Joseph who was 'the voice that was heard in Pharaoh's house,' then who was it? It could have been the interpreter, but the text barely mentions him, likely due to his insignificance to the story. More likely it was the brothers. Quite likely, they decided to go and deal with Pharaoh directly.

At this point, the idea that the brothers went to Pharaoh is only a **suspicion**. We still need to find confirmation of this point.

The first confirmation is the opening words of Pharaoh to Joseph, "And Pharaoh said to Joseph, say to your brothers, **do this**..." (Genesis 45:17). To instruct 'do this...' cannot be the opening of a conversation. It sounds more like **a final summary** of a long discussion. As if the commander is putting the final touch on all the ideas that were discussed during the strategy meeting.

Pharaoh's Proposal to Settle in Egypt

If Joseph's proposal were the only one on the table, things would have been simple. But the text tells us that Pharaoh intervened and suggested his own proposal.

The text says,

> And Pharaoh said to Joseph, say to your brothers, do this: load
> your livestock and go to the land of Canaan. And take your father
> and your households and come to me and I will give you the good
> of the land of Egypt and you shall eat the fat of the land. Now you
> are commanded to take for yourselves from the land of Egypt
> wagons for your little ones, and for your wives, and carry your
> father and come. And your eyes should not care for your goods,
> for the good of all the land of Egypt is yours. (45:17-20)

SCAN Rule: The first sentence in an open statement is the most
important one. In many cases the first sentence might include the reason
for the events that follow.

The fact is that Pharaoh started his proposal by stating, 'do this, load your
livestock…' Earlier, the text quotes the brothers talking about riding **asses**
into Egypt to get food. The Egyptians, on the other hand were using
horses for transportation. Since in this place the text quotes Pharaoh, it is
quite likely that the word **livestock** is the way the Egyptians looked upon
riding **asses**, and quite likely in a very demeaning way. Since this is likely
Egyptian language, it should indicate to us that the text is changing the
linguistic lens from Canaanite to Egyptian.

The fact that Pharaoh started his proposal by instructing the brothers to
load the livestock and go to Canaan might indicate that Pharaoh wanted
the livestock to be out of Egypt as soon as possible. It might even explain
why Pharaoh sent the wagons to bring the family back to Egypt, just to
make sure that the livestock would not return to Egypt.

Comparing Pharaoh's Proposal to Joseph's

There are differences between Joseph's proposal and Pharaoh's proposal.
The first difference is that Joseph is sending a message to his father,
talking to his father as the one who makes the decisions:

> …come down to me delay not. And **you** shall live in the land of
> Goshen, and **you** shall be near me, **you**, **your** sons, **your**
> grandchildren and **your** flocks, and **your** herds, and all that **you**

have. And there will I nourish **you**, for yet there are five years of famine, lest **you** and **your** household and all that **you** have come to poverty" (45:9-11).

Pharaoh's proposal, on the other hand, is directed to **the brothers**, and not to Jacob:

> [D]o this, load your[100] livestock and you should go and come to the land of Canaan. And take your father and your households, and come to me, and I will give **you** [plural] the good of the land of Egypt, and **you** [plural] shall eat the fat of the land. Now **you** [singular] are commanded to take for **yourselves** from the land of Egypt wagons for **your** little ones, and for **your** wives, and carry **your** father and come. And **your** eyes should not care for **your** goods for the good of all the land of Egypt is **yours**. (45:17-20)

The second difference we note is the order of listing of the family by Joseph and Pharaoh. While Joseph said, "...and you shall be near me, **you, your sons, your grandchildren and your flocks, and your herds**, and all that **you** have." (45:10). Joseph, naturally, listed his father first, and then moved on to list the family members, and then the possessions. Pharaoh, on the other hand, is listing Jacob the father **at the end of the list**, "...take for yourselves from the land of Egypt wagons **for your little ones, and for your wives, and carry your father** and come." (45:19). It is clear that Pharaoh is targeting the brothers and not the father. For him, Jacob was relegated to the end of the list.

We find twice in Pharaoh's proposal the connection between bringing the father to Egypt and the brothers 'coming to' Egypt. The first is, "And take your father and your households **and come to me**..." (45:18). The second is, "...and carry your father **and come**" (45:19). It seems that for Pharaoh, the fact that brothers 'came to' Egypt was not enough. For him, the idea was to bring Jacob down to Egypt. Or, in other words, to end the Israelite kingdom.

The third difference, and quite significant, between the two proposals is that while Joseph is suggesting his father live in the land of Goshen,

---

[100] "...your..." While in English the word 'your' does not distinguish singular or plural, the Hebrew text has Pharaoh using the plural form.

Pharaoh is talking in different terms, "…and **I will give you** the good of the land of Egypt…" (45:18).

We already saw in the linguistic journey on commerce and trade in Biblical language that the language of the text does not use the verb 'to pay.' Instead, the language uses the verb 'to give.' As the text says about Joseph selling the food to the Egyptians in exchange for the flocks, "And Joseph said **give** your cattle and I will **give** you food for your cattle if your money is gone" (47:16).

And Pharaoh is talking about 'giving.' The language of the text does not use the verb 'to give' when someone gets something for free. If so, the immediate question should be: what would the brothers 'give' Pharaoh in exchange?

The possible answer that comes to mind immediately is: land-for-land. I 'give' you '…the good of the land of Egypt…' in exchange for the land of Canaan. After all, it is clear that Pharaoh is not interested in their flocks, herds, and even other possessions, as he tells them that they can keep them for themselves, and he even said that they can leave possessions in the land of Canaan as they will get everything in Egypt.

Moreover, Pharaoh's proposal is divided into two parts. The first part is addressed to the brothers, "…do this, load your beasts and you should go and come to the land of Canaan. And take your father and your households, and come to me, and I will give you the good of the land of Egypt, and you shall eat the fat of the land" (45:17).

The second part starts with 'Now **you** are commanded…' and we should note that the 'you' here is the second person masculine singular.[101] This singular 'you' is targeting Joseph himself.

And there is a difference between these two parts. In order to see the difference, we need to take a long detour and discuss two linguistic journeys, one dealing with the verb 'to take,' and the other with the verb 'to carry.'

---

[101] In Hebrew there is a distinct pronoun for 'you' (*ata*) masculine and for 'you' (*at*) feminine. The one used here is *ata*. For the plural 'you' there is also distinction between the plural masculine (*atem*) and the feminine (*aten*).

Pharaoh's Proposal

The text says, "And take (*ukechu*) your father and your households, and come to me, and I will give you the good of the land of Egypt, and you shall eat the fat of the land. And you are commanded to take (*kechu*) for yourselves wagons from the land of Egypt for your little ones, and for your wives, and carry (*unesatem*) your father and come" (Genesis 45:18-19).

Linguistic Journey: To Take Someone

The verb 'to take' in Hebrew comes from the three-letter word *L-K-CH*. In this section we will examine the way the verb is used in the language of the text in the context of **taking** someone.

Instructions for the journey: in this linguistic journey we will deal with all the situations in which the text chooses to use the verb 'to take.' It might be that for the reader, who is involved with Pharaoh's proposal to the brothers, this linguistic journey would seem like a major detour and diversion from the issue at hand. However, we will not be able to grasp the deep meaning of Pharaoh's proposal without understanding the full meaning of the verb 'to take.' The reader should be patient, and enjoy the various issues discussed in this linguistic journey, starting with the concept of being chosen (Israel as the chosen people), the meaning of the concept of 'leadership,' and even an extensive discussion of the issue of marriage in the society of Biblical times. When we finish this linguistic journey we will be able to return to discuss Pharaoh's proposal, and to understand that it is not innocent at all. In summary, the reader needs to exercise patience.

Family Members

Abraham

We find that the head of the family, the one in **authority**, is the one who 'takes' the members of his family. For example, when Terah, Abraham's father starts his journey toward the land of Canaan, the text says, "And Terah **took** (*vayikach*) Abram his son, and Lot the son of Haran his grandson, and Sarai his daughter-in-law, his son Abram's wife..." (Genesis 11:31). We see the same when Abraham started his journey,

"And Abram **took** (*vayikach*) Sarai his wife, and Lot his brother's son, and all their possessions that they had gathered, and the souls that they had made in Haran..." (Genesis 12:5). When Abraham embarks on the circumcision 'project,' he "...**took** (*vayikach*) Ishmael his son, and all who were born in his house, and all who were bought with his money..." (Genesis 17:23).

When the angels rush Lot to leave Sodom before the destruction, they are quoted as saying, "...arise, **take** (*kach*) your wife and your two daughters who are here, lest you die in the iniquity of the city" (Genesis 19:15). The same form is used when the Almighty instructs Abraham to go and sacrifice Isaac, "And he said, **take** (*kach*) your son, your only son whom you love..." (Genesis 22:2). And indeed, Abraham went to do so, "...and **took** (*vayikach*) two of his lads with him, and Isaac his son..." (Genesis 22:3).

When they arrived at the location, the text says, "And Abraham **took** (*vayikach*) the wood of the burnt offering, and laid it upon Isaac his son, and he **took** the fire in his hand, and a knife, and they went both of them together" (Genesis 22:6). We should note that here the text does not say that Abraham **took** Isaac, as the text said at the beginning of the trip. And if the reader did not get the message, the text emphasizes, "...and they went both of them together."

Isaac

Of the three forefathers – Abraham, Isaac, and Jacob – Isaac is the only one to whom the text does not attribute the verb 'to take.' One might explain it by saying that unlike the other two, Isaac did not embark on a long-distance trip. However, the 'trip' that Abraham made on the way to sacrifice Isaac was a 3-day trip ("On the third day..." Genesis 22:4), which was not as long as a trip from one country to another. Moreover, Isaac did move around several times, and although the text does not say how long those trips were, he still had to move with his wife Rebecca and his two sons. And the text did not mention any 'taking' of family members by Isaac. Let's not forget that when the time came to bless his son before his death, Rebecca his wife was the one who took the initiative to decide who would get the blessing.

Jacob

When the time came for Jacob to return to his home country, the land of Canaan, after spending a long time in Haran, Jacob consulted his two wives, and practically asked them permission to do so. After all, they had to separate from their family, and to move to a far away country. The two wives' response was, "…Whatever Elohim has said to you, do" (Genesis 31:16). The text continues with describing Jacob embarking on his trip, "And Jacob rose up, and **carried** (*vayisa*) his sons and his wives upon the camels" (31:17). We should note that the text does not say that Jacob 'took' them. Jacob had their permission to move. Again, going back to Abraham and Isaac, as the text did not say, when Abraham and Isaac (along with the two lads) reached the location of the sacrifice, that Abraham 'took' Isaac, the conclusion should be that Abraham had Isaac's permission to do so.

For comparison, let's examine Moses' journey from Midian back to Egypt, after the revelation at the burning bush. The Almighty instructed him to go to Egypt and deliver the people out of Egypt.

The text says, "And Moses returned to Jethro his father-in-law and said to him, let me go and I will return to my brothers who are in Egypt and see whether they are still alive, and Jethro said to Moses, go in peace" (Exodus 4:18). As with Jacob, Moses asked his father-in-law permission to leave him and Midian, and go to Egypt. And Jethro gave that permission. And the text continues, "And Moses (*vayikach*) took his wife and his sons and rode them upon the ass…" (Exodus 4:20).

Moses asked for permission and it was granted, so why the use of the verb 'to take?' One should note that Moses asked permission from his **father-in-law**, and not, as Jacob, from his **wife**. And in fact, we find another difference between Jacob and Moses. While for Jacob the text lists first his sons and then his wives, for Moses the wife is listed first and the sons second. Generally speaking, the order of listing reflects the set of priorities for a person.

And in fact, we know that Moses' wife, Zippora, was quite an assertive wife. When they faced danger in the lodging on the way, Zippora took the initiative, and she "…took a sharp stone, and cut off the foreskin of her son, and threw it at his feet, and said, surely a bridegroom of blood are you to me" (Exodus 4:25). Zippora didn't wait for Moses to do it. She did it on her own. And Moses did not ask permission from Zippora to leave her father and her sisters, and go to a far-away country. And in fact, Zippora and Moses's sons vanished from the text until later on, when Jethro appears in the desert to visit Moses after the exodus, "And Jethro, Moses's father-in-law, took (*vayikach*) Zippora, Moses' wife, after her being sent away[102]" (18:2). One might wonder if Zippora 'being sent away' was due to the conflict created between the couple, due to Moses' neglecting to consult her before going back to Egypt.

Back to Jacob

However, before the important encounter with his brother Esau, the text says, "And he rose that night, and **took** (*vayikach*) his two wives, and his two women slaves, and his eleven sons..." (Genesis 32:23), "And he took (*vayikachem*) them and had them cross the brook..." (Genesis 32:24).

When Dinah was taken to the city of Shechem, and the father of the young man came to negotiate with her family, asking for her hand, the text quotes the brothers as saying, "And if you will not listen to us to be circumcised then we will **take** (*velakachnu*) our daughter and we will go" (Genesis 34:17). Although the text attributes the response to the brothers, still the fact that the response labels Dinah as 'our daughter' indicates that Jacob was the one who had the authority.

Joseph

When Joseph wanted his father Jacob to bless his two sons, the text says, "...and he **took** (*vayikach*) with him his two sons Menashe and Ephraim" (Genesis 48:1). And during the meeting, when his father asks, "Who are they?" the text quotes Joseph as saying, "...they are my sons whom *Elohim* has given me in this place..." (Genesis 48:9). Jacob instructs Joseph, "and he said, **take** (*kachem*) them please to me and I will bless them" (48:9). One should note that Jacob asserts his authority as the head of the family by saying to Joseph that he should be the one to take them and not Jacob. And the text continues, "And Joseph **took** (*vayikach*) them both, Ephraim in his right hand towards Israel's left, and Menashe in his left hand towards Israel's right hand..." (Genesis 48:13).

---

[102] 'Being sent away' is the terminology used in Biblical Hebrew for 'divorce.'

Siblings

We already saw that the text uses the verb 'to take' when the head of the family asserts authority over his family members. This is also the case for siblings.

After the attack on Shechem, the text says that Simeon and Levi, "…and **took** (*vayikchu*) Dinah out of Shechem's house and came out" (Genesis 34:26). We see the same when Jacob relented and allowed the brothers to take Benjamin to Egypt by saying, "And **take** (*kachu*) your brother and arise and return to the man" (Genesis 43:13). After Judah promised Jacob that he, Judah, would be responsible for Benjamin, the brothers could 'take' him. And when Judah talked to Joseph, before Joseph revealed himself to the brothers, Judah quoted Jacob as saying, "And you will **take** (*ulekachtem*) this also from my face, and harm befall him…" (Genesis 44:29). Later on, when Joseph wanted to introduce his brothers to Pharaoh as shepherds, the text says, "And from the periphery of his brothers he **took** (*lakach*) five men…" (Genesis 47:2), and we should note that he could exercise authority over only 'the periphery of his brothers.'

The Activity of Taking and Leadership

We saw earlier that before Jacob blessed Joseph's sons the activity of 'taking' took place. We see the same in other instances in the Tanach in which 'taking' precedes a blessing, or a high position, or the position of leadership.

'Taking' the people of Israel to be the people of the Almighty:

- "And I will **take** (*velakachti*) you to me for a people…" (Exodus 6:7),
- "And *Y-H-V-H* has **taken** (*lakach*) you and brought you out of the iron furnace, out of Egypt, to be for him a people of inheritance…" (Deuteronomy 4:20)
- "Or has *Elohim* ventured to go and **take** (*lakachat*) him a nation…" (Deuteronomy 4:34)

We see the same in the prophecy of redemption of the people:

- "I will **take** (*velakachti*) you from among the nations and gather you from all the countries and will bring you into your own land" (Ezekiel 36:24),
- "...I will **take** (*lokeach*) the sons of Israel from among the nations where they have gone, and will gather them from all around and bring them into their own land" (Ezekiel 37:21).

Before the priests and Levites are appointed to their service in the tabernacle, the text says that the Almighty said to Moses,

- "**Take** (*Kach*) Aaron and his sons with him..." (Leviticus 8:2).
- "And I, behold, I have **taken** the Levites from among the sons of Israel..." (Numbers 3:12),
- "And you shall **take** the Levites for me..." (Numbers 3:41),
- "**Take** (*kach*) the Levites instead of all the firstborn among the sons of Israel..." (Numbers 3:45),
- "**Take** (*kach*) the Levites from among the sons of Israel and cleanse them" (Numbers 8:6),
- "...instead of the firstborn of all the sons of Israel have I **taken** (*lakachti*) them to me" (Numbers 8:16), and
- "And I, behold, I have **taken** (*lakachti*) your brothers the Levites from among the sons of Israel..." (Numbers 18:6).

We find the same for other positions of leadership. For example, the chiefs of the twelve tribes, "And Moses and Aaron **took** (*vayikach*) these men who were pointed out by their names" (Numbers 1:17). When Moses complained that he could not bear the leadership by himself, the Almighty told him, "...gather to me seventy men of the elders of Israel, whom you know to be the elders of the people and officers over them, and **take** (*velakachta*) them to the Tent of meeting..." (Numbers 11:16).

The activity of 'taking' as relating to transfer of leadership is found with Moses and Joshua who succeeded him. The text says, "And *Y-H-V-H* said to Moses, **take** (*kach*) Joshua the son of Nun, a man in whom is spirit and lay your hand on him" (Numbers 27:18), and later on, the text says, "...and he **took** (*vayikach*) Joshua, and set him before Eleazar the priest..." (Numbers 27:22).

The bottom line is that the one who 'takes' another to a respectable or higher position is the one who is the leader who can act upon his wish to elevate the other. The one who is 'taken' by the other is the one who is 'chosen.' Note that 'taking' is in the active voice, and 'being chosen' is in the passive voice. In Biblical Hebrew, 'taking' is not 'choosing,' but 'being chosen' is the outcome of 'taking,' at least in the first five books of Moses. It is our understanding of what 'taking' is, but it is not explicitly in the language.

Abraham

When the Almighty addressed Abram and told him to leave his family, his homeland, and country to go to "...the land that I will show you" (Genesis 12:1), Abram indeed acts upon the Almighty's words and comes out of Haran. We should note at this point in time there is no mention of any 'taking.' If anyone takes anyone, it is Abram who takes his family with him, as we saw earlier, "And Abram **took** Sarai his wife..." (12:5).

Later on in life, Abraham sends his slave back to his homeland to bring a wife to his son Isaac. The slave asks Abraham what he should do if the woman would not like to move to the land of Canaan, "...should I return your son to the land from where you came?" (24:5). Abraham is in shock, and he responds, "...beware that you bring not my son there again" (24:6). And Abraham continues, *"Y-H-V-H* the G-d of heaven who **took** me (*lekachani*) from my father's house..." (Genesis 24:7).

Although Abraham tells his slave that the Almighty 'took' him from Haran, the fact is that the text did not say that when Abraham left Haran. What changed to bring Abraham to label his move from Haran to the land of Canaan as being 'taken?'

One only needs to read the earlier event – the binding of Isaac. After the angel appeared to Abraham and instructed him not to harm the lad, the angel appeared to him again and said, "...by myself have I sworn said *Y-H-V-H* for because you have done this thing, and you have not withheld your son, your only son. I will surely bless you..." (Genesis 22:16-17). Up to this point, Abraham had a covenant with the Almighty, the covenant of circumcision. But at this point it became an 'oath,' a lot stronger. The strength of the connection between the Almighty and Abraham brought Abraham to label his connection with the Almighty as being 'taken,' or, in effect, being 'chosen.'

Moses and Aaron

We see other Biblical figures who were taken – chosen – for the position of leadership. When the time came for Aaron to die, and to pass the mantle of leadership to his son Eleazar, the text says, "**Take** (*Kach*) Aaron and Eleazar his son and bring them up to Mount Hor" (Numbers 20:25), and on the top of the mountain, Moses took Aaron's garments, put them on Eleazar, and Eleazar succeeded his father Aaron.

Although Aaron and his son Eleazar were 'taken' by Moses for the position of priest, we should note that Moses was not 'taken.'

The text says that at the burning bush the Almighty says to Moses, "And now come now and I will **send** (*veshlachacha*) you to Pharaoh…" (Exodus 3:10). Note that the text does not say, "And now come now and I will **take** you and **send** you…" Later on, the Almighty instructs Moses to say to the people,

- "I AM **sent** (*shelachani*) me to you" (3:14),
- "…*Y-H-V-H* the G-d of you fathers, the G-d of Abraham, the G-d of Isaac, and the G-d of Jacob, **sent** me (*shelachani*) to you…" (3:15), and
- "…*Y-H-V-H* G-d of your fathers, the G-d of Abraham, of Isaac, and of Jacob, **appeared** to me…" (3:16).

Before the end of the encounter at the burning bush, the Almighty says to Moses in regard to Aaron his brother, "And you shall speak to him and put words in his mouth, and I will be with your mouth and with his mouth, and will instruct you what you shall do. And he shall talk to the people for you and he will be a mouth for you, and you will be *Elohim* for him" (Exodus 4:15-16).

The verbs used for Moses' mission are 'to send' and 'to appear.' And as for Aaron, Moses is not to be his leader, as he was not 'taken,' but he is to be his *Elohim*.

Aaron was 'taken' as we saw earlier, and his position was transferred to his descendants thereafter, just like a king. Moses, on the other hand, was not 'taken,' and therefore the question of who would succeed him was an open issue.

The Almighty said to Moses, "...you also shall be **gathered to your people**, as Aaron your brother was gathered" (Numbers 27:13).

We should note that the phrase 'gathered to your people' is the same phrase used for the three forefathers.

- "And Abraham expired, and died in a good old age, an old man, and full of years, and was **gathered to his people**" (Genesis 25:8).
- "And Isaac expired, and died and was **gathered to his people**..." (Genesis 35:29).
- "And Jacob finished commanding his sons, he gathered his feet into the bed, and expired, and was **gathered to his people**" (Genesis 49:33).

For the three forefathers the issue of inheritance was determined in their lifetime. For Abraham it was Isaac (not Ishmael); for Isaac it was Jacob (not Esau). For Jacob it was all his sons ("And Jacob finished commanding his sons..."). Not so with Moses.

Moses, who was not 'taken,' addressed the Almighty with a request,

Let *Y-H-V-H* the G-d of all spirits, set a man over the congregation. Who may go out before them, and who may go in before them, and who may lead them out, and who may bring them in, that the congregation of *Y-H-V-H* will not be as sheep which have no shepherd" (Numbers 27:16-17).

In response, the Almighty said, "...Take (*Kach*) Joshua the son of Nun..." (27:18). This should bring us to wonder why Joshua, who was indeed 'taken,' didn't transfer his position to his sons.

Jephthah

In the era of judges, the Ammonites were fighting Israel. The elders of Gilead who earlier expelled Jephthah from their midst now needed him for the battle. The text says, "...and the elders of Gilead went to **take** (*lakachat*) Jephthah from the land of Tob" (Judges 11:5). And, indeed, when they meet him they say, "...come and be our captain..." (11:6).

King Saul

The elders of Israel asked Samuel, "...you are old, and your sons walk not in your ways, now make a king for us to judge us like all the nations" (1 Samuel 8:5). Samuel was upset but the Almighty said to him, "...listen to the voice of the people in all that they say to you..." (8:7).

When the time came, the text says that the Almighty said to Samuel, "Tomorrow about this time I will send you a man from the land of Benjamin, and you shall anoint him to be ruler (*nagid*) over my people Israel..." (1 Samuel 9:16). And we should note that although the people asked for a 'king' (*melech*), the instruction is to anoint the man as 'ruler' (*nagid*). And indeed, the text says that the next day "Samuel took a vial of oil and poured it upon his head, and kissed him, and said, is it not because *Y-H-V-H* has anointed you to be a ruler (*nagid*) over his inheritance?" (10:1). Again, we should note that the text does not say that Saul was anointed to be 'king' but to be *nagid*, which is translated here as 'ruler.'

Later on, the text says that when Saul met his uncle "...but of the matter of the **kingdom**, about which Samuel spoke, he told him not" (10:16).

When Samuel introduced Saul to the people, the text says, "and all the people shouted and said, long live the king" (10:24).

After the victory over the Ammonites, the text says, "And Samuel said to the people, let us go to Gilgal, and renew the kingdom there. And all the people went to Gilgal, and there **they made Saul king** before *Y-H-V-H* in Gilgal..." (11:14-15).

The bottom line is that the text says that Saul became king due to the **people** making him king, and not because he was anointed to be so. The text does not say that Saul was 'taken.' The text does not say that Samuel anointed Saul to be 'king' (*melech*) but to be 'ruler' (*nagid*). In summary, the text diminishes Saul's right to be king, as he was not 'taken' by the Almighty.

King David

Unlike Saul, when the Almighty instructed Samuel to anoint Saul to be *nagid*, the case with David is different. The text says, quoting the

Almighty, "…and go, I will send you to Jesse the Bethlehemite for I have provided me a **king** among his sons" (1 Samuel 16:1).

And David appeared before Samuel, the text says, "…arise and anoint him, for this is he. And Samuel took the horn of oil, and anointed him…" (1 Samuel 16:12-13).

Although the text does not say that Samuel anointed David as king, the beginning of the chapter indicated that was the reason for anointing him.

And in fact, after King David took Uriah's wife Bathsheba, the prophet Nathan said to David, "And now so shall you say to my slave to David, thus said *Y-H-V-H* of hosts, I **took** (*lekachticha*) you from the sheepfold, from following the sheep, to be ruler (*nagid*) over my people over Israel" (2 Samuel 7:8; 1 Chronicles 17:7). It is true that David is mentioned here as being appointed a *nagid*, exactly like Saul; however, David was 'taken,' while Saul was not.

We even see the same with another king who is chosen by the Almighty to be the one to punish the sinning people of Israel, "…I will send and **take** (*velakachti*) Nebuchadrezzar the king of Babylon my slave and will set his throne upon these stones…" (Jeremiah 43:10).

Korach's Rebellion

With this knowledge, that the activity of 'taking' means assuming leadership, we can go back and examine a well-known place that has mystified a lot of commentators, the account of Korach who rebelled against Moses in the wilderness.

The text starts with, "And Korach, the son of Izhar, the son of Kohath, the son of Levi, **took** (*vayikach*) and Dathan and Abiram, the sons of Eliab, and On, the son of Peleth, sons of Reuben" (Numbers 16:1).

We should note that the text does not say that Korach 'took Dathan and Abiram and On.' After the text said that Korach 'took' we have the connecting word 'and' between Korach and the other three. So what did Korach take? By 'taking,' Korach **took** leadership. And if so, one should wonder how long this assumption of leadership took place. It had to be for a while.

How do we know that it was for a while? We only need to go to another place in the Tanach in which another man 'took,' and this was Absalom when he rebelled against his father King David.

> "And Absalom had **taken** (*lakach*) and erected for himself
> in his lifetime a pillar…" (2 Samuel 18:18).

We should note the sequence of events described in this verse. First, Absalom 'took,' which means Absalom rebelled and took the position of king instead of his father. Then Absalom erected a pillar, 'in his lifetime.' We know that the kingdom of Absalom ended when Absalom got killed during the war between him and King David's army. This means Absalom was a king for a period of at least the time it takes to erect a pillar, if not longer than that.

Returning to Korach, who lived many centuries before Absalom, and if we equate the two, because the two of them 'took' without saying what they 'took,' and we know they took leadership, then Korach quite likely was in leadership for at least the time it takes to erect a pillar.

Adam and the Garden of Eden

With the knowledge that 'taking' is 'choosing' and even elevating to a higher position, we should revisit the account of Adam being put into the Garden of Eden. The text says,

> "And *Y-H-V-H Elohim* planted a garden in Eden from the east
> and he put (*vayasem*) the man he formed" (Genesis 2:8).

A few verses later, the text says,

> "And *Y-H-V-H Elohim* **took** (*vayikach*) the man and
> put (*vayanichehu*) him into the Garden of Eden…" (Genesis 2:15).

Is the second verse a mere repetition? Or does it come to send a message?

We should note the following differences between the two verses. In the first verse, the content deals with the garden as it is mentioned first, and the man (*Adam*) is secondary as it is mentioned second. In the second verse, the order is reversed, as the man (*Adam*) is the focus of attention.

The second difference is the labeling of the garden itself. In the first introduction of the garden it is labeled 'garden **in** Eden,' and not 'Garden of Eden' as it is mentioned later. By the first verse, there is more to Eden than just the garden.

The third difference is that in the second verse Adam was 'taken' while he was not 'taken' in the first verse. No different from the sons of Israel who were 'taken' to be the Almighty's people, or the Levites to be priests, or Abraham after he 'passed the test' with the binding of Isaac. By the language, Adam was 'taken,' or in other words, he was 'chosen' for a certain position.

The fourth difference involves the verb for 'putting' the man, Adam, in the garden. In the first verse it is the verb *vayasem*; in the second verse it is the verb *vayanichehu*. The two of them are translated as 'put,' but Biblical Hebrew has two distinct verbs for what seems to be the same activity.

SCAN Rule: Change of language reflects a change in reality.

Background information: in most cases changes in language are due to emotions, or to some other dimension or atmosphere at the time of the activity.

Besides this place (Genesis 2:8) we find the verb *vayasem* in the following places:

- "…and *Y-H-V-H* put (*vayasem*) a mark upon Cain…" (4:15)
- "And Abraham took the wood of the burnt offering and put (*vayasem*) them upon Isaac his son…" (22:6)
- "…and he put (*vayasem*) him on the altar upon the wood" (22:9)
- "And the slave put (*vayasem*) his hand under Abraham's *yerech*…" (24:9)
- "…and he took of the stones of that place and put (*vayasem*) them under his head…" (28:11)
- "And he put (*vayasem*) three days' journey between himself and Jacob…" (30:36)

- "...and he put (*vayasem*) his face towards Mount Gilead" (31:21)
- "And Rachel had taken the teraphim and put (*vatesimem*) them in the camel's saddle..." (31:34)
- "And he put (*vayasem*) the female slaves and their children foremost..." (33:2)
- "And Jacob tore his clothes, and put (*vayasem*) sackcloth upon his waist..." (37:34)
- "...and he put (*vayasem*) a gold chain on his neck" (41:42)
- "...and he has put (*vayesimeni*) me a father to Pharaoh and lord of all his house..." (45:8)
- "...thus said your son Joseph, *Elohim* put (*samani*) me lord of all Egypt..." (45:9)
- "And Joseph put (*vayasem*) it into law over the land..." (47:26)
- "...in you shall Israel bless saying, *Elohim* will put (*yesimcha*) you as Ephraim and Menashe, and he put (*vayasem*) Ephraim before Menashe..." (48:20)

Besides 'putting' Adam in the Garden of Eden, we find the verb *lehaniach* in the following places:

- The angels rescuing Lot from Sodom, "...and they brought him out and put (*vayanichuhu*) him outside the city" (19:16)
- The wife of Joseph's master with the garment, "And she put (*vatanach*) his garment by her..." (39:16)

The verb *vayasem* appears 14 times in the book of Genesis; the verb *vayanach* in two more places, totaling three times. Numbers-wise, we can see that the verb *lehaniach* is rare.

When we examined the account of Joseph and his master's wife earlier, we saw the verse, "And she **put** (*vatanach*) his garment by her until his master came home" (Genesis 39:16). We saw that except for one place, all the other places in the Tanach the verb 'to put' is in the context of some holiness. And here the text said that Adam was 'put' (*vayanichehu*) into the Garden of Eden. Although the text says that he was put there, "...to work it and to guard it," but now that holiness is in the picture, and Adam was 'taken' ('chosen'), one should wonder if the Garden of Eden is a holy place. [See more about this in the chapter on the names of the Almighty.]

Back to Taking and Authority

The idea that the one who has the power, and in this case it is the Almighty, 'takes' the one under him, is repeated in another place in the Tanach. After the death of Saul the text says, "And Abner the son of Ner, captain of Saul's army, **took** (*lakach*) Ish-Bosheth the son of Saul, and brought him over to Mahanaim" (2 Samuel 2:8). And the text continues, "And **he made him king** over Gilead, and over the Ashurites, and over Jezreel, and over Ephraim, and over Benjamin, and over all Israel" (2:9). Although Ish-Bosheth is the king, the fact is that Abner is the one who made him king. If we have any doubt that Abner was the real power in that royal court, the text says, "And it came to pass while there was war between the house of Saul and the house of David, that **Abner made himself strong** for the house of Saul" (3:6).

'Taking' means assuming leadership, but the one who does the 'taking' is the one who has the power, and if there is no one to do the 'taking,' as we saw with Korach and Absalom, then we face a rebellion.

Other Examples of Taking as Leadership

When the sons of Israel were standing at the sea, seeing the water in front of them and the Egyptians behind them, they complained to Moses, "And they said to Moses, because there were no graves in Egypt have you **taken** (*lekachtanu*) us to die in the wilderness…" (Exodus 14:11). We should note that at the same time they acknowledged Moses' leadership, they also expressed the fact that they did not want to come out of Egypt. They were 'taken' out of there.

Balak and Balaam

Balak, the king of Moab, wanted Balaam to curse the people of Israel who were camping along his border. Balaam at first refused to go, and only after Balak sent a more distinguished delegation of ministers did Balaam go along with them. When Balak met Balaam he asked Balaam, "…why did you not come to me? Am I not able to honor you?" (Numbers 22:37). The point is that Balak knew that he was facing a 'hostile witness.'

In fact, each time the text brings us the background information before each curse turns out to be a blessing, the text mentions that Balak 'took'

Balaam. Before the first blessing, "And it came to pass on the next day that Balak **took** (*vayikach*) Balaam and brought him up the high places of Baal..." (22:41). And after the first blessing, "And Balak said to Balaam, what have you done to me, I **took** (*lekachticha*) you to curse my enemies..." (Numbers 23:11).

Before the second blessing, the text says, "And he **took** (*vayikachehu*) him to the field of Zophim to the top of Pisgah..." (Numbers 23:14).

After the second blessing the text says, "And Balak said to Balaam, please let me **take** (*ekachacha*) you to another place..." (23:27), and the text continues, "And Balak **took** (*vayikach*) Balaam to the top of Peor..." (23:28).

Before the second blessing we find the verb "...please **go** with me...," once, and the verb 'to take' once. But after the second blessing we find the verb 'to take' twice. The pressure on Balaam escalated.

After the third blessing, the text quotes Balak as saying to Balaam, "...I called (*keraticha*) you to curse my enemies..." (24:10). And at this point of time we encounter a change of language from before when Balak complained after the first blessing, "...I **took** (*lekachticha*) you to curse my enemies..." (23:11). We do not find the verb 'to take' after the third blessing. After three failed attempts in cursing, Balak got the message that Balaam did not accept the job. He was not 'taken.'

'Taking' as 'Being Responsible'

After Cain killed his brother Abel, the text quotes the Almighty as telling Cain, "And now you are cursed from the earth which has opened her mouth to **take** (*lakachat*) your brother's blood from your hand" (Genesis 4:11).

Does the earth actively take the blood of a murdered person? Or does the text come to tell us that the earth is 'responsible' and therefore it is involved in the event?

We see the same in the following place:

"If a man gives his fellow man an ass, or an ox, or a sheep, or any beast, to keep, and it dies, or is hurt, or taken away, and no one seeing it. An oath of *Y-H-V-H* shall be between them both, that he has not put his hand to his fellow man's goods, and its owner shall **take** (*velakach*) and he shall not pay" (Exodus 22:9-10).

If the goods were 'taken away,' and 'no one seeing it' what is left for the owner 'to take?' However, if one knows that 'to take' means 'to be responsible,' then it is understood that the one who was 'keeping' it is not 'responsible,' but the owner is.

Leadership in Warfare

We find the verb 'to take' as demonstrating authority in military leadership. When Laban is about to chase the fleeing Jacob, the text says, "And he **took** (*vayikach*) his brothers with him and pursued after him seven day's journey..." (Genesis 31:23). We find the same with Pharaoh pursuing the departing Israelites, "And he made ready his chariot and **took** (*lakach*) his people with him" (Exodus 14:6). Before the war with Jabin king of Canaan who reigned in Hazor, the prophetess Deborah called Barak the son of Avinoam and said to him, "...and **take** (*velakachta*) with you ten thousand men..." (Judges 4:6). The 'taking' of men comes to demonstrate 'taking leadership' and assuming responsibility.

Before the raid on Shechem to rescue Dinah, the text says, "...the two sons of Jacob, Simeon and Levi, Dinah's brothers **took** (*vayikchu*) each man his sword, and came upon the city boldly and slew all the males" (Genesis 34:25). In no other war mentioned in Genesis did the text need to say openly that the combatants took their weapons, and even which ones. However, knowing that the meaning of 'to take' is 'to take leadership,' we understand the reason for the use of the verb. Moreover, by specifying that they 'took' their weapons, the text comes to say that they didn't look to anyone else for leadership but themselves – 'each man his sword.'

In contrast, we find other leaders who did not 'take' the people to war. For example, Abraham who was about to launch a military expedition to rescue his nephew Lot who was taken captive. The text says, "...he armed (*vayarek*) his trainees who were born in his own house, three hundred and eighteen, and pursued to Dan" (Genesis 14:14). We should note that the text does not say that Abraham 'took' them to war. And in fact, after the war, when the king of Sodom offered Abraham the booty, Abraham said, "Save only that which the lads have eaten, and the share of the men who went with me, Aner, Eshkol, and Mamre, let them take their share" (14:24). And the text did say earlier, "…and these were with a covenant with Abraham" (14:13). Abraham didn't need to take them. They went of their own free will.

Another war in which we do not find the verb 'to take' is the war with Amalek. Moses said to Joshua, "…**choose** for us men, and go out, and fight with Amalek…" (Exodus 17:9). We should note that Moses did not tell Joshua to **take** men, but to **choose** them. And the description of the war clearly positioned Moses as the supreme commander, and not Joshua, "…when Moses held up his hand, that Israel prevailed, and when he let down his hand, Amalek prevailed" (17:11).

Another war without the verb 'to take' is the war with Midian. Moses tells the people, "…**extract** from yourselves men for the war, and let them go against the Midianites…" (Numbers 31:3). And the text continues, "And there **were delivered** out of the thousand of Israel, a thousand for every tribe…" (31:5). By using the passive voice, 'were delivered,' the text avoids using the verb 'to take.' The order was not given to one in charge but to the 'people.' And the order was not to 'take,' but to 'extract' them.

Taking Possession at War

The first one to use the verb 'to take' to indicate conquest in war is Jacob. When talking to Joseph before his death, the text quotes Jacob as saying, "And I have given you one portion above your brothers which I **took** (*lakachti*) from the hand of the Amorite with my sword and with my bow" (Genesis 48:22).

Later on, after the exodus, we find that the Israelites fought battles with two kings east of the Jordan. The text says, "And Israel **took** (*vayikach*) all these cities…" (Numbers 21:25), "…and he **took** (*vayikach*) all his land out of his hand…" (21:26).

In his words to the people before his death, Moses tells the people, "And we **captured** (*vanilkod*) all his cities at that time, there was not a city which we did not **take** (*lakachnu*) from them…" (Deuteronomy 3:4).

Here we find two different words to differentiate two different stages of conquest, the verb 'to capture' (*lilkod*) and the verb 'to take' (*lakachat*).

SCAN Rule: There are no synonyms in language.

Background information: One should take into consideration that no two different words express exactly the same meaning. Therefore, if we encounter two different words they must denote two different meanings. In mathematical terms we would say that X is X, but X is not Y.

In general, we can see that the activity of 'capturing' (*lilkod*) deals with the point in time during which the place is being conquered. However, conquering the place does not mean that the victors will actually settle in the place. We can see in the text several times in which 'capturing' is mentioned without settling the place. When 'settling' the place follows 'capturing' it, the text indicates so.

For example:

- "And Moses sent to spy out Jaazer and they **captured** (*vayilkedu*) its villages **and possessed** the Amorites who were there" (Numbers 21:32).
- "And the sons of Machir the son of Menashe went to Gilead and **captured** (*vayilekeduah*) **and possessed** the Amorite who was in it" (Numbers 32:39).
- "…the sons of Dan went up to fight against Leshem, and captured (*vayilkedu*) it and struck it with the sword **and possessed it and lived in it** and called Leshem Dan after the name of their father" (Joshua 19:47).
- "And David **captured** (*vayilkod*) the fortress of Zion, which is the City of David" (2 Samuel 5:7), and the text moves on to say, "And David lived in the fortress…" (2 Samuel 5:9).

Without saying it, the text perceives that 'capturing' is not enough. It is evident with the many battles that Joshua launched in the land, where 'capturing' took place without settling the places. And in the book of

Judges we find, "And it came to pass, when Israel was strong, that they put the Canaanites to tribute, **but they did not possess them**" (Judges 1:28).

Before returning to our linguistic journey relating to 'taking' we should note that the text relates to Saul's establishing himself as king of Israel with the verb 'to capture.' Thus we see, "And Saul **captured** (*vayilkod*) the kingdom over Israel..." (1 Samuel 14:47). If we understand that the verb 'to capture' relates only to the exact point of time in which conquering was done, should we understand that Saul only managed to **achieve** the kingdom, but the text does not say that Saul actually **held** the kingdom? This is in addition to the facts that the text does not say that Saul was 'taken' to be king, and that the people were the ones who made him king. These two points together reflect the negative attitude of the text towards the kingdom of Saul.

Back to Taking Possession at War

We find many times in which the verb 'to take' is used by the text to express the settlement of the tribes in the land.

For example,

- "For the tribe of the sons of Reuben according to the house of their fathers and the tribe of the sons of Gad according to the house of their fathers have **taken** (*lakchu*) their inheritance, and half the tribe of Menashe have **taken** (*lakchu*) their inheritance. The two tribes and the half tribe **took** (*lakchu*) their inheritance..." (Numbers 34:14-15),
- "With him the Reubenites and the Gadites have **taken** (*lakchu*) their inheritance..." (Joshua 13:8), and
- "...and Gad, and Reuben, and the half tribe of Menashe, have **taken** (*lakchu*) their inheritance..." (Joshua 18:7).

The same applies to others,

- "Jair the son of Menashe **took** (*lakach*) all the country of Argob..." (Deuteronomy 3:14), and

- "There was not a city that made peace with the sons of Israel, save the Hivites the inhabitants of Gibeon, all others they **took** (*lakchu*) in battle" (Joshua 11:19).

Later on, we see the same – the verb 'to take' relates to conquest:

- "And the king of the Ammonites answered to the messengers of Jephthah, because Israel **took** (*lakach*) my land when they came up from Egypt..." (Judges 11:13),
- "And said to him, thus said Jephthah, Israel did not **take** (*lakach*) the land of Moab nor the land of the Ammonites" (Judges 11:15),
- "...and the cities which the Philistines had **taken** (*lakchu*) from Israel..." (1 Samuel 7:14),
- "...the cities which my father **took** (*lakach*) from your father..." (1 Kings 20:34), and
- "...**took** (*vayikach*) again from the hand of Ben-Hadad the son of Hazael the cities..." (2 Kings 13:25).

Capturing Someone

After the war between the four kings and the five kings, the text says, "And they **took** (*vayikchu*) Lot, and his goods, the son of Abram's brother, and they went, and he lives in Sodom" (Genesis 14:12).

After the raid on Shechem, the text says,

> They **took** (*lakachu*) their sheep, and their oxen, and their asses, and that which was in the city, and that which was in the field. And all their armed ones, and all their little ones, and their wives they captured (*shavu*) and plundered (*vayavozu*) and all that was in the house. (Genesis 34:28-29)

We should note two points. The text separated the animals from the people in two different verses. Second, while for the animals the text uses 'to take' (*lakachat*), for the people the text uses the verbs 'to capture' (*lishbot*) and 'to plunder' (*laboz*). It seems that the text perceives 'taking' as more legitimate than 'capturing' or 'plundering.'

When Joseph faces his brothers, the text says, "...and he **took** (*vayikach*) from them Simeon and bound him before their eyes" (Genesis 42:24).

When the brothers were invited to Joseph's house to eat with him they were afraid because "…of the money that was returned in our sacks at the first time, that he may seek occasion against us and fall upon us, and **take** (*lakachat*) us for slaves…" (Genesis 43:18). We see the same centuries later when the woman cries to the prophet for help, saying, "…and the creditor has come to **take** (*lakachat*) to him my two children to be slaves" (2 Kings 4:1).

When at the time of Samuel the ark of *Elohim* was captured by the Philistines, the text consistently uses the verb 'was taken' to mean 'was captured.'

- *nilkach* (1 Samuel 4:11),
- *nilkacha* (4:17),
- *hilakach* (4:19),
- *hilakach* (4:21),
- *nilkach* (4:22),
- and in the active form, *lakchu* (5:1).

To mean 'conquest' the text says, "…for the king of Babylon had **taken** (*lakach*) from the river of Egypt to the river Euphrates…" (2 Kings 24:7).

There are many other examples.

Taking and Marriage

Introduction

Up to this point we saw that the verb 'to take' is used to describe the line of authority. The Almighty 'takes' Adam to be in the Garden of Eden. The Almighty 'takes' the sons of Israel to be his people. Moses 'takes' Aaron to serve as priests in the tabernacle. King David was 'taken' to serve as the leader of the nation. Korach and Absalom 'took' authority when they rebelled.

The verb 'to take' is also used to describe the act of marriage; a man 'takes' a woman to be his wife. However, a woman does not 'take' a man to be her husband. At least it is not in the language of the text.

Background Information

In the second account of the creation, in which the Almighty is 'introduced' as "*Y-H-V-H Elohim*," the text says,

> And *Y-H-V-H Elohim* made Adam fall into a deep sleep, and he slept, and He took one from his ribs, and closed up the flesh. And *Y-H-V-H Elohim* built the rib that He had taken from Adam, made he a woman and brought her to the Adam. And Adam said, this is now bone of my bones, and flesh of my flesh, she shall be called woman (*isha*) because she was **taken** (*lukacha*) out of man (*ish*). (Genesis 2:21-23)

The fact that the woman (*isha*) was taken (*lukacha*) from the man (*ish*) might be the explanation why the verb 'to take' is used for marrying a woman.

Taking a Wife

The Time Before Abraham

As the first one 'in the image of the Almighty,' Adam is the one who did not 'take' a woman. One might consider it as a bonus that he did not need to go and look for one, as the Almighty was the one who took care of this important job. But the fact is that we find that Adam did complain. After eating from the forbidden fruit, Adam is quoted as saying, "...the woman whom you **gave** to be with me..." (Genesis 3:12). And we should note that the woman both 'was taken' (*lukachah*) from Adam, and 'was given' (2:22) to him, by the text. We can look at 'giving' as the opposite of 'taking,' as Job is quoted as saying, "...*Y-H-V-H* **gave** and *Y-H-V-H* has **taken** away..." (Job 1:21).

After Adam, we find the first to be mentioned as 'taking' a wife is Lemech, "And Lemech **took** (*lakach*) for himself two wives..." (Genesis 4:19).

The next ones to be mentioned are the "the sons of *Elohim*." The text says, "...and they **took** (*vayikchu*) as wives **from all they chose**" (Genesis 6:2).

The phrase 'from all they chose' seems 'unnecessary' and as such it is very important. We will see in this linguistic journey, that free choice in 'taking' a wife was not that accepted.

We should note that although the text mentions Noah's wife, and the wives of Noah's sons, still there is no mention of the fact that Noah and/or his sons 'took' wives.

The Forefathers

Reality Check

Before we move to examine the language in the text describing the act of marriage among the three forefathers, we should note that all of them married within the extended family.

Abraham, at the time Abram, married Sarai. It is not that clear who Sarai was, but it is quite likely that she was the daughter, Iscah, of Abraham's oldest brother Haran.

Isaac, Abraham's son, married Rebecca who was Bethuel's daughter, the son of Abraham's youngest brother, Nahor. In fact, Rebecca was Isaac's first cousin once removed.

Jacob married Leah and Rachel who were his first cousins. Laban, the father of Leah and Rachel, was Rebecca's brother.

Language Check

For **Abraham**, the text says, "And Abram and Nahor **took** (*vayikach*) wives..." (Genesis 11:29). Later on, after Sarah's death, the text says, "And Abraham again **took** (*vayikach*) a wife and her name was Keturah" (Genesis 25:1).

For **Isaac**, Abraham sent his slave to bring Isaac a wife from his homeland, and the slave acted with the 'power of attorney.' We find that, "...and the slave **took** (*vayikach*) Rebecca and went" (Genesis 24:61). Still, we find later, "And Isaac brought her to his mother Sarah's tent, and **took** (*vayikach*) Rebecca and she became his wife, and he loved her..." (Genesis 24:67).

We should note that the text gives three stages in Rebecca's entrance into the family. First, 'Isaac brought her to his mother Sarah's tent,' second, 'and took Rebecca,' and third, 'she became his wife.' We should also note that 'he loved her' is after 'she became his wife.'

SCAN Rule: Change of language reflects a change in reality.

This means the each of these stages reflects different activities, and they do not overlap. Let's examine these three stages.

"...Isaac brought her to his mother Sarah's tent..."

This is before 'taking' her, and thus is not part of the marriage process. Once she arrived, she needed a place to stay before the marriage would take place. From later on, we learn that before Laban brought Leah to Jacob, the text says, "And Laban gathered all the men of the place, and made a feast" (Geneses 29:22). It is very unlikely that Isaac would marry Rebecca 'under the radar.' Marriage had to be done in public, and quite likely that's what Isaac was about to do. However, he didn't know the exact day Rebecca would arrive, or even if she would arrive, and therefore he needed time to arrange the 'feast.' In the meantime, modesty called for him to host Rebecca in a respectable and distinguished place, a place that would not start rumors that they cohabited before the marriage. His mother's tent was a good place for this purpose.

As a secondary benefit, we learn something about the way families lived at the time. Sarah had her own tent. This is not different from our learning of the search Laban did when he chased the fleeing Jacob, trying to find his missing gods. The text says there, "And Laban came into Jacob's tent, and into Leah's tent, and into the tent of the two women slaves, and he found them not, and he came out from Leah's tent, and came into Rachel's tent" (Genesis 31:33). The husband and the wife (or wives) had different tents. They did not sleep in the same tent. Exactly like Abraham and Sarah. At the time, there was separation between the husband and the wife, as it comes across in the text relating to the forefathers' living circumstances.

Let's check the story of Isaac calling his son Esau and informing him that he wants to give him the blessing after Esau brings his food from his hunting. The text says there, "And Rebecca heard when Isaac spoke to Esau his son..." (Genesis 27:5). The text does not say that she was present at the time Isaac talked to Esau. She 'heard,' but she was listening to it from outside Isaac's tent. And in fact, she called Jacob and told him to go and bring her the lamb so she could cook for Isaac, and then she said, "...And you shall bring it to your father that he may eat..." Rebecca was not talking in the presence of Isaac. She talked to Jacob in her own place, in her own tent.

We find the same with Laban searching after his stolen gods. The text says, "And Laban came into Jacob's tent, and into Leah's tent, and into the two maidservants' tents..." (31:33). Again, the husband and the wives, each one had a tent. And the maidservants had a tent as well.

"...and took Rebecca..."

This is the act of marriage. Quite likely it involved gathering the people of the place and making a feast, and most important of all, moving Rebecca from Sarah's tent into Isaac's tent, as she had to be 'taken' – removed from her previous non-marital accommodations.

"...she became his wife..."

Consummating the relationship.

These three components are mirrored in reverse in the process of divorce,

> When a man has taken (*yikach*) a wife, and consummated the relationship (*be'aalah*), and it comes to pass that she finds no favor in his eyes, because he has found some uncleanness in her, then let him write her a bill of divorcement, and give it in her hand, **and send her out of his house**. (Deuteronomy 24:1)

Giving her a 'bill of divorcement' is the exact opposite of the feast. If the feast is the announcement to the community that the woman is removed from the pool of available women, then the bill of divorcement is announcement to the community that she returned to the pool of available women. But this is not enough. Two more things need to take place; one is active, and one is passive. The passive one is that the man needs to refrain from 'coming to her.' And the active one is that she needs to be removed from his house, as she needs to be 'un-taken.'

For **Jacob**, the text does **not** say that Jacob **took** his two wives, Leah and Rachel.

For Jacob, the text says, "And Jacob said to Laban, let (*habah*) me have my wife, for my days are fulfilled, that I may come to her. And Laban gathered together all the men of the place, and made a feast. And it came to pass in the evening, that he took Leah his daughter, and brought her to him, and he came to her" (Genesis 29:21-23).

We should note that Jacob does not say to Laban, "…**give** (*tenah*) me my wife." If he were to say that, knowing that the verb 'to give' is used in Biblical Hebrew for commercial transactions, it would have amounted to Jacob cheapening his marriage.

In reality, as the text describes it, Jacob did work for Laban for seven years in exchange for his daughter Rachel. His work was the compensation for her. However, Jacob did not see it as a commercial transaction, but his work came to replace the dowry that was expected of him to give to the bride's family. We see it with Abraham's slave and Rebecca, and we see the talk between Shechem and Jacob over Dinah ("Ask me ever so much as dowry and gift…" (34:12)).

Instead, Jacob uses the word 'let' (*habah*), the same word that is used in the following places:

- regarding the tower of Babel, "…**let** (*habah*) us make bricks…" (Genesis 11:3),
- again the tower of Babel, "…**let** (*habah*) us build us a city and a tower…" (11:4),
- again the tower of Babel, "**Let** (*habah*) us go down…" (11:7),
- Rachel talking to Jacob, "…**let** (*habah*) me have sons…" (Genesis 30:1),
- Judah talking to Tamar, "**let** (*habah*) me please come to you…" (Genesis 38:16), and
- Egyptians talking to Joseph during the famine, "…**let** (*habah*) us have bread…" (Genesis 47:15).

Back to Jacob and Laban: we should note that in the marriage the text does not use the verb 'to take.' If anyone is 'taking' it is Laban, who 'took' Leah. And, again, Laban is not described as 'giving' Leah to Jacob, but 'bringing' her to him.

Jacob complained about the fraud, and then the marriage with Rachel is described, with a major change of language, "...and he **gave** (*vayiten*) him Rachel his daughter for a wife" (29:28). He 'brought' Leah and he 'gave' Rachel. We should remember that Rachel was a 'payment' for the work Jacob did for Laban. From Laban's point of view, it was a 'transaction.' And in fact, before fleeing Haran to go back to the land of Canaan, Jacob asked his wives permission to go. They said, "Are we not counted by him as strangers, for he has **sold** (*mecharanu*) us..." (Genesis 31:15).

The fact is that Jacob did not 'take' his two wives, at least not by the **language** of the text. The same applies to Moses. He also did not 'take' his wife Zipporah. The text says, "And Moses was content to dwell with the man, and he gave Moses Zipporah his daughter" (Exodus 2:21).

However, there is a difference between Laban and Jethro. For Laban the text says, "And it came to pass in the evening that he **took** (*vayikach*) Leah his daughter and **brought** her to him..." (Genesis 29:23). But for Jethro the text says, "...and he **gave** (*vayiten*) Moses Zipporah his daughter" (Exodus 2:21), exactly as the text says for Jacob and Rachel, "...and he **gave** (*vayiten*) him Rachel his daughter for a wife" (Genesis 29:28). We should ask the question: why did Leah have to be 'taken' before she was 'brought' to Jacob? Was she promised to another man?

We should note that the text in regard to Moses does not follow the regular formula, "...and he gave Zipporah his daughter **for a wife**." But the verse immediately following is, "And she bore him a son, and he called his name Gershom..." (2:22). We should also note that the text does not say that she 'conceived,' as it says in most other cases (unless the text deals with twins, where the word 'conceived' is missing for the second one).

Question: was Zipporah pregnant when she was 'given' to Moses?

The way the text relates to Moses' sons will support this suspicion. The text says, "...and the name of the **one** was Gershom... and the name of the **one** was Eliezer..." (Exodus 18:3-4). We should note that the text uses neither the formula – the name of the **first**, and the name of the **second**, nor the formula – the name of the **first**, and the name of **his brother**. Each one of them is 'one.' This is the only place in the entire Tanach that the text relates to two brothers in this fashion.

The idea that Moses divorced ('sent away') Zipporah, and then 'took' her back again, is supported by the following: "And Miriam and Aaron spoke against Moses because of the Cushite woman whom he had taken (*lakach*) for he had taken (*lakach*) a Cushite woman" (Numbers 12:1). We should note that the text repeats 'he had taken.' Actually, in reality, he did take her twice.

Back to Jacob

The first time in the text where it is mentioned that Jacob 'took' his wives is a long time later, "And he rose that night, and he **took** (*vayikach*) his two wives, and his two women slaves, and his eleven sons, and passed over the passage Jabok" (Genesis 32:23). We should note that passing over the passage Jabok is after Laban and Jacob reached a 'non-aggression' treaty, and Laban 'went and returned to his place' (Genesis 32:1).

Before the point in which Jacob separated from the household of his wives' father, his wives were not considered 'under his authority' but under their father's authority. With this understanding, we can read Jacob's reply to Laban, when Laban asked him why he didn't notify him of his wish to go back home to his father's household. The text says, "…because I was afraid, for I said, perhaps you would take by force your daughters from me" (Genesis 31:31).

This fear was not unfounded. We find other examples at that time, mentioned in the Tanach, in which a man's wife could have been given to someone else, if she was still in her father's household.

The text says, "And Samson went down to Timnath, and saw a woman in Timnath of the daughters of the Philistines" (Judges 14:1). Samson asked his parents to arrange the marriage for. him. Although his parents protested, they went down to Timnath, and Samson made a feast (14:10). The text continues to say that Samson "went up to his father's house" (14:19), and, "And Samson's wife was given to his companion who was his friend" (14:20). When Samson wanted to 'come to' his wife, who still lived in her father's household, her father did not let him (15:1), saying, "I truly thought you greatly hated her, therefore I gave her to your companion" (15:2), and offered him her younger daughter.

One might say that this was the Philistine culture, and not the Israelite culture, but the fact is that Jacob still expressed the fear that Laban could have taken his wives from him.

Moses Like Jacob

As we find Jacob taking his wives only very late in the text (only upon separating himself from the household of his father-in-law), so is the case with Moses. Once Moses accepted the mission by the Almighty to go to Egypt and get the sons of Israel out of Egypt, Moses notified his father-in-law that he was going to Egypt, and his father-in-law sent him in peace. Only then does the text say, "And Moses **took** (*vayikach*) his wife and his sons…" (Exodus 4:20).

Taking: Removing a Wife From her Father's House

This late entrance of 'taking' for Jacob and Moses should bring us to check other places in the text to give us the full picture of the act of marriage.

The first place is with Lot and his daughters. After the angels informed Lot that the city was going to be destroyed, the text says, "And Lot came out and spoke to his sons-in-law, who **took** (*lokchei*) his daughters…" (Genesis 19:14).

The idea that there were two stages in the act of marriage – the first is to actually consummate the relationship by 'coming to' the woman. But that was not enough for the woman to be considered 'taken.' Only when the woman was removed from the household of her father and moved to the household of her husband, was she considered a married woman, under her husband's authority, and not under her father's.

Judah and Tamar

After Judah's two sons died after being married to Tamar, the text says,

> And Judah said to Tamar his daughter-in-law, live as a widow **at your father's house**, till Shelah my son be grown, for he said, lest perhaps he die also, as his brothers did, and Tamar went **and lived in her father's house**. (Genesis 38:11)

By Tamar being removed from Judah's house, she was 'un-taken,' or, in other words, she was 'sent away.' It is no different from Moses and his wife Zipporah. The text there says, "And Jethro, Moses' father-in-law, took Zipporah, Moses' wife, **after he had sent her away**" (Exodus 18:2). By Zipporah being back at her father's house, she was 'sent away,' or, in Biblical Hebrew, they were 'divorced.'

And in regard to Judah, the text continues, "...and he said let (*habah*) me come to you for **he knew not that she was his daughter-in-law...**" (Genesis 38:16). The text does not say that he did not know that she was Tamar. The text only says that Judah didn't know that she was his 'daughter-in-law.' If she was removed from his house, she was 'sent away' (divorced), and if so, she was a free woman.

Back to Abraham

We already dealt with the question of who Sarai/Sarah was. And the question arises, if Sarai was the daughter of Haran, and all of them were from Terah the father, and his three sons lived together, and it is expected that this would be the case, how come Abraham 'took' Sarai, but Jacob did not 'take' Leah and Rachel?

The text says, "And Haran died before his father Terah in the land of his birth, in Ur of the Chaldeans" (Genesis 11:28). The verse immediately after is, "And Abram and Nahor **took** (*vayikach*) wives..." (11:29). Once Haran died, and the father of the bride was not in possession of her, the bridegroom, even though he was a relative, and even though they lived together within the extended family, could still 'take' the woman.

The Role of the Parents in Marriage

We are reading about a very conservative society, in which a couple could get married, and still live in the household of the bridegroom's parents, or even with the bride's parents, and yet such a woman would not be considered 'taken.' This idea should bring us to conclude that the parents did have a major role in the process of marriage. And in fact, we find this to be true.

When the time came for Isaac to get married, the text brings us Abraham, Isaac's father, who summoned the "oldest slave of his house, who ruled over all that he had" (24:2) and gave him the mission of going to his home country to get a wife for Isaac. Throughout this description there is no indication that Isaac was involved in the process. Abraham, the father, was the one in charge of picking the wife, and Abraham delegated to his slave this important 'project.' This would explain why the text told us that Isaac loved Rebecca after he 'took' her. Unlike Jacob, for whom the text starts the story by telling us that Jacob fell in love with Rachel at the very beginning. Only then did Jacob approach her father Laban, offering to work for him for the hand of his daughter. In this sense, Jacob was very independent.

Still, Jacob did not go to Haran before his father formally instructed him to do so, "Arise, go to Padan-Aram to the house of Bethuel your mother's father, and take a wife from there of the daughters of Laban your mother's brother" (Genesis 28:2).

We should note that Esau, unlike Jacob, did not wait for any instruction from his father before marrying; at least the text does not say so. The text says only, "And Esau was forty years old when he took a wife, Judith the daughter of Beeri the Hittite, and Basemath the daughter of Elon the Hittite. And they made life bitter for Isaac and for Rebecca" (Genesis 26:34-35).

Dinah in Shechem

The text says, "And Shechem the son of Hamor the Hivite, prince of the country, saw her; he **took** (*vayikach*) her and lay with her, and afflicted her" (Genesis 34:2).

The text says that Shechem already 'took' Dinah, as he removed her from her father's house, but without the father's permission. And in order to get the father's permission, Shechem is quoted as telling his father, "...**take** (*kach*) for me this child for a wife" (34:4). According to custom, Shechem had to ask his father to talk with Dinah's father, Jacob.

We see the same with Samson. The text says, "And Samson went down to Timnath and saw a woman in Timnath of the daughters of the Philistines" (Judges 14:1). Samson, the independent man, as it comes across by the text, roaming the land and fighting the Philistines, goes back to his parents and says, "...I have seen a woman in Timnath of the daughters of the Philistines, now **take** (*kechu*) her for me as a wife" (14:2). Going by the custom, the parents had to be the ones to 'take' the woman for the son.

Judah and Tamar

The text says, "And Judah **took** (*vayikach*) a wife for Er his firstborn, whose name was Tamar" (Genesis 38:6).

Again, the father is the one who 'takes' the wife for the son.

Who is Tamar?

Besides Sarah, where the text actively hides her true identity, and does so by commission, as the text changes her name, Tamar is the only one in the book of Genesis about whose identity the text does not give us any details. Unlike Sarah, the text conceals her identity by omission.

Three points should lead us to start to suspect (and the emphasis is on 'suspicion,' as it is not enough to be considered linguistic 'evidence') that Tamar is quite likely a descendant of the lineage of Lot. The first one is that there are only two women in the book of Genesis whose identity is murky. One woman is Sarah. As we saw earlier, in the section dealing with Abraham and Lot in the chapter on the brothers, the text actively moved to change her name without notifying the reader, and quite likely because of Lot's behavior in Egypt. Lot, who was Sarah's older brother, quite likely when he was in Egypt, a society that advocated marital relationships between first blood relatives, made a move on Sarah, which quite likely brought Abraham to initiate separation between them. And the second woman is Tamar, about whose lineage the text neglects to tell us anything. If Sarah's identity is murky because of Lot, one should wonder if Tamar's murky identity is also because of Lot.

The second point is that the text tells us that Judah 'took' Tamar as a wife for his older son. Knowing that 'taking a woman' cannot be if she is a niece (unless her father is dead, e.g., Abraham taking Sarah), should tell us that she was not from Judah's extended family, or from Judah's older siblings. She was 'removed' from her father's household.

The third and most decisive point is Tamar's behavior. There are only three examples in the entire Tanach in which a woman or women take the initiative to initiate a relationship with a man. The first example is Lot's daughters who initiated a sexual encounter with their father. Out of these sexual encounters two were born, **Moab** to the older, and Ben-Ami to the younger.

Fast forward to the third example which is Ruth **the Moabite** who was instructed by her mother-in-law to sneak into Boaz's place at night and request/demand that he marry her.

The second in chronological order is Tamar, who positioned herself on the road, pretending to be a prostitute, a fact that brought Judah to approach her and to suggest having sex with her.

This should bring us to suspect that Tamar might be one of Lot's descendants, and quite likely from Moab. He was still considered family as he was Abraham's nephew. And Moab's children would have been the same age as Judah's children.

If indeed Tamar was from Moab, then it would be an attempt by the text to suppress her true identity, quite likely **because** she was from Moab.

'Taking' With no Father in the Picture

We have an example of a case where the father is not the picture: Ishmael. Ishmael, Abraham's son, was expelled from his father's house, and he was about to get married, and the text says, "And he lived in the wilderness of Paran, and his mother **took** (*vatikach*) for him a wife from the land of Egypt" (Genesis 21:21).

The History of the Word 'Marriage'

In Modern Hebrew 'marriage' is *nisuyim*. This comes from the three-letter root word *N-S-A*, which actually means 'to carry.' One might ask how the language evolved to use the word 'to carry' for 'marriage.' Moreover, if in Biblical Hebrew the word used for 'marriage' is 'to take,' how do we get from the literal 'to take' to the literal 'to carry' to indicate marriage?

Knowing that marriage meant that the man 'takes' the woman, and knowing that the parents played a role in the setting up of the marriage, we can now go back in time to examine a major event in the history of the Israelite tribes in the land.

The Concubine on the Hill

The Tanach reports to us a major civil war among the tribes. More accurately, the war was between the tribe of Benjamin and the other eleven tribes. This war started with what is called the 'concubine on the hill.' A man with his concubine came to visit their family who resided in the tribe of Benjamin. During the night, some villains murdered the woman. The grieving man raised a commotion over this crime. The other tribes called upon the tribe of Benjamin to surrender the murderers, and the tribe of Benjamin refused. A war started and dozens of thousands were killed from both sides. Eventually, the tribes of Israel prevailed against the tribe of Benjamin. At the end of the war, the Israeli tribes took an oath not to give any of their women to the tribe of Benjamin as wives. That oath, which was taken in the heat of the battle, created a major danger that one of the tribes of Israel, the tribe of Benjamin, would be eradicated. And the other tribes regretted making that oath. But then they faced a problem of how they could help the tribe of Benjamin get married, raise families, and have children, and thus secure the future of the tribe.

The text outlines the solution they found:

> And they commanded the sons of Benjamin, saying go and lie in wait in the vineyards. And see, and behold, if the daughters of Shiloh come out to dance in the dances, then come out of the vineyards, and grab (*vachataftem*) every man his wife of the daughters of Shiloh, and go to the land of Benjamin. And if their

fathers or their brothers come to argue with us, that we will say to them, they found grace with us, because we did not take a wife for every man in the war, for you did not give to them, and now you will be guilty. And the sons of Benjamin did so, and **carried** (*vayis'u*) women from those who danced that they robbed, according to their number, and they went and returned to their inheritance and built the cities and lived in them. (Judges 21:20-23)

If anyone has any doubt what the verb *lachatof* means in Biblical Hebrew, one only has to go to one verse in Psalms, "He lies in wait secretly, like a lion in his den, he lies in wait to **grab** (*lachatof*) the poor, he **grabs** (*yachtof*) the poor, when he draws him into his net" (Psalms 10:9).

The tribes of Israel instructed the men of the tribe of Benjamin to actually 'grab,' and even 'kidnap' innocent women dancing at the time of the festival in Shiloh where the tabernacle was located. And we should note that the sons of Benjamin did so, and the text said that they 'carried' (*vayis'u*) the women with them. This very strict and conservative society in which the family of the bride and groom had a say in marriage, went 'outside the box' and instructed men to go against the system, and disregard the fathers and the brothers of the women, in order to preserve the line of Benjamin.

We should note that this is the first time in the Tanach where the word *laset* ('to carry') was used for a man getting a woman for a wife. If this was not enough, reflecting the fact that the man got 'possession' of the woman at the time they got married, in the case of the 'concubine on the hill,' the word 'to carry' was used, to reflect that the woman was 'taken' against her will, **and against the will of her own family**.

We have to go through many books in the Tanach before we see the word 'to carry' used for marriage. We see it in a few places, starting in the book of Ruth, "And they **married** (*vayis'u*) for them women of Moab..." (Ruth 1:4). The other examples are very late in the last books of the Tanach, the two books of Chronicles:

- "And Eleazar died, and had no sons, but daughters and their brothers, the sons of Kish **married** (*vayisa'um*) them" (1 Chronicles 23:22),

- "And Abijah grew mighty and **married** (*vayisa*) fourteen wives…" (2 Chronicles 13:21), and
- "And Jehoiada **married** (*vayisa*) two wives…" (2 Chronicles 24:3).

It would be interesting to know if the custom found in literature and in movies of the bridegroom carrying his bride over the threshold when they enter their house for the first time is derived from the 'carrying' described here with the tribe of Benjamin and the young women of Shiloh.

Women 'Taking'

In general, we see that women **take** someone in very few instances. For example, when a mother relates to her own son, like Hagar with Ishmael (Genesis 21:21). Or when Rebecca says to Jacob that he should flee to Haran to be with her brother Laban, to wait for Esau's anger to dissipate. And the text says, "…and I will send and I will **take** (*lekachticha*) you from there…" (Genesis 27:45).

We find other women who 'took' **children**. For example, Moses' mother, "…and the woman **took** (*vatikach*) **the child** and nursed him" (Exodus 2:9). Later on, we see a woman saving a small boy from being killed, "And Jehosheba the daughter of king Joram sister of Ahaziah took (*vatikach*) **Joash the son of Ahaziah** and stole him from among the king's sons who were killed…" (2 Kings 11:2). Even in a metaphor we see the same, "And when she saw that though she had waited her hope was lost, she **took** (*vatikach*) another of her **cubs** and made him a young lion" (Ezekiel 19:5), and in the book of Ruth, after Ruth bore a son, the text says, "And Naomi **took** (*vatikach*) **the child** and laid him in her bosom and became his nurse" (Ruth 4:16).

When the two women came in front of King Solomon in the well-known case of 'splitting the baby in two,' the text quotes the woman as saying, "And she arose in the middle of the night and **took** (*vatikach*) **my son** from my side…" (1 Kings 3:20).

Besides children, we can see two examples in which a woman 'takes' her woman slave,

- "And Sarai Abram's wife **took** (*vatikach*) Hagar her Egyptian **slave** after Abram had lived ten years in the land of Canaan, and gave her to her husband to be his wife" (Genesis 16:3), and
- "And Leah saw that she had ceased bearing, and she **took** (*vatikach*) Zilpah her **slave** and gave her to Jacob as a wife" (Genesis 30:9).

It is interesting to note that the text does not use the verb 'to take' when Rachel gives her maidservant Bilhah to Jacob, for her to deliver sons "on her knees" (30:3). Instead, the text says, "And she **gave** him Bilhah..." (30:4).

In summary, as we saw earlier, in which the text attributes the title 'the second' only to women, children, and slaves, here also. We can see that women 'take' only children or slaves. The hierarchy in society is maintained.

There is only one place in the entire Tanach in which a woman 'takes' **men**. Before attacking Jericho, Joshua sent two spies to scout the land. The text says, "...and they went, and came to a harlot's house, named Rahab, and lodged there" (Joshua 2:1).

The king of Jericho got the news that two men from the sons of Israel came to spy on the city, and he sent to Rahab to surrender these two men. And the text says, "And the woman **took** (*vatikach*) the two men and hid him..." (Joshua 2:4).

We should note two points. Only when the text talks about a 'harlot,' a woman outside the social order, would the text mention that she 'took' men. The text does not say that she hid 'them,' but that she hid 'him.' One of the two was not 'hiding.' If so, where was he? And if she 'took' them, should we suspect that the one who was not in hiding was in some other place? With Rahab?

In Conclusion

'Taking' someone is an issue of exercising power and authority. In the conservative society of that time a man 'took' a woman, and not vice versa.

And the text quotes Pharaoh as saying, "And **take** (*kechu*) your father and your households and come to me..." (Genesis 45:18). Without knowing the meaning of the word 'to take' we would not realize that Pharaoh's instructions meant to 'take' Jacob, to take possession of him, maybe even against his own will, and to bring him to Egypt.

If Pharaoh's instructions to the brothers 'to take' their father Jacob and to bring him to Egypt is not enough for us to know that Pharaoh was conspiring with the brothers against Jacob's status in the land of Canaan, then the continuation of Pharaoh's proposal is evidence that in fact it was a 'conspiracy.'

And the text continues,

> "And you are commanded to take for yourselves
> wagons from the land of Egypt for your little ones, and for your wives,
> and carry (*unesatem*) your father and come" (Genesis 45:19).

Linguistic Journey – the Verb to Carry

The three-letter root word *N-S-A* is used in Biblical Hebrew to mean 'lifting' or 'raising' and 'carrying' as well. Note that the text does not use a different word for the act of 'lifting,' and for the following act of 'carrying' the item that was 'lifted.'

In this journey we will concentrate on 'carrying people.'

Carrying Dead People

We find numerous times in the Tanach places where 'carrying' a dead body is mentioned. The first one is when Jacob is speaking to Joseph, "And I will lie with my fathers and you shall carry me (*unesatani*) from Egypt and bury me in their burial place..." (Genesis 47:30). After Jacob's death, "And his sons carried (*vayis'u*) him to the land of Canaan and buried him..." (50:13).

When Aaron's sons died in a fire, "And they went near and carried (*vayisa'um*) them in their coats..." (Leviticus 10:5).

In Leviticus we find several laws in regard to the impurity of one who touches a dead body,

- "And whoever carried (*hanosey*) anything of the carcass…" (Leviticus 11:25),
- "And he who carries (*vehanosey*) their carcass…" (Leviticus 11:28), and
- "…and he who carries (*vehanosey*) the carcass…" (Leviticus 11:40).

In the rest of the Tanach:

- "And his brothers and the house of his father came down, and **carried** (*vayis'u*) him and brought him up and buried him…" (Judges 16:31),
- "And they **carried** (*vayis'u*) up Asahel and buried him in the sepulcher of his father…" (2 Samuel 2:32),
- "And the prophet **lifted** (*vayisa*) up the carcass of the man of the *Elohim* and laid it upon the ass…" (1 Kings 13:29),
- "…and now lift (*sa*) and throw him in the plot of ground…" (2 Kings 9:26),
- "And they carried (*vayis'u*) him on the horses and he was buried…" 2 Kings 14:20),
- "And they stripped him, and **lifted** (*vayis'u*) his head and his armor…" (1 Chronicles 10:9),
- "And all brave men arose and **carried** (*vayis'u*) the body of Saul…" (1 Chronicles 10:12).
- "And they carried (*vayisa'uhu*) upon the horses and buried him…" (2 Chronicles 25:28).

Carrying Children

We find in the Tanach several examples of carrying **children**. For example, "And Jacob rose up and **carried** (*vayisa*) his sons and his wives on the camels" (Genesis 31:17). Moses speaks of the Almighty carrying the people in the wilderness, "…where the *Y-H-V-H* your G-d **carried** (*nesa'acha*) you like a man carries (*yisa*) his son…" (Deuteronomy 1:31).

Later on, we find more examples of carrying **children**,

- "And Jonathan, Saul's son, had a son who was lame in his feet. **He was five years old** when the news came of Saul and Jonathan from Jezreel, and his nurse **carried** (*vatisa'ehu*) him and fled..." (2 Samuel 4:4),
- "And he said to his father, my head, my head, and he said to the lad, **carry** (*sa'ehu*) to his mother. And he **carried** (*vayisa'ehu*) him and brought him to his mother and he sat on her knees till noon and he died" (2 Kings 4:19-20), and
- "...and she **carried** (*vatisa*) up her son and went out" (2 Kings 4:37).

When it comes to **adults,** we have an example where a man is carried, and it is at a time of danger – when Jonah is in the ship and the sailors are about to throw him into the sea, "And they **carried** (*vayis'u*) Jonah up and threw him into the sea..." (Jonah 1:15).

There are two other places where adults are 'carried/lifted;' however, it is in regard to an action by one of higher stature in relation to people of lesser stature:

- "...and he lifted up (*vayisa*) the head of the chief butler and of the chief baker among his servants" (Genesis 40:20).
- "Lift up (*sa*) the head of the booty that was taken both of man and of beast..." (Numbers 31:26).

Back to Pharaoh's Proposal

The only place in the entire Tanach in which an **adult** is mentioned as being carried by **his own children** is when Pharaoh instructs Joseph, "Now you are commanded to take for yourselves wagons from the land of Egypt for your little ones and for your wives and **carry** (*unesatem*) your father and come" (Genesis 45:19).

We saw earlier the verb 'to take,' when Pharaoh says 'Take your father...' indicates that Pharaoh is telling the brothers **to take possession** of their father. In a similar way, the text attributes to Pharaoh the use of the verb 'to carry.' Children are 'carried,' but not adults. By suggesting that Jacob be 'carried,' the language of the text is telling the reader that in Pharaoh's eyes Jacob is like a child or a dead man.

And the text continues, "And Jacob rose up from Beersheba and the sons of Israel **carried** (*vayis'u*) Jacob their father and their little ones and their wives in the wagons which Pharaoh had sent to carry (*laset*) him" (Genesis 46:5).

In summary, the verb 'to carry someone' relating to adults is used almost exclusively for a funeral procession, or for times in which there is a life-threatening situation, like Jonah being thrown into the sea. If so, one should wonder if the text, language-wise, is sending us the message that this journey of Jacob to Egypt is like a funeral procession, for the burial of a live man.

Confirmation of the 'Land-for-Land' Exchange

We find confirmation of the 'land-for-land' exchange in the way Joseph dealt with the people coming to buy food during the famine.

The text starts with, "And there was no bread in all the land, for the famine was very severe, so that **the land of Egypt and the land of Canaan** got tired because of the famine" (47:13).

The text continues with, "And Joseph gathered up all the money that was found **in the land of Egypt and in the land of Canaan** for the grain which they bought…" (47:14).

And the text continues, "And the money was all spent **in the land of Egypt and in the land of Canaan**…" (47:15), and at this point the text moves on with one glaring omission: "…**all the Egyptians** came to Joseph and said, give us bread…" (47:15). The Canaanites vanished from the text. And the text continues to inform us how Joseph bought the land of the Egyptians for Pharaoh in exchange for the food, and he actually made all the Egyptians vassals to the king, obliging them to give the king one fifth of the harvest each year to the king. It was a major accomplishment for Pharaoh.

With all the details of this plan of buying the Egyptians' land, and moving the people from one land to another, the reader tends to forget the vanishing Canaanites. They didn't sell their land for food. Why not? There were still five years of famine ahead. The answer is quite likely that they **couldn't** sell the land, because Pharaoh was not interested in buying their land, as he already owned it anyway, via the exchange with Jacob's family, the land of Goshen in exchange for the land of Canaan.

This would explain why Jacob after five years of famine could not return to the land of Canaan, as he had no place to return to. The land of Canaan already belonged to the Egyptian king who ruled the land of Canaan as his own.

Back to Pharaoh's Proposal

It is no wonder that Pharaoh approached the brothers and not Jacob. Pharaoh had to put a wedge between Jacob the father, the king of Israel, who was very likely to refuse to leave his throne, in spite of the heavy famine. Pharaoh had to get the brothers on his side against their father.

And we find confirmation that the brothers indeed went along. The wagons, which were offered by Pharaoh, and not by Joseph, are the confirmation of this point.

The text separated the instructions to bring their father and their houses from the instruction to take wagons by adding, "Now **you** (singular) are commanded, do (plural)[103] this..." (45:19). The **wagons** constitute the first time that Pharaoh asserts authority over Joseph.

The text continues, "...and Joseph gave them wagons **according to the commandment of Pharaoh**..." (45:21). However, when the brothers came to the land of Canaan and delivered the message to Jacob, the text says, "...and he saw the wagons **which Joseph had sent to carry him**..." (45:27). But we know that the wagons were sent 'according to the commandment of Pharaoh' and not by Joseph. Were the brothers misleading their father about the wagons? The text continues, "...and the sons of Israel carried Jacob their father and their little ones and their wives in the wagons **which Pharaoh had sent to carry him**" (46:5). The 'sons of Israel' knew exactly who sent the wagons. Joseph knew who sent the wagons, "...and Joseph gave them wagons **according to the commandment of Pharaoh**..." Jacob was the only one who did not know who sent the wagons. The message Jacob received was that Joseph was the one who sent the wagons.

---

[103] In Hebrew the pronoun is part of the verb. The verb here, "Do this," is in the second person plural.

Confirmation of the Brothers Misleading Jacob

Upon returning home the text describes the delivery of news in two verses. In the first one, the brothers report to their father, "And they told him saying Joseph is still alive and he is governor over all the land of Egypt. And Jacob's heart fainted for he believed them not" (45:26).

This verse is not talking about the idea to move to Egypt. It is just a report of the facts. Joseph was indeed alive, and he was indeed the ruler of Egypt. The text brings us Jacob's reaction to the news: 'his heart fainted' as he didn't believe them.

In the next verse, the brothers delivered not the facts, but Joseph's proposal to move to Egypt. We should note that the text uses two different words to describe these two segments of the conversation. The factual segment starts with the verb *vayagidu* (translated as 'they told him'). For the second part, the part that quoted Joseph's words, the text uses the verb *vayedabru* (translated as they 'talked' to him), "And they talked to him all the words of Joseph which he had said to them..." (45:27).

We should note that the text says that they told Jacob 'all the words of Joseph.' What is missing here is 'all the words of Pharaoh.' They just skipped over that part, that the source of the wagons was Pharaoh himself. If they were to reveal that part, then they would have needed to reveal also the land-for-land deal. They preferred that Jacob would think he was going to Egypt just to see his son Joseph.

Back to Jacob

The text quotes Jacob as saying, "And **Israel** said, it is enough, Joseph my son is yet alive, I will go and see him before I die" (45:28). By the text using the title 'Israel' it comes across that Jacob had no intention of abdicating his throne. He saw the trip to Egypt as just uniting with his lost son. Jacob did not know that this trip to Egypt was actually leaving the throne.

The text gives us Jacob's reaction to the wagons, "...and when he saw the wagons which Joseph had sent to carry him, the spirit of Jacob their father revived" (45:27).

The fact is that the brothers misled their father Jacob not by what they told him, but by what they didn't tell him, by what they concealed from him. This is a great example for a rule in SCAN.

SCAN Rule: Total Belief in the Subject.

Background information: Total Belief in the Subject means that the reader/listener should not ask if the statement is true or not. The main effort in analyzing a statement is not to find deception, but to find out what the person conceals in the statement. The fact is that in most cases guilty people prefer to give 'an incomplete truthful statement' rather than to create a statement describing events that didn't happen. What the person does not say in the statement is more important than what the person does say. The reader/listener should be able to distinguish between what the person does not say because the person considered it 'unimportant' enough to enter the statement, and what the person does not say because the person considered it important enough to conceal.

What was it about the 'wagons' that revived the spirit of 'Jacob their father?'

Linguistic Journey – Modes of Transportation

The Ass

Generally speaking, we can see that the ass is the common vehicle for people in the Biblical era. Starting with Abraham, the text says, "And Abram rose up early in the morning and saddled his **ass**…" (Genesis 22:2). We see the same with Balaam in the book Numbers, "And Balaam rose up in the morning, and saddled his [female] **ass**…" (Numbers 22:21).

In the era of the judges we see, "…having the servant with him and **a couple of asses**…" (Judges 19:3). And, "…but he rose up and went and came opposite Jebus which is Jerusalem and there were **with him two asses saddled** and his concubine also was with him" (Judges 19:10); and later, "Then he took her upon **the ass**…" (Judges 19:28).

We find that the ass served not only men, but women as well, and even women of high class. For the daughter of Caleb who received Hebron as a prize for his behavior at the time of the spies in the desert, "…as she came to him that she urged him to ask her father for a field, **and she alighted off her ass** and Caleb asked her what do you want?" (Joshua 15:18, Judges 1:14). We see the same with Abigail, a wealthy woman, from the time of David before he became king, "And when Abigail saw David, she hurried **and alighted off the ass**…" (1 Samuel 25:23).

When the people ask for a king, the prophet Samuel warns them with the following: "And he will take your slaves and your female slaves and your best young men **and your asses** and put them to his work" (1 Samuel 8:16). This should not surprise us. When Korach and his people rebelled against Moses in the desert, Moses is quoted as saying to the Almighty, "And Moses was very angry and said to the Lord, do not respect their offering, **I have not taken one ass from them**…" (Numbers 16:15). It comes across that the right of the ruler was to appropriate the asses of the population.

We see that the ass was even the vehicle for the king's household. And the king said to Ziba, what do you mean by these, and Ziba said, the asses are for the king's household to ride on…" (2 Samuel 16:2). The king's advisor was also riding an ass, "And Ahithophel saw that his counsel was not followed, he saddled **his ass**…" (2 Samuel 17:23).

At later times, we see that the price of an ass was used as the benchmark for market prices: "And there was a great famine in Samaria and behold they besieged it until an ass' head was sold for eighty pieces of silver…" (2 Kings 6:25). We see a slightly different inflation index from that of today.

The Mule

The mule starts to show up as a royal vehicle at the time of Absalom's rebellion, "And the slaves of Absalom did to Amnon as Absalom had commanded, then all the king's sons arose **and every man rode on his mule** and fled" (2 Samuel 13:29).

The ultimate is the description of the coronation of King Solomon. King David on his dying bed instructed his people, "And the king said to them, take with you the slaves of your lord, **and have Solomon my son ride upon the mule that I have** and bring him down to Gihon" (1 Kings 1:33), and indeed they did so, "…and had **Solomon ride upon King David's mule** and brought him to Gihon" (1 Kings 1:38).

The Chariot

In Genesis we find the wagon as a vehicle mentioned only in the context of Egypt, and even then only for the royal court.

For Joseph after his appointment as vice-royal, "And he made him ride in his second **chariot** and they cried before him bow the knee…" (Genesis 41:43), "And Joseph made ready his **chariot** and went up towards Israel his father to Goshen…" (Genesis 46:29). Later on, we find in Exodus when Pharaoh is pursuing the Israelites who exited Egypt, "And he made ready his **chariot** and took his people with him" (Exodus 14:6), and at the Red Sea, "And took off their **chariot** wheels that they drove heavily…" (Exodus 14:25), and in the song after the victory, "Pharaoh's **chariots** and his army has He thrown into the sea…" (Exodus 15:4)

We find the chariot used for war also by the Canaanites, "And the Lord said to Joshua, be not afraid because of them for tomorrow about this time will I deliver them up all slain before Israel, you shall lame their horses and burn their **chariots** with fire" (Joshua 11:6).

We should note that the only one who made a chariot for himself was Absalom, at the beginning of his rebellion against his father, King David. The text says, "And it came to pass after this that Absalom made himself a **chariot** and horses and fifty men to run before him" (2 Samuel 15:1). Not only is the chariot rare in the text in regard to the Israelites, but also rare is the use of horses. We find them only in regard to Egypt. Knowing that Absalom was the grandson of the King of Geshur, a non-Israelite King whose daughter King David married quite likely for political alliance, it can be understood that Absalom was not acting according to Israelite customs.

The Camel

The ass was the vehicle for short rides, but the camel was the vehicle for long rides, especially when one had to cross the desert from one country to another. The text tells us about Abraham's slave who goes to Haran (Mesopotamia), "And the slave took ten of his master's **camels**…"

(Genesis 24:10). We see the same with Jacob on his way back from Haran to the land of Canaan, "And Jacob rose up and set his sons and his wives upon the camels" (Genesis 31:17).

When Jacob sends the gifts ahead of him to greet his brother Esau, the text describes what Jacob sent him: "Two hundred female goats, and twenty male goats, two hundred ewes and twenty rams. Thirty milch camels with their colts, forty cows and ten bulls, twenty female asses and ten foals" (Genesis 32:15-16). The first verse deals with smaller animals and the second verse deals with larger animals.

The Wagon

In the Israelite camp, we find the **wagon** mentioned only in connection either with the tabernacle in the desert, or with the Ark of G-d in the era of the Judges and King David.

In the desert, it is said that the chiefs of the tribes brought offerings to the dedication of the tabernacle: "And they brought their offering before the Lord, six covered **wagons**, and twelve oxen, a wagon for two of the princes and for each one an ox and they brought them before the tabernacle" (Numbers 7:3).

In a later time, when the Ark of G-d was taken by the Philistines during the war, and the Philistines wanted to return it to the Israelites, the text says, "And therefore make a new **wagon** and take two heavy cows on which there has never been a yoke and tie the cows to the wagon and bring their calves home from them" (1 Samuel 6:7). We see the same later, at the time of King David, "And they set the ark of G-d upon a new **wagon** and brought it from the house of Abinadab that was in Geba and Uzza and Ahio the sons of Abinadab drove the new wagon" (2 Samuel 6:3).

Back to Jacob

The text quotes Pharaoh saying, "You are commanded to take **wagons** out of the land of Egypt..." (45:19), and then the text emphasizes, "...and Joseph gave them wagons according to the commandment of Pharaoh..." (45:21).

The wagons were not only a vehicle to carry the old and the little. The wagons were a symbol of the respect that Pharaoh gave to Jacob. No wonder the wagons revived Jacob's spirit: "...the spirit of **Jacob their father** revived" (45:27).

Jacob – Israel - Jacob

We should revisit the encounter between Jacob and his sons Reuben and Judah, when the two tried to convince him to allow Benjamin to go with them to Egypt to abide by the ruler's demand that their little brother show up, so they can purchase the needed food.

Upon the brothers' return from their first journey to Egypt, the text says, "And **Jacob their father** said to them me have you bereaved of my children..." (42:36), and we should note that the text used the formal language formula of "name + title." Reuben came with his offer to kill his sons if he did not return Benjamin. This offer is preceded by, "And Reuben spoke to his father..." (42:37).

There was a stalemate between the father and the sons. And the text continues with, "...**their father** said to them, go again buy us a little food" (43:2). Judah intervened, which brought the text to change the language to, "And **Israel** said why did you deal so ill with me..." (43:6). Judah continued with giving himself as surety to his father for Benjamin, and his proposal is preceded by "And Judah said to **Israel his father** send the lad with me..." (43:8). Again, we should note that the text used the formal language formula of "name + title." Once Jacob agreed to Judah's proposal, the text 'upgraded' Jacob to, "And **Israel their father** said to them..." (43:11). Not only is Jacob Judah's father, but the father of all his sons. The text continues, saying that Jacob gave his sons instructions how to proceed.

Fast forward. The sons are back in Canaan, and their report to their father ends with, "...the spirit of **Jacob their father** revived" (45:27). First, we should note that the text is returning to use '**Jacob** their father' and not '**Israel** their father' as it was before the journey with Benjamin. We should consider it as 'downgrading' from the national title (Israel) to the private person (Jacob). It would be interesting to know if the return to use the first name of Jacob indicates some tension between the father and the sons in discussing Joseph's proposal to relocate to Egypt, or it is only the perception of the text looking upon the sequence of events.

Back to Pharaoh's Proposal

We need to go back to Pharaoh's proposal to realize how misleading the wagons were.

The text says of Pharaoh's proposal, "Now you are commanded to take for yourselves from the land of Egypt wagons for your little ones, and for your wives, and **carry** your father and come" (45:19).

The wagons were meant to give the appearance of royal treatment accorded to Israel the king of the land of Canaan, but they were also meant to dismantle the kingdom entirely, and to bring everything to Egypt. Jacob's going down to Egypt was not just a visit to see his lost son. It was meant to end his kingdom altogether. And, indeed, the wagons did the trick. They convinced Jacob to come to Egypt.

Linguistic Bias

It comes across very strongly from the language of the text, supported by several points, that Joseph's brothers misled their father Jacob by bringing him down to Egypt thinking that he was going only to see his son Joseph, using this pretense to deprive him of his own country, his own realm.

Again, this finding is not present in the **content**, but in the **language** of the text. We should consider it a 'linguistic bias' of the text, concealing this fact from the reader.

The Journey to Egypt

> "And **Israel** traveled with all that he had
> and came to Beersheba…" (46:1)

We already saw earlier that Jacob as Israel, the frequent traveler in the language, is now taking his last trip, and the verb 'to travel' indicates trouble.

The Almighty appears to Jacob as Israel, "And G-d spoke to Israel in the visions of the night and said Jacob, Jacob, and he said here I am" (46:2). We should note that the text labels Jacob as 'Israel' while the text quotes the Almighty as calling him 'Jacob.' The text brings us the Almighty's encouragement to Jacob, "fear not to go down to Egypt for I will there make of you a great nation" (46:3).

And the text continues, "And Jacob rose up from Beersheba..." (46:5). Before the appearance of the Almighty he is 'Israel' and thereafter he is 'Jacob.' The 'downgrading' is complete.

"...And **the sons of Israel** carried **Jacob their father**..." (46:5)

As we saw earlier, the title 'the sons of Israel' was first used when Jacob's sons went down to Egypt the first time to purchase food; so here, when they embark on their journey to Egypt, and this time with their father, they are labeled 'the sons of Israel.' And they carried 'Jacob their father.' The text used the formal language formula of 'name + title.'

But we should note that by saying "...And **the sons of Israel** carried **Jacob their father**...," the text emphasizes two points in language.

First, the text does not say that 'Jacob was carried by his sons...' listing Jacob before his sons. Instead, the text listed the sons before the father, indicating to us the change in status between the father and the sons. The sons, as seen by the text, took command of the situation, and 'Jacob their father' is listed second, relegated to second place.

Second, the text does not say 'the sons of Israel **and** Jacob their father...' By the text saying 'the sons of Israel **carried** Jacob their father,' the text talks about Jacob and his sons as two different entities. In short, there is a missing 'we'/'they' in the sentence.

We find an additional signal of the split between the father and the sons. In continuing the story of the journey to Egypt, the text says, "...and came to Egypt, Jacob and all his seed with him. His sons, and his grandsons with him, his daughters and his sons' daughters, and all his seed brought he with (*et*) him to Egypt" (46:6-7). We should note the use of the distant *et* instead of the close *im* for the word 'with.'

The Census

The text says, "And these are the names of the sons of Israel who came to Egypt…" (Genesis 46:8). And the text ends by saying, "All the souls who came[104] with[105] Jacob to Egypt who came from his *yerech*,[106] besides the wives of Jacob's sons, all the souls were **sixty six**. And the sons of Joseph, who were in Egypt, were two souls, all the souls of the house of Jacob who came[107] to Egypt **were seventy**" (46:26-27).

We should note that the text does its best to avoid stating that Jacob came to Egypt. The text many times says that Jacob's descendants or household came to Egypt. And it is not only in this place that text avoids saying that Jacob came to Egypt. Nowhere in Genesis will we find any attribution of the verb 'coming to' in relation to Jacob and Egypt. Moreover, the text does not say that Jacob settled (*lashevet*) in Egypt, nor does it say he resided (*lagur*) in Egypt, nor does it say that he was present (*lishkon*) in Egypt. Jacob was carried or brought to Egypt and he lived (*lichyot*) there, or in other words, he only breathed the air of Egypt.

A lot has been said about the apparent contradiction between the two numbers – 66 and 70. However, there are two points that solve this alleged mystery.

First, the text counts seventy 'souls' in the house of Jacob, excluding Jacob. The text counts how many souls there were per each mother out of the four, Leah, Rachel, Bilhah and Zilpah. The text tells us that Leah had 33 including her sons, her daughter, and grandsons. The text says that Zilpah had 16 souls. Rachel had 14 souls, and Bilhah had 7. 33+16+14+7 brings the total to 70. So the number 70 is not wrong at all. It is accurate and the numbers support it.

[Note: the text counts the two dead sons of Judah among the offspring of Leah. They are still counted among the 70.]

---

[104] One should note that in Hebrew the present tense is used, "…who come to Egypt…"

[105] Remember we noted before that in Hebrew the word 'with' is not used. Instead the word 'to' is used, "…who came to Jacob to Egypt…"

[106] At this point of time we leave the word *yerech* in the original Hebrew, as we will shortly go on a linguistic journey to determine the exact meaning of the word.

[107] Again, the present tense is used, "…who come to Egypt…"

The question is the number 66, which is stated as being those who came from Jacob's *yerech*. And to understand this, we need to go now on a linguistic journey to identify the meaning of the word *yerech*. And once we determine the meaning, even the number 66 will be accurate and there will be no mystery there either.

Linguistic Journey – the Meaning of the Word *Yerech*

It is common to translate the word *yerech* as the thigh. Not only English, but in Modern Hebrew as well. But is it correct? There are several places in the text that this is not the case in Biblical Hebrew.

The Menorah

The text lists for us the different parts of the menorah, or the 'lampstand' as it is translated, "…its *yerech,* and its stem, its cups, its bulbs, and its flowers shall come from it" (Exodus 25:31). This order is repeated twice, once in Exodus (37:17) and once in Numbers (8:4). The order seems to be going from the bottom to the top. If so, the *yerech*, at least for the menorah, is the bottom, or the stand upon which the menorah is positioned. Incidentally, in English we call the part upon which something is placed 'the stand' while in Hebrew we call it 'the seat.'

The Tabernacle

We find the same with the tabernacle. The text says in regard to the table, "…and he put the table in the tent of meeting upon the *yerech* of the tabernacle northward outside the veil" (40:22). The typical translation of the word *yerech* in this context is 'side.' But one does not put a table on the side, but on the floor. So, again, the *yerech* will be the place upon which an item is placed. If the item is a table, then the *yerech* is the floor.

The same applies to the following:

- To the menorah in the tabernacle, "And he put the lampstand in the tent of meeting opposite the table on the south *yerech* of the tabernacle" (40:24).
- To slaughtering, "And he shall slaughter it on the northern *yerech* of the altar before the Lord…" (Leviticus 1:11).

- To the place where different groups camp, "The families of the sons of Kohath shall camp on the south *yerech* of the tabernacle" (Numbers 3:29), and "And the chief of the house of the father of the families of Merari was Zuriel the son of Abihail; these shall camp on the north *yerech* of the tabernacle" (3:35).

Even in the temple we see the *yerech* quite likely to be the floor, "And he brought also the bronze altar which was before the Lord, and he brought near from the front of the house from between the altar and the house of the Lord and put it <u>on</u> the north *yerech* of the altar" (2 Kings 16:14).

The Human Body

Realizing that the *yerech* is the bottom of the Menorah, and the floor of the Tabernacle, we can move on to the human body. And we can do no better than to check the place where a warrior places his sword.

The text says that Moses instructed the tribe of Levi:
- "…put every man his sword on his *yerech*…" (Exodus 32:27).

We see the same with the judge Ehud:

- "And Ehud made for himself a dagger which had two edges of a cubit length and he put it under his garments upon his right *yerech*" (Judges 3:16), and,
- "And Ehud sent forth his left hand and took the dagger from above his right *yerech* and thrust it into his belly" (3:21).

Even in later books we find the *yerech* as the place for the sword,

- "Gird your sword upon your *yerech*…" (Psalms 45:4), and,
- "…every man has his sword at his *yerech* because of the fear in the nights" (Song of Songs 3:8).

Is the *yerech* the waist around which one puts his belt? One place in the text will help us narrow it down. When talking about the priests' clothing, the text tells us that there should be one more item to their clothing, "And you shall make them linen breeches to cover their nakedness from the waists and to the *yerechayim*[108] they shall reach" (Exodus 28:42). Now we know that the area of 'nakedness' is surrounded by two parts of the body, the waist and the *yerech*.

The suspicion is now that the *yerechayim* of a person are the parts of the body upon which a person sits, meaning the two buttocks along with the upper thighs that are positioned on the seat.

This will explain the place where Jacob was injured at the time he struggled with the man (angel) during the night he passed the river Jabbok. The text says, "And when he saw that he prevailed not against him, he touched **the palm** (*kaf*) **of his *yerech*…**" (32:26).

In Hebrew, we have 'the palm of the hand' (*kaf hayad*), 'the palm of the foot' (*kaf haregel*) and 'the palm of the *yerech*' (*kaf hayerech*). All three are areas where there is some concavity in the flesh. When one bends one's hand, one creates the *kaf*, like the arch in the foot, and the *kaf hayerech* is the concavity created by joining the leg with the butt.

Back to Jacob's injury. "And as he passed Penuel the sun rose upon him and he was limping upon his *yerech*" (32:32). Jacob was limping because his butt was injured. The fact is that biologically, the buttocks are the body parts that move the legs, and if there is injury in the buttocks, this injury will cause limping. And the text concludes, "Therefore the sons of Israel do not eat of the sinew of the vein which is in the palm of the *yerech* to this day because he touched Jacob's palm of the *yerech* in the sinew of the vein" (32:33).

Knowing that the *yerech* is the buttocks along with the upper thighs, one can understand the warning the priest gave the woman suspected of being involved in an adulterous relationship: "…when the Lord makes your *yerech* fall away and your belly swell" (Numbers 5:21, with similar wording at verses 22 and 27). Because the buttocks are surrounding the 'nakedness' of the body (the genitals), it is no wonder that the punishment should be in that same area.

---

[108] *yerechayim* – the dual form of *yerech*. In Hebrew there are three forms to indicate grammatical number – single, plural, and **dual**. And in Hebrew both the waist and the yerech take the **dual (two) form**, and not more than two, relative to the human body.

Putting the Hand Under the *Yerech*

There are two instances in Genesis in which one asks another to put his hand **under** his *yerech*. The first one is Abraham. The text says, "And Abraham said to his slave the oldest in his house who ruled over all that he had, please put your hand under my *yerech*" (Genesis 24:2).

The text starts by telling the reader how important the slave was. He was the oldest in Abraham's house, and he was the one who ruled over all that Abraham had. And before Abraham asked his slave to promise that he would take a wife for his Isaac from his homeland, and not from the land of Canaan, Abraham asked his slave 'to put his hand under his *yerech*.' Realizing that the *yerech* is 'the seat of power,' one can easily understand that Abraham is asking his slave for 'a pledge of obedience.' Moreover, if one has to put his hand under the buttocks and the upper thighs of a sitting man, one has to kneel down. No different from a knight kneeling down before his king.

And the text ends the event by saying, "And the slave put his hand under the *yerech* of Abraham **his master** and swore to him..." (24:9). By adding the title 'his master' to Abraham the text comes to emphasize that indeed the slave accepted his position 'under' Abraham. This goes along with the proud fashion in which that slave introduced himself to Rebecca's family before he started his words to them: "And he said I am Abraham's slave" (Genesis 24:34).

The second instance in which this 'pledge of obedience' is requested is between Jacob and Joseph. The text says that before asking Joseph to bury him in the land of Canaan, Jacob told Joseph, "...if I have found grace in your sight, please put your hand under my *yerech*..." (47:29).

We should note that the text does not say, as it did with Abraham's slave, that Joseph indeed put his hand under his father's *yerech*, but the text quotes Joseph as saying, "...and he said, I will do as you have said," (47:30). By doing so, Joseph accepted his father's request, and when his father asked him to take an oath to this pledge (burial in the land of Canaan), as Abraham asked his slave to take an oath, Joseph indeed did so. And the text ended the event by saying, "...and Israel bowed himself upon the bed's head" (Genesis 47:31). By bowing, Israel showed his respect to his son Joseph, the vice-royal who accepted his authority to request such a thing of him. By bowing, Israel also brought Joseph's dream – that the sun, the moon, and the eleven stars would bow down to him – to realization. Here the 'sun' (the father) indeed did so.

Putting the hand under the *yerech* as a symbol of obedience is found also at a later time, the time of King Solomon. In Chronicles we find the following verse, "And all the princes and the mighty men and likewise all the sons of King David, put a hand under Solomon the king" (1 Chronicles 29:24). Although the text here does not say that they put the hand under the *yerech*, still by putting the hand 'under' King Solomon they accepted his authority.

'Those who Came From his *Yerech*'

Knowing that to pledge obedience is to put the hand under the *yerech* of the one you pledge obedience to, we can understand that the phrase 'those who came from his *yerech*' is actually an expression to say 'those who were under his authority.'

We find this phrase three times in the Tanach. The third place is with Gideon the judge. The text there says, "And Gideon had seventy sons **who came from his *yerech*** for he had many wives" (Judges 8:30).

The first two are of interest to us, as they are in the context of Jacob's family.

The first is when the text gives us the count of the people who came down to Egypt with Jacob, "All the souls who came to Jacob to Egypt **who came from his *yerech*** besides the wives of Jacob's sons, all the souls were sixty six" (46:26).

The second is at the beginning of Exodus where the text again gives us the count of Jacob's family: "And all the souls who came from the *yerech* of Jacob were seventy souls…" (Exodus 1:5).

What happened between the end of the book of Genesis and the beginning of the book of Exodus? We only need to quote the text itself, which is the last verse in Genesis, "And **Joseph died** being 110 years old and they embalmed him and he was put in a coffin in Egypt" (Genesis 50:26).

Once Joseph died, the book of Exodus starts with, "And all the souls who came from the *yerech* of Jacob were seventy souls and Joseph was in Egypt" (Exodus 1:5). Once Joseph was no longer active in the domestic politics of the family, the family reached unity and from 66 under the yerech of Jacob they could be seventy under the *yerech* of Jacob. The bottom line is that the four (70 minus 66) who were not under the *yerech* of Jacob when the family came to Egypt had to do with Joseph one way or another.

Who is mentioned in the list of seventy in Genesis at the time of going down to Egypt that had any close connection to Joseph? They must be three, Joseph being one. If we go strictly by the list, there are three others, Joseph's two sons Ephraim and Menashe, and Joseph's full brother Benjamin.

At this point of time there is no other known corroborating evidence that Benjamin is the fourth one; however, it is the only logical conclusion based on the fact that Joseph's death changed the number from 66 under the *yerech* of Jacob in Genesis to 70 under the *yerech* of Jacob in Exodus. Based on the requirement of scientific methodology not to base oneself on a single observation to reach a conclusion, we are mandated to search for at least one more point that will confirm this suspicion. Let's wait and see if we will find another corroborating point that Benjamin is number four.

Settling in the Land of Goshen

The text says, "…and they came to the land of Goshen" (Genesis 46:28). We should note that here the text uses a special form of the word 'land.' Not the regular *eretz* ('land' in Hebrew) but *artza* which means 'to the land' of Goshen. The text uses the same format as it did with the migration of Abraham from Haran to Canaan, "…and they went out to go to the land (*artza*) of Canaan and they came to the land (*artza*) of Canaan" (Genesis 12:5). By using the same formula, the text strengthens the idea that the land of Canaan was exchanged for the land of Goshen.

Artza

The phrase 'to the land' (*artza*) in conjunction with the name of the place appears in the text in the following places:

- The land of Canaan – Genesis 11:31, 12:5, 31:18, 42:29, 45:17, 50:13, and Numbers 35:10
- Negev (south part of Canaan) – Genesis 20:1
- The sons of Kedem (east; meaning Haran) – Genesis 29:1
- Seir (Esau's place) – Genesis 32:4
- Goshen – Genesis 46:28
- Egypt – Exodus 4:20
- Zebulun and Naftali (2 of the 12 tribes of Jacob) – Isaiah 8:23

We should note that the phrase '*artza* Egypt' in Exodus appears in regard to Moses who returns after a long exile in Midian to the land where he was born, the land of Egypt. This should bring us to at least suspect that the word 'land' used in the form *artza* comes to indicate familiarity.

The Reunion Between Jacob and Joseph

> And Joseph made ready his chariot and went up to meet Israel his father to Goshen, and presented himself to him, and he fell on his neck and cried on his neck a good while. And Israel said to Joseph, now let me die, since I have seen your face because you are still alive. (Genesis 46:29-30)

We should note that the text attributes the title 'Israel' to Jacob twice in this meeting. It comes to tell us that unlike his brothers who deserted their father the king, and traded his land (Canaan) for a new land (Goshen), Joseph still perceived his father as the king of Israel, regardless of his location in Egypt.

The fact that Joseph was the one to cry on his father's neck, while Jacob did not cry, might be due to the **wagons** that were presented to Jacob as being sent by Joseph, and not by Pharaoh. At that point, Jacob might have felt that his son Joseph was the one who brought about his downfall.

Summary

It seems that the brothers bypassed Joseph, and went directly to Pharaoh to reach a deal with him instead of accepting Joseph's proposal. And Pharaoh and 'his house' went along with it, as he got as a reward the extension of his kingdom. The land of Canaan was not a great place, as the famine still had five more years to go. However, it was only for five more years, and then life would return to normal, and Egypt would have the land under its wing. It is even better than investing in the stock market, since there is no guarantee that stock prices will indeed go up.

Back to the Sequence of Events – the Family Came to Goshen

"…and they came to the land of Goshen" (46:28).

The text continues with describing the reunion between Joseph and Jacob, and then says the following:

> And Joseph said to his brothers, and to his father's house, I will go up and tell Pharaoh and say to him, my brothers and my father's house who were in the land of Canaan have come to me. And the men are shepherds for their trade has been to do with cattle, and they have brought their flocks and their herds and all that they have. And it shall come to pass, when Pharaoh shall call you and shall say what is your occupation? And you will say, your slaves have been keeping cattle from our youth until now, both we and also our fathers, that you may live in the land of Goshen, for every shepherd is an abomination to the Egyptians. (46:31-34)

We should note two points here. The first is the way the text lists the people to whom Joseph addresses his message. The brothers are listed first, before his father's house, and the text does it twice.

Second, telling them Pharaoh is going to give them the land of Goshen is practically selling them the place after they already got it. They already settled in Goshen! So what is the point in telling Pharaoh the brothers' trade? The last verse gives us the answer: 'for every shepherd is an abomination to the Egyptians.'

Why would Joseph want to tell Pharaoh that his family deals with what is abominable to the Egyptians? One might think that the opposite would be true. But if we know that the brothers bypassed Joseph and went to deal directly with Pharaoh, then we understand that this move on Joseph's part was his answer to their treachery.

And the text continues, "And Joseph came and told Pharaoh saying, my father and my brothers and their flocks and their herds, and all that they have, have come from the land of Canaan, and behold they are in the land of Goshen" (47:1).

While talking to his family, Joseph addressed his message to the brothers first. Here, when he talked to Pharaoh, the text listed the father first, as expected. We should also note that in Pharaoh's original proposal to settle in Egypt, Pharaoh is quoted as saying, "And take your father and your households and come **to me**…" (45:18). Here, when Joseph talked to Pharaoh he did not specify to whom the brothers came. Just that they 'have come.' Moreover, Joseph bypassed the idea that his family 'came to' Egypt. In his words, his family came 'from the land of Canaan,' and in a vacuum they ended up in the land of Goshen, without saying that they 'came to' Goshen. Joseph, true to his original idea, was for his family to live only temporarily in Goshen, but not to 'come to' Goshen.

And the text continues, "And from the periphery of his brothers he took five men and presented them to Pharaoh" (Genesis 47:2).

Five men from the periphery of his brothers can only be the four sons of the concubines, and his own full brother, leaving out the six brothers who were sons of Leah. This should remind us that before he was sold to slavery, the text said, "…and he was a lad with the sons of Bilhah and with the sons of Zilpah, his father's wives…" (37:2). And now we see that old alliances are returning.

And the text describes the meeting between Pharaoh and the five brothers. "And Pharaoh said to his brothers, what is your occupation? And they said to Pharaoh, your slaves are shepherds, both we and also our fathers. And they said to Pharaoh…" (47:3-4). The fact that the text repeats the phrase "And they said to Pharaoh…" without saying what Pharaoh said, tells us that Pharaoh did not say anything. He was in deep shock. They told him to his face that they were dealing with 'an abomination to the Egyptians.'

The end of the meeting tells us that Joseph achieved his objective. The text tells us that Pharaoh said to Joseph, "…your father and your brothers have come **to you**" (47:5). In his original proposal, Pharaoh said, 'come to **me**.' Now, knowing that they are an 'abomination,' Pharaoh basically tells Joseph the following: I don't want to deal with them. Keep them far away from me. And Pharaoh ends his message, "…and if you know any men of activity among them then make them rulers over my cattle" (47:6). Pharaoh actually tells Joseph, from now on, you are in charge of them. There is no more direct access for them to me. You will be the one to appoint them if necessary.

The brothers bypassed Joseph and traded Canaan for Goshen, and Joseph retaliated and cut their access to Pharaoh.

> "And Joseph **brought** Jacob his father
> and made him stand before Pharaoh…" (47:7).

Linguistic Journey – to Bring Someone

We find several times in Genesis that someone was brought to someone else. Three times we find that it has to be concerning bringing a woman to a man. The first time is in regard to the creation of Eve, "And the rib which the Lord G-d had taken from man made He a woman and **brought her** to the man" (Genesis 2:22). Second, in regard to Rebecca entering the family of Abraham, "And Isaac **brought her** (Rebecca) to his mother Sarah's tent, and took Rebecca…" (24:67), and third, in regard to Laban replacing Rachel with Leah, "…he took Leah his daughter and **brought her** to him…" (29:23). In all these three places we are facing the uniting of two people together.

We should note that in the first two times (Eve and Rebecca) the text uses the short form of 'brought her' (*vayevi'eha*), using the pronoun 'her' at the end of the verb. In the case of Laban, the text uses the long way of 'brought her' (*vayaveh ota*), separating the pronoun 'her' from the verb. We also know, that unlike in the first two places, in the third place (Laban) the text reports a case of fraud, when Laban defrauds Jacob, bringing him Leah instead of Rachel.

Knowing that in ancient times (and still today in some conservative societies in the Middle East) the woman was transferred at the time of marriage from the control of her father to the control of her husband, we can understand why the woman was 'brought' to the man (Eve) or to her husband (Rebecca and later Leah).

We also find that when Joseph's brothers return to Egypt with Benjamin, Joseph instructs the one in charge of his house, "…**bring** these men home..." (Genesis 43:16), and "...and the man **brought** the men into Joseph's house" (43:17). Realizing that this is the time in which Joseph is going to be united with his brother Benjamin with whom he shares the same mother, it is understood that we are facing a reunion between the two brothers. And, indeed, with the same instruction that Joseph gave to 'bring' the men to his house, he also instructs the one in charge to "slaughter plenty" (43:16), as he prepares a major feast to enjoy the occasion.

Later on, when the man brought the men to Joseph's house, the text says, "...and gave them water, and they washed their feet, and he gave their asses provender" (43:24). No different from Abraham's slave who came to Rebecca's family, "And the man came into the house and he ungirded his camels, and gave straw and provender for the camels, and water to wash his feet, and the feet of the men who were with him" (24:32). The only difference between Abraham's slave and Joseph's brothers, is that Abraham's slave gave priority to the 'transportation vehicles' (camels) while the Egyptian in charge did not.

Later on, the text goes out of its way to describe the meal that Joseph and his brothers had along with the presents Joseph gave his brothers (and they still did not know that he was Joseph) and much more to Benjamin. The description only confirms that 'bringing' the men to his house was meant to celebrate a family **reunion**.

In the rest of the Tanach, we find several places in which someone is brought before the king, and in most cases, the encounter with the king does not end well.

- "When David returned from the slaying of the Philistine, Abner took him and **brought him** before Saul..." (1 Samuel 17:57),
- "And they took Uriahu out from Egypt and **brought him** to Jehoiakim the king who slew him with the sword..." (Jeremiah 26:23),
- "...and Irijah took Jeremiah and **brought him** to the princes" (Jeremiah 37:14),
- "And they put him in a cage of hooks and **brought him** to the king of Babylon..." (Ezekiel 19:9), and

- "And he searched for Ahaziah and they caught him for he was hiding in Samaria and **brought him** to Jehu and they had slain him..." (2 Chronicles 22:9).

The only one who didn't end in trouble when he was 'brought' before the king was David, but as the story unfolds, the king did want to kill David.

> "And Joseph **brought** Jacob his father
> and made him stand before Pharaoh..." (47:7)

The fact that Joseph 'brought' Jacob (not Israel) before Pharaoh, the king of Egypt, can be read as a courtesy visit. But it can also be read with the implication that Joseph is transferring his father from his status as an independent king to being under the authority of the Egyptian king: a meeting between the ruling king (Pharaoh) and the deposed king (Jacob).

We will check now to see if there is any confirmation of this understanding (that Jacob is being transferred to Pharaoh's authority) from other observations.

> "And Joseph brought Jacob his father
> and **made him stand** before Pharaoh..." (47:7)

We should first note that while Joseph took five brothers and 'presented' (47:2) them to Pharaoh, when the text relates to his father, it uses the phrase 'made him **stand** before' (meaning 'in front of') Pharaoh.

Linguistic Journey – Authority Relationships in Biblical Language

All these places show that the preposition 'before' indicates the acceptance of authority and control.

'To Stand Before...'

The text uses different verbs to describe meetings between people and meetings between man and the Almighty. In Genesis, we find four times where someone 'stood before.' Twice Abraham 'stood before' the Almighty, in relation to Sodom, in Genesis 18:22 and 19:27. The other two times are in regard to Joseph. The first, when the text mentioned Joseph's age (30) when he 'stood before' (41:46) Pharaoh. And the second time is when the brothers return to Egypt with Benjamin, the present, and the money, 'and they stood before Joseph' (43:15). From these four places we learn that 'to stand before' is to give honor to a higher authority.

In the rest of the Torah we find similar cases. 'To stand before' the Almighty is mentioned in Leviticus, "And they took that which Moses commanded before the Tent of Meeting and all the congregation **stood before** the Lord" (Leviticus 9:5).

In Deuteronomy, Moses relates to the Mount Sinai revelation as, "The day when you **stood before** the Lord your G-d..." (Deuteronomy 4:10).

Later on, Moses relates to another event in which the people 'stood before' the Almighty, "But with him who **stands** here with us this day **before** the Lord our G-d..." (Deuteronomy 29:14).

For the tribe of Levi, the text talks several times about 'standing before' the congregation, before Aaron, and before the Lord. First, at the time of the Korach rebellion, Moses tells Korach and his people:

> Does it seem but a small thing to you that the G-d of Israel has separated you from the congregation of Israel, to bring you near to himself to do the service of the tabernacle of the Lord and to **stand before** the congregation to serve them? (Numbers 16:9)

We should note that by this verse the congregation is the authority over the Levites. In another place, the source of the authority is Aaron, "Bring the tribe of Levi near, and make them **stand before** Aaron the priest that they may serve him" (Numbers 3:6). We also find, "And you shall make the Levites **stand before** Aaron and **before** his sons..." (Numbers 8:13).

The book of Deuteronomy cites the source of the Levites' authority as the Almighty, "At that time the Lord set apart the tribe of Levi to carry the ark of the covenant of the Lord, to **stand before** the Lord to serve him and to bless in his name to this day" (Deuteronomy 10:8). In another place it says, "And he will serve in the name of the Lord his G-d as all his brothers the Levites do, who **stand before** the Lord" (Deuteronomy 18:7). We should note that usually when the phrase 'to stand before' appears, it is in conjunction with the verb 'to serve.'

We find 'to stand before' in other places. When Moses appears before Pharaoh during the plague of the boils, "And they took the ashes from the furnace and **stood before** Pharaoh..." (Exodus 9:10). From the language of the text we can understand that although Moses and Aaron were in the midst of the plagues to subdue Pharaoh, still they paid him respect.

For this plague the text also says, "And the magicians **could not stand before** Moses because of the boils..." (Exodus 9:11).

'To stand before' also appears in regard to the relationship between Moses and Joshua. The text says, "Joshua the son of Nun **who stands before you** he shall come there..." (Deuteronomy 1:38). When it is time to transfer leadership, the text says, "And you should make him **stand before** Eleazar the priest and **before** all the congregation and give him a charge in their sight" (Numbers 27:19). Since the text mentions here two sources of authority – Eleazar and the congregation – it goes on to clarify that the first one mentioned is the important one:

> And he shall **stand before** Eleazar the priest who shall ask counsel for him according to the judgment of Urim before the Lord, at his word shall they go out and at his word they shall come, both he and all the sons of Israel with him and all the congregation. (27:21)

We should note that here the text relegates 'the congregation' to third place, after Eleazar and after the sons of Israel, so there should be no doubt that Eleazar is the source of authority. And, indeed, this section ends with, "And Moses did as the Lord commanded him, and he took Joshua and made him **stand before** Eleazar the priest and **before** all the congregation" (27:22). Eleazar appears first (more important) and the congregation appears second.

We find 'to stand before' in the context of judgment:

> And the daughters of Zelophehad the son of Hepher the son of Gilead the son of Machir the son of Menashe of the families of Menashe the son of Joseph got near... And they stood before Moses and before Eleazar the priest and before the princes and all the congregation... (Numbers 27:1-2)

If we have any doubt that the text discusses here an issue of the court, the text says, "And Moses brought their cause[109] before the Lord" (Numbers 27:5).

In the test of the adulterous wife, the text says, "And the priest shall bring her near and make her **stand before** the Lord" (Numbers 5:16). We also find, "And they shall be to you cities of refuge from the avenger, that the man slayer should not die until he **stands before** the congregation in judgment" (Numbers 35:12). And, "And the two men between whom the controversy is shall **stand before** the Lord **before** the priests and the judges who shall be in those days" (Deuteronomy 19:17).

'To stand before' is also used in a very negative way, "…and a woman shall not **stand before** a beast to lie down to it…" (Leviticus 18:23). In using 'to stand before' the text emphasizes that a woman letting a beast control her is worse than the sexual activity itself, because 'standing before' the beast appears in the sentence before 'lie down to it.'

Moses' Relationship With the Almighty

According to the text, Moses is the only one before whom the Almighty stands, "Behold I will **stand before you** there upon the rock in Horeb and you shall strike the rock, and water shall come out of it…" (Exodus 17:6).

The people ask Moses, "Go near and hear all that the Lord our G-d shall say and speak to us all that the Lord our G-d shall speak to you…" (Deuteronomy 5:24). The Almighty responds positively and says, "And as for you, **stand** here **by** me and I will speak to you…" (5:28). Moses 'stands,' not 'before' the Almighty, but rather 'by' the Almighty. This change of language fits the words of the Almighty to Aaron and Miriam after they spoke against Moses, "With him I speak mouth to mouth, manifestly and not in dark speech and he behold the form of the Lord…" (Numbers 12:8).

To Stand Over/on

We saw that up to now the phrase 'to stand before' indicates acceptance of a higher authority. It is time to check if the text uses other prepositions

---

[109] In Hebrew that word for 'cause' is *mishpatan*. The word *mishpat* is law, in the sense of making judgment in court (case law).

with the verb 'to stand' when there is no acceptance of authority. And, indeed, we find that when there is no acceptance of authority there is no 'to stand before.'

The first case is the visit of Jethro, Moses' father-in-law, who sees Moses judging the people. The text says, "And it came to pass on the next day that Moses sat to judge the people, and the people **stood over**[110] Moses from the morning to the evening" (Exodus 18:13). The question is: what does 'to stand over' mean?

In the book Numbers we find, "And the princes of Israel, chiefs of the house of their fathers, who were the princes of the tribes, and who **stood over** the ones who were counted, offered" (Numbers 7:2). The text says that the princes are the ones who 'stood over' the ones who were counted. They were the authority figures. And in another place the text says, "...nor shall you **stand over** the blood of your neighbor..." (Leviticus 19:16).

We can understand why Jethro intervened by giving Moses his advice. From the behavior of the people Jethro understood that the people 'stood over' Moses and they did not 'stand before' Moses. The people behaved as if they were the ones in charge and not Moses. And after Jethro advised Moses how to build the legal system, Jethro said, "If you shall do this thing, and G-d command you so, then you shall be able to endure, and all this people shall also **go to their place** in peace" (Exodus 18:23). The people will accept their position.

To Come Near

There are several places where a meeting starts with the verb 'to come near.' We will start with the story about the spies, an event that brought about the wandering of the people for forty years. Moses described how the event started, "And **you came near me** every one of you and said, we will send men before us and they shall search us out the land and bring us word by which way we must go up and to what cities we shall come" (Deuteronomy 1:22). Moses adds that "And the word pleased[111] me well..." (1:23). But the question is, is it positive or negative that Moses started the description by saying that everyone 'came near me?'

---

[110] In Hebrew the preposition is 'on' (*aal*).
[111] In Hebrew it is literally 'it was good in my eyes.'

There are other places from which we can understand that the fact that the idea of spying starting with "you came near me" in Moses' description should have indicated to us that the issue was not simple at all. First, we will examine cases in which people 'came near' Moses, but then also 'stood before' him.

> The daughters of Zelophehad, the son of Hepher, the son of Gilead, the son of Machir, the son of Menashe, of the families of Menashe the son of Joseph **came near**, and these are the names of his daughters Mahlah, Noah, and Hoglah, and Milcah, and Tirzah. And they **stood before** Moses, and before Eleazar the priest and before the princes and all the congregation… (Numbers 27:1-2).

Although it said that the daughters of Zelophehad 'came near,' still text devotes one full verse to say that they 'stood before' all the leadership. They accepted the authority of the leadership even before pressing on with their issue.

We can compare the description of the daughters of Zelophehad to the description of the tribe of Menashe who later on complained about the decision regarding the daughters of Zelophehad, that a daughter can inherit from her father if there are no brothers in line to inherit. The text says, "And the chief fathers of the families of the son of Gilead, the son of Machir, the son of Menashe, of the families of the sons of Joseph, **came near** and **spoke before** Moses…" (Numbers 36:1). The text does not say that they 'stood before' but 'spoke before.' From the change of language we can learn of the tension present at this meeting, a lot more than what took place in the meeting with the daughters of Zelophehad. Here, the text deals with the chief fathers who were complaining, an issue that is different from several daughters of one family.

We can return now to the story of the spies that started with the verb 'you came near me.' From the language of the text, which does not use the phrase 'standing before' Moses, we can already feel the tension that existed at the time of the request. There is no positive angle to this request, even at this early stage. As the daughters of Zelophehad addressed Moses after they felt they were dispossessed of their inheritance, so we should understand that the request to send spies came after the people felt that something was not right.

When the spies returned from the mission, the text says,

> And they returned from searching the land after forty days. And they went and came to Moses and to Aaron and to all the congregation of the people of Israel to the wilderness of Paran to Kadesh and brought back word to them and to all the congregation and showed them the fruit of the land. (Numbers 13:25-26)

The text does not say that they 'stood before' Moses and the congregation. As they did not 'stand before' Moses upon embarking on their mission, so it is upon their return. From the language of the text we can already conclude that we are about to read their negative report of their visit to the land.

We find the verb 'to come near' in another place, "And the officers who were over thousands of the army, the captains of the thousands, and captains of the hundreds came near to Moses" (Numbers 31:48). If we remember that earlier the text says, "And Moses was angry with the officers of the army, with the captains over thousands, and captains over hundreds, who came from the battle. And Moses said to them, have you kept all the women alive" (Numbers 31:14-15). We can understand why the officers had 'to come near' to Moses. There is no 'coming near' unless there was some distance prior to it.

There is another place in which we find the verb 'to come near before,' but without 'standing.' The text says,

> And there were men who were defiled by the dead body of a man so that they could not keep the Passover on that day, and **they came near before** Moses and **before** Aaron on that day. And those men said to him, we are defiled by the dead body of a man, why are we kept back, so that we may not offer an offering to the Lord in his appointed season among the people of Israel? (Numbers 9:6-7)

Moses' reaction is notable: "And Moses said to them, **stand** and I will hear what the Lord will command concerning you" (9:8). The request to 'stand' indicates that the men's attitude was the right one, although not completely adequate. There was 'before' but without 'standing,' a point that Moses makes to correct it.

In another place we find the verb 'to come near' after a complaint, "And Moses spoke to Aaron, say to all the congregation of the people of Israel, **get near** before the Lord, for he has heard your murmurings" (Exodus 16:9). Again, we see that there is no 'coming near' without some distance prior to it.

Korach's Rebellion

"And they rose up before Moses... And they gathered themselves over Moses and Aaron..." (Numbers 16:2-3). Not only do we have the act of **'rising** before' and not **'standing** before' the upcoming turmoil, but we also have the act of 'gathering themselves over,' the same phrase used for all the people's complaints.

Later, Moses says, "And Moses said to Korach, **be** you and all your company **before** the Lord..." (16:16). 'Be before' and not 'stand before.' It is clear from the language of the text quoting Moses that the encounter is not going to end on a positive note. And later the text says, "And they took every man his censer and put fire in them, and laid incense on it, and **stood** at the entrance to the Tent of meeting with Moses and Aaron" (16:18). They 'stood,' but they did not 'stand before.'

The Tribes of Gad and Reuben

We find the same in the case of the tribes of Gad and Reuben who asked to settle the land east of the Jordan. The text says, "The sons of Gad and the sons of Reuben **came** and spoke to Moses and to Eleazar the priest and to the princes of the congregation saying..." (Numbers 32:2). They 'came' but they did not 'stand before,' and now we can understand the sharp rebuke they received from Moses, who compared them to the spies (32:8-9).

After Moses' rebuke, the text says, "And they **came near** to him and they said..." (32:16-17). As Judah 'came near to' Joseph, so the tribes 'came near to' Moses to pacify him. Still, they did not 'stand before' him.

In summary, we can see that 'to stand before' means to accept authority. 'To make someone stand before' is an activity used when there is transfer of power – Moses to Joshua – or, when there is clarification of the source of authority – who is above whom – Joshua is the one who 'stands before' Eleazar. However, when there is no acceptance of authority, or when we face a rebellion or a complaint, there is no 'standing before.'

Back to Jacob Standing before Pharaoh

> "And Joseph brought Jacob his father
> and **made him stand** before Pharaoh…" (47:7)

We are not facing here a simple meeting between the father of the vice-royal and the royal himself. We are facing here a very significant event in which Joseph is aiming to transfer his father to the authority of the Egyptian king.

We should note that the text does not say, 'And Joseph brought Jacob his father and he **stood** before Pharaoh.' Instead, the text says that Joseph '**made** him stand before' Pharaoh. The 'standing before' Pharaoh is initiated by Joseph and not by Jacob. Does Jacob accept this official transfer of authority? Does he accept the fact that he is no more king, and now he is under another king?

> "…and Jacob **blessed** Pharaoh" (47:7)

In Genesis we find the following blessings:

The Almighty blesses Adam and Eve (Genesis 1:28), Noah (9:1), Abraham (12:2-3), (18:18), (22:17-18), Sarah (17:16), Isaac (26:3-4, 12, 24), Ishmael (17:20), Jacob (28:14). We also find that Jacob receives a blessing from the one he struggled with during the night (32:30).

Rebecca's brothers bless her before she embarks on her journey to the land of Canaan to be married to Isaac (24:60). Isaac blesses Jacob (27:23), (28:3-4). Jacob blesses Ephraim and Menashe (48:20) and blesses his sons before his death (49:28). Among the sons, the word 'blessing' is mentioned specifically for Joseph (49:26).

We find two people who are blessed due to their proximity to Jacob and his family. The first one is Laban (30:27), and the house of Joseph's master in Egypt (39:5).

There are only two cases in which the blessing is not given by the Almighty, or by family relatives, or even by proximity to the Patriarch's family – the blessing of Abraham by the king of Shalem (14:19) and the blessing of Pharaoh by Jacob. The fact that Jacob blesses Pharaoh, and the king of Shalem blesses Abraham, should bring us to wonder if these two cases are parallel in some way, or they share a characteristic, or maybe even more than one. A king blesses the father of the nation – Abraham, and one of the fathers of the nation blesses a king – Pharaoh.

Between these two events, Jacob's blessing Pharaoh stands out. While we know what the blessing of king of Shalem to Abraham was, the text does not say what the blessing Jacob gave to Pharaoh was. From the text's point of view, the importance of the blessing is not its content, but the fact that it was given.

Very easily, we can regard this blessing as an attempt by Jacob to resist the fact that his son Joseph 'made him stand before' the Egyptian king. At this stage, Jacob does not see himself as an underling of Pharaoh, but as an equal.

The text continues the meeting between Jacob and Pharaoh, "And Pharaoh said to Jacob, how old are you?[112]" (Genesis 47:8).

It is quite likely that Pharaoh does not ask the question because he doesn't know. The possibility that Jacob's age was not raised in one of the conversations regarding such an extraordinary event – uniting the vice-royal with his family from the land of Canaan – is very remote. Pharaoh knew Jacob's age.

Moreover, to ask anyone for his/her age is not considered a polite question. Such a question is never asked by anyone in Genesis, and not found in other books either. Such a question will be tolerated only when there is a large gap in age between the one who asks the question, and the one who is being asked, when the one to ask is the older. Pharaoh's question is sending a clear message that the two are not equal.

---

[112] Literally, 'How many days are in the years of your life?'

The question quite likely came due to Jacob's blessing. Pharaoh, who considered himself a god, saw in Jacob's blessing a 'downgrading' or 'demotion.' He actually asks: who are you to bless me? If not for your status then maybe for your very old age.

And Jacob answers Pharaoh's question and in the context it was asked:

> "And Jacob said to Pharaoh, the days of the years of my residing are a hundred and thirty years, few and evil have the days of the years of my life been, and have not attained to the days of the years of the life of my fathers in the days of their residing" (47:9).

The text says 'the days of the years of my residing' and not 'the days of the years of my life' as Pharaoh asked. Later, Jacob talks about "...the days of the years of my fathers in the days of their residing." Jacob distinguishes between 'living' and 'residing.'

But the main point is that Jacob is comparing himself to both Abraham and Isaac. Abraham lived 175 years, and Isaac 180 years, and at the time Jacob is talking to Pharaoh he mentions his age of 130 years. How can he say that his 'days of the years of my life' did not 'attain the days of the years of the life of my fathers' when he is not yet dying? And he also labels his years as 'few and evil.'

Are we facing a whining man? Or, are we facing a king who lost his kingdom due to the heavy famine in the land, and as a result of his total despair he is summarizing his life?

And the text moves to end the meeting between Jacob and Pharaoh, "And Jacob blessed Pharaoh..." (47:10). It is quite likely that we are not facing a second blessing. However, Pharaoh interrupted Jacob when Jacob started blessing him, and Jacob insists on his right to bless Pharaoh. He might have lost his kingdom, but he only sees it as temporary, and therefore he sees himself as a king who can bless another king.

And the text ends with, "...and **came out** from before Pharaoh" (47:10).

Continuing the Linguistic Journey of Authority Relations in Biblical Language

To Come Out From Before

We find the verb 'to come out' in conjunction with the preposition 'from before' in several places in the text. In all these places it is clear that the phrase 'to come out from before' means acceptance of authority and acting accordingly.

For example, when Moses gathers the people and gives them a long list of how to build the tabernacle, the text ends with, "And the congregation of the people of Israel came out from the presence of Moses" (Exodus 35:20). We find the same at the end of Korach's rebellion, when there is a test of the staffs of all the tribes to see which staff would bloom, and when Aaron's staff bloomed, the text says, "And Moses **came out**[113] with all the staffs **from before** the Lord..." (Numbers 17:24).

We find the activity of 'coming out from before' twice in Genesis, first, Cain on whose forehead the Almighty put a sign so nobody would kill him. The text ends the encounter between the Almighty and Cain with, "And Cain **came out from before** the Lord..." (Genesis 4:16). Second, Joseph, "...and Joseph **came out from before** Pharaoh and went throughout all the land of Egypt" (Genesis 41:46).

We find the verb 'came out from before' at a time of trouble twice. First, with the death of Aaron's two sons, the text says, "And a fire **came out from before** the Lord and devoured them and they died before the Lord" (Leviticus 10:2). At another trouble point the text says, "...for anger has **come out from before** the Lord; the plague has begun" (Numbers 17:11).

Moses is the only one in which the text uses a different formula when talking about abiding by the Lord's command, although the word 'from before'[114] is still used. When the Almighty guides Moses to take the staff and to talk to the rock, the text says, "And Moses **took** the staff **from before** the Lord as He commanded him" (Numbers 20:9). The fact that the verb 'to come out' is not in use should already alert us that something

---

[113] Literally the word to 'come out' in Hebrew is *latzet*. It is from the three-letter root word *Y-TZ-A*. In this place the text says *vaYoTZe* which means that Moses 'brought out' the staffs.
[114] In Hebrew 'from before' is one word, *milifnei*.

is not right. This point will be discussed at length later on in the chapter on the names of the Almighty.

The text ended the meeting by saying that Jacob '**came out** from before Pharaoh' (47:10). Jacob was no different from Cain 'coming out from before' the Almighty when he got the sign on his forehead, and no different from Joseph who 'came out from before' Pharaoh when he got the mission to organize the food in Egypt. The ending of the meeting testifies that from the text's point of view, Jacob went from being 'Pharaoh' in his own land, to being 'Jacob' in the land of Pharaoh. The kingdom of Israel was over!

The Split Between Jacob and his Sons

When Joseph presents five of his brothers to Pharaoh, and Pharaoh asks them "what is your occupation?" (47:3), they answer that they are shepherds, and they add, "…to **reside** (*lagur*) in the land we have come… and now therefore please let your slaves **settle** (*yeshvu*) in the land of Goshen" (47:4).

The text quotes the brothers using two different verbs to relate to their stay in Egypt. First they use the verb *lagur* indicating it is a temporary stay, but then the text quotes them using the more permanent stay of 'settling" somewhere as part of the society, *lashevet*.

Is it a coincidence?

After the encounter between Jacob and Pharaoh, the text says, "And Joseph settled (*vayoshev*) his father and his brothers and gave them a **possession** (*achuza*) in the land of Egypt…" (47:11). We should note that the text uses the same word *achuza* as it uses later on in Exodus relating to the land of Canaan promised to the 'sons of Israel' as an everlasting **possession**.

And the text continues with, "And Joseph nourished his father and his brothers and all his father's household…" (47:12). The text moves on to describe in 14 long verses (47:13-26) how Joseph used the heavy famine to change the status of the people of Egypt from being independent, to being dependent on Pharaoh, and becoming practically 'residers' in the land of Pharaoh.

The text ends this section by saying two verses, "And **Israel** settled (*vayeshev*) in the land of Egypt in the country of Goshen and they had possessions in it and grew and multiplied exceedingly. And **Jacob** lived (*vayechi*) in the land of Egypt seventeen years..." (47:27-28).

We should note two points. The text devotes a separate sentence for 'Israel' and for 'Jacob' as they are two different entities. Second, the text uses a different verb for each of them. For 'Israel' the text uses the verb *lashevet* indicating permanent settlement, and for 'Jacob' the text uses the verb *lichyot*, which does not relate to the type of residence, but simply to living a life. Jacob, the person, was in total isolation.

If we sum up the situation, as Jacob saw it, we can see a very bleak picture. Jacob's sons deserted the Promised Land. They found a new land, the land of Goshen, and they didn't see themselves connected to the old country. What could Jacob do to influence the course of events? To talk to his sons would not help, as they were entrenched in their new country, Goshen/Egypt. But there was something Jacob could do, and he did.

The Request to be Buried in Canaan

Introduction

The fact is that a burial place is an important issue in the book Genesis.

The text devotes 16 verses to the negotiation that led to the purchase of the burial place in Hebron for Sarah, Genesis 23:3-18. The text says that upon Rachel's death, she was buried in Beth-Lehem, and Jacob positioned a *matzevah* on her burial place, making it a holy place. Later on, before his death, Jacob says to Joseph, "And as for me, when I came from Padan, Rachel died on me in the land of Canaan in the way, when yet there was but a little way to come to Ephrath, and I buried her in the way of Ephrath which is Beth-Lehem" (Genesis 48:7).

We should note that Jacob brought this point into the conversation with Joseph when he elevated his two sons to be two tribes among his other sons from Leah, Bilhah, and Zilpah. One might wonder if the reason Jacob brought Rachel's death into the picture upon elevating Joseph's two sons is due to the name Rachel gave Joseph, "And she called his name Joseph,[115] and said, the Lord shall add to me **another** son" (Genesis 30:24).

The Opening Sentence

"And the time drew near for **Israel** to die,
and he called **his son Joseph**…" (47:29)

We should note three points: first, the text labels Jacob 'Israel,' although he is no longer 'Israel in Canaan' but under the Egyptian Pharaoh in Egypt. Second, the use of 'Israel' is in conjunction with Joseph. Third, the text uses the personal language formula of 'title + name' for Joseph.

The Request

"…if I found grace in your sight, put please your hand
under my *yerech* and deal kindly and truly with me;
please bury me not in Egypt" (47:29).

First, as established earlier, Jacob asks Joseph for a pledge of obedience. Second, he asks him to deal 'kindly and truly'[116] with him. But the most important point, the first point on Jacob's mind is **not** where he will be buried, but where he will **not** be buried. Jacob did not want to be buried in Egypt.

Knowing what we know now, that the other sons of Jacob reached a deal with Pharaoh to exchange the land of Canaan for the land of Goshen, Jacob was concerned that the future of the Hebrews, as an independent nation, would come to a close. They were part of the Egyptian country now, and although settled in one distinct area of the country, still they were subjects of Pharaoh. They were actually Egyptian citizens living in Egypt. Jacob decided to use his dead body to make a statement. By his request not to be buried in Egypt, Jacob declared that he was not part of Egypt. He was still part of the land of Canaan.

---

[115] Joseph is the future tense of the verb 'to add' which is from three letter root word 'Y-S-F' and in Hebrew his name is *Yosef*.
[116] Literally, it is says 'and do for me kindness and truth.' The phrase 'kindness and truth' or 'kindness of truth' is an expression today in Hebrew to indicate the taking care of the dead to bury them. And it considered kindness in its ultimate form (truth), as the dead cannot reciprocate the favor.

And Jacob continued his request, "And I shall lie with my fathers, and you shall carry me out of Egypt and bury me in their burying place…" (47:30). And again, we see that the first priority on Jacob's mind is to be out of Egypt.

Joseph responded with, "I will do as you have said" (47:30).

We should compare Joseph's reaction to the reaction of the other sons, when Jacob, on his dying bed, commands them with the same point, to bury him in the family burial place in the land of Canaan. There, the text says, "And Jacob finished commanding his sons, he gathered up his feet into the bed and expired, and was gathered to his people" (49:33). The text does not give their response. Not like Joseph who said earlier, "I will do as you have said." The text is silent about their response. And if the text does not bring their response, it is quite likely that **they did not answer**.

And the text continues, "And Joseph fell upon his father's face and cried upon him and kissed him" (50:1). And where are the brothers?

Back to Jacob and Joseph

Although Joseph responded with, "I will do as you have said" (47:30), Jacob continued by asking, "And he said, swear to me and he swore to him…" (47:31).

Linguistic Journey – to Swear or Take an Oath

There are several places in the book of Genesis in which someone is asking another to swear, or take an oath, to guarantee that the other person will do his request. Can we find a common denominator between all these places where 'swearing' or 'taking an oath' is mentioned?

The best place to see the meaning of such an activity is by the difference in language in regard to the covenant between the Almighty and Abraham.

From the beginning we can see that the text considers the connection between the Almighty and Abraham a 'covenant,' and in numerous places:

- "On that day the Lord made a **covenant** with Abram saying to your seed I have given this land…" (15:18),
- "And I will make my **covenant** between me and you…" (17:2),
- "As for me behold my **covenant** is with you…" (17:4),
- "And I will establish my **covenant** between me and you…" (17:7),
- "And G-d said to Abram you shall keep my **covenant**…" (17:9),
- "This is my **covenant** which you shall keep between me and you and your seed after you…" (17:10),
- "And you shall circumcise the flesh of your foreskin and it shall be a sign of the **covenant** between me and you" (17:11),
- "…and my **covenant** shall be in your flesh for an everlasting **covenant**" (17:13),
- "…he has broken my **covenant**" (17:14),
- "…and I will establish my **covenant** with him for an everlasting **covenant**…" (17:19), and
- "And my **covenant** will I establish with Isaac…" (17:21).

However, we find a change in language in regard to the 'covenant' right at the event of binding Isaac at the altar. The text quotes the Angel of the Lord saying, "…by myself have I **sworn** said the Lord for because you have done this thing and have not withheld your son your only son" (22:16).

Once Abraham did something **against his own interest** – not sparing his own son, his only son, from the Almighty, the 'covenant' was 'upgraded' from one that was 'established' (*karat*) to one that was 'sworn' (*nishbaa*).

And, indeed, thereafter Abraham is quoted as saying to his slave, "The Lord G-d of heaven who took me from my father's house, and from the land of my family and who spoke to me and who swore (*nishbaa*) to me saying to your seed will I give this land…" (24:7).

The Almighty Himself is quoted as saying, "…and I will perform the **oath** (*shevua*) which I swore (*nishbaati*) to Abraham your father" (26:3). We see the same with Joseph talking to his brothers before his death, "…and bring you up from this land to the land which he **swore** (*nishbaa*) to Abraham to Isaac and to Jacob" (50:24).

At this point, we should check to see if in other places in the text we can see the idea of 'taking an oath' or 'swearing' is in the context of asking someone to do something against his own interest.

Abraham and Abimelech

After Abraham sent away Ishmael, and established Isaac, his son from Sarah his wife, as his heir, the text continues, "And it came to pass at that time that Abimelech and Phikol the chief captain of his army spoke to Abraham saying, G-d is with you in all that you do" (21:22).

This event starts with Abimelech, the king of the Philistines, and his military commander acknowledging that Abraham is the rising star in the region: G-d is with him in everything he does.

Abimelech continues, "Now **swear** to me here by G-d that you will not deal falsely with me nor with my son nor with my grandson but according to the kindness that I have done to you, you shall do to me, and to the land where you have resided" (21:23).

Abimelech is asking Abraham to 'swear' realizing that the tendency of a 'rising star,' at least, in the world of cold interests, is for everyone to act in his own interest. So Abimelech moves now to secure his front with Abraham, asking him to 'swear.' And Abraham indeed answers, "…I will **swear**" (21:24).

But Abraham is not willing to 'swear' without getting something in return. So the text moves on to bring us Abraham's demand that Abimelech and his people not steal the water from the well that Abraham's people dug.

And the text says, "And Abraham took sheep and oxen and gave them to Abimelech and both of them made a **covenant**" (21:27).

But this is not enough for Abraham. Making a 'covenant' is not as strong as 'swearing,' and Abraham wanted Abimelech to 'swear' as he (Abraham) was willing to do. And the text continues, "And Abraham set seven ewe lambs of the flock by themselves" (21:28). When Abimelech asked the reason for setting these lambs apart, Abraham answered "…they may be a witness for me that I have dug this well" (21:30).

And the event ends by the text saying, "Therefore he called that place Beersheba because there **they swore both of them**" (21:31). Not only did Abraham have to act against his interest as a 'rising star,' but Abimelech also had to give up his claim to the well, the source of water in the arid place. Therefore, 'they swore both of them.'

Abraham and Eliezer

The text brings us the story of Abraham's conversation with his slave, a conversation in which Abraham sends his slave away to Abraham's mother country to bring a wife to his son Isaac.

The text starts with,

"And Abraham was **old and well advanced in age**…" (Genesis 24:1)

Since the text started by saying that Abraham 'was old' why does it need to say that he was 'well advanced in age' also? The two different phrases cannot mean the same thing; we need to find out what the meaning of the phrase 'well advanced in age' is.

"…well advanced in age…"

In Hebrew the phrase 'well advanced in age' is literally, "comes in days." The phrase appears in the Tanach in the following places:

In regard to Abraham, when Abraham is informed by the three angels that within a year his wife Sarah will bear a son for him,

- "And Abraham and Sarah were old **and well advanced in age**, and it had ceased to be with Sarah after the manner of women" (18:11).

The phrase appears in regard to Joshua,

- "And Joshua was old **and well advanced in age**…" (Joshua 13:1),
- "And it came to pass a long time after the Lord had given rest to Israel from all their enemies on every side that Joshua became old **and well advanced in age**" (23:1), and

- "And Joshua called for all Israel, and for their elders and for their chiefs and for the judges and for the officers and said to them I am old **and well advanced in age**" (23:2).

And in regard to King David, the verse that opens the first book of Kings,

- "And king David was old **and well advanced in age**…" (1 Kings 1:1).

Returning to Abraham, the text tells us that the Almighty appeared to Abraham and said, "…Fear not Abraham I am your shield and your reward will be great" (Genesis 15:1).

Abraham responded with, "…what will you give me seeing I go childless and the steward of my house is Eliezer of Damascus. And Abram said, behold to me you have given no seed, and the man of my house is my heir" (15:2-3).

The Almighty responded, "…this shall not be your heir but he who shall come forth from your own bowels shall be your heir" (15:4).

And the text moved on to tell us of the birth of Isaac, and now the issue is how Isaac himself will continue the line of Abraham's family. If Isaac were to continue to be childless then by default Eliezer, whom Abraham mentioned as the one that might inherit from him if Abraham were to continue to be childless, Eliezer is returning to the picture. And according to tradition, this is the same one that Abraham appoints to bring a wife to Isaac, a wife that will bear children to Isaac, grandchildren to Abraham, and deprive Eliezer of the inheritance.

By the text saying, "And Abraham was old **and well advanced in age**…" (24:1), it is telling us that the issue of inheritance is in the forefront. Being old is a physical fact, but being 'come in days' means that the mind is preoccupied with the question of who is the one to continue the line – who is the one to 'come in days to come.'

The same applies to King David. The verse, "And king David was old **and well advanced in age**…" (1 Kings 1:1), starts the chapter that deals with the coronation of King Solomon.

Unlike Abraham and King David who were active in setting the heir to continue the line, Joshua was glaring in his passivity on this issue. Three times the text brings us the phrase 'well advanced in age.' However, Joshua does not deal with the leadership by designating someone to succeed him. Instead, Joshua only gives the people an ideological will. This is in sharp contrast to Moses who, along with the ideological wills he gave the people in Deuteronomy, also appointed Joshua to succeed him. One should wonder why Joshua did not take care of this important issue, and chose instead to leave a leadership vacuum, a vacuum that led to the era of the judges.

We should remember that Joshua was 'taken' by Moses to the position of 'leading' the people. We already saw in our linguistic journey dealing with the verb 'to take' that one who is 'taken' gives his position to his sons. Like Aaron and David. If so, we should ask if Joshua had sons. Note that the text does not mention any sons of Joshua. Did he have sons? Were they fit to lead, or were they maybe like the sons of Eli the priest, and Samuel?

Back to Abraham

Abraham said to Eliezer,[117]

> "And I will make you swear by the Lord
> the G-d of heaven and the G-d of the earth…" (24:3).

Realizing that Eliezer is on his way to embark on a mission to accomplish something that is totally against his own interest, we can understand why Abraham asks Eliezer to 'swear.' This against-his-own-interest-mission puts Eliezer in much higher regard than even we attribute to him. It is no wonder the text twice repeats the events in Haran by the well, once when they occur, and the second time when the text quotes Eliezer talking to Rebecca's family. Combined with the fact that the text changed its language from 'slave' to "man" when Eliezer's prayer is answered immediately, one can easily reach the conclusion that the text is in awe of Eliezer.

---

[117] As mentioned earlier, throughout this story the text does not identify the slave by name. To name him Eliezer is only an assumption, and not taken from the text.

Jacob and Esau

The next time we see someone asking another to 'swear' is in the event of selling the birthright by Esau to Jacob: "And Jacob said, swear to me this day and he swore to him and he sold his birthright to Jacob" (25:33).

Again, when we realize that Jacob asked Esau to do something against Esau's own interest, it is no wonder he asked him to swear.

Isaac and Abimelech

Isaac's relationship with the Philistines and their king Abimelech was gradually deteriorating. The text says that after the king released Isaac's wife, the Almighty blessed Isaac (26:12), and, "And the man became rich and gained more and more until he became very wealthy" (26:13), and the Philistines "envied him" (26:14). Their envy brought the Philistines to fill all the wells Abraham dug with earth (26:15). If Isaac didn't get the message that he was not welcome, the king himself told him, "Go from us for you are mightier than we" (26:16), and in fact, Isaac went from there and camped in the Valley of Gerar (26:18). At this stage, the war over water that went on in Abraham's time started again between Isaac and the Philistines (26:19-21). Finally, there was one well that there was no dispute over, a well that brought Isaac to say, "…the Lord has made room for us and we shall be fruitful in the land" (26:22). Isaac moved on to Beersheba where the Almighty appeared to him and promised him that his seed would multiply.

At this stage the king of the Philistines and his military commander show up at Isaac's camp. Surprised, Isaac asks them, "Why do you come to me seeing you hate me and have sent me away from you" (26:27). They responded, "We saw certainly that the Lord was with you…" (26:28). As in the time of Abraham, once Isaac became the rising power in the area, the others wanted to make sure that he would not attack them.

They asked Isaac "…let there be now an **oath** between us, and let us make a **covenant** with you" (26:28).

We should note that the Philistines asked for both an 'oath' (swearing) and a 'covenant.' However, the story ends with, "And they rose up in the morning and **swore** with one another…" (26:31). By omission, we can conclude that although they 'swore,' no 'covenant' was made between them.

Following the encounter between Abraham and Abimelech, the text continues with "And it came to pass after these things that G-d tested Abraham…" (22:1). We should note that no such 'test' is mentioned after the 'swearing' between Isaac and Abimelech. The difference is that Abraham and Abimelech had both a 'covenant' and 'swearing' between them, while Isaac and Abimelech had no 'covenant' between them. Although Abimelech requested a covenant, Isaac did not go along with it.

Taking into consideration that Abraham had to go through a 'test' after his 'covenant' with Abimelech, a 'test' that required binding Isaac on the altar and being ready to slaughter him, it is no wonder that the same Isaac refused this time to go along with a 'covenant' with Abimelech.

Jacob and Laban

After Laban reached the fleeing Jacob, and Laban searched Jacob's camp for his missing idols without finding them, the text says that Laban suggested, "Now let us make a covenant you and me and let it be for a witness between me and you" (31:44).

After they gathered stones and set them up as a monument for their covenant, Laban said,

> …the Lord watch between me and you when we are absent one from another. If you shall afflict my daughters, or if you shall take other wives beside my daughters although no man is with us, G-d is witness between me and you. (31:49-50)

And Laban continued,

> This heap shall be witness and this pillar (*matzevah*) shall be witness that I will not pass over this heap to you, and that you shall not pass over this heap and this pillar to me, for harm. The G-d of Abraham and the G-d of Nahor, the G-d of their father, judge between us… (31:52-53)

And the text concludes with, "And Jacob swore by the fear of his father Isaac" (31:53).

We should note that Laban only talked about a 'covenant' and he did not ask Jacob to 'swear,' but Jacob did 'swear.' We should also note that Laban requested that the G-ds of Abraham (Jacob's grandfather) and Nahor (Laban's grandfather) be witnesses to the 'covenant,' while Jacob 'swore' by the 'fear of his father Isaac,' and not by the G-d of Abraham, as Laban stated.

Knowing that 'swearing' takes place when one is requested to take a step against his own interest, we can zoom immediately to a request that Laban added to the covenant, "If you shall afflict my daughters, or **if you shall take other wives** beside my daughters..." (31:50). Laban, taking care of his own daughters, demanded a commitment from Jacob that in the future Laban's daughters would be Jacob's only wives. This demand had nothing to do with the 'covenant' between the two not to harm each other. This demand came to restrict Jacob in the future, even inside his own household, regardless of anything going on between him and Laban.

This is quite likely the reason that Jacob 'swore,' and in the name of his father Isaac – the only forefather that had only one wife, Rebecca.

A Point Important to the Text

The fact that the text tells us that Jacob 'swore,' and quite likely due to the commitment by Jacob not to take additional wives, should lead us to conclude that the text perceives such an act as a commitment against Jacob's own interest. Realizing that Jacob had four wives – two wives and two concubines (whom the text later upgrades to wives), we can conclude that only a man who had more than four wives would perceive such a commitment as being against the person's own self-interest. Restricting one's freedom to marry more than four wives should be perceived as a point important to the text.

Jacob and Joseph

Knowing that a request to 'swear' means to do something against one's own interest, we should wonder what is against Joseph's own interest in Jacob's request to be buried in the land of Canaan.

Realizing that his favorite son would like to have his father buried close to where he resides, so he can visit his grave at times, especially on the day of the anniversary of his death, Jacob asked Joseph not to do so. Therefore, he requested Joseph to 'swear,' and Joseph indeed "swore to him…" (47:31).

Joseph and his Brothers

Just as Jacob asked Joseph to take an oath not to bury him in Egypt, Joseph also asks his brothers to swear not to leave him behind when the Almighty takes them out of Egypt. And the text says, "**And Joseph made the sons of Israel swear** saying, G-d will surely visit you and you shall carry up by bones from here" (50:25).

By Joseph asking 'the sons of Israel' to 'swear,' we should conclude that Joseph perceived his request to be against the self-interest of 'the sons of Israel.' This request to 'swear' is mentioned in Exodus. The text says there, "And Moses took the bones of Joseph with him, for he had **solemnly sworn**[118] the sons of Israel…" (Exodus 13:19).

The text in Exodus, by doubling the verb, tells us that the request to 'swear' was extremely important to Joseph, and quite likely perceived by Joseph as being **strongly** against the self-interests of 'the sons of Israel.'

Knowing that the 'sons of Israel' connected their present and future to Egypt, we find it easy to understand why Joseph saw the need to ask them to swear. It was against their self-interest not to bury him in Egypt. They were 'Egyptians' or 'Goshenites,' and the request to be buried in the forsaken land of Canaan did not fit their goal.

The Ending Verse of Genesis

The text ends the book with, "And Joseph died being a hundred and ten years old, and they embalmed him, **and he was put in a coffin in Egypt**" (50:26). Ending the book with a body in a coffin sounds like a strange way to end any book. But if one knows the inside story of trading the land of Canaan for the land of Goshen, then one would understand that this

---

[118] "solemnly sworn" – again we find the verb is doubled, *hashbea hishbia*, for emphasis.

cryptic sentence tells the knowledgeable reader, 'The story is not over yet. To be continued...'

Evidence of the Land-for-Land Deal in Exodus

> And it came to pass in the course of those many days that the king of Egypt died, and the sons of Israel sighed by reason of the bondage, and they cried, and their cry rose up to G-d by reason of the bondage. And G-d heard their groaning and G-d remembered his covenant with Abraham, with Isaac, and with Jacob. And G-d looked upon the sons of Israel and G-d apprehended. (Exodus 2: 23-25)

We should note that there is no mention here of any longing to return to the land of Canaan. The 'groaning' of the people is only 'by the reason of the bondage.' If anyone had to remember the history of the people ever being in the land of Canaan, it was the Almighty himself, who remembered the covenant He 'signed' with the three forefathers. The people themselves couldn't even remember, as they were from a generation that was not even raised to remember such a connection.

When the Almighty appeared to Moses at the burning bush, the Almighty said that He came down 'to deliver them out of the hand of Egypt' (3:8), not by eliminating the bondage, as quite likely that was what the people were looking for as a solution, but "to bring them up out of that land to a good land..." (3:8). The land of Canaan.

And the Almighty told Moses how the people would come out of Egypt, "And I know that the king of Egypt will not let you go, if not by a mighty hand. And I will stretch out my hand and smite Egypt with all my wonders which I will do in their midst and after that he will send you away" (Exodus 3:19-20).

Was the objective of the plagues only to punish Egypt for the enslavement of the people? Or, were the plagues meant to bring Pharaoh to expel the people from the land? Otherwise, they wouldn't have gone. Their forefathers settled them there and they were part of the country. Abused and mistreated all over, but they were still part of the country. And in fact, the exodus out of Egypt did not take place until Pharaoh in the middle of the night called Moses and Aaron and said, "...Rise up and get you out from among my people both you and the sons of Israel…" (Exodus 12:31). The bottom line is: the people did not get out of Egypt. They were sent away and expelled. If they were to be asked, they would have said 'no.'

It is not an assumption that they would have said no. The text itself says, "And it came to pass when Pharaoh had sent the people away, that G-d led them not through the way of the land of the Philistines, although that was near, for G-d said, **lest perhaps the people regret when they see war and they return to Egypt**" (Exodus 13:17). The text openly says that the support for coming out of Egypt was very shallow.

The text quotes the people complaining when they saw the Egyptians chasing them, "because there were no graves in Egypt, have you taken us away to die in the wilderness? Why have you dealt thus with us, to bring us out of Egypt?" (Exodus 14:11).

In other complaints, over lack of water, the text quotes the people saying, "…Would to G-d we had died by the hand of the Lord in the land of Egypt, **when we sat by the meat pots**, and when **we did eat bread to the full**…" (Exodus 16:3).

In another place the people are quoted as saying, "We remember the fish which we ate in Egypt for nothing, the cucumbers, and the melons, and the leeks and the onions and the garlic (Numbers 11:5). The people simply glorified the life in Egypt. After all, they were raised to see themselves as 'Egyptians.'

The ultimate are the words of the people during the Korach revolt, "Is it a small thing that you have **brought us out of a land that flows with milk and honey** to kill us in the wilderness…" (Numbers 16:13).

The same expression used for the land of Canaan is attributed to the land of Egypt! The reader of today, when encountering such a blasphemy, is in shock. How could they? But they could. The land of Goshen did replace the land of Canaan. The land of Goshen was indeed the land that 'flowed with milk and honey.'

By the burning bush, Moses says to the Almighty, "…they will not believe me, nor listen to my voice…" (Exodus 4:1). Does Moses express doubt in the people's ability to believe him due to Moses' lack of connection to the people? Or, did Moses know the people well enough to know it was quite likely that they would not accept his mission of taking them out of Egypt?

But the people's attitude towards the land of Goshen/Egypt, and their lack of any connection to the land of Canaan, was not any consideration in the 'plan' set forth in the Covenant of the Splits. It was the right time by the Almighty's reckoning, and therefore it was the time for them to get out of there.

This point testifies that the connection between the land of Canaan and the 'sons of Israel' is not a connection generated **by the people**, but **by the Almighty** who moved to deliver the divine plan set forth 400 years earlier. At the generation of the exodus, the exodus was imposed on the people. And later the land of Canaan was imposed on them.

Back to Jacob and Joseph

The text says, "And it came to pass after these things that one told Joseph behold your father is sick, and he took his two sons Menashe and Ephraim" (Genesis 48:1).

And the text continues, "And one told **Jacob** and said behold **your son Joseph** comes to you…" (48:2). Note that at this point the text labels Jacob 'Jacob.' And the text quotes the 'one' using the personal language formula of 'title + name.' This personal formula was quite likely used by a relative, maybe even one of the sons, or the grandsons attending him.

Once 'Jacob' gets the information that 'his son Joseph' is coming, the text changes the language, "…and **Israel** strengthened himself and sat upon the bed" (48:2). As we saw before, the text gives 'Jacob' the title 'Israel' when Joseph is in the picture.

The text continues with, "And **Jacob** said to Joseph…" (48:3). However, when Jacob moves on to bless Joseph's sons, the text changes the language again, and says, "And **Israel** saw Joseph's sons and said who are these" (48:8). From now on, throughout the story Jacob is 'Israel:'

- "And the eyes of **Israel** were dim…" (48:10),
- "And **Israel** said to Joseph…" (48:11),

- "…towards **Israel**'s left hand… towards **Israel**'s right hand…" (48:13),
- "And **Israel** stretched out his right hand…" (48:14),
- "…in you shall **Israel** bless…" (48:20), and
- "And **Israel** said to Joseph…" (48:21).

In summary, the **language** of the text tells us that Joseph was the only one who perceived Jacob to be 'Israel' until the last minute of his life.

Jacob's Words to his Sons

The words start with, "And **Jacob** called **his sons** and said gather yourselves together that I may tell you that which shall befall you in the last days. Gather yourselves together[119] and hear you **sons of Jacob**, and listen to **Israel your father**" (49:1-2).

We should compare the way Jacob started his blessing to the way Moses started his before his death. There, the text says, "And this is the blessing with which Moses the man of G-d blessed the people of Israel before his death. And he said…" (Deuteronomy 33:1-2). There is no request by Moses to the people to listen to his blessing. Earlier, when Moses sang the song to the heavens and earth he said, "Give ear O you heavens and I will speak, and hear O earth the words of my mouth" (32:1). But he did not need to command the people to listen to him. He knew they did.

We should also note that the text labels Moses' words a 'blessing,' while the text does not do so when Jacob speaks to his sons. Only upon the end of his words does the text say, "…And this is it what their father spoke to them and blessed them, every one according to his blessing he blessed them" (Genesis 49:28).

> "Gather yourselves together and hear you **sons of Jacob**,
> and listen to **Israel your father**" (49:2)

Why the repetition? If they are 'the sons of Jacob' it would be understood that he is their father. But the fact is that they were first 'the sons of Jacob,' and they relegated 'Israel' to second place. It was important for

---

[119] The verb used for the 'gather yourselves together' in the first verse is *he'asfu* while the verb used in the second verse (translated also as 'gather yourselves together') is *hikavtzu*. This point will be discussed later, not in this analysis.

Jacob that they not only be 'his sons,' but that he also be 'Israel' their father. Exactly as Joseph accepted him, with all the honor of a king, which he still felt he deserved.

Jacob's Blessing to Dan

When Jacob blesses Dan, the text quotes him as saying, "Dan shall be a serpent by the road, an adder in the path, that bites the horse heels, and his rider fell backward" (49:17). The immediately following verse is, "For your salvation I have waited O Lord" (49:18).

However, ending the previous verse, "…and his rider fell backward," and if we understand that Jacob is the one who was 'riding the horse' (a metaphor for a king with all his might in the land of Canaan), and his end was to fall from the horse (a metaphor for losing his kingdom) and even backward (going to exile in Egypt), then we can understand Jacob's words to the tribe of Dan were a metaphor that describes his own situation. And when he comes to this point, from the depth of his heart he cries, "For your salvation I have **waited** O Lord." Waited in past tense, and now at my death I can see that my request has not been answered.

Jacob's Death

After talking to his sons, the text says,

> "And **Jacob** finished commanding **his sons**, he gathered his feet to the
> bed, and expired, and was gathered unto his people" (49:33).

In conjunction with Joseph he was mostly 'Israel;' in conjunction with 'his sons' he was 'Jacob.'

There are two points in the language of the text that are in this description, and are different from the descriptions of Abraham and Isaac. One point is well known. The text does not say that Jacob 'died.' The other one, less noticed, is that the text added a very specific activity: "…**he gathered his feet** to the bed…" (49:33).

Does the text come to tell us that when he talked to his sons he was in a sitting position? As he was when he talked to Joseph earlier? Or, maybe there is some other meaning to 'gathering the feet.'

Linguistic Journey – the Feet in Biblical Language

In many places we can see that the feet are the symbol of power. When Pharaoh commissions Joseph to be in charge of the land of Egypt, Pharaoh is quoted as saying, "And Pharaoh said to Joseph I am Pharaoh and without you shall no man lift up his hand **or foot** in all the land of Egypt" (41:44). In his words to Judah, Jacob says, "The staff shall not depart from Judah, nor the scepter **from between his feet**…" (49:10).

Later on, in Exodus, Moses speaks to Pharaoh saying, "And all these your slaves shall come to me and bow down to me saying get out and all the people who are **in your feet**…" (Exodus 11:8). We see the same, when the text gives us the description of the Almighty, as seen by the people, "And they saw the G-d of Israel, and there **was under his feet**…" (Exodus 24:10). Did the people see God's actual feet? Or is the text talking in a metaphor about the symbol of power?

In Deuteronomy we find, "Every place where **the soles of your feet** shall tread shall be yours…" (Deuteronomy 11:24). 'The soles of the feet' are the symbol of possession.

If there is any evidence that the feet are the symbol of power, then it is the name that the text gives to the three main festivals of the year – Passover (*Pesach*), Pentecost (*Shavuot*), and Tabernacles (*Sukkot*) – *Regalim* ('feet').

The text says, "Three times (*peamim*) in the year all your males shall appear before the Master G-d" (Exodus 23:17; 34:23). In another place the word *peamim* (times) is substituted with *regalim* (feet), "Three times (*regalim*) you shall keep a feast to me in the year" (Exodus 23:14). And indeed today in Modern Hebrew we relate to these three festivals as *regalim* (feet) and the act of going to Jerusalem for the festival as 'ascending to the *regel* (foot).' People think that the word *regel* was chosen because of the fact that people walked to Jerusalem. But the fact is that most Biblical personalities did have the 'vehicle' of the time, which was the ass. The word *regel* for the festival comes from the concept of authority. As the text says, "…appear before the **Master** G-d" (Exodus 23:17). The *regel* is the idea of submission to the Almighty by ascending to Jerusalem.

After his dream in which he saw the ladder with angels going up and down, and the Almighty appeared to him and promised to guard him on his way, the text says, "And Jacob **lifted his feet** and went to the land of the people of the east" (Genesis 29:1). Did he physically 'lift his feet,' or does the text mean that he felt more confident, more in control of his own destiny after the events of the preceding night?

Back to Jacob's Death

> "And Jacob finished commanding his sons,
> **he gathered his feet** to the bed, and expired,
> and was gathered unto his people" (49:33).

As he 'lifted his feet' after the dream before going to Haran, so he 'gathered his feet' before expiring. The text comes to tell us that Jacob felt that he had the authority of a king until his last breath. That he was king until he expired.

The Funeral

Introduction

The funeral procession of Jacob takes seven verses (50:7-13) ending with reminding the reader/listener that, "…and buried him in the cave of the field of Machpelah which Abraham bought with the field for a possession of a burying place of Ephron the Hittite, before Mamre" (50:13).

If we look for confirmation that the brothers deserted the land of Canaan, and saw themselves as citizens of the land of Goshen, we can find it in the way the text described the people who went up from Egypt to Jacob's funeral in the land of Canaan.

Going to the Funeral

The text devotes three verses to count the people who 'went up' to the funeral.

In the first verse, the text says, "And Joseph **went up** to bury his father, and with him **went up** all the slaves of Pharaoh, the elders of his house, and all the elders of the land of Egypt" (50:7).

In this verse, the text uses the verb 'to go up' twice, once for Joseph, and once for all the Egyptian dignitaries.

In the second verse, the text says, "And all the house of Joseph, and his brothers, and his father's house, only the little ones, and their flocks, and their herds, they left in the land of Goshen" (50:8).

We should note that in this verse the text avoids using the verb 'to go up.' It might seem a coincidence, but the third verse confirms it: "And there **went up** with him both chariots and horsemen and it was a very great company" (50:9).

Two points we should note. The first point is the location of Joseph's brothers in the list. They show up after listing the Egyptian court. One might say that this is due to the importance that the royal court deserved. However, we find out that this not the case on the return from the funeral. There, the text says, "And Joseph **returned** to Egypt, **he, and his brothers**, and all who went up with him to bury his father..." (50:14). Now, when the text talks about 'returning,' the brothers are listed second, and all the important royal court are listed in one pile, 'and all who went up with him.'

Second, on the way to the funeral, and even on the way back, the text avoids using 'went up' for Joseph's brothers. The others are the ones "...and all who **went up** with him..."

Moreover, as the text described the royal court on the way to the funeral, the text should have listed 'And all the house of Joseph' right after listing Joseph. But the text moves 'all the house of Joseph' to the second verse, to conceal the fact that the brothers are not attributed the activity of 'going up.'

Getting to the Land of Canaan

The text avoided saying that the funeral 'came to' the land of Canaan. After all, it was not their land anymore, and therefore in Biblical language there was no way to say that they 'came to' Canaan. 'Coming to' a land is only by a resident or even an owner. The text managed to do as follows:

"And they **came to** the threshing floor of Atad which is beyond the Jordan..." (50:10), there they had the period of mourning of seven days, and only then the text said, "And his sons **carried** him to the land of Canaan and buried him..." (50:13). As they carried him from the land of Canaan, now they carried him to the land of Canaan. But they did not **come to** the land of Canaan. It was not theirs to do so.

One should also note that the period of mourning of seven days usually starts after the burial. However, here the period of mourning is before the burial, and across the Jordan. The permission that Pharaoh gave was only to bury the father in the land of Canaan, but the period of mourning had to be done outside the land of Canaan, and before the burial.

Summary

In different ways the text tells us, language-wise, that the brothers were not owners, and not even residents, in the land of Canaan. They were Goshenites and not Canaanites.

The Apology

After the funeral, and upon their return to Egypt, the brothers sent a delegation to Joseph to make peace with him. This is interesting, taking into consideration that when he revealed himself, he told them that they were not the ones who sold him to slavery, as it was the hand of the Almighty, to bring about the redemption of the family at the time of the famine. So, the issue of them selling him to slavery was settled.

Moreover, Jacob came to Egypt two years into the famine, and he lived in Egypt for seventeen years. His death was twelve years after the famine was over. What would be the reason for the brothers to apologize now?

When Joseph revealed himself to the brothers he was quoted as saying, "Now therefore be not grieved, not angry with yourselves that you sold me here, for G-d sent me before you to preserve life" (45:5).

When the brothers apologized to Joseph after Jacob's death, he was quoted as saying, "But you thought evil against me, but G-d meant it good, to bring about as it is this day a large people alive" (50:20).

There are two differences between these two times he forgave them. While in the first forgiveness, Joseph mentioned selling him to slavery, in the second one he does not. In the first one, Joseph talks about 'preserving life,' in the second one he talks about reaching a point of having a large people (*aam rav*). In the second forgiveness, talking with the perspective of time ('as it is this day'), Joseph acknowledges that, in retrospect, the move to Goshen did bring about growing the people into a 'large people.'

The Text of the Apology

If we need any more evidence that Joseph's brothers bypassed Joseph and went to Pharaoh directly, then the text of the apology serves as evidence.

The text says that before the brothers sent their delegation to Joseph they said, "...Joseph will perhaps hate us and will certainly pay us back for all the evil which *gamalnu* him" (Genesis 50:15), and the apology itself said. "...for the evil they *gemalucha*..." (50:17)

The root *G-M-L* is actually the activity of 'reciprocating,' or, in other words, doing something for something which was done for you. For example, the text says that when King Saul apologized to David for pursuing him, Saul said, "...you are more righteous than I, for you *gemaltani* the good while I *gemalticha* evil" (1 Samuel 24:17). And Isaiah said, "...Woe to their soul for they have *gamlu* them evil" (Isaiah 3:9), and, "I will mention the grace of *Y-H-V-H*, for all that *Y-H-V-H gemalanu*..." (Isaiah 63:7).

Incidentally, nowadays, the Israeli military operations against Arab attacks are called *tagmul* operations.

Summary

Being a reactive verb, the verb *ligmol* cannot start a chain of events. It can only be a second, or later, step in the sequence of events. This is to say that the brothers being quoted as 'they *gamlu*' something to Joseph can only be done after Joseph did something for, or to, them. If we go strictly by the text, Joseph did only one main thing for the brothers – he offered them shelter and food during the famine. And this offer was without any request for payment. It was based only upon Joseph's sense of responsibility to his family. What did the brothers do in return for this offer, which they later described using the verb *ligmol*? We found that they went to deal directly with Pharaoh. Just not to have to deal with Joseph. Or in other words, he offered them his good heart and they returned with the same evil behavior they used when they sold him to slavery. And now they come to apologize for going to Pharaoh behind his back. And why did they wait until after Jacob died? They didn't want to apologize, and they figured that as long as Jacob was alive, Joseph would not retaliate for their behavior. But now the insurance policy was removed, they, projecting their evil ways on Joseph, figured he would behave as they did, and therefore, they needed to apologize. Till this point, they still didn't figure Joseph out. They didn't get it.

Summary

We have plenty of linguistic signals to confirm that there was a land-for-land deal between Joseph's brothers and Pharaoh. The land of Canaan was given to Pharaoh in a bartered deal for the land of Goshen.

Linguistic Bias

There is enough evidence in the language of the text that there was a deal of land-for-land, the land of Canaan for the land of Goshen. Jacob's family not only went down to Egypt/Goshen, but they also gave up the land of Canaan to the Egyptian king. This information is not present in the **content** of the text, but in the **language** of the text. It should be considered a 'linguistic bias' of the text that wants to conceal this information from the reader.

The Kingdom of Israel

The Borders

Before Joseph's brothers sold him to slavery, the text says that Jacob said to Joseph, "…Are not your brothers shepherding in Shechem? Come, and I will send you to them, and he said to him, here I am. And he said to him, go please see whether it is well with your brothers and well with the flocks and bring me word again…" (Genesis 37:13-14).

Understand that the text says that Jacob sent Joseph on an inspection tour with the expectation of getting a report from him. And the text continued the same verse, "…and he sent him from **the valley of Hebron** and he came to **Shechem**" (37:14).

Hebron is the southern side of the mountain ridge known today as Judea. Shechem, on the other hand, is on the north side of that same mountain ridge, known today as Samaria. This mountain ridge divides the land from east to west. From this mountain ridge one can only go down – either to the Jordan valley to the east, or to the west towards the coastal area. The width of the plateau on the top of this mountain ridge is estimated to be around 2-3 km or 1.5-2 miles in the area near Jerusalem of today, but it can extend to a little bit more in other areas. The distance between the two points – Hebron and Shechem – is 80 km or 50 miles. Considering that the pace of an ass ride is 30 km a day, it is over a two-day ride just to reach the destination.

"…and he **came** to Shechem" (37:14)

We already established that 'coming to' a place is not 'visiting.' One has to be a resident, citizen, or even an owner to be able to 'come to.' We should not forget that Shechem is the place where Jacob bought land. Shechem is also the place that was raided by two sons of Jacob. And Joseph 'came to' Shechem.

While Joseph was in Shechem, and not finding his brothers, he met a man who informed him that he heard the brothers saying, "…let us go to Dothan…" (37:17), which is even further north than Shechem.

From this story alone we can conclude that Jacob and his family extended their reach from Hebron in the south to Shechem in the north, practically covering all the area of the mountain ridge.

How did it all Start?

Innocently!

Introduction

Unlike Abraham who 'came to' the land of Canaan only once, Jacob, upon his return from Haran, 'came to' three places in the land of Canaan: Shechem, Luz, and Hebron. These three places are in one direct line from north to south. Abraham, after he 'came to' the land, moved around within it various times, and the text changed from using the verb 'settle' to using 'was present' a verb used for someone who is infrequently in the place, and thus a downgrade.

Another point: before he left the land of Canaan to go to his uncle Laban, the text says that Jacob made a vow,

> And Jacob vowed a vow saying, if G-d will be with me and will keep me in this way that I go and will give me bread to eat and garment to put on, and I will come back to my father's house in peace, then shall the Lord be my G-d. (28:20-21)

We should note that this vow was taken in Luz, the second place to which Jacob arrived in the land of Canaan upon his return, after the attack on Shechem.

Shechem

The text brings us the description of Jacob's return to the land by saying,

> And Jacob came to Shalem, a city of Shechem which is in the land of Canaan when he came from Padan-Aram, and pitched his tent before the city. And he bought a parcel of a field where he had spread his tent, at the hand of the sons of Hamor, Shechem's father, for a hundred pieces of money. (Genesis 33:18-19)

What would have happened if Shechem, the son of Hamor the Hivite, prince of the country, hadn't lusted for Jacob's daughter Dinah, and hadn't abducted her into his house? It is a nice game of what if, and maybe without this event, Jacob would have lived in peace, happily ever after, close to Shechem, a place where he had invested money in real estate. But the facts are that Shechem did lust for Dinah and he did abduct her. And these actions changed the course of events.

Dinah's brothers attacked the city and rescued her. The text brings us the intensity of this attack, "…and came upon the city boldly and slew all the males. And they slew Hamor and Shechem his son with the edge of the sword, and took Dinah out of Shechem's house and went out" (34:25-26).

If the attack had ended there, one might have been able to call it 'retribution' or even 'revenge.' But the text continues to describe the savagery of the attack,

> The sons of Jacob came upon the slain and plundered the city because they had defiled their sister. They took their sheep, and their oxen, and their asses, and that which was in the city, and that which was in the field. And all their wealth, and all their little ones, and their wives took they captive and carried off all that was in the houses. (34:27-29)

This savagery brought Jacob to complain,

> You have brought trouble on me to make me odious among the inhabitants of the land, among the Canaanites and the Perizzites, and I being few in number, they shall gather together against me and slay me and I shall be destroyed, I and my house. (34:30)

At this point, the Almighty told Jacob to go up to Beth-El and to build an altar to the G-d "…who appeared to you when you fled from the face of Esau your brother" (35:1). In preparation, the text says that Jacob said to "his household and to all who were with him" (35:2) to remove all the idols in their midst and to purify themselves and change their garments. The people indeed gave Jacob all the idols and Jacob "hid them under the oak which was by Shechem" (35:4).

The fact that Jacob did not destroy these idols, and instead hid them under an oak by the city of Shechem, testifies that it was his intent not to abandon the place altogether, but to return to it sometime in the future.

And the text continued, "And they journeyed and the terror of G-d was upon the cities that were around them, and they did not pursue after the sons of Jacob" (35:5).

We are facing a sentence in the negative. The text tells us what the 'cities that were around them' didn't do. But the text does not say what they did do, at least not in the **content** of the text. However, in the **language** we do get a clue what happened.

The text continues, "And Jacob came to Luz which is in the land of Canaan that is Beth-El, he and all the **people** who were with him" (35:6).

At this point in time, we need to go to the original Hebrew. The fact is that the text does not say 'people' in the sense of 'men and women.' The text uses the word 'people' in the sense of 'nation' – *aam*. When the text quotes Pharaoh at the beginning of Exodus, "…the people (*aam*) of the sons of Israel are more and mightier than we" (Exodus 1:9). When people say 'the American people' they don't mean 'the American men and women.' They clearly mean 'the American **nation**.' And this is the word used in the text right here.

When Jacob told the people of 'his house and to all who were with him' to remove the idols from among them, the text describes them as 'all who were with him.' However, by the time they reached Luz, Jacob was heading a 'nation.' What brought this change of language?

The 'cities around them' did not pursue Jacob and his family. However, the savagery of the attack on Shechem did not go unnoticed. It is quite likely that the cities all around moved to come and plead allegiance to this new guy on the block, out of fear that this savagery would be directed at them. From just 'a few' before the attack on Shechem, the text refers to a 'nation' after the attack on Shechem.

The text continues with saying that Jacob built an altar and called its name, again, El Beth-El. Then the text moves to bring us a sentence out of the blue: "And Deborah, Rebecca's nurse, died, and she was buried beneath Beth-El under an oak, and the name of it was called Allon Bachuth[120]" (Genesis 35:8).

We should realize that a burial place is an important point in the book of Genesis. Abraham purchased land to bury his wife Sarah; Jacob erected a pillar on Rachel's grave; and Jacob requested that Joseph not bury him in Egypt. Mentioning the fact that Deborah, Rebecca's nurse is buried

---

[120] Allon Bacuth – *allon* means 'oak' and *bacuth* means 'crying.'

'under an **oak**' (and remember Jacob hid the idols under an **oak** by Shechem) in Beth-El comes to signify to us, again, that Beth-El is not just a place for Jacob to visit. He put his stake in the land in Luz which is Beth-El 'which is in the land of Canaan,' as the text comes to specify to us again and again.

If we have any doubt that this burial of Rebecca's nurse in Beth-El was significant, and quite likely as a claim of Jacob to the land, then the text moves to tell us about another appearance of the Almighty to Jacob. This appearance deserves very careful scrutiny.

The text starts with, "And G-d appeared to Jacob again, **when he came from Padan-Aram** and blessed him (35:9).

This is an interesting sentence, as the text says Jacob came from Padan-Aram into the land of Canaan by 'coming to' Shechem. But for the Almighty, Shechem was not the closing of the chapter. Luz was.

Let's go back to the appearance of the Almighty to Jacob in Luz **before** going to Haran. There, the Almighty said to Jacob, "And behold I am with you, and will keep you in all places where you go, and will bring you back to this ground,[121] for I will not leave you, until I have done that about which I have spoken to you" (Genesis 28:15).

The Almighty's promise, given many years ago on the way to Haran, was finally fulfilled. Jacob indeed came to that same 'ground' (Luz) in one piece.

And the text continues with informing us of the Almighty giving Jacob a new name.

Jacob Gets the Name Israel

There are four people in the book of Genesis that are given new names. The first two are Abraham and Sarah.

---

[121] The regular translation of 'land' or 'country' is wrong as the text uses the Hebrew word *adamah* from which the word *Adam* is derived. Since Jacob is lying on his back on the ground, the promise relates to return him in peace to that same spot – Luz, or Beth-El.

For Abraham, the text says, "Neither shall your name any more be Abram, but your name shall be Abraham..." (Genesis 17:5). For Sarah, the text does the same ten verses later, "...As for Sarai your wife, you shall not call her Sarai, but Sarah shall her name be" (17:15).

For both Abraham and Sarah, the text is not saying anything about 'calling' them a new **additional** name. The text simply states that their name from now on will be another name – Abraham for Abram, and Sarah for Sarai. And indeed, from that point on we cannot find the old names in use by the text. The text relates to Abraham and Sarah using only their new names.

However, for Jacob the text deviates from this pattern, saying the following:

"Your name is Jacob, your name shall not be **called** any more Jacob, but Israel shall be your name, and he **called** his name Israel" (35:10). There is no simple statement of giving Jacob a new name. Instead, the text is talking about 'calling' Jacob with a new name. Moreover, for Jacob, the text uses the same formula it uses everywhere else for giving a name to a newborn baby: 'and he **called** his name Israel.' Language-wise, the text is reporting to us the 'birth' of Israel. And indeed, we find from now on that the two names are in use – the old one as well as the new one. The old name did not die. There is only the birth of a new name.

The fourth person in Genesis who got a new name, also using the formula of 'calling,' is Joseph: "And Pharaoh called Joseph's name Zaphnath-Paaneah[122]..." (41:45). And like Jacob, we find that Joseph did not lose his old name. The text still relates to him by his name Joseph.

The fact that the text brings us the 'birth' of Israel right after it changes its language from 'all who were with him' to the 'people (nation) that were with him' testifies that a significant change took place in Beth-El which is Luz, 'which is in the land of Canaan.'

The Promise

The text continues to inform us that after the change of name from Jacob to Israel the Almighty repeats the promise of giving Jacob/Israel the land

---

[122] *Zaphnath* is 'mystery' and *Paaneah* is 'solving.'

of Canaan. The text says, "And the land which I gave Abraham and Isaac to you I will give it, and to your seed after you will I give the land" (35:12).

At first glance it seems that everything is fine. Like his predecessors Abraham and Isaac, who got the same promise, Jacob is continuing in their shoes and receives the same promise. However, if we compare all the instances in which this promise was given to Abraham and Isaac, and even to Jacob himself, when he was in Luz on his way to Haran, we see that things were not that rosy.

Linguistic Journey - the Promise

The promise is given to Abraham four times.

- "…to your seed I will **give** this land…" (Genesis 12:7)
- "For all the land which you see, to you I will **give** it, and to your seed forever" (13:15)
- "…to your seed have I **given** this land…" (15:18)
- "And I will **give** to you and to your seed after you the land where you reside, all the land of Canaan for everlasting possession…" (17:8)

The text gives the promise to Isaac only once.

- "…for to you and to your seed I will **give** all these countries…" (26:3).

As for Jacob, the promise he received on his way to Haran is,

- "…the land on which you lie to you I will **give** it and to your seed" (28:13).

Upon his return to the land of Canaan, and at the same place he received the promise initially – Beth-El which is Luz –

- "And the land which I gave Abraham and Isaac to you I will **give** it, and to your seed after you will I **give** the land" (35:12).

The difference between all the previous places and this last place is that in this last place the text uses the verb 'will give' twice, while earlier it is only once. Up to this point, the text does not distinguish between the one receiving the promise and his seed. However, literally, the text speaks of two different 'givings.' One is to the one who receives the promise, and in this case it is Jacob/Israel, and the other is to his seed. If one thinks about it, then two 'givings' means that **the land will be taken away in-between**.

This appearance of the Almighty ends with the following sentence, "And G-d went up from him in the place where he spoke with him" (35:13).

There are many appearances of the Almighty to the three forefathers, and most of them end without any concluding sentence. The text just continues with the sequence of events, assuming the reader knows that the encounter is over. However, there are three places in which there is a concluding sentence. The first two are with Abraham.

The first time is when the Almighty changes Sarah's name from Sarai to Sarah, and informs Abraham that within a year he, Abraham, will have a son with Sarah. The text continues, saying, "And Abraham fell upon his face and laughed and said in his heart, shall a child be born to him who is hundred years old? And shall Sarah who is ninety years old bear?" (17:17). And Abraham suggests that Ishmael might serve as his son (17:18). The Almighty insists that the son will be from Sarah and his covenant with Abraham will continue with Isaac (17:21). The Almighty also promises Abraham that Ishmael will receive a consolation gift, "...and will make him fruitful, and will multiply him exceedingly, twelve princes shall he father, and I will make him a great nation" (17:20).

Although the text does not say it openly, the fact is that Abraham did express disbelief in the Almighty's ability to produce a son to a couple in which the wife is ninety years old, and the husband is one hundred years old.

And indeed the text ends by saying, "And he finished talking with him **and G-d went up from Abraham**" (Genesis 17:22).

The second time in which the text brings us a concluding sentence is after Abraham negotiates with the Almighty on how many righteous people need to be present in the city of Sodom before the city will be spared from destruction. The negotiations started with the number fifty, and through 45, 40, 30 and 20, it reached 10. When the number reached 10, Abraham stopping pleading.

This description of a human being arguing with the Almighty about the justice of his actions sounds as if Abraham equates himself to the position of the Almighty. One only needs to go and read the book of Job to know that humans should not doubt divine justice. Humans with their finite knowledge cannot follow the infinite. But Abraham did dare to challenge the Almighty.

The text ends this encounter by saying, "And the Lord went his way as soon as he had concluded talking to Abraham **and Abraham returned to his place**" (Genesis 18:33).

Note here that the Almighty doesn't go back **up**. He just goes on His way. If we go back to the beginning of the encounter about Sodom, it says, "And the men rose **up** from there… and Abraham went with them" (18:16). Abraham was already **up**, and at the end of the conversation he returned to his place. 'Returning to his place' can be in reality, but at the same time it can be a metaphor. Abraham returned **down** to his place as a human being.

Back to Jacob

After changing his name to Israel, and doing it in a way that does not exclude the use of his old name Jacob, the Almighty talked about giving the land two times, once to Jacob, and once '…to your seed **after you** will I give the land.' And the text ended this encounter by saying, "And G-d went up from him **in the place where he spoke with him**" (35:13).

The first two times in which a concluding sentence was used with Abraham, it testifies to some displeasure, maybe even by the Almighty, or by the text itself, about the preceding events. Realizing this, we can easily conclude that the same applies to Jacob on the ground at Luz. And indeed we find that this is the last time the Almighty appeared to Jacob until the time before he left the land of Canaan to go down to Egypt. At which time the Almighty appeared to Jacob promising him, "I will go down with you to Egypt, and I will also surely bring you up again, and Joseph shall put his hand upon your eyes" (46:4). There was no mention of the promise to give him, or his seed, the land of Canaan at that point.

Before his death, Jacob talked to his son Joseph saying, "G-d Almighty appeared to me at Luz in the land of Canaan and blessed me. And said to me, behold, I will make you fruitful, and multiply you, and I will make you a multitude of people, and will give you this land to your seed after you **for an everlasting possession**" (48:4).

We should note that the promise 'for an everlasting possession' is not quoted in the promise given to Jacob, not in the first appearance at Luz before going to Haran, and not in the second appearance at Luz upon returning from Haran. This promise – everlasting possession – is actually given to Abraham: "And I will give to you, and to your seed after you, the land where you reside, all the land of Canaan, **for an everlasting possession**..." (17:8). How come the Jacob misquoted the Almighty?

"And G-d went up from him **in the place where he spoke with him**" (35:13).

We should remember the initial promise delivered in the first appearance at Luz – to return you to the **ground** you are on right now. The text tells us that the Almighty tells Jacob – I delivered on my promise!

And the text continues, "And Jacob set up a pillar (*matzevah*) **in the place where he talked with him**, a pillar of stone, and he poured a drink offering on it, and he poured oil on it" (35:14).

In the first appearance we read that Jacob only poured oil on the *matzevah*; here, we find that he also poured 'a drink offering.'

The Death of Rachel

Upon departing Beth-El the text brings us several verses (35:16-20) describing Rachel giving birth to Benjamin, a birth that brings on her death, and her burial on the way. Again, we see a burial place, a significant point, also testifying to a claim to the land.

This event of Rachel's death is brought to us right after the concluding sentence in which the Almighty gave Jacob/Israel the message that He delivered on His promise to bring Jacob back safely to the exact same spot where he was before. Jacob is also the one who said to Laban his father-in-law, when Laban was searching for his stolen idols, "With whom you will find your gods, **let him not live**…" (31:32), not knowing that Rachel was the one who stole them.

The proximity of these two events should bring us to recognize that the text connects these two points thematically: the Almighty delivered on His promise, and now it is time for Jacob to deliver on his 'promise.'

Rachel's death devastated Jacob, as we saw in an earlier discussion. It brought him to abdicate his position as the head of the family.

After the description of Rachel's death and burial, the text indicates Israel journeyed and spread his tent beyond the tower of Edar (35:21), and that is where Reuben slept with Bilhah, Jacob's concubine (35:22).

The History Game: What if…?

What would have happened if Abner, the military commander of the house of King Saul, hadn't slept with Rizpah the daughter of Aiah, who was King Saul's concubine? The text in 2 Samuel says that after the death of Saul on the battlefield, Abner was getting stronger in the house of Saul, and slept with Rizpah. The son of Saul reprimanded Abner for doing so. In retaliation, Abner decided to "transfer the kingdom from the house of Saul and to set up the throne of David over Israel and over Judah, from Dan to Beersheba" (2 Samuel 3:10).

If Abner hadn't slept with Rizpah, David might have remained the king over one tribe, the tribe in Judah, staying in the capital of the tribe in Hebron, and the united kingdom of David over all the twelve tribes would not have been established. Maybe.

What would have happened if Reuben hadn't slept with Bilhah, Jacob's concubine? Maybe the kingdom of Jacob/Israel wouldn't have been established. Maybe.

But the fact is that Reuben did sleep with Bilhah. And this event was indeed a major significant point. How do we know?

Counting Jacob's Sons

There are two places in which the text gives us the **number** of Jacob's sons. The first is here, right after the text says that Reuben slept with his father's concubine. And the second is upon the descent of the family to Egypt.

If the second counting is at the time the first Israeli kingdom is coming to a close, then the first counting is at the time the first Israeli kingdom began.

It is no different from a passage in the book Samuel 2. The text says,

> And there was a long war between the house of Saul and the house of David, but David became stronger and stronger, and the house of Saul became weaker and weaker. And to David were sons born in Hebron, and his firstborn was Amnon... (2 Samuel 3:1-2)

The text connects the strengthening of the 'House of David' to the counting of sons.

Implications for Jacob

Up to this point, the story presents to us one man and how he established himself by getting married, bringing up children, and accumulating wealth. However, once Jacob couldn't function as a leader because of his beloved wife's death, and the firstborn took over, the message to the society was it is not a one-man show. It is a dynasty. It is no different from the time Abimelech showed up at Abraham's place after Abraham sent Ishmael away and established Isaac as his heir. Once the line of ascension was established, Abimelech said to Abraham, "...G-d is with you in all that you do" (Genesis 21:22).

And indeed the text connected the death of Rachel and Jacob's mourning for her to Reuben sleeping with Bilhah, not only by the **context** (proximity to each other), but also **language**-wise. The text says,

> And **Israel** journeyed and spread his tent beyond the tower of Eder. And it came to pass when **Israel** lived in that land that

Reuben went and lay with Bilhah his father's concubine and **Israel** heard it, and the sons of Jacob were twelve. (Genesis 35:21-22)

This is the first time since the change of name by the Almighty that the text relates to Jacob as 'Israel,' using the national title.

And the text continues, "And Jacob **came to** Isaac his father, to the city of Arba, which is Hebron, where Abraham and Isaac resided" (35:27).

This is third time in which Jacob 'came to' since he returned to the land of Canaan. And the text emphasizes to us that Jacob 'came to' the place where his two predecessors 'resided.' He was not 'residing' there. He 'came to' the place.

And after this point the text moves to discuss the family line of Esau and the kings of Edom, and then the text continues with, "And Jacob **settled** in the land where his father **resided** in the land of Canaan" (37:1). As earlier, where Jacob 'came to' Hebron, now he 'settles' there while his father 'resided' there. And then the story of Joseph and his father begins.

Summary

The places in the land of Canaan – Shechem, Luz, and Hebron – were important to the creation of the kingdom of Israel by Jacob. The first place was the city of Shechem that was his entrance to the land. There he bought a piece of land, and planned on settling. The abduction of Dinah, and the savage attack on the city by Dinah's brothers, forced a change in Jacob's plans. He didn't plan to establish a kingdom, but it was imposed on him. However, he didn't reject it, and he even contributed to it, by launching more wars against the Amorites.

Luz was very likely the religious center of this kingdom. Out of the three places that the text says that Jacob 'came to' in the land of Canaan – Shechem, Luz, and Hebron – Luz is the one that gets the most religious activity in both numbers and significance.

The Almighty appeared to Jacob twice in Luz. The first time was right after the dream of the angels on the ladder. And the second time was upon his return from Haran when the Almighty appeared to him and changed his name from Jacob to Israel.

As for religious practices that at the time were manifested by either building an altar or erecting a *matsevah*, we have no mention of any establishment of an altar or a *matzevah* in Hebron. The text mentions once that Jacob erected an altar in Shechem (33:20). As for Luz, we have both a *matzevah* and an altar. A matzevah is mentioned twice, once on Jacob's way to Haran (28:18), the same time that he declared the place "the gate of the heaven" (28:17), and a second time upon his return from Haran, after the attack on Shechem to rescue Dinah and after the Almighty appeared to Jacob in Luz changing his name (35:14). He built an altar in Luz (35:7), and this altar was built on the express request of the Almighty.

Hebron was very likely his capital, the city where he located himself most of the time. This was the place from which he sent Joseph on the 'inspection tour' that brought about the selling of Joseph to slavery, Joseph going down to Egypt, and gradually rising in Egyptian society, to be able to help his father when the famine took the kingdom down.

The fact that Hebron was the capital of Jacob/Israel might explain why Caleb the son of Jephunneh wanted Hebron to be his 'inheritance' in the land. Caleb addressed Joshua and said, "…give me this mountain…" (Joshua 14:12). "And Joshua blessed him and gave Caleb the son of Jephunneh Hebron for an inheritance" (14:13). And the text continued in the book of Joshua, "Hebron therefore became the inheritance of Caleb the son of Jephunneh the Kenazite to this day…" (14:14).

What was the Character of the First Israeli Kingdom?

Introduction

The label 'kingdom' might be a little bit inappropriate. Although we have enough linguistic evidence that Jacob, as Israel, functioned as a king, still it is disputable if the title 'king' was even used at the time he ruled over the land.

The evidence of this possible lack of title is the way the brothers responded to Joseph's dream that their sheaves would bow down to Joseph's sheaf. The brothers are quoted by the text as saying, "Shall you indeed **reign**[123] over us? Or shall you indeed have **dominion**[124] over us?" (Genesis 37:8).

The fact that the text quotes the brothers as not sure which verb to use to describe the activity of bowing in front of someone raises the suspicion that it was not that clear if their father was a *melech* ('king') or a *moshel* ('ruler').

Comparing Abraham to Jacob/Israel

When Abraham migrated from Haran to the land of Canaan, the text says, "And Abram took Sarai his wife, and Lot his brother's son, and all their possessions that they had gathered, **and the souls that they had acquired in Haran**…" (Genesis 12:5).

By comparison, when Jacob and his family went down to Egypt due to the famine, the text says, "….and the sons of Israel carried Jacob their father and their little ones, and their wives in the wagons which Pharaoh had sent to carry him. And they took their cattle and their goods which they had acquired in the land of Canaan…" (Genesis 46:5-6). And missing from the description is 'the souls that they had acquired in the land of Canaan.' Unlike his grandfather Abraham, Jacob was not in the business of trying to win over souls.

If there was any achievement that Jacob listed in his language, it was his military conquest: "And I have given you one portion above your brothers, which I took from the hand of the Amorite **with my sword and with my bow**" (Genesis 48:22).

Foreign Affairs

Israel, being a tiny sliver of land between the large country of Egypt to the west and the rising powers of Assyria and Babylonia to the east, had to create alliances with the nearby countries. The first book of Kings describes the way King Solomon went about establishing his kingdom,

---

[123] "…indeed reign…" – the verb is doubled for emphasis. The Hebrew word for king is *melech*, and the related form *limloch* is the verb. In Hebrew the brothers are saying, "shall you *maloch timloch* over us?"
[124] "…indeed have dominion…" – Again doubling the verb. The word in Hebrew for the verb 'to rule' over someone is *limshol*. The text quotes the brothers as saying, "…or shall you *mashol timshol* over us?"

> And Solomon made a marriage alliance with Pharaoh king of Egypt and took Pharaoh's daughter and brought her into the city of David until he had made an end of building his own house, and the house of the Lord, and the wall of Jerusalem round about. (1 Kings 3:1)

The first act of King Solomon was to secure the western border with Egypt. None of this is mentioned in Genesis about Jacob. It might be that Jacob could not do so, as he swore to Laban his father-in-law and uncle not to take more wives than he already had (Genesis 31:50, 53). Still, Jacob was not into 'foreign affairs.'

Actually, the eastern border of his kingdom was already secured by a non-aggression pact he had with his father-in-law Laban – that the two will not cross the demarked line against each other for evil cause. Even his southeastern border was relatively quiet, as he had reached an understanding with his brother Esau who lived to the southeast of him. If Jacob/Israel had any problem with others, it was with the Amorite people residing in the land, and against them he launched battles, with his sword and his bow.

This point alone might explain why Joseph did not contact his father and his family for so long, even after he became vice-royal. Although there was no warfare between the two countries, still there was no peace either. Joseph could not do anything that would endanger his position in Egypt. This would also explain why the text says that Pharaoh, and the house of Pharaoh were so pleased when they got the news that Joseph's brothers 'came to' Egypt. Not because they cared for Joseph the person, but they got the chance to take down the hostile country to the east. That's why Pharaoh insisted that the brothers bring their father with them. Joseph's brothers were not important to Pharaoh, but dismantling the kingdom of Israel was definitely an objective. And this is the reason that the brothers had to mislead their belligerent father about trading the land, and about the wagons, so they could secure their position in Egypt.

Warfare

The text says that the one who abducted Dinah was Shechem the son of Hamor **the Hivite**..." (34:2). By saying to Joseph that he took land from the Amorite, Jacob was not talking about the attack on Shechem. Remember, it was his two sons Levi and Simeon who carried out the attack on Shechem. And Jacob even criticized them for it. Therefore, the land that Jacob took from the Amorite must have been another battle that Jacob was talking about, a battle that he launched against the Amorites. There is no mention of this battle or war anywhere else, but it did happen. Between Shechem, Luz and Hebron, the three places the text mentions as the places went from north to south, there was more to the story than the text reveals. The settling of the land did not go peacefully. Wars started and battles were conducted, and won.

Moreover, if the 'sword' is the weapon of close encounter, the bow is the weapon of more distant encounter. Jacob talked about these two types of warfare. Jacob was not only a shepherd, taking care of the sheep. Jacob was a warrior.

Domestic Affairs

The only negative point in the picture was internal – within the family, and not outside. We already saw that the fact that the firstborn Reuben slept with his father's concubine means that he took control over the operation once Jacob couldn't function due to his heavy mourning for his dead wife. And in fact, the text attributes to this event the point that the family established itself as permanent and not a one-man show. The text started counting Jacob's sons right after this event. Reuben did function well, and indeed delivered the reign back to his father when his father came out of his deep depression.

But instead of keeping Reuben as his heir apparent, Israel chose Joseph to be his heir. The text tells us that "Israel loved Joseph more than all his sons" (37:3), but the fact is that Joseph was the firstborn of Rachel the 'wife' of Jacob (Leah is not mentioned as his wife). Joseph got the coat with the stripes (37:3) that later on, in the time of David, symbolized the garments of the king's daughters. Joseph was the shepherd of his brothers with the sheep (37:2) and he was sent later on an inspection tour to check on his brothers. For Israel, Joseph was the one in line to inherit his position and the entire family. And Joseph's dreams testified that he saw himself being groomed to be the heir.

This fact did not go well with the six sons of Leah, Reuben heading them. This preference of the younger brother from the other wife produced a lot of internal strife in the family. It brought Leah's sons to the point they wanted to kill Joseph, only to be prevented by Judah who found a compromise, selling him to slavery instead of killing him. They got rid of the problem, but unknowingly they started the wheels moving towards a future solution to the family distress at the time of the upcoming famine.

Question

Why does the text say, and at the same time, not say, that Jacob was the first king of Israel? Why do we need to go and dig deeply into the language of the text to find that Jacob was indeed a king? What prevented the text from openly attributing the title 'king' to Jacob? It is similar to the question that we asked earlier, why doesn't the text attribute the title 'firstborn' to Joseph?

Possible Answer

The fact that there were famines in the land of Canaan is mentioned the Tanach several times. At the time of Abraham the text says, "And there was a famine in the land; and Abram went down to Egypt to reside there; for the famine was severe in the land" (Genesis 12:10). The same is true at the time of Isaac, "And there was a famine in the land, beside the first famine that was in the days of Abraham…" (26:1).

Besides the time of Jacob and his sons, we find other times in which there was a famine.

- "And there was a famine in the days of David three years year after year…" (2 Samuel 21:1)
- at the time of Ahab, "…and there was a severe famine in Samaria" (1 Kings 18:2)
- at the time of Elijah the prophet, "And there was a famine in the lands…" (2 Kings 4:38)

When Solomon dedicated the temple he listed all the possible troubles that might arise, "If there is a famine in the land, if there is pestilence…" (1 Kings 8:37) and he listed famine as trouble number one.

When David counted the people and aroused the Almighty's anger towards him, the prophet appeared to him and said,

…three alternatives I offer you, choose one of them that I may do it to you… Shall seven years of famine come to you in your land? Or will you flee three months before your enemies while they pursue you? Or should there be three days' pestilence in your land…" (2 Samuel 24:12-13).

David chose the third option – pestilence for three days.

We know that David already experienced the second option in the past. David had to run away from King Saul while King Saul pursued him constantly, and David had to run away from Absalom his son after he rebelled against him. We have no report of how long the rebellion lasted.

But what about the first option mentioned in the prophet's message, 'Shall seven years of famine come to you in your land?' Did David try this option? The text does not mention anything about such a long famine. The text only mentions a famine of three years, and emphasizes 'a year after a year.' But where do we find a famine of seven years? The famine in Jacob's time.

The book of Genesis repeats the oppression of the famine during Jacob's time many times:

- "And the seven years of **famine** began to come according as Joseph had said, and the **famine** was in all the lands…" (Genesis 41:54),
- "And the **famine** was over all the face of the earth…" (41:56),
- "…because the **famine** was so severe in all the earth" (41:57),
- "…for the famine was in the land of Canaan" (42:5),
- "And the **famine** was severe in the land" (43:1),
- "For these two years has the **famine** been in the land, and yet there are five years when there shall be neither plowing nor harvest" (45:6),
- "…for your slaves have no pasture for their flocks for the **famine** is severe in the land" (47:4), and
- "And there was no bread in all the land, for the **famine** was very severe so that the land of Egypt and the land of Canaan were tired because of the **famine**" (47:13).

Moreover, the text tells us that the famine at that time changed the administration system in the land of Egypt, "And Joseph bought all the land of Egypt for Pharaoh for the Egyptians sold every man his field because the famine prevailed over them so the land became Pharaoh's" (47:20).

In other lands, and in other times, a heavy famine brought the downfall of kingdoms and even empires. One of the theories to explain the downfall of the Mayan culture was a heavy famine that decimated all the agriculture in the region and brought the destruction of the kingdom. The heavy famine at the time of Joseph in Egypt brought the first Israeli kingdom to be destroyed. This memory had to be engraved very strongly in the history of the people. It is no wonder that King David did not choose the first option of famine for seven years. David knew that he could survive a famine of three years, but seven years of famine would be the destruction of the kingdom right after its inception.

In summary, there is no problem for the text to bring us the famine at the time of Abraham, and at the time of Isaac, and even the famine at the time of Jacob. What the text does not want to bring to our knowledge is the destruction of the kingdom – the first Israeli kingdom. The text prefers to portray this destruction as a 'family' going into exile down to Egypt, without detailing the loss of independence, the loss of prestige, and the loss of real estate.

Why does the text conceal this fact? After all, Genesis is not a book that conceals the failures of people. The book does not conceal the fact that Abraham had to leave the land of Canaan and move to Egypt for a while to live there. The same applies to Isaac who went to live in the land of the Philistines at the time of the famine. So why does the text conceal this fact, the failure of the first Israeli kingdom?

We need go back in time to the Covenant of the Splits in which the Almighty told Abraham the future of his family.

The text says there,

> And he said to Abram, know for a certainty that your seed shall be
> a stranger in a land that is not theirs, and shall enslave them and
> they shall afflict them four hundred years. And also that nation,

whom they shall serve, will I judge and afterwards shall they come out with great wealth. And you shall go to your fathers in peace, you shall be buried in a good old age. But in the fourth generation they shall come here again, for the iniquity of the Amorites is not yet full. (Genesis 15:13-16)

The 'plan' is for Abraham's **seed** is to live as 'a stranger in a land that is not theirs.' We know that when Sarah demanded to expel Ishmael and his mother Hagar, the Almighty told Abraham, "…for in Isaac shall your seed be called" (Genesis 21:12).

The 'plan' was activated from the time Isaac, Abraham's seed, was born. And the idea is that anyone from Isaac on must be living as 'a stranger in a land that is not theirs.' That includes the land of Canaan, and the reason is, 'for the iniquity of the Amorites is not yet full.'

Jacob, in spite of this 'plan,' decided to take charge and live in the land, not as 'a stranger,' as the 'plan' prescribes, but as an owner, as a king. Before his death, Jacob says to Joseph, "And I have given you one portion above your brothers, which I took from the hand of the Amorite with my sword and with my bow" (Genesis 48:22).

It is very likely that Jacob knew of the Almighty's 'plan.' His grandfather and his father did not keep it a secret. But he still went ahead and established his kingdom, Israel. It was a kingdom created against the will of the Almighty. It is no wonder that it had to go down. It was established before the right time – as the Amorite did not deserve yet to be ejected from the land – their iniquity was 'not yet full.'

There are other sinners in the book of Genesis, but all the others sinned in a personal way, and did not go directly against the will of the Almighty on a national level. Jacob did.

If we were dealing with regular historical research, we would have read books and books on 'The Rise and Fall of the First Israeli Kingdom.' However, here we are facing sensitivity on the part of the text that tries to suppress this fact.

Linguistic Biases

1. The language of the text exposes sensitivity and attempts to suppress the fact of the downfall of the first Israeli kingdom.
2. The text conceals the fact that Judah headed the faction advocating migration to Egypt while Reuben headed the faction advocating staying in the land of Canaan.
3. The text conceals the fact that Joseph's brothers misled their father Jacob to bring him down to Egypt thinking that he was going only to see his son Joseph, using this pretense to deprive him of his own country.
4. The text perceives Jacob's being forbidden from taking more than four wives to be a commitment against Jacob's self-interest. Only one who had more than four wives would perceive it as such.
5. The text conceals the land-for-land deal made by the brothers and Pharaoh – the land of Canaan for the land of Goshen. Jacob's family not only went down to Egypt/Goshen, but they also gave up the land of Canaan to the Egyptian king.

Point in Language to Consider:

1. Biblical language uses several key words and phrases to describe the concept of authority: 'under the *yerech*,' 'standing before,' 'gathering the feet,' and *regel* ('foot') used to mean the three festivals.

NAMES OF THE ALMIGHTY

Introduction

The text mainly uses two names for the Almighty. The first by the order of appearance is *Elohim*, which in translation is 'gods' in the plural. The second is the tetragrammaton, or the word *Y-H-V-H*, which in Hebrew actually merges the three tenses – past, present, and future – of the verb 'to be.' It is forbidden in the Jewish religion to pronounce this word by one of the Ten Commandments. Therefore, it is usually referred to in Hebrew as 'The Name,' or in Hebrew, *Hashem*.

In the text we find another 'name' for the Almighty, *Adonai*. Note that this 'name' is not found in the language of the text itself (the narration), but only in quotes of what people say. Therefore, we should perceive this 'name' as only a respectful address to the Almighty by a human who addresses his/her creator.

Note: Because the traditional chapters of Genesis do not necessarily correspond to the natural divisions of the events described, we will define sections for this particular analysis.

Section	From	To
1	Chapter 1, verse 1	Chapter 2, verse 3
2	Chapter 2, verse 4	Chapter 3, verse 24
3	Chapter 4, verse 1	Chapter 4, verse 26
4	Chapter 5, verse 1	Chapter 5, verse 32
5	Chapter 6, verse 1	Chapter 6, verse 8

Background

From our discussion of the social introduction we saw two changes in language in regard to the name of the Almighty. For Leah, who was given by her father Laban to Jacob instead of Rachel, there is a change of language between *Y-H-V-H* and *Elohim*. The text used the name *Y-H-V-H* for the first four sons and the name *Elohim* for the last two sons. For Joseph, we see that the text uses the name *Y-H-V-H* when it relates to Potiphar, Joseph's master, but the text does not use the name *Y-H-V-H* when giving us quotations attributed to Joseph. The fact that we find that changes in language for the names of the Almighty are 'content-based changes' should bring us to check the system behind the changes in language throughout the book of Genesis, and in later books.

A point that can guide us in the search of the meaning of the use of the title *Y-H-V-H* versus the title *Elohim* can be found in Exodus at the scene of the burning bush. Moses gets the instruction from the Almighty, "…and you shall come, you and the elders of Israel, to the king of Egypt, and you shall say to him, **Y-H-V-H the G-d of the Hebrews** has met with us…" (Exodus 3:18). This instruction is given to Moses, fifth generation after Jacob, while the book of Genesis ends at the end of Jacob's life.

The linguistic journey for the names of the Almighty in the book of Genesis might bring us the sequence of events that brings about '*Y-H-V-H* the G-d of the Hebrews' in Exodus.

General

In the book of Genesis we find four different linguistic forms for the name of the Almighty – *Elohim, Y-H-V-H Elohim, Y-H-V-H,* and *El Shaddai.*

The book starts with the section about the creation, which starts, "In the beginning *Elohim* created…" (1:1), and ends with the verse, "…because that in it He had rested from all His work which *Elohim* created and made" (2:3). In this section there is only the use of the name *Elohim,* 34 times.

The second section starts with the verse, "These are the *toldot* of the heavens and of the earth when they were created, in the day that **Y-H-V-H Elohim** made the earth and the heavens" (2:4). This section ends with the end of chapter three, including the penultimate verse, "And **Y-H-V-H Elohim** sent him out from the Garden of Eden, to till the ground from where he was taken…" (3:23). In this section the title *Y-H-V-H Elohim* is used in the language of the text 20 times. On the other hand, when the text brings us quotes by the serpent and the woman (3:1-5), the text uses the title *Elohim* three times by the serpent and once by the woman. Starting from the account of the serpent and the woman, we can see that the text distinguishes between the way the Almighty is seen by mankind, in this case by the woman (or even the serpent), and the way the text itself perceives the Almighty, as the text here calls the Almighty *Y-H-V-H Elohim.*

The first two sections describe to us the physical creation, connecting the creation of the human to the physical creation. The second section ends with the ascension of man on the stage of history and his settlement of the earth.

After the first two sections, the text moves on to describe human history upon the earth, by describing the life a regular couple would experience – building a home and giving birth to children. Here, for the first time, the title *Y-H-V-H* as an independent word appears, in a quote attributed to Eve who gives birth to Cain, "…and she conceived and bore Cain and said I have acquired a man from *Y-H-V-H*" (4:1). The fact that *Y-H-V-H* appears in conjunction with the birth of the first son to Adam should guide us in continuing the search for the meaning of *Y-H-V-H*.

The third section is chapter four, the account of Cain and Abel. This section starts with the verse, "And Adam knew Eve his wife…" (4:1), and ends with the verse, "And to Seth, to him also there was born a son; and he called his name Enosh; then was it begun to call in the name of *Y-H-V-H*" (4:26). This section brings us to extreme opposites in the life of humans. First, the section describes how a human being worships *Y-H-V-H*, "…and Cain brought of the fruit of the ground an offering to *Y-H-V-H*" (4:3). Almost in the same breath, the text brings us the first murder in written history, the killing of Abel by Cain. In this section the text uses only the name *Y-H-V-H* except a quote in one verse, in the birth of Seth after the killing of Abel, "…and she bore a son and called his name Seth for **Elohim** appointed[125] me another seed instead of Abel whom Cain slew" (4:25). Then at the birth of Seth's son Enosh the text returns to use the name of *Y-H-V-H*, "then was it begun to call in the name of *Y-H-V-H*" (4:26). As we saw in the birth of Cain, for at his birth the text starts to use the name of *Y-H-V-H*, and by doing so, it skips over the first generation of Adam and Eve, so here we see that after the killing of Abel, the text quotes Eve as using the name of *Elohim*, as opposed to the way she named Cain – using the name of *Y-H-V-H*. The text connects the use of *Elohim* in Eve's words to the fact that Cain killed Abel. Cain killed, and the text uses the name *Y-H-V-H*, and we find a 'jump' over the next generation, avoiding the name *Y-H-V-H*. In summary, a trend (and it is not definite; we need to confirm it) starts to emerge: once the generation sins, the title *Y-H-V-H* skips over the next generation.

---

[125] In Hebrew the verb used for 'appointed' (gave) is *shaht* while the name is ***Shet***.

The fourth section deals with the history of humanity from the creation of Adam to Noah. The section starts with, "This is the book of *toldot* of Adam in the day when **Elohim** created Adam in the image of **Elohim** he made him" (5:1). In the course of describing the generations we find three times the name of *Elohim* in describing Enoch. The description of the generations ends with the birth of Noah, "And he called his name Noah saying this shall comfort us concerning our work and toil of our hands, because of the ground which **Y-H-V-H** has cursed" (5:29), and we find that the name of *Y-H-V-H* appears in conjunction with the **birth** of Noah. This should remind us of the appearance of the name *Y-H-V-H* with the **birth** of Cain.

In summary, the fact is that the text brings to the fore the name *Y-H-V-H* with the birth of an offspring – Cain the son of Adam, and Noah the son of Lemech. Until the birth of Lemech we do not see the name *Y-H-V-H* that many times – 9 times in total – 8 times in the case of Cain and Abel, and once in the case of Noah's birth.

After the birth of Noah the text continues with the same formula it used for the description of the generations from Adam to Noah, "And Noah was five hundred years old and Noah fathered Shem, Ham and Japheth" (5:32). This verse ends section four.

At this point, the text takes a detour from the life of Noah and starts section five, a section that can be classified as an 'out-of-sequence' section. This section deals with the corruption of humans upon earth. This section starts with, "And it came to pass when men began to multiply on the face of the earth…" (6:1), and ends with, "And Noah found grace in the eyes of **Y-H-V-H**" (6:8).

In this relatively short section we find the name of *Y-H-V-H* five times. We also see in this section the verse, "And **Y-H-V-H** said my spirit shall not strive with Adam forever, for he is also flesh…" (6:3), and the name *Y-H-V-H* appears in the context of the presence of the spirit of *Y-H-V-H* in mankind. The section quotes *Y-H-V-H*, saying, "I will destroy man…" (6:7), and ends by saying that, "Noah found grace in the eyes of *Y-H-V-H*" (6:8).

SCAN Rule: 'Out-of-sequence' information is only 'out-of-sequence' to the reader, not to the one who gives the information.

Section five gives us essential information needed to understand the name *Y-H-V-H* in the eyes of the text: the presence of the spirit of *Y-H-V-H* in mankind. Up to this point *Y-H-V-H* expected that all mankind would have the spirit of *Y-H-V-H*, but the end of this section paves the way to find one person who merits the presence of the spirit of *Y-H-V-H* inside. And at this point the text continues to describe Noah's life.

From this point on, the search will continue to find the one who merits this reward: having the presence of the spirit of *Y-H-V-H* inside.

Noah

In the section dealing with Noah we find the title *Y-H-V-H* seven times, while the title *Elohim* appears 16 times. Although it is not statistically significant, still we should note that in the case of Cain and Abel the title *Y-H-V-H* appears eight times, while for Noah it is seven times.

The section about Noah starts with, "These are the *toldot* of Noah..." (6:9), and ends with the verse, "And all the days of Noah were nine hundred and fifty years and he died" (9:29). The title *Y-H-V-H* appears relatively infrequently in this section compared to the title *Elohim*; this should bring us to check the places where *Y-H-V-H* appears.

SCAN Rule: We should analyze the text by examining the extraordinary and not by the ordinary way the language of the text describes events.

This means that the SCAN analyst needs to determine the regular way the text gives information. After this regular way is well established, then it is possible to find the deviations from the regular way, and by doing so to understand the meaning of the text. In statistical terms, we should establish the **average** and search for the **deviation**.

The title *Y-H-V-H* appears for Noah in the following places:

- "And **Y-H-V-H** said to Noah come you and all your house into the ark, for you have I seen righteous before me in this generation" (7:1).
- "And Noah did according to all that **Y-H-V-H** commanded him" (7:5).

- "And those who went in, went in male and female of all flesh, as **Elohim** had commanded him, and **Y-H-V-H** closed him in" (7:16),
- "And Noah built an altar to **Y-H-V-H**..." (8:20).
- "And **Y-H-V-H** smelled the pleasing odor, and **Y-H-V-H** said in his heart..." (8:21).
- "And he said blessed be **Y-H-V-H** G-d of Shem..." (9:26).

The first two verses in this list set a boundary around a subsection that seems repetitive of an earlier subsection that starts with, "And **Elohim** said to Noah the end of all flesh has come before me..." (6:13), and ends with, "And Noah did according to all that **Elohim** commanded him, so did he" (6:22).

If so, what does the text come to tell us in this alleged repetition? The subsection that starts and ends with the title *Y-H-V-H* deals with the 'pure' animal and with the 'impure' animal (7:2). It is clear that the 'pure' animal relates to the worship of *Y-H-V-H*, and indeed we see after the flood, "And Noah built an altar to **Y-H-V-H**..." (8:20). So this subsection using the title *Y-H-V-H* deals with the personal connection between mankind and the Almighty.

Moreover, the first verse (7:1) brings the title *Y-H-V-H* in conjunction with the word 'righteous.' Up to this point the text brings us two men who had some connection to *Elohim*; first: "And Enoch walked[126] with (*et*) the **Elohim**..." (5:22), and "And Enoch walked with (*et*) the **Elohim** and he was not for **Elohim** took him" (5:24). The second is Noah: "These are the *toldot* of Noah, Noah was a righteous and perfect man in his generations, **Noah walked with (*et*) the Elohim**" (6:9).

[For comparison, note: while for Enoch and Noah the text says that they walked with (*et*) the *Elohim*, we find that for Abraham the text says, "...And **Y-H-V-H** appeared to Abram and said to him, I am *El Shaddai* walk **before** me and be perfect" (17:1). Later on, Abraham's slave in his words to Rebecca's family quotes his master Abraham, "And he said to me *Y-H-V-H* **before** whom I went..." (24:40).]

---

[126] In Hebrew the verb *lalechet* comes from the three-letter-root word *H-L-CH*. And has the primary meaning 'to walk.' But since there is no other verb in Hebrew for 'to go,' this verb is also used for 'to go.' Here the text uses the reflexive form *hithalech*, which is introspective, relating to an activity that is projected inward.

The last verse in our list, "And he said blessed be **Y-H-V-H** G-d of Shem…" (9:26), is the first time that any human blessed the Almighty. Up to this point we find the opposite, that the Almighty blessed the human:

- "And **Elohim** blessed them saying be fruitful and multiply…" (1:22)
- "And **Elohim** blessed them…" (1:28)
- "…and blessed them and called their name Man…" (5:2)
- "And **Elohim** blessed Noah and his sons…" (9:1)

The text gives Noah the status of being the first to give a blessing that goes the other direction, from man to the Almighty. And we see, again, that the title *Y-H-V-H* appears when man, from his point of view, perceives a personal connection with the Almighty.

At this point we can deal with one verse in the description of Noah's life in which both titles of the Almighty are in use, *Elohim* and *Y-H-V-H*: "And those who went in, went in male and female of all flesh, as **Elohim** had commanded him, and **Y-H-V-H** closed him in" (7:16). The text brought us two subsections. The first was to build the ark, saving Noah and his family along with two from all living forms, a physical rescue of men and animals. The second subsection was to give the instruction about the seven from the pure animals and two from the impure animals, saving the connection between man and the Almighty. The text moves on to inform us that Noah did both. And to express this point the text, in its language, uses both titles *Elohim* and *Y-H-V-H*.

The end of the section dealing with Noah's life brings us the incident between Noah and his youngest son Ham, and the curse that Noah put on Ham's son Canaan. Immediately the text ends the life of Noah and informs us of his death (9:29).

As we saw after the killing of Abel by Cain, in which the title *Y-H-V-H* vanishes for Seth and returns only at the time of Enosh, so here, with the account of Noah, we witness the vanishing of the title of *Y-H-V-H* after Noah's death, and for several generations the title *Y-H-V-H* appears only twice.

Nimrod

We find the title *Y-H-V-H* comes twice in connection with Nimrod, "He was a mighty hunter before ***Y-H-V-H***; therefore it is said, as Nimrod the mighty hunter before ***Y-H-V-H***" (10:9). The fact that the title *Y-H-V-H* is mentioned twice for Nimrod is a positive note for Nimrod. But the fact that there is no continuation of that use of the title after Nimrod testifies that it was only a temporary appearance with no real and strong hold. We have to read the whole book of Genesis before we can return to this verse and understand that the text is telling us that being 'a mighty hunter' is not the way for one to merit that the spirit of *Y-H-V-H* be in him/her.

Tower of Babel

> And the whole earth was of one language and of one speech. And it came to pass as they journeyed from the east that they found a plain in the land of Shinar and they lived there. And they said one to another, come let us make bricks and burn them thoroughly, and they had brick for stone and slime had they for mortar. (11:1-3)

In these three verses we do not see the name of the Almighty even once. And now the text brings us the verse that changes the course of events: "And they said, come let us build us a city and a tower, whose top may reach to heaven; and let us make us a name, lest we be scattered abroad upon the face of the whole earth" (11:4). At this stage, the text brings us the response of the Almighty, and with it the name *Y-H-V-H* reappears.

> And ***Y-H-V-H*** came down to see the city and the tower that the sons of men built. And ***Y-H-V-H*** said, behold, the people are one, and they have all one language, and this they begin to do, and now nothing will be restrained from them, which they have schemed to do. Come let us go down and there confuse their language that they may not understand one another's speech. And ***Y-H-V-H*** scattered them abroad from there upon the face of the earth, and they left off the building of the city. Therefore is the name of it called Babel because ***Y-H-V-H*** did there confuse the language of all the earth, and from there did ***Y-H-V-H*** scatter them abroad upon the face of all the earth. (11:5-9)

The text does not say that the behavior of the people building the tower mandated immediate punishment. The text says that *Y-H-V-H* saw a need to 'come down' to see what was going on. This reminds us of the verse before the decision to destroy Sodom and Gomorrah, "**I will go down** now and see whether they have done altogether according to the cry, which has come to me, and if not, I will know" (18:21). In the end, the people of Babel do not receive the same punishment, total annihilation, as the people of Sodom. Their punishment was confusing the language of all the earth, "And *Y-H-V-H* scattered them abroad from there upon the face of the earth, and they left off the building of the city" (11:8).

Remember that the phrase 'And *Y-H-V-H*' appears in conjunction with the verse, "And *Y-H-V-H* said my spirit shall not always strive with man..." (6:3). We can view the fact that the people built a tower "...whose top may reach to heaven..." as their attempt to have a connection with heaven. However, like Nimrod who is mentioned before them, they wanted to do it using physical means, Nimrod by hunting, and the people of Babel by a tower. Moreover, at the time of Enosh the text said "...then was it begun to call in the **name** of *Y-H-V-H*" (4:26), while the people of Babel talked about "...and let us make **us a name**..." (11:4). The name the people of Babel were talking about was their own, therefore the appearance of the title *Y-H-V-H* in this section, and the response of *Y-H-V-H* to the idea. The connection to *Y-H-V-H* cannot be by this method.

In summary, as the killing of Abel resulted in the disappearance of the title *Y-H-V-H* for one generation, the generation of Seth (*Elohim*), so the incest that Ham committed on Noah brought about the disappearance of the title of *Y-H-V-H* for several more generations. The text brings us two types of behavior that do not coincide with the title *Y-H-V-H* – spilling blood (Cain) and incest (Ham).

The text continues with the description of the generations from Noah to Abraham. And at the time Abraham ascended the stage of Biblical history we find several changes.

Abraham

The description of human history in Genesis from the creation to Noah was relatively short. To the life of Noah – from his birth to his death – including the flood, the text devotes four chapters. Then the text expedites the pace, and within two chapters reaches the birth of Abraham. At this point, the text slows down the pace again, and for the life of Abraham the text devotes fourteen chapters, starting with the verse, "...and fathered Abram, Nahor and Haran..." (11:26), and ending with the verses, "...there was Abraham buried, and Sarah his wife. And it came to pass after the death of Abraham..." (25:10-11).

Abraham is different from the other figures in Genesis by two points. First, Abraham is the only one in Genesis to whom the text gives the title 'prophet,[127]' in a quote of the Almighty's words, when the Almighty speaks to Abimelech, after Abimelech took Sarah to his palace, "Now therefore restore the man his wife for he is a **prophet**..." (20:7). Besides Abraham, there are only three other figures in the five books of Moses who received the title *navi* ('prophet'):

- Moses: "And there has not arisen since in Israel a *navi* like Moses..." (Deuteronomy 34:10).
- Aaron: "...and Aaron your brother will be your *navi*" (Exodus 7:1).
- Miriam (Moses' sister): "And Miriam the *neviah*..." (Exodus 15:20).

Abraham is also the only one in Genesis about whom the text brings us a quote by the Almighty, "For **I knew him** that he will command his sons and his house after him..." (Genesis 18:19). The only other figure who received such a connection with the Almighty is Moses, "...and you said **I knew you** by name and you have also found grace in my eyes" (Exodus 33:12).

With the appearance of Abraham we also witness a change in the ratio of appearance between the two titles of the Almighty, *Y-H-V-H* and *Elohim*. In the case of Noah the text used the title *Elohim* 16 times, and used the title *Y-H-V-H* only seven times, representing a ratio of 70% for *Elohim* and 30% for *Y-H-V-H*. For Abraham the ratio changes significantly; the title *Y-H-V-H* is used 50 times and the title *Elohim* is used only 31 times, a ratio of 62% for *Y-H-V-H* and 38% for *Elohim*. In addition, *Y-H-V-H* is used five times in connection with Lot, Abraham's nephew, thirteen times

---

[127] In Hebrew the word for 'prophet' is *navi*, which is derived from the word 'to bring.' The idea of *navi* is not to predict the future but to bring the word of the Almighty to the people.

in connection with Abraham's slave, and three times in connection with Laban and his father Bethuel.

The section about Abraham starts with, "And *Y-H-V-H* said to Abram, go..." (Genesis 12:1). We should note that *Y-H-V-H* does not introduce himself to Abram at this point. Later on, beginning the account of the covenant of the splits, the text says, "And he said to him I am *Y-H-V-H* who brought you out of Ur of the Chaldeans..." (15:7). This means that *Y-H-V-H* must have already appeared to Abram even before His appearance telling him to leave his family and country and go to the land of Canaan. Therefore, there was no need for any 'introduction.'

The text says that *Y-H-V-H* instructs Abraham what to do, and indeed Abraham does it. Later on, we can see that the title *Y-H-V-H* is used in a quote by Laban, "And he said, come in, you blessed of *Y-H-V-H*..." (24:31). We can conclude that the title *Y-H-V-H* was known in Haran even before the appearance of *Y-H-V-H* to Abraham in Haran, and even after Abraham went to the land of Canaan.

In the case of Noah, where the language of the text used the title *Elohim* in the majority and *Y-H-V-H* in the minority, the way to find the meaning was to check the content inside the sentence where the title *Y-H-V-H* was used in the minority seven verses.

As a matter of fact, this is the way to go any time we find a change in language in any statement. We should look carefully at the places where the text deviates from the 'average' (majority) versus the 'deviation' (minority) usage. The context inside the sentence where the change of language occurs should guide us to the meaning of the use of that particular language in the person's speech.

The same should apply to the case of Abraham where the minority (38%) usage is the title *Elohim*, and therefore the scrutiny should be focused on these cases.

In the case of Abraham we can get help from two almost identical events described in the text, although the language of the text is different. The two cases are the two times in which Hagar, Sarah's slave who was given by Sarah to Abraham to bear a son for him, found herself in the desert. In the first case the text says, "...and Sarai dealt hardly with her and she fled from her face" (16:6). Hagar found herself "…by a fountain of water in the wilderness by the fountain in the way of Shur" (16:7). In the second case, Abraham listens to Sarah who demanded, "Expel this slave and her son…" (21:10), and Abraham indeed sent her away (21:14), and "…she got lost in the wilderness of Beersheba" (21:14).

In the two events an angel appears to Hagar and speaks to her. In the first event the language of the text labels the angel as the 'angel of *Y-H-V-H*' (16:7-11) four times, and at the end of the event, the text says, "And she called the name of *Y-H-V-H* who spoke to her You G-d see me…" (16:13). In contrast, in the second event the language of the text labels the angel as the 'angel of *Elohim*' (21:17). The description of the second event, from start to end, uses the title *Elohim*: "And **Elohim** heard the voice of the lad…" (21:17), and, "And **Elohim** opened her eyes…" (21:19).

What is the difference between the two events that brought the text to change the language? The answer is that in between these two events Hagar was expelled, or sent away, from the house of Abraham. As long as she was connected with the house of Abraham, even though she ran away from there, as described in the first event, the text used the title *Y-H-V-H*. Once the connection was severed, the text used the title *Elohim*.

From this comparison it seems that the title *Y-H-V-H* is used in regard to Abraham and the people of his household. The title *Elohim* is for people outside this circle. At this point we will search for corroboration of this understanding.

The text brings us two instances in which a conversation is held between Abraham and the Almighty. The first instance says,

> …and **Y-H-V-H** appeared to Abram and said to him, I am *El Shaddai*, walk before me and be perfect. And I will give my covenant between me and you, and will multiply you exceedingly. And Abram fell on his face and **Elohim** talked with (*et*) him saying… (17:1-3)

The text narration starts the section with the use of the title *Y-H-V-H*, and immediately moves to use the title *Elohim* throughout the conversation until its end in the verse, "And He finished talking with (*et*) him and **Elohim** went up from above Abraham" (17:22).

The second conversation starts with, "And **Y-H-V-H** said shall I hide from Abraham that thing which I do?" (18:17). In this famous conversation, in which Abraham argues with *Y-H-V-H* on the justice of collective punishment, the language of the text uses the title *Y-H-V-H* seven times, and at the end of the conversation, "And **Y-H-V-H** went when he finished talking to Abraham and Abraham returned to his place" (18:33).

Besides the change in language between the two conversations in regard to the title *Elohim* vs. the title *Y-H-V-H*, we also see that the first conversation ends with a summary that *Elohim* spoke with (*et*) Abraham, while the second conversation ends with a summary that *Y-H-V-H* spoke **to** Abraham. We already saw that the preposition *et* indicates some distance, and indeed there is some distance between *Elohim* and Abraham, a distance that does not exist between *Y-H-V-H* and Abraham. What is the reason for such distance between Abraham and *Elohim*?

In order to answer the question we need to examine the content of the conversation that started with the title *Y-H-V-H* and immediately moved on to use the title *Elohim*, Genesis 17:1-22.

The conversation starts with, "As for me behold my covenant is with you, and you shall be a father of many nations" (17:4). We should note that the promise of covenant is not limited to one nation but is with many nations – in the plural. The conversation continues with promising Abraham and his seed after him the land of Canaan (verses 5-8), with calling for circumcision (verses 9-14), with promising Abraham a son from Sarah (verses 15-19), and with promising to make Ishmael "a great nation" (verse 20). Before the ending verse we find, "and my covenant will I establish with Isaac whom Sarah shall bear to you at this set time in the next year" (17:21). The text continues saying that Abraham indeed entered the covenant of circumcision, he and all the people of his household. And by doing so, Abraham distinguished himself from all the nations around him.

Thus, the main part of the conversation is the covenant of circumcision, which distinguishes Abraham from his environment, and a promise that from Abraham "many nations" will come and that Ishmael will be 'a great nation.' The conversation deals with the connection (or more accurately, severing the connection) between Abraham's household and the other nations.

This linguistic pattern remains stable. The next time the title *Elohim* appears is, "And it came to pass when *Elohim* destroyed the cities of the plain..." (19:29). As long as the text deals with Lot and his rescue, and Lot was from Abraham's family, the text uses the title *Y-H-V-H*. When the angels talk to Lot the text quotes them as saying, "...because their cry has grown great before the face of *Y-H-V-H*..." (19:13), "...*Y-H-V-H* being merciful to him..." (19:16), "And *Y-H-V-H* rained upon Sodom and upon Gomorrah brimstone and fire from *Y-H-V-H* out of heaven" (19:24), "And Abraham got up early in the morning to the place where he stood before *Y-H-V-H*" (19:27). But when the text moves to talk about the destruction of 'the cities of the plain,' the text uses the title *Elohim*. In this section we can see that the title *Y-H-V-H* is used both for mercy, as in '...*Y-H-V-H* being merciful to him...' (19:16), and for cruelty, as in 'And *Y-H-V-H* rained upon Sodom...'(19:24). The change in titles does not come due to a different characteristic of the Almighty. The change comes due to a different focus on the subject of destruction. If it deals with Abraham and the people of his household, and in this case a relative of Abraham (Lot), then the title in use is *Y-H-V-H*. However, if the text focuses on people out of the circle of Abraham and his household – 'the cities of the plain' – the title in use is *Elohim*.

We find the same in the account of Abimelech, the king of the Philistines, who takes Sarah into his household (Genesis 20:2-18). Throughout the account the text uses the title *Elohim*, "And *Elohim* came to Abimelech in the dream by night..." (20:3), "And *Elohim* said to him..." (20:6). The text uses the title *Elohim* even when Abraham speaks to Abimelech – "...because I thought surely the fear of *Elohim* is not in this place..." (20:11), "And it came to pass when *Elohim* caused me to wander from my father's house..." (20:13), and "And Abraham prayed to *Elohim* and *Elohim* healed Abimelech and his wife and his maidservants..." (20:17). And when the text returns to talk about Sarah, "For *Y-H-V-H* had fast closed up all the wombs of the house of Abimelech because of Sarah Abraham's wife" (20:18). The title *Y-H-V-H* appears in the language of the text when the text relates to 'Sarah Abraham's wife.'

We find the same linguistic structure in the encounter Abraham had with Abimelech and the treaty over the seven ewe lambs (Genesis 21:22-33).

The text quotes Abimelech twice in the description using the title *Elohim*, "...*Elohim* is with you in all that you do" (21:22), and, "Now therefore swear to me by *Elohim* that..." (21:23). Once the text says that Abimelech and Phicol his commander rose up and "returned to the land of the Philistines" (21:32), the text ends by saying, "And Abraham planted a grove in Beersheba and called there in the name of **Y-H-V-H**, the everlasting G-d" (21:33). *Elohim* is the language of the text when it describes Abimelech's activities, and *Y-H-V-H* is the language of the text when it describes Abraham's activities.

At this point, we can return to the beginning of chapter 21 to see how the language changes during the course of events. The chapter starts with, "And **Y-H-V-H** considered Sarah as he had said and **Y-H-V-H** did to Sarah as he had spoken. And Sarah conceived and bore Abraham a son in his old age, at the set time of which *Elohim* had spoken to him" (21:1-2). While the first verse relates to the connection between the Almighty and Abraham and Sarah, the second verse brings us back to the encounter that ended with the concluding sentence, "And he finished talking with (*et*) him and *Elohim* went up from above Abraham" (17:22), the same encounter in which *Elohim* promised Abraham that the covenant between him and *Elohim* would continue with the son born to Sarah and not with Ishmael. Note in that conversation *Elohim* promised Abraham a 'consolation prize,' for Ishmael, "And as for Ishmael I have heard you, behold, I have blessed him, and will make him fruitful and will multiply him exceedingly, twelve princes shall he father and I will make him a great nation" (17:20).

The change from the title *Y-H-V-H* in the first verse to the title *Elohim* in the second verse teaches us that the description in front of us does not deal only with the birth of Isaac, but the fate of Ishmael is also on the scale. And continuing, we see the text quotes Sarah as saying, "...*Elohim* has made me laugh so that all who hear will laugh with me" (21:6). And the reader who pays attention to the language of Sarah needs to understand that at that point of time Ishmael's fate was on her mind. And indeed, as we continue, we find the title *Elohim* also when *Elohim* speaks to Abraham, "And *Elohim* said to Abraham, let it not be grievous in your eyes because of the lad and because of your slave..." (21:12).

The Binding of Isaac

"And it came to pass after these things…" (22:1)

We already saw in an earlier chapter that the phrase 'after these things' appears six times in Genesis, and in all these places, the phrase appears after the person reached an agreement or an understanding with the ruler of the land. In order to understand the linguistic background of the account of the binding, we need to go back to what was said earlier.

When *Elohim* changed Abram's name to Abraham, *Elohim* also added the promise, "And I will give to you, and to your seed after you, the land where you reside, all the land of Canaan, for an everlasting possession, and I will be their ***Elohim***" (17:8). Then the text continues with the following details: the duty of circumcision, another notification of the upcoming birth of Isaac, the destruction of Sodom and Gomorrah, Abimelech taking Sarah, the birth of Isaac, and the expulsion of Ishmael.

The text brings us the preceding event to the binding of Isaac. In this event Abimelech says to Abraham, "…***Elohim*** is with you in all that you do. Now therefore swear to me here by ***Elohim***…" (21:22-23), and the text brings us Abraham's response, "I will swear" (21:24).

We should note that all during the description of this event – the covenant between Abraham and Abimelech – the text uses the title *Elohim*.

And then the text continues with the test of the binding of Isaac, "…that ***Elohim*** tested Abraham…" (22:1). In Deuteronomy we find the reason to test a human, "…to test you to know what is in your heart whether you would keep his commandments or not" (Deuteronomy 8:2).

If Abraham swore to Abimelech by *Elohim*, then he had to be faithful to the god of Abimelech, as Abimelech worshipped his god. The text says how the people of Canaan worshipped their gods, "…for even their sons and their daughters they have burned in the fire to their gods" (Deuteronomy 12:31).

And the text continues with the binding of Isaac using the title *Elohim*, "…and rose up and went to the place of which ***Elohim*** had told him" (Genesis 22:3), "And Abraham said, my son, ***Elohim*** will provide himself a lamb for a burnt offering…" (22:8), and, "And they came to the place which *Elohim* had told him…" (22:9).

When the decisive moment arrives, "And Abraham stretched out his hand and took the knife to slay his son. And the angel of *Y-H-V-H* called to him from heaven…" (22:10-11). The angel of *Y-H-V-H* tells Abraham, "…for now I know that you fear *Elohim*…" (22:12), in order to tell us that Abraham passed the test that *Elohim* demanded of him, but from that point on the text moves to use the title *Y-H-V-H* in the rest of the description, "And Abraham called the name of that place Adonai-Yireh[128] as it is said to this day, in the mount of *Y-H-V-H* it shall be seen" (22:14), "And the angel of *Y-H-V-H* called to Abraham from heaven…" (22:15), and, "By myself have I sworn, said *Y-H-V-H*…" (22:16).

From the time of this change of language from *Elohim* to *Y-H-V-H*, the text does not use the title *Elohim* for Abraham, not in describing the course of events and not in quotes, either from Abraham's words, or from the words of Eliezer, Abraham's slave. The title *Elohim* vanishes from the language of the text until the death of Abraham.

The test of the binding comes to emphasize the distinction in the language of the text between *Elohim,* relating to the other nations and the way they worship their gods, and *Y-H-V-H*, relating to Abraham. Unlike Enoch and Noah who walked with (*et*) *Elohim*, Eliezer quotes Abraham as saying, "And he said to me, *Y-H-V-H* before whom I went…" (24:40).

Y-H-V-H and *Elohim* – Conclusion

The importance, language-wise, of the test of the binding of Isaac in the life of Abraham, is the distinction in the **language** of the text between the use of the titles *Y-H-V-H* and *Elohim* **before** the test, and the use of the titles **after** the test. While both titles are used **before** the test, only the title *Y-H-V-H* is used **after** the test. It seems from this conclusion that the two titles *Y-H-V-H* and *Elohim* are two names of the same creator. *Y-H-V-H* is the title used when the Creator is looking towards Abraham and his household, and *Elohim* is the title used when the Creator is looking upon anyone else outside the household of Abraham.

---

[128] *Adonai* is used in the text as an expression of respect for anyone who is above the speaker. It is used extensively when one approaches the Almighty in a prayer. *Yireh* is the future tense, third person of the verb 'to see.' Combined together, the phrase means, 'He will see the Almighty.'

Isaac

The number of chapters in Genesis dealing with Isaac (two) is relatively low compared to Abraham (14). Even if we add the verses dealing with his birth, and the verses dealing with the recruitment of Rebecca to be his wife, we do not reach even half of the number of chapters dealing with Abraham. **Quantity-wise** we can conclude that Isaac is only a link connecting Abraham to Jacob, without any significance himself.

However, **language-wise**, Isaac constitutes a bright light in the language of the text. The title *Y-H-V-H* (connection between the Almighty and humanity) appears ten times compared to only three times for the title *Elohim* – a ratio of 77% for *Y-H-V-H* vs. 23% for *Elohim*. If we compare Isaac to Abraham who had a ratio of 62% for *Y-H-V-H* and 38% for *Elohim*, we can see that Isaac wins the competition with Abraham.

As we did with Noah and Abraham, we will examine the minority usage, the three places in which the text used the title *Elohim* in proximity to Isaac.

The first time is right after the death of Abraham. The text says, "And it came to pass after the death of Abraham that ***Elohim*** blessed his son Isaac, and Isaac lived by the well Lahairoi" (Genesis 25:11). If we examine the course of events, we see that immediately after this verse, the text moves on to deal with Ishmael, to whom the text devotes six verses (25:12-18). The section starts with "And these are the *toldot* of Ishmael the son of Abraham..." (25:12), and ends with the death of Ishmael and adds a verse on the expansion of Ishmael's offspring all over the region, "And they lived from Havilah to Shur that is before Egypt as you go toward Assyria, and he fell upon the face of all his brothers" (25:18). Immediately the text moved on with "And these are the *toldot* of Isaac the son of Abraham..." (25:19).

It is easy to attribute the use of the title *Elohim* in verse 11 in connection with Isaac to the fact that Ishmael is still in the picture. Once Ishmael leaves the **content** of the text, the title *Elohim* leaves the **language** of the text as well, and it shows up only later in Isaac's blessing of Jacob.

Throughout the life of Isaac the text uses the title *Y-H-V-H*:

- "And Isaac prayed to **Y-H-V-H** in the presence of his wife because she was barren and **Y-H-V-H** granted his prayer…" (25:21),
- "…and she went to inquire of **Y-H-V-H**. And **Y-H-V-H** said to her…" (25:22-23),
- "And **Y-H-V-H** appeared to him…" (26:2),
- "…and **Y-H-V-H** blessed him" (26:12),
- "…and he said, for now **Y-H-V-H** has made room for us…" (26:22),
- "And **Y-H-V-H** appeared to him the same night…" (26:24), and
- "And he built an altar there and called on the name of **Y-H-V-H**…" (26:25).

Even when the text quotes Abimelech speaking with Isaac, it uses the title *Y-H-V-H*:

- "And they said, we saw certainly that **Y-H-V-H** was with you…" (26:28), and
- "…and we have sent you away in peace, you are now the blessed of **Y-H-V-H**" (26:29).

For comparison, when Abimelech speaks with Abraham, in the conversation preceding the test of the binding, we see, "…that Abimelech and Phicol, the chief captain of his army, spoke to Abraham saying, *Elohim* is with you in all that you do. And now therefore swear to me by *Elohim*…" (21:22-23). After the test of the binding, and the establishment of *Y-H-V-H* as the G-d of Abraham and his household, Abimelech, the foreign king, is quoted using the name of the G-d of Abraham as well.

The text quotes Isaac using the title *Elohim* in the two blessings he gave to Jacob. The first blessing is when Jacob got the blessing while pretending to be his brother Esau,

…and said, see the smell of my son is like the smell of a field which **Y-H-V-H** has blessed. And **Elohim** shall give you of the dew of the heaven, and the fatness of the earth, and plenty of grain and wine. Let people serve you and nations bow down to you, be lord over your brothers, and let your mother's sons bow down to you... (27:27-29).

The blessing starts using the title *Y-H-V-H* and continues using the title *Elohim*. When the text talks of other nations then *Elohim* is in the picture.

In the second blessing, when Isaac knows that he is blessing Jacob, Isaac relates to the blessing of Abraham by *Elohim*,

> And G-d Almighty[129] bless you and make you fruitful and multiply you that you may be a multitude of people. And give the blessing of Abraham to you, and to your seed with you, that you may inherit the land where you reside which **Elohim** gave to Abraham. (28:3-4)

Since the text dealing with the blessing of Abraham used the title *Elohim*, so here, the text uses the same title. A linguistic inner completeness.

Jacob

Jacob enters the stage in Genesis at the time of his birth in Chapter 25. Immediately, the text brings us the description of selling the birthright by Esau to Jacob. The description of Jacob's life starts before the description of Isaac's life ends, and actually of the two chapters that Genesis devotes to Isaac, one chapter deals with getting the blessing from Isaac by fraud. Starting with the verse "And Jacob came out of Beersheba and went to Haran," (28:10) to the end of the book, 22 chapters, we have the description of Jacob's life. The description of the life of each of the first two forefathers – Abraham and Isaac – was one literary unit; however, we find that the description of Jacob's life is spread out with intervening stories. This fact alone testifies to his uniqueness.

The chapters in Genesis that deal with Jacob start with chapter 27, about receiving the blessing, and end with chapter 35 – nine chapters. Then Genesis moves on to deal with Esau's generations in chapter 36, and then the description of Joseph's life starts in chapter 37. And indeed the text tells us, "These are the *toldot* of Jacob: Joseph..." (37:2). The fates of the two – Jacob and Joseph – are intertwined. The description of Joseph's life continues over eleven chapters, with a break of one chapter to deal with

---

[129] G-d Almighty – *El Shaddai*. *El Shaddai* is discussed later in this chapter.

the case of Judah and Tamar – chapter 38. Then Genesis again picks up the description of Jacob's life with two chapters dealing with his words to his sons before his death, and the account of his funeral in the land of Canaan. In total, Genesis devotes eleven chapters to the life of Jacob.

Jacob is different from his two predecessors also language-wise. After we saw that Isaac won first place in the division between the title *Y-H-V-H* (77%) and *Elohim* (23%), the ratio reverses itself when dealing with Jacob. The title *Y-H-V-H* appears 8 times (25%) while the title *Elohim* appears 24 times (75%). And this division does not count the words of Leah, Rachel, and Laban. This ratio of the title *Y-H-V-H* to *Elohim* is even less than the ratio that appears for the life of Noah, 70% for *Elohim* and 30% for *Y-H-V-H*. Quantity-wise, Jacob is at the bottom of the league in the race to merit the title *Y-H-V-H* and be flag bearer of the connection of the Almighty to humanity.

Dealing With the Wife Being Barren

Jacob is different from his two predecessors also behavior-wise. Let's take for example the way the husband relates to the fact that his wife is barren. In all three generations the husband had to deal with his wife being barren – Abraham with Sarah, Isaac with Rebecca, and Jacob with Rachel.

For Abraham we see that the text brings us Abraham's appeal to the Almighty, "And Abram said, behold to me you have given no seed, and lo, one in my household is my heir" (15:3). Abraham does not blame Sarah for the fact that he has no seed. He sees everything as coming from the Almighty, and if he doesn't have seed, then it means the Almighty didn't give him seed.

For Isaac, the text says, "And Isaac prayed to *Y-H-V-H* in the presence of his wife because she was barren and *Y-H-V-H* granted his prayer and Rebecca his wife conceived" (25:21). The text does not bring us the content of Isaac's prayer, but the structure of the sentence shows that the appeal to the almighty is the main point of the sentence, and the fact that Rebecca was barren is only the reason for his appeal to the Almighty.

It is different in the case of Jacob. From the dream of "The Ladder and the Angels" to the time right before his return to the land of Canaan, a period of more than twenty years, the text does not bring us any appeal of Jacob to the Almighty. No wonder that there are few places that the title *Y-H-V-H* appears in the life of Jacob. And when Rachel appeals to him, "…give me children, or else I die" (30:1), does Jacob appeal to the Almighty as his father did with his mother? No. The text brings us Jacob's response: "And Jacob's anger was kindled against Rachel and he said, am I in *Elohim's* place who has withheld from you the fruit of the womb?" (30:2).

Dealing With the Difficulties of Life

There is another difference between Jacob on one hand, and Abraham and Isaac on the other. Jacob is the only one among the forefathers who complains about his life,

> And Jacob said to Pharaoh the days of the years of my sojourning are a hundred and thirty years, **few and evil** have the days of the years of my life been, and have not attained to the days of the years of the life on my fathers in the days of their sojourning. (47:9)

In contrast, when Abraham is called to answer the king Abimelech, he is quoted as saying, "And it came to pass when *Elohim* caused me to wander from my father's house…" (20:13). Compared to Jacob, Abraham's own reflection on his life is hardly a complaint at all. And we find no complaints from Isaac about his life.

The lives of Abraham and Jacob were similar. Both of them had to go away from their fathers' houses, Abraham from his father Terah in Haran, and Jacob from his father Isaac in the land of Canaan. Both of them had to go into exile in Egypt due to a famine in the land of Canaan. However, while Abraham had the challenge of dealing with Sarah being taken by the Egyptians into the palace, and the same with the Philistine king taking Sarah to his palace, Jacob arrived in Egypt when his son was the ruler. Both of them lost their wives; Abraham buried his wife Sarah in Hebron, and lived 50 years after that. Jacob buried his wife Rachel when she gave birth to Benjamin. It is true that Abraham lived longer than Jacob, but Jacob complained to Pharaoh not only that his days were few, but also that they were evil. And here one can ask the question: does the fact that the text says about Abraham, "and he believed in *Y-H-V-H* and he counted it to him for righteousness" (15:6), something that was not said about Jacob, have anything to do with Abraham's optimistic view of life?

The ratio between the title *Y-H-V-H* and the title *Elohim*, and the comparison between the behavior of the forefathers in relation to the same problems – the wife being barren, and the reflection about their lives – should bring us to examine carefully the differences in activities (as opposed to differences in language) between Jacob and the other two forefathers.

Building Altars

The first two forefathers built altars, while Jacob put up *matzevah*s (pillars). For Abraham the text says,

- "…and there he built an **altar** to *Y-H-V-H*…" (12:7),
- "…and there he built an **altar** to *Y-H-V-H*…" (12:8),
- "…And built there an **altar** to *Y-H-V-H*" (13:18), and
- "…and Abraham built the **altar**…" (22:9) for the binding of Isaac.

For Isaac the text says, "And he built an **altar** there…" (26:25).

On the other hand, for Jacob the text says:

- "…and took the stone that he had put under his head, and set it up for a **pillar** (*matzevah*) and poured oil upon its top" (28:18),
- "And Jacob set up a **pillar** (*matzevah*) in the place where he talked with him, a **pillar** (*matzevah*) of stone, and poured a drink of offering on it, and he poured oil on it" (35:14).

There are only two places where the text mentions an altar for Jacob. The first place is, "And he erected there an **altar** and called it G-d, the G-d of Israel" (33:20). In this verse, the text changes its language, and instead of the verb 'built,' as commonly used for the first two forefathers, the text uses here the verb 'erected' (*vayatzev*), a verb that is derived from the three-letter root word of *matzevah* and not an altar.

The second place in which an altar is mentioned for Jacob is unique in the whole of Genesis. This is the only place in which an 'altar' is not built by the man worshipping his Creator, but by the initiative of the creator who asks the man to build him an altar, "And **Elohim** said to Jacob, arise and go up to Beth-El and live there and make there an altar to the G-d who appeared to you when you fled from the face of Esau your brother" (35:1). Jacob tells the people of his house, "And let us arise and go up to Beth-El and I will make there an altar to the G-d who answered me in the day of my distress and was with me in the way which I went" (35:3). Later, the text says, "And he built there an altar and called the place El Beth-El[130]..." (35:7).

We should note three points. First, the text changed the language again. Before, the text used either the verb 'built' (*vayiven*) or 'erected' (*vayatzev*), but now the text quotes Jacob as saying to the people of his house, "I will **make** (*ve'esseh*) there an altar..." (35:3), as *Elohim* asked him to do in verse 35:1.

Second, while Elohim asked him to make an altar, in fact the text says he built this one. Moreover, while Elohim spoke of the G-d who appeared to him when he fled from Esau, Jacob spoke of the G-d who answered him in his distress and was with him on his way.

Third, the pace of the text changed in relation to the altars built by the two first forefathers, and the one built by Jacob. Slowing the pace of the account in regard to building this altar by Jacob indicates that quite likely Jacob delayed in building the altar. It is clear that Jacob did not initiate the building of the altar, but even after he was asked to do so by the Almighty, it seems from the slow pace that he really did not want to do so.

We can see another difference between the first two forefathers and Jacob, once the altar is built. For Abraham the text says, "...and there he built an altar to **Y-H-V-H** and called upon the name of **Y-H-V-H**" (12:8). For Isaac the text says, "And he built an altar there and called upon the name of **Y-H-V-H**..." (26:25). On the other hand, for Jacob the text says, "And he erected there an altar and called it G-d, G-d of Israel" (33:20). The text does not say that Jacob called 'upon the name of **Y-H-V-H**.' The text says that Jacob gave a name to the altar itself, 'G-d, G-d of Israel.' Even the second time in which Jacob built an altar, not on his own initiative, but by the initiative of the Almighty, the text says, "And he built there an altar and called **the place** El Beth-El..." (35:7). Again, the 'calling' or 'naming' is for the place and not for *Y-H-V-H*.

---

[130] El Beth-El – *El* means 'G-d' and *Beth* means 'house of.'

The Connection to the Almighty

The way the Almighty appeared to the forefathers is also a point to distinguish Jacob from the first two forefathers.

For Abraham the text says, "After these things the word of *Y-H-V-H* came to Abram **in a vision** saying..." (15:1), and in continuing the appearance of the Almighty to Abram, the text says, "and when the sun was going down a deep sleep fell upon Abram..." (15:12).

[We should note that the Almighty appears in a 'vision' two more times, and both of them are in relation to Balaam, "The speech of him who heard the words of G-d who saw the **vision** of the Almighty..." (Numbers 24:4), and, "The speech of one who heard the words of G-d, and knew the knowledge of the most High, who saw the **vision** of the Almighty..." (24:16).]

The text never says that any other conversation between the Almighty and Abraham was held in a 'vision,' during 'sleep,' or in a 'dream.' Moreover, when the three angels appear to Abraham, the text says, "And *Y-H-V-H* appeared to him in the plains of Mamre and he sat in the tent door **in the heat of the day**" (Genesis 18:1). Note it was in the middle of the day, and not during the night. This should remind us the words of the Almighty to Aaron and Miriam, after they criticized Moses, "With him I speak mouth to mouth, manifestly, and not in dark speech..." (Numbers 12:8).

For Isaac we find one place in which the text says, "And *Y-H-V-H* appeared to him **that night**..." (Genesis 26:24). In another encounter between the Almighty and Isaac the text does not say that it was at night (26:2).

As for Jacob, we find out that the first encounter he had with the Almighty was at night, "...and remained there **all night** because the sun was set, and he took of the stones of that place, and put them under his head and lay down in that place. And he **dreamt**..." (28:11-12). Other encounters between the Almighty and Jacob were also at night. For example, before he returned from Haran to the land of Canaan, the Almighty appeared to Jacob and instructed him to return, "And *Y-H-V-H* said to Jacob return to the land of your fathers and to your family and I will be with (*im*) you"

(31:3). However, when Jacob reports on this instruction to his wives, he says, "And the angel of *Elohim* spoke to me **in a dream** saying, Jacob, and I said, here I am... now arise, get out from this land and return to the land of your family" (31:11-13). We should note that while the text labels the angel who talked with Jacob as 'the angel of *Y-H-V-H*,' Jacob himself, when talking to his wives, labels the angel as 'the angel of *Elohim*.'

Before Jacob went down to Egypt to meet Joseph we find, "And *Elohim* spoke to Israel **in the visions of the night**..." (46:2). The struggle between Jacob and the 'man,' after which the 'man' informs Jacob that his name will be changed from Jacob to Israel, is also during the night, "...and there wrestled a man with him **until the breaking of the day**" (32:25).

The only time in which the text says that the Almighty spoke to Jacob, without saying that it was at night, is when the Almighty instructs Jacob to build an altar, "And *Elohim* said to Jacob, arise, go up to Beth-El, and live there, and make there an altar to the G-d who appeared to you when you fled from the face of Esau your brother" (35:1).

We should note that in this appearance of the Almighty to Jacob, the instruction is not to build an altar to either *Elohim* or *Y-H-V-H*. The instruction leaves it open for Jacob to decide to whom he should build the altar. Although *Elohim* gives the instruction, still the intended G-d is 'to the G-d who appeared to you.' One might wonder if the change of language from *Y-H-V-H* when He appeared to him, instructing him to return to his family, to *Elohim* when he reported it to his wives, has anything to do with the Almighty leaving Jacob to decide.

The fact that most of the time the Almighty appeared to Jacob at night should remind us that the appearance of the Almighty at night mentioned in Biblical text is usually reserved for people who are not from Abraham's family, "And *Elohim* came to Abimelech **in the dream by night**..." (20:3), "And *Elohim* came to Laban the Aramean **in the dream by night**..." (31:24). Pharaoh's **dream** which predicted the seven years of plenty vs. the seven years of famine was at night as well (41:1-7). The same applies to Balaam, the prophet of the other nations, for whom the text says, "And he said to them, lodge here this **night** and I will bring back word to you...And *Elohim* came to Balaam..." (Numbers 22:8-9), and, "And *Elohim* came to Balaam **at night**..." (Numbers 22:20).

We can see that the text considers the quality of the connection between Jacob and the Almighty to be a different quality from the one the two forefathers Abraham and Isaac enjoyed. And the ratio of the text's use of *Y-H-V-H* vs. *Elohim* for Jacob is even less than the ratio for Noah.

With this finding, we can now examine the places where the text used the title *Y-H-V-H* in relation to Jacob, in other words, the minority usage.

Jacob and *Y-H-V-H*

The first time the text brings us the title *Y-H-V-H* in a quote attributed to Jacob is when Jacob appears to his father Isaac while pretending to be his brother Esau, in order to get the blessing. Isaac asks Jacob, "...how is it that you have found it so quickly my son?" (Genesis 27:20); to which Jacob answers, "...because *Y-H-V-H* your G-d brought it to me" (27:20).

One can argue that Jacob says 'your G-d' because he wants to pretend to be Esau. However, if we examine Jacob's language later on, as the text quotes him, we can see that Jacob does not connect the Almighty to himself. When he talks with Rachel and Leah, the text quotes him as saying, "...but the G-d of my father has been with (*im*) me" (31:5). Later on, when he reached a covenant with Laban, after Laban chased him, "Except for the G-d of my father, the G-d of Abraham and the fear of Isaac..." (31:42). And where is 'my G-d' in Jacob's complaint?

Throughout the life of Jacob the text uses the title *Y-H-V-H* eight times, out of which half of the times are in the dream of 'the ladder and the angels' when Jacob is setting out on his way to Haran. This fact alone should bring us to concentrate on this event.

Jacob and the "Ladder and Angels" Dream

The event starts with the text saying,

> "And *vayifgaa* upon the place and remained there all night
> because the sun was set, and he took of the stones of that place,
> and put them under his head and lay down in that place" (28:11).

First we need to check the meaning of the word *vayifgaa*, which even in Modern Hebrew presents a challenge in this place.

Linguistic Journey – the Verb *Lifgoaa*

The verb *lifgoaa* comes from three-letter root word *P-G-AA* . (The letter '*AA*' is the single letter *ayin* in Hebrew. It is the sound 'A' coming from throat and not from the front of the mouth. This letter does not exist in English). In Modern Hebrew, the verb is used with the meaning to hit someone.

In the Biblical text, we find the verb *lifgoaa* in the following places: When Abraham approached the people of Heth in a request to purchase a burial plot, he is quoted by the text as saying, "…if your mind is that I should bury my dead out of my sight, hear me, and ***ufigu*** for me to Ephron the son of Zohar" (23:8). In this sentence, it seems that the meaning is "…and connect me to Ephron the son of Zohar." After the reunion between Jacob and his brother Esau, the text says, "And Jacob went on his way, ***vayifgu*** him the angels of *Elohim*" (32:2). And here the meaning is that the angels of *Elohim* met him. In both places, it is clear that the text is not dealing with a hostile encounter. In the case of Abraham and the people of Heth, it even sounds like an 'invitation' to a meeting.

After the officers of the sons of Israel complain to Pharaoh about the severity of the new measurements enacted against them, the text says, "***Vayifgu*** Moses and Aaron who stood towards them as they came out from Pharaoh" (Exodus 5:20). In another place in Exodus we find, "If you ***tifgaa*** your enemy's ox or his ass going astray, you shall surely return it to him" (23:4). In both places it seems that the verb *lifgoaa* has the meaning of 'a chance encounter' with someone or something. Although it is not a 'friendly' encounter, neither is it a 'hostile' encounter.

When the text talks about the one who killed someone with no intention to do so, who runs away from the refuge city, "The avenger of blood shall himself slay the murderer, ***befigo*** him, he shall slay him" (Numbers 35:19), and then, "…the avenger of blood shall slay the murderer when ***befigo*** him" (35:21). Here, we should remember that the text uses the verb 'to hit' when talking about the murder. And here the verb *lifgoaa* appears before the verb 'to slay.' In this instance, the verb *lifgoaa* sounds like an attempt by the 'avenger of blood' to find the murderer.

From all the above-mentioned places, it can be understood that the verb *lifgoaa* has the meaning 'to meet' or 'to find.' Abraham asks to meet with Ehpron and asks the people of Heth to help him find Ephron. The angels of *Elohim* met or found Jacob. When the officers of the sons of Israel came out from Pharaoh they met Moses and Aaron by chance, as someone happens to find his enemy's ox.

The only place in which the verb *lifgoaa* comes with a definite negative meaning is when Moses and Aaron refuse Pharaoh's proposal for them to worship in the land of Egypt, "And they said, the G-d of the Hebrews has met with us, let us please go three days' journey into the desert, and sacrifice to *Y-H-V-H* our G-d, lest he **yifgaa'enu** with pestilence or with the sword" (Exodus 5:3).

The fact that in this place Moses and Aaron use the verb *lifgoaa* comes to indicate to us that there is a wrong use of the verb. This is a classic example of 'average' vs. 'deviation.'

SCAN Rule: when the SCAN analyst encounters a one-time deviation from the 'average' use of language throughout the rest of the text, the SCAN analyst should suspect that deception is present at the time of the deviation.

This deviation from the average use of the verb *lifgoaa* should indicate to us that Moses and Aaron knew that there was no way that the Almighty would send pestilence or the sword. However, this is what they told Pharaoh.

Back to Jacob

"And *vayifgaa* upon **the place**..." (Genesis 28:11).

We should note that the text does not talk about just any place, but of '**the** place' – a 'known' place.

The word 'the place' – a known place – appears for the first time in Biblical text in the account of the binding of Isaac to the altar. The text says, "And Abraham rose up early in the morning, and saddled his ass, and took two of his lads with him, and Isaac his son, and broke the wood for the burnt offering, and rose up, and went to **the place** of which *Elohim* had told him" (22:3). We also find, "On the third day Abraham lifted up his eyes and saw **the place** from far away" (22:4). Then, "And they came to **the place** which *Elohim* had told him…" (22:9). At the end of the event, "And Abraham called the name of **that place** Adonai-Yireh, as it is said to this day, in the mount of *Y-H-V-H* it shall be seen" (22:14). The fact that Abraham gave a name to the place indicates that the place got to be a permanent place, as Abraham gave a name to Beersheba (21:31).

When Jacob woke up from his sleep, the text says, "And Jacob awoke from his sleep and he said, **indeed** there is *Y-H-V-H* in this place and I didn't know" (28:16).

The word 'indeed' (*achen*) should 'wake us up' to wonder what it is doing there. The word 'indeed' sounds as if it relates to some knowledge that Jacob had about the place before he got there. The word *achen* can be found in Exodus, "And he said, who made you a prince and a judge over us? Do you intend to kill me, as you killed the Egyptian? And Moses feared and said, *achen* this thing is known" (Exodus 2:14). The word *achen* indicates that Moses expected that the killing of the Egyptian would indeed be found out.

"…indeed there is *Y-H-V-H* in this place and **I didn't know**" (28:16).

'Didn't Know' – Background Information

When we come to analyze a statement in modern times, whether it is a witness or a suspect, we should know if the answer is given to a specific question, or is it an answer to an 'open question,' making the answer an 'open statement.' For example, if we ask a person, 'Do you know if such-and-such took place?' and the person answers, 'I don't know,' this might be a legitimate answer. When we direct the person's attention to a particular point and the person says, 'I don't know' (or 'I don't remember') such an answer cannot bring us to conclude anything.

However, when we deal with an 'open statement,' for example, when we ask a person to give us 'what happened' on a particular day, then in the person's mind the 'editing process' starts to determine what should be included in the 'open statement' and what should not be included. The person needs to bring the event to the front of his mind and to ask himself or herself one question all the time: 'Is it important enough for me to include in my answer?' If the person answers in the affirmative, the person includes it in the open statement. However, if the person answers in the negative, the person does not include it in the open statement.

We should note two major points in regard to this 'editing process.' One, it is a very innocent process. The truthful person does it as well. Two, it is **a very quick** process in the person's mind, to the point that after giving the statement, if the person is asked about a certain point in the text, the person is not able to reconstruct the event that was present in the mind at the time of delivering the statement. This quick pace of the mind brings the feeling that the process is subconscious, but the fact is that it is not subconscious. If the SCAN analyst were to bring this information derived from the text to the attention of the person, the person would confirm it.

The 'editing process' means that any information a person includes in an 'open statement' is labeled 'important enough to enter the statement.' This also means that the sentence 'I don't know' or 'I don't remember' is **illegitimate** when it is found in an 'open statement.' If a person does not know something, the person does not include it in an 'open statement.' However, if a person knows that he/she doesn't know, it should be considered a signal of concealing information.

When we come to analyze Biblical text we should distinguish between two situations. One, the text tells us that someone 'didn't know.' This is a statement of a fact by the text itself. Second, the text quotes the person himself, saying that he/she 'didn't know.' In both cases we should check the place carefully. However, it is more important when it is in a quote by someone.

"…indeed there is *Y-H-V-H* in this place and **I didn't know**" (28:16).

Did Jacob 'bump' into '**the** place' (*hamakom*)? Or, did Jacob maybe 'find' the place he was looking for, the same place he knew from his grandfather Abraham was the place where "*Y-H-V-H* will see" (Genesis 22:14)? It is quite likely that the encounter Abraham had with the angel, at the time of binding Isaac at the altar, did not remain a secret in the family. It is very likely that this incident in the family history passed from father to son and grandson, and would have singled out the place where the angel of the Almighty appeared to Abraham. It is also very likely that on the way to Haran, Jacob decided to visit the same place that he was told was the place where the Almighty appeared. When Jacob woke up in the morning and said, "...indeed there is *Y-H-V-H* in this place and **I didn't know**" (28:16), it doesn't come to say that Jacob didn't know, but to say that Jacob didn't accept it or didn't believe it. Therefore, when the Almighty approached him in that place, Jacob realized that what he was told earlier 'indeed' was true.

Now that we have dealt with what Jacob 'didn't know,' we should go to another place in Genesis where the text (not Jacob himself) says that Jacob didn't know. And that 'lack of knowledge' has an impact on our discussion of Jacob and his connection to the Almighty.

Jacob, Rachel and the *Teraphim*

> "...and Jacob **did not know** that
> Rachel had stolen them" (Genesis 31:32).

The text says,

> And Jacob rose up, and carried his sons and his wives on the camels. And he led all his cattle, and all his goods, which he had acquired, the cattle of his getting, which he had acquired in Padan-Aram, to go to Isaac his father in the land of Canaan. And Laban went to shear his sheep, **and Rachel had stolen the *teraphim* that were her father's**. (Genesis 31:17-19)

When Laban reached Jacob, Laban finished his emotional address to Jacob by saying, "And now that you are surely gone, because you so long after your father's house, **why have you stolen my gods?**" (31:30). Jacob responded by saying, "With whom you will find your gods, let him not live. Before our brothers point out what is yours with me, and take it with you. And Jacob **didn't know** that Rachel had stolen them" (31:32).

What didn't Jacob know? Or, more accurately, what did Jacob know?

Checking the language used by the text to quote both Laban and Jacob shows that both of them used the word 'gods.' Laban asked Jacob why did he steal his **gods**, and Jacob answered, "With whom you will find your

gods…" But the text does not tell us that Rachel stole Laban's gods. The text says that she stole Laban's *teraphim*.

Are the *teraphim* really statues?

In the book Judges we find the following verse, "…do you know that there is in these houses an *ephod*, and *teraphim*, and a statue and a mask…" (Judges 18:14).

It is not easy to know what the nature of the *teraphim* was, but from this verse it is clear that *teraphim* are not statues, and they are not the *ephod*, and they are not masks.

SCAN Rule: There are no synonyms in an 'open statement.'

'Change of language reflects a change of reality.' This means that X cannot be Y and Y cannot be Z. Each one of them should reflect a different point in reality.

Moreover, the order of listing in the verse indicates that the *ephod* is the most important one, being listed first, the *teraphim* are listed second, the statue is listed third, and the mask is listed last. And by being listed at the end, quite likely it was the least important.

In an earlier chapter of Judges we find, "And the man Micah had a house of *Elohim* and made an *ephod* and *teraphim* and consecrated one of his sons who became the priest" (Judges 17:5). In this verse we see that the statue and the mask are not mentioned at all. To Micah the *ephod* and *teraphim* were enough to start running the house of *Elohim*.

To know for what the *teraphim* served, we have to go to another place in the Tanach, to the prophet Ezekiel. We find there, "For the king of Babylon stood at the parting of the way, at the head of the two ways, to use divination, he shook the arrows, **he asked the *teraphim***, he looked in the liver" (Ezekiel 21:26). In Zechariah we find, "**For the *teraphim* have spoken vanity** and the diviners have seen a lie and the dreams have told falsehoods…" (Zechariah 10:2).

These two verses are taken from a very late time (Ezekiel and Zechariah) compared to Rachel and Laban, but we can see that the *teraphim* were used to predict the future. People were asking the *teraphim*, and the *teraphim* were 'talking' to them, although they talked 'vanity' (nonsense), as Zechariah said.

Returning to Jacob, Rachel and the *teraphim*, we can see that Rachel did not steal her father's gods, but she stole the device that would enable her to know the future, assuming a person believes in it. But why would Rachel steal the *teraphim*?

To answer this question we have to go back and look upon the people in the sequence of events – Jacob, Rachel, and Leah.

Jacob woke up from his sleep and said, "…indeed there is *Y-H-V-H* in this place and **I didn't know**" (Genesis 28:16). Then Jacob took a vow saying, "…If *Elohim* will be with me and will guard me in this way that I go, and will give me bread to eat and garment to wear. And I come back to my father's house in peace, then shall *Y-H-V-H* be my *Elohim*" (28:20-21). As the vow goes, *Y-H-V-H* will be Jacob's *Elohim* only after he returns safely to his father's house. Not before that time. Jacob does not see himself committed to *Y-H-V-H* before returning safely. At this stage it is difficult to see Jacob as a great believer in *Y-H-V-H*, definitely not like his grandfather Abraham.

Earlier, we saw a change in Leah's language, from *Y-H-V-H* in the birth of the first four sons, to *Elohim* in the birth of the last two sons. We should also take into consideration that in naming the first four sons, Leah gave them Hebrew names: Reuben ('see, it is a son'), Simeon ('the Almighty heard (*shamaa*)'), Levi ('my husband will accompany (*yilaveh*) me, and Judah (thanking the Almighty). However, when naming the two last ones she used Aramaic names, Issachar and Zebulon. In naming Zebulon, Leah used two Aramaic verbs – *zebadani* and *yizbeleni*. Combining the change from *Y-H-V-H* to *Elohim* in giving Hebrew names to the four oldest and Aramaic names to the last two, one can easily reach a conclusion that Leah quite likely returned to the culture and religion of her father Laban, once she felt rejected by Jacob.

With Rachel, as with Leah, we find a change in language, but in the opposite direction, from *Elohim* to *Y-H-V-H*. When her maid Bilhah gives birth to a son, Rachel is quoted as saying, "…*Elohim* has judged (*danani*) me and also heard my voice and has given me a son, therefore she called his name Dan" (Genesis 30:6). When Naphtali is born, "...with the wrestlings (*naftulei*) of *Elohim* have I wrestled with my sister, and I have prevailed, and she called his name Naphtali" (30:8).

When Rachel gave birth to Joseph, "...*Elohim* has taken away my reproach. And she called his name Joseph and said, *Y-H-V-H* shall add to me another son" (30:23-24). The text quotes Rachel as using the name of *Y-H-V-H* at the time of the birth of Joseph. The birth of Joseph brought her to use the name of Jacob's G-d.

We should note that Joseph is the only son among Jacob's twelve sons for whom the two forms of the name of the Almighty are present at his naming – *Elohim* and *Y-H-V-H*.

Only after the attack that Simeon and Levi launched against the city of Shechem because of Dinah, did Jacob tell "his household and to all who were with him" (35:2), "Remove all the foreign gods that are among you, and purify yourselves and change your garments" (35:2). Up to this point, Jacob's household was full of idols and idolatry.

As long as Rachel and Leah lived in their father's house, and they could worship the idols that were in Laban's house, Rachel didn't need the *teraphim*. However, when she understood that she was going to move far away from her father's house and culture (and religion), she had to take the *teraphim* with her. But why specifically Rachel? Why not Leah or the two maids? We have to remember at that time Rachel was the only one of Jacob's four wives (counting the maids as wives) with only one son. And very soon we will see that the *teraphim* had to do with Rachel and fertility.

When Laban searched for his gods the text says, "And Laban came into Jacob's tent and into Leah's tent, and into the two maids' tents... then he went out from Leah's tent and came into Rachel's tent" (31:33). According to which order did Laban choose to run the search? We should remember that at the time Leah had six sons, the two maids had two sons each, and Rachel had only one son. Jacob is the father of all the sons. Therefore, Laban searched according to the fertility of each one of them. Jacob – as the father of all eleven, was the most fertile. Therefore, he was the first to be searched. Leah the second, having six. The maids, having two each, were next in line, and Rachel with only one was the last.

We should note that Laban, believing in the *teraphim*, did not go according to who **needed** the *teraphim* the most, but according to who **benefited** from them the most.

If we have any doubt that the *teraphim* had to do with fertility, we can go to another place in the Tanach where the *teraphim* are mentioned. When the text talks about King Saul chasing David to kill him, the text says, "And Michal let David down through the window and he went and fled and escaped. And Michal took the *teraphim* and laid them on the bed and put a pillow of goats' hair at its head, and covered it with a cloth" (1 Samuel 19:13).

Why would Michal have the *teraphim* at her house? Later on, the text tells us, "And Michal the daughter of Saul had no child to the day of her death" (2 Samuel 6:23). The one who didn't have a child was also the one who had the *teraphim* at home. No different from Rachel, Jacob's wife. One has to conclude that the *teraphim* have to do with fertility.

Returning to Laban's search of Jacob's household, while Laban is in the midst of the search, the text says, "And Rachel had taken the *teraphim* and put them in the camel's saddle, and sat upon them..." (Genesis 31:34). Until this point the *teraphim* were in plain sight for everyone to see. Rachel didn't hide them, as she had no reason to do so. Jacob didn't have any reason to suspect that something was wrong when his beloved wife, known to him to be an idol worshipper, and to be totally preoccupied with fertility, and to be jealous of her sister, would be connected to the *teraphim*. The only thing Jacob didn't know was that the exposed *teraphim* were stolen.

When Laban asked Jacob, "Why did you steal my gods?" Jacob didn't think that Laban was talking about the *teraphim*. After all, *teraphim* and gods were two different things. And when the text says that Jacob didn't know that Rachel stole them, the text is telling us the truth. We need to read between the lines. He knew she had the *teraphim*. He just didn't know that she had stolen them.

We can examine now other places in which the text uses the title *Y-H-V-H* in Jacob's life.

The first place, "And **Y-H-V-H** saw that Leah was hated, he opened her womb, and Rachel was barren" (Genesis 29:31). The text attributes the birth of the sons to *Y-H-V-H* and not to *Elohim*. This is also the way the two mothers Leah and Rachel saw it.

The next place where the text quotes Jacob as using the title *Y-H-V-H* shows up in, "…and **Y-H-V-H** has blessed you for my sake…" (Genesis 30:30). We should take into consideration that in this event Jacob and Laban are negotiating over the compensation for Jacob's work, and Laban is the first one to use the title *Y-H-V-H*: "…if I have found favor in your eyes, I guess that **Y-H-V-H** has blessed me for your sake" (Genesis 30:27). This should remind us of the account of Joseph and his Egyptian master, a case in which the text attributes the title *Y-H-V-H* to Joseph's master, while Joseph himself does not do so, at least not by the text. Later on, the text quotes Laban as saying, "…for he said **Y-H-V-H** watch between me and you when we are absent from one another" (Genesis 31:49).

The next place where the text uses the title *Y-H-V-H* is, "And **Y-H-V-H** said to Jacob, return to the land of your fathers and to your family and I will be with you" (Genesis 31:3). As *Y-H-V-H* appeared to Jacob in the dream of the ladder and the angels, in which He promised him that He would be with him all the way, so now *Y-H-V-H* appears and tells Jacob that it is time to return home. It would be interesting to know what would have happened if *Y-H-V-H* hadn't told Jacob to return home. Would he have returned? Or, maybe he would have stayed, even though he suffered his uncle/father-in-law's ill treatment.

The next time the text uses the title *Y-H-V-H* is during the wait for Esau's visit. The text says, "And Jacob was greatly afraid and distressed…" (Genesis 32:8). Jacob divides his household into two camps, and then he prays to the Almighty, "And Jacob said, O G-d of my father Abraham and G-d of my father Isaac, **Y-H-V-H** who said to me, return to your country and to your family and I will deal well with you" (Genesis 32:10). This is the last time Jacob used the title *Y-H-V-H* until his last words to his sons before his death. There, we find in his words to Dan, "I have hoped for your salvation, O **Y-H-V-H**" (Genesis 49:18).

In summary, we find the title *Y-H-V-H* in Jacob's language, as the text quotes him, when Jacob is in danger: when he went into exile in Haran (the dream of the ladder and the angels), when he negotiated with Laban, when he was about to meet his brother Esau, and when he blessed Dan just before his death (in conjunction with the word 'salvation').

We cannot summarize the content on one hand, and the language on the other hand, relating to Jacob without dealing with him blessing Joseph's sons: "And he blessed Joseph and said the *Elohim* before whom my fathers Abraham and Isaac walked themselves[131], the *Elohim* who shepherded me all my life long to this day..." (Genesis 48:15).

There are two parts to the verse. The first is, '...the *Elohim* before whom my fathers Abraham and Isaac walked themselves.' We should note that Jacob, who is now facing his death, and according to the text he died at the age of 147, a long life, does not include **himself** among those who 'walked before the *Elohim*.' Instead, he mentions only his fathers. In comparison, we can bring Abraham's slave who talks to Rebecca's family and quotes his master Abraham as saying, "And he said to me, *Y-H-V-H* before whom I walked..." (Genesis 24:40). Note also that, while Abraham 'walked before *Y-H-V-H*,' Jacob didn't walk before *Elohim*. And finally, note that in saying this, Jacob does not rule out the existence of other *elohim* before whom his fathers did not walk.

Now to the second part of the verse:

> "...the *Elohim* who **shepherded** me
> all my life long to this day." (48:15)

We should return now to the dream of the ladder and the angels and read what *Y-H-V-H* promised Jacob, "And behold I am with you, and I will **guard** you in all places where you go, and will bring you back to this land, for I will not leave you, until I have done that about which I have spoken to you" (Genesis 28:15). Later on, when Jacob woke from his sleep, he took a vow, "If *Elohim* will be with me, and will **guard** me in this way that I go, and will give me bread to eat and garment to wear, and I come back to my father's house in peace, then shall *Y-H-V-H* be my *Elohim*" (Genesis 28:20-21).

---

[131] "...walked themselves..." The verb in Hebrew is *hitalchu*, the reflexive form of the verb *lalechet*, which has the primary meaning 'to walk.' But since there is no other verb in Hebrew for 'to go,' this verb is also used for 'to go.'

Jacob was a shepherd. We know that Jacob was Laban's shepherd for over twenty years. But we also know that all Abraham's family were mainly shepherds. Even in the beginning of his life, the text introduces Jacob as "…and Jacob was a perfect man living in tents" (Genesis 25:27). The word 'tents' indicates the fact that the stay was temporary, a major component of the life of shepherds. Later on, when Jacob acts to increase the percentage of sheep to be born "striped, speckled and spotted" (Genesis 30:39), Jacob demonstrates a deep understanding of the genetics of sheep. Later on, when Laban reached Jacob who ran away from Haran, Jacob gave the 'shepherd speech' (Genesis 31:36-42) indicating how important shepherding was in Jacob's life. This fact should bring us to check the language of shepherds. Jacob is the first one to guide us in this search.

The Language of Shepherds

When Jacob negotiated with Laban concerning his compensation, Jacob is quoted as saying, "…you shall not give me anything. If you will do this thing for me, I will again **shepherd** and **guard** your flock" (Genesis 30:31). The text quotes Jacob as engaging in two different activities, 'to shepherd' and 'to guard.' Later on, the text brings us a verse to explain these two activities: "And he set three days' journey between himself and Jacob, **and Jacob shepherded the rest of Laban's flock**" (30:36). From this, we learn that until that point of time, Jacob was the shepherd of Laban's flock along with his own flock. During the negotiation over his compensation, Jacob suggested that not only would he shepherd Laban's flock, but also that he would do it himself, 'I will again **shepherd** and **guard** your flock.' The text comes to clarify this issue by mentioning the separation of the two tasks. It means that the profession of shepherding included two different jobs, 'the shepherd' and 'the guard.' The shepherd was the one who was responsible for the flock, but not necessarily with the flock every single minute. On the other hand, 'the guard' was the one whose duty was to be with the flock all the time, to make sure that no wild animal or a thief hurt the flock. We find in the Tanach another case dealing with another shepherd, David. When Jesse, David's father, tells David to go and bring food to his brothers who are at the front line, the text says, "And David rose up early in the morning **and left the sheep with a guard**, and carried, and went…" (1 Samuel 17:20).

The fact that the shepherd was not necessarily with the flock all the time is also expressed in the case of Joseph, "…Joseph being seventeen years old was **shepherding** his brothers with the flock…" (Genesis 37:2). We know that Joseph was not with his brothers all the time. And in fact, his father told him, "…Are not your brothers shepherding the flock in Shechem? Come, and I will send you to them…" (Genesis 37:13). The 'shepherd' was the leader, the one responsible for the flock.

With this knowledge, we can read the exchange between the Almighty and Cain, after Cain killed his brother Abel. The text says, "And *Y-H-V-H* said to Cain, where is Abel your brother? And he said, I know not, am I my brother's **guard**?" (Genesis 4:9).

Cain's defense was that his brother was a shepherd, which means moving from one place to another. Cain, on the other hand, was a farmer, one who is attached to his land and does not move at all. In many words, Cain said, 'do you expect me, the one who is in one place, to be attached to my brother more than my brother the **shepherd** is attached to his flock? The guard is more mobile than the shepherd, and I am the farmer who does not move at all.' In summary, we can conclude that while the 'shepherd' is responsible for the flock a little bit from afar, the 'guard' is closer to the flock, a lot more than the 'shepherd.'

Back to Jacob

Now we can return to the dream of the ladder and the angels. The Almighty promised Jacob that He would 'guard' him. Jacob, when he took a vow, used the term "…and will guard me," meaning guarding Jacob from nearby and all the time.

And when Jacob blessed Joseph's sons, he is quoted as saying, "…the *Elohim* who **shepherded** me all my life long to this day" (48:15). Jacob did not say, '…the *Elohim* who **guarded** me all my life long to this day' as the Almighty promised him, and as he took a vow at that time. Jacob used the title 'shepherd.' From the language of the quote we should wonder if Jacob is complaining about the quality of the connection between him and the Almighty. He did not receive 'guarding.' He received 'shepherding.'

Summary

We can see that the text uses the title *Y-H-V-H* in the context of the connection between the Almighty and the human being. And the closer the connection, the more the text uses the title *Y-H-V-H*. According to this, Isaac, although he is only a transition figure between Abraham and Jacob, received first place in the 'competition' for the best connection with the Almighty. Jacob, on the other hand, is in last place, even behind Noah.

El Shaddai – G-d Almighty

Abraham is the first one for whom the title 'G-d Almighty' enters the text: "And Abram was ninety nine years old and *Y-H-V-H* appeared to Abram and said to him, I am G-d Almighty (*El Shaddai*) walk[132] before me and be perfect[133]" (Genesis 17:1). This verse comes to start the section in which the Almighty changes Abraham's name from Abram to Abraham, adding one more letter to his name, and the section comes to give the instruction about circumcision. The section ends with,

> And Abraham was ninety years old and nine when he was circumcised in the flesh of his foreskin. And Ishmael his son was thirteen years old when he was circumcised in the flesh of his foreskin. In the midst of this day Abraham was circumcised and Ishmael his son. And all the men of his house, born in the house, and bought with money from the foreigner, were circumcised with him. (Genesis 17:24-27)

If we position the verse that starts chapter 17 with the verse that ends the previous chapter, we get the following content: "And Abram was eighty six years old when Hagar bore Ishmael to Abram. And Abram was ninety nine years old..." (Genesis 16:16 - 17:1).

Times and Missing Time in an Open Statement

Background information: An 'open statement' means that the person giving the statement has the freedom to decide what to include in the

---

[132] The verb 'walk' in the command form is *lech*. The form used here is not the regular *lech* but the reflexive form of the verb, *hithalech*.
[133] The word *tamim* or *tam* means 'complete,' 'whole.'

statement, and what not to include. This means that the reader/listener cannot impose on the person to include times in the 'open statement.' Including times is a matter of personal priorities. We find that some people include many times, some include a few times, and some do not even include any times. From the point of view of the analysis, there is no significance if there are times or there are no times.

'The editing process governing the open statement' means that if the person giving the statement includes time in the text, the time mentioned in the statement is an important time for the person, and the SCAN analyst should consider it as such.

When the person puts two times adjacent to each other, without mentioning any activity between them, the person brings to the attention of the reader/listener 'missing time.' Such 'missing time' should be considered extremely important. In a statement of today, the SCAN analyst should consider such 'missing time' a signal of concealing information.

At this stage, one might ask: why would a person who wants to conceal information leave a signal indicating so? The answer to this question is: Everyone wants to tell everyone everything.

> "And Abram was eighty six years old when Hagar bore
> Ishmael to Abram. And Abram was ninety nine years old…"
> (Genesis 16:16-17:1).

What happened in these thirteen years that the text prefers to put aside? We know what happened at the beginning of these thirteen years – Ishmael was born. And we know what happened at the end of these thirteen years – Ishmael, Abraham's son, was circumcised. And indeed the text devotes one verse to mentioning Ishmael's age at the time he was circumcised. And in between we have "missing time."

We need to go back in time to the birth of Ishmael. After Sarah didn't bear any son to Abraham, Sarah approached Abraham and said, "…come to my maid, it may be that I may be built[134] from her…" (Genesis 16:2). We find the same with Rachel who gives her maid Bilhah to Jacob,

---

[134] Literally, the text quotes Sarah as saying that she will be 'built' by the fact that Hagar would bear a son to Abraham.

"...come to her and she shall bear upon my knees that I may also be **built** by her" (Genesis 30:3).

When Bilhah bears a son, Rachel says, "...*Elohim* judged me and also heard my voice and has given me a son..." (Genesis 30:6). Rachel sees the birth of Dan as her own delivery – *Elohim* has given her a son.

Comparison of the two events, Sarah and Hagar, and Rachel and Bilhah, brings two points to our attention. First, Rachel said, 'that I may **also** be built by her.' By saying 'also' Rachel must be relating to an earlier event, and quite likely it is the case of Sarah and Hagar. Second, while Sarah says, "...**it may be** that I may be built from her," and the word 'may be' indicates doubt, Rachel has no doubt at all that she will be 'built' by the son born to her husband Jacob and her slave Bilhah. Rachel was sure of her position in Jacob's household, and sure that Bilhah would not act against her after the birth. This is not the case for Sarah, and the word 'may be' expresses concern and doubt about Hagar. And in fact later on Sarah finds out that Hagar took ownership of the son born to her, and Sarah was left aside.

In contrast, the sequence of events in the birth of Ishmael was different. The text says, "And he came to Hagar and she conceived and when she saw that she had conceived her mistress was diminished in her eyes" (Genesis 16:4). After Hagar ran away from Sarah, and returned by the Angel's encouragement, the text says, "And Hagar bore Abram a son and Abram called **his son**'s name, whom Hagar bore, Ishmael" (Genesis 16:15). Hagar bore a son to Abram, and Ishmael was Abram's son, and not Sarah's son, unlike the case with Rachel and Dan.

At this point in time, the text stops the sequence of events, and using a 'time machine' the text 'jumps' over thirteen years and brings us the verse, "And Abram was ninety nine years old and *Y-H-V-H* appeared to Abram and said to him, I am G-d Almighty (*El Shaddai*) walk before me **and be perfect**" (Genesis 17:1). What was the situation that brought the Almighty to tell Abraham 'to be perfect?' In order to understand it, we have to go to the book of Deuteronomy, to know the meaning of the word 'perfect,' or, indeed, what is the opposite of 'perfect?'

"For you come into the land which *Y-H-V-H* your G-d gives you,
you shall not learn to do after the abominations of those nations.

> There shall not be found among you any one who makes his son or his daughter pass through the fire, or who uses divination, or a soothsayer, or an enchanter, or a witch or a charmer, or a medium, or a wizard, or a necromancer. For all that do these things are abomination to *Y-H-V-H*, and because of these abominations *Y-H-V-H* your G-d drives them out from before you. You shall be **perfect** (*tamim*) with *Y-H-V-H* your G-d. (Deuteronomy 18: 9-13)

It is quite likely that the fact that the text specifies that Ishmael was Abraham's son and not Sarah's son, meant that the responsibility for Ishmael's upbringing rested on the shoulders of his **Egyptian** mother. And in these thirteen years that Hagar raised Ishmael in Abraham's household, she quite likely raised him in the same way she was raised by her Egyptian parents. And the Egyptian way of life, with everything that it entails, entered Abraham's household. As a result, there was a reduction in the quality of the connection between Abraham and the Almighty. There was a need to open a new chapter, to reach a new covenant between the Almighty and Abraham, one to preserve the connection with *Y-H-V-H*: "…and *Y-H-V-H* appeared to Abram and said to him, I am G-d Almighty (*El Shaddai*) walk before me and be perfect" (Genesis 17:1).

The fact is that among the three forefathers – Abraham, Isaac, and Jacob – the Almighty appears as "G-d Almighty" (*El Shaddai*) only to Abraham and Jacob, but not to Isaac. Isaac uses the title *El Shaddai* when he gives the blessing to Jacob, "…and *El Shaddai* will bless you…" (Genesis 28:3), but this is not a quote by the Almighty Himself, but a quote by Isaac. As noted before, Isaac is the top among the forefathers for the proportion of the title *Y-H-V-H* to the title *Elohim* – 77% for the title *Y-H-V-H* as opposed to 23% for the title *Elohim*. And Jacob, to whom Isaac gives the 'G-d Almighty' blessing, got the opposite ratio of 75% for *Elohim* and 25% for the title *Y-H-V-H*. Therefore, it should not be a surprise that Isaac gives Jacob the blessing of G-d Almighty before he goes away to Haran, to remind Jacob to be strong in faith to his G-d while in the midst of people who practiced idolatry. Isaac very likely knew Jacob wasn't as strong in allegiance to *Y-H-V-H*, the G-d of his fathers Abraham and Isaac.

If we compare the places in which the title 'G-d Almighty' appears in a quote by the Almighty to Abraham and Jacob, we can see that the two of them are identical in nature. In both of them there is a change of name. For Abraham, it is from Abram to Abraham, and from Sarai to Sarah. For

Jacob it is from Jacob to Israel. In both of them there is a significant addition. For Abraham we find the covenant of circumcision, which signifies the house of Abraham. For Jacob we find the request to build an altar to "…the G-d who appeared to you when you fled from the face of Esau your brother" (Genesis 35:1). Before building the altar Jacob says to all the people of his house, "…Put away the foreign gods that are among you; purify yourselves and change your garments" (35:2).

Content-wise, the change of name for Abraham comes after the 'missing time' of 13 years from the birth of Ishmael and his upbringing by his Egyptian mother, and ends with the circumcision of Abraham and Ishmael. Ishmael received an independent verse for his circumcision. We learn that at that point of time there was a need to separate the house of Abraham from the customs of the surrounding nations, who acted the opposite of *tamim* (perfect), customs that were brought into Abraham's house by the Egyptian Hagar and her son Ishmael. As we saw earlier, the verb *letzahek* meant activity that had to do with sex in the framework of idolatry. The circumcision, a covenant 'signed' into the male sexual organ, came to distinguish the house of Abraham, and his descendants after him, from the other nations.

One can say that with the circumcision Ishmael was put on 'probation,' receiving a 'grace period,' to test if he was worthy to remain in the house of Abraham or not. The fact that later on Sarah saw him *metzahek* (Genesis 21:9) sealed his fate to be removed from the house of Abraham. The Egyptian behavior did not fit the behavior of worshipping the Almighty – *Y-H-V-H*.

Jacob and *El Shaddai*

"…I am **G-d Almighty**, be fruitful and multiply, a nation and a company of nations shall be of you, and kings shall come from your loins" (Genesis 35:11).

The appearance of 'G-d Almighty' and the change of name from Jacob to Israel comes after Jacob's stay in Haran for over 20 years and his exposure to the idolatry that was common there, not only in the outside environment, but even inside his own house.

Language-wise, in the two appearances of 'G-d Almighty' – both to Abraham and Jacob – the text uses the title *Elohim* and not *Y-H-V-H*. All the identical components should bring us to the conclusion that the title 'G-d Almighty' comes to distinguish between both *Elohim* and *Y-H-V-H* and the other idols that have no strength, no *Shaddai,* no 'might.'

We should note that the title 'G-d Almighty' appears twice more in Genesis, and both of them in regard to Joseph. First, when Jacob promises Joseph two tribes, the benefit of the firstborn, "And Jacob said to Joseph, G-d Almighty (*El Shaddai*) appeared to me at Luz in the land of Canaan and blessed me" (Genesis 48:3). And second, when Jacob blessed Joseph before his death, "By the G-d of your father who shall help you, and by the Almighty[135] who shall bless you with blessing of heaven above, blessings of the deep that lies under, blessing of the breasts and of the womb" (49:25). For one reason or another, no other brother among the twelve needed the title *El Shaddai* to appear for him. One might wonder if it has anything to do with the fact that Joseph was a priest for idolatry while in Egypt.

Abraham and *El Shaddai*

"…**walk** before me and be perfect" (Genesis 17:1)

Note: as footnoted earlier, the verb 'walk' or 'go' is not used in the regular form, but in the form of doing activity geared inward and not outward (reflexive). The text does not say *lech* but *hithalech.*

We can understand the form *hithalech* in another verse talking about one who is hurt by another, "If he rises and goes (*hithalech*) out with his staff, then shall he who struck him be acquitted, only he shall pay for the loss of his time and shall cause him to be thoroughly healed" (Exodus 21:19). From this place it comes across that the verb *hithalech* means to walk or go **independently**, without any help by anyone or anything. When the Almighty tells Abraham, "Arise, go (*hithalech*) through the land in its length and in its breadth, for I will give it to you" (Genesis 13:17), the Almighty tells Abraham to feel independent and free to *hithalech* in the land.

"…walk **before me** and be perfect" (Genesis 17:1)

---

[135] In the Hebrew text it does not show up as *El Shaddai*, but as *et Shaddai*, one letter different.

The text brings us two people who 'walked' in this reflexive form. The first is Enoch, "And Enoch walked (*vayithalech*) with (*et*) the *Elohim*..." (Genesis 5:22), and Noah, "...with (*et*) the *Elohim* walked Noah (*hithalech*)" (6:9).

We should immediately notice the difference in the way the text positions *Elohim* in the sentence. While for Enoch, the *Elohim* is second, for Noah, the *Elohim* is first. Just by the order we should conclude that the connection between Noah and *Elohim* was closer than the connection Enoch had. No wonder that the verse for Noah starts with, "...Noah was a just man and perfect in his generations," a description missing for Enoch.

As we saw earlier, the preposition 'with' in Biblical Hebrew has two varieties, *im,* which is closer than *et*. And both Enoch and Noah are described as *hithalech*, with *et* indicating some distance between them and the Almighty. When the Almighty speaks to Abraham and tells him to walk (*hithalech*), He is not asking him to walk with (*et*) Him. He asks him to walk 'in front' of Him. We already saw earlier that the word 'in front of' (in Hebrew it is one word) relates to accepting authority. In summary, by the Almighty telling Abraham, 'walk before me' the Almighty says, 'be independent and free with your movements and stand on your own two feet, but at the same time accept my authority as the Creator.' This is not different at all from the summary by the prophet Micah of the demands of *Y-H-V-H* from the human being, "What does *Y-H-V-H* demand of you, but to do justice, and to love mercy, and to walk humbly with (*im*) your G-d" (Micah 6:8).

We know that Abraham accepted the Almighty's demands of him. When Abraham's slave speaks to Rebecca's family he quotes his master as telling him, "And he said to me, *Y-H-V-H* **in front** of Whom I walked (*hithalachti*)..." (Genesis 24:40).

It seems to us that the covenant of circumcision was an event that influenced the house of Abraham, and was a significant activity within the family. But from the text this is not the case. The environment did not receive the covenant of circumcision easily. The text says, "...and circumcised the flesh of their foreskin **in the midst of this day**..." (Genesis 17:23) and the text repeats it, "**In the midst of this day** Abraham was circumcised and Ishmael his son" (17:26).

The phrase 'in the midst of this day' appears once more in Genesis, "**In the midst of this day** entered Noah and Shem, Ham and Japheth, the sons of Noah, and Noah's wife, and the three wives of his sons with them, into the ark" (Genesis 7:13). Noah's entrance into the ark ends with, "…and Y-H-V-H closed him in" (7:16). Closing the door appears in the account of the Angels and Lot in Sodom, when the people of the city are crowding around the house, "The men put forth their hand and pulled Lot into the house to them and closed the door" (19:10). As the people of Sodom crowded around the house, so it is quite likely that the people crowded around the ark when Noah and his family entered it. And Abraham circumcised himself and the men of his household "in the midst of this day," and quite likely in spite of resistance from the people around.

We should note that the phrase 'in the midst of this day' appears in regard to the exodus out of Egypt, "…for **in the midst of this day** have I brought your armies out of Egypt…" (Exodus 12:17, 41, and 51).

In English it would be appropriate to understand the phrase 'in the midst of this day' as meaning 'in broad daylight.'

Summary

The title 'G-d Almighty' (*El Shaddai*) is in the picture when there is a need to call the people of the house of Abraham to order. It may be Abraham himself, when Hagar and Ishmael brought Egyptian idolatry into his house, or it may be Jacob who received the blessing of 'G-d Almighty' from his father before going away to Haran, and the appearance of 'G-d Almighty' to Jacob upon his return, after a long stay in his idol worshipping uncle's house. And it may be Joseph who was surrounded by Egyptian idolatry while in slavery.

Elohim vs. *Y-H-V-H* in Other Books

As the book of Genesis ends with a ratio leaning strongly to the title *Elohim*, and few for the title *Y-H-V-H*, so starts the book Exodus. The text starts entirely with the title *Elohim*:

- "And the midwives feared ***Elohim***…" (Exodus 1:17),
- "And ***Elohim*** dealt well with the midwives…" (1:20), and

- "And it came to pass because the midwives feared *Elohim*..." (1:21).

When the text talks of the sons of Israel's cry from enslavement, we see, "...and their cry came up to *Elohim*..." (2:23). We should note that the text does not say, '...and the sons of Israel sighed because of the slavery and they cried to *Elohim*...' The text says only that they 'cried,' but not necessarily to *Elohim*. Their cry went up to *Elohim*, without their specifically directing it. And the text continues, "And *Elohim* heard their groaning and *Elohim* remembered his covenant..." (2:24), and the same with, "And *Elohim* saw the sons of Israel and *Elohim* knew" (2:25).

Up to this point we see only the use of *Elohim* in the language of the text. And the text continues with the encounter between Moses and the Almighty at the burning bush.

The Burning Bush

Moses, while shepherding the sheep of Jethro, his father-in-law (remember Jacob and Laban), took the sheep to the wilderness, "...and came to the mountain of *Elohim*, to Horeb" (3:1).

The text continues, "And the angel of *Y-H-V-H* appeared to him in the flame of fire out of the midst of a bush..." (3:2). This is the first time that the book of Exodus uses the title *Y-H-V-H*, and the reader who is tuned to the language of the text can figure that we are about to see the renewal of the connection between *Y-H-V-H* and the descendants of the house of Abraham.

Moses, who is in awe of "this great sight" (3:3), turns aside to see "why the bush is not burnt" (3:3). And the text continues, "And *Y-H-V-H* saw that he turned aside to see..." (3:4). Up to this point, we can see twice that the text brings to the reader's knowledge that *Y-H-V-H* is the one behind the events. And the text continues, "...and *Elohim* called to him out of the midst of the bush and said Moses, Moses and he said, here I am" (3:4). The reader knows that *Y-H-V-H* is the one who is 'running the show,' but to Moses *Y-H-V-H* appears as *Elohim*.

In Genesis we saw that the Almighty appeared to Abraham and Jacob, and within the appearance the text uses both titles – *Y-H-V-H* and *Elohim*. For

Abraham the text said, "…And *Y-H-V-H* appeared to Abram and said to him I am the Almighty G-d, walk before Me and be perfect. And I will make My covenant between Me and you, and will multiply you exceedingly. And Abram fell on his face, and *Elohim* talked to him saying" (Genesis 17:1-3). In this appearance the Almighty informs Abram of the change of his name and the covenant of circumcision.

We also saw for Jacob, "And *Elohim* said to Jacob, arise, go up to Beth-El and live there and make there an altar to the G-d who appeared to you when you fled from the face of Esau your brother" (35:1). And the reader knows that "the G-d who appeared to you when you fled…" is *Y-H-V-H* in chapter 28. In this appearance (35:10), the Almighty informs Jacob of the change of his name and his demand to build an altar to him.

We should note that the Almighty appeared to Isaac, but in this appearance there is no combination of the title *Y-H-V-H* and *Elohim*, "And *Y-H-V-H* appeared to him and said, do not go down to Egypt…" (26:2). Unlike the other two forefathers, when the Almighty changed their names, for Isaac there is no need to do so. He is the only forefather for whom the Almighty himself gave him a name even before his birth: "And *Elohim* said, Sarah your wife shall bear you a son and you shall call his name Isaac…" (17:19).

The Title *Y-H-V-H Elohim* in Exodus

In the description of creation in Genesis that starts with, "These are the *toldot* of the heavens and of the earth when they were created, in the day that *Y-H-V-H Elohim* made the earth and the heavens" (2:4), and ends with the expulsion of Adam from the Garden of Eden, "And *Y-H-V-H Elohim* sent him out from the Garden of Eden…" (3:23), the text uses the combination of the two titles as one name, *Y-H-V-H Elohim*. There is only one more place in the entire Torah where this title is used, in Exodus. After the plague of hail, Moses says to Pharaoh – "But as for you and your slaves, I know that you still do not fear *Y-H-V-H Elohim*" (Exodus 9:30).

These are the only two places in the five books of Moses in which the title *Y-H-V-H Elohim* is used, and therefore these two places are connected: the creation and the plague of hail in Egypt, which was a natural disaster (weather).

We should note that there are only four events in the entire five books of Moses where the text uses the verb *lehamtir* (to cause to rain).

- The creation account, "And every plant of the field before it was in the earth, and every herb of the field before it grew, for **Y-H-V-H Elohim** had not caused it to rain (*lo himtir*) upon the earth…" (Genesis 2:5)
- The destruction of Sodom, "And *Y-H-V-H* caused to rain (*himtir*) upon Sodom and Gomorrah brimstone and fire from *Y-H-V-H* out of heaven" (Genesis 19:24)
- The plague of hail, "Behold, tomorrow about this time I will cause to rain (*mamtir*) a very severe hail…" (Exodus 9:18), and "…and *Y-H-V-H* caused to rain (*vayamter*) hail upon the land of Egypt" (9:23)
- The delivery of manna, "And **Y-H-V-H** said to Moses, behold I am causing to rain (*mamtir*) bread from heaven for you…" (16:4)

It is no wonder that the plague of hail brought Pharaoh to admit, "…I have sinned this time; **Y-H-V-H** is righteous and I and my people are wicked" (9:27).

The Almighty says to Moses, "And I appeared to Abraham, to Isaac, and to Jacob, by the name of G-d Almighty (*El Shaddai*), and I was not known to them by my name *Y-H-V-H*" (Exodus 6:3). Indeed, the Almighty did appear to Abraham and Jacob by the title *El Shaddai* (G-d Almighty). But we know the Almighty did also appear to the forefathers by his title *Y-H-V-H*. The text quotes the Almighty saying to Abraham, "…I am *Y-H-V-H* who brought you out of Ur of the Chaldeans…" (Genesis 15:7). If so, how can the text say, "…and I was not known to them by my name *Y-H-V-H*?"

When Moses asks at the burning Bush, "…and they shall say to me what is his name, what shall I say to them?" (Exodus 3:13), the answer that Moses gets is not the title of *Y-H-V-H* (or in modern language, first name + last name), but something altogether different, "…I will be what I will be…" (Exodus 3:14). The Almighty answers Moses by giving his **nature**, his **character**, and not his title.

Language-wise, Genesis comes to describe to us the development of the connection between the Almighty and humanity. After the flood, the search was on to find who would be the 'flag bearer' of the **name** (nature, character) of the Almighty among humanity, and the winner in this 'competition' was Abraham and his descendants. The plagues of Egypt, described in Exodus, beyond coming to force Pharaoh to send the sons of Israel out of Egypt, had the objective to show the other nations, and in this case it was Egypt, that '*Y-H-V-H* the G-d of the Hebrews' appears not only to Abraham's family and his descendants, but also to the whole world, by declaring that the nation of Israel is his chosen. And indeed, we find in the description of the plagues that the text says the following:

- After the plague of the frogs, "…that you may know that there is no one like *Y-H-V-H* our G-d" (Exodus 8:6)
- Before the plague of the swarms of flies, "…that you may know that I am *Y-H-V-H* in the midst of the earth" (8:18)
- Before the plague of hail, "And for this I raised you up, to show you My power and that My **name** be proclaimed throughout all the earth" (9:16)

Y-H-V-H and *Elohim* Appear Together

In Exodus we find two places that the text uses both titles in the same place – *Y-H-V-H* and *Elohim* – at the burning bush, as we saw in verses 3:1 and 3:2, and at the revelation of Mount Sinai: "And *Elohim* spoke all these words saying I am *Y-H-V-H* your G-d…" (Exodus 20:1-2).

Back to the Burning Bush

After Moses is told "…take off your shoes from your feet…" (3:5), the Almighty 'introduced' himself to Moses, "…I am the G-d of your father, the G-d of Abraham, the G-d of Isaac, and the G-d of Jacob and Moses hid his face, for he was afraid to look upon the *Elohim*" (3:6). Even when the Almighty introduced himself as the G-d of the forefathers, Moses did not relate to the Almighty as *Y-H-V-H* but as *Elohim*. Still, Moses' response showed respect and fear of the Almighty. "And *Y-H-V-H* said I have surely seen…" (3:7). Moses' reaction of respect and fear 'encourages' the Almighty to appear to Moses as *Y-H-V-H*. The text brings us the Almighty's words spread over four verses, and ends with, "Come now, I will send you to Pharaoh…" (3:10). The text brings us Moses' refusal not only **content-wise**, "…Who am I that I should go to Pharaoh…" (3:11), but also **language-wise,** "...Moses said to the ***Elohim*...**" (3:11). Moses responds to *Elohim* and not to *Y-H-V-H*.

The Almighty promises Moses, "I will be with you" (3:12), but here as well, Moses' response, "And Moses said to the ***Elohim*...**" (3:13), and Moses asks for the name of the Almighty. Here, the text shows us the retreat of the Almighty, "And ***Elohim*** said to Moses, I will be what I will be, and he said, thus shall you say to the sons of Israel, I will be[136] has sent me to you" (3:14). Twice, Moses does not respond. Does the lack of response come from shock, or from misunderstanding? The lack of response by Moses brings the Almighty to guide Moses how to introduce the Almighty to the people,

> And ***Elohim*** said more to Moses, thus shall you say to the sons of Israel, *Y-H-V-H* the G-d of your fathers, the G-d of Abraham, the G-d of Isaac, and the G-d of Jacob, has sent me to you, this is my name forever, and this is my memorial to all generations. (3:15)

If we compare the initial 'introduction' of the Almighty to Moses in verse 6, to the one mentioned here in verse 15, we see an important addition. It is not only "...the G-d of your fathers, the G-d of Abraham, the G-d of Isaac, and the G-d of Jacob," but now it is "...***Y-H-V-H*** the G-d of your fathers, the G-d of Abraham, the G-d of Isaac, and the G-d of Jacob...." In the next verse the Almighty repeats this formula, and now in the guidance how to talk to the elders of Israel, "...***Y-H-V-H*** G-d of your fathers appeared to me, the G-d of Abraham, Isaac and Jacob..." (3:16). The Almighty's words are spread over eight verses (3:15-22). Moses responds, "And Moses answered and said, but behold they will not believe me, nor listen to my voice, for they will say, ***Y-H-V-H*** has not appeared to you" (4:1).

Even if Moses does not express resistance, and expresses lack of faith in the Israelites' ability to believe in his mission, still the text brings us a major change of language in Moses' words: this is the first time that Moses uses the title *Y-H-V-H*. From this point on, the title *Elohim* vanishes from the language of the text, and only the title *Y-H-V-H* is used. Later on, when the text brings us the Almighty's anger at Moses' refusal

---

[136] "I will be" in Hebrew is *A-H-Y-H*, which is similar to *Y-H-V-H*. While the first is in the first person (starting with the letter *A*) the second is in the third person (starting with the letter *Y*).

to go, still there is use of the title *Y-H-V-H*, "And the anger of **Y-H-V-H** was kindled against Moses…" (4:14). It is still *Y-H-V-H*, and not *Elohim*.

The fact that there is a connection between Moses' language and the language of the Almighty, as it is quoted by the text, shows us the close, intimate connection between Moses and the Almighty. We also learn that the Almighty appears as *Y-H-V-H* to a human of the sons of Israel (here it is Moses) only when the human himself uses *Y-H-V-H* and not *Elohim*. The language of the Almighty is influenced by the language of the human who approaches the Almighty.

The Exodus out of Egypt

> "And it came to pass when Pharaoh had sent the people away, that **Elohim** led them not through the way of the land of the Philistines, although that was near, for **Elohim** said, lest perhaps the people repent when they see war, and they return to Egypt. And **Elohim** led the people around through the way of the wilderness of the Red Sea, and the sons of Israel went up armed out of the land of Egypt. And Moses took the bones of Joseph with him, for he had solemnly sworn the sons of Israel saying, **Elohim** will surely visit you and you shall carry up my bones from here with you" (Exodus 13:17-19).

The section starts with the verb 'to send' (*beshalach*). The text does not deal with the sons of Israel 'coming out' of Egypt, but with Pharaoh sending them away. The section focuses on the time of departure, and the language of the text is *Elohim*. But when the text starts to describe the sons of Israel who are distancing themselves from Egypt, and their journey in the wilderness, it uses the title *Y-H-V-H*, "And **Y-H-V-H** went before them by day…" (13:21).

We see the same when they are by the Sea of Reeds,

> And the Egyptians shall know that I am **Y-H-V-H** when I have gotten honor over Pharaoh, over his chariots, and over his horsemen. And the angel of the **Elohim**, who went before the camp of Israel, moved and went behind them, and the pillar of the cloud went from before their face, and stood behind them. And it

came between the camp of the Egyptians and the camp of Israel… (14:18-20)

When the objective of the angel is to be a buffer between the Egyptians and the Israelites, either before them, to separate them from others who might be on the way ahead, or behind them, to separate them from the Egyptians, it is the angel of the *Elohim*.

The Israelites' Complaints

The first 'complaint' of the sons of Israel comes when they are standing by the Sea of Reeds:

> And Pharaoh drew near, and the sons of Israel lifted up their eyes and behold, the Egyptians marched after them, and they were very afraid, and the sons of Israel cried out to *Y-H-V-H*. And they said to Moses, because there were no graves in Egypt, have you taken us away to die in the wilderness? Why have you dealt thus with us, to carry us forth out of Egypt? Is not this the word that we did tell you in Egypt, saying, let us alone that we may serve the Egyptians? For it had been better for us to serve the Egyptians than that we should die in the wilderness. (14:10-12)

We find similar complaints later on in the journey in the wilderness, with the same words, more or less: it would have been better for us to serve the Egyptians than to die in the wilderness. The reaction to the complaint is dependent on the language of the complaint, as it is quoted by the text. In this case, the text says, "… and the sons of Israel cried out to *Y-H-V-H*" (14:10). And Moses responded, "And Moses said to the people, do not fear…" (14:13).

The next complaint is one month after the departure from Egypt, "…and all the congregation of the sons of Israel came to the wilderness of Sin, which is between Elim and Sinai, on the fifteenth day of the second month after their departing out of the land of Egypt" (16:1).

The text continues,

> And the sons of Israel said to them, let it be that we had died by the hand of *Y-H-V-H* in the land of Egypt, when we sat by the meat

pots, and when we did eat bread to the full, for you have brought us forth unto this wilderness to kill this whole assembly with hunger. (16:2-3)

And the Almighty's response was, "And **Y-H-V-H** said to Moses, behold I am causing to rain (*mamtir*) bread from heaven for you…" (16:4).

We see twice that the content of the complaint is not the reference point upon which the response of the Almighty or Moses is dependent. The fact that in both places the people are addressing *Y-H-V-H*, or use the title *Y-H-V-H* in their language, is enough to bring a response that is designed to address the issue presented in the complaint.

In the third complaint in Exodus, we do not find that the sons of Israel used the title *Y-H-V-H*. And indeed the text started the section by saying, "And the people quarreled with Moses…" (17:2). We should note that only Moses is mentioned in the text, without his brother Aaron.

And the text continues, "…give (*tenu*[137]) us water that we may drink…" (17:2). Even though the sons of Israel do not use the title *Y-H-V-H*, they still use the plural 'give us' and not the singular. By using the plural pronoun, as the text quotes the complaint, the sons of Israel recognize that Moses is not alone, and they actually address both Moses and the Almighty. And Moses indeed answers, "…why do you quarrel with **me**? Why do you test **Y-H-V-H**?" (17:2)

In continuing the complaint the text says, "And the people thirsted there for water, and the people complained against Moses, and said, why have you brought us up out of Egypt, to kill us and our children and our cattle with thirst" (17:3). Here, the complaint is addressed to Moses, and '**brought** us up' is in the singular and not in plural. At this point, Moses feels helpless, "And Moses cried to **Y-H-V-H** saying, what shall I do to this people? They are almost ready to stone me" (17:4).

The response of the Almighty addresses the lack of water,

> And **Y-H-V-H** said to Moses, go on before the people, and take with you the elders of Israel, and your staff with which you struck the Nile, take in your hand and go. Behold, I will stand before you

---

[137] *tenu* – this is the command form for the verb 'to give' in the second person **plural**.

there upon the rock in Horeb, and you shall strike the rock, and water shall come out of it, that the people may drink. (17:5-6)

The text starts the section by saying, "And the people quarreled with Moses…" and ends by saying, "And he called the name of the place Massah and Meribah…" (17:7). We should note that the complaint started as addressing both Moses and the Almighty together, and deteriorated to addressing only Moses. Still, the complaint produced a solution.

Summary

There are only three complaints mentioned in Exodus, and that is a very small sample. Still, we can see that when the complainants used the title *Y-H-V-H* with its meaning – accepting the authority of the Almighty – they received a solution to their complaint. In the only complaint in which the text attributes to it the title 'quarrel,' and at its end the text mentions that the place received the title 'test and quarrel' (*massah* and *meribah*), we still can see that the sons of Israel received a solution to their need. They did not use the title *Y-H-V-H*, but at the same time they did not express in their language any rebellion against the Almighty. This complaint, void of the title *Y-H-V-H*, can be classified as 'neutral.'

In the same place – Rephidim – that received the name 'test and quarrel,' we also see the war with Amalek, "And Amalek came and fought with Israel in Rephidim" (17:8). The text continues, "And Moses said to Joshua, choose for us men, and go out, fight with Amalek; tomorrow I will stand on the top of the hill with the staff of the *Elohim* in my hand" (17:9).

The fact is that the text connects, by proximity (the context), the complaint of lack of water and Amalek's appearance to fight Israel. Is there a linguistic connection between the fact that the sons of Israel did not use the title *Y-H-V-H* in their complaint, and the fact that Moses brought with him 'the staff of the *Elohim*' with him to the war?

The War With Amalek

If we compare the war with Amalek mentioned briefly in Exodus, to other wars mentioned in the Torah, we see one major difference. The war with Amalek starts with, "And Moses said to Joshua, choose for us men, and go out, fight with Amalek, tomorrow I will stand on the top of the hill and the staff of the ***Elohim*** in my hand" (Exodus 17:9). Moses included himself in conducting the war, and the 'staff of the ***Elohim***' is in his hand. And the text indeed says, "And it came to pass when Moses held up his hand, that Israel prevailed, and when he let down his hand, Amalek prevailed" (17:11).

Another war mentioned briefly is the war with the Canaanite king of Arad who was in the Negev, a war mentioned in the book of Numbers (21:1-3). There are few details of the war. The text brings us this war without the leader of the war, "And **Israel** vowed a vow to ***Y-H-V-H*** and said, if you will indeed deliver this people into my hand, then I will utterly destroy their cities..." (Numbers 21:2).

We find the same in the Israelite war with Sihon the Emorite king, "And Israel struck him with the edge of the sword, and possessed his land..." (Numbers 21:24). So it is with the war with Og the king of Bashan, where there are few details of conducting the war, "And they struck him and his sons, and all his people, until none was left alive, and they possessed his land" (Numbers 21:35). The fact that Moses was the 'commander-in-chief' is only expressed in the verse, "And ***Y-H-V-H*** said to Moses, fear him not, for I have delivered him into your hand and all his people..." (21:34).

When Moses is quoted in describing these two wars in Deuteronomy – Sihon and Og – the text does not give us any details on how the war was conducted. For Sihon, "And ***Y-H-V-H*** our G-d delivered him before us..." (Deuteronomy 2:33), and for Og, "And ***Y-H-V-H*** our G-d delivered into our hands Og also..." (3:3).

On the other hand, the most talked-about war is the war with Midian, mentioned in Numbers: "And Moses sent them to the war, a thousand for every tribe, them and Phinehas the son of Eleazar the priest, to the war, with the holy instruments and in his hand the trumpets to blow" (Numbers 31:6). And at the conclusion of the war, the text says, "And they brought the captives and the booty and the plunder to Moses and Eleazar the priest and to the congregation of the sons of Israel to the camp..." (31:12).

Moses was not personally involved in the war. And the text gives a very detailed report of the plunder and how it was divided between the warriors and the tribe of Levi.

In summary, the war with Amalek is the only war in which Moses takes active part in conducting the war, and the text says that Moses' behavior influenced the success of the Israelites. This is also the war in which Moses takes the 'staff of *Elohim*' with him to the battlefield.

The Appearance of Jethro

The next event mentioned in Exodus where the title *Elohim* and the title *Y-H-V-H* are both in use is in the description of the visit that Jethro, Moses' father-in-law, paid to Moses in the desert.

If we examine the structure of the book of Exodus, we can see that the appearance of Jethro is right before the Revelation of Mount Sinai. After the revelation the book continues with a section that is clearly 'out-of-sequence,' chapters 21, 22 and 23, dealing with the laws about behavior between humans. These chapters could have easily been placed anywhere else in the Torah, for example, in the book Numbers, or even better, in the book Deuteronomy that is full of tort law. Indeed, we see that chapter 24 continues directly after the revelation at Mount Sinai, "And to Moses He said, come up to *Y-H-V-H*, you and Aaron, Nadab and Abihu, and seventy of the elders of Israel, and bow down from far away" (Exodus 24:1). Later in the chapter we find, "And *Y-H-V-H* said to Moses, come up to me into the mountain and be there and I will give you the tablets of stone and the Torah and the commandment which I have written that you may teach them" (24:12). The text continues with Moses going up the mountain for forty days and forty nights.

Examining the time line, we can see in the book Numbers that Moses addresses his father-in-law and asks him to remain with the sons of Israel. This appeal comes right before the sons of Israel departed from the 'Mountain of *Y-H-V-H*.' The text says, "And when you go with us, that whatever goodness *Y-H-V-H* shall benefit us, we will benefit you. And they journeyed from the mountain of *Y-H-V-H*..." (Numbers 10:32-33). Therefore, the text places the visit of Jethro from before the revelation until the departure from Mount Sinai.

At the end of the appearance of Jethro mentioned in Exodus, the text says, "And Moses sent his father-in-law away and he went his way to his land" (Exodus 18:27). Take into consideration that Mount Sinai, the place where the Almighty revealed Himself to Moses at the burning bush, was not far away from Jethro's location, "And Moses shepherded the flock of Jethro his father-in-law, the priest of Midian, and he led the flock into the wilderness and came to the mountain of *Elohim* to Horeb" (Exodus 3:1). It is quite unlikely that Moses took the flock very far away from where they lived. Quite likely they were still in relatively close proximity. Jethro could have easily been able to come and go while the Israelites were camping by Mount Sinai.

We should note that when Moses' father-in-law comes to visit Moses, he is introduced by the text as 'Jethro.' No different from the way the text introduces him at the beginning of Exodus, when Moses settled in Midian, helped Jethro's daughters at the well, and later on married Jethro's daughter, Zipporah. However, before his departure from the 'Mountain of Y-H-V-H,' Moses' father-in-law is introduced as "And Moses said to Hobab, the son of Reuel the Midianite, Moses' father-in-law..." (Numbers 10:29).

Not only did his name change, but also his title. In Exodus he is introduced as 'the priest of Midian;' in Numbers he is introduced only as 'the Midianite,' and the text omitted the title 'priest.' These two changes in language, taking place at the same time, change of name and change of title, should signal that although he didn't join the sons of Israel as a full member, he still accepted the authority of Y-H-V-H in his life, and therefore decided to quit his 'job' as 'the priest of Midian.' Another point that supports this 'suspicion' is Jethro's own words, "...but I will go to my land and my homeland" (Numbers 10:30), words that are identical to Abraham's words to his slave, "But you shall go to my land and to my homeland..." (Genesis 24:4). For the text to use the exact same words for Jethro as the words used by the first forefather of the nation is quite remarkable. We should note that the book Numbers does not say Jethro indeed went back to his land and his homeland, a fact mentioned only in Exodus.

Back to Jethro's Visit

The fact that Jethro is not from the sons of Israel, although related to one of them, should bring us to expect that the title *Elohim* should be in use, and quite frequently.

The text starts the sequence of events before Jethro's journey to the camp of the Israelites, "And Jethro, the priest of Midian, Moses' father-in-law heard of all that **Elohim** had done for Moses, and for Israel his people, that **Y-H-V-H** had brought Israel out of Egypt" (Exodus 18:1). While the beginning of the verse talks from Jethro's point of view, and therefore *Elohim* is in use, the second part is the text's point of view, and as such *Y-H-V-H* is in use.

The text starts the sequence of events of Jethro's visit, "And Jethro, Moses' father-in-law, came with his sons and his wife to Moses to the wilderness where he camped there at the mountain of **Elohim**" (Exodus 18:5). Upon his arrival, Moses tells his father-in-law all the great events, "…all that **Y-H-V-H** had done to Pharaoh and to Egypt…" (18:8). And as Moses uses the title *Y-H-V-H*, so does Jethro, "And Jethro rejoiced for all of the goodness which **Y-H-V-H** had done to Israel…" (18:9), "And Jethro said, Blessed be **Y-H-V-H**…" (18:10), and, "Now I know that **Y-H-V-H** is greater than all the **elohim**…" (18:11). This last verse does not rule out the existence of other *elohim*, but only praises *Y-H-V-H* as being greater than the others. And indeed, the text continues, "And Jethro, Moses' father-in-law, took a burnt offering and sacrifices to **Elohim**, and Aaron came, and all the elders of Israel to eat bread with Moses' father-in-law before the **Elohim**" (18:12). It can be understood that Jethro would offer burnt offering and sacrifices to *Elohim*, as he is not committed to *Y-H-V-H* the G-d of Israel, but we should note that Aaron and the elders of Israel come to eat bread before *Elohim* and not *Y-H-V-H*.

When Jethro talks with Moses about the way Moses deals with the people, we see copious use of the title *Elohim*, not only as a quote from Jethro, but also as a quote by Moses, "And Moses said to his father-in-law for the people come to me to inquire of **Elohim**" (18:15). Jethro responds with, "…I will give you advice and **Elohim** shall be with you, you should be for the people in front of **Elohim**, and you bring the things to **Elohim**" (18:19). When Jethro gives guidelines how to choose judges, he is quoted as saying, "and you should see from the people able men, fearing

Elohim…" (18:21), and Jethro ends his advice by saying, If you shall do this thing, *Elohim* will command you and you shall be able to endure…" (18:23).

And the description ends with, "And Moses chose able men from all Israel…" (18:25). There is a lot said about the list that Jethro gave, "able men, fearing *Elohim*, men of truth, hating unjust gain" while Moses chose only by the first characteristic, "able men." One might ask why Moses. couldn't find *Elohim*-fearing people. Or maybe Moses didn't want *Elohim*-fearing people, but rather *Y-H-V-H*-fearing people.

The Sinai Revelation

There are four times in which the Almighty appeared to the first Israelites with both titles *Elohim* and *Y-H-V-H* in the same account, and at times even in the same sentence. The four incidents are (1) the appearance to Abraham to inform him of the change of his name and informing him of the covenant of circumcision, (2) the appearance to Jacob informing him of his change of name from Jacob to Israel and commanding him to build an altar, (3) the appearance to Moses at the burning bush, and (4) the revelation at Mount Sinai. We have discussed the first three already.

For the revelation at Mount Sinai, the text says, "And Moses went up to the *Elohim* and *Y-H-V-H* called to him from the mountain saying…" (Exodus 19:3). Moses returned to the elders of the people:

- "…and laid before them all these words which *Y-H-V-H* commanded him" (19:7)
- "And all the people answered together and said, all that *Y-H-V-H* has spoken we will do…" (19:8)
- "…Moses returned the words of the people to *Y-H-V-H*' (19:8)
- "And *Y-H-V-H* said to Moses…" (19:9)
- "…and Moses told the words of the people to *Y-H-V-H*' (19:9)
- "And *Y-H-V-H* said to Moses…" (19:10)
- "…for the third day *Y-H-V-H* will come down in the sight of all the people upon Mount Sinai" (19:11)

Until now we saw several consecutive verses in which the text used the title *Y-H-V-H*, but as we get closer to the revelation itself, the language changes and both titles, *Elohim* and *Y-H-V-H*, are used together,

- "And Moses brought the people out of the camp towards the ***Elohim*** and they stood at the lower part of the mount" (19:17),
- "And Mount Sinai was altogether in smoke because ***Y-H-V-H*** descended upon it in fire…" (19:18),
- "And the voice of the shofar sounded long and became louder and louder, Moses spoke and the ***Elohim*** answered him by a voice" (19:19),
- "And ***Y-H-V-H*** came down upon Mount Sinai, on the top of the mountain, and ***Y-H-V-H*** called Moses up to the top of the mountain…" (19:20),
- "And ***Y-H-V-H*** said to Moses…" (19:21),
- "…lest they break through to ***Y-H-V-H*** to gaze…" (19:21),
- "And Moses said to ***Y-H-V-H*** …" (19:23),
- "And ***Y-H-V-H*** said to him…" (19:24), and,
- "…let not the priests and the people break through to come up to ***Y-H-V-H***…" (19:24).

The Ten Commandments start with, "And ***Elohim*** spoke all these words saying. I am ***Y-H-V-H*** your G-d…" (20:1-2). At the end of the Ten Commandments we find the title *Elohim* as well, "And they said to Moses, speak with us, and we will hear, but let not ***Elohim*** speak with us, lest we die" (20:16), "And Moses said to the people, fear not, for the ***Elohim*** has come to test you…" (20:17), and, "And the people stood far away, and Moses drew near to the thick darkness where the ***Elohim*** was" (20:18).

If we put together all the verses in which the title *Elohim* is in use, we get the following picture:

- "And Moses went up to the ***Elohim***…" (Exodus 19:3),
- "And Moses brought the people out of the camp towards the ***Elohim***…" (19:17),
- "…Moses spoke and the ***Elohim*** answered him by a voice" (19:19),
- "And ***Elohim*** spoke all these words saying." (20:1),
- "but let not ***Elohim*** speak with us, lest we die" (20:16),
- "…for the ***Elohim*** has come to test you…" (20:17), and
- "…and Moses drew near to the thick darkness where the ***Elohim*** was" (20:18).

In these seven verses the title *Elohim* appears in the context of the Almighty's appearance – 'went up,' 'towards,' 'come,' and 'drew near' – the act of getting closer prior to the Almighty's appearance itself, and the appearance itself – 'answered him' and 'spoke.' Most of the use of the title '*Y-H-V-H*' occurs while Moses is preparing the people for the revelation to come, and in the first verse of the Ten Commandments, "I am *Y-H-V-H*…," a verse in which the Almighty introduces Himself to the people of Israel. However, the actual communication between the Almighty and the people is using the title *Elohim*.

When the book Exodus brings us the description of Moses' ascension to the mountain to receive the stone tablets, we find the title "And he gave to Moses, when he finished talking with him upon Mount Sinai two tablets of testimony, tablets of stone, written by the finger of *Elohim*" (31:18), and, "…the tablets were the work of *Elohim*, and the writing was the writing of *Elohim*, engraved upon the tablets" (32:16).

We also find, "And upon the nobles of the sons of Israel he laid not his hand, and they saw the *Elohim* and ate and drank" (24:11).

The idea that the title *Elohim* is in use for the appearance of the Almighty is also manifested in conjunction with the name of Mount Sinai. The title 'the mountain of Elohim' appears several times in Exodus. When Aaron goes towards his brother Moses, the text says, "…and he went and met him in the mountain of *Elohim*…" (4:27). When Jethro comes to visit Moses, "And Jethro, Moses' father-in-law, came with his sons and his wife into the wilderness where he encamped at the mountain of *Elohim*" (18:5). When Moses goes up the mountain to receive the stone tablets, "And Moses rose up, and his servant Joshua, and Moses went up to the mountain of *Elohim*" (24:13). In the appearance of the Almighty at the burning bush we find the combination of 'mountain' and *Elohim* although in a reversed order, "…and this shall be a sign to you, that I have sent you. When you have brought the people out of Egypt, you shall serve *Elohim* on this *mountain*" (3:12).

In the first book of Kings we find that Elijah went to the mountain of Horeb, "And he arose, and ate and drank, and went in the strength of that meal forty days and forty nights to the mountain of *Elohim*, Horeb" (1 Kings 19:8).

In contrast, the title 'mountain of *Y-H-V-H*' appears in the Tanach in regard to Mount Moriah, the Temple Mount, the mountain upon which Abraham bound his son Isaac to the altar:

- "…as it is said to this day, in the mountain of **Y-H-V-H** it shall be seen" (Genesis 22:14)
- "…to come to the mountain of **Y-H-V-H**, to the Rock of Israel" (Isaiah 30:29)
- "And many nations hall come and say, come, and let us go up to the mountain of **Y-H-V-H**…" (Micah 4:2)
- "…and the mountain of **Y-H-V-H** of hosts the holy mountain" (Zechariah 8:3)
- "Who shall ascend in the mountain of **Y-H-V-H**…" (Psalms 24:3)

In the entire Tanach we find the title 'mountain of *Y-H-V-H*' related to Mount Sinai in only one place, "And they journeyed from the mountain of **Y-H-V-H** three days' journey…" (Numbers 10:33). Mount Sinai receives the title 'mountain of *Y-H-V-H*' only after the end of the appearance of *Elohim* at the top of the mountain, when the sons of Israel depart the mountain, 'And they journeyed from the mountain of **Y-H-V-H** …'

The Sinai Revelation – Summary

Language-wise, the Sinai revelation is no different from the binding of Isaac on the altar. Language-wise, each of these two events constitutes a pivotal point in the language of the text. In Genesis we see the use of both titles – *Y-H-V-H* and *Elohim* in Abraham's life until the binding of Isaac, and after the binding only the title *Y-H-V-H* is in use. We see the same in Exodus. Before the Sinai revelation we see both titles – *Y-H-V-H* and *Elohim* – and after the revelation we have only the use of *Y-H-V-H* in the language of the text. The title *Elohim* appears at times, but its appearance is explained easily by the sequence of events in the surrounding text.

Therefore, it can be said that **language-wise**, the book Exodus is structurally a replica of the book Genesis.

Chapters 21-23

This section starts with "And these are the judgments which **you** shall set before them" (Exodus 21:1). It should be noted that this 'you' starts a section including three chapters, 21, 22, and 23, in which Moses is not mentioned. This section ends with "And to Moses he said…" (24:1). Note that by starting the verse with "And to Moses he said," and not with the regular formula "And *Y-H-V-H* spoke to Moses saying," and by putting Moses before the speaker, the text comes, quite likely, to compare it to what was said in the preceding verses, which was *not* said to Moses. This should bring us again to wonder to whom the 'you' in the beginning verse of chapter 21 refers.

As we saw earlier, these three chapters seem like they are 'out-of-sequence.' Out-of-sequence information is only 'out-of-sequence' for the reader, but it is 'in-sequence' for the text. For the text, it is 'in-sequence' by the mere fact that it is located there. Therefore, we need to check what the connection is among these three chapters located between the Mount Sinai Revelation and Moses ascending to the mountain in, "And to Moses he said, come up to *Y-H-V-H*…" (24:1).

At first glance, it seems that there is a connection, at least language-wise. The revelation at Mount Sinai, the appearance of the Almighty to the people at the top of the mountain, reflects the transfer from using both titles (*Y-H-V-H* and *Elohim*) **before** the revelation, to using only *Y-H-V-H* **after** the revelation.

The three chapters, 21, 22, and 23, show the use of both titles:

- "And his master shall bring him to the *Elohim*…" (21:6),
- "If the thief is not found, then the master of the house shall be brought to the *Elohim*…" (22:7),
- "…to the *Elohim* shall come the cause of both parties, and who the *Elohim* shall condemn, he shall pay double to his fellow man" (22:8),
- "The oath of *Y-H-V-H* shall be between them both…" (22:10),
- "He who sacrifices to the *Elohim* shall be destroyed except for *Y-H-V-H*" (22:19),
- "You shall not revile *Elohim*, nor curse the ruler of your people" (22:27), and
- "Three times in the year all your males shall appear before the master *Y-H-V-H*" (23:17).

Note: This book focuses on Genesis. The sections in Genesis that are out-of-sequence will be dealt with later in this analysis. The out-of-sequence chapters 21-23 located in Exodus are not the focus of this analysis, and will have to wait for some other time to be dealt with. Saying that, one should recognize that the fact that this section is 'out-of-sequence' should bring us to conclude that it is extremely important.

Building the Tabernacle

The only place in Exodus after the Sinai revelation in which we find the title *Elohim* is in regard to Bezalel, the 'architect' who built the tabernacle, "See, I have called by name Bezalel the son of Uri, the son of Hur, of the tribe of Judah. And I have filled him with the spirit of ***Elohim***, in wisdom, and in understanding, and in knowledge, and all kinds of workmanship" (Exodus 31:2-3), and, "And he has filled him with spirit of ***Elohim***, in wisdom, in understanding, and in knowledge, and in every kind of workmanship" (Exodus 35:31).

When we come to explain the rare use of the title *Elohim* we should remember that language-wise, the text compares the building of the tabernacle to the creation of the world. The creation described at the beginning of Genesis ends with,

> Thus the heavens and the earth were **finished**, and all the host of them. And *Elohim* **finished** on the seventh day His **work** that he had **made**, and He rested on the seventh day from all His **work** that He had **made**. And *Elohim* **blessed** the seventh day, and sanctified it, because that in it He had rested from all His **work** which *Elohim* created to **make**. (Genesis 2:1-3)

The building of the tabernacle ends with,

> Thus all the work of the tabernacle of the Tent of Meeting **finished**, and the sons of Israel did according to all that *Y-H-V-H* commanded Moses, so did they," and, "And Moses looked upon all the **work** and, behold, they had **made** it as *Y-H-V-H* had commanded, so had they **made** it, and Moses **blessed** them. (39:43)

We find four verbs used in both places – the creation and the building of the tabernacle – 'to make,' 'to work,' 'to bless,' and 'to finish.'

Linguistically, the creation of the world and the building of the tabernacle are equivalent; therefore, if there was a period of chaos before the creation, then the period before the building of the tabernacle can be considered chaotic as well. "And the earth was without form, and void, and darkness was upon the face of the deep. And a spirit of *Elohim* is hovering upon the face of the water" (Genesis 1:2). The spirit of *Elohim* exists before the creation, and the title of *Elohim* is present before the revelation and building of the tabernacle.

Besides the period before the creation, the phrase 'spirit of *Elohim*' appears two other times. The first is when the text quotes Pharaoh who is overwhelmed after Joseph solved his dream for him, "And Pharaoh said to his slaves, can we find such a man whom the **spirit of *Elohim*** is in him?" (Genesis 41:38). The second place is in Balaam, "And Balaam lifted up his eyes and he saw Israel dwelling according to his tribes, and the **spirit of *Elohim*** came upon him" (Numbers 24:2). In both places the text relates to two people who are not from 'the sons of Israel.'

It is interesting to note that in the first two times in which Balaam blesses the Israelites, the text quotes him as using the title *Y-H-V-H*. In the first place, "…or how shall I be angry when *Y-H-V-H* has not been angry" (Numbers 23:8). In the second blessing, "He has not seen iniquity in Jacob, nor has he seen perverseness in Israel, *Y-H-V-H* his G-d with him, and the trumpet blast of a king is among them" (Numbers 23:21). In contrast, in the third blessing, which started with the 'spirit of *Elohim*' descending upon him, the title *Y-H-V-H* does not appear in his language. On the other hand, in the third blessing we find a component that does not appear in the first two blessings, "How goodly are your tents O Jacob and your dwellings O Israel" (Numbers 24:5). When Balaam speaks of the structures that the Israelites live in, 'tents' and 'dwellings,' the title *Elohim* appears in the language of the text.

We should remember the words of Noah after the incident with his son Ham, "*Elohim* shall enlarge Japheth, and he shall live in the tents of Shem…" (Genesis 9:27). When there is a need to build a structure (the tabernacle), a profession that the descendants of Shem did not excel in, there was a need for the 'spirit of *Elohim*.' The same is true for the building of the temple later on, when King Solomon needed the help of Hiram the king of Tyre.

The Sin of the Golden Calf

The sin of the golden calf brought a civil war in which the tribe of Levi killed three thousand people (Exodus 32:28). Aaron, whom the text says was the one to make the mask of the calf, the symbol of idolatry, was not punished. The most he received was a 'reprimand,' according to the text, "And Moses saw that the people were exposed[138] for Aaron had made them exposed to their shame among their enemies" (Exodus 32:25).

To understand why Aaron was not punished, we should go back to the beginning. When the people asked Aaron, "Arise, make us ***Elohim***…" (32:1), Aaron responds to them by saying, "…take off the golden earrings which are in your ears of your wives, of your sons, and of your daughters, and bring them to me" (32:2)

Golden earrings are mentioned for the first time in Genesis as related to idolatry. After the incident with Dinah in Shechem, Jacob said to the people of his household, "…put away the foreign gods that are among you, and purify and change your garments" (Genesis 35:2), and the text continued with, "And they gave to Jacob all the foreign gods which were in their hand, **and all the rings which were in their ears**, and Jacob hid them under the oak which was by Shechem" (35:4). One way or another, earrings served in idol worshipping.

In the 'out-of-sequence' section in Exodus (chapters 21-23) discussed earlier, the text says, "And if the slave shall plainly say, I love my master, my wife, and my children, I will not go out free. And his master shall bring him to the ***Elohim*** and he shall also bring him to the door, or to the door post, and his master shall bore his **ear** through with an awl, and he shall serve him forever" (Exodus 21:5-6). The verse in which the text uses the title ***Elohim*** is the same verse in which the text speaks of boring the ear, a practice that was related to idolatry.

---

[138] The word used in Hebrew is *pharuaa*, and later *phearaoh*. This verb is used by the text to describe the priest who exposes the hair of the woman suspected of adultery. Note that the letters used in the text are identical to the letters creating the word *Pharaoh*, the king of Egypt.

When Aaron heard the demand to make *Elohim* for the people, he used the opportunity to collect from them all the jewelry that testified in the past to idolatry. If he had to make *Elohim*, then at least he would remove from them the foreign gods that were among them, exactly as Jacob did in Shechem.

Moreover, once the golden calf was made, the text says, "And Aaron saw it, and he built an altar before it, and Aaron called and said, tomorrow is a feast to *Y-H-V-H*" (32:5). Aaron did everything for the sake of *Y-H-V-H*. As the sons of Israel were not punished when they complained if they used the name of *Y-H-V-H*, so Aaron was not punished.

The Book of Numbers

The first complaint mentioned is in regard to the people who could not take part in the sacrifice of Passover,

> …and they came near before Moses and before Aaron on that day. And those men said to him, we are impure by the dead body of a man, why are we kept back, so that we many not offer an offering to *Y-H-V-H* in his appointed time among the sons of Israel? (Numbers 9:6-7)

Not only do the complaining men use the title *Y-H-V-H*, but the text also starts with 'they came near.' Just the use of this verb should tell us that the intent of the men was to give respect to Moses. And, indeed, Moses responded by saying, "Stand, and I will hear what *Y-H-V-H* will command concerning you" (9:8).

We can see the same with the daughters of Zelophehad, "And the daughters of Zelophehad **came near**…" (Numbers 27:1), "And they **stood before** Moses…" (27:2), and the preposition 'before' testifies to their acceptance of his authority. And the text quotes the language of the women, "Our father died in the wilderness and he was not in the company of those who gathered themselves together against *Y-H-V-H* in the company of Korach…" (27:3). We see that they use the title *Y-H-V-H*. And thus, "And Moses brought[139] their case before *Y-H-V-H*" (27:5).

---

[139] Note that the word used in Hebrew to indicate that the daughters of Zelophehad 'came near' (*vatikravnah*) to Moses is the same word the text used to say that Moses brought (*vayakrev*) their case before the Almighty.

Unlike the impure men who could not take part in the Passover sacrifice, and the complaint of Zelophehad's daughters, the text starts the account of the sons of Gad and the sons of Reuben in a different way:

> The sons of Gad and the sons of Reuben **came** and spoke to Moses, and to Eleazar the priest, and to the princes of the congregation saying. Ataroth, and Dibon, and Jazer, and Nimrah, and Heshbon, and Elealeh, and Shebam, and Nebo, and Beon. The land which *Y-H-V-H* struck before the congregation of Israel is a land of cattle, and your slaves have cattle. (Numbers 32:2-4)

Even though the text does not use the verb 'to come near' but instead uses the verb 'to come,' we still see that they use the title *Y-H-V-H*, and therefore the response is a reprimand, but it is not a penalty. After reprimanding them, the text continues, "And they came near to him and said, we will build sheepfolds here for our cattle and cities for our little ones. And we will go ready armed…" (32:16-17). 'And they came near' should remind us of Judah who 'came near' to Joseph (Genesis 44:18). As Judah approached Joseph with the objective of reaching a meeting of the minds, so here the fact that the sons of Reuben and Gad came near indicated that they were willing to go along with Moses' demands.

There are other complaints. For example,

> And the people complained evil in the ears of *Y-H-V-H*, and *Y-H-V-H* heard and his anger was kindled, and the fire of *Y-H-V-H* burnt among them, and consumed in the outlying parts of the .camp. And the people cried to Moses, and Moses prayed to *Y-H-V-H* and the fire quenched. And he called the name of the place *Taberah*[140] because the fire of *Y-H-V-H* burnt among them. (Numbers 11:1-3).

The text does not say what the complaint was about, but the text tells us that they complained in 'the ears of *Y-H-V-H*.' In fact, this complaint brought the anger of *Y-H-V-H*, and the fire of *Y-H-V-H*, but the text does not say if there were any casualties. And if the text does not say it, as it does in other places, it is quite likely that there were no casualties.

Another complaint:

---

[140] *Taberah* – 'fire starting.'

And the mixed multitude that was among them had a strong craving, and also the sons of Israel went back to crying, and said, who shall give us meat to eat? We remember the fish that we ate in Egypt for nothing, the cucumbers, and the melons, and the leeks, and the onions, and the garlic. And now our soul is dried away, there is nothing at all, beside this manna before our eyes. (Numbers 11:4-6)

This complaint, of lack of meat to eat, does not use the title *Y-H-V-H*. One can classify it as neutral – not for *Y-H-V-H*, and not against Him. And the response of *Y-H-V-H* and Moses was, "…and the anger of **Y-H-V-H** was kindled greatly and it was bad in Moses' eyes" (11:10), but the people do not get punished for their complaint. The opposite is true. The complaint brings a solution,

And say to the people, sanctify yourselves for tomorrow, and you shall eat meat, for you have wept in the ears of **Y-H-V-H** saying, who shall give us meat to eat, for it was well with us in Egypt, and **Y-H-V-H** will give you meat and you shall eat. (11:18)

Another complaint, after the sin of the spies:

And all the sons of Israel complained against Moses and against Aaron, and the whole congregation said to them, let us die in the land of Egypt or die in this wilderness. And why has **Y-H-V-H** brought us to this land to fall by the sword, that our wives and our little ones should be a prey, were it not better for us to return to Egypt? (14:2-3)

The text uses the title *Y-H-V-H* for the complaint. Moses' response is, "And Moses and Aaron fell on their faces before all the assembly of the congregation of the sons of Israel" (14:5).

We find two additional complaints, and both of them by relatives of Moses. The first is the complaint of Miriam and Aaron,

And Miriam and Aaron spoke against Moses because of the Cushite woman whom he had married, for he had married a Cushite woman. And they said has **Y-H-V-H** indeed spoken only by Moses? Has he not spoken also by us? And *Y-H-V-H* heard it. (12:1-2)

The language of the text uses the title *Y-H-V-H*, and Miriam received a relatively light punishment, "...let her be shut out from the camp seven days, and after that let her be returned" (12:14).

The second complaint is the complaint of Korach,

> And they gathered together against Moses and against Aaron, and said to them, you take too much upon you, seeing all the congregation is holy, every one of them, and *Y-H-V-H* is among them, and why then do you raise yourselves up above the congregation of *Y-H-V-H?* (16:3)

The language of the complaint uses the title *Y-H-V-H*, and it is no different from the complaint of the people after the sin of the spies. And Moses' response is the same, "And Moses heard and fell upon his face" (16:4). Moses addresses Korach,

> Does it seem but a small thing to you that the G-d of Israel separated you from the congregation of Israel, to bring you near to Himself to do the service of the tabernacle of *Y-H-V-H* and to stand before the congregation to minister to them? And he has brought you near to Him, and all your brothers, the sons of Levi with you, and do you also seek the priesthood? Therefore you and all your congregation gathered against *Y-H-V-H*, and what is Aaron that you complain against him? (16:9-11)

At this point, the text does not bring us Korach's response. It would be an interesting exercise to guess what the course of events would have been if the complaint were to have ended at this stage.

The text continues and we see an escalation, not by Korach but by Dathan and Abiram,

> And Moses sent to call Dathan and Abiram, the sons of Eliab, and they said, we will not come up. Is it a small thing that you have brought us out of a land that flows with milk and honey, to kill us

in the wilderness, that you also make yourself a ruler over us? (16:12-13)

Not only do Dathan and Abiram not use the title *Y-H-V-H*, as Korach did, but they accuse Moses of a personal attempt to grab power, without any mention of *Y-H-V-H*. This escalation brought upon the dramatic event in which the earth opened and swallowed them. We should note that later the text says, "And the sons of Korach did not die" (26:11).

After the punishment of Korach and his congregation the text brings us another complaint, "On the next day all the congregation of the sons of Israel complained against Moses and against Aaron saying, you have killed the people of *Y-H-V-H*" (17:6). Although their language uses the title *Y-H-V-H*, still they relate to Moses as an outsider, not one of the 'people of *Y-H-V-H*.' And later a plague starts and strikes the people.

There are two additional complaints about lack of water, and the response to each is very different. We will start with the second one mentioned in Numbers,

> ...and the soul of the people was diminished by the journey. And the people spoke against **Elohim** and Moses, why have you brought us out of Egypt to die in the wilderness? For there is no bread, nor is there any water, and our soul loathes this light bread. And **Y-H-V-H** sent into the people the venomous serpents, and they bit the people, and many people of Israel died. And the people came to Moses and said, we have sinned, for we have spoken against **Y-H-V-H** and you, pray to **Y-H-V-H**, and Moses prayed for the people." (Numbers 21:4-7)

This is the only complaint that the text quotes the people using the title *Elohim*, and indeed the response was swift and harsh, and does not deal with the substance of the complaint. Just the punishment is mentioned, "...And **Y-H-V-H** sent into the people the venomous serpents." When the people repent and say that they are sorry, the text quotes them as using the title *Y-H-V-H*, "...we have sinned, for we have spoken against **Y-H-V-H** and you..." (21:7).

Hitting the Rock

In contrast, another complaint produced many questions as to the punishment Moses received,

> And the people quarreled with Moses, and spoke saying, let us die with our brothers who died before *Y-H-V-H*. And why have you brought the congregation of *Y-H-V-H* into this wilderness, that we and our cattle should die there? (Numbers 20:3-4)

In the language of the complaint we find twice the title *Y-H-V-H*. And the response of the Almighty is,

> Take the staff and gather the assembly together you and Aaron your brother, and speak to the rock before their eyes, and it shall give forth its water, and you shall bring out for them water and you should cause the congregation and their beasts to drink.[141] (20:8)

The instructions that Moses received came to answer the real need of the people for water. And the question is: what is the difference between a similar complaint mentioned in Exodus, when Moses was instructed to 'hit' the rock? And then there is another question. If Moses is instructed to speak to the rock, why is he instructed to take the staff with him?

The Timing

The complaint in Exodus starts with, "And all the congregation of the sons of Israel journeyed from the wilderness of Sin, to their journeys according to the commandments of *Y-H-V-H* and camped in Rephidim, and there was no water for the people to drink" (Exodus 17:1). The book Numbers brings us the order of the journeys:

> …and passed in the sea into the wilderness, and went three days journey in the wilderness of Etham, and camped in Marah. And they journeyed from Marah and came to Elim, and in Elim were twelve fountains of water, and seventy palm trees and they camped there. And they journeyed from Elim and camped by the Red Sea.

---

[141] 'Cause to drink' in Hebrew is one word. As the verb to 'eat' is what one does, the verb to 'feed' is 'causing one to eat,' or, actually bringing the food to his/her mouth. In Hebrew these two verbs 'to eat' and 'to feed' are two different forms of the same verb. The same applies with 'drinking;' the verb to 'cause to drink' is the equivalent of 'feeding' food.

And they journeyed from the Red Sea and camped in the wilderness of Sin. And they journeyed from the wilderness of Sin and camped in Dophkah. And they journeyed from Dophkah and camped in Alush. And they journeyed from Alush and camped in Rephidim, and there was no water there for the people to drink. And they journeyed from Rephidim and camped in the wilderness of Sinai. (Numbers 33:8-15)

By the order of the journeys, Rephidim appears before the wilderness of Sinai. If so, the complaint mentioned in Exodus was **before** the revelation of Mount Sinai, while the complaint in Numbers is **after** the revelation of Mount Sinai.

We should not forget that the Sinai Revelation is a major milepost in the language of the text. Before the Sinai Revelation we find both titles in use – *Y-H-V-H* and *Elohim* – and after the Sinai Revelation we find almost completely the title *Y-H-V-H*, and where the title *Elohim* appears, it can be explained easily by the location in the sentence, or the sequence of events.

The Instructions

> "Take the staff and **gather** the congregation together
> you and Aaron your brother…" (Numbers 20:8).

To Gather People

The noun *kahal* in Hebrew is translated 'assembly.' In Modern Hebrew *kahal* is 'assembly' as well (many people get together in an auditorium for a lecture, and the lecturer addresses the *kahal*). It also stands for 'crowd.' Since in Hebrew words are connected, the noun *kahal* has also a related verb *lehakhil* or 'to assemble the assembly,' or 'to gather people together.'

The verb *lehakhil* appears several times in the Torah. Five times it appears during complaints in the desert:

- In the sin of the golden calf "And the people saw that Moses delayed to come down from the mountain, the people gathered themselves (*vayikahalu*) on Aaron…" (Exodus 32:1).
- In the Korach rebellion, "And they gathered themselves together (*vayikahalu*) on Moses and Aaron…" (Numbers 16:3),

- "and Korach gathered (*vayakhel*) on them all the congregation…" (16:19),
- "And it came to pass when the congregation was gathered (*behikahel*) on Moses and Aaron…" (17:7)
- And in this complaint about the water, "…and they gathered themselves together (*vayikahalu*) on Moses and Aaron" (20:2).

The text uses the verb *lehakhil* ('to gather') in regard to Moses in the following places:

- In the Sinai revelation: "The day when you stood before *Y-H-V-H* your G-d in Horeb, when *Y-H-V-H* said to me, **gather** (*hakhel*) the people together and I will make them hear my words…" (Deuteronomy 4:10).
- In building the tabernacle: "And Moses **gathered** (*vayakhel*) all the congregation of the sons of Israel and said to them, these are the words that *Y-H-V-H* has commanded that you should do them" (Exodus 35:1).
- In sanctifying the Levites: "And **gather** (*hakhel*) all the congregation together to the entrance of the Tent of Meeting. And Moses did as *Y-H-V-H* commanded him and the congregation was **gathered** (*vatikahel*)…" (Leviticus 8:3-4).
- "And you shall bring the Levites near before the Tent of Meeting, and you shall **gather** (*vehikhalta*) the whole congregation of the sons of Israel" (Numbers 8:9).
- In taking the census: "And they **gathered** (*hikhilu*)…" (Numbers 1:18).
- In the commandment for the future tabernacle (*Sukkot*) festival in the Sabbatical year: "**Gather** (*hakhel*) the people together…" (Deuteronomy 31:12).
- In the details of the commandment to gather the people: "And when the assembly (*kahal*) is to be **gathered** (*vehakhil*) together, you shall blow, but you shall not sound an alarm" (Numbers 10:7).

Back to Hitting the Rock

In this case when the people complained about the lack of water, Moses was instructed to gather (*lehakhil*) the people. There is no other complaint about water for which Moses was told to gather the people. Not even at the time that he hit the rock and got the water flowing. The instruction to gather the people elevated the importance of this event comparing it to other events like the Sinai revelation, building the tabernacle, sanctifying the Levites, and taking the census, and even the future assembly in the sabbatical year. The importance that the Almighty attributed to this event should have told Moses that the Almighty wanted to use this event to educate the people, no less than the Sinai revelation or building the tabernacle. Moses should have known that this was not just a simple address of a serious need for water. And the instructions that Moses received started with him taking the staff with him.

After receiving the instructions, the following was Moses' response, "And Moses took the staff from before *Y-H-V-H* as He commanded him" (Numbers 20:9).

There is one more time in which Moses 'took' the staff with him, "And Moses took his wife and his sons and set them upon the ass, and he returned to the land of Egypt, and Moses took the staff of *Elohim* in his hand" (Exodus 4:20). And here we see that it is not just a 'staff,' but it is the 'staff of *Elohim*.' The 'staff of *Elohim*' appears also in the war with Amalek, "…tomorrow I will stand on the top of the hill with the staff of *Elohim* in my hand" (Exodus 17:9).

> "And Moses took the staff **from before *Y-H-V-H***
> as He commanded him" (Numbers 20:9)

The phrase 'from before *Y-H-V-H*' appears in connection with Moses twice. The first time, in the Korach Rebellion, when Moses put to the test Aaron's staff and the staffs of the other tribes, "And Moses brought out all the staffs **from before** *Y-H-V-H* to all the sons of Israel, and they looked, and took every man his staff" (Numbers 17:24). The second time is here in Numbers 20:9. Throughout the first five books of Moses, there are no other times in which Moses comes out 'from before *Y-H-V-H*.' And the two times involve the staff.

Moreover, all other places where the word 'from before' appears deal with acceptance of authority, and they come in conjunction with the word 'to go out.'

- "And Cain **went out from before** *Y-H-V-H*…" (Genesis 4:16),
- "…and Joseph **went out from before** Pharaoh…" (Genesis 41:46),

- "And Jacob blessed Pharaoh and **went out from before** Pharaoh" (47:10),
- "And all the congregation of the sons of Israel **went out from before** Moses" (Exodus 35:20),
- and in the case of Korach, "And Moses **brought out**[142] all the staffs **from before** Y-H-V-H to all the sons of Israel, and they looked, and took every man his staff" (Numbers 17:24).

The only time in which the word 'from before' comes **without** the verb 'to go out' is in the case of the complaint about the water in the case in front of us, "And Moses **took** the staff **from before** Y-H-V-H as He commanded him" (Numbers 20:9). We should note the change of verb from 'bringing out' to 'taking.' The fact that we face a rare linguistic combination should indicate to us that we are facing a unique case. Should we understand that Moses **did not** 'go out from before Y-H-V-H' and therefore it means that Moses did not accept the authority of the Almighty in this case?

"And Moses and Aaron gathered **the assembly** (*kahal*)
before the rock…" (Numbers 20:10).

This is the first 'deviation' from the instruction of the Almighty. While Moses was commanded to gather the 'congregation' (*edah*), he gathered the 'assembly' (*kahal*). Note that before the Sinai revelation, Moses was commanded to gather the 'people.' In building the tabernacle, it was 'all the **congregation** of the sons of Israel.' In sanctifying the Levites, it was 'the congregation,' and 'the congregation of the sons of Israel.' In the census, it was 'the congregation.' For the future gathering during the Sukkot festival at the Sabbatical year, it was 'the **people**, the men and the women and the little ones….' Even though the text gives the instruction for blowing the silver trumpet (Numbers 10:7) at the time of gathering the 'assembly' (*kahal*), according to the text, Moses and Aaron gathered the 'assembly' (*kahal*) **only once** – at the water dispute in our case.

"…and he said to them, **please hear,** you the rebels, shall we
cause water to go out of this rock for you?" (Numbers 20:10).

---

[142] In Hebrew this 'brought out' is a form of the verb 'to go out.' The form of the verb is 'to cause someone or something to do the activity' (the causal form). So the word 'brought out' is literally 'caused to go out.'

The phrase 'please hear' appears in the Torah in the following other places:

- Joseph talked to his brothers, "And he said to them **please hear** this dream that I have dreamed" (Genesis 37:6).
- The Almighty talked to Aaron and Miriam after they complained about Moses, "And he said **please hear** my words, if…" (Numbers 12:6).
- Moses speaks to Korach and his congregation, "And Moses said to Korach, **please hear** the sons of Levi" (Numbers 16:8).

In these three places it is clear that the phrase 'please hear' indicates anger and quarrel. The phrase with Joseph comes after the previous verse ended with, "…and they hated him even more" (Genesis 37:5). And Moses addressed the assembly with 'please hear.' Just from this phrase we should understand that Moses perceived the situation as adversarial.

> "…and he said to them, please hear, **you the rebels**, will we
> fetch you water out of this rock?" (Numbers 20:10).

The present complaint came after the death of Miriam, and the text says, "And there was no water for the congregation…" (Numbers 20:2). The tendency among many is to perceive this complaint as an expression of lack of faith by the people. Whoever thinks so should travel to the Sinai desert for just one day to see the moving sands shining in the sun. A place where one cannot look at the sand as it is a mirror reflecting the sun's rays. The glare from the sun might seriously hurt a person's eyes. And if we examine the language of the complainants, as they are quoted by the text, we can see that twice they used the title Y-H-V-H. In this complaint it is difficult to see the complainants as 'rebels.' Again, it seems as if Moses perceived them as 'rebels' more than they were indeed. The lack of water was a legitimate complaint.

> "…and he said to them, please hear, you the rebels, **will we**
> **fetch you water out of this rock?**" (Numbers 20:10)

This sentence is an open challenge to 'the assembly.' The people didn't talk about a specific rock, but about the lack of water. Not only did Moses gather the 'assembly' instead of the 'congregation;' not only did he start his address by saying, 'please hear,' an indication of a quarrel, but Moses also addressed the 'assembly' and challenged them.

> "And Moses **lifted up his hand**…" (Numbers 20:11).

The activity of lifting the hand is mentioned in other places in the Torah.

- When the king of Sodom approached Abraham and said, "…give me the soul, and take the goods for yourself" (Genesis 14:21), Abraham answered with, "…I have **lifted my hand** to Y-H-V-H most high G-d, the possessor of heaven and earth that I will not take…" (Genesis 14:22-23).
- Later in Genesis, "And Pharaoh said to Joseph I am Pharaoh and without you shall no man **lift his hand** or foot in all the land of Egypt" (Genesis 41:44).

In the first example, the king of Sodom was trying to dictate the disposition of the spoils of war, and Abram lifts his hand, acknowledging the supreme authority of G-d, but also exerting his own authority over the Sodomite king to overrule him in the disposition of the spoils of war. In the second example, Pharaoh gives Joseph the ability to control the movements of the hands or legs of others, or in other words absolute authority, over all others in Egypt.

The text says that Moses 'lifted his hand' when there was no instruction to do so.

At the time of the war with Amalek, the text says, "And it came to pass, when Moses **lifted his hand** Israel prevailed, and when he let down his hand Amalek prevailed" (Exodus 17:11). Did Moses perceive himself to be at war with the 'assembly' as he had been at war with Amalek? Moses himself in the song before his death says, "…and lest they say, our hand **has been lifted**[143] and Y-H-V-H has not done all this" (Deuteronomy 32:27). Lifting the hand was enough to send the 'assembly' the message that 'Y-H-V-H has not done all this.'

> "…and twice he struck the rock **with his staff**
> and a lot of water came out, and the congregation

---

[143] The verb to lift the hand is *leharim*. The word used in the text is *ramah*, which is the passive form of the verb. It can be translated as 'high,' or it can be translated as 'has been lifted.'

and their beasts drank" (Numbers 20:11).

This staff is introduced for the first time at the burning bush, and other times the staff is mentioned in connection with Moses follow:

- The Almighty says to Moses, "And this staff you shall take in your hand, with which you shall do the signs" (Exodus 4:17).
- The text says "…and Moses took the staff of the *Elohim* in his hand" (Exodus 4:20).
- Moses says to Pharaoh, "…behold I will strike with the staff that is in my hand upon the water which is in the Nile and they shall be turned to blood" (Exodus 7:17).
- The text says, "…And he lifted the staff and struck the water…" (7:20).
- For the plague of hail the text says, "And Moses stretched out his staff toward heaven…" (Exodus 9:23),
- For the plague of locust, "And Moses stretched out his staff over the land of Egypt…" (Exodus 10:13).

Note that Moses started the ten plagues by using '**the** staff,' without any possession attributed to the staff; then as the plagues progressed, Moses felt more and more connected to the staff. For the plagues of hail and locust it became '**his** staff.'

During the war with Amalek, which took place before the Sinai revelation, the text says, "…tomorrow I will stand on the top of the hill with the staff of the *Elohim* in my hand" (Exodus 17:9).

The next and last time the staff is mentioned in the Torah is here in the dispute over the water:

> Take the staff and **gather** the assembly together you and Aaron your brother, and speak to the rock before their eyes, and it shall give forth his water, and you shall bring out to them water out of the rock, so you shall let the congregation and their beasts drink. And Moses took the staff from before *Y-H-V-H* as He commanded him. (Numbers 20:8-9)

The instruction was to take the staff, but to speak to the rock. Moses indeed took the staff, but in the event itself, the text says, "…and twice he struck the rock with **his staff**…" (Numbers 20:11). The instruction to take the staff but not to use it, and instead to speak to the rock, which came after the Sinai revelation, was to get away from the components in the faith of *Elohim*, and to give up on the staff which was the 'staff of *Elohim*.' However, Moses was emotionally attached to the staff ('**his** staff'), and he could not give it up.

Now we can understand why the Almighty labels Moses' action with the staff 'rebellion' twice in the text.

- "…because you **rebelled against my word** at the water of quarrel" (Numbers 20:24)
- "As you **rebelled against my commandment** in the desert of Zin, in the strife of the congregation to sanctify me at the water before their eyes, that is the water of quarrel in Kadesh in the wilderness of Zin" (Numbers 27:14).

Moses labeled the 'assembly' as 'rebels' when they did not rebel against *Y-H-V-H*; they only wanted water. But the Almighty himself considered Moses' actions before the assembly rebellion. Moses rebelled against the word of *Y-H-V-H*, and lost an opportunity, equal in its importance to the Sinai revelation and to the building of the tabernacle based on the use of *lehakhil* ('to gather'), to show the sons of Israel that after the Sinai revelation *Y-H-V-H* is G-d and not the *Elohim* represented by the staff.

Summary

We see that the language the people use at the time of their complaint determines the response. If the complainants use the title *Y-H-V-H* with all its meaning of acceptance of the authority of *Y-H-V-H*, then the response is according to the complaint. When the complaint uses the title *Y-H-V-H* but not in the right way, a punishment is due. But if the complaint uses the title *Elohim* then the punishment is swift and harsh. It is no different from the burning bush when the title *Y-H-V-H* appears only after Moses uses the same title. The response of the Almighty is dependent on the language of the human. And no human is spared, even Moses himself. What would have been the punishment, or would there even be a punishment, if Moses had used the 'staff of *Y-H-V-H*' and not the 'staff of *Elohim*?' But if we realize that only in the dimension of *Elohim* are there physical symbols, such as the staff, then just to imagine the existence of the 'staff of *Y-H-V-H*' would be a mere intellectual exercise, and not a realistic option.

Jethro's Departure

While the language of the text used the title *Elohim* extensively when Jethro came to visit Moses in the desert, we find that by the time Jethro departed there was extensive use of the title *Y-H-V-H*.

> And Moses said to Hobab,[144] the son of Reuel the Midianite, Moses' father-in-law, we are journeying to the place about which **Y-H-V-H** said, I will give it to you, come with us, and we will do you good, for **Y-H-V-H** has spoken good concerning Israel. And he said to him, I will not go, but I will go to my own land and to my homeland. And he said, please leave us not, for you know how we are to camp in the wilderness, and you may be eyes to us. And it shall be, if you go with us, it shall be, that whatever goodness **Y-H-V-H** shall do to us, the same will we do to you. (Numbers 10:29-32)

While Jethro came to visit before the Sinai revelation, it is quite likely that he departed after it. This is likely to be the reason that he came as 'Jethro' and departed as 'Hobab.' The Sinai revelation impressed him enough to bring him to join the faith in *Y-H-V-H*, although not enough to join the nation of *Y-H-V-H*.

Balaam

When the ministers of Balak invite Balaam to come and curse Israel, Balaam is quoted as saying to them, "...lodge here this night and I will bring back word to you, as *Y-H-V-H* shall speak to me..." (Numbers 22:8). Balaam presents himself to Balak's ministers as having a connection to the G-d of Israel. By doing so, Balaam strengthens his apparent ability to curse Israel. However, when the Almighty appears to Balaam during the night, the text says, "And **Elohim** came to Balaam and said who are those men that are with (*im*) you?" (22:9). The text tells the reader that regardless of the way that Balaam presented himself to Balak's ministers, it was not *Y-H-V-H* who appeared to him but *Elohim*. If we have any

---

[144] *Hobab* in Hebrew comes from the word *habib*, which is 'one who is liked.' It is a word for 'friend' or 'mate.'

doubt that Balaam himself knew of this difference, then the text continues the conversation with, "And Balaam said to the *Elohim*, Balak the son of Zippor, king of Moab, has sent for me" (22:10). The text does not say, 'and Balaam said to *Y-H-V-H*;' Balaam knew to whom he was talking. The text continues, "And *Elohim* said to Balaam you shall not go with (*im*) them…" (22:12). Balaam, with the idea of strengthening his closeness to the G-d of Israel, answers Balak's ministers in the morning, "…go to your land, for *Y-H-V-H* refuses to give me leave to go with (*im*) you" (22:13).

When the second delegation of ministers appears, "more honorable" (22:15) than the previous ones, Balaam is quoted as saying to them, "…if Balak would give me his house full of silver and gold, I would not go beyond the word of *Y-H-V-H* my G-d, to do less or more" (22:18). And then, "And now please remain you also here this night that I may know what *Y-H-V-H* will say further to me" (22:19). As before, "And *Elohim* came to Balaam at night…" (22:20).

When Balaam goes with (*im*) them although he was only allowed to go with (*et*) them (see *im* vs. *et* discussed earlier), "And *Elohim's* anger was kindled because he went…" (22:22). At this point, the text changes the language in the very same verse, saying, "…and the angel of *Y-H-V-H* stood in the way as an adversary[145] against him…" (22:22). *Elohim* is the one who appeared to Balaam, but the angel of *Y-H-V-H* is the one who comes to defend Israel.

From this point on, the text continues using the title *Y-H-V-H*:

- "And the ass saw the angel of *Y-H-V-H*…" (22:23),
- "And the angel of *Y-H-V-H* stood in the path of the vineyards…" (22:24),
- "And the ass saw the angel of *Y-H-V-H*…" (22:25),
- "And the angel of *Y-H-V-H* went further…" (22:26),
- "And the ass saw the angel of *Y-H-V-H*…" (22:27),
- "And *Y-H-V-H* opened the mouth of the ass…" (22:28), and
- "And *Y-H-V-H* opened the eyes of Balaam, and he saw the angel of *Y-H-V-H*…" (22:31).

Here, for the first time, the angel of *Y-H-V-H* (and not *Elohim*) appears to Balaam. And the text continues,

---

[145] In the Hebrew the word is actually 'Satan.'

- "And the angel of **Y-H-V-H** said to him why did you strike your ass…" (22:32),
- "And Balaam said to the angel of **Y-H-V-H** I have sinned…" (22:34), and
- "And the angel of **Y-H-V-H** said to Balaam, Go with (*im*) the men…" (22:35).

When at last Balaam comes to Balak, he is quoted as saying, "…behold I came to you. Have I now any power at all to say any thing? The word that *Elohim* puts in my mouth shall I speak" (22:38). When there is no need for any misrepresentation of his power, as the mission has already started and he is already there, there is no need for Balaam to use the title *Y-H-V-H* and instead he is quoted as using the title *Elohim*, which is more to be expected by two people outside the nation of Israel.

Before the first blessing, Balaam is saying to Balak, "…Stand by your burnt offering and I will go perhaps **Y-H-V-H** will come to meet me and whatever he shows me I will tell you…" (23:3). Again, we see that Balaam presents himself to Balak as connected to the G-d of Israel. Is it due to the meeting with the angel of *Y-H-V-H*? And immediately the text continues, "And *Elohim* met Balaam…" (23:4). However, when he is instructed to go and bless Israel, the text says, "And **Y-H-V-H** put a word in Balaam's mouth…" (23:5). And in fact, in the first blessing we can see that Balaam uses the title *Y-H-V-H*, "How shall I curse he whom **Y-H-V-H** has not cursed? Or how shall I be angry, he with whom **Y-H-V-H** has not been angry?" (23:8). When Balak complains, Balaam answers him, "…must I not take heed to speak that which **Y-H-V-H** has put in my mouth?" (23:12).

Before the second blessing the text says, "And **Y-H-V-H** met Balaam and put a word in his mouth…" (23:16). When Balaam gets to Balak, Balak asks him, "…what has **Y-H-V-H** spoken?" (23:17). And Balaam starts with the second blessing, "He has not seen iniquity in Jacob, nor has he seen perverseness in Israel, **Y-H-V-H** his G-d is with (*im*) him and the trumpet blast of a king is among them" (23:21). When Balak complains, Balaam answers, "…did I not tell you saying, all that **Y-H-V-H** speaks I must do?" (23:26).

Balak tries another way to allow Balaam to curse Israel. This time he addresses Balaam while using the title *Elohim*, "...please come, I will bring you to another place, perhaps it will please the ***Elohim*** that you may curse them for me from there" (23:27). Balaam, on the other hand, understands that *Y-H-V-H* is standing in his way, "And Balaam saw that it pleased ***Y-H-V-H*** to bless Israel..." (24:1). He saw that before the blessing, "...and the spirit of ***Elohim*** came upon him" (24:2). This is the only blessing in which Balaam does not use the title *Y-H-V-H*.

When Balak complains again, Balaam answers, quoting what he told the ministers who came to invite him, "If Balak would give me his house full of silver and gold, I would not go beyond the command of ***Y-H-V-H***, to do either good or bad of my own mind; but what ***Y-H-V-H*** said, that will I speak" (24:13).

Summary

We can see that the changes in language between the title *Y-H-V-H* and *Elohim* are guided by the sequence of events. The complete harmony between the **content** of the text and the **language** used to describe the events, testify that one 'engine' guides the **content** and the **language**. There is no coincidence in the 'changes in language.' Actually they are not 'changes in language.' 'Changes in language' is only the terminology used in the SCAN technique to enable the analyst to deal with the language. But for the text itself, the different titles of the Almighty constitute a 'linguistic code' guided by the sequence of events. This harmony is the strongest signal that **memory** is guiding the text. It gives **reliability** to the description of the events. We know that based upon linguistic evidence (the harmony between the language and the content) that we are not facing a 'story' (fiction), but we are facing a text based upon memory, or, in other words, history.

Y-H-V-H, *Elohim*, and *El Shaddai*

The text starts with the description of the physical creation using the title *Elohim*. This section ends with the creation of Adam. From this point, the text starts to use the combined title ***Y-H-V-H Elohim*** when the text starts to focus on Adam and his relation to his creator. The combined title is in use until Adam is expelled from the Garden of Eden.

From this point on, there is an attempt by the Creator to connect to the human upon earth. Would it be Adam himself? We find that the killing of Abel by Cain prevented Adam from being the 'flag bearer' of the connection between the Creator and humanity. Would it be Noah? We find that the behavior of Ham, Noah's youngest son, prevented Noah from being the 'flag bearer.' It is a very narrow sample of only two people. But it is apparent that it is not the behavior of the human himself that counts, but **the behavior of his sons**. And the test of who merits being the 'flag bearer' is based upon two different behaviors that the Creator is not pleased with, murder (Cain) and incest (Ham).

At this point Abraham enters the picture. The text says that Abraham merited being the 'flag bearer' because, "For I know him, that he will command his sons and his household after him…" (Genesis 18:19).

When *Y-H-V-H* and *Elohim* appeared to Abraham at the same time it was to symbolize the point of separation between Abraham being part of the general environment surrounding him, and Abraham's first step on an independent path, different from all the other nations around him. The fact that Egyptian and Canaanite idolatry was ridden with incest and other promiscuous activities mandated that the symbol of this covenant between Abraham and the Creator be circumcision.

Circumcision did not cause a total separation between Abraham and his environment, as Ishmael and Hagar still lived in Abraham's household, and the Creator who looked from above on the events intervened to rectify the situation, so that the 'flag bearer' would be able to continue in his position. At this point of time, *El Shaddai* appears to Abraham and corrects his way, and the correction mandated removal of the followers of idolatry from his house.

If the 'flag bearer' is tempted to reach a covenant with a local king, as Abraham did with Abimelech, then there is a need to test if the 'flag bearer' decided to give up his position as such, and therefore Abraham was tested in the binding of Isaac. Since Abraham passed the test, he merited that from that point on until his death only *Y-H-V-H* would be the one to appear to him.

The fact that the three names attributed to the Creator are used in full harmony throughout the text, without even one exception, indicates that

language-wise, we are dealing with **one unified** text. The perception of the Creator as it is expressed by the text is not random or any coincidence; rather it is an expression of a very basic view of the world.

The book of Genesis (and of Exodus – the two books are one linguistic unit) deals with the creation of the connection between the Creator and humanity. First, the Creator had an expectation that all humanity would be connected. This expectation brought disappointment and there was a need to reorganize. Therefore, the flood came. After the flood, a thorough search started to find the few who would be the messengers of the divine word – *naviim* ('prophets') – to humanity. The first one who received this title was Abraham.

This thorough search was not a simple one. We can see that there were ups and downs in the process. While Abraham was, all in all, okay (60% for *Y-H-V-H* and 40% for *Elohim*), we see that his son Isaac was even better than he was. However, in the third generation we witness a downfall between *Y-H-V-H* and the messengers of His word.

There was a need to wait until the Sinai revelation to reach a total separation from the foreign influence that was present in 'the house of Abraham' (and at that time the text talks of 'the sons of Israel'), and to determine decisively that *Y-H-V-H* is the G-d of Israel, the G-d of the Hebrews.

The burning bush event shows that *Y-H-V-H* appears to someone from the house of Abraham only after the person himself uses the title *Y-H-V-H*. If the person himself does not do so, the revelation, quite likely, uses the title *Elohim*. It is the same Creator, but with a different approach to the person. 'Attitude brings attitude.'

One can look upon the book of Genesis, at least **language-wise** when it relates to the names of the Almighty, as a description of the process of development or evolution of the connection between the Creator and the chosen few. It was not easy, and it did not come in one step. It took many generations. We should note that this process does not show up in the **content** of the text, but in the **language** of the text.

In summary, the names of the Almighty do not correlate either to worshipping G-d or to its opposite, idolatry. The language of book of

Genesis does not perceive idolatry as influencing the choice of the 'flag bearer.' The Creator knew that humanity was ignorant of His existence, and therefore there was no need to complain. The test was not in theology or in opinion, but in **behavior towards one's fellow man**. Murder and incest constituted a 'red line' that the Creator did not see as behavior befitting the messenger of His word. Therefore, *Y-H-V-H* and *Elohim* can appear together to Abraham, to Jacob, and even to Moses.

When Rebecca prevented Esau from killing his brother Jacob by sending Jacob away to be with her brother Laban, Rebecca guaranteed the position of Isaac as 'the flag bearer' of the connection of the Almighty to humanity.

When Judah prevented the murder of Joseph by the brothers, Judah insured Jacob's position as the one to continue the path of Abraham and Isaac. When Jacob blessed Judah before his death, he said, "…from the prey, my son, you are gone up…" (Genesis 49:9). As Cain's killing of Abel influenced the position of Adam, as the behavior of Ham influenced the position of Noah, so was it in the power of the brothers' behavior to influence the position of Jacob as the "flag bearer" of the connection between the Creator and humanity. This is so, even though the connection of Jacob with the Creator was not as strong as the connection of his father Isaac and his grandfather Abraham with the Creator. Jacob was 'rescued' by Judah's behavior, and therefore Judah merited being the leader of the 'flag bearers' of the Almighty's connection to humanity. Or, in other words, Judah merited that he would be the father of the kingdom of the nation of 'flag bearers,' the Jewish people, and that the nation would be named after him – Judah.

Points in Language to Consider:

1. There is a connection between the change of names of the Almighty – *Y-H-V-H* and *Elohim* – dependent on the birth of the sons – for both Leah and Rachel.
2. The text brings to the front the name *Y-H-V-H* with the birth of an offspring – Cain the son of Adam, and Noah the son of Lemech.
3. The 'name' of the Almighty does not relate to the modern concept of 'name' (first name + last name), but to the concept of character and attributes, as with Moses at the burning bush.

4. The language of the human who approaches the Almighty influences the language of the Almighty. The Almighty appears as *Y-H-V-H* to a human of the sons of Israel (for example, Moses) only when the human himself uses the title *Y-H-V-H* and not *Elohim*.

THE CREATION OF MAN

Introduction

As we saw earlier when we discussed the names of the Almighty, there are two descriptions of creation. The first one, the physical creation with the title of the Almighty *Elohim*, and the second description, more focusing on the creation of Man, with the title of the Almighty *Y-H-V-H Elohim*. We also found that each title of the Almighty relates to a different dimension of the Almighty. The title *Elohim* (gods, in the plural) relates to the face of the Almighty toward the nations, while the title *Y-H-V-H* relates to the face of the Almighty toward the house of Abraham.

We also saw that the book of Genesis, **language-wise,** is actually a description of the **evolution** of the connection of the Almighty to human beings. It was a long journey that started with the Almighty expecting to have a connection to **all** humanity, only to be disappointed and to search for **one** "flag bearer" to be the messenger of this connection.

With this idea of facing **the evolution** of the connection between the Almighty and humanity, let's examine now the description of the creation of man in the first chapter of Genesis.

The Creation of Man

The text says, "And *Elohim* said, let us make man in our image (*betzalmeinu*) after our likeness *(kidmuteinu)*…" (Genesis 1:26), and the verse immediately after is, "And *Elohim* created the man in His own image (*betzalmo),* in the image of (*betzelem) Elohim* He created him, male and female He created them" (1:27).

This last verse (27) sounds like an unnecessary repetition. The first part, "And *Elohim* created the Man in His own image (*betzalmo)* is 'necessary,' as the previous verse speaks only about the intent of the Almighty to do so, and without the text saying that the Almighty actually did it, we wouldn't know. But the second part of the text, '…in the image of (*betzelem) Elohim* He created him,' clearly sounds unnecessary. We can understand the third part, '…male and female He created them' as necessary because it brings us new information, but why the second part? The first part already includes this information.

SCAN Rule: There is no 'unnecessary information' in an 'open statement.' It is only unnecessary to the reader/listener, but it is necessary to the writer/speaker. When the reader/listener understands the statement completely, everything is 'necessary.'

Before moving into our linguistic journey, we should note one linguistic point that is missing from the English translation, and even Hebrew speaking people do not notice at all. The fact is that the first part of the 'unnecessary' clause is different grammatically from the other two parts.

Tenses in Biblical Hebrew

In Biblical Hebrew there are two tenses that are at issue for our discussion. First is the regular past tense, and second is the future tense with what is labeled by many as 'the turning vav' (the letter v in Hebrew standing for the word 'and'). This 'future + vav' is considered past tense. This is the reason that so many sentences/verses in the Tanach start with the word 'And…' This discussion is not going to deal comprehensively with this point, as it is on the agenda for future examination. But for the time being, for the sake of full disclosure of the text, we should know that the text of the 'unnecessary sentence' is literally, "**And** *Elohim* **will** create the Man in His own image (*betzalmo*), in the image of (*betzelem*) *Elohim* He creat**ed** him, male and female He creat**ed** them" (1:27). We understand that the first part relates to the past as well, but **tense-wise,** the first part of the verse is distinguished from the other two.

Back to the Unnecessary Clause

Are we facing an unnecessary clause, or are we facing some information that is not understood right now? In order to understand what the sentence really speaks of, let's accumulate some more information.

We already saw these two verses in the creation of man in the first chapter. But after this description of the creation of man, the text moves on to describe the creation of man by *Y-H-V-H Elohim*. The text gives us the creation of man (Adam and Eve), the story of eating the forbidden fruit, and the expulsion of Adam and Eve from the Garden of Eden. Then the text moves on with the birth of Cain and Abel, and the killing of Abel by Cain. Then the text moves on with the birth of Seth, and him having a son Enosh, and the text says, "then was it begun to call in the name of *Y-H-V-H*" (Genesis 4:26). The verse immediately after is, "This is the book of the *toldot* of man on the day of *Elohim*'s creation of man; in the likeness (*bidmut*) of *Elohim* He made him" (Genesis 5:1).

Summary

The plan the Almighty expressed in the first chapter, as stated by the text, was to make man "...in our image (*betzalmeinu*) after our likeness (*kidmuteinu*)..." (Genesis 1:26). The first description speaks of creating man "...in His own image (*betzalmo*)(1:27). The second description speaks about the creation of man "...in the likeness (*bidmut*) of *Elohim* He made him" (Genesis 5:1).

To this picture we should add that there is a change in language between the two verses – the one in 1:27, and the one in 5:1. While the verse in 1:27 talks of 'creating,' the verse in 5:1 talks of 'making.'

We should also add to this mix the following verse, "And Adam lived a hundred and thirty years and fathered a son in his own likeness (*bidmuto*) after his image (*ketzalmo*) and he called his name Seth (Genesis 5:3). And in this last verse we see a reversal of order from the initial plan: the *demut* is first, and the *tzelem* is second.

So, while the plan talked about two dimensions to the expected creation, *betzalmeinu* and *kidmuteinu,* the creation that *Elohim* did was with *betzelem* and the creation that *Y-H-V-H Elohim* did was with *bidmut*.

Moreover, while the creation of man by *Elohim* is described using the verb 'to create' (*vayibra*), the creation of man by *Y-H-V-H Elohim* is described using the verb 'to form' (*vayitzer*).

Bottom line, we are facing several changes in language from the first description to the second description. Coincidence? After all the linguistic journeys that we have had in this research of the text, we should already know better. There are no changes in language. The term 'changes in language' is only a phrase used in the SCAN technique to relate to what is going on in the text. However, for the writer/speaker they are not changes in language. Each word has a distinct meaning, different from the other.

Before we start two linguistic journeys to find the difference in meaning between *betzelem* and *demut*, we need to know one additional point about the language. The word *tzelem* comes with the preposition *b'* while the word *demut* comes with the preposition *k'*. Generally speaking, the difference between the two is that the preposition *b'* indicates a more direct connection. It stands for the preposition 'in.' On the other hand, the preposition *k'* indicates a more indirect connection. It has the meaning of 'like,' and does not mean an exact identical comparison.

With this knowledge we can start our linguistic journey to deal first with the word *tzelem*, and then with the word *demut*.

The Word *Tzelem*

We find the word *tzelem* in regard to idolatry. For example, "...and destroy all their figured pavements and destroy all their molten images (*tzalmei*), and devastate all their high places" (Numbers 33:52). When the Philistines captured the ark of *Y-H-V-H*, and they were plagued by the ark being in their midst, and they decided to return the ark to the Israelites, "And they put the ark of *Y-H-V-H* to the wagon, and the box and the mice of gold and their images (*tzalmei*) of swellings" (1 Samuel 6:11). In two other places we see, "And all the people of the land came to the house of Baal, and broke down its altars, and its images (*tzelamav*) they broke into little pieces, and killed Matan the priest of Baal before the altars..." (2 Kings 11:18; and a very similar version in 2 Chronicles 23:17). In Ezekiel we find, "...and you made for yourself images (*tzalmei*) of a male and played the harlot with them" (Ezekiel 16:17).

We should recognize that the word *tzelem*, traditionally translated as 'image,' is a concrete physical representation of the deity, like a statue. This fits with the preposition *b'*.

The Word *Demut*

While the word *tzelem* relates to the physical attribute of the Almighty, we find that the word *demut* relates to the 'likeness' of the Almighty. For example, "The noise of a multitude in the mountains, the likeness (*demut*) of large people" (Isaiah 13:4). In Isaiah, we find also a verb derived from the word *demut* – *ledamyen*, which means 'to liken:' "To whom then will you imagine (*tedamyun*) god, and which likeness (*demut*) will you construct for him?" (Isaiah 40:18).

The word *demut* is used extensively in Ezekiel's description of his vision of the Almighty:

- "And from its midst came the likeness (*demut*) of four animals and this was their appearance, they had the likeness (*demut*) of a man" (Ezekiel 1:5).
- "And the likeness (*demut*) of their face the face of man..." (Ezekiel 1:10).
- "And above the firmament that was over their heads was the appearance of the sapphire stone, the likeness (*demut*) of a chair, and on the model of the chair a model that appears as a man from above" (Ezekiel 1:26).
- "And the appearance of the rainbow that is in the cloud in the day of rain so was the appearance of the brightness around, it was the appearance of the likeness (*demut*) of the glory of *Y-H-V-H*, and I saw and I fell on my face, and I heard a voice speaking" (Ezekiel 1:28).
- "And I saw and there was a likeness (*demut*) in the appearance of fire..." (Ezekiel 8:2).

In the second book of Kings we find that King Ahaz who visited Damascus sent to the priest of Jerusalem his impression of the altar he saw there, "...and King Ahaz sent to Uriah the priest the *demut* of the altar, and its pattern (*tabnito*), according to all its workmanship" (2 Kings 16:10). We can see that while the *tabnit* relates to the exact technical details, the *demut* relates to more **overall** terms – 'likeness.'

Back to the Creation

The text says, "And *Elohim* said, let us make man in our image (*betzalmeinu*) after our likeness (*kidmuteinu*)..." (Genesis 1:26), and the verse immediately after is, "And *Elohim* created the Man *betzalmo, betzelem Elohim* He created him..." (1:27).

The text speaks of two different attributes of the Almighty, the concrete, physical one, the *tzelem*, and the *demut*, the 'likeness,' or in other words, the more abstract and spiritual one. And although the initial plan was to have the man created with both dimensions, the first stage of the creation of man was only the physical one. This is the stage in which the Almighty functiones as *Elohim*, and deals with the creation of the physical world, starting with the creation of the heavens and the earth. And man was no different from any other physical creation described in the first chapter.

Once this creation was completed, the second stage started, and this time the Almighty functioned with the title *Y-H-V-H Elohim*. As we saw earlier, this title relates to the connection of the Almighty to humans. And here, we don't have the verb 'to create' (*libroa*) but the verb 'to form' (*litzor*). While 'creation' means to produce something from nothing, the verb 'to form' means taking some material and making something out of it. For example, "What use is there in a statue whose maker (literally form-er, *yotzro*) shaped him..." (Habakkuk 2:18).

We find in Isaiah, "And now thus says *Y-H-V-H* who created (*bora'acha*) you Jacob and formed you (*yotzrecha*) Israel..." Isaiah 43:1. While Jacob (the man) was 'created' (born), Israel (the national name of Jacob) was 'formed.'

Isaiah is listing for us the three stages of creation, "All who are called in my name, for my glory I have created (*berativ*), I have formed (*yetzartiv*) him and I even made (*asitiv*) him" (Isaiah 43:7). We have creating, forming, and making. And in fact, we find these three verbs in use in the story of creation. 'To create' and 'to make' are in the story of creation by *Elohim*, and 'to form' is in the story of creation by *Y-H-V-H Elohim*.

We can conclude that what is often labeled the 'second story of creation' is actually the second stage of creation – the progression from the physical to the spiritual. This is the reason that after the text says that at the time of Enosh, "...was it begun to call in the name of *Y-H-V-H*" (Genesis 4:26). The text continues with, "This is the book of the *toldot* of man on the day of *Elohim*'s creation of man, in the likeness (*bidemut*) of *Elohim* He made him" (Genesis 5:1). The text comes to conclude that now, after calling in the name of *Y-H-V-H*, the man was created in the *demut* of the Almighty.

Realizing that the text of Genesis is talking about two different stages of creation of man, the first created by *Elohim* with the physical attributes, and the second, created by *Y-H-V-H Elohim*, with the 'likeness' (more spiritual attributes), we can move on to read a section which has puzzled many. "And the sons of *Elohim* saw the daughters of the man that they were good, and they took as wives all those whom they chose" (Genesis 6:2). The text speaks of the product of the first creation (sons of *Elohim*) marrying the product of the second creation (the daughters of the man).

Summary

The beginning of Genesis is not two different stories of creation. **Language**-wise, the beginning of the book speaks of the **evolution** of the creation of man. It was not done in one stage. This is the reason that the **names** of the Almighty are different in these two descriptions, and this is the reason that the **verbs** are different. *Elohim* corresponds to creation while *Y-H-V-H Elohim* corresponds to formation. And this is the reason that the **products** are different. While the first creation used the word *tzelem* (representing the physical), the second stage used the word *demut* (representing the spiritual).

The bottom line is the book of Genesis, language-wise, does not speak only of the **evolution** of the connection between the Almighty and humans. The book also describes very clearly the **evolution** of the creation of humans.

If we don't pay attention to the language of the text, we are oblivious to this knowledge. It is not in the **content** of the text, but in the **language** of the text.

I would like to end this journey by admitting that I did not see this point myself before. I wondered about the 'unnecessary' sentence in Genesis 1:27, but I couldn't figure it out. Only when I went into the actual language of the text, and copied the verses, and sorted them and put them all together, only then could I see how the changes in language in relation to both the product (*tzelem* or *demut*), and the verbs (creating vs. forming), coincide with the different names of the Almighty. Then I understood that the 'unnecessary part' in verse 1:27 is not 'unnecessary' at all. It comes to emphasize to the reader/listener that although the initial plan was to create the man in one step, in reality, it was not so. In reality, there were two stages. The first was the physical (*tzelem*) and the second was the spiritual (*demut*), or the connection between the Creator, and the one who was created. The 'unnecessary' part comes for emphasis, in case we neglect to realize it.

NAME CALLING

Introduction

The first person in the book of Genesis does not get the 'ceremony' of being given a name. The text says, "And *Elohim* said, let us make man (*adam*) in our image…" (1:26), and then the text continues, "And *Elohim* created the man in His own image…" (1:27), and then, "And *Elohim* blessed them…" (1:28).

In the second description of the creation we find the activity of calling names. The text says, "And the man **gave names** to all animals and to the bird of the sky, and to every beast of the field…" (2:20)

Once the woman came into existence, the text says, "And the man said, this is now bone of my bones, and flesh of my flesh, she **should be called woman** because she was taken out of man" (2:23).

We should note that although by the content, the man gave the name to the woman, still language-wise, the text does not use the formula that we encounter later, '…and he/she called him/her…' Instead, the text uses the passive voice, '…she should be called woman…' without actually saying who gave her the name.

In summary, the first man does not get the ceremony of being 'called' by name. His companion, the woman, gets a name; however, the man does not 'take possession' of giving her the name because of the passive voice.

Naming Babies

Introduction

This survey of the text is checking the **language** of the text and not the **content**. This means that in this survey we are not interested if the text gives us the name of someone. We are interested if the text actually mentions the activity of 'naming' someone. Or, in other words, does the text actually say, '…and he/she **called his name**…'

The Survey

The first babies to be born are Cain and Abel. The text says, "And Adam knew Eve his wife and she conceived and bore Cain, and said, I have acquired a man with *Y-H-V-H*" (Genesis 4:1).

We should note that the text says that Cain was practically born with his name 'built in.' Thereafter, the text says, '…and said I have acquired a man with *Y-H-V-H*' but the text does not use either 'because' or 'therefore' to connect her saying it to the name. The **content** implies it, but the **language** does not say it.

As for Abel the text says, "And she again bore his brother Abel…" (4:2), without any saying attached to the name. The name Abel means 'vanity' and does not call for any explanation. Still, the text does not actually mention the activity of 'calling' the name.

If we go by the order of the text, we find that after Cain and Abel the text describes the birth of three more babies without 'name calling.' The text mentions Lemech and his two wives. The text says, "And Adah bore Jabal he was the father of those who live in tents and those who have cattle" (4:20); "And his brother's name was Jubal…" (4:21); and third, "And Zillah, she also bore Tubal-Cain…" (4:22); "and the sister of Tubal-Cain was Naamah" (4:22).

The first one to get a 'name calling' citation is Seth. The text says, "And Adam knew his wife again, and she bore a son, **and she called his name** Seth, because *Elohim* has appointed me another seed instead of Abel whom Cain slew" (4:25). And the text continues, "And to Seth, to him also there was born a son and **he called his name** Enosh…" (4:26).

Enosh is the first one for whom the text says that his father (Seth) was the one to give him his name. Until Enosh, we see that the mother (Eve) is the one to give the name, whether it is Cain, for whom Eve gives the reason for the name although without 'name calling,' or it is Seth, for whom we have both 'name calling' and giving a reason for the name.

And we can see that the text connects Eve's calling the name to the reason for the name by using the word 'because.' This combination of calling the name and giving the reason for the name makes Seth a milepost in terms of 'name calling.'

Enosh, Seth's son, the second generation that gets 'name calling,' is also the generation for which the text says, "…then was it begun to call in the name of *Y-H-V-H*" (4:26). As we saw in the chapter on the Names of the Almighty, the second generation determines if the first generation merits the status of 'flag bearer.' Here, too, we see that there must be two consecutive generations 'calling a name' before we encounter the 'calling the name' of the Almighty. This proximity of the activity of 'naming a baby' to the activity of calling in the name of the Almighty should bring us to wonder if the birth of a baby was the cause for religious practice, for humans to see the 'hand' of the Almighty intervening in events on earth, and to wonder about the meaning of life.

Another important milepost. The text attributes the name calling of the Almighty, using the name of *Y-H-V-H* to Enosh, the first human according to the text who recognized the existence of *Y-H-V-H*.

After Seth and Enosh, we have to wait for quite a while before the text returns to 'calling names' and even giving the reason for the name.

The Dark Age of Calling Names

The 'dark age' of no 'name calling' includes Jabal, Jubal, and Tubal-Cain above, then a brief respite with Seth and Enosh. In chapter five the 'dark age' continues. There we find the ten generations from Adam to Noah, in which the text uses the formula, "and he fathered." This goes on from Enosh to Noah. Then for Noah the text says, "And Lemech lived a hundred and eighty two years and fathered a son. And **he called his name** Noah saying, this shall comfort us concerning our work and toil of our hands…" (5:29).

We should note that Noah is the first one after Seth whose 'name calling' gives a reason for the name.

Noah

And the text moves on with the birth of Noah's sons (5:32) without 'name calling,' like the ones before Noah.

The text continues in chapter 10, giving us the offspring of Noah's sons without any 'name calling.' The same applies to the ten generations between Noah and Abraham, including Abraham himself and his family.

Ishmael

After a very long time since Noah had his name calling, the next one to get name calling, and from the Almighty Himself, is Ishmael. The text says that the angel of *Y-H-V-H* tells Hagar, Sarah's slave who ran away, "…behold you conceive and you shall bear a son, and you shall call him Ishmael because *Y-H-V-H* has heard your affliction" (16:11). And later on, when Ishmael is born, the text says, "And Hagar bore Abram a son, and **Abram called his son's name**, whom Hagar bore, Ishmael" (16:15). The text also gives Abraham's age at the time Ishmael was born, "And Abram was eighty six years old at Hagar's bearing Ishmael to Abram" (16:16).

We should note that Ishmael, like Noah, received a reason for his name.

Isaac

Like Ishmael, the text says that Isaac got his name directly from the Almighty, "And Elohim said but Sarah your wife shall bear you a son and you shall call his name Isaac…" (17:19). When he was born, "And Abraham **called the name** of his son who was born to him, whom Sarah bore to him, Isaac" (21:3), and, like Ishmael, the text adds Abraham's age when Isaac was born, "And Abraham was one hundred years old when Isaac his son was born to him" (21:5).

Unlike Ishmael, the text does not say openly (using 'because…') the reason for the name Isaac. But from the context the reason is apparent and clear. Two verses before the Almighty's announcement cited above, the Almighty said of Sarah, "And I will bless her and give you also a son from her…" (17:16), and Abraham, "…fell upon his face and laughed…" (17:17).

The text repeats the idea of laughing, and this time by Sarah. When the three angels appear to Abraham and inform him again of the upcoming birth of a son to Sarah, the text says, "…And Sarah was hearing it at the entrance to the tent…" (18:10), and, "And Sarah laughed within herself…" (18:12). After the birth of Isaac, the text says that Sarah said, "…*Elohim* has made laugh of me that all who hear will laugh at me" (21:6). Isaac merited his name respectfully, as his two parents laughed before his birth, and his mother even talked about laughing after his birth.

Isaac, which in Hebrew is Yitzhak, means 'he will laugh.'

Lot and his Daughters

After the destruction of Sodom, Lot is stranded in the mountain with his two daughters. The daughters initiated marital relations with their father, believing that there was no 'man' (likely meaning 'important man') to marry them. After they made their father drunk, they slept with him, and they got pregnant.

The text says, "And the firstborn bore a son and **she called his name** Moab; he is the father of Moab till today" (19:37). The text goes on, "And the young one, she also bore a son, and **called his name** Ben-Ami (the son of my people); he is the father of the sons of Ammon till today" (19:38).

We should note that the text does not give the reason for the names chosen for the sons, although the names speak for themselves. 'Moab' means "from father," and it is a point to note that the daughter did not see anything wrong with naming the son with a name testifying that he is the son of her own father. The second son – Ben-Ami – means 'son of my people' in Hebrew. But we should note that it can also mean 'cousin,' if we consider the comparative language Arabic. We find *aam* in modern Arabic is 'uncle' and 'my uncle's son' is 'my cousin.'

Esau and Jacob

The text says, "And the first came out red, all over like a hairy garment, and **they called his name** Esau" (25:25). "And after that came his brother out, and his hand holding on Esau's heel, and he **called his name** Jacob and Isaac was sixty years old at the time of bearing them" (25:26).

We should note that although the text does not give the reason for the name of Esau, the reason for Jacob is clear. In Hebrew, the word 'heel' is *aakev*, and the name Jacob in Hebrew is *Yaacov*, which means 'he will follow the heel.'

Jacob's Children

All the twelve sons, and one daughter, of Jacob received the formula, '...and she (mostly) or he called his or her name...' Thus, we find Reuben (29:32), Simeon (29:33), Levi (29:34), Judah (29:35), Dan (30:6), Naphtali (30:8), Gad (30:11), Asher (30:13), Issachar (30:18), Zebulun (30:20), Dinah (30:21), Joseph (30:24), and Benjamin (35:18).

We should note that all the sons received a reason for their name; only the daughter Dinah received 'name calling' without a reason.

We should also note that Benjamin is the son who received a name from each one of his parents. His mother called his name *Ben Oni*, 'son of my strength,' though it was in proximity to her death. On the other hand, his father Jacob called him Benjamin, 'son of my right hand,' (Genesis 35:18) and later referred to Reuben as his strength, "you are my firstborn, *oni*" ('my strength') in proximity to his (Jacob's) death (Genesis 49:3).

Judah's Children

All Judah's sons also receive the formula of '...called his name...' The firstborn was Er (38:3), followed by Onan (38:4), Shelah (38:5), and two sons from Tamar, Peretz (38:29), and Zerach (38:30).

We should note that the first three did not receive any reason for their names. However, the sons from Tamar did receive a reason for their names. Peretz got his name for coming out before his brother. And Zerach got his name for the scarlet thread that was put on his hand when his hand came out first.

Joseph's Sons

Both Joseph's sons received the formula 'called his name,' Menashe (41:51), and Ephraim (41:52); and both of them receive a reason for their names.

Name Calling by the Almighty

We cannot close this list without saying that in Genesis we have several people who received 'name calling' by the Almighty – Adam (5:2), all the forefathers – Abraham (Abram to Abraham), Sarah (Sarai to Sarah), Isaac (before his birth), And Jacob (Jacob to Israel). Ishmael received his name before his birth, but by the angel of *Y-H-V-H*, and not *Y-H-V-H* Himself.

Summary

The book of Genesis mentions 'name calling' for the following people: Seth, Enosh, Noah, Ishmael, Isaac, Lot's sons from his daughters, Esau and Jacob, Jacob's children, Judah's children, and Joseph's children.

Discussion

Since we have already completed the analysis of the names of the Almighty, we can easily figure out why Seth is the first one to receive 'name calling,' and even getting a reason for his name. Reading the text is self-explanatory.

The text says,

> And Adam knew his wife again, and she bore a son, **and she called his name** Seth, because *Elohim* has appointed me another seed instead of Abel whom Cain slew. And to Seth, to him also there was born a son and **he called his name** Enosh, then was it begun to call the name of *Y-H-V-H*. (4:25-26)

In the chapter on the names of the Almighty we saw that the test to determine who would be the 'flag bearer' of the name of the Almighty among humanity was the way the sons behave. Seth is mentioned in the text because his son is the one that in his time the name of the Almighty began to be used in 'calling.' We already saw in the story of the wife of Joseph's master that 'calling the name' of the deity was a major practice in pagan idolatry. It is no wonder that the fourth saying in the "Ten Commandments" is "You shall not raise (*tisa*) the name of *Y-H-V-H* your God in vain..." (Exodus 20:7). This prohibition is so severe that even today many Jewish people do not say the actual name of the Almighty, and instead use the substitute 'The Name' (*Hashem*).

We should note that the text tells us Enosh was the first one in human history to introduce the name of *Y-H-V-H* into society. Not the name of *Elohim*, but the name of *Y-H-V-H*. And the name of *Y-H-V-H* enters the text as the first time in which **religious worship** started with 'calling the name' of the Almighty.

[Incidentally, in Modern Hebrew the word 'humanity' is *Enoshut*, derived from the name Enosh.]

Although the text does not actually say that Enosh himself is the one who called the name of *Y-H-V-H*, as the text used passive voice for the calling of the name, ('then was it begun to call the name of *Y-H-V-H*'), still Enosh received 'name calling' since he lived in the era that this practice started. Not Abraham. Enosh. And Enosh received 'name calling' at birth, while Abraham did not.

Noah: Noah is the next one to be mentioned with 'name calling' and a reason for the name. He was a major candidate for the 'flag bearer' only to be eliminated by the behavior of his youngest son.

Abraham: It is interesting to note that Abraham, the first forefather of the 'flag bearer' people, gets neither 'name calling' nor a reason for his name. 'Name calling' at birth bypassed Abraham. We do find 'name calling' for Abraham, but not when he was born, to receive his name by his father Terah. On the other hand, Abraham merited receiving a name from the Almighty, when he changed his name from Abram to Abraham.

Ishmael: Ishmael could have been Abraham's son for all purposes, including inheritance and being the 'flag bearer,' but he was disqualified by his behavior, engaging in Egyptian idolatrous sexual practices in Abraham's household.

Isaac, **Jacob** and **Jacob's children** all received 'name calling' with reasons for their names.

The ones that stand out in the book are Judah's sons and Joseph's sons. They are the only grandsons of Jacob who received 'name calling' with reasons for their names. If we continue our line of thinking, based upon the test of who would be the 'flag bearer,' it means that these children participated in the competition to be the 'flag bearer.' Moreover, Joseph's sons were elevated to the level of 'sons' and not 'grandsons.' Jacob considered them as his own sons, and later on, they were tribes as all the others. As for Judah's sons, we know in retrospect that Peretz, the firstborn son from Tamar, is the forefather of the Judean kingdom.

The only real questions outstanding are Lot's sons from his daughters. Lot was out of the race long before he fathered these two sons. Ishmael, who received 'name calling' for himself, and even got his name from an angel of the Almighty, did not receive 'name calling' for his sons. It is understood, as he was out of the race. The same applies to Esau, who removed himself, on his own initiative, from the land of Canaan, and did not get any 'name calling' for his sons. So why do Lot's sons from his daughters get 'name calling?' And the first one even has Lot himself inserted into his name – Moab. Something in the perception of the text brought these two sons to merit entering the text, even with the not-so-nice circumstances. We should consider it a **content** bias of the text.

Moab and Ammon

Lot's two sons from his daughters call for our attention. And in fact there is another point, **language**-wise, that makes these two unique as well.

In the first five books of Moses (the Torah) and in the book of Joshua there are nineteen places in which the phrase 'till this day' appears in the text. Note that this phrase does not show up in any book of the Tanach after these six books. There are two variations of the phrase. The first is 'till this day,' where *aad* means 'till,' *hayom* means 'the day,' and *hazeh* means 'this.' The second is a shorter version, 'till today' (*aad* + *hayom*). It seems that, like other changes in language in the book, we are facing **formal** language in contrast to **familiar** language. Quite likely, 'till today' is familiar language, while 'till this day' sounds more formal. Note that the phrase 'till today' appears only three times, while the other version, 'till this day' appears 16 times.

A listing of all the occurrences of "till this day" can be found in Appendix E. As we did in other linguistic searches, we will examine carefully the minority cases, the phrase 'till today.'

Two of the three deal with the two sons of Lot from his daughters, "And the firstborn bore a son, and called his name Moab; he is the father of Moab **till today**" (Genesis 19:37). "And the younger one also bore a son, and called his name Ben Ami (the son of my people); he is the father of the sons of Ammon **till today**" (Genesis 19:38).

The third place deals with the burial place of Rachel, "And Jacob set a pillar upon her grave that is the pillar of Rachel's grave **till today**" (Genesis 35:20).

Language-wise, these three places are connected. The question is what is the common denominator among these three? What does Rachel's grave have to do with Moab and Ammon?

We know from the text that Rachel was buried close to Beth-Lehem. First, when she dies giving birth to Benjamin, the text says, "And Rachel died and was buried in the way to Ephrath which is Beth-lehem" (Genesis 35:19). Second, later on, when before his death Jacob talks with Joseph, the text says, "And as for me when I came from Padan Rachel died on me in the land of Canaan in the way when yet there was but a little way to come to Ephrath and I buried her there in the way of Ephrath which is Beth-Lehem" (48:7). Beth-Lehem receives a personal touch, familiar **language** in the text.

And what would bring the text to use familiar language for Moab and Ammon? These two were elevated in the language of the text on a pedestal, not more and not less than Rachel the foremother.

We should consider this a linguistic bias in favor of Beth-Lehem, Moab, and Ammon.

Note that there is one verse in the entire Tanach that connects Beth-Lehem to Moab, "And Naomi returned, and Ruth the **Moabite**, her daughter-in-law with her, who returned from the fields of **Moab**, and they came to **Beth-Lehem** at the beginning of the barley harvest" (Ruth 1:22).

Ruth the Moabite who married Boaz from the tribe of Judah. The book of Ruth ends with, "…and Boaz fathered Obed. And Obed fathered Jesse, and Jesse fathered David" (Ruth 4:22). Boaz and Ruth (the Moabite) were the great-grandparents of King David.

Summary

Not only do Moab and Ammon stand out in the list of people for whom the text attributes 'name calling,' (although they are not part of the race to be the 'flag bearer' of the connection between the Almighty and humanity), but they also receive familiar language by the text.

We should not forget that, as we saw earlier in our linguistic analysis, the first daughter, who bore Moab, received more respectable language for sleeping with her father than her younger sister.

Linguistic Biases

The two sons of Lot from his daughters are equal in importance to the people from Abraham's family, whom the text considers to be in the 'race' for becoming the 'flag bearer' of the connection of humanity to the Almighty.

Beth-Lehem receives familiar language by the text indicating some connection between the text and the place.

Points in Language to Consider:

1. According to the text, 'calling the name' of a newborn baby is equivalent in importance to 'calling the name' of the Almighty. The two of them enter the text in the same place.

2. According to the text, Enosh is the first one in human history to introduce the name of Y-H-V-H into society. Not the name *Elohim*, but the name *Y-H-V-H*.

Before we recap and discuss all the linguistic biases that show up in the text of Genesis and what they tell us, we should check a few more points that will help us find out what is behind these biases. We will deal with three issues:

- Speeches in Genesis
- Out-of-sequence sections
- Language and knowledge of a shepherd

571

SPEECHES IN GENESIS

Introduction

The book of Genesis brings to the reader many conversations between people, and the text quotes the two participants in the conversation. At times, we find even a relatively long conversation, for example, the negotiation that Abraham has with the Almighty before the destruction of Sodom. In this discussion we will examine only speeches, when the text brings us a long quote spread over several verses. Although it is an arbitrary definition, for this examination of the text we define a 'speech' as a long quote that lasts at least five verses.

The following are the speeches in the book of Genesis, listed according to their length, from the longest to the shortest:

32 verses: Jacob's words to his sons before his death, from "…gather yourselves and I will tell you that which shall befall you at the end of the days" (Genesis 49:1), to "…the purchase of the field and of the cave that is in it was from the sons of Heth" (49:32).

17 verses: Judah's words to Joseph before Joseph reveals himself to his brothers, from "…O my lord, please let your slave speak in my lord's ears…" (44:18), to "…lest perhaps I see the evil that shall come on my father" (44:34).

16 verses: the words of Abraham's slave to Rebecca's family, from "…I am Abraham's slave" (24:34), to "And now if you will deal kindly and truly with my master, tell me, and if not, tell me, that I may turn to the right or to the left" (24:49).

12 verses: Joseph's words interpreting Pharaoh's dream, from "…the dream of Pharaoh is one, the *Elohim* has revealed to Pharaoh what he is about to do" (41:25), to "…and the land perish not in the famine" (41:36).

10 verses: Joseph's words to his brothers after he revealed himself, from "I am Joseph your brother whom you sold to Egypt" (45:4), to "…and you shall hurry and bring down my father" (45:13).

9 verses: Jacob's words to Rachel and Leah, from "...I see your father's face that he is not towards me as before..." (31:5), to "I am the G-d Beth-El where you anointed there a pillar, and you made a vow to me, now arise, get out from this land, and return to the land of your family" (31:13).

8 verses: Pharaoh reporting his dream to Joseph, from "...in my dream..." (41:17), to "...and I told this to the magicians but there was none who would tell me" (41:24).

7 verses: Jacob's words to Laban, from "...what is my trespass, what is my sin that you have so hotly pursued after me" (31:36), to "...G-d has seen my affliction and the labor of my hands, and rebuked you last night" (31:42).

5 verses: Laban's words to Jacob, from "...what have you done, that you have stolen away my heart..." (31:26), to "And now that you are surely gone because you so longed after your father's house, why have you stolen my gods" (31:30).

The Common Denominator

Except for one speech, Judah's words to Joseph, all the other speeches discuss divine intervention in the sequence of events. Either the **content** discusses divine intervention, or the **language** of the text does. First, in Jacob's last words to his son, we find "I have waited for your salvation O *Y-H-V-H*" (49:18), and, "By the G-d of your father who shall help you and by the Almighty who shall bless you..." (49:25). The speech of Abraham's slave, the third in length, shows the intervention of heaven in the action of humans. The slave asks for divine help and receives it right away. As we saw earlier, the **language** of the text upgraded him from a 'slave' to a 'man.' Joseph's words, which interpret Pharaoh's dream, show the word of G-d as it appeared to Pharaoh in his dream. The same applies to Pharaoh's words when he reports his dream to Joseph.

Joseph's words to his brothers, after he revealed himself, say clearly that "And now it was not you who sent me here but the *Elohim*..." (45:8). Later on, at another time, Joseph is quoted as saying "And you thought evil against me, but *Elohim* meant it to good..." (50:20).

Jacob's words to Rachel and Leah bring the words of the Angel of *Y-H-V-H* telling him to return to his country. The speech of Laban to Jacob in the Mount of Gilead and the speech of Jacob to Laban also deal with the intervention of the Almighty. The Almighty appears to Laban in the dream of the night and warns him not to harm Jacob, and Laban reports this intervention. Jacob, in his answer, says that without the intervention of the Almighty he would have been sent away empty.

The Exception

The only speech, the second in length, that does not deal with the intervention of the Almighty in everyday life, and does not mention the name of the Almighty, not even once, is the speech of Judah to Joseph. This speech reports to Joseph the surety promise that Judah gave his father for Benjamin. Although there is no divine intervention, still it is a very important issue, family unity.

Discussion

Two points we learn from these speeches. The first: divine intervention in everyday life is of great importance to the writer. The second: Judah is in splendid isolation in the book. The flag bearer of family unity surpasses even divine intervention when it comes to dealing with Judah. We should consider this point as a **content bias** of the text towards Judah.

OUT-OF-SEQUENCE

SCAN Rule: 'Out-of-sequence' is only 'out-of-sequence' for the reader. For the one who gives the statement, it is right where it should be. When the reader understands the statement in full, the 'out-of-sequence' portion becomes 'in-sequence.'

Background Information: When we approach an open statement we should realize that the text does not describe the whole reality. For example, when the writer/speaker says, 'I got up, took a shower, got dressed, and had breakfast,' the reader/listener should not conclude that these are all the activities done during that time. The reader/listener should not forget that the open statement goes through an editing process. It might be that between each two activities there is some gap of time that is unknown to the reader/listener in which something else occurred. For example, between 'I got up' and 'took a shower' there were 5 minutes, 10 minutes, an hour, or maybe even two hours. And still the writer/speaker is truthful. The information included in the statement is only what the writer/speaker considered important enough to be included.

Let's go now over the book of Genesis and see which sections seem unrelated to the sequence of events, or in other words, out-of-sequence.

The first section appears in the description of the war that Abraham waged to rescue his nephew Lot from his captors. After the decisive victory, Abraham returned with Lot and all the people of Sodom who were captives.

And the text continues, "And the king of Sodom came out towards him after his return from the slaughter of Kedarlaomer and of the kings who were with him, at the valley of Shaveh which is the king's valley" (Genesis 14:17).

At this point we face in the text an out-of-sequence section of three verses:

> And Melchizedek[146] king of Shalem brought forth bread and wine and he was the priest of the most high G-d. And he blessed him and said, blessed be Abram of the most high G-d, possessor of heaven and earth. And blessed be G-d the Most High, who has

---

[146] *Melchizedek* -- In Hebrew, *Malchi* means 'king of,' and *tzedek* means 'justice.'

delivered your enemies into your hand. And he gave him a tenth of all. (Genesis 14:18-20)

And the text continues what started in verse 17, "And the king of Sodom said to Abram, give me the soul, and take the goods for yourself" (14:21).

What does the appearance of Melchizedek king of Shalem have to do with the encounter between Abraham and the king of Sodom? At first glance, it seems out of place, as if it comes in a vacuum.

In order to understand the meaning of this appearance of Melchizedek the king of Shalem, we need to check two points:

First, the meaning of the activity of 'coming out towards someone.' This is an activity that is mentioned numerous times in the Tanach. The following are the places in the first five books:

- "…And Edom **came out towards** him with much people, and with a strong hand" (Numbers 20:20),
- "…and Sihon gathered all his people and **came out towards** Israel to the wilderness and he came to Jahaz, and fought Israel" (Numbers 21:23),
- "And Balak heard that Balaam had come, and he **came out towards** him to a city of Moab…" (Numbers 22:36),
- "And the Emorites who lived in that mountain **came out towards** you and chased you, as bees do, and destroyed you in Seir…" (Deuteronomy 1:44),
- "And Sihon **came out towards** us, he and all his people, to fight at Jahaz" (Deuteronomy 2:32),
- "…and Og the king of Cashan **came out towards** us, he and all his people to battle at Edrei" (Deuteronomy 3:1), and
- "…and Sihon the king of Heshbon, and Og the king of Bashan, **came out towards** us to battle, and we defeated them" (Deuteronomy 29:6).

Except for Balak, the other places are used in conjunction with coming out to war. Even for Balak and Balaam we can see that the conversation between them upon their meeting is about Balak's complaint why Balaam didn't show up earlier.

In the rest of the Tanach we find 'coming out towards' in the following places:

- "And Benjamin **came out towards** them from Geba the second day and slew eighteen thousand men of the sons of Israel..." (Judges 20:25),
- "...and Israel **came out towards** the Philistines to battle..." (1 Samuel 4:1),
- "And it came to pass, that as soon as he had finished offering the burnt offering, behold Samuel came, and Saul **came out towards** him to bless him" (1 Samuel 13:10),
- "And Ishmael the son of Nethaniah **came out towards** them from Mizpah..." (Jeremiah 41:6), and
- "...Necho king of Egypt came up to fight in Carchamish by Euphrates, and Josiah **came out towards** him" (2 Chronicles 35:20).

Again, we find that in these places the expression 'coming out towards' relates to coming out in the context of war. Even the coming out of Saul towards Samuel is not in a friendly atmosphere. And indeed, during the encounter, which took place in a war camp, Samuel criticized Saul and informed him the end of his kingdom was near.

We can deal now with two encounters in the Tanach in which 'coming out towards' is not in the context of coming out to war.

The first, Leah 'hires' Jacob for the night in exchange for her son Reuben's mandrakes. The text says, "And Jacob came from the field in the evening, and Leah **came out towards him** and said, to me you come for I have hired you with my son's mandrakes, and he lay with her that night" (Genesis 30:16) and we see that in spite of the fact that she said 'to me you come,' the text describes it as 'he lay with her.' In this case we see clearly that Leah was challenging Jacob. She didn't ask what he wanted, and he reacted accordingly.

Another encounter is the meeting between Moses and his father-in-law Jethro. The text says, "And Moses **came out towards his father-in-law,** and bowed and kissed him and they asked each other about their welfare[147] and they came into the tent" (Exodus 18:7). The phrase 'came out

---

[147] Literally, the Hebrew text says, "...and they asked each other for peace..."

towards' attributed to Moses might indicate that Moses did expect some conflict with his father-in-law.

And, indeed, the text found it necessary to state that they met in a friendly atmosphere, and that they even '…asked each other about their welfare.' It is quite reasonable that something like this would occur and there is no need to even mention it. But the text, for one reason or another, does state this 'unimportant' point.

SCAN Rule: Unimportant information is doubly important.

Background information: The editing process mandates that only what is important in the writer/speaker's view enters the text. Therefore, whenever the reader/listener encounters what seems to be unimportant, it means that the reader/listener's logic does not follow the writer/speaker's logic. As a result, the reader/listener should consider such information doubly important.

Question: is it possible that before the meeting between Moses and Jethro, there was an expectation that it would not be a friendly meeting?

Let's return to the encounter between Abraham and the king of Sodom who 'came out towards' Abraham. In order to understand the complaint of the king of Sodom, we have to skip the first part describing the victory (Genesis 14:15), and deal with the second part describing the rescue of the captives and the possessions. "And he returned all the goods, and also returned his brother Lot, and his goods, and also the women and the people" (14:16).

The text notes clearly that Abraham returned 'all the goods,' and he returned Lot and his goods. The text does it by using the verb 'return' twice. However, the text does not say that Abraham 'returned' the women and the people. The verb 'to return' is strikingly missing in relation to the women and the people.

We should not be surprised that Abraham refused to return the women and the people. Abraham's objective was to rescue his nephew Lot. It is quite likely that Abraham hesitated to return them to the king of Sodom. If he were to do so, he would be endangering the women and the people by returning them to their evil and brutal king.

Suddenly Melchizedek the king of Shalem appeared on the scene. Then the verse that comes after the section about Melchizedek's appearance completes the picture, "And the king of Sodom said to Abram, give me the soul, and take the goods for yourself" (14:21). We should note that the king of Sodom does not ask for the women and the people. He wants the 'soul.' The struggle is for the souls of those rescued. The rest of the conversation between Abraham and the king of Sodom does not deal with the 'soul' but with the possessions. Abraham refuses to receive any of the possessions as a reward for the war. We should note that the text does not say if Abraham gave in to the demand presented by king of Sodom.

The text does not say that a war was about to start between Abraham and the king of Sodom. But in fact, from two linguistic points we can see that there was a lot of tension between the two. First is the fact that the king of Sodom 'came out towards' Abraham, and second is the missing word 'returned' for the captives. If one doesn't know that there were clouds of war between Abraham and the king of Sodom, then the appearance of Melchizedek the king of Shalem is out-of-sequence. This appearance has to do with the attempt to prevent the upcoming war. There was a need to put peace between the two, Abraham and the king of Sodom. And Shalem ('complete') sounds a lot like *shalom* ('peace'). But in Biblical language the broader meaning of *shalem* also includes peace.

The question can be asked, was there really a need to mention the intervention by the king of Shalem to put peace between the two sides? The sequence of events would have flowed nicely even without him. This section dealing with Melchizedek gets its explanation from the text itself. **Language**-wise, the importance of this section is that it is the first time in the Tanach in which the city of Shalem is mentioned in relation to kings and kingdoms. The city of Shalem, which is identified with Jerusalem, appears for the first time as a place of the seat of a king, who is a 'priest to *El Elion*' (Genesis 14:18).

From the two kings mentioned in the description of Abraham's war (the king of Sodom and the king of Shalem), we can move now to a section about which many readers wonder why the text devotes so many verses to deal with something that seems unrelated to the sequence of events (out-of-sequence). Is it really out-of-sequence? "And these are the kings who reigned in the land of Edom before there reigned any king over the sons of Israel" (Genesis 36:31).

We should note that the second section that is out-of-sequence also deals with kings, although not Israelite kings. Let's add it to our list, and continue to the next (third) section.

Chapter 37 starts with "And Jacob lived in the land where his father sojourned, in the land of Canaan. These are the *toldot* of Jacob Joseph being seventeen years old..." (Genesis 37:1-2), and the text continues with the description of Joseph, his dreams, the brothers' and the father's reaction, and continues with the description of selling Joseph to slavery, the rise of Joseph to power, the famine, and the move of the family to Egypt. The descent of the family to Egypt fulfills the promise to Abraham in the Covenant of the Splits.

But right after the sale of Joseph and his arrival in Egypt, the text moves on with an out-of-sequence section, a whole chapter, chapter 38, dealing with Judah. "And it came to pass at that time that Judah went down from his brothers and spread till an Adullamite man whose name was Hirah" (Genesis 38:1).

The fact that the text itself views chapter 38 as out-of-sequence is clear because chapter 37 ends with, "And the Medanim sold him to Egypt to Potiphar, Pharaoh's eunuch and captain of the guard" (Genesis 37:36), and chapter 39 starts with the verse, "And Joseph was brought down to Egypt, and Potiphar, Pharaoh's eunuch, captain of the guard, an Egyptian man, bought him from the Ishmaelites who brought him down there" (Genesis 39:1), almost a repetition of the ending verse of chapter 37.

Chapter 38 deals with Judah's sons who died, Tamar who is left a "widow at her father's house" (38:11), Tamar's actions that bring her to conceive from Judah, and ultimately giving birth to two sons:

> And it came to pass when she labored, that one put out his hand, and the midwife took and bound upon his hand a scarlet thread saying, this came out first. And it came to pass, as he drew back his hand, that behold, his brother came out, and she said, what a breach you have made for yourself. Therefore he named him

Peretz. And afterwards came his brother who had the scarlet thread on his hand, and he named him Zerach. (Genesis 38:28-30)

It seems that the mention of the birth of the two sons Peretz and Zerach is the reason for the inclusion of this whole out-of-sequence chapter dealing with Judah and Tamar. We should not disregard the fact that Peretz is the forefather of the kingdom established centuries later by King David.

At this point we can move on to the fourth and last section that is out-of-sequence. At the time Jacob's family descended to Egypt, the text counts the people in Jacob's family starting with, "And these are the names of the sons of Israel who came to Egypt, Jacob and his sons, the firstborn of Jacob, Reuben" (Genesis 46:8). The section ends with, "...all the souls of the house of Jacob who came to Egypt were seventy" (Genesis 46:27).

Jacob had twelve sons, and the sons of these twelve are also counted. However, the text deviates twice and counts two grandsons of Jacob's two sons Judah and Asher. Judah's grandsons, "and the sons of Peretz were Hezron and Hamul" (Genesis 46:12). The same Peretz, to whom the text devoted a whole chapter to bring to our knowledge his birth, here gives us Peretz's sons, Hezron and Hamul. We should note that Hezron is the connecting link between Judah, Leah's son, and the kingdom later on.

But the text mentions two more grandsons, Asher's grandsons, "...and the sons of Beriah were Heber and Malchiel" (Genesis 46:17).

What is the reason that these two deserved to be mentioned? Content-wise, we know for a fact that Asher, or the tribe of Asher later on, was not important or significant in any way. Not at the time of Jacob, and not later on, at the time of settlement in Joshua's time. If so, is there anything in their names that gave them the distinction of being mentioned right here in the text?

Heber is mentioned first, and Malchiel is second. And we should note that Malchiel comprises *Malchi* ('king of') and *El* ('G-d'). It is no different from *Malchi* ('king of') *zedek* ('justice'), who deserved to be mentioned at the encounter between Abraham and the king of Sodom.

Summary

All the sections that are out-of-sequence in the book of Genesis deal with kings or kingdom or kings' lineage. The first is Melchizedek the king of Shalem. The second, the Edomite kings. The third, the birth of Peretz, the forefather of the Israelite kingdom, and Zerach. And the fourth and last – the grandsons of Asher – Heber and Malchiel ('king of G-d').

SHEPHERD LANGUAGE AND INFLUENCE

"...and guard (*ushemarani*) me in this way..." (Genesis 28:20).

When Jacob blessed Joseph's sons, he said, "...the Elohim who shepherds (*haro'eh*) me all my life to this day" (48:15). As we saw earlier, the shepherd (*ro'eh*) and the guard (*shomer*) are two different occupations in the shepherding business. The shepherd is the one in charge, and the guard is the one who is present with the sheep all the time. When Jacob said to Laban, "...I will again shepherd (*ereh*) and guard (*eshmor*) your sheep" (30:31), Jacob suggested to Laban that he, Jacob, would be in the field with Laban's sheep.

It is not only by the **content** that the forefathers were shepherds, "And the men are shepherds for their trade has been to shepherd cattle..." (46:34). Even the **language** of the text is the language of a shepherd. After all, a 'shepherd's vocabulary' is in use, and that might indicate a linguistic bias towards shepherding.

We see it not only language-wise, but also context-wise, or, in other words, the way the text divides the sentences.

The text says for Cain and Abel, "...and she conceived and bore Cain and said I have acquired a man from *Y-H-V-H*. And she again bore his brother Abel..." (4:1-2). At this point we can expect to see that the text will continue informing us about Cain and Abel according to their order of birth – Cain was the first and Abel was the second. But the text does not go by the order of birth. The text said, "And she again bore his brother Abel and Abel was a shepherd and Cain was tiller of the earth" (4:2). The text positioned Abel before his brother Cain, even **before** the differences in their offerings to the Almighty.

The text continues with, "And in process of time it came to pass that Cain brought of the fruit of the earth an offering to *Y-H-V-H*" (4:3). At this point a new verse starts, "And Abel also brought of the firstlings of his flock and of the fat of it and *Y-H-V-H* accepted Abel and his offering" (4:4). And in the next verse, "And for Cain and for his offering He did not accept..." (4:5).

The text could have had easily divided the sentences as follows: "And in process of time it came to pass that Cain brought of the fruit of the earth an offering to Y-H-V-H, and Abel also brought of the firstlings of his flock and of the fat of it." And now the text would continue with the next verse informing us of the Almighty's response to both offerings, "And Y-H-V-H accepted Abel and his offering, and for Cain and for his offering He did not accept."

As the reader of the text in the scroll, when there is no sentence division and no punctuation, I can testify that when I prepare myself for this section I need to be on alert that the division of the sentences does not follow my expectation, and I need to be careful not to fall into the trap of expectations, but to go according to the traditional divisions of the sentences as passed down through the centuries, a division that is clearly biased towards the shepherd. And how do we know that the traditional division of sentences in the text is correct? Because before it was written, it was spoken, and that is the way it was spoken. The fact that the text uses the sound of words to send messages reinforces the understanding that we face text that was told to listeners, and not read by people.

The order of listing the property of the forefathers also indicates the importance of the sheep. When the text lists Abraham's property, the text says, "And he treated Abram well for her sake, and he had sheep and oxen and male asses and men slaves and female slaves and female asses and camels" (12:16). When Abraham's slave speaks with Rebecca's family, and lists Abraham's property, the slave says, "And Y-H-V-H has blessed my master greatly and he has become great and he has given him flocks, and herds and silver and gold and men slaves and female slaves and camels and asses" (24:35). In both instances, the sheep are 'starring' in first place. In the list by Abraham's slave, the sheep are even before the silver and the gold.

The only time that the sheep are not listed first is in Jacob's words in his message to his brother Esau. Jacob instructs his messengers to tell his brother, "And I have oxen and asses, flocks and male slave and female slave..." (32:6). Here, we can see that the oxen and the asses are relegating the sheep to third place.

Earlier, when the text lists Jacob's property, it says, "And the man increased exceedingly and had many sheep and female slaves and male slaves and camels and asses" (30:43). Unlike Jacob's words that listed the oxen first, when the text itself is listing the property, the sheep are first on the list.

As we saw earlier among the speeches in Genesis, we find the shepherd speech (Genesis 31:36-42), and it describes very vividly, and very poetically, the difficulties of the shepherd who has to face the heat of the day and the cold of the night – the extremes present in the desert. The speech actually rhymes like a song!

Genetics and Imprinting

In the book we find a description of bringing the animals to mate in a way that would produce multi-colored offspring.

When Jacob and Laban were discussing what Jacob's compensation would be for taking care of Laban's sheep, Jacob suggested that his salary would be all the cattle and goats that were speckled and spotted, and the brown sheep, including the ones that would be born from then on (Genesis 30:31-34). Laban agreed, but immediately removed from the herd all the male goats that were striped and spotted, and all the female goats that were speckled and spotted, and the brown sheep, and put a distance of three days between them and the sheep that Jacob was shepherding (Genesis 30:35-36). By doing so, Laban wanted to guarantee that no goats that were speckled and spotted, or sheep that were brown, would be born from then on.

Would Jacob be content with what was left? Or, would Jacob do his best to bring about more speckled and spotted animals and brown sheep, from those that were not speckled and spotted or brown, that were under his responsibility while working for Laban?

The text tells us the plan that Jacob devised:

> And Jacob took rods of green poplar, and of the almond and plane tree, and peeled white streaks in them, and made the white appear which was in the rods. And he set rods that he had peeled before the flocks in the gutters in the watering troughs when the flocks came to drink, that they should conceive when they came to drink.

And the flocks conceived before the rods, and brought forth flocks that were striped, speckled and spotted" (Genesis 30:37-39).

What was this plan? Was it a mystery? Or some voodoo practice? Or maybe it was a very clever plan exposing knowledge of imprinting and genetics that Jacob had observed, long before Gregor Mendel derived his laws of genetic inheritance from peas.

Let's not forget that Jacob was shepherding Laban's sheep for more than fourteen years, enough time to pass two generations of sheep. Although Laban removed the parents from the herd, and distanced them from the young ones, still Jacob knew that at times a non-speckled sheep might deliver a speckled sheep. It was a question of dealing with inheritance that was not one-to-one, or, in modern scientific language, recessive genes. Jacob also knew that the young sheep are imprinted with the way their parents looked, and removing them was not enough to erase that imprinting. All he had to do was to create similarity to the parents at the time the sheep were in heat. By creating spotted and speckled rods, Jacob invited all the young sheep that remembered how their parents looked to come to the water in groups. And when they mated, they mated with the same sheep that also had the same recessive genes as themselves. By doing so, Jacob dramatically increased the chances that these sheep would produce speckled and spotted ones. No mystery, and no voodoo practice. Just knowledge of a shepherd who observed his herd over a very long time, and saw what was going on over generations.

In summary, Jacob had vast knowledge in shepherding sheep. In front of us there are two options – either Jacob is the one who wrote this description, or another shepherd who was in the business at least fourteen years, enough time to follow the creation of offspring among sheep, and this shepherd was the one who brought us this knowledge in the text.

WHO WROTE THE BOOK?

Let's first re-examine the list of biases and other points we have found in our analysis.

Recap of Biases in the Text

Up to this point we are facing the following biases:

Order of Birth

1. Peretz and Zerach, Judah's sons from Tamar, are compared linguistically to Isaac's sons Esau and Jacob.
2. The text wants to prevent disrespect towards Judah by not giving him the title 'the fourth.'
3. Although Joseph gets all the benefits of being a firstborn to Jacob and Rachel, the text does not give him the title 'firstborn.'
4. Ephraim, Joseph's younger son, is the only man in Genesis who gets a title indicating disrespect: 'the second.'
5. The elder of Lot's daughters, the one who gave birth to Moab, gets more respectable language in the text ('she came' and 'lay with' (*et*), while the young 'arose' and 'lay with' (*im*)).
6. There is a possible linguistic bias in favor of Judah due to use of respectable language ('come please, let me **come to** you') in an encounter between a man and a harlot.

Order of Social Introduction

7. Caleb the son of Jephunneh from the tribe of Judah is equated language-wise to Moses: 'Moses My slave' and 'Caleb My slave.'
8. Caleb the son of Jephunneh from the tribe of Judah is equated language-wise to King Solomon: '*lemale* after.'
9. Caleb the son of Jephunneh from the tribe of Judah is equated content-wise to King Saul: offering his daughter to the victor in battle.
10. In describing the births, by relating to the birth of his brother, the text equates three pairs of brothers: Cain and Abel, Jacob and Esau, and Peretz and Zerach. Cain is the firstborn of humanity. Jacob, later Israel, is the father of the nation. Peretz, Judah's son, is the father of the Judean tribe that later got the kingdom.

Joseph in Egypt

11. The text conceals the fact that Joseph was a priest of Egyptian idolatry.
12. Unlike the text commenting on Abraham in regard to the binding of Isaac, where the text openly stated that Abraham passed the test, the text does not state that Joseph passed with flying colors the test of allegiance – allegiance to his culture, people, and religion.
13. The fact that Joseph did not buy the lands of the Egyptian priests at the time of the famine is the most sensitive point in the book of Genesis.

Brothers

14. The text does not perceive Haran, or Aram, as equivalent to Egypt, a place to where people 'go down' from Canaan, or from where people 'go up' to Canaan. Going to or from Haran is no different from moving around within Canaan.
15. The text conceals the fact that Jacob was out of commission due to Rachel's death at the time Reuben took over leadership.
16. The text avoids giving Jacob the title 'king,' although Jacob (or Israel) functioned according to all the trappings of kingdoms commonly known in that era. We learn it from quotes by Jacob, Judah and Reuben.
17. The language of the text exposes sensitivity and attempts to suppress the fact of the downfall of the first Israeli kingdom.

Status of Jacob

18. The text conceals the fact that Judah headed the faction advocating migration to Egypt while Reuben headed the faction advocating staying in the land of Canaan.
19. The text conceals the fact that Joseph's brothers misled their father Jacob to bring him down to Egypt thinking that he was going only to see his son Joseph, using this pretense to deprive him of his own country.

20. The text perceives Jacob's being forbidden from taking more than four wives as being a commitment against Jacob's self-interest. Only one who had more than four wives would perceive it as such.
21. The text conceals the land-for-land deal made by the brothers and Pharaoh – the land of Canaan for the land of Goshen. Jacob's family not only went down to Egypt/Goshen, but they also gave up the land of Canaan to the Egyptian king.

Name Calling

22. The two sons of Lot from his daughters are equal in importance to the people from Abraham's family who are considered by the text as competing in the race to become the 'flag bearer' of the name of the Almighty.
23. Beth-Lehem receives familiar language by the text, indicating some connection between the text and the place.

Content Biases

24. The speech that Judah gave before Joseph acknowledged himself to his brothers is the only speech in the book of Genesis that does not relate to the Almighty's intervention in everyday life.
25. The out-of-sequence sections in the book of Genesis deal with kings or kingdom or the lineage of kings. The first is Melchizedek the king of Shalem. The second is the kings of Edom. The third is the birth of Peretz, the forefather of the Judean kingdom, and Zerach. The fourth is the grandsons of Asher, Heber and Malchiel, 'king of G-d.'
26. The text uses the language of a shepherd.

Recap of Other Points in Language to Consider

1. The connection of the human to the Almighty is important for the text. The Mount Sinai revelation separates the Biblical text into two separate eras, at least from the point of view of using the word *toldot*.
2. The building of a city is an important point for the text. This is due to the unity between the content and the language in regard to this point.

3. The connection of the human to the Almighty is important for the text. This is due to the 'promotion' in language in regard to Joshua.

4. The use of familiar language vs. formal language might indicate that the writer has a public persona along with a personal one.

5. The connection of the human to the Almighty is important for the text. The ability to ask something from the Almighty, and have an immediate positive response by the Almighty to the request, changed the language of the text in regard to Abraham's slave from 'slave' to 'man.'

6. The connection of the human to the Almighty is important for the text. The ability to ask something from the Almighty, and have an immediate positive response by the Almighty to the request is granted to Rebecca, the only foremother who appeals to the Almighty, and the Almighty answers her immediately and directly, and tells her of upcoming events.

7. The text perceives that the flow of history is divinely guided. The use of 'After these things' indicates when the Almighty promises something to a human, the human should trust the promise of the Almighty, and not rely upon a pact with another human to guarantee the results already promised by the Almighty.

8. The connection of the human to the Almighty is important for the text. Rebecca's love for Jacob – a mother's love for her son – is mentioned in an open statement as this love testifies to Rebecca's connection to the Almighty.

9. The language of the text uses the **sound** of words to send messages – *vayazed* vs. *vayazid, sheni* vs. *shani, and biglal* vs. *gilulim.*

10. The fact that the text uses the **sound** of the words, the way they register in the listener's ear, should bring us to wonder if the text was more read to **listeners** than read by **readers**.

11. Throughout the text of Genesis the word 'brother,' either in the singular or in the plural, is **not** used in a positive context.

12. To the text, 'calling the name' of a newborn baby is equivalent in importance to 'calling the name' of the Almighty. The two of them enter the text in the same place.

13. The text recognizes Enosh as the first one in human history to introduce the name of Y-H-V-H into society. Not the name of *Elohim*, but the name of *Y-H-V-H.*

So Who Wrote the Book of Genesis? – Discussion

Language-wise, Judah merits first place in the list of linguistic biases. First, the text avoids disrespect towards Judah by avoiding listing his order of birth among the siblings, Judah being the fourth (Bias 2). The text also favors Judah by attributing to him the use of respectable language ('come please, let me come to you...') in an encounter between a man and a harlot (Bias 6).

There are other places in which the text avoids diminishing the reputation of Judah, by avoiding mentioning activities that Judah was involved in. For example, the text conceals the fact that Judah headed the faction advocating migration to Egypt during the famine, while Reuben headed the faction advocating staying in the land of Canaan (Bias 18). The text conceals the land-for-land deal made by the brothers and Pharaoh – the land of Canaan for the land of Goshen. Jacob's family not only went down to Egypt/Goshen, but they also gave up the land of Canaan to the Egyptian king (Bias 21). Quite likely the text conceals this fact due to Judah being the head of the faction advocating this move. Since the text had to conceal Judah's role in the land-for-land deal, the text had to further conceal the fact that Joseph's brothers misled their father Jacob to bring him down to Egypt thinking that he was going only to see his son Joseph, using this pretense to deprive him of his own country (Bias 19).

Judah's sons Peretz and Zerach are compared linguistically to Isaac's sons, Jacob and Esau (Bias 1). Peretz and Zerach (Peretz being, later on, **the forefather of the kingdom**) are compared linguistically to the sons of Adam, **the father of humanity**, and to the sons of Isaac, Jacob and Esau, Jacob being **the forefather of the nation** (Bias 10).

The idea of 'kingdom' dominates the linguistic biases. First, although Jacob functioned as a king, and his language was a king's language, the text avoids giving him the title 'king' (Bias 16). The text avoids telling the reader that the fact that Jacob's family went down to Egypt was actually the destruction of the first Israeli kingdom (Bias 17). The text conceals the fact that Jacob was out of commission due to mourning for the death of his beloved wife Rachel, and Reuben had to take over leadership at the time, a fact that is described in only one verse (Bias 15), and therefore sensitive for the text.

Content-wise, we find that kingdom also dominates the content biases. The sections that are out-of-sequence deal with kings or their lineage – Melchizedek, Peretz, the Edomite kings, and Malchiel (Bias 25).

There is another point in language that supports that a man in authority is writing the text. The use of formal language as opposed to familiar language might indicate that the writer has a personal persona along with a public one (Point 4).

There is one major point that adds more information about the profile of the writer – the relationship of the writer to Lot and Moab.

Let's start with Lot. The language of the writer gives preference to the oldest daughter of Lot (Bias 5) who fathered Moab. The two sons of Lot from his daughters, Moab and Ammon, stand out in importance by the text mentioning them with 'name calling' at the time of their birth. They are equal in this point to the rest of the descendants of Abraham's family (Bias 22).

Language-wise, Moab and Ammon are connected to Beth-Lehem by the change of language from 'till this day' to 'till today' (Bias 23). And the only verse in the entire Tanach that connects Moab and Ammon to Beth-Lehem is the verse in Ruth (1:22), mentioning Ruth the Moabite and Beth-Lehem in one breath.

Although they are not listed as linguistic or content biases, as they are only suspicions, possibly valid, we should note additional points in regard to Lot and his descendants.

By the context (positioning of different components within the sentence), it is exposed that quite ikely something happened between Lot and Sarah while they were in Egypt, an event that brought Abraham to separate from Lot. This might explain why Sarah is the only person whose name the text changes from birth (from Iscah to Sarai) without stating it openly, as the text did with other name changes. This lack of mentioning the name change might reflect the text attempting to honor either the reputation of Sarah, or even the reputation of Lot. To add to this point, another woman about whose lineage the text neglects to provide any information is Tamar, the woman who bore two sons to Judah, and one of them is the forefather of the Judean kingdom. Again, quite likely it is because she was a descendant of Lot/Moab.

Another point to consider is that the text uses the language of a shepherd (Bias 26). The language and the context in which the text is written support strongly that a shepherd, or a man with considerable experience in shepherding, is writing the text.

In summary, all the above should bring us to list the following main characteristics in the profile of the writer of the text:

- The writer has to be a king.
- The writer is from the tribe of Judah.
- The writer quite likely is a descendant of Moab.
- The writer quite likely has been a shepherd for at least 14 years (two life cycles of sheep).

At this stage of the discussion, these four major points point the finger to one Biblical figure who fits this profile – King David. King David, from the tribe of Judah, who came from Bethlehem, was a shepherd many years before he ascended to the stage of history by slaying Goliath the Philistine. He reigned in Hebron as the king of Judah, as did Caleb the son of Jephunneh before him. King David is a descendant of Ruth the Moabite who married Boaz, who was the forefather of Jesse, David's father.

King David's connection to the King of Moab was not only due to the historical connection between Boaz from the tribe of Judah and Ruth the Moabite. In 1 Samuel 22:3 we find that when David ran away from King Saul who was pursuing him, trying to kill him, David 'deposited' his parents with the king of Moab. Quite likely, he did so in order to prevent King Saul from hurting them, or using them as leverage to get to him. It is no different from Absalom who ran away from David to his grandfather, the king of Geshur. This connection to the king of Moab points to the fact that the king of Moab saw himself related to David, not only on a historical basis, but as matter of blood relationship, valid even at that time.

Additional Characteristics

The Intervention of the Almighty in Human Life

The connection of human to the Almighty is a point that surfaces throughout the book of Genesis. It has the power to change the language of the text. Abraham's slave was upgraded from a 'slave' to a 'man' once his request from the Almighty to help him find a wife for his master's son was granted right away (Point 5). Rebecca gets quite a lot of attention just by the fact that she is the only foremother who talked directly to the Almighty, and the Almighty talked to her and even told her the future of her two sons (Point 6). The text mentions her love for her son only because it was love guided by the Almighty (Point 8).

The writer perceives the flow of events in history as divinely guided. The transitional phrase 'after these things' shows up when a human does not trust in the promise of the Almighty and reaches a covenant with a foreign king (Point 7).

We also saw that the changes in the names of the Almighty are not merely changes in language, they are the product of a very deep and significant theology. The book of Genesis is not only history detailing the lives of the forefathers of the nation. Language-wise, Genesis is a description of **the evolution of the connection between the Almighty and humanity**. This evolution may not be apparent in the **content**, but it is definitely present in the **language** of the text.

It is appropriate at this point to quote King David himself.

> And these are the last words of David. David the son of Jesse said, and the man who was raised up on high, the anointed of the G-d of Jacob, and the sweet singer of Israel said, The spirit of *Y-H-V-H* spoke by me, and His word was in my tongue. (2 Samuel 23:1-2)

The Sweet Singer of Israel

Although there are not that many points to prove it, one can still see that the text plays with words by their **sound** (Point 9). For example, the word *vayazed* vs. the word *vayazid* relating to knowingly doing something one should not do. The word *shani* (scarlet thread) that was on the hand of

Zerach at the time of birth hints of Zerach being the *sheni* (second) born. The word *biglal* (because) is only used in relation to idolatry (*gilulim*).

The writer of the text has experience in writing while emphasizing the sound of the words. True. At this point, only three examples are listed, and statistically it is not significant enough to become proof. Still it fits the fact that the writer has experience in music and singing as well as in writing. In writing songs and music there is attention not only to the content, but also to the way the words sound, and to rhyme and meter. We should note that David is introduced in the Bible in the following way: When King Saul looked for someone who could play the lyre, one of his lads said: "…I have seen a son of Jesse the Bethlehemite, **who knows how to play**, and a fine warrior man, and a man of war, and **prudent in speech**, and a handsome man, **and *Y-H-V-H* is with him**" (1 Samuel 16:18).

Up to this point, we are zooming to King David, but we also find biases against Joseph, the firstborn of Rachel, Jacob's wife. First, the text does not give him the title 'firstborn' (Bias 3). The text actively diminishes the reputation of Ephraim, the youngest son of Joseph (who was chosen by Jacob, Joseph's father, to be the one to lead the tribe) by giving him the title 'the second' (Bias 4). On the other hand, the fact that the text conceals that Joseph was a priest of Egyptian idolatry (Bias 11) is a point that relates to the time of writing the text. Joseph in his role as a priest of Egyptian idolatry is the most sensitive point in the book of Genesis by the scale of 'negative + reason' sentences, because of the fact that Joseph did not force the Egyptian priests to forfeit their land during the famine (Bias 13). Quite likely the book was written at the time the writer did not want to irritate the tribes of Joseph, Menashe and Ephraim. Note that after the Absalom rebellion, King David confronted another rebellion by Sheba the son of Bichri to separate the tribe of Ephraim from David's kingdom.

Summary

In scientific methodology it is said the shortest explanation that explains the most data is the best explanation. Based upon the observations in this analysis, the shortest explanation that explains all the linguistic and content biases throughout Genesis is that King David is the writer of Genesis.

There are additional points supporting that King David is the writer. Besides the importance of the connection of humans to the Almighty, which is so evident in the book, we have a few points relating directly to King David.

First, the text perceives Jacob's being forbidden from taking more than four wives as being a commitments against his own interest (Bias 20). Only one who had more than four wives would perceive it as such, and King David had more than four wives.

We find two points fitting King David from our list of other points important to the text. Throughout the text of Genesis the word 'brother,' either in the singular or in the plural, is **not** used in a positive context (Point 11). The first book of Samuel describes an incident in which David's older brother reprimanded him. When David came to the war zone, as his father asked him to do, his brother told him, "…I know your presumption and the evil of your heart…" (1 Samuel 17:28).

The building of a city is an important activity (Point 2). The text in the second book of Samuel says, "David lived in the fortress and called it the city of David. And David built around from the Millo inward" (2 Samuel 5:9).

Reading the Text Knowing That King David is the Writer

Knowing that King David is the writer of the book of Genesis, let's examine now a few points, looking at them in a different way.

There are several places in which the text says that someone who was born was the father of …" For example, "And Adah bore Jabal; he was the father of those who live in tents and those who have cattle (Genesis 4:20). Also, "And his brother's name was Jubal; he was the father of all who handle the harp and pipe" (4:21).

We should note the order of listing: the father of shepherds is listed first while the father of musicians is listed second. One can attribute it to the order of birth, but it might still reflect the preference of the writer, who was a shepherd before he became a musician.

In another place, in relation to Lot's two daughters giving birth to their sons, the text says, "And the firstborn bore a son and called his name Moab; he is the father of Moab till today. And the younger, she also bore a son, and called his name Ben-Ami; he is the father of the sons of Ammon till today" (Genesis 19:37-38).

We should note that for the two sons of Lemech, the text says, "...he **was** the father of ..." using past tense. But for the two sons of Lot from his daughters, the text does not use past tense. The text says, "...he **is** the father of ..." using present tense. For the text, these two are closer in time, or maybe even closer emotionally.

Additional Points Supporting King David as the Author

In this section we will examine six points found in the **language** and the **content** of Genesis. All six points fit the conclusion that King David is the author of Genesis:

- The title "the second"
- Building a city
- Haran/Aram equal to Canaan
- The scale of sensitivity regarding priests
- The restriction on taking more than four wives
- The title "brother"/"brothers"

The Title "The Second"

In the first chapter, "The Social Introduction – Order of Birth," we found that there is a linguistic bias against Ephraim who received the title "the second," a title used only for women, children, and slaves. In the chapter "Joseph in Egypt" we saw that in contrast to Abraham in the test of binding Isaac on the altar, a test that Abraham passed with flying colors as the text expresses it openly, for Joseph, Ephraim's father, the text conceals the fact that Joseph passed the test of loyalty – loyalty to his culture, people, and religion.

We will examine the tribe of Ephraim in the era of the Judges, with the knowledge that David came from the tribe of Judah, and let's see if the ascension of David to the throne was likely to be accepted easily by the tribe of Ephraim.

Ephraim in the Era of Judges and the Kingdom

This era started after Joshua succeeded Moses in the leadership of the people. Joshua himself was from the tribe of Ephraim.

The second judge after Joshua's death was Ehud the son of Gera the Yemini. After he killed the king of Moab, the text says, "...he blew a shofar in the mountain of Ephraim and the people of Israel went down with him from the mount, and he before them" (Judges 3:27). The first tribe mentioned in the song of Deborah, "Out of Ephraim was there a root of them against Amalek, after you Benjamin with your tribes..." (Judges 5:14). After Ephraim, Benjamin is mentioned, the sons of Machir (Menasheh), Zebulun, Issachar, Reuben, Dan, Asher, and again Zebulun, and Naphtali. Ephraim is the first entry in the list of tribes, while the tribe of Judah is noticeably missing. The fact that Ephraim is listed first should not surprise us since Deborah herself was from the tribe of Ephraim, "And she lived under the palm tree of Deborah between Ramah and Beth-El **in Mount Ephraim**, and the people of Israel came up to her for judgment" (Judges 4:5).

The tribe of Ephraim stars again in the life of two different judges, first, in the story of Gideon. After Gideon won the war with Midian, the tribe of Ephraim addresses him with a complaint: "...Why have you served us thus that you called us not when you went to fight with the Midianites? And they quarreled with him strongly" (Judges 8:1).

The tribe of Ephraim lodges the same complaint to Jephthah after his war with the Ammonites: "...Why did you pass over to fight against the Ammonites and did not call us to go with you? We will burn your house upon you with fire" (Judges 12:1).

The complaint by the tribe of Ephraim starts a civil war between the people of Gilead and the people of Ephraim. The text sums up this war by saying, "...and there fell at that time of the Ephraimites forty two thousand" (Judges 12:6).

The book of Judges brings us the exact number of casualties in the civil wars between the tribe of Benjamin and the other tribes in the incident of "the concubine on the hill." The tribe of Benjamin enlisted twenty six thousand to confront four hundred thousand. If we sum up all the casualties from all the tribes, including Benjamin, it was a war that killed sixty eight thousand people.

It is true that the war of the tribes with Benjamin was the bloodiest civil war. The war of Ephraim with Gilead takes second place in casualties.

Not only does Deborah list the tribe of Ephraim first, but also the tribe of Ephraim finds the right to criticize two judges after they went to war without calling them. In other words, the tribe of Ephraim expected every judge, or even any other tribe that goes to war, to notify the tribe of Ephraim of his/their intent to do so.

If we look upon the map of the settlement of Israelite tribes after entering the land we can see that the tribe of Ephraim is located right in the center of the land occupied by the tribes. If we remember that Ephraim is the one Jacob preferred to get preference over his brother Menasheh, and if we remember that these two tribes are descendants of Joseph "...the crown of the head of him who was separate from his brothers" (Genesis 49:26 and Deuteronomy 33:16), then we can understand why Ephraim saw it as his right to criticize judges who were not from his own tribe.

Ephraim in the Era of David

Since the prophet Samuel is the one who anointed David to be king, we should note that Samuel himself was from the tribe of Ephraim. The book Samuel starts with introducing us to Samuel's father: "And there was one man of Ramathaim-Zophim, of Mount Ephraim, and his name was Elkanah, the son of Jeroham, the son of Elihu, the son of Tohu, the son of Zuph, an Ephrathite" (1 Samuel 1:1).

After his birth, Samuel is given to the Tabernacle in Shiloh, which was located in the tribe of Ephraim. This religious center served the Israelite tribes as their place of worship for 369 years.

And now to King David's reign. The mount of Ephraim is the place where the war between King David and his son Absalom was lodged, "And the people went out into the field against Israel and the battle was **in the wood of Ephraim**" (2 Samuel 18:6). In this battle Joab killed Absalom against a direct order by King David not to kill Absalom who had rebelled against his father the king. The death of Absalom brought King David to mourn saying, "...O my son, my son Absalom! Would I had died for you, O Absalom, my son, my son" (2 Samuel 19:1).

Ephraim after the Kingdom of David

Jeroboam the son of Nebat, the one who established the northern Israelite kingdom, was from the tribe of Ephraim. In Solomon's kingdom the text tells us that Solomon "...made him ruler over all the labor of the house of Joseph" (1 Kings 11:28). The text even tells us, "Solomon sought to kill Jeroboam. And Jeroboam arose and fled to Egypt to Shishak king of Egypt and was in Egypt until the death of Solomon" (1 Kings 11:40).

The text says that Jeroboam, "...built Shechem in Mount Ephraim..." (1 Kings 12:25), to be his capital. Jeroboam immediately moved to lead the people to worship "two calves of gold" (12:28), declaring "...behold your gods O Israel which brought you out of the land of Egypt," an identical declaration to the one made in the desert at the time of the sin of the golden calf.

The fact that Jeroboam the son of Nebat was from the tribe of Ephraim the son of Joseph brought "Ephraim" to be the name of the northern kingdom. The prophet Isaiah says, "Because Aram, **Ephraim**, and the son of Remaliah, have taken evil counsel against you saying, let us go up against Judah..." (Isaiah 7:5-6), and, "...the head of **Ephraim** is Samaria, and the head of Samaria is Remaliah's son..." (7:9), and, "...since the day **Ephraim** departed from Judah..." (7:17).

We also find, "The envy also of Ephraim shall depart, and the adversaries of Judah shall be cut off..." (11:13). The prophet Ezekiel compares Ephraim to Israel,

> ...take one stick and write upon it for Judah, and for the people of Israel his companions; then take another stick and write upon it for Joseph, the stick of Ephraim, and for the house of Israel his companions. And join them one to the other into one stick..." (Ezekiel 37:16-17)

Summary

It is quite likely that the tribe of Ephraim, the younger son of Joseph, the son who was elevated by his grandfather Jacob to be above his older brother Manasseh, perceived itself to be the most suitable to lead the other tribes, starting from the era of the judges and thereafter. The tribe of Ephraim did not easily accept the kingdom of David, and when the tribe saw the time was right, after the death of Solomon, the tribe rebelled and separated itself from the Judaic kingdom. Jeroboam from the tribe of Ephraim established the northern kingdom, the kingdom of Israel, or, in the words of the prophets, the kingdom of "Ephraim."

The book of Genesis, by the using the title "the second" for Ephraim, clearly shows the anger that King David had towards this tribe. This linguistic bias should be a beacon when we deal with the question of when the book was written.

Building a City

In "The Order of Social Introduction" we saw that building a city is an important point in the text. This is based upon the harmony between the **content** and the **language** in regard to Cain building a city, "...and he built a city, and called the name of the city as the name of **his son Enoch**" (Genesis 4:17). The text uses the informal formula of social introduction, "title + name," to talk about building a city.

As for King David, the book of Samuel says, "And David lived (*vayeshev*) in the fortress and called it the City of David. And David built around from the Millo inward" (2 Samuel 5:9). The text also says, "And Hiram the king of Tyre sent messengers to David, and cedar trees, and carpenters, and masons, and they built David a house" (2 Samuel 5:11).

In summary, as a person who built his capital city, David when coming to talk about someone else (Cain) building a city, feels kinship with the builder. Therefore, we see harmony between the content (building a city), and using the personal language formula "title + name" when talking about Cain naming the city after "his son Enoch."

Haran/Aram as Equal to the Land of Canaan

In the chapter on "Joseph in Egypt" we found that the verbs "to go down" and "to go up" are used for traveling from the Land of Canaan to Egypt and back. The text does not use these verbs when talking about traveling between Canaan and Haran. This linguistic similarity equates Haran to the Land of Canaan in status.

In Samuel, the text reports to us about David, "And the Arameans of Damascus came to help Hadadezer king of Zobah, David slew of the Arameans twenty two thousand men. And David put garrisons in Aram of Damascus and the Arameans became slaves to David and brought tribute…" (2 Samuel 8:5-6).

Later on, the text says,

> And Hadadezer sent and brought out the Arameans who were beyond the river, and they came to Helam, and Shobach the captain of the army of Hadadezer went before them. And when it was told to David, he gathered all Israel, and crossed the Jordan and came to Helam. And the Arameans set themselves in array against David and fought with him. And the Arameans fled from before Israel, and David slew the men of seven hundred chariots of the Arameans, and forty thousand horse soldiers, and struck Shobach the captain of their army who died there. And when all the kings who were slaves to Hadadezer saw that they were defeated before Israel, they made peace with Israel, and served them… (2 Samuel 10:16-19)

In summary, David's era was the era in which the lands of Canaan and Aram were under one rule, David's rule, even "the Arameans who were beyond the river" (2 Samuel 10:16). Politically, in David's time, Haran and Canaan were one, but we also see that in the language of Genesis, one does not "go up" from Aram to Canaan, nor does one "go down" from Canaan to Aram, unlike Egypt. So in David's time, the **language** of the text in Genesis coincides with the political **reality**.

Scale of Sensitivity in Genesis

The scale of sensitivity includes two components – negative sentences (what didn't happen) and giving a reason. This scale of sensitivity shows that the most sensitive point to the text in the entire book is the fact that the priests in Egypt did not sell their lands to Joseph at the time of the famine.

Knowing that King David is the author of Genesis, we should go to the book of Samuel, which helps us understand why the priests in Egypt were the most sensitive point.

After King David defeated Edom in the war, the text gives us a summary of David's kingdom:

> "And David reigned over all Israel and David executed judgment and justice to all his people. And Joab the son of Zeruiah was over the army, and Jehoshaphat the son of Ahilud was recorder (secretary). And Zadok the son of Ahitub and Ahimelech the son of Abiathar were priests (*kohanim*), and Seraiah was the scribe. And Benaiah the son of Jehoiada and the Kerethites and the Pelethites, and the sons of David were priests (*kohanim*)" (2 Samuel 8:15-18).

The text does say that Zadok the son of Ahitub and Ahimelech the son of Abiathar were priests. However, at the end of the list, the text adds, "and the sons of David were priests." We know that Zadok and Ahimelech were from the tribe of Levi, the tribe that was chosen to minister in the tabernacle, and their priesthood was granted to them for generations. The sons of David, as David himself, were from the tribe of Judah. How did they serve as priests?

It is quite likely that the appointment of David's sons to be priests was not welcomed by the tribe of Levi, as they felt the priesthood was due them simply by their heritage. And in fact, this point – the priests of Egypt – is the most sensitive point in the text, by the scale of sensitivity – negative sentences combined with giving a reason.

More Than Four Wives

In "Status of Jacob/Israel" we found that the text uses the verb "to swear/to take an oath" when Jacob swears to Laban that he will not take any more wives, and stay married only to Laban's daughters (and their two slaves). In doing so, language-wise, the text perceives Jacob's commitment as an act against Jacob's own interest. Only a man who had more than four wives would see such a commitment as against the self-interest of the one who takes the oath.

As for David, the text says,

> And to David were sons born in Hebron, and his firstborn was Amnon of **Ahinoam the Jezreelitess**. And next to him was Kileab of **Abigail the wife of Nabal the Carmelite**, and the third Absalom the son of **Maachah the daughter of Talmai king of Geshur**. And the fourth Donijah the son of **Haggith**, and the fifth Shephatiah the son of **Abital**. And the sixth Ithream by **Eglah** David's wife. These were born to David in Hebron. (2 Samuel 3:2-5)

In summary, in Hebron, when David was king over only the tribe of Judah, David had six wives.

Later on, the text says,

> And David took more concubines and wives from Jerusalem after he came from Hebron, and there were more sons and daughters born to David. And these are the names of those who were born in Jerusalem, Shammuah and Shobab, and Nathan and Solomon. And Ibhar and Elishua and Nepheg and Japhia. And Elishama and Eliadah and Eliphalet. (2 Samuel 5:13-16)

Solomon is listed among the ones who were born in Jerusalem and was the son of Bath-Sheba the wife of Uriah the Hittite. In addition, during Absalom's rebellion the text says, "…and the king left ten women who were concubines to keep the house" (2 Samuel 15:16).

In summary, David had a lot more wives than just four, the number of wives that Jacob had. Therefore, David, looking back to the time of

Jacob, would be very likely to perceive having *only* four wives as a restriction.

The Relationship with Brothers

The most important feature in Genesis is the fact that throughout the book of Genesis the word "brother," or even "brothers" in the plural, is almost entirely used in a negative context.

David and "Brothers"

In Samuel we find the following description: Jesse, David's father tells David, "…take now for your brothers an ephah of this parched grain, and these ten loaves, and run to the camp to your brothers. And carry these ten cheeses to the captain of their thousand, and look how your brothers fare (*ve'et* **achecha** *tifkod* **leshalom**)…" (1 Samuel 17:17-18).

Jesse's request that David bring food to his brothers in the military camp before the battle with the Philistines should remind us of Jacob's request that Joseph go and check how his brothers are doing with the sheep at Shechem, "…see whether it is well with your brothers (**shelom achecha**)…" (Genesis 37:14).

Although David was not sold to slavery by his brothers when he met them, the text brings us the words of Eliab "his big brother" (not the firstborn) who tells David,

> …and Eliab's anger was kindled against David, and he said, why did you come here? And with whom have you left those few sheep in the wilderness? **I know your presumption, and the evil of your heart** for you have come down that you might see the battle. (1 Samuel 17:28)

The clause, "…I know your presumption, and the evil of your heart…" must relate to some earlier conflicts between David and his "big" brother. The text does not bring us these issues, but from Eliab's words we can conclude that there were such issues.

The text also tells us that David's three older brothers went to Saul's camp. This was after Samuel passed over them and anointed David in front of his family to be king, "And the three eldest sons of Jesse **followed Saul** to the battle..." (1 Samuel 17:13). The unnecessary phrase, "followed Saul," might indicate that not only did they go to the battle, but they also took sides with Saul against David.

David and the Sons of his Sister Zeruiah

Introduction

The book of Chronicles brings us the siblings in Jesse's family,

> And Jesse fathered his firstborn Eliab, and Abinadab the second and Shimma the third. Nethaneel the fourth and Raddai the fifth. Ozem the sixth David the seventh. And their sisters **Zeruiah** and Abigail and the sons of Zeruiah, Abishai, Joab, and Asahel three." (1 Chronicles 2:13-16)

Zeruiah's Sons

The first of Zeruiah's sons appearing in the text is Abishai. The text says, "And David answered and said to Ahimelech the Hittite and to Abishai the son of Zeruiah, brother to Joab saying, who will go down with me to Saul to the camp? And Abishai said, I will go down with you" (1 Samuel 26:6). The fact that Abishai appears not only as "the son of Zeruiah" but also as "brother to Joab" might indicate the importance of Joab, either at the time, or at the time of the writing.

When David and Abishai are in Saul's camp, the text brings the words of Abishai to David,

> ...God has delivered your enemy into your hand this day, now please let me strike him once with the spear to the earth, and I will not strike him a second time. And David said to Abishai destroy him not, for who can stretch forth his hand against the Lord's anointed and be guiltless. (Samuel 1 26:8-9)

This is not the only time that Abishai suggests to David to kill someone who is a threat to David. When David ran away from Absalom, Shimei the son of Gera from Saul's family cursed David. Abishai said to David, "...why would this dead dog curse my lord the king? Let me go over please and take off his head" (2 Samuel 16:9). David responded, "...what have I to do with you, the sons of Zeruiah? Let him curse because the Lord has said to him curse David. Who shall then say, why have you done so" (2 Samuel 16:10).

Calling them by their relation to their mother, "the sons of Zeruiah," should remind us of Saul's anger towards David, when Saul asked his son Jonathan, "...why does not **the son of Jesse** come to the meal..." (1 Samuel 20:27).

Two points to consider: Not even once did Saul label David to his face with the title "the son of Jesse." All instances in which Saul used this title were when David was not present. In contrast, we can see that David uses this kind of title to the person himself. Second, while David is talking to Abishai, still David uses the plural "sons of Zeruiah" including here quite likely Joab and maybe his brother Asahel.

When David returns to Jerusalem, Shimei the son of Gera comes to greet him and to apologize. "...[W]hat have I to do with you, **Sons of Zeruiah**, that you should this day be Satan to me? Shall there any man be put to death this day in Israel..." (2 Samuel 19:23).

Abner the son of Ner, the military commander of Mephibosheth, son of Saul, came to David in Hebron and offered him the loyalty of the ten tribes who were still loyal to Saul's dynasty. Joab, who wanted revenge against Abner for killing his brother Asahel, killed Abner. The text tells us that because of this murder, "When Saul's son heard that Abner was dead in Hebron his hands were feeble and the Israelites were frightened" (2 Samuel 4:1).

When David hears of Abner's death, David tells his people, "...do you not know that a prince and a great man has fallen this day in Israel. And I am this day weak and anointed king, and these men **the sons of Zeruiah** are too hard for me, the Lord shall reward the doer of evil according to his evil" (2 Samuel 3:38-39).

Absalom and Amnon

After Amnon, David's firstborn, rapes his half-sister Tamar, full sister to Absalom (2 Samuel 13:14), Absalom waits two years. Then during the shearing of the sheep celebration, Absalom instructs his people to kill Amnon. After Amnon's death, Absalom runs away to his grandfather, the king of Geshur.

Absalom and Joab

David instructs his people not to strike Absalom at the decisive battle. After all, David's own son conducted the rebellion against him. Joab, whose mother was Zeruiah, David's sister, does not abide by this instruction and kills Absalom. It is true that David's throne was more secure by killing the rebel son, but we should not forget that Joab and Absalom were first cousins.

Joab and Amasa

During the rebellion, Absalom dismisses Joab the son of Zeruiah (David's sister), who presided over David's military, and instead Absalom appoints Amasa the son of Abigail (David's other sister) to be the military commander.

After the end of the rebellion and the killing of Absalom, Sheba the son of Bichri starts another rebellion. During the pursuit of Sheba son of Bichri, the text says,

> And Joab said to Amasa, are you well my brother? And Joab took Amasa by the beard with his right hand to kiss him. And Amasa took no heed of the sword that was in Joab's hand, and he struck him with it in the belly, and shed out his bowels to the ground, and did not strike him again, and he died… (2 Samuel 20:9-10)

Although the text is talking about Joab, David's military commander, who kills Amasa, Absalom's military commander, we should realize the text is dealing with two first cousins.

David and Joab

It is not surprising that David would choose a relative to be the commander of the military. In a royal regime, the king has to take care that the one who can rebel against him, and has the power to do so, will be one from his own family. Blood relative guarantees loyalty, at least to a point.

If we examine the relationship between David and Joab, we can see that in the decisive majority of the cases, if not in all of them, Joab acts with complete loyalty to David, from Joab's point of view.

When Abner the son of Ner comes to David in Hebron to offer him the loyalty of the other tribes, Joab says, "You know Abner the son of Ner that he came to deceive you, and to know your going out and your coming in, and to know all that you do" (2 Samuel 3:25).

In the case of Bathsheba we see that David completely trusted Joab to act in David's personal interest. When David wanted to get rid of Uriah the Hittite, Bathsheba's husband, David wrote a letter to Joab, and gave the letter to Uriah. In the letter, David instructed Joab to position Uriah "…in the front of the hottest battle" (2 Samuel 11:15) so Uriah would die. Joab did so.

During the war against the Ammonites, when Joab is about to achieve total victory over the city, Joab was willing to give up on the honor that the victory would give him, and instead to give the honor to David, "And gather the rest of the people and encamp against the city and take it, lest I take the city and it be called after my name" (2 Samuel 12:28).

After Absalom killed Amnon, Absalom ran into exile and spent three years in Geshur. The text says, "And Joab the son of Zeruiah knew that the king's heart was towards Absalom" (2 Samuel 14:1). Joab sent a wise woman from Tekoah to give David the story of the two brothers of whom one killed the other. David knew that Joab was the one who sent the woman, he called Joab and said, "…behold now I have done this thing, go and bring back the lad Absalom" (2 Samuel 14:21). In response, "And Joab fell to the ground on his face and bowed and blessed the king and Joab said, today your slave knows that I have found grace in your sight my lord, O king, in that the king has fulfilled the request of his slave" (2 Samuel 14:22).

The fact that Joab said "…today your slave knows that I have found grace in your sight my lord, O king, in that the king has fulfilled the request of his slave" should bring us to ask if there were other instances in which David did not listen to Joab's advice.

And indeed, later on, we find that David did not accept Joab's view, and this non-acceptance brings evil to the land.

The text brings us David's wish to count the population of the kingdom, "And the king said to Joab the captain of the army who was with him, go now through all the tribes of Israel, from Dan to Beersheba, and count the people, that I may know the number of the people" (2 Samuel 24:2).

Joab responded, "…may the Lord your God add to the people, how many they may be, a hundredfold, and the eyes of my lord the king should see it, but why does my lord the king desire this thing?" (2 Samuel 24:3).

David insisted on having the census. The text continues, "And the king's word prevailed against Joab and against the captains of the army, and Joab and the captains of the army went from the presence of the king to count the people of Israel" (2 Samuel 24:4).

This census brought upon the plague of pestilence for three days (2 Samuel 24:15).

The only instance in which Joab didn't abide by David's order was the killing of Absalom.

David instructed his military people before the decisive battle, "…for my sake deal gently with the lad Absalom" (2 Samuel 18:5).

When Joab was informed that Absalom's head was caught in the thick boughs of the oak (2 Samuel 18:9), Joab instructed the one who informed him to kill Absalom, and even offered him monetary reward. The man refused citing the king's order.

Joab had to do it himself, "…he took three darts in his hand and thrust them through the heart of Absalom while he was still alive in the midst of the oak. And ten lads who carried Joab's armor surrounded and struck Absalom and slew him" (2 Samuel 18:14-15).

Joab saw it necessary to disobey a direct order of David and to kill the son who rebelled against his father David. David's order was a personal order of a father, and not a king's order to guarantee his reign. Joab, who was loyal to the king and the kingdom, saw it as right to disobey the father and to act according to the interests of the king and the kingdom.

When David mourns his son Absalom, Joab says to David,

> ...You have shamed this day the faces of all your slaves who this day saved your life and the lives of you sons and of your daughters and the lives of your wives and the lives of your concubines. In that you love your enemies and hate your friends, for you have declared this day that you regard neither princes nor slaves, for this day I know that if Absalom had lived, and we had all died this day, then it would have pleased you well. (2 Samuel 19:6-7)

Joab's words, calling for David to act like a king and not like a father mourning his rebellious son, bring David to come out to the people and return to acting like a king.

Joab's actions show that Joab's policy was "to love your friends and to hate your enemies." This policy brought him to kill Abner son of Ner, the military commander of Saul's army (on top of his revenge for Abner's killing his brother), and to kill Amasa, the military commander of Absalom's army during the rebellion. After all, a blood relationship cannot guarantee the safety of the person who rebels against the authority of the throne. The authority of the king and the sovereignty of the kingdom are above all, even if it involves a relative, be it a brother, a nephew, or a cousin.

Before his death we see that David instructs his son Solomon how to deal with Joab,

> And also you know what Joab the son of Zeruiah did to me, and what he did to the two captains of the armies of Israel, to Abner the son of Ner and to Amasa the son of Jether, whom he killed, and shed the blood of war in peace, and put the blood of war upon his girdle around his waist, and his shoes that were on his feet. And do according to your wisdom and let not his grey head go down to Sheol in peace. (1 Kings 2:5-6)

It is interesting that David does not mention openly the killing of Absalom by Joab. He refers to it by his words "…did to me…" Openly, David mentions the commanders of only two militaries hostile to David, Saul's army and Absalom's army.

It is quite likely that Joab, David's nephew by David's sister, was strong in David's kingdom just as Abner the son of Ner was strong in Saul's kingdom. Therefore, if Solomon were to guarantee his rule, he had to take care that there would be nobody strong enough in his kingdom to threaten his authority. But we should not forget that David instructs his son Solomon to kill his nephew Joab, Solomon's first cousin.

The question can be asked: if David instructed Solomon to kill his nephew Joab, and Solomon did so, what prevented David from doing it himself, after Joab killed Abner the son of Ner, or after he killed Amasa the son of Abigail, David's sister? Is it possible that at the time Joab killed Abner the son of Ner, or Amasa the son of Abigail, that Zeruiah, Joab's mother and David's sister, was still alive, and David did not want to sadden her? And after her death, before David's death, David could act as a king and not as a relative? It would be no different from Esau who wanted to kill his brother Jacob, after Jacob fraudulently received the blessing, and Esau said, "…when the days of mourning for my father are at hand, then I will slay my brother Jacob" (Genesis 27:41).

Summary

The fact that any king in ancient times had to guarantee his rule by surrounding himself with blood relatives, combined with the fact that at the time a king had several, if not many, wives producing sons from different mothers, created an explosive formula within the family. Sons from different mothers competed against each other (Absalom killing Amnon), and cousins or even nephews had no problem eliminating their opposition, even though this opposition was within the extended family (Joab killing Amasa or David ordering Joab killed). With this environment surrounding him, king David sat down to write the book of Genesis.

One can look at the situation not only in one direction, but as a two-way street. The picture portrayed to us in the book of Genesis of the families of the forefathers might indicate that both Isaac and Jacob functioned as kings. Esau wanted to kill his brother not just because of a blessing. The issue of the blessing was really who would take over after the death of the patriarch (*i.e.*, the king or lord). And when Joseph's brothers wanted to kill him, and settled on selling him to slavery, it was not only due to simple jealousy over paternal preference of a brother over his other brothers. It was a struggle for inheritance within the royal house. No different from Solomon killing his half-brother Adonijah, after Adonijah requested to have his father David's servant Abishag to himself.

This similarity would support the finding that Jacob was the first king of Israel, with all the rights of a king, but with all the problems of a royal house. A royal house meant that the brothers were a source of struggle and conflict over inheritance. Thus we can see that the content supports the SCAN finding that the title "brothers" carries a negative connotation.

EPILOGUE

Total Belief in the Subject

When people ask me to give them the most basic point in the SCAN technique, the foundation of all other rules used in this analysis, my answer is: 'Total Belief in the Subject.'

At first, most investigators, who deal with so many deceptive people, receive this news with major skepticism, thinking how can it be? They know from their experience that so many people lied to them in the past, so how can I come to them and say that they should approach the open statement by accepting it at face value? And I even emphasize to them, that even if I know for a fact that the subject is lying, I still look upon the statement as if the statement is absolutely true.

This point actually brought me to move from polygraph (lie detection) into statement analysis. It didn't take me long into my polygraph experience to realize that for most subjects who came deceptive on the charts coming out of the machine, and later confessed to the crime, their confessions did not contradict their initial statements. The confession complements the initial statement, but does not contradict it. And there were people who even said after their confession, "But I want you to know that I didn't lie to you in my initial statement." And in fact, when I share this experience of mine with my students, and some of them are polygraph examiners, I see many of them nodding their heads, and some of them even say openly that this is their experience as well.

Once, one realizes that the initial open statement, in the worst-case scenario, is only an incomplete truthful statement, the person is on his/her way to analyze the statement.

'Total belief in the subject' means that the subject has a 'copyright' on the text. That the 'open statement' is like Jericho in the bible: 'nobody goes in, and nobody comes out.' The text is one unit and indivisible, and one is not allowed to choose what one can accept, and what one can reject.

And if the reader/listener encounters a point in the open statement that the reader/listener does not understand, that does not mean that the statement is deceptive. It only means that the reader/listener does not understand it.

And in fact, in many cases, the reader/listener needs to first understand the choice of words used in the statement, before moving any further.

At this point, when you are reaching the end of this book, you realize that in many cases I took you (and myself) on a linguistic journey to understand the language, and once the language was clarified, we understood the story a lot better.

And as in any other scientific field, there is no way to reach a conclusion based upon just one point. Scientific methodology mandates that we corroborate our findings in **different ways**, and the more points we find, the more solid the conclusion is. And once different points lead to the same conclusion, we face a **definite** conclusion.

Moreover, the fact that the more we go into the text, the more we find linguistic evidence of the same conclusion, the more we realize that the conclusion is accurate. It is not different from a sudoku puzzle. Everything must fit. And if something does not fit, we know that we are wrong, and quite likely we messed up a lot earlier. SCAN analysis is actually a 'verbal sudoku.' And at the end of this analysis, we can still say everything fits.

When a detective sends me a statement, and I finish the analysis, and everything fits, I know that the analysis is accurate. And in fact, rarely if ever, would a detective report that the analysis sent him the wrong way. And in most cases, the analysis finds information that the detective didn't know, and after receiving the analysis, the detective continues his investigation, and finds confirmation of the points exposed in the analysis.

Unlike **empirical** evidence found in the scientific method, SCAN analysis produces many times **clinical** evidence, or, in other words, evidence **from within**, and not from the outside.

What is the Meaning of our Findings?

We found several points that are exposed by the **language** of the text, but they are not present in the **content**. But the bottom line, as an investigator (and I label myself a 'language detective') the question is: what is the meaning of our findings?

In other words, once one goes over an open statement and finds out that there are signals of concealing information, with the emphasis on concealing and not on lying, the immediate conclusion is that **memory** is the engine behind the statement. Common sense tells us that one cannot conceal unless one has something in memory to conceal. And in fact, concealing information gives credibility to the information in the statement. True, the investigator has a problem, because the person giving the statement does not tell everything he/she knows. At the same time, the investigator should conclude that the statement is not fiction. The statement reflects reality as experienced by the person.

There are many investigators who equate concealing information with deception. But this is the wrong approach. Actually, concealing information is the opposite of deception. And as a matter of fact, around 70% of truthful people conceal information. In my classes, I ask students to write statements describing a day of theirs. When we come to address the signals of concealing information, we find that many in the group raise their hands confirming that they have these signals in their statements. Nothing is wrong with it. Most people do not want everything to come out.

By finding all the hidden information behind the text, we are sealing that the text in the book of Genesis is not literature or fiction. It is a text coming directly, non-stop, from the memory of the writer. We should not criticize others more than we criticize ourselves. And therefore, we should not consider the fact that the book conceals information from us a fault of the book or of the writer. Actually, it is a major asset of the book, bringing us to conclude **professionally** that the book is a product of memory, as the writer knew it at the time.

Personal Meaning

As an orthodox Jew, whenever the Torah scroll is placed back inside the ark, I raise my hand and testify "This is the Torah that Moses put in front of the sons of Israel according to the word of Hashem (The Name)." Does this analysis change anything in my view of the Torah? Definitely not. This analysis, in my view, does not reduce my faith that there is a divine Supreme Being that is behind everything in life. Finding that Moses was not the one who wrote Genesis does not mean that the book is talking less to me. If anything, realizing now the depth of the knowledge presented in the book, I am more in awe than ever by the book.

I was practically raised on the book of Genesis, and the other books of the Torah. When I was a kid, our Friday night dinner was not only food. During the meal, we read aloud the Biblical portion of the week, and everyone read his share. We even discussed the stories and commented on them. Friday night dinner was an educational experience of immersion in the text. And over the years the stories became part of our lives. It is not rare, when we come to a certain story, for example, the Korach rebellion against Moses, that people comment, "Does he not learn from experience not to rebel? Why is he so stupid as to rebel again?" And a similar comment is made for other stories as well, "What, again? Won't they ever learn?"

As I said in the introduction to this analysis, and I wrote the introduction before I started this journey that lasted close to two years, I didn't know that I would find what I found. And in the course of this analysis I came to many other points that enrich my knowledge of the text. However, I decided to restrict this analysis to dealing with the 'social introduction' of people, and as you already saw, with the 'social introduction' of the Almighty. It is my plan to move on to other points in the language of the text.

Over the years, many students asked me if I plan to write a textbook for the SCAN technique. It didn't appeal to me. After so many years, I found that the way I want to present the SCAN technique to the public is by showing the SCAN technique in use on Biblical text. This analysis brings together my two main dimensions in life – the Bible first, and the SCAN technique second. This is the product you have before you.

I would like to end by thanking both my parents for giving me the love of the text. Without them, and without the upbringing they provided me, I don't think that I would have been able to reach this point where I can present a complete and coherent product – the SCAN technique in the book of Genesis.

Appendix A: Social Introduction – Name + Title

Genesis

- "And Adam knew **Eve his wife**…" (Genesis 4:1)
- "And Terah took **Abram his son**, and **Lot the son of Haran his grandson**, and **Sarai his daughter-in-law, his son Abram's wife**…" (Genesis 11:31)

Abraham

For Sarah –
- "And Abram took **Sarai his wife**…" (12:5)
- "…he said to **Sarai his wife**…" (12:11)
- "And Abraham said of **Sarah his wife**…" (20:2)
- "…and returned to him **Sarah his wife**" (20:14)
- "And after this Abraham buried **Sarah his wife**…" (23:19)
- "…there was Abraham buried and **Sarah his wife**" (25:10)
- "There they buried Abraham and **Sarah his wife**…" (49:31)

For Ishmael –
- "And Abraham took **Ishmael his son**…" (17:23)
- "And **Ishmael his son** was thirteen years old…" (17:25)
- "…and **Ishmael his son**" (17:26)

For Isaac –
- "And Abraham circumcised **Isaac his son**…" (21:4)
- "And Abraham was a hundred years old when **Isaac his son** was born to him" (21:5)
- "…and took two of his lads with him and **Isaac his son**…" (22:3)
- "…and laid it upon **Isaac his son**…" (22:6)
- "…and bound **Isaac his son**…" (22:9)
- "…and *Elohim* blessed **Isaac his son**…" (25:11)

When both Isaac and Ishmael are present –
- "And **Isaac and Ishmael his sons** buried him…" (25:9)

Isaac

For Rebecca –
- "…and **Rebecca his wife** conceived" (25:21)
- "…and Isaac was *metzahek* **Rebecca his wife**" (26:8)
- "…there they buried Isaac and **Rebecca his wife**…" (49:31)

For Esau –
- "…he called **Esau his big son**…" (27:1)
- "…and Rebecca heard when Isaac spoke to **Esau his son** (27:5)

For Jacob we should note that the text does not attribute the title "his son" to Jacob –
- "And Isaac called **Jacob** [*]…" (28:1)
- "And Isaac sent away **Jacob** [*]…" (28:5)

For comparison see the language of the text for Rebecca and her two sons.

For Rebecca's family –
- "…go to Padan-Aram to the house of **Bethuel your mother's father**, and take from there a wife from the daughters of **Laban your mother's brother**" (28:2)

Rebecca

- "And Rebecca spoke to **Jacob her son** saying behold I heard your father speak to **Esau your brother** saying…" (27:6)
- "And Jacob said to **Rebecca his mother**…" (27:11)
- "And Rebecca took the best garments of **Esau her big son** which were with her in the house and put them on **Jacob her little son**" (27:15)
- "And she gave the savory food and the bread which she had prepared to the hand of **Jacob her son**" (27:17)
- "And these words of **Esau her big son** were told to Rebecca and she sent and called **Jacob her little son**…" (27:42)
- "…flee to **Laban my brother**…" (27:43)

Jacob

For Esau –
- "…behold **Esau my brother** is a hairy man…" (27:11)
- "And Jacob sent messengers before him to **Esau his brother**…" (32:4)
- "…a present for **Esau his brother**" (32:14)
- "…when **Esau my brother** meets you…" (32:18)

Later, there are places where the order changes to "title + name" for Esau.

For Rachel –
- "The sons of **Rachel Jacob's wife**…" (46:19).

There are numerous places where the name appears before the title. For example,

- "And **Shechem the son of Hamor the Hivite prince of the country** saw her…" (34:2)
- "And Judah said to **Tamar his daughter-in-law**…" (38:11)

Name + Title in the Rest of the Tanach

Moses

For Aaron and his sons –
- "…and **Aaron your brother** shall speak to Pharaoh…" (Exodus 7:2)
- "And bring close to you **Aaron your brother**…" (Exodus 28:1)
- "Take Aaron **and Eleazar his son**…" (Numbers 20:25)
- "…and put them upon **Eleazar his son**…" (20:26)
- "…and put them upon **Eleazar his son**…" (20:28)
- "…and **Eleazar his son** ministered…" (Deuteronomy 10:6)

For Jethro –
- "And **Jethro the priest of Midian Moses' father-in-law** heard…" (Exodus 18:1)
- "And **Jethro Moses' father-in-law** took…" (18:2)
- "And **Jethro Moses' father-in-law** came…" (18:5)

- "And **Jethro Moses' father-in-law** took…" (18:12)

Books of Joshua and Judges

- "And **Eleazar the son of Aaron** died and they buried him in a hill that belonged to **Pinehas his son**…" (Joshua 24:33)
- "And **Deborah a prophetess the wife of Laqpidoth**…" (Judges 4:4)
- "…to the tent of **Yael the wife of Heber the Kenite**… peace between **Jabin the king of Hazor** and…" (Judges 4:17)
- "…he gave to **Peninna his wife**…" (1 Samuel 1:4)
- "And Eli called Samuel and said **Samuel my son**…" (1 Samuel 3:16)
- "…**Kish Saul's father** …and Kish said to **Saul his son**…" (1 Samuel 9:3)

Saul – Jonathan – David

- "And Saul and **Jonathan his son**…" (1 Samuel 13:16)
- "…with Saul and **Jonathan his son**" (1 Samuel 13:22)
- "…and Saul said to **Jonathan his son**…" (1 Samuel 20:27)
- "…and Saul and **Jonathan his son** are dead also" (2 Samuel 1:4)
- "…how do you know that Saul and **Jonathan his son** as dead" (2 Samuel 1:5)
- "…for Saul and for **Jonathan his son**…" (2 Samuel 1:12)
- "And David lamented with this lamentation over Saul and over **Jonathan his son**" (2 Samuel 1:17)
- "…and took the bones of Saul and the bones of **Jonathan his son**…" (2 Samuel 21:12)
- "And he brought from there the bones of Saul and the bones of **Jonathan his son**…" (2 Samuel 21:13)
- "…and said send me **David your son**…" (1 Samuel 16:19)
- "…and sent them with **David his son**…" (1 Samuel 16:20)
- "And Saul had given **Michal his daughter David's wife**…" (1 Samuel 25:44)
- "And Toi sent **Joram his son**…" (2 Samuel 8:10)
- "…and the king of the Ammonites died and **Hanun his son** reigned in his place" (2 Samuel 10:1)
- "And the rest of the people he gave in the hand of **Abishai his brother**…" (2 Samuel 10:10)

- "...return to the city in peace and **Ahimaaz your son**..." (2 Samuel 15:27)
- "...and the Lord has given the kingdom to the hand of **Absalom your son**..." (2 Samuel 16:8)

Solomon

- "...**Solomon your son** shall reign after me..." (1 Kings 1:17; 1:30)
- "...and he charged **Solomon his son** saying" (1 Kings 2:1)
- "And it was in the heart of **David my father**..." (1 Kings 8:17)
- "And the Lord said to **David my father**..." (1 Kings 8:18)
- "...and was buried in the city of **David his father**..." (1 Kings 11:43)

The Kings of Judah and Israel

- "...and **Nadab his son** reigned in his place" (1 Kings 14:20)
- "...and **Abijam his son** reigned in his place" (1 Kings 14:31)
- "...and **Asa his son** reigned in his place" (1 Kings 15:8)
- "...and **Jehoshaphat his son** reigned in his place" (1 Kings 15:24)
- "...and **Elah his son** reigned in his place" (1 Kings 16:6)
- "...and **Ahab his son** reigned in his place" (1 Kings 16:28)
- "...and **Ahaziah his son** reigned in his place" (1 Kings 22:40)
- "...and **Jehoram his son** reigned in his place" (1 Kings 22:51)
- "...and **Ahaziah his son** reigned in his place (2 Kings 8:24)
- "...and **Jehoahaz his son** reigned in his place (2 Kings 10:35)
- "...and **Amaziah his son** reigned in his place (2 Kings 12:22)
- "...and **Joash his son** reigned in his place (2 Kings 13:9)
- "...and **Ben-Hadad his son** reigned in his place (2 Kings 13:24)
- "...and **Jeroboam his son** reigned in his place (2 Kings 14:16)
- "...and **Zechariah his son** reigned in his place (2 Kings 14:29)
- "...and **Jotham his son** reigned in his place (2 Kings 15:7)
- "...and **Pekahiah his son** reigned in his place (2 Kings 15:22)
- "...and **Ahaz his son** reigned in his place (2 Kings 15:38)
- "...and **Hezekiah his son** reigned in his place (2 Kings 16:20)
- "...and **Manasseh his son** reigned in his place (2 Kings 20:21)
- "...and **Amon his son** reigned in his place (2 Kings 21:18)
- "...and **Josiah his son** reigned in his place (2 Kings 21:26)
- "...and **Jeoiachin his son** reigned in his place (2 Kings 24:6)

Appendix B: *Litzok* – Crying for Help

Biblical Hebrew uses the verb *litzok* to express a cry for help. Following are examples.

Genesis

- "What have you done? The voice of your brother's bloods *tzoakim* to me from the ground" (Genesis 4:10)
- "I will go down and see *haketzaakata* (according to her cry), whether they have done altogether…" (18:21)
- "…because *tzaakatam* has grown great before the face of the Lord…" (19:13)
- "When Esau heard the words of his father *vayitzaak tzeaaka* great and very bitter…" (27:34)
- "And all the land of Egypt was famished and *vayitzaak* the people to Pharaoh…" (41:55)

Exodus

- "I have surely seen the affliction of my people who are in Egypt and have heard their *tzaakatam*…" (3:7)
- "And now behold the *tzaakat* of the people of Israel has come to me…" (3:9)
- "…therefore they *tzoaakim* saying let us go and sacrifice to our G-d" (5:8)
- "The officers of the people of Israel came and *vayitzaaku* to Pharaoh…" (5:15)
- "…And Moses *vaitzaak* cried to the Lord…" (8:8)
- "And there shall be a great *tzaaka* throughout the land of Egypt…" (11:6)
- "….and there was a great *tzeaaka* in Egypt…" (12:30)
- "…and the people of Israel *vayitzaaku* out to the Lord" (14:10)
- "…Why do you *titzaak* to me?…" (14:15)
- "And he *vayitzaak* to the Lord…" (15:25)
- "And Moses *vayitzaak* to the Lord…" (17:4)
- "…if you afflict him and they *tzaok yitzaak* to me I will surely hear *tzaakato*" (22:22)
- "…when he *yitzaak* to me that I will hear…" (22:26)

Numbers

- "And the people *vayitzhak* to Moses…" (11:2)
- "And Moses *vayitzaak* to the Lord saying…" (12:13)
- "And we *vanitzaak* to the Lord…" (20:16)

Deuteronomy

- "…because she has *tzaaka* not…" (22:24)
- "…and the betrothed girl *tzaaka*…" (22:27)
- "And we *vanitzaak* to the Lord G-d of our fathers…" (26:7)

Appendix C: *Likro* – to Call

To Name a Person

Genesis: 2:23, 3:20, 4:25, 4:26, 5:2, 5:3, 5:29, 16:11, 16:15, 17:5, 17:15, 17:19, 19:37, 19:38, 21:3, 25:25, 25:26, 25:30, 27:36, 29:32, 29:33, 29:34, 29:35, 30:6, 30:8, 30:11, 30:13, 30:18, 30:20, 30:21, 30:24, 35:10, 35:18 (2), 38:3, 38:4, 38:5, 38:29, 38:30, 41:45, 41:51, 41:52
Exodus: 2:10, 2:22
Numbers: 13:16
Deuteronomy: 25:10, 28:10

To Name a Location

Genesis: 4:17, 11:9, 16:14, 19:22, 21:31, 22:14, 26:18, 26:20, 26:21, 26:22, 26:33, 28:19, 31:47 (2), 31:48, 32:3, 32:31, 33:17, 33:20, 35:7, 35:8, 35:15, 50:11
Exodus: 15:23, 17:7, 17:15, 33:7
Numbers: 11:3, 11:34, 13:24, 21:3, 32:38, 32:41, 32:42
Deuteronomy: 3:9 (2), 3:13, 3:14

To Call Someone

Genesis: 3:9, 12:18, 19:5, 20:8, 20:9, 21:17, 22:11, 22:15, 24:57, 24:58, 26:9, 27:1, 27:42, 28:1, 31:4, 31:54, 39:14, 41:8, 41:14, 46:33, 47:29
Exodus: 1:18, 2:7, 2:8, 2:20, 3:4, 7:11, 8:4, 8:21, 9:27, 10:16, 10:24, 12:21, 12:31, 19:3, 19:7, 19:20, 24:16, 34:15, 34:31, 36:2
Leviticus: 1:1, 9:1, 10:4
Numbers: 12:5, 16:12, 22:5, 22:20, 22:37, 24:10, 25:2
Deuteronomy: 25:8, 29:1, 31:7, 31:14

To Call the Festivals

Exodus: 12:16 (2)
Leviticus: 23:2, 23:3, 23:4, 23:7, 23:21, 23:24, 23:27, 23:35, 23:36, 23:37, 25:10
Numbers: 28:18, 28:25, 28:26, 29:1, 29:7, 29:12

To Call to (*el*)

- "And the Lord **called to** Adam and said to him where are you." (Genesis 3:9)
- "And they **called to** Lot and said to him where are the men who came in to you this night?" (19:5)
- "...and the angel of G-d **called to** Hagar from heaven..." (21:17)
- "And the angel of the Lord **called to** him from heaven and said Abraham Abraham, and he said here I am." (22:11)
- "And the angel of the Lord **called to** Abraham from heaven the second time." (22:15)
- "And Isaac **called to** Jacob and blessed him..." (28:1)
- "...G-d **called to** him out of the midst of the bush..." (Exodus 3:4)
- "And Pharaoh **called to** Moses and Aaron..." (8:21)
- "And Pharaoh **called to** Moses and said go serve the Lord..." (10:24)
- "...and the Lord **called to** him from the mountain saying..." (19:3)
- "...and he **called to** Moses on the seventh day from the midst of the cloud." (24:16)
- "And Moses **called to** them and Aaron and all the chiefs of the congregation returned to him..." (34:31)
- "And Moses **called to** Bezalel and Aholihab..." (36:2)
- "And he **called to** Moses and the Lord spoke to him..." (Leviticus 1:1)
- "And Moses **called to** Mishael and Elzaphan the sons of Uzziel the uncle of Aaron..." (10:4)
- "And Moses **called to** all Israel and said to them..." (Deuteronomy 29:1)
-

To call (*l'*)

Genesis

- "And Pharaoh called Abram and said what is this that you have done to me?" (Genesis 12:18)
- "...and he called all his slaves..." (20:8)
- "And Abimelech called Abraham and said to him what have you done to us?" (20:9)

- "And they said we will call the girl and inquire at her mouth." (24:57)
- "And they called Rebecca and said to her will you go with this man and she said I will go." (24:58)
- "And Abimelech called Isaac and said behold certainly she is your wife and why did you say she is my sister?" (26:9)
- "...and she sent and called Jacob her little son..." (27:42)
- "And Jacob sent and called Rachel and Leah to the field to his flock." (31:4)
- "...and he called his brothers to eat bread..." (31:54)
- "And she called the people of her house and spoke to them..." (39:14)
- "And it shall come to pass when Pharaoh shall call you and shall say what is your occupation." (46:33)
- "And the time drew nearer for Israel to die and he called his son Joseph..." (47:29)

Exodus

- "And the king of Egypt called the midwives and said to them..." (Exodus 1:18)
- "And his sister said to Pharaoh's daughter shall I go and call you a nurse of the Hebrew women..." (2:7)
- "And he said to his daughters and where is he? Why is it that you have left the man? Call him that he may eat bread." (2:20)
- "And Pharaoh also called the wise men and the sorcerers..." (7:11)
- "And Pharaoh called Moses and Aaron..." (8:4)
- "And Pharaoh sent and called Moses and Aaron and said to them..." (9:27)
- "And Pharaoh hurriedly called Moses and Aaron and he said..." (10:16)
- "And Moses called all the elders of Israel and said to them..." (12:21)
- "And he called Moses and Aaron by night and said..." (12:31)
- "And Moses came and called the elders of the people..." (19:7)
- "And the Lord came down upon Mount Sinai on the top of the mount and the Lord called Moses up to the top of the mount and Moses ascended." (19:20)
- "...and he will call you and you will eat of his sacrifice." (34:15)

Leviticus

- "And on the eighth day Moses called Aaron and his sons and the elders of Israel." (Leviticus 9:1)

Numbers

- "And Moses sent to call Datan and Abiram the sons of Eliab..." (Numbers 16:12)
- "And he sent messengers to Balaam the son of Beor to Pethor, which is by the river of the land of his people to call him..." (22:5)
- "...if the men came to call you rise up and go with (*et*) them..." (22:20)
- "...did I not send to you to call you?" (22:37)
- "...I called you to curse my enemies..." (24:10)
- "And they called the people to their sacrifices for their gods..." (25:2)

Deuteronomy

- "And the elders of his city shall call him and speak to him..." (25:8)
- "And Moses called Joshua and said to him in the sight of all Israel..." (31:7)

To Call (*et*)

- "And when Isaac was old and his eyes were dim so that he could not see he called (*et*) Esau his big son..." (Genesis 27:1)
- "And in the morning his spirit was troubled and he sent and called (*et*) all the sorcerers of Egypt and all its wise men..." (41:8)
- "And Pharaoh sent and called (*et*) Joseph and they rushed him out of the dungeon..." (41:14)
- "...and the maiden went and called (*et*) the child's mother." (Exodus 2:8)
- "And the Lord said to Moses behold your days approach to die call (*et*) Joshua and present yourselves in the Tent of Meeting..." (Deuteronomy 31:14)

To Call + Name

- "And the Lord came down in the pillar of cloud and stood at the entrance to the tent and called Aaron and Miriam and they both came out." (Numbers 12:5)

To Call the Name of G-d

- "...then it was begun to call in the name of the Lord." (Genesis 4:26)
- "...and called in the name of the Lord." (12:8)
- "...and there Abram called in the name of the Lord." (13:4)
- "And he built an altar and he called in the name of the Lord..." (26:25)
- "And the Lord descended in a cloud and stood there with him and he called in the name of the Lord." (Exodus 34:5)
- "Because the name of the Lord I will call; ascribe greatness to our G-d." (Deuteronomy 32:3)

To Call the Lord

- "For what nation is which so great who has G-d so near to it, as the Lord our G-d is whenever we call him." (Deuteronomy 4:7)
- "...and your eye be evil against your poor brother and you will not give him and he will call on you to the Lord and it be sin in you." (15:9)
- "...lest he will call on you to the Lord and it be sin in you." (24:15)
-

To Call + Content

- "...and he called get out every man from me..." (Genesis 45:1)
- "...and Aaron called and said tomorrow is a festival to the Lord." (Exodus 32:5)
- "And the Lord passed by before him and he called the Lord the Lord..." (34:6)
- "...and he should call unclean, unclean." (Leviticus 13:45)
- "...that you may use them for calling the congregation..." (Numbers 10:2)

- "...because it is called Sabbatical year for the Lord." (Deuteronomy 15:2)
- "When you come near to a city to fight against it, you should call to it for peace." (Deuteronomy 20:10)
- "They shall call peoples to the mountain..." (Deuteronomy 33:19)

To Read From a Book

- "And he took the Book of the Covenant and read it and read in the ears of the people..." (Exodus 24:7)
- "...and he shall read in it all the days of his life..." (Deuteronomy 17:19)
- "...you shall read this Torah against all Israel in their ears." (Deuteronomy 31:11)

Appendix D: Clusters of Negative + Reason

Double Clusters

- "And he moved from there and dug another well and for that <u>they strove not</u> and he called the name of it Rehoboth and he said **because** now the Lord has made room for us and we shall be fruitful in the land" (Genesis 26:22)
- "And he <u>discerned him not</u> **because** his hands were hairy..." (27:23)
- "...and they were very angry **because** he had done a vile deed in Israel in lying with Jacob's daughter which thing <u>ought not to be done</u>" (34:7)
- "And the lad <u>was not late to do the thing</u> **because** he desired Jacob's daughter..." (34:19)
- "...let me come to you **because** <u>he did not know</u> that she was his daughter-in-law..." (38:16)
- "And Joseph fathered grain as the sand of the sea, very much, until he stopped counting **because** <u>there was no number</u>" (41:49)
- "And Benjamin, Joseph's brother, Jacob <u>sent not</u> with his brothers, **because** he said lest perhaps harm befall him" (42:4)
- "And Joseph <u>could not</u> refrain himself before all those who stood by him and he called take out every man from me. And there <u>stood no man</u> with him while Joseph made himself known to his brothers" (45:1)
- "...and his brothers <u>could not</u> answer him **because** they were afraid of him" (45:3)
- "...And Jacob's heart fainted **because** he <u>didn't believe</u> them" (45:26)
- "And <u>there was no bread</u> in all the land **because** the famine was very severe..." (47:13)

Triple Clusters

- "And the land <u>was not</u> able to sustain them to live together **because** their possessions were great and they <u>could not</u> live together" (13:6)
- "**Therefore** the people of Israel <u>do not eat</u> the sinew of the vein which is in the hollow of the thigh to this day **because** he touched the hollow of Jacob's thigh..." (32:33)

- "**Because** their possessions were greater from living together and the land of their residence <u>could not sustain</u> them **because** of their cattle" (36:7)
- "And they served him by himself and for them by themselves and for the Egyptians who are with him by themselves **because** the Egyptians <u>may not eat bread</u> with the Hebrews **because** it is abomination to the Egyptians" (43:32)

Appendix E: *Ad Hayom Hazeh* – Till This Day

- "And he called it Sheba therefore the name of the city is Beersheba **till this day**" (Genesis 26:33)
- "Therefore the sons of Israel do not eat the sinew of the vein which is in the hollow of the thigh **till this day**…" (Genesis 32:33)
- "And Joseph made it a law over the land of Egypt **till this day**, that Pharaoh should have the fifth part…" (Genesis 47:26)
- "…the Elohim which shepherded me all my life **till this day**" (Genesis 48:15)
- "…which neither your fathers, nor your grandfathers have seen since the day that they were upon the earth **till this day**…" (Exodus 10:6)
- "And the ass said to Balaam, am not I your ass upon which you have ridden ever since I was yours **till this day**…" (Numbers 22:30)
- "Like he did to the sons of Esau, who lived in Seir, when he destroyed the Horim from before them, and they succeeded them and lived in their place even **till this day**" (Deuteronomy 2:22)
- "…and he called the Bashan after his own name Havoth-Jair **till this day**" (Deuteronomy 3:14)
- "At that time *Y-H-V-H* set apart the tribe of Levi, to carry the ark of the covenant of *Y-H-V-H*, to stand before *Y-H-V-H* to minister to him, and bless in his name, **till this day**" (Deuteronomy 10:8)
- "…how he made the water of the Red Sea overflow them as they pursued after you, and how *Y-H-V-H* has destroyed them **till this day**" (Deuteronomy 11:4)
- "And *Y-H-V-H* has not given you a heart to perceive, and eyes to see, and ears to hear, **till this day**" (Deuteronomy 29:3)
- "…but no man knows his grave **till this day**" (Deuteronomy 34:6)
- "And Joshua set twelve stones in the midst of the Jordan, in the place where the feet of the priests who carried the ark of the covenant stood, and they are there **till this day**" (Joshua 4:9)
- "…therefore he called the name of the place Gilgal **till this day**" (Joshua 5:9)
- "And Joshua saved Rahab the harlot alive, and her father's household, and all that she had, and she lives among Israel **till this day**…" (Joshua 6:25)

- "And they raised over him a heap of stones **till this day**. So *Y-H-V-H* turned from the fierceness of his anger, therefore he called the name of the place the Valley of Achor **till this day**" (Joshua 7:26)
- "And Joshua burned Ai, and made it a heap forever, a desolation **till this day**" (Joshua 8:28)

Appendix F: SCAN Rules Used in This Analysis

SCAN Rule: The person is dead. The statement is alive!

SCAN Rule: Total Belief in the Subject

SCAN Rule: We need to analyze the text according to the extraordinary, not according to the usual or average and accepted way the language goes about describing the events.

SCAN Rule: 'Out-of-sequence' information is only 'out-of-sequence' to the reader/listener. However, it is 'in-sequence' for the writer/speaker, and the writer/speaker positioned it at the place it should be. When the reader/listener understands the statement completely, everything will be 'in-sequence.'

SCAN Rule: 'Out-of-sequence' information indicates that the writer/speaker took some significant information out of the 'open statement,' but left in the 'open statement' the effects of the missing information. Once the missing information will be brought back into the 'open statement,' everything will be 'in-sequence.'

SCAN Rule: The first sentence in an open statement is the most important sentence. It is the point at which the subject decided to start the statement. In many cases the first sentence includes the reason for the events that follow.

SCAN Rule: The location in the "open statement," or in the sentence, is connected to the change of language.

SCAN Rule: The shortest way to give a sentence is the best way. Any deviation from the shortest way is meaningful.

SCAN Rule: Doubling an activity in an "open statement" indicates a signal of concealing information.

SCAN Rule: In an "open statement" there is no "unnecessary" sentence. It is only "unnecessary" for the reader/listener, but it is the "necessary for the subject. When the reader/listener encounters an "unnecessary" sentence, the reader/listener should realize that the sentence is extremely important.

SCAN Rule: A word, a sentence, or a phrase that connects two different events might indicate that there was a stop in the delivery of the information, and might indicate that some information was ejected from the statement at this point of time.

SCAN Rule: when a certain event in an "open statement" is surrounded by two "unnecessary connections" the reader/listener should relate to that event as extremely sensitive. In an "open statement" of modern times the SCAN analyst should guide the investigator to focus on this point in the follow-up investigation, even if the analyst does not see anything sensitive, according to his/her point of view.

SCAN Rule: The sequence of events inside the sentence should reflect the sequence of events in reality in the past.

SCAN Rule: 'Unimportant information' is only 'unimportant' to the reader/listener, but it is important for the one who gives the statement, since only what is 'important' will enter the open statement. When the reader/listener encounters 'unimportant information' it should be considered by the reader/listener as 'extremely important.'

SCAN Rule: Change of language reflects a change in reality.

SCAN Rule: An 'unnecessary connection' comes to indicate that some information might be missing at this point of time.

SCAN Rule: There are no synonyms in language.

SCAN Rule: We should analyze the text by the 'extraordinary' and not by the regular way the language of the text describes the events.

SCAN Rule: When the SCAN analyst encounters a one-time deviation from the 'average' use of language throughout the rest of the text, the SCAN analyst should suspect that deception is present at the time of the deviation.

SCAN Rule: There is no 'unnecessary information' in an 'open statement.' It is only unnecessary to the reader/listener, but it is necessary to the writer/speaker. When the reader/listener understands the statement completely, everything is 'necessary.'

SCAN Rule: Unimportant information is doubly important.

About the Author

Avinoam Sapir

Born in Tel-Aviv, Israel, in 1949, he studied Psychology and Criminology at Bar-Ilan University and did his master's thesis on Interrogation in Jewish Law at Tel-Aviv University. After military service he began his career with the Israeli Police as a polygraph examiner. In 1978 he started teaching interviewing to various Israeli government agencies, moving to the U.S. in 1985. He developed the SCAN technique based on these experiences and has taught it in eleven countries on six continents.